"I'm really impressed with how functional my software has become because of Expect. Thanks for a wonderful program!!!!!!"

—*John Conti, Cisco Systems*

"Expect has become a necessary tool for system administration. In a short time, we have used Expect in six areas and have cut out seven hours a week in tedious and repetitive tasks."

—*Thomas Naughton, Hull Trading Company*

"I'd been using Expect for automating various grubby day-to-day system tasks for a long time. During the procurement for EPA's supercomputer, we found that we needed a portable way to quantify interactive response time for the benchmark. Using Expect we were able to 'drive' the standard vi editor to produce an average of seconds/command keystroke."

—*Frank Terhaar-Yonkers, Martin Marietta Technical Services/U.S. EPA*

"Thanks for Expect. It just made an impossible project possible."

—*Bruce Barnett, GE Corporate Research and Development Center*

"My Expect scripts function perfectly. The original problem defeated several people here (including those much more expert in Unix than myself), so it is a relief to have found such a simple solution."

—*Richard Gartner, Bodleian Library, Oxford University, United Kingdom*

"Expect is great! We at DEC have to go through ftp-gateways to get to the real world. I've written an Expect script that is easier and more reliable than a previously cobbled together system using perl -> mail -> perl -> kermit. The whole thing is now one small Expect script."

—*Rob Urban, Migration Consultant, Digital Equipment GmbH, Munich, Germany*

"Thank you so much!!! Expect is not only a timesaver but a lifesaver, too!"

—*Stephen Campos, University of Texas at Austin*

"Thanks to Expect, we've solved many problems that would have otherwise needed a lot of programming—meaning we would not have had time to do them!"

—*Pekka Kytölaakso, Centre for Scientific Computing, Espoo, Finland*

"I'm changing passwords on over 600 hosts, and BOY! am I glad that Expect's passmass script exists! Now *there's* an indispensable tool!"

—*Win Bent, University Comp. Services, University of Southern California*

"Expect is a lifesaver for a project that I am currently involved with. I have only been working with Expect for the last couple of days, but it has already shaved about 6 months off of the completion time of the project."

—*Ron Young, System Computing Services, University of Nevada*

"Thanks for making my life easier. This program has really helped me shorten the cycle time for software Q.A. Expect is like a dream come true for automation. My productivity has really increased."

Brian F. Woodson, 3Com NSD Software Q.A.

"What I really like about Expect is that it lets you shift in and out of interactive and automated mode as you are driving programs."

—*Lloyd Zusman, Master Byte Software, Inc.*

"Expect is exactly what I needed to automate some telnet procedures here at Motorola. I had been pulling my hair out thinking that there HAD to be a way to get my shell script to work, but you just can't do it. Luckily somebody in my group clued me in to Expect!"

–*Marjorie Cartwright, RISC Design Group, Motorola*

"Expect helped me to achieve what I first didn't think possible."

—*Hennie Rautenbach, Sabinet, Pretoria, South Africa*

Exploring Expect

Other books by Don Libes

Life With UNIX (Prentice-Hall, co-author Sandy Ressler)

Obfuscated C and Other Mysteries (Wiley)

Exploring Expect

A Tcl-Based Toolkit for Automating Interactive Programs

Don Libes

O'Reilly & Associates, Inc.

Cambridge · Köln · Paris · Sebastopol · Tokyo

Exploring Expect: A Tcl-Based Toolkit for Automating Interactive Programs
by Don Libes

Editor: Tim O'Reilly

Production Editor: Don Libes

Printing History:

> January 1995: First Edition.
>
> April 1995: Minor corrections.
>
> November 1996: Minor corrections.

ISBN: 1-56592-090-2   [2/98]

To Sue

Brief Table of Contents

	Brief Table of Contents	*ix*
	Extended Table Of Contents	*xi*
	Preface	*xxiii*
	How To Read This Book	*xxxi*
1.	*Introduction — What Is Expect?*	*1*
2.	*Tcl — Introduction And Overview*	*23*
3.	*Getting Started With Expect*	*71*
4.	*Glob Patterns And Other Basics*	*87*
5.	*Regular Expressions*	*107*
6.	*Patterns, Actions, And Limits*	*129*
7.	*Debugging Patterns And Controlling Output*	*165*
8.	*Handling A Process And A User*	*185*
9.	*The Expect Program*	*213*
10.	*Handling Multiple Processes*	*233*
11.	*Handling Multiple Processes Simultaneously*	*247*
12.	*Send*	*271*
13.	*Spawn*	*287*
14.	*Signals*	*307*
15.	*Interact*	*323*
16.	*Interacting With Multiple Processes*	*349*

17. *Background Processing*   *371*

18. *Debugging Scripts*   *403*

19. *Expect + Tk = Expectk*   *429*

20. *Extended Examples*   *465*

21. *Expect, C, And C++*   *491*

22. *Expect As Just Another Tcl Extension*   *513*

23. *Miscellaneous*   *523*

    Appendix—Commands and Variables   *531*

    Index Of Scripts   *537*

    Index   *541*

Extended Table Of Contents

Brief Table of Contents..*ix*

Extended Table Of Contents...*xi*

Preface ....*xxiii*
Expect—Why Another Tool? xxiv
Tcl—A Little History xxv
Acknowledgments xxvii

How To Read This Book...*xxxi*
Notational Conventions xxxii
Exercises xxxiii

1: Introduction — What Is Expect?................................ *1*
Ouch, Those Programs Are Painful! 1
A Very Brief Overview 3
A First Script—dialback 3
Total Automation 4
Differing Behavior When Running Non-Interactively 7
Partial Automation 8
Dangerous, Unfriendly, Or Otherwise Unlikable User Interfaces ... 9
Graphical Applications 10
A Little More About Tcl 11

Job Control 12

Background Processes 12

Using Expect With Other Programs 13

Using Expect On UNIX 13

Using Expect On Other Operating Systems 13

Using Expect In Real Applications 14

Using Expect In Commercial Applications—Legalese 15

Obtaining Expect And The Examples 16

Expect And Tcl Resources 19

Exercises 22

2: Tcl—Introduction And Overview *23*

Everything Is A String 23

Quoting Conventions 25

Expressions 27

Braces—Deferring Evaluation 29

Control Structures 29

More On Expressions 37

Lists 38

More Ways To Manipulate Strings 46

Arrays 49

Indirect References 51

Handling Errors 53

Evaluating Lists As Commands 56

Passing By Reference 57

Working With Files 60

File I/O 61

Executing UNIX Commands 66

Environment Variables 67

Handling Unknown Commands 68

Libraries 68

Is There More To Tcl? 69

Exercises 70

3: Getting Started With Expect *71*

The send Command 71

The expect Command 72

Anchoring 73

What Happens When Input Does Not Match 74

Pattern-Action Pairs 75

Example—Timed Reads In The Shell 77

The spawn Command 78

The interact Command 82

Example—Anonymous ftp 83

Exercises 85

4: Glob Patterns And Other Basics 87

The * Wildcard 87

More Glob Patterns 91

Backslashes 91

Handling Timeout 94

Handling End Of File (eof) 98

Hints On The spawn Command 99

Back To Eof 100

The close Command 101

Programs That Ignore Eof 103

The wait Command 105

Exercises 106

5: Regular Expressions 107

Regular Expressions—A Quick Start 107

Identifying Regular Expressions And Glob Patterns 109

Using Parentheses To Override Precedence 110

Using Parentheses For Feedback 111

More On The timed-read Script 112

Pattern Matching Strategy 113

Nested Parentheses 115

Always Count Parentheses, Even Inside Of Alternatives 116

Example—The Return Value From A Remote Shell 117

Matching Customized Prompts 120

Example—A Smart Remote Login Script 122

What Else Gets Stored In expect_out 124

More On Anchoring 125

Exercises 126

6: Patterns, Actions, And Limits 129

Matching Anything But 129

Really Complex Patterns 131

Really Simple Patterns 134

Matching One Line And Only One Line 135

Tcl's string match Command 136

Tcl's regexp Command 137

Tcl's regsub Command 138

Ignoring Case 139

All Those Other String Functions Are Handy, Too 140

Actions That Affect Control Flow 140

Example—rogue 141

Character Graphics 142

More Actions That Affect Control Flow 143

Matching Multiple Times 145

Recognizing Prompts (Yet Again) 147

Speed Is On Your Side 148

Controlling The Limits Of Pattern Matching Input 149

The full_buffer Keyword 151

Double Buffering 152

Perpetual Buffering 154

The Politics Of Patterns 154

Expecting A Null Character 155

Parity 157

Length Limits 158

Comments In expect Commands 158

Restrictions On expect Arguments 159

eval—Good, Bad, And Ugly 160

Exercises 162

7: Debugging Patterns And Controlling Output 165

Pattern Debugging 165

Enabling Internal Diagnostics 171

Logging Internal Diagnostics 173

Disabling Normal Program Output 174

The log_user Command 175

Example—su2 178

Recording All Expect Output 180

Sending Messages To The Log 182

About File Names 182

Log And Diagnostic State 182

Exercises 183

8: Handling A Process And A User *185*

The send_user Command 185

The send_error Command 187

The expect_user Command 192

Dealing With Programs That Reprompt 193

Dealing With Programs That Miss Input 196

Sleeping 196

Line Versus Character–Oriented And Other Terminal Modes 197

Echoing 199

Prompting For A Password On Behalf Of A Program 201

Security And Insecurity 202

Resetting The Terminal Upon Exit 204

More On The stty Command 204

The system Command 207

Redirecting The Standard Input Or Output 209

The expect_tty Command 210

The send_tty Command 210

Exercises 211

9: The Expect Program *213*

Expect—Just Another Program 213

Invoking Scripts Without Saying "expect" 215

Rewriting The #! Line 216

The .exp Extension 217

The –– And Other Flags 217

The –c Flag 218

The –f Flag 220

Writing The #! Line 221

The –i Flag 221

The –n And –N Flags 221

The –d Flag 223

The –D Flag 223

The –b Flag 224

The – Flag 224

The interpreter Command 225

Exercises 232

10: Handling Multiple Processes *233*

The spawn_id Variable 233

Example—chess Versus chess 234

Example—Automating The write Command 237

How exp_continue Affects spawn_id 238

The Value Of spawn_id Affects Many Commands 238

Symbolic Spawn Ids 239

Job Control 240

Procedures Introduce New Scopes 241

How Expect Writes Variables In Different Scopes 243

Predefined Spawn Ids 245

Exercises 246

11: Handling Multiple Processes Simultaneously *247*

Implicit Versus Explicit Spawn Ids 247

Waiting From Multiple Processes Simultaneously 249

Example—Answerback 250

Which Pattern Goes With Which Spawn Id 252

Which Spawn Id Matched 253

Spawn Id Lists 254

Example—Connecting Together Two Users To An Application 255

Example—Timing All Commands 256

Matching Any Spawn Id Already Listed 259

The expect_before And expect_after Commands 259

Indirect Spawn Ids 268

Exercises 270

12: Send 271

Implicit Versus Explicit Spawn Ids 271
Sending To Multiple Processes 272
Sending Without Echoing 273
Sending To Programs In Cooked Mode 274
Sending Slowly 275
Sending Humanly 278
Sending Nulls 281
Sending Breaks 281
Sending Strings That Look Like Flags 282
Sending Character Graphics 283
Comparing send To puts 283
Exercises 285

13: Spawn 287

The Search Path 287
Philosophy—Processes Are Smart 288
Treating Files As Spawned Processes 289
Opening Ttys 290
Bugs And Workarounds 291
Process Pipelines And Ptys 291
Automating xterm 293
Checking For Errors From spawn 296
spawn –noecho 298
Example—unbuffer 299
Obtaining Console Output 300
Setting Pty Modes From spawn 300
Hung Ptys 302
Restrictions On Spawning Multiple Processes 303
Getting The Process Id From A Spawn Id 304
Using File I/O Commands On Spawned Processes 304
Exercises 305

14: Signals.. 307

Signals 307
Signals In Spawned Processes 310
Notes On Specific Signals 311
When And Where Signals Are Evaluated 318
Overriding The Original Return Value 320
Using A Different Interpreter To Process Signals 321
Exit Handling 321
Exercises 322

15: Interact 323

The interact Command 323
Simple Patterns 324
Exact Matching 327
Matching Patterns From The Spawned Process 328
Regular Expressions 328
What Happens To Things That Do Not Match 331
More Detail On Matching 332
Echoing 333
Avoiding Echoing 335
Giving Feedback Without –echo 335
Telling The User About New Features 336
Sending Characters While Pattern Matching 337
The continue And break Actions 339
The return Action 339
The Default Action 341
Detecting End-Of-File 342
Matching A Null Character 343
Timing Out 343
More On Terminal Modes (Or The –reset Flag) 344
Example—Preventing Bad Commands 346
Exercises 347

16: Interacting With Multiple Processes 349

Connecting To A Process Other Than The Currently Spawned Process 349
Connecting To A Process Instead Of The User 350

Example—rz And sz Over rlogin 351

Redirecting Input And Output 353

Default Input And Output 354

Controlling Multiple Processes—kibitz 355

Combining Multiple Inputs Or Outputs 358

Which Spawn Id Matched 359

Indirect Spawn Ids 359

An Extended Example—xkibitz 361

Exercises 369

17: Background Processing 371

Putting Expect In The Background 371

Running Expect Without A Controlling Terminal 372

Disconnecting The Controlling Terminal 373

The fork Command 374

The disconnect Command 375

Reconnecting 378

Using kibitz From Other Expect Scripts 380

Mailing From Expect 383

A Manager For Disconnected Processes—dislocate 384

Expect As A Daemon 392

Example—Automating Gopher And Mosaic telnet Connections 397

Exercises 401

18: Debugging Scripts 403

Tracing 403

Logging 404

Command Tracing 405

Variable Tracing 406

Example—Logging By Tracing 407

UNIX System Call Tracing 408

Tk And tkinspect 409

Traditional Debugging 410

Debugger Command Overview And Philosophy 412

Stepping Over Procedure Calls 413

Stepping Into Procedure Calls 415

Where Am I 416

The Current Scope 416

Moving Up And Down The Stack 417

Returning From A Procedure 418

Continuing Execution 418

Defining Breakpoints 419

Help 426

Changing Program Behavior 426

Changing Debugger Behavior 426

Exercises 428

19: Expect + Tk = Expectk 429

Tk—A Brief Technical Overview 430

Expectk 432

The send Command 433

An Extended Example—tkpasswd 434

Using Tk Widgets To Prompt For Passwords 444

The expect Command And The Tk Event Loop 445

The expect_background Command 446

Multiple Spawn Ids In expect_background 447

Background Actions 447

Example—A Dumb Terminal Emulator 447

Example—A Smarter Terminal Emulator 448

Using The Terminal Emulator For Testing And Automation 458

Exercises 462

20: Extended Examples 465

Encrypting A Directory 465

File Transfer Over telnet 467

You Have Unread News—tknewsbiff 475

Exercises 489

21: Expect, C, And C++ 491

Overview 492

Linking 493

Include Files 493

Ptys And Processes 494

Allocating Your Own Pty 498

Closing The Connection To The Spawned Process 499

Expect Commands 500

Regular Expression Patterns 502

Exact Matching 504

Matching A Null 504

What Characters Matched 504

When The Number Of Patterns Is Not Known In Advance 506

Expecting From Streams 507

Running In The Background 507

Handling Multiple Inputs And More On Timeouts 508

Output And Debugging Miscellany 509

Pty Trapping 510

Exercises 510

22: Expect As Just Another Tcl Extension............................513

Adding Expect To Another Tcl-based Program 513

Differences Between Expect And The Expect Extension In Another Program 515

Adding Extensions To Expect 516

Adding Extensions To Expectk 517

Creating Scriptless Expect Programs 518

Functions And Variables In The Expect Extension 518

Exercises 522

23: Miscellaneous...523

Random Numbers 523

Example—Generating Random Passwords 524

The Expect Library 526

Expect Versions 527

Timestamps 528

The time Command 529

Exercises 530

Appendix — Commands and Variables.................................531

Commands And Flags 531

Variables 535

Index Of Scripts 537

Index 541

In The Preface:
- *About This Book*
- *The Origin And Early Days Of Expect*
- *Acknowledgments*

Preface

This book is a tutorial for Expect, a software suite for automating interactive tools.

Expect has turned out to be very popular. This is good and bad. It's good because people are able to do things more easily than before and in some cases do things that they would never have even tried. Expect is not simply another language. It is a completely new type of tool that addresses problems that were not even recognized as problems in the past.

The bad news is that since writing Expect, I've been plagued by people asking me questions about it. While it was not originally intended to be a rich or complex piece of software, it has admittedly become more sophisticated as various features have been added. But more importantly, the nature of automating interactive programs involves dealing with issues that are quite unlike the issues involved in traditional programming.

While Expect comes with a "man page" (which is quite a misnomer at 25 pages), I continue to get requests for information that does not properly belong there. Often the requests are for examples. Sometimes they are simply for advice. This book is an attempt to write down all of these things *and* to describe everything in the man page in a tutorial fashion.

This book draws upon the thousands of Expect applications that people have described to me, the common and not-so-common problems that people have discussed with me—and explanations of the limitations—what you can't do with Expect.

I pull no punches. Expect is not meant to do everything for everyone, and I am quite frank about discussing its limitations. While some may represent my own limitations, others mirror my beliefs about how UNIX should work rather than what can be accomplished. Indeed, I have resisted requests for enhancements that do not add anything specifically useful to the original intent of Expect or that can already be done more easily by another program. Expect is not yet-another kitchen-sink language.

I am convinced[†] that Expect is very easy to use for the majority of applications that users put it to. And I am convinced that many people can learn to do useful Expect scripting in an hour or two.

Nevertheless, I recognize that the language is substantial. Using it is one thing. Mastering it is quite another. Just reading through the 500+ pages in this book may be an onerous task for some. However, as I said above, I believe that much of the reason for the length of this book is due to the unique nature of automating interactive programs. No matter how you accomplish it—whether using Expect, a commercial product, or a home-grown set of kludges—automating interactive programs is a task that is full of surprises. And while the examples in this book are specific to Expect, the knowledge you gain from them can be taken and applied to other interaction automation tools.

Indeed, Expect represents only the tip of the iceberg in the field of interactive automation. Already, GUI automators are on the market. Eventually, hypermedia automators will make their debut, combining simulations of human voice, images, and all sorts of other sensory data.

Expect—Why Another Tool?

I initially did not view Expect as something that would last very long. It struck me as solving a very simple problem but not in the best way possible. Indeed, I originally wrote Expect as an experiment to demonstrate the need for a general way of handling interaction automation. I expected that, having shown the utility of it, the popular shells of the day would all soon incorporate these functions, allowing Expect-like things to be accomplished from the shells without requiring the use of another tool.

But to my surprise that has not been the case. Some shells (e.g., Korn shell, Z shell) provide co-processes but offer no access to pseudo-terminals and no in-line stream pattern matching. Most shells don't even provide co-processes. Thus, Expect remains very important to shell programmers.

Expect is also useful with environments that have limited or baffling Expect-like functions. For example, Emacs, a popular editor, has actually had the ability to do Expect-like processing for years. However, Emacs is a fairly unusual programming environment and few people do real Emacs programming. Perl is another unusual programming environment, again, with its own Expect-like functionality; however, the implementation is

---

† Meaning that I have no proof.

difficult to use and many Perl programmers find it easier to call Expect scripts for these tasks. Perl is also a large language, which makes its use for Expect-like programming all the more formidable for the casual user.[†]

By comparison, Expect is simple. It really only does one thing. But it does it very well. Everything in Expect is optimized to help you automate interactive programs.

That doesn't mean it can't do other things. These other things simply aren't the focus of Expect. But you can use Expect to work with non-interactive applications. Expect rests on top of Tcl which provides a very pleasant environment in which to work. I have implemented and used a number of complex software packages that use Tcl as a scripting language, and I look forward to using any other application that does similarly.

Tcl — A Little History

Underneath Expect is Tcl, a small and simple language designed to be embedded in applications. Much of the reason Expect appears so coherent and well thought out is actually due to Tcl.

Tcl is a tour de force. It is powerful yet elegant, drawing a fine line between primitives and extensibility, and between simplicity and overkill. Tcl allowed *me* to concentrate on the application requirements of Expect. Tcl will allow *you* to call and mix the Expect primitives in all sorts of interesting ways to control your applications.

The intent behind Tcl matches Expect's philosophy perfectly. Expect doesn't need a specialized language. Any generic but extensible control language would have sufficed. However, at the time that I was thinking about writing Expect, no such extensible control language existed. I was irritated at the thought of having to create a language specifically for such a simple application. There was simply no justification for designing yet another language.

I had been thinking about writing an Expect-like program after helping Scott Paisley write a program to automate the initial login and command in a telnet session. The program understood only a few simple commands. For instance, `find` waited for a single fixed string to arrive. Every session ended in a permanent sort of `interact` with a single telnet process. There were no variables and no flow control commands such as `if`. And the program used pipes instead of ptys. The program solved our immediate problem, but it had a lot of special-case coding and I thought it could be generalized. This was in 1987.

---

† Although *Exploring Expect* is based on Tcl, programmers attempting to automate interactive programs using Emacs, Perl, Python, Scheme, C, or any other tool will find this book helpful because many of the concepts underlying Expect-like programming are common to all of those tools.

For a long time I considered borrowing a shell, integrating the Expect primitives into it, and then re-releasing it. However, shells are not intended to be used this way and I did not have any interest in maintaining a shell once I had stuck my hands in it. At that time, shells were renowned for being messy beasts. For example, the C shell was well known for not having consistent and robust parsing. And the Bourne shell had stimulated the Obfuscated C Code Contest—a contest that actually celebrates and revels in torturous code. I wanted something else.

I was fortunate to be able to attend the 1990 Winter USENIX Conference in Washington DC (January 22-26). I had been thinking about writing something like Expect for several years, and I decided to go there and ask some wizards about what they did for portable language facilities. To my delight, there was a talk at the conference addressing that very topic.

John Ousterhout, a professor at the University of California at Berkeley, had designed a language for embedding into applications—my very need! By the middle of the talk, I knew I wanted to try using it. At the end of talk, when he said it was freely available, I swooned.

Four days later, I had a copy of Tcl. I couldn't believe it. It was not only everything John had promised, it was also easy to use and well documented. By February 7 (eight days after first downloading Tcl), I had a working, albeit primitive, Expect. It had the core of what Expect has today: `send`, `expect`, `spawn`, `interact`, plus a logging function. At that time, the compiled Tcl code was about 48K, while Expect added on another 12K. The idea of a control language being larger than the application seemed peculiar, but it worked too well to go back to the old ways of designing ad hoc interfaces.

Even with minimal functionality, it clearly suggested some interesting uses and I thought that it might be nice to inform others. I had a USENIX Call-For-Papers hanging next to my workstation. It said:

> *The final deadline for receipt of submissions is February 7, 1990.*
> *Abstracts received after this deadline will not be considered.*

It was February 8, one day after the deadline. I sat down, banged out the requested extended abstract, and sent it in on the 9th.[†] It was accepted with top marks by all the referees and appeared at the very next conference. No person was more astonished by this rapid publication describing a Tcl-based application than John. (John published

---

† The abstract was finished in a couple of hours, but I delayed a day to contemplate several different names for the software. While "Expect" has worked out well, another leading contender was "Sex" (for either "Super Exec" or "Send-Expect") which was obviously much more memorable—a key factor for audience attendance in a multi-track conference—plus "intercourse with other programs" seemed reasonably descriptive of what the software did.

another Tcl-related paper at the 1991 Winter USENIX Conference—leading to Tcl papers at three consecutive USENIX conferences and a high profile very early in its life.)

During 1990 and 1991, my local ftp server distributed over 2500 copies of Tcl, all for the purpose of running Expect. I like to think that Expect was a catalyst in the success of Tcl, but even without Expect, Tcl would have caught on eventually. Tcl is now used by thousands of applications and millions of users. Some of the Tcl extensions (Tk, in particular) stand on their own, and like Expect, allow people to do things more easily than before and in many cases things that they would never even have tried.

Since writing Expect, I've used Tcl to build several other applications and extensions. While none of them are as general purpose as Expect, the results are wonderful. Even for building specialized tools, Tcl is a joy to work with. I hope never to go back to yacc and lex again.

While the focus here is Expect, not Tcl, I believe that this book is worth reading even if you are learning Tcl for other reasons—perhaps contemplating putting it to use in your own applications. Expect is a good example of what can be accomplished with Tcl. Plus there are many techniques—such as the debugger and the signal handler—that while invented for Expect, can be applied to just about any other Tcl application. By reusing my efforts (and in some cases, avoiding my mistakes), it will be that much easier when designing your own Tcl-based applications.

Acknowledgments

I owe a large amount to the many people that used Expect and gave me excellent feedback. There are literally hundreds of people who made contributions. Many suggestions, although cavalierly made, developed into important aspects of Expect. Some people donated sizable chunks of code while yet others debated with me on philosophical aspects.

Thanks to Scott Paisley who initially sowed the seeds for the idea and then ended up listening to me rave on about it for several years before I took any action. Scott also wrote the dialback script that appears in Chapter 1 (p. 4).

I would also like to thank (in no particular order) John Conti, Mike Gourlay, Frank Terhaar-Yonkers, Jerry Friesen, Brian Fitzgerald, Mark Diekhans, Kevin Kenny, Rob Nagler, Terrence Brannon, Ken Manheimer, Steve Clark, Keith Eberhardt, Brian Woodson, Pete Termaat, Sandy Ressler, Hal Peterson, Mike O'Dell, Steve Legowik, Scott Hess, David Vezie, Adrian Mariano, Keith Hanlan, Rick Lyons, Jeff Okamoto, Tom Tromey, Phil Shepherd, Michael Grant, Bob Proulx, Marty Leisner, Ting Leung, Karl Lehenbauer, Przemek Klosowski, Bill Tierney, Steve Summit, Rainer Wilcke, Alon Albert, Jay Schmidgall, Corey Satten, Konrad Haedener, Tor Lillqvist, Pasi Kaara, Kartik

Subbarao, Steve Ray, Karl Vogel, Seth Perlman, Dave Mielke, Brian Bebeau, Bob Bagwill, Dan Bernstein, Pascal Meheut, Rusty Wilson, Jonathan Kamens, Bill Houle, Todd Richmond, Mark Weissman, Chris Matheus, Lou Salkind, Bud Bach, R.K. Lloyd, Chip Rosenthal, david d 'zoo' zuhn, John Rouillard, Steven Diamond, Bert Robben, Rick Cady, Enzo Michelangeli, Josef Sachs, Stephen Fitzpatrick, and numerous others whose names litter my log books and change files. Of special note are Rob Savoye, who automated the Expect configuration procedure; the people who wrote Autoconf on which Rob's work rests; Henry Spencer, who wrote the regular expression engine used by Expect and Tcl; and Arnold Robbins, who wrote the POSIX date formatter.

And thanks to John Ousterhout for Tcl and for Tk. It is difficult to describe the amount of work that he has put into making them possible, making them so usable, and then making them freely available. John is a renaissance computer scientist. He programs with great style—his code is a pleasure to read, and it is documented in a thoughtful and readable fashion. Tcl is a great accomplishment, yet it is only one of many for John. John is a continuing source of excellent ideas followed up by gargantuan amounts of effort.

A significant amount of support for the development of Expect was provided by the National Institute of Standards and Technology (NIST). The development of Expect fit in well with the charter of NIST, an agency of the U.S. Department of Commerce, whose goal is, after all, to promote commerce and assist industry in the development of technology. Even though Expect was never specifically funded as a separate project at NIST, I was permitted to work on Expect to the extent that it directly aided projects at NIST because it kept solving problems that would crop up. Thanks to Cita Furlani, Selden Stewart, Jeane Ford, and Howard Bloom for allowing the flexibility and freedom in the technical work to explore Expect.

Much of the funding for Expect actually came out of my own pocket. But the person who really paid the steepest price is Susan Mulroney. She has been especially patient ("Isn't that thing done yet?!"), allowing me to give up lots of quality time ("Please come home, the toilet is overflowing!") even after I decided the software wasn't enough and I had to write a book on it. ("What? Another book!?") Even worse, she has to put up with my sense of humor.

Writing a book is no simple task. Getting permission from the government alone took eleven months. (Getting permission for the previous sentence took three of them.) With a full-time job in the way (and fixing bugs, making enhancements, and answering everyone's questions—all after hours), the writing took another two years. This was also delayed by changes in Tcl, Tk, and Expect themselves.

The secret to successful writing is getting the most dedicated, anal, and brutally honest reviewers. My readers nitpicked the manuscript to death, pointing out flaws and incorrect or missing reasoning or explanations. I thank the readers for finding all these problems and keeping me on my toes. Thanks to W. Richard Stevens, Henry Spencer, Brian Kernighan, Gerard Holzmann, Thomas Accardo, Bennett Todd, Miguel Angel Bayona, Tim O Reilly, Frank Willison, Brent Welch (now writing a Tcl book of his own!), Danny Faught, Paul Kinzelman, Barry Johnston, Rob Huebner, Todd Bradfute, David Dodd, Will Morse, Thomas Brown, Sam Shen, Adrian Mariano, Ken Lunde, Marc Rovner, Jeffrey Friedl, David Rosenfeld, Stavros Macrakis, Jeremy Mathers, Larry Virden, Keith Neufeld, Nelson Beebe, and Jeff Moore. Thanks also to Lennie, Sol, and Susan Libes for proofreading yet another manuscript, evidently under the belief that due to a freak biological accident many years ago, they are guaranteed the right to be my critics forever. Due to a more recent biological event, I must also thank Sue Baughman and Lenore Mulroney for babysitting the Kenna.

Finally, thanks to Sheryl Avruch, Frank Willison, and Clairemarie Fisher O Leary for production help, Edie Freedman for typography advice as well as a most appropriate and appealing cover, Tanya Herlick and Jessica Perry Hekman for system administration, Brian Erwin and Linda Walsh for creative and inspired sales and marketing (yes, they do more than make t-shirts), Seth Maislin for copyediting, Mike Sierra for FrameMaker assistance, Jennifer Niederst for Nutshell design standards, Michael Kalantarian and Celinda Bormeth for numerous sordid little details, and Tim O Reilly, who listened patiently to all my questions and solved them with wisdom and common sense.

We'd Like to Hear From You

We have tested and verified all of the information in this book to the best of our ability, but you may find that features have changed (or even that we have made mistakes!). Please let us know about any errors you find, as well as your suggestions for future editions, by writing:

O'Reilly & Associates, Inc.
101 Morris Street
Sebastopol, CA 95472
1-800-998-9938 (in the U.S. or Canada)
1-707-829-0515 (international/local)
1-707-829-0104 (FAX)

You can also send us messages electronically. To be put on the mailing list or request a catalog, send email to:

nuts@oreilly.com

To ask technical questions or comment on the book, send email to:

bookquestions@oreilly.com

How To Read This Book

This book can be read from front to back. Each chapter flows naturally into the next, and examples in each chapter only use the concepts that have been introduced up to that point. Of course, you can skip chapters or jump around if you like. But I recommend you come back and read everything eventually. This book is chock-full of examples—and they are really worth seeing. To further stimulate you, exercises at the end of each chapter hint at additional thoughts and applications.

Expect draws together a lot of concepts from different programs and even different operating systems. For this reason it is likely that you are familiar with some pieces but not others. The book is laid out so that it is easy to skip things with which you are already familiar. The Preface provides mostly historical notes, setting the scene for Expect and describing how it came into existence. This is not critical to the use of Expect but it makes interesting reading. You may want to read it later.

Chapter 1 is an overview of Expect, giving a taste of what it can do, why it is worth your attention, who uses it, and how it fits into the world. If you know little or nothing about Expect and would like to quickly know what it is all about, read this chapter rather than flipping through the book.

Chapter 2 is an overview of Tcl, the language that Expect uses. Tcl is used by many other software packages so you may already know it—I encourage you to read Chapter 2 anyway. Even if you know Tcl already, you will find that aspects of the language that Expect relies upon are different than in other Tcl tools. Chapter 2 emphasizes these aspects and at the same time puts the rest of Tcl into a consistent framework so that it all fits together.

After Chapter 2 comes the meat of the book—chapters that focus on different parts of Expect starting with automating simple interactions and ending with sophisticated and complex applications that use multiple processes and graphic front-ends. The chapter names are suggestive of the main concepts covered in each chapter; however, all of the chapters include many other concepts that are easier to explain in the context of the chapters they are in. This makes the titles a little less helpful, but the Extended Table Of Contents lists all of the concept headings of each chapter.

Near the end of the book are several chapters on subjects that may not be of interest to everyone. For instance, one such chapter is how to use Expect with Tk; another is how to use Expect from C or C++ (without Tcl). There is also a chapter on embedding Expect in with your own Tcl extensions. That particular chapter assumes that you have read the Tcl reference documentation on the C interface.

The last chapter contains some topics that did not deserve their own chapters nor did they fit in any others. The concepts there are not that important but may be useful nonetheless.

I believe strongly in thorough indexes and there are two in this book so that you can find any item even if it is not in the Extended Table of Contents. The general index cross-references all concepts, commands, examples, and figures. Many of the examples in the book are interesting in their own right and you will want to use them as tools on their own. In order to find your way back to them, another index lists the substantive examples. Most of these are also available in machine-readable form with the Expect distribution itself. I will describe how to obtain the distribution in Chapter 1 (p. 16).

There is also an appendix that contains a list of all of the Expect commands and variables. Each entry has a brief description and a page number back to the body of the book where you can get the full explanation. I recommend you turn to page 531 and dog-ear it right now!

Most of the chapters are heavily illustrated with code fragments. Code-reading is essential to see how things look in context. And the more code to which you are exposed, the more ideas you can learn. It is also important to see larger pieces of code, and I have provided several significantly bigger programs in chapters towards the rear of the book. Unlike most programs found in the Tcl archives, the ones in this book are extensively and carefully described.

Finally, a gentle warning before you start reading—this book describes how to use Expect, but it is not a reference manual. While terse and lacking in background and examples, the man page that comes with the Expect software is always the latest and most accurate documentation. If Expect changes, it will be reflected there.

Notational Conventions

Body text is set in ITC Garamond Light. Terms being defined or emphasized are *italicized*. Parameterized input or output (i.e., rm *filename*) appears as *Courier Italic*.

`Courier` is used for source code, files, hostnames, literal I/O, or anything that is computer input or output. Characters typed by a person are in **`Courier Bold`**. Due to the nature of Expect, it may sometimes appear that a person has typed something when in reality it was typed by Expect. Thus, the boldness of the font will be helpful in these otherwise misleading situations.

Straight quotes (` or " or ') are used when they are literally part of the characters or strings. Curly quotes ("") are occasionally used to distinguish literal text from the surrounding text or nearby punctuation if it might not otherwise be obvious (or for consistency with other strings in the same sentence).

Inter-chapter references such as "Chapter 1 (p. 19)" include page numbers describing exactly where in the chapter the referenced topic appears. In this example, the discussion of Expect and Tcl resources appears in the first chapter and the discussion itself begins on page 19.

Exercises

At the end of each chapter are exercises. These exercises are well worth reading—*even if you do not do them*. The exercises are not of the form "now repeat the examples shown but with slightly changed parameters". You do not need busy work. You want to apply Expect immediately to your problems.

Instead, the exercises are deliberately meant to be thought provoking. Many of them suggest entirely different ideas than the examples elsewhere in the book. One of the problems with a tool like Expect is that it is *so* different, it is hard to recognize certain things are possible without actually being told or seeing an example.

Alas, without making the book significantly bigger, there was a limit to the examples I could include. Rather than devoting another two or three pages to explaining each one (or saying "you can do XYZ but I don't have the space to explain it"), I have left them as exercises. All of them are possible with Expect.

Again, do not approach the exercises as lessons to be done. Rather, think about them and use them as stimulation for discovering other problems you can solve. Together, the examples and exercises in this book are only a tiny fraction of what you can do with Expect.

In This Chapter:
- *What Expect Does And Does Not Do*
- *Simple Examples*
- *Who Uses Expect And How*
- *How to Get Expect*
- *How Expect Fits Into UNIX And Other Operating Systems*

1

Introduction — What Is Expect?

Expect is a program to control interactive applications. These applications interactively prompt and expect a user to enter keystrokes in response. By using Expect, you can write simple scripts to automate these interactions. And using automated interactive programs, you will be able to solve problems that you never would have even considered before.

Expect can save you hours of drudgery, and this book will start you on your way. This first chapter is an overview of Expect. I will describe some simple applications and present some short scripts. However, *the explanations are not intended to be complete* but rather to whet your appetite and give you a taste of the good things to come. In the following chapters, I will revisit all of the concepts mentioned in this chapter and cover them in more detail.

Ouch, Those Programs Are Painful!

fsck, the UNIX file system check program, can be run from a shell script only with the −y or −n options. The manual defines the −y option as follows:

> *Assume a yes response to all questions asked by fsck; this should be used with extreme caution, as it is a free license to continue, even after severe problems are encountered.*

The −n option is safer, but almost uselessly so. This kind of interface is inexcusably bad, yet many programs have the same style. ftp, a file transfer program, has an option that disables interactive prompting so that it can be run from a script. But it provides no way to take alternative action should an error occur.

Expect is a tool for controlling interactive programs. It solves the `fsck` problem, providing all the interactive functionality non-interactively. Expect is not specifically designed for `fsck` and can handle errors from `ftp` as well.

The problems with `fsck` and `ftp` illustrate a major limitation in the user interface offered by shells such as `sh`, `csh`, and others (which I will generically refer to as "the shell" from now on). The shell does not provide a way of reading output from and writing input to a program. This means the shell can run `fsck`, but only by missing out on some of its useful features. Some programs cannot be run at all from a shell script. For example, `passwd` cannot be run without a user interactively supplying the input. Similar programs that cannot be automated in a shell script are `telnet`, `crypt`, `su`, `rlogin`, and `gdb`. A large number of application programs are written with the same fault of demanding user input.

Expect was designed specifically to interact with *interactive* programs. An Expect programmer can write a script describing the dialogue. Then the Expect program can run the "interactive" program non-interactively. Expect can also be used to automate only parts of a dialogue, since control can be passed from the script to the keyboard and vice versa. This allows a script to do the drudgery and a user to do the fun stuff.

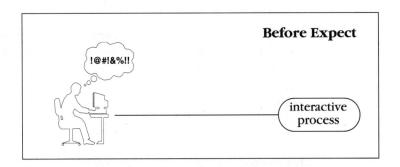

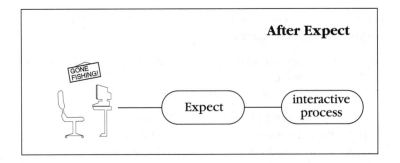

A Very Brief Overview

Expect programs can be written in C or C++, but are almost always written using Tcl.[†]
Tcl is an interpreted language that is widely used in many other applications. If you
already use a Tcl-based application, you will not have to learn a new language for
Expect.

Tcl is a very typical-looking shell-like language. There are commands to set variables
(set), control flow (if, while, foreach, etc.), and perform the usual math and string
operations. Of course, UNIX programs can be called (exec). I will provide a quick
introduction to the language in Chapter 2 (p. 23).

Expect is integrated on top of Tcl and provides additional commands for interacting
with programs. Expect is named after the specific command that waits for output from a
program. The expect command is the heart of the Expect program. The expect
command describes a list of patterns to watch for. Each pattern is followed by an
action. If the pattern is found, the action is executed.

For example, the following fragment is from a script that involves a login. When
executed, the script waits for the strings "welcome", "failed", or "busy", and then it
evaluates one of the corresponding actions. The action associated with busy shows
how multiple commands can be evaluated. The timeout keyword is a special pattern
that matches if no other pattern matches in a certain amount of time.

```
expect {
    "welcome" break
    "failed"  abort
    timeout   abort
    "busy" {
        puts "busy"
        continue
    }
}
```

A First Script — dialback

It is surprising how little scripting is necessary to produce something useful. Below is a
script that dials a phone. It is used to reverse the charges so that long-distance phone
calls are charged to the computer. It is invoked with the phone number as its argument.

---

† Tcl is pronounced "tickle". Some people are uncomfortable using this particular word in a formal setting. In
that case, I recommend either saying the letters (i.e., "tee cee ell") or coming up with a name suitable to your
audience (e.g., "macho stud language"). Whatever works for you.

```
spawn tip modem
expect "connected"
send "ATD$argv\r"
# modem takes a while to connect
set timeout 60
expect "CONNECT"
```

The first line runs the `tip` program so that the output of a modem can be read by `expect` and its input written by `send`. Once `tip` says it is connected, the modem is told to dial using the command `ATD` followed by the phone number. The phone number is retrieved from `argv`, which is a variable predefined to contain the original argument with which the script was called.

The fourth line is just a comment noting that the variable being set in the next line controls how long `expect` will wait before giving up. At this point, the script waits for the call to complete. No matter what happens, `expect` terminates. If the call succeeds, the system detects that a user is connected and prompts with "`login:`".

Actual scripts do more error checking, of course. For example, the script could retry if the call fails. But the point here is that it does not take much code to produce useful scripts. This six-line script replaced a 60Kb executable (written in C) that did the same thing!

In Chapter 16 (p. 351), I will talk more about the dialback concept and show a different way to do it.

Total Automation

Earlier I mentioned some programs that cannot be automated with the shell. It is difficult to imagine why you might even want to embed some of these programs in shell scripts. Certainly the original authors of the programs did not conceive of this need. As an example, consider `passwd`.

`passwd` is the command to change a password. The `passwd` program does not take the new password from the command line. Instead, it interactively prompts for it—twice. Here is what it looks like when run by a system administrator. (When run by users, the interaction is slightly more complex because they are prompted for their old passwords as well.)

```
# passwd libes
Changing password for libes on thunder.
New password:
Retype new password:
```

This is fine for a single password. But suppose you have accounts of your own on a number of unrelated computers and you would like them all to have the same password. Or suppose you are a system administrator establishing 1000 accounts at the beginning of each semester. All of a sudden, an automated `passwd` makes a lot of sense. Here is an Expect script to do just that—automate `passwd` so that it can be called from a shell script.

```
spawn passwd [lindex $argv 0]
set password [lindex $argv 1]
expect "password:"
send "$password\r"
expect "password:"
send "$password\r"
expect eof
```

The first line starts the `passwd` program with the username passed as an argument. The next line saves the password in a variable for convenience. As in shell scripts, variables do not have to be declared in advance.

In the third line, the `expect` command looks for the pattern "`password:`". `expect` waits until the pattern is found before continuing.

After receiving the prompt, the next line sends a password to the current process. The `\r` indicates a carriage-return. (Most of the usual C string conventions are supported.) There are two `expect–send` sequences because `passwd` asks the password to be typed twice as a spelling verification. There is no point to this in a non-interactive `passwd`, but the script has to do it because `passwd` assumes it is interacting with a human who does not type consistently.

The final command "`expect  eof`" causes the script to wait for the end-of-file in the output of `passwd`. Similar to `timeout`, `eof` is another keyword pattern. This final `expect` effectively waits for `passwd` to complete execution before returning control to the script.

Take a step back for a moment. Consider that this problem could be solved in a different way. You could edit the source to `passwd` (should you be so lucky as to have it) and modify it so that given an optional flag, it reads its arguments from the command line just the way that the Expect script does. If you lack the source and have to write `passwd` from scratch, of course, then you will have to worry about how to encrypt passwords, lock and write the password database, etc. In fact, even if you only modify the existing code, you may find it surprisingly complicated code to look at. The `passwd` program does some very tricky things. If you do get it to work, pray that nothing changes when your system is upgraded. If the vendor adds NIS, Kerberos, shadow passwords, a different encryption function, or some other new feature, you will have to revisit the code.

Testing

Despite all the reasons against it, suppose you decide to make changes to the passwd source anyway. After recompiling, it is a good idea to test your changes, right? You want to make sure passwd operates correctly when used interactively. Oh, but you cannot test the old interactive half of your new passwd program in a simple shell script—that is the whole reason you modified it in the first place!

This idea of testing interactive programs for correct behavior is another reason why Expect is useful. Even if you never want to automate a program, you may want to test it. passwd is just one example. Your own programs are another. Suppose you write a program that responds immediately to each command or keystroke. You cannot test it simply by piping a file of commands at it. It may discard characters that arrive before they are wanted, it may want a terminal in raw mode, it may want keystrokes such as ^C to activate signals, or you may need to see its responses in order to know how to phrase each subsequent command.

For example, suppose you are writing a debugger. The debugger may lay out a program in memory differently each time the program is recompiled, but the debugger should otherwise function the same (apart from any bugs you are fixing). If you are trying to verify that the debugger correctly handles the symbol table, you might ask for the value of all variables, verifying that each value is the same whether asked by memory address or variable name.

There is no way to embed the commands in a script because the script itself must change each time as elements are laid down in memory differently. For example, gdb, the GNU debugger, accepts the command "print &var" to print the address of var. Here is what an interaction might look like.

```
(gdb) print &var
$1 = (int *) 0xe008
```

In response, gdb numbers the output and then prints an equal sign followed by the type and value. It is possible for Expect to ask for and then print the type and value with the following code:

```
send "print &var\r"
expect "0x*\r" {
    send_user "$expect_out(0,string)\n"
}
```

The pattern 0x*\r is a pattern that matches the output 0xe008 followed by a carriage return. The "*" in the pattern is a wildcard meaning "match anything". This is a convenient shortcut to specifying patterns. Later on, I will demonstrate how to be more precise in what you are asking for.

Following the pattern is an action—triggered when the pattern matches. Here the action is just one command, but it could be more than one, even including another `expect` command.

`send_user` sends the quoted string back to the user rather than to `gdb`. The `$` in the string indicates that a variable reference follows and that its value is to be substituted in the string. Specifically, the variable `expect_out` is an array that contains the results of the previous `expect`. In this case, the results are just what matched the beginning of the pattern "`0x*`" up to and including the return character.

Expect is useful for more than just testing a debugger. It can be used to test all of the same programs that it automates. For example, the script used to automate `passwd` can be extended to test it, checking `passwd` with regard to improper passwords, unusually slow response, signals, and other sorts of problematic behavior.

Differing Behavior When Running Non-Interactively

Some programs behave differently when run interactively and non-interactively, and they do so intentionally. For example, most programs prompt only when running interactively. Non-interactively, prompting is not needed.

A more serious problem occurs when dealing with programs that change the way they buffer output depending on whether they are running interactively or not. Programs using the standard I/O library provided by UNIX automatically buffer their output when running non-interactively. This causes problems when you need to see the output immediately. Expect can make the programs think they are running interactively, thereby resolving the buffering problem.

As another example, shells force the user to press control characters (^Z, ^C) and keywords (`fg`, `bg`) to switch jobs. These cannot be used from shell scripts. Similarly, the shell running non-interactively does not deal with history and other features designed solely for interactive use. This presents a similar problem as with `passwd` earlier. Namely, it is impossible to construct shell scripts which test certain shell behavior. The result is that these aspects of the shell will inevitably not be rigorously tested. Using Expect, it is possible to drive the shell using its interactive job control features. A spawned shell thinks it is running interactively and handles job control as usual.

Partial Automation

Expect's interact command turns control of a process over to you so that you can type directly to the process instead of through send commands.

Consider fsck, the UNIX program I mentioned earlier, which checks file system consistency. fsck provides almost no way of answering questions in advance. About all you can say is "answer everything yes" or "answer everything no".

The following fragment shows how a script can automatically answer some questions differently than others. The script begins by spawning fsck and then in a loop answering yes to one type of question and no to another. The \\ prevents the next character from being interpreted as a wildcard. In this example, the asterisk is a wild card but the question mark is not and matches a literal question mark.

```
while 1 {
    expect {
        eof                     {break}
        "UNREF FILE*CLEAR\\?"   {send "y\r"}
        "BAD INODE*FIX\\?"      {send "n\r"}
        "\\? "                  {interact +}
    }
}
```

The last question mark is a catch-all. If the script sees a question it does not understand, it executes the interact command, which passes control back to you. Your keystrokes go directly to fsck. When done, you can exit or return control to the script, here triggered by pressing the plus key. If you return control to the script, automated processing continues where it left off.

Without Expect, fsck can be run non-interactively only with very reduced functionality. It is barely programmable and yet it is the most critical of system administration tools. Many other tools have similarly deficient user interfaces. In fact, the large number of these is precisely what inspired the original development of Expect.

The interact command can be used to partially automate any program. Another popular use is for writing scripts that telnet through a number of hosts or front-ends, automatically handling protocols as encountered. When such a script finally reaches a point that you would like to take over, you can do so. For example, you could browse through remote library catalogs this way. Using Expect, scripts can make a number of different library systems seem like they are all connected rather than different and disconnected.

The interact command also provides arbitrarily complex macros. If you find yourself repeatedly typing out long names, you can create a short character sequence to type instead. A simple example is the following interact command, which sends the (meaningless but long and hard to type) string "set   def   qwk/term=vt100 yhoriz=200" when (the short and easy to type) "y2" is entered. This ability to abbreviate is useful when dealing with interactive programs that require you to enter the same gobbledegook over and over again.

```
interact {
    "y2" {send "set def qwk/term=vt100 yhoriz=200"}
    "~~d" {send [exec date]}
}
```

This fragment also sends the current date if you press "~~d". Arbitrary actions can be invoked, including other **expect** and **interact** commands. This example uses the **exec** command to run the UNIX **date** command.

Macros can be used in the other direction, too. If the program you are dealing with prints things out that you do not want to see or want to see but in a different way, you can change the appearance entirely.

Dangerous, Unfriendly, Or Otherwise Unlikable User Interfaces

The **interact** command is just a shorthand for the simplest and most common types of filtering that can be done in interactions. It is possible to build arbitrarily sophisticated mechanisms using the tools in Expect.

For example, commands can be filtered out of interfaces to prevent users from entering commands that you would prefer they not enter. Programs can also be wrapped even more tightly. The **adb** program, for instance, can crash a UNIX system with a slip of the finger or, more likely, inexperience. You can prevent this from happening by securely wrapping the **adb** program in a script. Not only does this increase the safety of your system, but your system administrators no longer all have to be masters of its intricacies.

The UNIX **dump** program is another program with an unlikable interface. For example, **dump** often guesses incorrectly about the length of a tape and will prompt for a new tape even if one is not needed. An Expect script can be used to respond to **dump** so that it can continue automatically. A script can answer just this question or any question from **dump**.

Expect can, in general, be applied to interfaces that you simply do not like for whatever reason. For example, you might like to automate sequences of your favorite game, perhaps because you have long since mastered some of it and would like to practice the end game but without laboriously replaying the beginning each time.

It is possible to customize exactly how much of the underlying programs show through. You can even make interactions entirely invisible so that users do not have to be irritated by underlying programs that they have no interest in anyway. Their attitude is "Use any tool. Just get the job done." And they are right.

Graphical Applications

Expect can be combined with Tk, a toolkit for the X Window System. The combination of Expect and Tk is called Expectk.[†] Using Expectk, it is possible to take an existing interactive application and give it a Motif-like X interface without changing any of the underlying program. No recompiling is necessary, and because the underlying programs are not changed, there is no need to retest them again. All your efforts can be focused on the graphical user interface. Making it look pretty is all you have to do.

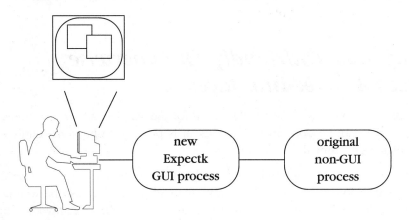

While Expectk will allow you to *build* X applications, it is limited in the amount it can *automate* existing X applications. Currently, Expect can automate `xterm` and other applications that specifically provide automation support, but Expect cannot automate any arbitrary X application.

Expect is also limited in its knowledge of character graphics such as is done by Curses. Nonetheless, with a little scripting, testing and automation of character graphics can be accomplished, and in Chapter 19 (p. 458), I will describe one way of doing this. Ultimately, I believe that Expect will do best with this capability built in rather than provided via scripts. However, the requirements and interfaces are not obvious, and further experimentation and design is required. ExpecTerm is an example implementa-

---

† Tk is pronounced "tee kay´". Expectk is pronounced "ek spec´ tee kay".

tion of a built-in character-graphic capability based on an earlier version of Expect. ExpecTerm is available from the Tcl archive (see page 20).

A Little More About Tcl

Expect's language is general-purpose. It has control structures and data structures so that you can do just about anything. This can make up for the lack of programmability in other programs. For example, most debuggers do not provide very sophisticated methods of programmed control. Typically, you cannot declare variables and are restricted to simple loops.

The core of Expect's language facilities are provided by Tcl, a language used by many other tools. "Tcl" stands for Tool Command Language. It comes as a library intended to be embedded in applications, providing a generic language facility to any application. Tcl solves a long-standing problem in designing application languages.

Actually, most tools do not have very sophisticated internal control languages. The shell represents the extreme—it has a very rich language and can even call upon other programs. Start-up scripts such as .cshrc and .profile can be very complex. Few programs have such flexibility. And that is just as well. Such programs each have their own language and it is daunting to master each new one.

In the middle of the spectrum are programs such as ftp that have a limited ad hoc language—such as permitted in the file .netrc—not very flexible but better than nothing. A lot of programs are designed like ftp—their languages are limited, not extensible, and different from one tool to the next.

At the far end are programs such as telnet which have no control language whatsoever. The bulk of all interactive programs are like ftp and telnet—severely lacking in programmability.

This lack of programmability is understandable. Consider writing an application that controls the printer. It is not worth writing a big language that requires a scanner, a parser, symbol table, etc. The application alone might only be 10Kb. However, it is impossible to predict what uses you might put your program to in the future. Suppose you get another printer. Then your program needs to understand this. Suppose you give your program to someone else and they have two printers but they are of two different types. Suppose they want to reserve one printer for printouts of a special kind for a day—printing checks on payday, for example. You can see that the possibilities are endless. So rather than customizing the application each time and extending the language as required (if you have not boxed yourself into a corner already), it makes sense to use a general-purpose language from the beginning.

Programs that already use Tcl are all set. They have a nice language from the outset. But many tools we are blessed with were written before Tcl existed. And most of them will not be rewritten. Development of most of these programs has stopped long ago (although for $$$ you can buy new versions). Fortunately, Expect allows you to layer Tcl on top of any interactive program without making any changes whatsoever to the original program. In effect, Expect makes nonprogrammable programs programmable.

Job Control

Just as you personally can interact with multiple programs at the same time, so can Expect. Analogous to the way you can say fg and bg to switch between processes in a shell, Expect can also switch its attention. Of course, Expect does it a lot more quickly than you can. The result is that Expect can act as "glue" for programs that were never designed to operate with other programs. An amusing example is the original chess program distributed with V7 and BSD UNIX written by Ken Thompson. It was designed to interact with a user—it prompts for moves and echoes user input in algebraic notation. Unfortunately, it does not accept its own output as input. Even if it did, there is no way to pipe both inputs and outputs between two processes simultaneously from the shell.

With a few lines of Expect, it is possible to make one chess process play another, including both the communication and the massaging of the output so that it is acceptable as input. I will show this in Chapter 10 (p. 233), along with some more serious uses for these techniques.

Background Processes

Expect is useful for automating processes in the background such as through cron. By using Expect with cron, you can not only automate the interactions but also automate starting the process in the first place. For example, you might want to copy over files each night between two networked but otherwise unrelated systems. And you can be arbitrarily selective about choosing files. You might want to copy over only executables that are less than 1 Mb and were created on a Saturday unless the current load exceeds 2.5 and the previous transfer took less than 5 seconds, or some other such complicated set of rules. There are no ftp clients that have such complex front-ends. But you can write Expect scripts to make whatever decisions seem appropriate while driving ftp.

It is even possible to have a cron process interactively contact you while it is in the background. For example, an ftp script may need a password to continue what it is doing. It can search the network for you and then ask you for it. Or you can have it look for a set of users. After getting the password, Expect will go back and use it to complete the task. By having Expect query for passwords, you do not need to embed them in scripts.

Doing backups from `cron` is another common reason to use Expect. If the backup program needs another tape, an Expect script can tell it to go on (for example, if your tapes are physically longer than the backup program thinks), or it can, again, contact you for assistance.

Using Expect With Other Programs

Most of the examples in this chapter use programs that are common to all UNIX systems. But Expect is not restricted to these programs. You can apply Expect to other programs. Even (gasp!) programs that *you* have written.

In the previous section, I described how you might automate `ftp`. But if you have a different program on your system to do file transfer, that's fine. Expect can use it. Expect does not have a built-in mechanism for file transfer, remote login, rebooting your colleague's workstation, or a million other useful things. Instead, Expect uses whatever local utilities you already have. This means that you do not have to learn a new file transfer protocol or a new host-to-host security system. If you use "`.rhosts`", then that is what Expect will use when it does remote host operations. If you use Kerberos, then Expect will use that. And so on.

Using Expect On UNIX

I have mentioned a number of UNIX programs that can be controlled by Expect. Expect can run any UNIX program, not just interactive ones. So you can invoke programs like `cat` or `ls` if you need them too.

Expect can do just about anything that any shell script can do. But that is not the point of Expect. Indeed, Expect scripts are meant to be small. By wrapping badly behaving programs with Expect scripts, you can use them from other scripting languages, such as the shell. The resulting scripts behave just like any UNIX program. Users have no way of knowing that the programs are just scripts.

Using Expect On Other Operating Systems

Expect makes use of a number of features that are present in all UNIX systems. The family of standards known as "POSIX" describes most but not all of these features. So while Expect can run on any UNIX system, it may have trouble providing all of its features on non-UNIX systems that nonetheless claim strict POSIX compliance. While

Expect works just fine on some non-UNIX POSIX systems and can work in a limited way on all POSIX systems, I prefer to be conservative in my claims, so I use the phrase "UNIX systems" when referring to the systems on which Expect runs.

Fortunately, Expect can be used to control other operating systems indirectly. Since Expect is capable of making network connections (through `telnet`, `rlogin`, `tip`, etc.), it can remotely contact other computers even while running on a UNIX computer. In this way, it is very common to use Expect scripts to control non-UNIX computers such as Lisp machines, PostScript printers, modems, pagers, etc.

Testing and setting modems and other network devices (routers, bridges, etc.) is a particularly popular use of Expect. It is possible to write scripts that regularly test sets of modems to make sure that they are functional and that previous users have not left them in a bad state. Such scripts can even simulate a real user—placing a phone call, connecting to a remote host, and even logging in. An Expect script can remember the port numbers and other trivia that users do not bother to note until they have scrolled off the screen. So if a line turns out to be faulty, the script can record this and other information to a log.

Using Expect In Real Applications

Expect is a real program used in real applications. In my own environment, my colleagues depend on many Expect scripts to do important and critical tasks. We also use Expect to whip up demos and to automate ad hoc programs.

I have already mentioned lots of other uses for Expect. Many more cannot be described without also going into detail about proprietary or one-of-a-kind programs that people are stuck with using every day. But I will mention some companies and examples of how each uses Expect to give you a warm fuzzy feeling that Expect is widely accepted.

3Com does software quality assurance with Expect. Silicon Graphics uses it to do network measurements such as echo response time using `telnet`. The World Bank uses it to automate file transfers and updates. IBM uses it as part of a tape backup production environment. HP uses it to automate queries to multiple heterogenous commercial online databases. Sun uses it to sweep across their in-house network testing computer security. Martin Marietta uses it to control and extract usage statistics from network routers. Tektronix uses it to test software simulations of test instruments. The National Cancer Institute uses it to administer accounts across multiple platforms. Cisco uses it for network control and testing. Xerox uses it for researcher collaboration. Motorola uses it to control and backup multiple commercial databases. Data General uses it for software quality engineering. The Baha'i World Centre uses it to automate and coordinate data collection and storage from different telephone exchange locations. Amdahl uses it to automatically retrieve stock prices. CenterLine Software uses it for software quality assurance. Encore Computer uses it to simulate 500 users logging into one system at the same time. AT&T uses it to copy files between internal hosts through a firewall to and from external Internet hosts. Sandia National Laboratories uses it to control unreliable processes that need to be watched constantly. Schlumberger uses it to manage a network environment including routers, repeaters, bridges, and terminal servers all from different manufacturers. ComputerVision built an automated testbed using it. This is just a fraction of some of the users and uses of Expect. The whole list is truly astonishing, and it continues to grow rapidly.

In addition to this list of internal applications, companies such as IBM, AT&T, and Data General have incorporated Expect into applications that they sell. One of the best known commercial products utilizing Expect is DejaGnu, written by Rob Savoye for Cygnus Support. DejaGnu is a software testing utility designed to simplify the running of large collections of regression tests. Using Tcl and Expect, DejaGnu provides a framework in which tests can be written, run, and analyzed quickly and easily. Due to the power of Expect, DejaGnu is capable of testing both interactive and non-interactive applications, including embedded applications and applications on other hosts to support cross-platform and remote target board development. Cygnus has created freely available DejaGnu test suites for the GNU C and C++ compiler, debugger, assembler, and binary utilities. These test suites can be used to test any similar program or port of such a program, whether it is freely available or proprietary. According to the Free Software Report, Vol. 3, No. 1, "Cygnus supports over 70 platform configurations of the GNU compilers fully tested by DejaGnu. DejaGnu executes 8000 test cases in 16,000,000 documented tests for a typical release."

Using Expect In Commercial Applications — Legalese

It is not necessary to license Expect. Most of Expect is in the public domain, but two parts of it have copyrights. The Tcl core and the regular expression engine inside Expect are copyrighted but otherwise freely available, allowing the software to be used for any purpose and without fee, and with few restrictions on the code other than maintaining the copyright internally. The full copyright notices follow:

documentation, even if the University of California has been advised of the possibility of such damage.

The University of California specifically disclaims any warranties, including, but not limited to, the implied warranties of merchantability and fitness for a particular purpose. The software provided hereunder is on an "as is" basis, and the University of California has no obligation to provide maintenance, support, updates, enhancements, or modifications.

Copyright (c) 1986 by University of Toronto.
Written by Henry Spencer. Not derived from licensed software.

Permission is granted to anyone to use this software for any purpose on any computer system, and to redistribute it freely, subject to the following restrictions:

1. The author is not responsible for the consequences of use of this software, no matter how awful, even if they arise from defects in it.

2. The origin of this software must not be misrepresented, either by explicit claim or by omission.

3. Altered versions must be plainly marked as such, and must not be misrepresented as being the original software.

The following notice is required on the NIST-authored portions of Expect:

This software was produced by the National Institute of Standards and Technology (NIST), an agency of the U.S. government, and by statute is not subject to copyright in the United States. Recipients of this software assume all responsibility associated with its operation, modification, maintenance, and subsequent redistribution.

So you can use Expect in other freely-redistributable or commercial packages. You can even use pieces of the code in other software products. Just don't blame the authors for any problems encountered with the software.

Obtaining Expect And The Examples

Expect may already be installed on your system, typically in /usr/local/bin. If you cannot find Expect, ask your system administrator. If you do not have a system administrator, you can obtain Expect by following the instructions below. Expect requires no special permissions to install, nor does it have to be installed in any particular place. You can even try it out in your own directory.

Expect includes a number of examples, several of which are useful as tools in their own right. Indeed, quite a few have man pages of their own and can be installed along with Expect. If the examples are not installed, you can find them in the example directory of the Expect distribution. Ask your local system administrator where the distribution is.

The examples provided with Expect are subject to change, but below is a list of just a few of the examples. The README file in the example directory contains a complete list as well as full explanations about each of the examples:

chess.exp	play one chess game against another
dislocate	allow disconnection from and reconnection to background processes
dvorak	emulate a Dvorak keyboard
ftp-rfc	retrieve an RFC from the Internet via anonymous ftp
kibitz	let several people control a program at the same time for remote assistance, group editing, etc.
lpunlock	unhang a printer waiting for a lock
mkpasswd	generate a good random password and optionally run passwd with it
passmass	set a password on many machines simultaneously
rftp	allow recursive get, put, and list from ftp
rlogin-cwd	rlogin with the same current working directory
rogue.exp	find a good game of rogue
timed-read	limit the amount of time a read from the shell can take
timed-run	limit the amount of time for which a program can run
tkpasswd	change passwords in a GUI
tknewsbiff	pop up a window (or play sounds, etc.) when news arrives in selected newsgroups
tkterm	emulate a terminal in a Tk text widget
unbuffer	disable output buffering that normally occurs when program output is redirected
weather	retrieve a weather forecast from the Internet

These and additional examples are available with the Expect distribution. The README file in the distribution also describes the location of the Expect archive which holds even more scripts. You can also contribute your own scripts to the archive. Particularly large or sophisticated applications (such as those which combine Expect with other extensions) can be found separately in the Tcl archive (see page 20).

There is a high probability that you already have Expect on your system. Expect is shipped by many vendors with their operating system utilities. Expect can also be found on many software distributions including GCT from Testing Foundations, USENET Software from UUNET, the Sun User Group CD-ROM, the Prime Time Freeware CD-ROM, the Lemis CD-ROM, and others. Even if you do not have one of these, some other user on your system may have already retrieved Expect from an Internet repository.

The entire Expect distribution can be obtained from many sites around the Internet. Your best bet to finding a nearby site is to use an Archie server. Archie maintains a data-base of thousands of computers across the Internet and what programs they are willing to supply. If you do not know how to use Archie, you can obtain instructions by sending email to `archie@archie.sura.net` with the word `help` as the contents of the message.[†]

As this book is being written, Archie reports at least one site in the following countries where Expect can be obtained:

Country	Internet site
Australia	`minnie.cs.adfa.oz.au`
Austria	`ftp.tu-graz.ac.at`
Canada	`julian.uwo.ca`
England	`unix.hensa.ac.uk`
France	`ftp.imag.fr`
Germany	`ftp.informatik.tu-muenchen.de`
Greece	`pythia.csi.forth.gr`
Ireland	`walton.maths.tcd.ie`
Israel	`cs.huji.ac.il`
Japan	`akiu.gw.tohoku.ac.jp`
Netherlands	`svin02.info.win.tue.nl`
Norway	`ftp.eunet.no`
Sweden	`ftp.sunet.se`
Switzerland	`ftp.switch.ch`
United States	`ftp.cme.nist.gov`

Currently, the site `ftp.cme.nist.gov` always contains the latest version of Expect (or a pointer to it). To retrieve it from there, you can use anonymous `ftp` or request auto-matic email delivery.

To get Expect from `ftp.cme.nist.gov` via `ftp`, retrieve the file `pub/expect/README`. This will tell you what other files you need to retrieve and what to do after that. Typically, you need a copy of Expect and a copy of Tcl. You may also want to get a copy of Tk. These can be found in the same directory as Expect.

---

† All hostnames and filenames in this chapter are subject to change.

If you are not directly on the Internet but can send mail, you can request email delivery of the files. Send a message to "`library@cme.nist.gov`". The message body should be:

```
send pub/expect/README
```

The site `ftp.smli.com` always contains the latest releases of Tcl and Tk. This site permits anonymous `ftp`. If you would like to request email from that site, any of the other sites listed above, or any other anonymous `ftp` sites, you can use an "ftp by mail" agent, such as the one provided by Digital Equipment's Western Research Laboratories. Complete instructions for using `ftp-mail` may be retrieved by emailing to `ftpmail@decwrl.dec.com`. The subject should be "`ftpmail`" and the message body should be "`help`".

Expect And Tcl Resources

This book contains a great deal of information about Expect and Tcl. Yet there are other resources that you may find useful. I will occasionally refer to some of these resources. The others are just for extra reading on your own.

Important Reading Material

The software for Expect, Tcl, and related packages include online manuals often called *man pages*. This is the definitive reference material. I will occasionally use the phrase *Tcl reference material*, for example, to refer to the Tcl man pages. As with most references, the reference material does not provide a lot of background or examples. Nevertheless, it is the most crucial documentation and therefore comes with the software itself.

I encourage you to use TkMan for reading man pages. Written by Tom Phelps at the University of California at Berkeley, TkMan provides an extremely pleasant GUI for browsing man pages. I cannot describe all the nice features of TkMan in this small space. Instead I will merely say that I now actually look forward to reading man pages as long as I can do it with TkMan. TkMan is written in Tcl and Tk and offers a splendid example of their power. Instructions on how to obtain TkMan can be found in the Tcl FAQ (see page 20).

Authoritatively written by the author of Tcl and Tk, John Ousterhout's *Tcl and the Tk Toolkit* (Addison-Wesley, 1994) is really four books in one, all written in a very readable and balanced style. Two of the books introduce Tcl and Tk. The other two describe how to write extensions for Tcl and Tk. If you find yourself writing many Expect scripts or becoming interested in applying Tcl to other projects, I strongly recommend you read this book.

Although Ousterhout's book does not cover all the features of Tcl and Tk, it nonetheless may be the place to turn for your questions left unanswered by *Exploring Expect.* For example, *Tcl and the Tk Toolkit* provide a more thorough treatment of some of the exotic features of Tcl. Ousterhout also provides a number of fascinating historical asides as well as some philosophical notes that contrast interestingly with my own.

Other Books

Software Solutions in C edited by Dale Schumacher (Academic Press, to appear) includes a chapter by Henry Spencer on the implementation of his regular expression pattern matcher which is used by Tcl and Expect. His explanation of how pattern matching is actually accomplished is lucid and fascinating. This book is intended for C programming experts, but it may provide additional insight on designing efficient patterns and otherwise using patterns effectively.

Practical Programming in Tcl and Tk by Brent Welch (Prentice Hall, 1995) focuses on the more useful parts of Tcl, Tk, and several important extensions. With his own perspective, Welch provides very good explanations of topics that have proven tricky to people even after reading Ousterhout's book. Welch also illustrates Tcl scripting and C programming issues by way of numerous program fragments, providing many building blocks that can be used in your own applications.

Other Online Documentation

The Tcl Frequently Asked Questions List (*FAQ*) contains many common questions and answers that somehow do not belong in either the manual pages or books. For example, the FAQ contains lists of Tcl extensions, documents, `ftp` sites, and of course common questions and answers. The FAQ was created by Larry Virden and is available from the Tcl archive on the Internet site `ftp.aud.alcatel.com` as `tcl/docs/tcl-faq.part`*XXX*, where *XXX* represents part numbers and file types. The file `Index` in the same directory lists the literal file names. The Tcl archive is maintained by Sam Kimery.

The Tcl FAQ can also be found on a number of other Internet sites. For example, it can be found on `rtfm.mit.edu`, which contains many other FAQs. The FAQ is also available through World Wide Web (WWW) as `http://www.cis.ohio-state.edu:80/hypertext/faq/usenet/tcl-faq/top.html`. The World Wide Web also provides access to other information on Tcl and Tk. The link `http://www.sco.com/IXI/of_interest/tcl/Tcl.html` contains links to other Tcl material with a focus on World Wide Web-related information such as browsers and HTML converters. Created by Mike Hopkirk, this link contains much other interesting and useful information as well. Another useful link is `http://web.cs.ualberta.ca/~wade/`

HyperTcl. Created by Wade Holst, this link concentrates on Tcl extensions. Included are a jobs database and an idea database. You can register ideas that you are working on and read what others are doing with Tcl. Many other Tcl-related WWW pages can be found in the Tcl FAQ.

A large number of scholarly papers on Expect and Tcl have appeared in journals and conference proceedings. These papers are not useful for people writing simple Expect scripts. Most of these papers are intended for computer scientists and cover topics such as implementation, performance, and comparisons to other methodologies. A Tcl bibliography is available on the Internet site `ftp.aud.alcatel.com` in the directory `tcl/docs`. The same directory contains other miscellaneous documents such as quick reference cards and essays on miscellaneous topics.

Support

A number of companies and individuals sell support for Tcl. These are described in the Tcl FAQ. Cygnus Support and Computerized Processes Unlimited sell support for Expect as well, and it is likely that other companies and individuals would also offer support if approached. This is not to mean that you will need support if you use Expect; however, it is not uncommon to find that management requires software be commercially supported before it is acceptable. As an aside, it may well be cost effective to have a professional support service solve your problems for you. Support can include modifications at your request, round-the-clock consulting by phone, site visits, and other services.

> Cygnus Support
> 1937 Landings Drive
> Mountain View, CA 94043
> +1 (415) 903-1400
> `info@cygnus.com`

> Computerized Processes Unlimited
> 4200 S. I-10 Service Rd., Suite 205
> Metairie, LA 70006
> +1 (504) 889-2784
> `info@cpu.com`

Many questions can be also be answered with the help of the Usenet newsgroup `comp.lang.tcl`. This newsgroup contains announcements for new releases of Tcl and Tcl extensions. The newsgroup is the right place to post bug reports, fixes, observations, and, of course, humor. Many of the people who read it are experts at Tcl and Expect, and they will answer questions. Simple questions that can be found in a book or the FAQ are discouraged. But challenging problems or requests for advice are welcomed.

The `comp.lang.tcl` newsgroup can be subscribed to by mail. In addition, there are dozens of mailing lists on particular extensions and aspects of Tcl. All of these are documented in the FAQ.

Exercises

1. Using `.netrc` or `<<` redirection in a shell script, have `ftp` retrieve a file. Make the script retry if the remote site is too busy but not if the file cannot be found.

2. Count the number of times that people have rewritten `ftp` to make it more flexible. Use Archie if you need help.

3. Count the number of programs you use that each have a different language for writing scripts or `.rc` files.

4. Find Expect's **example** directory online and try out some of the examples. Rewrite one in your favorite language.

5. Think about each keystroke that you press today. How much is the same from one session to the next? How much can be automated?

6. UNIX existed for over 20 years—without Expect. What did people do before? Which of those solutions still make sense today?

2

Tcl — Introduction And Overview

Expect does not have its own special-purpose language. Expect uses Tcl, a popular language for embedding in applications. Tcl provides lots of basic commands such as if/then/else, while, and set. Expect extends the language with commands such as expect and interact.

This chapter is an introduction and overview of Tcl. While not covering all of Tcl, this chapter does provide everything that the rest of the book depends on, and this is enough to write virtually any Expect script. Even if you already know Tcl, you may find it helpful to read this chapter. In this chapter, I will emphasize things about Tcl that you may not have thought much about before.

You probably want to get on with using Expect, and I can understand the urge to skip this chapter in the hopes of learning as little Tcl as possible so you can put Expect to work for you now. Please be patient and it will all fit together that much more easily.

If you do skip this chapter and you find yourself wondering about points in the other chapters, turn back to this chapter and read it.

A few concepts will not be covered here but will be explained as they are encountered for the first time in other chapters. The index can help you locate where each command is first defined and used.

I will occasionally mention when a particular Tcl command or feature is similar to C. It is not necessary that you know C in order to use Tcl, but if you do know it, such statements are clues that you can rely on what you already know from that language.

Everything Is A String

The types of variables are not declared in Tcl. There is no need since there is only one type: string. Every value is a string. Numbers are strings. Even commands and variables are strings! The following commands set the variable `name` to the string value "Don", the variable `word` to the value "`foobar`", and the variable `pi` to "`3.14159`".

```
set name Don
set word foobar
set pi 3.14159
```

Variable names, values, and commands are case sensitive. So the variable "name" is different than "Name".

To access a variable's value, prefix the variable name with a dollar sign ($). The following command sets the variable `phrase` to `foobar` by retrieving it from the variable `word`.

```
set phrase $word
```

Variable substitutions can occur anywhere in a command, not just at the beginning of an argument. The following command sets the variable `phrase2` to the string "`word=foobar`".

```
set phrase2 word=$word
```

You can insert a literal dollar sign by prefixing it with a backslash. The following command sets the variable `money` to the value "`$1000`".

```
set money \$1000
```

The backslash is also a useful way to embed other special characters in strings. For example, "`\t`" is a tab and "`\b`" is a backspace. Most of the Standard C backslash conventions are supported including `\` followed by one to three octal digits and `\x` followed by any number of hex digits.[†] I will mention more of these escapes later.

```
# stick control-Z in a variable
set controlZ \032
# define control-C
set controlC \x03
# define string with embedded control-Z and tab
set oddword foo\032bar\tgorp
```

A command beginning with "#" is a comment. It extends to the end of the line. You can think of "#" as a command whose arguments are discarded.

Multiple commands can be strung together if they are separated by a semicolon. A literal semicolon can be embedded by prefacing it with a backslash.

```
set word1 foo; set word2 bar     ;# two commands
set word3 foo\;bar               ;# one command
```

---

† The use of `\0` by itself to represent the null character is the only escape not supported. I will describe how to handle nulls in Chapter 6 (p. 155).

The "`;#`" sequence above is a common way of a tacking comments on the end of a line. The "`;`" ends the previous command and the "`#`" starts the comment. Writing the "`;#`" together avoids the possibility of having your comment unintentionally accepted as additional arguments because of a forgotten semicolon.

Commands are normally terminated at the end of a line, but a backslash at the end of a line allows multi-line commands. The backslash-newline sequence and any following whitespace behaves as if it were a single space. Later, I will show other ways of writing multi-line commands.

```
set word \
        really-long-string-which-does-not-quite-fit-on-previous-line
```

Quoting Conventions

Tcl separates arguments by whitespace (blanks, tabs, etc.). You can pass space characters by double quoting an argument. The quotes are not part of the argument; they just serve to keep it together. Tcl is similar to the shell in this respect.

```
set string1 "Hello world"
```

Double quotes prevent ";" from breaking things up.

```
set string2 "A semicolon ; is in here"
```

Keeping an argument together is all that double quotes do. Character sequences such as $, \t, and \b still behave as before.

```
set name "Sam"
set age 17
set word2 "My name is $name; my age is $age;"
```

After execution of these three commands, `word2` is left with the value "`My name is Sam; my age is 17;`".

Notice that in the first command `Sam` was quoted, while in the second command 17 was not quoted, even though neither contained blanks. When arguments do not have blanks, you do not have to quote them but I often do anyway—they are easier to read. However, I do not bother to quote numbers because quoted numbers simply look funny. Anyway, numbers never contain whitespace.

You can actually have whitespace in command names and variable names in which case you need to quote them too. I will show how to do this later, but I recommend you avoid it if possible.

Return Values

All commands return values. For example, the `pid` command returns the process id of the current process. To evaluate a command and use its *return value* as an argument or inside an argument, embed the command in brackets. The bracketed command is replaced by its return value.

```
set p "My pid is [pid]."
```

The `set` command returns its second argument. The following command sets b and a to 0.

```
set b "[set a 0]"
```

When it comes to deciding what are arguments, brackets are a special case. Tcl groups everything between matching brackets, so it is not necessary to quote arguments that already have all their whitespace enclosed entirely within brackets. The following are all legal.

```
set b [set a 0]
set b "[set a 0]"
set b "[set a 0]hello world"
set b [set a 0]hello
```

After execution of this last command, a is set to "0" and b is set to "0hello".

With only one argument, `set` returns the value of its first argument.

```
set c [set b]
```

Calling `set` with one argument is similar to using the dollar sign. Indeed, the previous command can be rewritten as "set c $b". However they are not always interchangeable. Consider the two commands:

```
set $phello
set [set p]hello
```

The first returns the value of the variable `phello`. The second returns the value of the variable p concatenated with the string "hello".

The $ syntax is shorter but does not automatically terminate the end of the variable. In the rare cases where the variable just runs right into more alphanumeric characters, the one-argument `set` command in brackets is useful.

The one-argument `set` command is also useful when entering commands interactively. For example, here is what it looks like when I type a command to the Tcl interpreter:[†]

[†] When Tcl is installed, it creates a program called `tclsh` (which stands for "Tcl shell" but is usually pronounced "ticklish"). `tclsh` is a program that contains only the Tcl commands and interpreter. Typing directly to `tclsh` is not the usual way to use Tcl, but `tclsh` is convenient for experimenting with the basic Tcl commands. `tclsh` actually prompts with a bare "%", but I show it here as "`tclsh>` " so that you cannot confuse it with the C-shell prompt.

```
tclsh> set p
12389
```

After entering "set p", the return value was printed. When using Tcl interactively, you will always see the return value printed. When executing commands from a script, the return values are discarded. Inside scripts, use the puts command to print to the standard output.

Puts

You can print values out with the puts command. In its simplest form, it takes a single string argument and prints it followed by a newline.

```
puts "Hello world!"
puts "The value of name is $name"
```

Expressions

Strings can be treated as expressions having mathematical values. For example, when the string "1+1" is treated as an expression, it has the value 2. Tcl does not automatically treat strings as expressions, but individual commands can. I will demonstrate this in a moment. For now, just remember that expressions are not complete commands in themselves.

Expressions are quite similar to those in the C language. The following are all valid expressions:

```
1 + 5
1+5
1+5.5
1e10+5.5
(5%3)*sin(4)
1 <= 2
(1 <= 2) || (2 != 3)
```

All of the usual mathematical operators are available including +, −, *, /, and % (modulo). Many functions exist such as sin, cos, log, and sqrt. Boolean operators include || (or), && (and), and ! (not). The usual comparison operators are available (<= (less than or equal), == (equal), != (not equal), etc.). They return 0 if the expression is false and 1 if it is true.

Whitespace may be used freely to enhance readability. A number of numeric forms are supported including scientific notation as well as octal (any number with a leading 0) and hexadecimal (any number with a leading 0x). Functions such as floor, ceil, and round convert from floating-point to integral values.

Precedence and associativity follow C rules closely. For instance, the expression "1-2*3" is interpreted as "1-(2*3)" because multiplication is of higher precedence than subtraction. All binary operators at the same level of precedence are left-associative. This means, for instance, that the expression "1-2-3" is interpreted as "(1-2)-3". Since Tcl expressions rarely become complex, I will omit a lengthy discussion of the numerous levels of precedence, and instead note that you can always use parentheses to override a particular precedence or associativity.[†] See the Tcl reference material for the complete list of operators and their precedences.

Variable values may also be used in expressions.

```
1 + $age
$argc < 10
```

Return values can be used in expressions using the bracket notation. For example, an expression to compare the current process id to 0 is:

```
[pid] == 0
```

If the process id is 0, the expression equals 1; otherwise it equals 0.

Expressions are not commands by themselves. Rather, certain commands treat their arguments as expressions, evaluating them in the process of command execution. For example, the `while` command treats its first argument as an expression. I will describe `while` and similar commands later.

The `expr` command takes any number of arguments and evaluates them as a single expression and returns the result.

```
set x "The answer is 1 + 3"
set y "The answer is [1 + 3]"
set z "The answer is [expr 1 + 3]"
```

After evaluation of the first command, x has the value "The answer is 1 + 3". The last command leaves z with the value "The answer is 4". The middle command causes an error. "1 + 3" is not a valid command because 1 is not a command.

Here is a more complicated-looking command (legal this time). It computes a result based on the current process id value and the value of the variable mod.

```
set x [expr (5 % $mod) + ( 17 == [pid])]
```

---

† I have long considered numerous levels of precedence to be more a hindrance than a benefit. I am reminded of this whenever I switch back and forth between languages that have differing precedence tables, each with dozens of levels. To avoid mental anguish, I frequently use more parentheses than necessary. In *Tcl and the Tk Toolkit*, Ousterhout echoes my sentiments when he says: "*Except in the simplest and most obvious cases you should use parentheses to indicate the way operators should be grouped; this will prevent errors by you and by others who modify your programs.*"

Braces—Deferring Evaluation

Braces are similar to double quotes. Both function as a grouping mechanism; however, braces defer any evaluation of brackets, dollar signs, and backslash sequences. In fact, braces defer everything.

```
set var1 "a$b[set c]\r"
set var2 {a$b[set c]\r}
```

After evaluation of these two commands, `var1` contains an "a" followed by the values of b and c, terminated by a return character. The variable `var2` contains the characters "a", "$", "b", "[", "s", "e", "t", " ", "c", "]", "\", and "r".

As with double quotes, the braces are not part of the argument they enclose. They just serve to group and defer. The primary use of braces is in writing control commands such as `while` loops, `for` loops, and procedures. These commands need to see the strings without having $ substitutions and bracket evaluations made.

Control Structures

Control structures are commands that direct the flow of control. Many of the control structures in Tcl are patterned directly after their C equivalents. Tcl gives you the power to write your own control structures, so if you do not like those of C, you may yet find happiness. I will not describe how to do it, but it is surprisingly easy. (The hard part is designing something that makes sense.)

The while Command

The `while` command loops until an expression is false. It looks very similar to a `while` in the C language. The following `while` loop computes the factorial of the number stored in the variable `count`.

```
set total 1

while {$count > 0} {
    set total [expr $total * $count]
    set count [expr $count-1]
}
```

The body of the loop is composed of the two `set` commands between the braces. The body is executed as long as $count is greater than 0.

Taking a step back, the `while` command has two arguments. The first is the controlling expression. The second is the body. Notice that both arguments are enclosed in braces. That means that no $ substitutions or bracket evaluations are made. For instance, this `while` command literally gets the string "`$count > 0`" as its first argument. Similarly, for the body. So how does anything happen?

The answer is that the `while` command itself evaluates the expression. If true (nonzero), the `while` command evaluates the body. The `while` command then re-evaluates the expression. As long as the expression keeps re-evaluating to a nonzero value, the `while` command keeps re-evaluating the body.

It is useful to compare this with the `set` command. The `set` command does not do any evaluation of its second argument. Consider this command:

```
set count [expr $count-1]
```

The `[expr ...]` part is evaluated *before* the `set` command even begins. If `count` is 7, the `set` command sees an argument of 6. In contrast, the `while` command sees the argument "`$count > 0`". It would not make any sense to evaluate that expression before the `while` command, since it has to change every time through the loop.

Using braces this way is fundamental toward the correct use of Tcl's control structures. You will see that all the other ones follow easily from this.

The incr Command

Many loops use a counter of some sort. Incrementing or decrementing a counter is so common that there is a command to simplify it. It is called `incr`. It modifies the variable given as its first argument. With no other argument `incr` adds one, otherwise `incr` adds the remaining argument.

The two commands are equivalent:

```
set count [expr $count-1]
incr count -1
```

The for Command

The `for` command is similar to the `while` command. The `for` command has a controlling expression and a body. However, before the expression is a "start" argument, and after the expression is a "next" argument.

```
for start expression next {
    # commands here make up
    # the body of the for
}
```

Both the start and next arguments are commands. The start argument is executed before the first evaluation of the controlling expression. The next argument is evaluated immediately after the body of the loop.

The code shown earlier to compute a factorial can be simplified using the `incr` command and a `for` loop as follows:

```
for {set total 1} {$count > 0} {incr count -1} {
    set total [expr $total * $count]
}
```

Either of the start or next argument can be empty, but you have to leave a placeholder. For example, you could express an infinite loop as:

```
for {} {1} {} {
    ... some command ...
}
```

The if Command

In its simplest form, the `if` command takes a controlling expression and a body to execute if the expression is nonzero. It looks a lot like a `while` command, but the body is executed at most once.

```
if {$count < 0} {
    set total 1
}
```

If present, an optional `else` fragment is executed only if the expression evaluates to zero. Here is an example:

```
if {$count < 5} {
    puts "count is less than five"
} else {
    puts "count is not less than five"
}
```

It is also possible to add more conditions using `elseif` arguments. Any number of `elseif` arguments may be used.

```
if {$count < 0} {
    puts "count is less than zero"
} elseif {$count > 0} {
    puts "count is greater than zero"
} else {
    puts "count is equal to zero"
}
```

In the `while` and `for` commands, the controlling expressions are written with braces to defer their evaluation. Their evaluation is deferred because they need to be re-evaluated repeatedly. The expression in an `if` is not re-evaluated and so it does not need to be deferred. The braces are still useful to group the arguments of the expression together but if the grouping behavior is not needed, then the braces can be omitted entirely. For example, the following two commands are equivalent:

```
if $a {incr a}
if {$a} {incr a}
```

The following two commands are *not* equivalent.

```
while $a {incr a}
while {$a} {incr a}
```

It does not hurt to write braces around all expressions; however, if you frequently read other people's code, you must get used to seeing the braces omitted in some expressions.

The switch Command

The `switch` command is similar to the `if` command but is more specialized. Instead of evaluating a mathematical expression, the `switch` command compares a string to a set of patterns. Each pattern is also associated with a body of Tcl commands. The first pattern that matches has its associated body evaluated.

Here is a fragment that sets the variable `type` depending on the value of `count`. For example, if `count` is the string `big`, then `type` is set to `array`. If `count` matches none of the choices, the special `default` body is used.

```
switch -- $count \
  1 {
    set type byte
} 2 {
    set type word
} big {
    set type array
} default {
    puts "$count is not a valid type"
}
```

By default, a pattern must match the string exactly. But the `switch` command can match patterns in several different ways. For example, shell-style pattern matching is used when the `switch` command starts out with the `-glob` flag:

```
switch -glob -- $count \
```

With shell-style pattern matching, "?" matches any single character and "*" matches any string. The `-regexp` flag indicates that patterns are interpreted as regular expressions. I will describe all of these different types of pattern matching in more detail later.

Since the `switch` command supports several flags, you must always use the `--` as the final flag to prevent inadvertent interpretation of your string as a flag.

Continuation Lines

By default, commands do not continue beyond the end of a line. However, there are several exceptions to this. One exception is that a backslash at the end of a line continues the command. I used this in the previous example where the first line of the switch had a backslash to continue the command. Without it, the command would have ended after $count and the 1 on the next line would have mistakenly been interpreted as another command.

Another exception is that open braces cause commands to continue across lines. This is precisely how I have written all of the other multi-line examples so far. Fortunately, this style looks a lot like another common style—the C language. Even if you are not used to C, it will be helpful if you adopt the C formatting style—just leave an open brace at the end of the current line and you can omit the backslashes.

Consider the following three if commands:

```
if {$count < 0} {
    puts "count is less than zero"
}

if {$count < 0} \
    { puts "count is less than zero"
}

if {$count < 0}
{
    puts "count is less than zero"
}
```

The first two examples are correct. The third one is incorrect—the if command is missing a body.

Open braces nest, so this guideline works if you write braced commands inside of braces. Later in this chapter and in the next, I will return to the subject of braces and how to use them effectively.

Double quotes and brackets also cause commands to continue across lines. As before, a \n or literal newline is retained and a backslash-newline-whitespace sequence is replaced by a single space. Compare the following two commands:

```
set oneline "hello\
    world"
set twolines "hello
    world"
```

After execution, oneline is set to "hello<space>world", while twolines is set to "hello<newline><space><space><space><space>world".

The break And continue Commands

The break and continue commands change the normal flow inside looping control structures such as for and while.

The break command causes the current loop command to return so that the next command after the loop can run. For example, the following would loop infinitely except for the break command in the middle. If a ever equals three, the break command will execute and the while command will return.

```
set a 0
while {1} {
    incr a
    if {$a == 3} break
    puts "hello"
}
```

The continue command drives control back to the top of the loop so that no more commands are executed during the current iteration. In the following example, the continue is executed whenever the value of a modulo three is not equal to zero. This has the effect of printing "hello" three times for every "there" printed.

```
set a 0
while {1} {
    incr a
    puts "hello"
    if {$a%3 != 0} continue
    puts "there"
}
```

The proc And return Commands

It is possible to create your own commands using the proc command. Such commands are called *procedures* but they behave the same as if they were built-in commands.

The proc command takes three arguments. The first argument is a command name. The second argument is a list of variables, each initalized to an argument of the procedure when it is called. (The variables are occasionally called *formal parameters* or just *parameters* to distinguish them from the actual arguments to which they are set.) The third argument of proc is a body of code.

The following command defines a procedure called fib that computes the nth Fibonacci number given any two starting numbers. Fibonacci numbers are sequences of numbers where each new number in the sequence is generated by adding the most recent two together. The starting two numbers are the first two arguments. The last argument defines which element of the sequence to return.

```
proc fib {pen ult n} {
    for {set i 0} {$i<$n} {incr i} {
        set new [expr $ult+$pen]
        set pen $ult            ;# new penultimate value
        set ult $new            ;# new ultimate value
    }
    return $pen
}
```

The `return` command in the last line takes its argument and makes the procedure `fib` itself return with that value. Once defined, `fib` can then be used as a command. For example, it could be called as:

```
set m [fib 0 1 9]
```

Although `fib` always returns a number, any string can be returned using `return`. A lot of procedures do not have a need to return anything—they just need to return. In this case, it is not necessary to provide `return` with an argument. The `return` command itself may be omitted if it would otherwise be the last command executed in a procedure. Then, the procedure returns with whatever is returned by the last command executed within the procedure.

You can force a single procedure to return by using `return`. In contrast, use the `exit` command to make the script (i.e., process) end and return to the shell (or whatever invoked the original script). The `exit` command works even inside of a procedure. The `exit` command can only return a number because that is all that UNIX permits. For example:

```
exit 1
```

Procedures can be called only after they are defined. Procedures share a single namespace with no name scoping. That means that once a procedure is defined, it can be called from any procedure, including itself. Here is another version of `fib`. This one is *recursive*—it calls itself.

```
proc fib {pen ult n} {
    if {$n == 0} {
        return $pen
    }
    return [fib $ult [expr $pen+$ult] [expr $n-1]]
}
```

Earlier I noted that the `return` command may be omitted if it is the last command executed in a procedure. Based on this, the previous procedure can be simplified:

```
proc fib {pen ult n} {
    if {$n == 0} {
        return $pen
    }
```

```
        fib $ult [expr $pen+$ult] [expr $n-1]
    }
```

In contrast to procedures, variables are usually local to the current procedure. In the example above, the variables ult, pen, and n, are not visible to any procedures that call fib such as expr. They are not even visible to other invocations of the fib procedure. The fib procedure calls expr, passing it the value of ult but not the string "ult". The expr command cannot modify the variable ult. Computer scientists call this *pass by value*.

It is possible for a procedure to change a variable in the caller's scope. The set and incr commands handle their first argument this way. This technique is called *pass by reference*, and I will explain how to write procedures that do this on page 57. Another technique to communicate values between commands is to use global variables. Using a lot of global variables can be confusing, but since most scripts are short, global variables are a very popular technique.

The global command identifies variables to consider *global*. This means that references to those variables inside the procedure are the same as references to those variables outside all the procedures.

For example, you could define the constant pi as a global variable outside any procedure. A procedure that needed the value would then access it using the global command. For example:

```
    proc circumference_of_circle {radius} {
        global pi

        expr 2*$pi*$radius
    }
```

You can list additional variable names as arguments to a global command, and you can have multiple global commands in a procedure.

```
    global pi e golden_ratio
```

The source Command

Procedures and variables that are used in numerous scripts can be stored in other files, allowing them to be conveniently shared. A file of commands can be read with the source command. Its argument is the name of a file to read. Tcl understands the tilde convention from the C shell. For example, the following command reads the file definitions.tcl from your home directory:

```
    source ~/definitions.tcl
```

As the file is read, the commands are executed. So if the file contains procedure definitions, the procedures will be callable after the source command returns. Tcl's source command is similar to the C shell's source command.

Tcl's library facility provides a way to automatically source files as needed. It is described on page 68.

The return command can be used to make a source command return. Otherwise, source returns only after executing the last command in the file.

More On Expressions

In the while and if command examples, I enclosed the expressions in braces and said that the expressions were evaluated by the commands themselves. For example, in the while command, the expression was

```
$count > 0
```

Because the expression was wrapped in braces, evaluation of $count was deferred. During expression evaluation, a $ followed by a variable name is interpreted in just the same way it is done with arguments that are not wrapped in braces. Similarly, brackets are also interpreted the same way in both contexts. For this reason, commands like the following two have the same result. But in the first command, $count is evaluated before expr executes, while in the second command, expr itself evaluates $count.

```
expr $count > 0
expr {$count > 0}
```

The expr command can perform some string operations. For example, quoted strings are recognized as string literals. Thus, you can say things like:

```
expr {$name == "Don"}
```

Unquoted strings cannot be used as string literals. The following fails:

```
expr {$name == Don}
```

Unquoted strings are not permitted inside expressions to prevent ambiguities in interpretation. But strings in expressions can still be tricky. In fact, I recommend avoiding expr for these implicit string operations. The reason is that expr tries to interpret strings as numbers. Only if they are not numbers, are they treated as uninterpreted strings. Consider:

```
tclsh> if {"0x0" == "0"} {puts equal}
equal
```

Strings which are not even internally representable as numbers can cause problems:

```
tclsh> expr {$x=="1E500"}
floating-point value too large to represent
    while executing
"expr {$x=="1E500"}"
```

On page 47, I will describe the "string compare" operation which is a better way of comparing arbitrary strings. However, because many people do use expr for string operations, it is important to be able to recognize and understand it in scripts.

Lists

In the proc command, the second argument was a list of variables.

```
proc fib {ult pen n} {
```

The parameter list is just a string containing the characters, "u", "l", "t", " ", "p", "e", "n", " ", and "n". Intuitively, the string can also be thought of as a list of three elements: ult, pen, and n. The whitespace just serves to separate the elements.

Lists are very useful, and Tcl provides many commands to manipulate them. For example, llength returns the length of a list.[†]

```
tclsh> llength "a b c"
3
tclsh> llength ""
0
tclsh> llength [llength "a b c"]
1
tclsh> llength {llength "a b c"}
2
```

In the next few sections, I will describe more commands to manipulate lists.

Selecting Elements Of Lists

The lindex and lrange commands select elements from a list by their index. The lindex command selects a single element. The lrange command selects a set of elements. Elements are indexed starting from zero.[‡]

```
tclsh> lindex "a b c d e" 0
a
tclsh> lindex "a b c d e" 2
c
```

---

† That is not a misspelling—all of the list manipulation commands start with an "l".
‡ When I use ordinal terms such as "first", I mean "index 0".

```
tclsh> lrange "a b c d e" 0 2
a b c
tclsh> llength [lrange "a b c d e" 0 2]
3
```

You can step through the members of a list using an index and a `for` loop. Here is a loop to print out the elements of a list in reverse.

```
for {set i [expr [llength $list]-1]} {$i>=0} {incr i -1} {
    puts [lindex $list $i]
}
```

Iterating from front to back is much more common than the reverse. In fact, it is so common, there is a command to do it called `foreach`. The first argument is a variable name. Upon each iteration of the loop, the variable is set to the next element in the list, provided as the second argument. The third argument is the loop body.

For example, this fragment prints each element in `list`.

```
foreach element $list {
    puts $element
}
```

After execution, the variable `element` remains set to the last element in the list.

Varying Argument Lists

Usually procedures must be called with the same number of arguments as they have formal parameters. When a procedure is called, each parameter is set to one of the arguments. However, if the last parameter is named `args`, all the remaining arguments are stored in a list and assigned to `args`. For example, imagine a procedure `p1` definition that begins:

```
proc p1 {a b args} {
```

If you call it as "p1 red box cheese whiz", a is set to red, b is set to box, and args is set to "cheese whiz". If called as "p1 red box", args is set to the empty list.

Here is a more realistic example. The procedure `sum` takes an arbitrary number of arguments, adds them together, and returns the total.

```
proc sum {args} {
    set total 0
    foreach int $args {
        incr total $int
    }
    return $total
}
```

I will show another example of a procedure with varying arguments on page 59.

Lists Of Lists

List elements can themselves be lists. This is a concern in several situations, but the simplest is when elements contain whitespace. For example, there must be a way to distinguish between the list of "a" and "b" and the list containing the single element "a b".

Assuming an argument has begun with a double quote, the next double quote ends the argument. It is possible to precede double quotes with backslashes inside a list, but this is very hard to read, given enough levels of quoting. Here is a list of one element.

```
set x "\"a b\""                        ;# correct but ugly
```

As an alternative, Tcl supports braces to group lists inside lists. Using braces, it is easy to construct arbitrarily complex lists.

```
set a "a b {c d} {e {f g {xyz}}}"
```

Assuming you do not need things like variable substitution, you can replace the top-level double quotes with braces as well.

```
set a {a b {c d} {e {f g {xyz}}}}
```

This looks more consistent, so it is very common to use braces at the top level to write an argument consisting of a list of lists.

The reason braces work so much better for this than double quotes is that left and right braces are distinguishable. There is no such thing as a right double quote, so Tcl cannot tell when quotes should or should not match. But it is easy to tell when braces match. Tcl counts the left-hand braces and right-hand braces. When they are equal, the list is complete.

This is exactly what happens when Tcl sees a for, while, or other control structure. Examine the while command below. The last argument is the body. There is one open brace on the first line and another on the fourth. The close brace on the sixth line matches one, and the close brace on the last line matches the other, terminating the list and hence the argument.

```
while {1} {          ;# one open brace
    incr a
    puts "hello"
    if {$a%3 != 0} { ;# two open braces
        continue
    }                ;# one open brace
    puts "there"
}                    ;# zero open braces
```

Double quotes and brackets have no special meaning inside of braces and do not have to match. But braces themselves do. To embed a literal brace, you have to precede it with a backslash.

Here are some examples of lists of lists:

```
set x  { a b c }
set y  { a b {Hello world!}}
set z  { a [ { ] } }
```

All of these are three-element lists. The third element of y is a two-element list. The first and second elements of y can be considered one-element lists even though they have no grouping braces around them.

```
tclsh> llength $y
3
tclsh> llength [lindex $y 2]
2
tclsh> llength [lindex $y 0]
1
```

The second and third elements of z are both one-element lists.

```
tclsh> lindex $z 1
[
tclsh> lindex $z 2
 ]
```

Notice the spacing. Element two of z is a three-character string. The first and last characters are spaces, and the middle character is a right bracket. In contrast, element one is a single character. The spaces separating the elements of z were stripped off when the elements were extracted by lindex. The braces are not part of the elements.

The braces are, however, part of the *string* z. Considered as a string, z has eleven characters including the inner braces. The outer braces are not part of the string.

Similarly, the string in y begins with a space and ends with a right brace. The last element of y has only a single space in the middle.

```
tclsh> lindex $y 2
Hello world!
```

The assignment to y could be rewritten with double quotes.

```
tclsh> set y2 { a b "Hello world!" }
 a b "Hello world!"
tclsh> lindex $y2 2
Hello world!
```

In this case, the last element of y2 is the same. But more complicated strings cannot be stored this way. Tcl will complain.

```
tclsh> set y3 { a b "My name is "Goofy"" }
 a b "My name is "Goofy""
tclsh> lindex $y3 2
list element in quotes followed by "Goofy""" instead of space
```

There is nothing wrong with y3 as a string. However, it is not a list.

This section may seem confusing at first. You might want to come back to it after you have written some Tcl scripts.

Creating Lists

With care, lists can be created with the set command or with any command that creates a string with the proper structure. To make things easier, Tcl provides three commands that create strings that are guaranteed to be lists. These commands are list, lappend, and linsert.

The list And concat Commands

The list command takes all of its arguments and combines them into a list. For example:

```
tclsh> list a b "Hello world"
a b {Hello world}
```

In this example, a three-element list is returned. Each element corresponds to one of the arguments. The double quotes have been replaced by braces, but that does not affect the contents. When the third element is extracted, the braces will be stripped off.

```
tclsh> lindex [list a b "Hello World"] 2
Hello World
```

The list command is particularly useful if you need to create a list composed of variable values. Simply appending them is insufficient. If either variable contains embedded whitespace, for example, the list will end up with more than two elements.

```
tclsh> set a "foo bar \"hello\""
foo bar "hello"
tclsh> set b "gorp"
gorp
tclsh> set ab "$a $b"    ;# WRONG
foo bar "hello" gorp
tclsh> llength $ab
4
```

In contrast, the list command correctly preserves the embedded lists. The list command also correctly handles things such as escaped braces and quotes.

If you want to append several lists together, use the concat command.

```
tclsh> concat a b "Hello world"
a b Hello world
```

The concat command treats each of its arguments as a list. The elements of all of the lists are then returned in a new list. Compare the output from concat (above) and list (below).

```
tclsh> list a b "Hello world"
a b {Hello world}
```

Here is another example of concat. Notice that whitespace inside elements is preserved.

```
tclsh> concat a {b {c d}}
a b {c d}
```

In practice, concat is rarely used. However, it is helpful to understand concat because several commands exhibit concat-like behavior. For example, the expr command concatenates its arguments together before evaluating them—much in the style of concat. Thus, the following commands produce the same result:

```
tclsh> expr 1 - {2 - 3}
-4
tclsh> expr 1 - 2 - 3
-4
```

Building Up Lists With The lappend Command

Building up lists is a common operation. For example, you may want to read in lines from a file and maintain them in memory as a list. Assuming the existence of commands get_a_line and more_lines_in_file, your code might look something like this:

```
while {[more_lines_in_file]} {
    set list "$list [get_a_line]"
}
```

The body builds up the list. Each time through the loop, a new line is appended to the end of the list.

This is such a common operation that Tcl provides a command to do this more efficiently. The lappend command takes a variable name as its first argument and appends the remaining arguments. The example above could be rewritten:

```
while {[more_lines_in_file]} {
    lappend list [get_a_line]
}
```

Notice that the first argument is not passed by value. Only the name is passed. Tcl appends the remaining arguments *in place*—that is, without making a copy of the original list. You do not have to use set to save the new list. This behavior of modifying the list in place is unusual—the other list commands require the list to be passed by value.

The linsert Command

Like its name implies, the linsert command inserts elements into a list. The first argument is a list. The second argument is a numeric index describing where to insert into the list. The remaining arguments are the arguments to be inserted.

```
tclsh> set list {a b c d}
a b c d
tclsh> set list [linsert $list 0 new]
new a b c d
tclsh> linsert $list 1 foo bar {hello world}
new foo bar {hello world} a b c d
```

The lreplace Command

The lreplace command is similar to the linsert command except that lreplace deletes existing elements before inserting the new ones. The second and third arguments identify the beginning and ending indices of the elements to be deleted, and the remaining arguments are inserted in their place.

```
tclsh> set list {a b c d e}
a b c d e
tclsh> lreplace $list 1 3 x y
a x y e
```

The lsearch Command

The lsearch command is the opposite of the lindex command. The lsearch command returns the index of the first occurrence of an element in a list. If the element does not exist, -1 is returned.

```
tclsh> lsearch {a b c d e} "c"
2
tclsh> lsearch {a b c d e} "f"
-1
```

The lsearch command interprets the element as a shell-style pattern by default. If you want an exact match, use the -exact flag:

```
tclsh> lsearch {a b c d ?} "?"
0
tclsh> lsearch -exact {a b c d ?} "?"
4
```

The lsort Command

The lsort command sorts a list. By default, it sorts in increasing order.

```
tclsh> lsort {one two three four five six}
five four one six three two
```

Several flags are available including -integer, -real, and -decreasing to sort in ways suggested by their names.

It is also possible to supply lsort with a comparison procedure of your own. This is useful for lists with elements that are lists in themselves. However, lists of more than a hundred or so elements are sorted slowly enough that it is more efficient to have them sorted by an external program such as the UNIX sort command.[†]

The split And join Commands

The split and join commands are useful for splitting strings into lists, and vice versa—joining lists into strings.

The split command splits a string into a list. The first argument is the string to be split. The second argument is a string of characters, each of which separates elements in the first argument.

For example, if the variable line contained a line from /etc/passwd, it could be split as:

```
tclsh> split $line ":"
root Gw19QKxuFWDX7 0 1 Operator / /bin/csh
```

The directories of a file name can be split using a "/".

```
tclsh> split "/etc/passwd" "/"
{} etc passwd
```

Notice the empty element because of the / at the beginning of the string.

---

† Alternatively, you can write your own Tcl command to do this in C, C++, or any other faster language.

The `join` command does the opposite of `split`. It joins elements in a list together. The first argument is a list to join together. The second argument is a string to place between all the elements.

```
tclsh> join {{} etc passwd} "/"
/etc/passwd
```

With an empty second argument, `split` splits between every character, and `join` joins the elements together without inserting any separating characters.

```
tclsh> split "abc" ""
a b c
tclsh> join {a b c} ""
abc
```

More Ways To Manipulate Strings

There are a number of other useful commands for string manipulation. These include `scan`, `format`, `string`, and `append`. Two more string manipulation commands are `regexp` and `regsub`. Those two commands require a decent understanding of regular expressions, so I will hold off describing `regexp` and `regsub` until Chapter 6 (p. 137). Then, the commands will be much easier to understand.

The scan And format Commands

The `scan` and `format` commands extract and format substrings corresponding to low-level types such as integers, reals, and characters. `scan` and `format` are good at dealing with filling, padding, and generating unusual characters. These commands are analogous to `sscanf` and `sprintf` in the C language, and most of the C conventions are supported.

As an example, the following command assigns to `x` a string composed of a ^A immediately followed by "`foo      ==1700.000000`" (the number of zeros after the decimal point may differ on your system). The string "`foo`" is left-justified in an eight-character field.

```
set x [format "%1c%-8s==%f" 1 foo 17.0e2]
```

The first argument is a description of how to print the remaining arguments. The remaining arguments are substituted for the fields that begin with a "`%`". In the example above, the "`-`" means "left justify" and the 8 is a minimum field width. The "c", "s", and "f" force the arguments to be treated as a character, a string, and a real number (f stands for float), respectively. The "`==`" is passed through literally since it does not begin with a "`%`".

The `scan` command does the opposite of `format`. For example, the output above can be broken back down with the following command:

```
scan $x "%c%8s%*\[ =]%f" char string float
```

The first argument, `$x`, holds the string to be scanned. The first character is assigned to the variable `char`. The next string (ending at the first whitespace or after eight characters, whichever comes first) is assigned to the variable string. Any number of blanks and equal signs are matched and discarded. The asterisk suppresses the assignment. Finally, the real is matched and assigned to the variable `float`. The `scan` command returns the number of percent-style formats that match.

I will not describe `scan` and `format` further at this point, but I will return to them later in the book. For a complete discussion, you can also consult the Tcl reference material or any C language reference.

The string Command

The `string` command is a catchall for a number of miscellaneous but very useful string manipulation operations. The first argument to the `string` command names the particular operation. While discussing these operations, I will refer to the remaining arguments as if they were the only arguments.

As with the list commands, the string commands also use zero-based indices. So the first character in a string is at position 0, the second character is at position 1, and so on.

The `compare` operation compares the two arguments lexicographically (i.e., according to the underlying hardware alphabet of the machine). The command returns -1, 0, or 1, depending on if the first argument is less than, equal to, or greater than the second argument.

As an example, this could be used in an `if` command like so:

```
if {[string compare $a $b] == 0} {
    puts "strings are equal"
} else {
    puts "strings are not equal"
}
```

The `match` operation returns 1 if the first argument matches the second or 0 if it does not match. The first argument is a pattern similar in style to the shell, where * matches any number of characters and ? matches any single character.

```
tclsh> string match "*.c" "main.c"
1
```

I will cover these patterns in more detail in Chapter 4 (p. 87). The `regexp` command provides more powerful patterns. I will describe those patterns in Chapter 5 (p. 107).

The `first` operation searches for a string (first argument) in another string (second argument). It returns the first position in the second argument where the first argument is found. -1 is returned if the second string does not contain the first.

```
tclsh> string first "uu" "uunet.uu.net"
0
```

The `last` operation returns the last position where the first argument is found.

```
tclsh> string last "uu" "uunet.uu.net"
6
```

The `length` operation returns the number of characters in the string.

```
tclsh> string length "foo"
3
tclsh> string length ""
0
```

The `index` operation returns the character corresponding to the given index (second argument) in a string (first argument). For example:

```
tclsh> string index "abcdefg" 2
c
```

The `range` operation is analogous to the `lrange` command, but `range` works on strings. Indices correspond to character positions. All characters between the indices inclusive are returned. The string "end" may be used to refer to the last position in the string.

```
tclsh> string range "abcdefg" 2 3
cd
```

The `tolower` and `toupper` operations convert an argument to lowercase and uppercase, respectively.

```
tclsh> string tolower "NeXT"
next
```

The `trimleft` operation removes characters from the beginning of a string. The string is the first argument. The characters removed are any which appear in the optional second argument. If there is no second argument, then whitespace is removed.

```
string trimleft $num "-"     ;# force $num nonnegative
```

The `trimright` operation is like `trimleft` except that characters are removed from the end of the string. The `trim` operation removes characters from both the beginning and the end of the string.

The append Command

The following command appends a string to another string in a variable.

```
set var "$var$string"
```

Appending strings is a very common operation. For example, it is often used in a loop to read the output of a program and to create a single variable containing the entire output.

Appending occurs so frequently that there is a command specifically for this purpose. The append command takes a variable as the first argument and appends to it all of the remaining strings.

```
tclsh> append var "abc"
abc
tclsh> append var "def" "ghi"
abcdefghi
```

Notice that the first argument is not passed by value. Only the name is passed. Tcl appends the remaining arguments *in place*—that is, without making a copy of the original list. This allows Tcl to take some shortcuts internally. Using append is much more efficient than the alternative set command.

This behavior of modifying the string in place is unusual—none of the string operations work this way. However, the lappend command does. So just remember that append and lappend work this way. It might be helpful to go back to the lappend description (page 43) now and compare its behavior with append.

Both append and lappend share a few other features. Neither requires that the variable be initialized. If uninitialized, the first string argument is set rather than appended (as if the set command had been used). append and lappend also return the final value of the variable. However, this return value is rarely used since both commands already store the value in the variable.

Arrays

Earlier, I described how multiple strings can be stored together in a list. Tcl provides a second mechanism for storing multiple strings together called *arrays*.

Each string stored in an array is called an element and has an associated name. The element name is given in parentheses following the array name. For example, an array of user ids could be defined as:

```
set uid(0)    "root"
set uid(1)    "daemon"
set uid(2)    "uucp"
```

```
set uid(100)  "dave"
set uid(101)  "josh"
. . .
```

Once defined, elements can then be accessed by name:

```
set number 101
puts var "User id $number is $uid($number)"
```

You can use any string as an array element, not just a number. For example, the following additional assignments allow user ids to be looked up by either user id or name.

```
set uid(root)     0
set uid(daemon)   1
set uid(uucp)     2
set uid(dave)     100
set uid(josh)     101
```

Because element names can be arbitrary strings, it is possible to simulate multi-dimensional arrays or structures. For example, a password database could be stored in an array like this:

```
set uid(dave,uid)        100
set uid(dave,password)   diNBXuprAac4w
set uid(dave,shell)      /usr/local/bin/zsh
set uid(josh,uid)        101
set uid(josh,password)   gS4jKHp1AjYnd
set uid(josh,shell)      /usr/local/bin/tcsh
```

Now an arbitrary user's shell can be retrieved as `$uid($user,shell)`. The choice of a comma to separate parts of the element name is arbitrary. You can use any character and you can use more than one in a name.

It is possible to have element names with whitespace in them. For example, it might be convenient to find out the user name, given a full name. Doing it in two steps is easy and usually what you want anyway—presumably, the name variable is set elsewhere.

```
set name "John Ousterhout"
set uid($name) ouster
```

If you just want to embed a literal array reference that contains whitespace, you have to quote it. Remember, any string with whitespace must be quoted to keep it as a single argument (unless it is already in braces).

```
set "uid(John Ousterhout)" ouster
```

This is not specific to arrays. Any variable containing whitespace can be set similarly. The following sets the variable named "a b".

```
set "a b" 1
```

This may seem strange at first, but it just a natural result of the few simple rules that describe Tcl commands and arguments.

From now on when I want to explicitly talk about a variable that is not an array, I will use the term *scalar variable*.

Earlier, I described how to pass scalar variables into procedures—as parameters or globals. Arrays can be accessed as globals, too. (Name the array in a `global` command and all of the elements become visible in the procedure.) Arrays can be passed as parameters but not as easily as scalar variables. Later in this chapter (page 58), I will describe the `upvar` command that provides the means to accomplish this.

Indirect References

On page 26, I described how the single-argument `set` command is useful to separate variable names from other adjacent characters. This can be used for arbitrarily complex indirect references. For example, the following commands dynamically form a variable name from the contents of b and a literal c character. This result is taken as another variable name, and its contents are assigned to d.

```
set xc 1
set b x
set d [set [set b]c]       ;# sets d to value of xc
```

This type of indirection works with array names too. For example, the following sequence stores an array name in a and then retrieves a value through it.

```
set a(1) foo
set a2 a
puts [set [set a2](1)]
```

In contrast, replacing either of the `set` commands with the $ notation fails. The first of the next two commands incorrectly tries to use a2 as the array name.

```
tclsh> puts [set $a2(1)]
can't read "a2(1)": variable isn't array
tclsh> puts $[set a2](1)
$a(1)
```

In the second command, the dollar sign is substituted literally because there is not a variable name immediately following it when it is first scanned.

Variable Information

Tcl provides the `info` command to obtain assorted pieces of internal information about Tcl. The most useful of the `info` operations is "`info exists`". Given a variable name, "info exists" returns 1 if the variable exists or 0 otherwise. Only variables accessible from the current scope are checked. For example, the following command shows that haha has not been defined. An attempt to read it would fail.

```
tclsh> info exists haha
0
```

Three related commands are "info locals", "info globals", and "info vars". They return a list of local, global, and all variables respectively. They can be constrained to match a subset by supplying an optional pattern (in the style of the "string match" command). For example, the following command returns a list of all global variables that begin with the letters "mail".

```
info globals mail*
```

Tcl has similar commands for testing whether commands and procedures exist. "info commands" returns a list of all commands. "info procs" returns a list of just the procedures (commands defined with the proc command).

"info level" returns information about the stack. With no arguments, the stack depth is returned. "info level 0" returns the command and arguments of the current procedure. "info level -1" returns the command and arguments of the calling procedure of the current procedure. -2 indicates the next previous caller, and so on.

The "info script" command returns the file name of the current script being executed. This is just one of a number of other information commands that give related types of information useful in only the most esoteric circumstances. See the Tcl reference material for more information.

Array Information

While the info command can be used on arrays, Tcl provides some more specialized commands for this purpose. For example, "array size b" returns the number of elements in an array.

```
tclsh> set color(pavement) black
black
tclsh> set color(snow) white
white
tclsh> array size color
2
```

The command "array names" returns the element names of an array.

```
tclsh> array names color
pavement snow
```

Here is a loop to print the elements of the array and their values.

```
tclsh> foreach name [array names color] {
    puts "The color of $name is $color($name)."
}
The color of snow is white.
The color of pavement is black.
```

Unsetting Variables

The unset command unsets a variable. After being unset, a variable no longer exists. You can unset scalar variables or entire arrays. For example:

```
unset a
unset array(elt)
unset array
```

After a variable is unset, it can no longer be read and "info exists" returns 0.

Tracing Variables

Variable accesses can be traced with the trace command. Using trace, you can evaluate procedures whenever a variable is accessed. While this is useful in many ways, I will cover trace in more detail in the discussion on debugging (Chapter 18 (p. 406)) since that is almost always where trace first shows its value. In that same chapter, I will also describe how to trace commands.

Handling Errors

When typing commands interactively, errors cause the Tcl interpreter to give up on the current command and reprompt for a new command. All well and good. However, you do not want this to happen while running a script.

While many errors are just the result of typing goofs, some errors are more difficult to avoid and it is easier to react to them "after the fact". For example, if you write a procedure that does several divisions, code before each division can check that the denominator is not zero. A much easier alternative is to check that the whole procedure did not fail. This is done using the catch command. catch evaluates its argument as another command and returns 1 if there was an error or 0 if the procedure returned normally.

Assuming your procedure is named `divalot`, you can call it this way:

```
if [catch divalot] {
    puts "got an error in divalot!"
    exit
}
```

The argument to `catch` is a list of the command and arguments to be evaluated. If your procedure takes arguments, then they must be grouped together. For example:

```
catch {puts "Hello world"}
catch {divalot some args}
```

If your procedure returns a value itself, this can be saved by providing a variable name as the second argument to `catch`. For example, suppose `divalot` normally returns a value of 17 or 18.

```
tclsh> catch {divalot some args} result
0
tclsh> set result
17
```

Here, `catch` returned 0 indicating `divalot` succeeded. The variable `result` is set to the value returned by `divalot`.

This same mechanism can be used to get the messages produced by an error. For example, you can compute the values of x for the equation $0 = ax^2 + bx + c$ by using the quadratic formula. In mathematical notation, the formula looks like this:

$$\frac{-b \pm \sqrt{b^2 - 4ac}}{2a}$$

Here is a procedure for the quadratic formula:

```
proc qf {a b c} {
    set s [expr sqrt($b*$b-4*$a*$c)]
    set d [expr 2*$a]
    list [expr (-$b+$s)/$d] \
         [expr (-$b-$s)/$d]
}
```

When run successfully, `qf` produces a two-element list of values:

```
tclsh> catch {qf 1 0 -2} roots
0
tclsh> set roots
1.41421 -1.41421
```

When run unsuccessfully, this same command records the error in `roots`:

```
tclsh> catch {qf 0 0 -2} roots
1
tclsh> set roots
divide by zero
```

By using `catch` this way, you avoid having to put a lot of error-checking code inside `qf`. In this case, there is no need to check for division by zero or taking the square root of a negative number. This simplifies the code.

While it is rarely useful in a script, it is possible to get a description of all the commands and procedures that were in evaluation when an error occurred. This description is stored in the global variable `errorInfo`. In the example above, `errorInfo` looks like this:

```
tclsh> set errorInfo
divide by zero
    while executing
"expr (-$b+$s)/$d"
    invoked from within
"list [expr (-$b+$s)/$d]..."
    invoked from within
"return [list [expr (-$b+$s)/$d]..."
    (procedure "qf" line 4)
    invoked from within
"qf 0 0 -2"
```

`errorInfo` is actually set when the error occurs. You can use `errorInfo` whether or not you use `catch` to, well, . . . catch the error.

Causing Errors

The `error` command is used to create error conditions which can be caught with the `catch` command. `error` is useful inside of procedures that return errors naturally already.

For example, if you wanted to restrict the `qf` routine so that the variable "a" could not be larger than 100, you could rewrite the beginning of it as:

```
proc qf {a b c} {
    if {$a > 100} {error "a too large"}
    set s [expr sqrt($b*$b-4*$a*$c)]
    . . .
```

Now if "a" is greater than 100, "`catch {qf ...}`" will return 1. The message "`a too large`" will be stored in the optional variable name supplied to `catch` as the second argument.

Evaluating Lists As Commands

Everything in Tcl is represented as a string. This includes commands. You can manipulate commands just like any other string. Here is an example where a command is stored in a variable.

```
tclsh> set output "puts"
puts
tclsh> $output "Hello world!"
Hello world!
```

The variable `output` could be used to select between several different forms of output. If this command was embedded inside a procedure, it could handle different forms of output with the same parameterized code. The Tk extension of Tcl uses this technique to manipulate multiple widgets with the same code.

Evaluating an entire command cannot be done the same way. Look what happens:

```
tclsh> set cmd "puts \"Hello world!\""
puts "Hello world!"
tclsh> $cmd
invalid command name "puts "Hello world!""
```

The problem is that the entire string in `cmd` is taken as the command name rather than a list of a command and arguments.

In order to treat a string as a list of a command name and arguments, the string must be passed to the `eval` command. For instance:

```
tclsh> eval $cmd
Hello world!
```

The `eval` command treats each of its arguments as a list. The elements from all of the lists are used to form a new list that is interpreted as a command. The first element becomes the command name. The remaining elements become the arguments to the command.

The following example uses the arguments "append", "v1", "a b", and "c d" to produce and evaluate the command "append v1 a b c d".

```
tclsh> eval append v1 "a b" "c d"
abcd
```

Remember the `concat` command from page 43? The `eval` command treats it arguments in exactly the same was as `concat`. For example, notice how internal space is preserved:

```
tclsh> eval append v2 {a b} {c {d e}}
abcd e
```

The list command will protect any argument from being broken up by eval.

```
tclsh> eval append v3 [list {a b}] [list {c {d e}}]
a bc d e
```

When the arguments to eval are unknown (because they are stored in a variable), it is particularly important to use the list command. For example, the previous command is more likely to be expressed in a script this way:

```
eval append somevar [list $arg1] [list $arg2]
```

Unless you want your arguments to be broken up, surround them with list commands.

The eval command also performs $ substitution and [] evaluation so that the command is handled as if it had originally been typed in and evaluated rather than stored in a variable. In fact, when a script is running, eval is used internally to break the lines into command names and arguments, and evaluate them. Commands such as if, while, and catch use the eval command internally to evaluate their command blocks. So the same conventions apply whether you are using eval explicitly, writing commands in a script, or typing commands interactively.

Again, the list command will protect unwanted $ substitution and [] evaluation.

These eval conventions such as $ substitution and [] evaluation are *only* done when a command is evaluated. So if you have a string with embedded dollar signs or whitespace, for example, you have to protect it only when it is evaluated.

```
tclsh> set a "\$foo"
$foo
tclsh> set b $a
$foo
tclsh> set b
$foo
```

Passing By Reference

By default, you can only refer to global variables (after using the global command) or variables declared within a procedure. The upvar command provides a way to refer to variables in any outer scope. A common use for this is to implement *pass by reference*. When a variable is passed by reference, the calling procedure can see any changes the called procedure makes to the variable.

The most common use of upvar is to get access to a variable in the scope of the calling procedure. If a procedure is called with the variable v as an argument, the procedure associates the caller's variable v with a second variable so that when the second variable is changed, the caller's v is changed also.

For example, the following command associates the variable name stored in name with the variable p.

```
upvar $name p
```

After this command, any references to p also refer to the variable named within name. If name contains "v", "set p 1" sets p to 1 inside the procedure and v to 1 in the caller of the procedure.

The qf procedure from page 54 can be rewritten to use upvar. As originally written, qf returned a list. This is a little inconvenient because the list always has to be torn apart to get at the two values. Lists are handy when they are long or of unknown size, but they are a nuisance just for handling two values. However, Tcl only allows procedures to return a single value, and a list is the only way to make two values "feel" like one.

Here is another procedure to compute the quadratic formula but written with upvar. This procedure, called qf2, writes its results into the caller's fourth and fifth parameters.

```
proc qf2 {a b c name1 name2} {
    upvar $name1 r1 $name2 r2
        set s [expr sqrt($b*$b-4*$a*$c)]
    set d [expr $a+$a]
    set r1 [expr (-$b+$s)/$d]
    set r2 [expr (-$b-$s)/$d]
}
```

The qf2 procedure looks like this when it is called.

```
tclsh> catch {qf2 1 0 -2 root1 root2}
0
tclsh> set root1
1.41421
tclsh> set root2
-1.41421
```

A specific caller can be chosen by specifying a level immediately after the command name. Integers describe the number of levels up the procedure call stack. The default is 1 (the calling procedure). If an integer is preceded by a "#", then the level is an absolute level with #0 equivalent to the global level. For example, the following command associates the global variable curved_intersection_count with the local variable x.

```
upvar #0 curved_intersection_count x
```

The upvar command is especially useful for dealing with arrays because arrays cannot be passed by value. (There is no way to refer to the value of an entire array.) However, arrays can be passed by reference.

For example, imagine you want to compute the distance between two points in an xyz-coordinate system. Each point is represented by three numbers. Rather than passing six numbers, it is simpler to pass the entire array. Here is a procedure which computes the distance assuming the numbers are all stored in a single array:

```
proc distance {name} {
    upvar $name a

    set xdelta [expr $a(x,2) - $a(x,1)]
    set ydelta [expr $a(y,2) - $a(y,1)]
    set zdelta [expr $a(z,2) - $a(z,1)]
    expr {sqrt(
        $xdelta*$xdelta +
        $ydelta*$ydelta +
        $zdelta*$zdelta)
    }
}
```

Evaluating Commands In Other Scopes

The `uplevel` command is similar in spirit to `upvar`. With `uplevel`, commands can be evaluated in the scope of the calling procedure. The syntax is similar to `eval`. For example, the following command increments `x` in the scope of the calling procedure.

```
uplevel incr x
```

The `uplevel` command can be used to create new control structures such as variations on `if` and `while` or even more powerful constructs. I will describe such a construct in Chapter 19 (p. 459). However, a full discussion of this topic is beyond the scope of this book.

As a simple example, the following procedure (written by Karl Lehenbauer with a modification by Allan Brighton) provides static variables in the style of C. Like variables declared `global`, variables declared `static` are accessible from other procedures. However, the same `static` variables cannot be accessed by procedures in different files. This can be helpful in avoiding naming collisions between two programmers—both of whom unintentionally choose the same names for global variables that are private to their own files.

```
proc static {args} {
    set unique [info script]
    foreach var $args {
        uplevel 1 "upvar #0 static($unique:$var) $var"
    }
}
```

The procedure makes its arguments be references into an array (appropriately called static). Because of the uplevel command, all uses of the named variable after the static call become references into the array. The array elements have the file name embedded in them. This prevents conflicts with similarly-named variables in other files. By setting unique to "[lindex [info level -1] 0]", static can declare persistent variables that cannot be accessed by any other procedure even in the same file.

If you have significant amounts of Tcl code, you may want to consider even more sophisticated scoping techniques. For instance, [incr Tcl], written by Michael McLennan, is a Tcl extension that supports object-oriented programming in the style of C++. [incr Tcl] provides mechanisms for data encapsulation within well-defined interfaces, greatly increasing code readability while lessening the effort to write such code in the first place. The Tcl FAQ describes how to obtain [incr Tcl]. For more information on how to get the FAQ, see Chapter 1 (p. 20).

Working With Files

Tcl has commands for accessing files. The open command opens a file. The second argument determines how the file should be opened. "r" opens a file for reading; "w" truncates a file and opens it for writing; "a" opens a file for appending (writing without truncation). The second argument defaults to "r".

```
open "/etc/passwd" "r"
open "/tmp/stuff.[pid]" "w"
```

The first command opens /etc/password for reading. The second command opens a file in /tmp for writing. The process id is used to construct the file name—this is an ideal way to construct unique temporary names.

The open command returns a *file identifier*. This identifier can be passed to the many other file commands, such as the close command. The close command closes a file that is open. The close command takes one argument—a file identifier. Here is an example:

```
set input [open "/etc/passwd" "r"]     ;# open file
close $input                           ;# close same file
```

The open command is a good example of a command that is frequently evaluated from a catch command. Attempting to open (for reading) a nonexistent file generates an error. Here is one way to catch it:

```
if [catch {open $filename} input] {
    puts "$input"
    return
}
```

By printing the error message from open, this fragment accurately reports any problems related to opening the file. For example, the file might exist yet not allow permission to read it.

The open command may also be used to read from or write to pipelines specified as /bin/sh-like commands. A pipe character ("|") signifies that the remainder of the argument is a command. For example, the following command searches through all the files in the current directory hierarchy and finds each occurrence of the word book. Each matching occurrence can be read as if you were reading it from a plain file.

```
open "| find . -type f -print | xargs grep book"
```

The argument to open must be a valid list. Each element in the list becomes a command or argument in the pipeline. If you needed to search for "good book", you could do it in a number of ways. Here are just two:

```
open "| find -type f -print | xargs grep \"good book\""
open {| find -type f -print | xargs grep {good book}}
```

File I/O

Once a file is open, you can read from it and write to it.

Use the puts command to write to a file. If you provide a file identifier, puts will write to that file.

```
set file [open /tmp/stuff w]
puts $file "Hello World"          ;# write to /tmp/stuff
```

Remember that puts writes to the standard output by default. Sometimes it is convenient to refer to the standard output explicitly. You can do that using the predefined file identifier stdout. (You can also refer to the standard input as stdin and the standard error as stderr.)

The puts command also accepts the argument -nonewline, which skips adding a newline to the end of the line.

```
puts -nonewline $file "Hello World"
```

If you are writing strings without newlines to a character special file (such as a terminal), the output will not immediately appear because the I/O system buffers output one line at a time. However, there are strings you want to appear immediately and without a newline. Prompts are good examples. To force them out, use the flush command.

```
puts -nonewline $file $prompt
flush $file
```

Use the `gets` command or `read` command to read from a file. `gets` reads a line at a time and is good for text files in simple applications. `read` is appropriate for everything else.

The `gets` command takes a file identifier and an optional variable name in which to store the string that was read. When used this way, the length of the string is returned. If the end of the file is reached, -1 is returned.

I frequently read through files with the following code. Each time through the loop, one line is read and stored in the variable `line`. Any other commands in the loop are used to process each line. The loop terminates when all the lines have been read.

```
while {[gets $file line] != -1} {
    # do something with $line
}
```

The `read` command is similar to `gets`. The `read` command reads input but not line by line like `gets`. Instead, `read` reads a fixed number of characters. It is ideal if you want to process a file a huge chunk at a time. The maximum number to be read is passed as the second argument and the actual characters read are returned. For example, to read 100000 bytes you would use:

```
set chunk [read $file 100000]
```

The characters read may be less than the number requested if there are no more characters in the file or if you are reading from a terminal or similar type of special file.

The command `eof` returns a 1 if the end of the file has been encountered (e.g., by a previous `read` or `gets`). Otherwise `eof` returns a 0. This can be used to rewrite the loop above (using `gets`) to use `read`.

```
while {![eof $file]} {
    set buffer [read $file 100000]
    # do something with $buffer
}
```

If you omit the length, the `read` command reads the entire file. If the file fits in physical memory, you can read things with this form of `read` much more efficiently than with `gets`.[†] For example, if you want to process each line in a file, you can write:

```
foreach line [split [read $file] "\n"] {
    # do something with $line
}
```

There are two other commands to manipulate files: `seek` and `tell`. They provide random access into files and are analogous to the UNIX `lseek` and `tell` system calls.

[†] If the file is larger than physical memory, algorithms that require multiple passes over strings will cause thrashing.

They are rarely used, so I will not describe them further. See the Tcl reference material for more information.

File Name Matching

If a file name starts with a tilde character and a user name, the open command translates this to the named user's home directory. If the tilde is immediately followed by a slash, it is translated to the home directory of the user running the script. This is the same behavior that most shells support.

However, the open command does not do anything special with other metacharacters such as "*" and "?". The following command opens a file with a "*" at the end of its name!

```
open "/tmp/foo*" "w"
```

The glob command takes file patterns as arguments and returns the list of files that match. For example, the following command returns the files that end with .exp and .c in the current directory.

```
glob *.exp *.c
```

An error occurs if no files are matched by glob unless you use the –nocomplain flag.

The result of glob can be passed to open (presuming that it only matches one file). Using glob as the source in a foreach loop provides a way of opening each file separately.

```
foreach filename [glob *.exp] {
    set file [open $filename]
    # do something with $file
    close $file
}
```

The characters understood by glob are ~ (match a user's home directory), * (match anything), ? (match any single character), [] (match a set or range of characters), {} (match a choice of strings), and \ (match the next character literally). I will not go into details on these—they are similar to matching done by many shells such as csh. Plus I will be talking about most of them in later chapters anyway.

Setting And Getting The Current Directory

If file names do not begin with a "~" or "/", they are relative to the current directory. The current directory can be set with cd. It is analogous to the cd command in the shell. As in the open command, the tilde convention is supported but all other shell metacharacters are not. There is no built-in directory stack.

Here is an example of cd and pwd:

```
tclsh> cd ~libes/bin
tclsh> pwd
/usr/libes/bin
```

cd with no arguments changes to the home directory of the user running the script.

File Name Manipulation

The file command does a large number of different things all related to file names. The first argument names the function and the second argument is the file name to work on.

Four functions are purely textual. The same results can be accomplished with the string functions, but these are particularly convenient.

The "file dirname" command returns the directory part of the file name. (It returns a ". " if there is no slash. It returns a slash if there is only one slash and it is the first character.) For example:

```
tclsh> file dirname /usr/libes/bin/prog.exp
/usr/libes/bin
```

The opposite of "file dirname" is "file tail". It returns everything after the last slash. (If there is no slash, it returns the original file name.)

The "file extension" command returns the last dot and anything following it in the file name. (It returns the empty string if there is no dot.) For example:

```
tclsh> file extension /usr/libes/src/my.prog.c
.c
```

The opposite of "file extension" is "file rootname". It returns everything but the extension.

```
tclsh> file rootname /usr/libes/src/my.prog.c
/usr/libes/src/my.prog
```

While these functions are very useful with file names, they can be used on any string where dots and slashes are separators.

For example, suppose you have an IP address in addr and want to change the last field to the value stored in the variable new. You could use split and join, but the file name manipulation functions do it more easily.

```
tclsh> set addr
127.0.1.2
tclsh> set new
42
tclsh> set addr [file rootname $addr].$new
127.0.1.42
```

When you need to construct arbitrary compound names, consider using dots and slashes so that you can use the file name commands. You can also use blanks, of course, in which case you can use the `string` commands. However, since blanks are used as argument separators, you have to be much more careful when using commands such as `eval`.

File Information

The `file` command can be used to test for various attributes of a file. Listed below are a number of predicates and their meanings. Each variation returns a 0 if the condition is false for the file or 1 if it is true. Here is an example to test whether the file `/tmp/foo` exists:

```
tclsh> file exists /tmp/foo
1
```

The predicates are:

`file isdirectory` *file*	true if *file* is a directory
`file isfile` *file*	true if *file* is a plain file (i.e., not a directory, device, etc.)
`file executable` *file*	true if you have permission to execute *file*
`file exists` *file*	true if *file* exists
`file owned` *file*	true if you own *file*
`file readable` *file*	true if you have permission to read *file*
`file writable` *file*	true if you have permission to write *file*

All the predicates return 0 if the file does not exist.

While the predicates make it very easy to test whether a file meets a condition, it is occasionally useful to directly ask for file information. Tcl provides a number of commands that do that. Each of these takes a file name as the last argument.

The "`file size`" command returns the number of bytes in a file. For example:

```
tclsh> file size /etc/motd
63
```

The "`file atime`" command returns the time in seconds when the file was last accessed. The "`file mtime`" command returns the time in seconds when the file was last modified. The number of seconds is counted starting from January 1, 1970.

The "`file type`" command returns a string describing the type of the file such as `file`, `directory`, `characterSpecial`, `blockSpecial`, `link`, or `socket`. The "`file readlink`" command returns the name to which the file points to, assuming it is a symbolic link.

The "file stat" command returns the raw values of a file's inode. Each value is written as elements in an array. The array name is given as the third argument to the file command. For example, the following command writes the information to the array stuff.

```
file stat /etc/motd stuff
```

Elements are written for atime, ctime, mtime, type, uid, gid, ino, mode, nlink, dev, size. These are all written as integers except for the type element which is written as I described before. Most of these values are also accessible more directly by using one of the other arguments to the file command. However, some of the more unusual elements (such as nlink) have no corresponding analog. For example, the following command prints the number of links to a file:

```
file stat $filename fileinfo
puts "$filename has $fileinfo(nlink) links"
```

If the file is a symbolic link, "file stat" returns information about the file to which it points. The "file lstat" command works similarly to "file stat" except that it returns information about the link itself. See the UNIX stat documentation for more information on stat and lstat.

All of the non-predicate file information commands require the file to exist or else they will generate an error. This error can be caught using catch.

Executing UNIX Commands

In the previous section, I described many commands for working with files. Yet, you may have noticed some omissions. For example, there are no Tcl commands to remove files or make directories. These commands already exist outside of Tcl. In order to take advantage of them, Tcl provides a way of calling existing UNIX commands. This makes Tcl simpler to learn and use. You can reuse commands that you are already familiar with such as rm and mkdir. There is little point in having Tcl duplicate these.

UNIX commands can be executed by calling exec. The arguments generally follow the same /bin/sh-like conventions as open including ">", "<", "|", "&", and variations on them. Use whitespace before and after the redirection symbols.

```
tclsh> exec date
Thu Feb 24  9:32:00 EST 1994
tclsh> exec date | wc -w
      6
tclsh> exec date > /tmp/foo
tclsh> exec cat /tmp/foo
Thu Feb 24  9:32:03 EST 1994
```

Unless redirected, the standard output of the exec command is returned as the result. This enables you to save the output of a program in a variable or use it in another command.

```
tclsh> puts "The date is [exec date]"
The date is Thu Feb 24  9:32:17 EST 1994
```

Tcl assumes that UNIX programs return the exit value 0 if successful. Use catch to test whether a program succeeds or not. The following command returns the exit value from mv which could, for example, indicate that a file did not exist.

```
catch {exec mv oldname newname}
```

Many programs return nonzero exit values even if they were successful. For example, diff returns an exit value of 1 when it finds that two files are different. Some UNIX programs are sloppy and return a random exit value which can generate an error in exec. An error is also generated if a program writes to its standard error stream. It is common to use catch with exec to deal with these problems.

Tilde substitution is performed on the command but not on the arguments, and no globbing is done at all. So if you want to delete all the .o files in a directory, for instance, it must be done as follows:

```
exec rm [glob *.o]
```

Beyond the /bin/sh conventions, exec supports special redirections to reference open files. In particular, an @ after a redirection symbol introduces a file identifier returned from open. For example, the following command writes the date to an open file.

```
set file [open /tmp/foo]
exec date >@ $file
```

The exec command has a number of other esoteric features. See the reference documentation for more information.

Environment Variables

The global array env is pre-initialized so that each element corresponds to an environment variable. For example, the path is a list of directories to search for executable programs. From the shell, the path is stored in the variable PATH. When using Tcl, the path is contained in env(PATH). It is manipulated just like any other variable.

```
tclsh> set env(PATH)
/usr/local/bin:/usr/bin:/bin
tclsh> set env(PATH) ".:$env(PATH)"      ;# prepend current dir
.:/usr/local/bin:/usr/bin:/bin
```

Modifications to the env array do not affect the parent environment, but new processes that are created (using exec, for instance) will inherit the current values (including any new elements that have been created).

Handling Unknown Commands

The unknown command is called when another command is executed which is not known to the Tcl interpreter. Rather than simply issuing an error message, this gives you the opportunity to handle the problem and recover in an intelligent way. For example, you could attempt to re-evaluate the arguments as an expression. This would allow you to be able to evaluate expressions without using the expr command.

```
set a [1+1]
```

To make unknown do what you want, simply define it as a procedure. The list of arguments is available as a parameter to the unknown command. Here is a definition of unknown which supports expression evaluation without having to specify the expr command:

```
proc unknown {args} {
    expr $args
}
```

By default, Tcl comes with a definition for unknown that does a number of things such as attempt history substitution. I will only go into detail on the most useful action that unknown takes—retrieving procedure definitions from libraries.

Libraries

By default, the unknown command tries to find procedure definitions in a library. A library is simply a file that contain procedure definitions. Libraries can be explicitly read using the source command. However, it is possible to prepare an index file which describes the library contents in such a way that Tcl knows which library to load based on the command name. Once a library is loaded, the unknown command calls the new procedure just defined. After the procedure completes, unknown completes and it appears as if the procedure had been defined all along.

As an example, one of Tcl's default libraries defines the parray procedure. parray prints out the contents of an array. It is a parameterized version of the code on page 53.

The `info` command shows that `parray` is not defined before it is invoked, but it is defined afterwards:

```
tclsh> info command parray
tclsh> parray color
color(pavement) = black
color(snow)     = white
tclsh> info command parray
parray
```

You can add procedures to the libraries or create new libraries. See the Tcl reference material for more information on using libraries.

Is There More To Tcl?

This chapter has covered most of the Tcl commands and data structures. I will expand on a few of these descriptions later in the book, but for the most part, you have now seen the entire Tcl language.

Even though Tcl is a small language, it is capable of handling very large and sophisticated scripts. However, Tcl was originally designed for writing small scripts with most of the work being done in the underlying commands themselves. Indeed, Tcl supports the ability to add additional commands written in other languages such as C and C++. This is useful for commands that must be very fast or do something unusual (such as the Expect commands do).

Fortunately, the need to resort to implementing your own commands is becoming increasingly unnecessary. People have already written commands for just about anything you can imagine. They are packaged into collections called *extensions* and are available from the Tcl archive. I have already mentioned [incr Tcl] which provides commands for object-oriented programming. Another popular extension is TclX, which provides commands for most of the UNIX system and library calls. There are a variety of extensions to support different databases (e.g., SQL, Oracle, Dbm). And there are many extensions to support graphics (e.g., GL, PHIGS, SIPP, YART). These extensions and others are described in the Tcl FAQ (page 20). In Chapter 22 (p. 513), I will describe how to add existing extensions to Expect.

If none of these extensions provides what you are looking for, you can always write your own. Tcl has always supported this way of adding new commands and it is surprisingly easy to do. If you are interested in learning more about this, I recommend Ousterhout's *Tcl and the Tk Toolkit*.

Exercises

1. Is Tcl like any other language you know? Bourne shell? C shell? Lisp? C?

2. As best as you can remember (or guess), write down the precedence table for Tcl expressions. Now look it up in the reference material. How close were you? Repeat this exercise with Perl, C, Lisp, and APL.

3. What is the best thing about Tcl? What is the worst thing about Tcl? (That bad, eh?)

4. Try putting comments where they do not belong—for instance, between the parameters of a procedure. What happens?

5. Write a procedure to reverse a string. If you wrote an iterative solution, now write a recursive solution or vice versa.

6. Repeat the previous exercise but with a list instead of a string.

7. Write a procedure to rename all the files in a directory ending with `.c` to names ending in "`.cc`".

8. Write a procedure that takes a list of variable names and a list of values, and sets each variable in the list to the respective value in the other list. Think of different alternatives to handle the case when the lists are of different lengths.

9. Write a procedure that creates a uniquely-named temporary file. Make sure it works even if you run it multiple times in the same process.

10. Write a procedure that can define other procedures that automatically have access to global variables.

In This Chapter:

• *The Basic Expect Commands*

• *Starting Processes*

• *Sending Input*

• *Waiting For Output*

• *Interacting*

3

Getting Started With Expect

Three commands are central to the power of Expect: send, expect, and spawn. The send command sends strings to a process, the expect command waits for strings from a process, and the spawn command starts a process.

In this chapter, I will describe these commands and another one that is very useful: interact. To best understand this chapter, it will help to have some basic familiarity with Tcl. If you are wondering about a command that is not explained, look it up in the index for a reference in the previous chapter and read about it there.

The send Command

The send command takes a string as an argument and sends it to a process. For example:

```
send "hello world"
```

This sends the string "hello world" (without the quotes). If Expect is already interacting with a program, the string will be sent to that program. But initially, send will send to the standard output. Here is what happens when I type this to the Expect interpreter interactively:

```
expect1.1> send "hello world"
hello worldexpect1.2>
```

The send command does not format the string in any way, so after it is printed the next Expect prompt gets appended to it without any space. To make the prompt appear on a different line, put a newline character at the end of the string. A newline is represented by "\n".

```
expect1.1> send "hello world\n"
hello world
expect1.2>
```

If these commands are stored in a file, `speak`, the script can be executed from the UNIX command line:

```
% expect speak
hello world
%
```

With a little magic it is possible to invoke the file as just "`speak`" rather than "`expect speak`". On most systems it suffices to insert the line "`#!/usr/local/bin/expect --`" and say "`chmod +x speak; rehash`". I will explain this in more detail in Chapter 9 (p. 215). For now, just take it on faith.

The expect Command

`expect` is the opposite of `send`. The `expect` command waits for a response, usually from a process. `expect` can wait for a specific string, but more often `expect` is used to wait for any string that matches a given pattern. Analogous to `send`, the `expect` command initially waits for characters from the keyboard[†]. Using them, I can create a little conversation:

```
expect "hi\n"
send "hello there!\n"
```

When run, the interaction looks like this:

```
hi
hello there!
```

I typed the string `hi` and then pressed return. My input matched the pattern "`hi\n`". Ideally, a return would be matched with "`\r`"; however, the UNIX terminal driver translates a return to "`\n`".[‡] As you will see later on, it is rarely necessary to have to worry about this mapping because most of Expect's interactions occur with programs not users, anyway. Nonetheless, it is occasionally useful to expect input from people. Plus, it is much easier to experiment with Expect this way.

If `expect` reads characters that do not match the expected string, it continues waiting for more characters. If I had typed `hello` followed by a return, `expect` would continue to wait for "`hi\n`".

---

† It actually reads from standard input which is typically the keyboard. For now, I will treat them as if they were the same thing.
‡ You can disable this behavior by saying "`stty -icrnl`" to the shell, but most programs expect this mapping to take place so learn to live with it.

When the matching string is finally typed, `expect` returns. But before returning, `expect` stores the matched characters in a variable called `expect_out(0,string)`. All of the matched characters plus the characters that came earlier but did not match are stored in a variable called `expect_out(buffer)`. `expect` does this every time it matches characters. The names of these variables may seem odd, but they will make more sense later on.

Imagine the following script:

```
expect "hi\n"
send "you typed <$expect_out(buffer)>"
send "but I only expected <$expect_out(0,string)>"
```

The angle brackets do not do anything special. They will just appear in the output, making it clear where the literal text stops and the variable values start. When run the script looks like this:

```
Nice weather, eh?
hi
you typed <Nice weather, eh?
hi>
but I only expected <hi>
```

I typed "Nice weather, eh?" <return> "hi" <return>. `expect` reported that it found the hi but it also found something unexpected: "Nice weather, eh?\n".

Anchoring

Finding unexpected data in the input does not bother `expect`. It keeps looking until it finds something that matches. It is possible to prevent `expect` from matching when unexpected data arrives before a pattern. The caret (^) is a special character that only matches the beginning of the input. If the first character of the pattern is a caret, the remainder of the pattern must match starting at the beginning of the incoming data. It cannot skip over characters to find a valid match. For example, the pattern `^hi` matches if I enter "hiccup" but not if I enter "sushi".

The dollar sign ($) is another special character. It matches the end of the data. The pattern `hi$` matches if I enter "sushi" but not if I enter "hiccup". And the pattern `^hi$` matches neither "sushi" nor "hiccup". It matches "hi" and nothing else.

Patterns that use the ^ or $ are said to be *anchored*. Some programs, such as `sed`, define anchoring in terms of the beginning of a line. This makes sense for `sed`, but not for `expect`. `expect` anchors at the beginning of whatever input it has received without regard to line boundaries.

When patterns are *not* anchored, patterns match beginning at the earliest possible position in the string. For example, if the pattern is hi and the input is philosophic, the hi in philo is matched rather than the hi in sophic. In the next section, this subtlety will become more important.

What Happens When Input Does Not Match

Once expect has matched data to a pattern, it moves the data to the expect_out array as I showed earlier. The matched data is no longer eligible to be matched. Additional matches can only take place with new data.

Consider the following fragment:

```
expect "hi"
send "$expect_out(0,string) $expect_out(buffer)"
```

If I execute these two commands, Expect waits for me to enter hi. If I enter philosophic followed by a return, Expect finds the hi and prints:

```
hi phi
```

If I execute the two commands again, Expect prints:

```
hi losophi
```

Even though there were two occurrences of hi, the first time expect matched the first one, moving it into expect_out. The next expect started from where the previous one had left off.

With simple patterns like these, expect always stops waiting and returns immediately after matching the pattern. If expect receives more input than it needs, that input is remembered for the possibility of matching in later expect commands. In other words, expect *buffers* its input. This allows expect to receive input before it is actually ready to use it. The input will be held in an *input buffer* until an expect pattern matches it. This buffer is internal to expect and is not accessible to the script in any way except by matching patterns against it.

After the second expect above, the buffer must hold c\n. This is all that was left after the second hi in philosophic. The \n is there, of course, because after entering the word, I pressed return.

What happens if the commands are run again? In this case, expect is not going to find anything to match hi. The expect command eventually *times out* and returns. By default, after 10 seconds expect gives up waiting for input that matches the pattern. This ability to give up waiting is very useful. Typically, there is some reasonable amount of time to wait for input after which there is no further point to waiting. The choice of 10 seconds is good for many tasks. But there is no hard rule. Programs almost never guarantee that "if there is no response after 17 seconds, then the program or computer has crashed".

The timeout is changed by setting the variable `timeout` using the Tcl `set` command. For example, the following command sets the timeout to 60 seconds.

```
set timeout 60
```

The value of `timeout` must be an integral number of seconds. Normally timeouts are nonnegative, but the special case of -1 signifies that `expect` should wait forever. A timeout of 0 indicates that `expect` should not wait at all.

If `expect` times out, the values of `expect_out` are not changed. Therefore, the commands above would have printed:

```
hi losophi
```

even though only `c\n` remained in the buffer.

Pattern-Action Pairs

You can directly associate a command with a pattern. Such commands are referred to as *actions*. The association is made by listing the action immediately after the pattern in the `expect` command itself. For example:

```
expect "hi" {send "You said $expect_out(buffer)"}
```

The command "`send "You said $expect_out(buffer)"`" will be executed if and only if `hi` is matched in the input.

Additional pattern-action pairs can be listed after the first one:

```
expect "hi"    { send "You said hi\n" } \
    "hello"    { send "Hello yourself\n" } \
    "bye"      { send "That was unexpected\n" }
```

This command looks for "hi", "hello", and "bye" simultaneously. If any of the three patterns are found, the action listed immediately after the first matching pattern is executed. It is possible that none of them match within the time period defined by the timeout. In this case, `expect` stops waiting and execution continues with the next command in the script. Actions can be associated with timeouts, and I will describe that in Chapter 4 (p. 94).

In the `expect` command, it does not matter how the patterns and actions visually line up. They can all appear on a single line if you can fit them, but lining up the patterns and actions usually makes it easier for a human to read them.

Notice how all the actions are embedded in braces. That is because expect would otherwise misinterpret the command. What is the problem with the following command?

```
expect "hi" send "You said hi\n"      ;# wrong!
```

In this case, hi is taken as a pattern, send is the associated action and "You said hi\n" is taken as the next pattern. This is obviously not what was intended! If the action is more than a single argument, you must enclose it in braces.

Because Tcl commands normally terminate at the end of a line, a backslash is used to continue the command. Since all but the last line must end with a backslash, it can be a bit painful to cut and paste lines. You always have to make sure that the backslashes are there. The expect command supports an alternate syntax that lets you put all the arguments in one big braced list. For example:

```
expect {
    "hi" { send "You said hi\n"}
    "hello" { send "Hello yourself\n"}
    "bye" { send "That was unexpected\n"}
}
```

The initial open brace causes Tcl to continue scanning additional lines to complete the command. Once the matching brace is found, all of the patterns and actions between the outer braces are passed to expect as arguments.

Here is another way of writing the same expect commands:

```
expect "hi" {
        send "You said hi\n"
    } "hello" {
        send "Hello yourself\n"
    } "bye" {
        send "That was unexpected\n"
    }
```

Each open brace forces more lines to be read until a close brace is encountered. But on the same line that the close brace appears, another open brace causes the search to continue once again for a mate. Even though all the arguments are not enclosed by yet another pair of braces, the whole command is nonetheless read as one. This style has the advantage that it is easier to have multi-line actions, and the actions can be moved around more easily because they are not on the same line as their patterns (presuming your editor can cut and paste by lines more easily than half-lines). If you want to further separate the patterns, you can rewrite it as:

```
expect {
    "hi" {
        send "You said hi\n"
    }
    "hello" {
        send "Hello yourself\n"
    }
    "bye" {
        send "That was unexpected\n"
    }
}
```

While this looks like it wastes a lot of space, you can now cut and paste the first action (hi) without disturbing the "expect   {". You can decide for yourself which style is appropriate. Depending on the context, I may use any one of these. If commands are very short, I may even pack them all on a line. For example, the following command has two patterns, "exit" and "quit". Their actions are listed immediately to the right of each pattern.

```
expect "exit" {exit 1} "quit" abort
```

Example — Timed Reads In The Shell

I have shown how to wait for input for a given amount of time and how to send data back. I will wrap this up in a script called timed-read.

```
#!/usr/local/bin/expect --
set timeout $argv
expect "\n" {
    send [string trimright "$expect_out(buffer)" "\n"]
}
```

The timeout is read from the variable argv which is predefined to contain the arguments from the command line. I will describe argv further in Chapter 9 (p. 213). The next command waits for a line to be entered. When it is, "string trimright ... "\n"" returns the string without the newline on the end of it, and that is returned as the result of the script.

You can now call this script from a shell as follows:

% timed-read 60

This command waits 60 seconds for the user to type a line and then it returns whatever the user typed. This ability is very useful. For example, suppose your system reboots automatically upon a crash. You could set up your system so that it gives someone the opportunity to log in to straighten out any problems before coming up all the way. Of course, if the machine crashes when no one is around, you do not want the computer to wait until someone comes in just to tell it to go ahead. To do so, just embed this in your shell script:

```
echo "Rebooting..."
echo "Want to poke around before coming up all the way?"
answer=`timed-read 60`
```

Now you could test to see if the answer is yes or no. If no one is around, the script will just time out after 60 seconds and the answer will be empty. The shell script could then continue with the rebooting process.

Surprisingly, there is no simple way for a shell script to wait for a period of time for an answer. The standard solution is to fork off another shell script that sends a signal back to the original shell script that catches the signal and tries to recover. This sounds easy but is fairly difficult to code. And if you are already in a forked process or have forked other processes, it is very tricky to keep everything straight.

By comparison, the Expect solution is straightforward. In the next chapter, I will show how to make the **expect** command strip off the newline automatically. This will make the script even simpler.[†]

The spawn Command

While interacting with a person is useful, most of the time Expect is used to interact with programs. You have already seen enough to get a feeling for **send** and **expect**. There is more to learn about them, but now I want to explore the **spawn** command.

The **spawn** command starts another program. A running program is known as a *process*. Expect is flexible and will view humans as processes too. This allows you to use the same commands for both humans and processes. The only difference is that processes have to be spawned first.[‡]

The first argument of the **spawn** command is the name of a program to start. The remaining arguments are passed to the program. For example:

```
spawn ftp ftp.uu.net
```

This command spawns an ftp process. ftp sees ftp.uu.net as its argument. This directs ftp to open a connection to that host just as if the command "ftp ftp.uu.net" had been typed to the shell. You can now send commands using **send** and read prompts and responses using **expect**.

---

† Shell backquotes automatically strip trailing newlines, so the script could be simplified in this scenario just by omitting the "string trimright" command. However, in other contexts it is useful to strip the newlines.
‡ Admittedly, humans have to be spawned as well; however, this type of spawning is probably best left to the confines of the bedroom.

It is always a good idea to wait for prompts before sending any information. If you do not wait, the program might not be ready to listen and could conceivably miss your commands. I will show examples of this in a later chapter. For now, play it safe and wait for the prompt.

`ftp` begins by asking for a name and password. `ftp.uu.net` is a great place for retrieving things—they let anyone use their anonymous `ftp` service. They ask for identification (you must enter your e-mail address at the password prompt) but it is primarily for gathering statistics and debugging.

When I run `ftp` by hand from the shell, this is what I see:

```
% ftp ftp.uu.net
Connected to ftp.uu.net.
220 ftp.UU.NET FTP server (Version 6.34 Thu Oct 22 14:32:01 EDT
    1992) ready.
Name (ftp.uu.net:don): anonymous
331 Guest login ok, send e-mail address as password.
Password:
230-                    Welcome to the UUNET archive.
230-    For information about UUNET, call +1 703 204 8000...
230-    Access is allowed all day...

             < a lot of stuff here omitted >

230 Guest login ok, access restrictions apply.
```

To automate this interaction, a script has to wait for the prompts and send the responses. The first prompt is for a name, to which the script replies "anonymous\r". The second prompt is for a password (or e-mail address) to which the script replies "don@libes.com\r". Finally, the script looks for a prompt to enter `ftp` commands. This looks like "ftp> ".

```
expect "Name"
send "anonymous\r"
expect "Password:"
send "don@libes.com\r"
expect "ftp> "
```

Notice that each line sent by the script is terminated with \r. This denotes a return character and is exactly what you would press if you entered these lines at the shell, so that is exactly what Expect has to send.

It is a common mistake to terminate `send` commands to a process followed by \n. In this context, \n denotes a linefeed character. You do not interactively end lines with a linefeed. So Expect must not either. Use "\r".

Contrast this to what I was doing earlier—sending to a user, or rather, standard output. Such strings were indeed terminated with a \n. In that context, the \n denotes a newline. Because standard output goes to a terminal, the terminal driver translates this to a carriage-return linefeed sequence.

Similarly, when reading lines from a program that would normally appear on a terminal, you will see the carriage-return linefeed sequence. This is represented as \r\n in an expect pattern.

This may seem confusing at first, but it is inherent in the way UNIX does terminal I/O and in the representation of characters and newlines in strings. The representation used by Tcl and Expect is common to the C language and most of the UNIX utilities. I will have more to say on the subject of newlines and carriage returns in Chapter 8 (p. 185).

Running this script produces almost the same output as when it was run by hand. The only difference is when the program is spawned. When you manually invoke ftp, you normally see something like:

```
% ftp ftp.uu.net
```

Instead **expect** shows:

```
spawn ftp ftp.uu.net
```

The difference is that there is no shell prompt and the string **spawn** appears. In Chapter 13 (p. 298), I will show how to customize this string or get rid of it entirely.

The remainder of the output is identical whether run interactively via the shell or automated via Expect.

Uunet is a very large repository of public-access on-line information. Among other things stored there are the standards and other documents describing the Internet. These are called RFCs (Request For Comments). For instance RFC 959 describes the FTP protocol and RFC 854 describes the Telnet protocol. These RFCs are all in separate files but stored in one common directory. You can go to that directory using the following commands:

```
send "cd inet/rfc\r"
```

Each RFC is assigned a number by the publisher. Uunet uses this number to name the file containing the RFC. This means that you have to know the mapping from the title to the number. Fortunately, Uunet has such an index stored as a separate document. You can download this with the following additional commands:

```
expect "ftp> "
send "binary\r"
expect "ftp> "
send "get rfc-index.Z\r"
expect "ftp> "
```

The first line waits to make sure that the `ftp` server has completed the previous command. The `binary` command forces `ftp` to disable any translation it might otherwise attempt on transferred files. This is a necessity because the index is not a text file but a compressed file. This format is implied by the `.Z` extension in the name.

The RFCs are named `rfc###.Z`, where `###` is the RFC number. Along with the index, they are all stored in the directory `inet/rfc`. By passing the RFC number as an argument, it is possible to add two more commands to download any RFC.

```
send "get rfc$argv.Z\r"
expect "ftp> "
```

This extracts the number from the command line so that you could call it from the shell as:

```
% ftp-rfc 1178
```

Notice that after the `get` command is another `expect` for a prompt. Even though the script is not going to send another command, it is a good idea to wait for the prompt. This forces the script to wait for the file to be transferred. Without this wait, Expect would reach the end of the script and exit. `ftp` would in turn exit, and the file transfer would almost certainly not be completed by then.

`ftp` actually has the capability to tell if there were problems in transferring a file, and this capability should be used if you want a robust script. In the interest of simplicity I will ignore this now, but eventually I will start presenting scripts that are more robust.

However, there is one change for robustness that cannot be ignored. The default timeout is 10 seconds, and almost any `ftp` transfer takes at least 10 seconds. The simplest way to handle this is to disable the timeout so that the script waits as long as it takes to get the file. As before, this is done by inserting the following command before any of the `expect` commands:

```
set timeout -1
```

So far this script simply retrieves the RFC from Uunet. As I noted earlier, the file is compressed. Since you usually want to uncompress the RFC, it is convenient to add another line to the script that does this. The `uncompress` program is not interactive so it can be called using `exec` as:

```
exec uncompress rfc$argv.Z
```

You could certainly `spawn` it, but `exec` is better for running non-interactive programs— you do not have to mess around with `send` and `expect`. If `uncompress` has any problems, Expect reports them on the standard error.

The final script looks like this:

```
#!/usr/local/bin/expect --
# retrieve an RFC (or the index) from uunet via anon ftp

if {[llength $argv] == 0} {
    puts "usage: ftp-rfc {-index|#}"
    exit 1
}
set timeout -1
spawn ftp ftp.uu.net
expect "Name"
send "anonymous\r"
expect "Password:"
send "don@libes.com\r"
expect "ftp> "
send "cd inet/rfc\r"
expect "ftp> "

send "binary\r"
expect "ftp> "
send "get rfc$argv.Z\r"
expect "ftp> "

exec uncompress rfc$argv.Z
```

I have added a comment to the top describing what the script does, and I have also added a check for the arguments. Since the script requires at least one argument, a usage message is printed if no arguments are supplied.

More checks could be added. For example, if a user runs this script as "ftp-rfc 1178 1179", it will not find any such file—the get will try to get a file named rfc1178 and save it locally as 1179.Z—obviously not what the user intended. How might you modify the script to handle this case?

The interact Command

All of the uses of Expect so far have been to totally automate a task. However, sometimes this is too rigid. For a variety of reasons you may not want to completely automate a task. A common alternative is to automate some of it and then do the rest manually.

In the previous example, anonymous ftp was used to retrieve files automatically from the site ftp.uu.net. At the beginning of that script was some interaction to identify myself to the `ftp` server. This consisted of entering the string `anonymous\r` followed by my email address. Here was the Expect fragment to do it:

```
expect "Name"
send "anonymous\r"
expect "Password:"
send "don@libes.com\r"
```

Now consider doing this manually. If you like to browse through the many computers that support anonymous `ftp`, repeating this little identification scenario can be a nuisance. And it seems rather silly since your computer is perfectly capable of supplying this information. This so-called password is not really a *secret* password—it is just an email address. Let Expect do this part while you do the browsing.

Expect provides a command that turns control from the script over to you. It is named `interact` and called as:

```
interact
```

When this command is executed, Expect stops reading commands from the script and instead begins reading from the keyboard and the process. When you press keys, they are sent immediately to the spawned process. At the same time, when the process sends output, it is immediately sent to the standard output so that you can read it.

The result is that you are effectively connected directly to the process as if Expect was not even there. Conveniently, when the spawned process terminates, the `interact` command returns control to the script. And if you make `interact` the last line of the script, then the script itself terminates as well.

Example — Anonymous ftp

The `interact` command is ideal for building a script I call `aftp`. This script consists of the user/password interaction from the previous example and an `interact` command. The complete `aftp` script is shown below.

Anytime you want to begin anonymous `ftp`, you can use this little script. It will automatically supply the appropriate identification and then turn control over to you. When you type `quit` to `ftp`, `ftp` will exit, so `interact` will exit, and then the script will exit.

```
#!/usr/local/bin/expect --
spawn ftp $argv
expect "Name"
send "anonymous\r"
expect "Password:"
send "don@libes.com\r"
interact
```

Notice that the script does not wait for "ftp> " before the `interact` command. You could add another `expect` command to do that, but it would be redundant. Since the `interact` waits for characters from the process as well as the keyboard simultaneously, when the "ftp> " finally does arrive, `interact` will then display it. Presumably, a user will wait for the prompt before typing anyway so there is no functional benefit to using an explicit `expect`.

With only a little more work, this script can be jazzed up in lots of ways. For example, rather then embedding your name in the script, you can pull it out of the environment by using the expression `$env(USER)`. The full command in the script would be:

```
send "$env(USER)@libes.com\r"
```

It is a little more difficult to make this script portable to any machine because there is no standard command to retrieve the domain name (presuming you are using domain-name style email addresses, of course). While many systems have a command literally called `domainname`, it often refers to the NIS domain name, not the Internet domain name. And the `hostname` command does not dependably return the domain name either.

One solution is to look for the domain name in the file "`/etc/resolv.conf`". This file is used by the name server software that runs on most UNIX hosts on the Internet. Here is a procedure to look up the domain name:

```
proc domainname {} {
    set file [open /etc/resolv.conf r]
    while {[gets $file buf] != -1} {
        if {[scan $buf "domain %s" name] == 1} {
            close $file
            return $name
        }
    }
    close $file
    error "no domain declaration in /etc/resolv.conf"
}
```

The `domainname` procedure reads `/etc/resolv.conf` until it encounters a line that begins with the string `domain`. The rest of the line is returned. If no string is found, or the file cannot be read, an error is generated.

The full command in the script can now be written as:

```
send "$env(USER)@[domainname]\r"
```

Exercises

1. The `ftp-rfc` script does not understand what to do if the user enters multiple RFC numbers on the command line. Modify the script so that it handles this problem.

2. Modify `ftp-rfc` so that if given an argument such as "`telnet`", the script first retrieves the index, then looks up which RFCs mention the argument in the title, and downloads them. Cache the index and RFCs in a public directory so that they do not have to be repeatedly downloaded.

3. Most `ftp` sites use a root directory where only `pub` is of interest. The result is that "`cd pub`" is always the first command everyone executes. Make the `aftp` script automatically `cd` to `pub` and print the directories it finds there before turning over control to `interact`.

4. Make the `aftp` script `cd` to `pub` only if `pub` exists.

5. Write a script to dial a pager. Use it in the error handling part of a shell script that performs a critical function such as backup or `fsck`.

6. The `domainname` procedure on page 84 is not foolproof. For example, the file `resolv.conf` might not exist. Assume the procedure fails on your system and ask `nslookup` for the current domain name.

7. Write a script that connects to a modem and dials phone numbers from a list until one answers.

4

Glob Patterns And Other Basics

In the last chapter, I showed some simple patterns that allow you to avoid having to specify exactly what you want to wait for. In this chapter, I will describe how to use patterns that you are already probably familiar with from the shell—glob patterns. I will also describe what happens when patterns do not match. I will go over some other basic situations such as how to handle timeouts. Finally I will describe what to do at the ends of scripts and processes.

The * Wildcard

Suppose you want to match all of the input and the only thing you know about it is that hi occurs within it. You are not sure if there is more to it, or even if another hi might appear. You just want to get it all. To do this, use the asterisk (*). The asterisk is a wild-card that matches any number of characters. You can write:

```
expect "hi*"
send "$expect_out(0,string) $expect_out(buffer)"
```

If the input buffer contained "philosophic\n", expect would match the entire buffer. Here is the output from the previous commands:

```
hilosophic
 philosophic
```

The pattern hi matched the literal hi while the * matched the string "losophic\n". The first p was not matched by anything in the pattern so it shows up in expect_out(buffer) but not in expect_out(0,string).

Earlier I said that `*` matches any number of characters. More precisely, it matches the longest string possible while still allowing the pattern itself to match. With the input buffer of "philosophic\n", compare the effects of the following two commands:

```
expect "hi*"
expect "hi*hi"
```

In the first one, the `*` matches losophic\n. This is the longest possible string that the `*` can match while still allowing the hi to match hi. In the second expect, the `*` only matches losop, thereby allowing the second hi to match. If the `*` matched anything else, the entire pattern would fail to match.

What happens with the following command in which there are two asterisks?

```
expect "*hi*"
```

This could conceivably match in two ways corresponding to the two occurrences of "hi" in the string.

	* matches	hi matches	* matches
possibility (1)	philosop	hi	c\n
possibility (2)	p	hi	losophic\n

What actually happens is possibility (1). The first `*` matches philosop. As before, each `*` tries to match the longest string possible while allowing the total pattern to match, but the `*`'s are matched from left to right. The leftmost `*`'s match strings before the rightmost `*`'s have a chance. While the outcome is the same in this case (that is, the whole pattern matches), I will show cases later where it is necessary to realize that pattern matching proceeds from left to right.

At The Beginning Of A Pattern Is Rarely Useful

Patterns match beginning at the earliest possible character in a string. In Chapter 3 (p. 74), I showed how the pattern hi matched the first hi in philosophic. However, in the example above, the subpattern hi matched the second hi. Why the difference?

The difference is that hi was preceded by "`*`". Since the `*` is capable of matching anything, the leading `*` causes the match to start at the beginning of the string. In contrast, the earliest point that the bare hi can match is the first hi. Once that hi has matched, it cannot match anything else—including the second hi.

In practice, a leading `*` is usually redundant. Most patterns have enough literal letters that there is no choice in how the match occurs. The only remaining difference is that the leading `*` forces the otherwise unmatched leading characters to be stored in `expect_out(0,string)`. However, the characters will already be stored in `expect_out(buffer)` so there is little merit on this point alone.[†]

* At The End Of A Pattern Can Be Tricky

When a * appears at the right end of a pattern, it matches everything left in the input buffer (assuming the rest of the pattern matches). This is a useful way of clearing out the entire buffer so that the next `expect` does not return a mishmash of things that were received previously and things that are brand new.

Sometimes it is even useful to say:

```
expect *
```

Here the * matches anything. This is like saying, "I don't care what's in the input buffer. Throw it away." This pattern *always* matches, even if nothing is there. Remember that * matches anything, and the empty string is anything! As a corollary of this behavior, this command always returns immediately. It never waits for new data to arrive. It does not have to since it matches everything.

In the examples demonstrating * so far, each string was entered by a person who pressed return afterwards. This is typical of most programs, because they run in what is called *cooked mode*. Cooked mode includes the usual line-editing features such as backspace and delete-previous-word. This is provided by the terminal driver, not the program. This simplifies most programs. They see the line only after you have edited it and pressed return.

Unfortunately, output from processes is not nearly so well behaved. When you watch the output of a program such as `ftp` or `telnet` (or `cat` for that matter), it may seem as if lines appear on your screen as atomic units. But this is not guaranteed. For example, in the previous chapter, I showed that when `ftp` starts up it looks like this:

```
% ftp ftp.uu.net
Connected to ftp.uu.net.
220 ftp.UU.NET FTP server (Version 6.34 Thu Oct 22 14:32:01 EDT
    1992) ready.
Name (ftp.uu.net:don):
```

Even though the program may have printed "`Connected to ftp.uu.net.\n`" all at once—perhaps by a single `printf` in a C program—the UNIX kernel can break this into small chunks, spitting out a few characters each time to the terminal. For example, it might print out "Conn" and then "ecte" and then "d to" and so on. Fortunately, computers are so fast that humans do not notice the brief pauses in the middle of

---

[†] The more likely reason to see scripts that begin many patterns with "*" is that prior to Expect version 4, all patterns were anchored, with the consequence that most patterns required a leading "*".

output. The reason the system breaks up output like this is that programs usually produce characters faster than the terminal driver can display them. The operating system will obligingly wait for the terminal driver to effectively say, "Okay, I've displayed that last bunch of characters. Send me a couple more." In reality, the system does not just sit there and wait. Since it is running many other programs at the same time, the system switches its attention frequently to other programs. Expect itself is one such "other program" in this sense.

When Expect runs, it will immediately ask for all the characters that a program produced only to find something like "Conn". If told to wait for a string that matches "Name*:   ", Expect will keep asking the computer if there is any more output, and it will eventually find the output it is looking for.

As I said, humans are slow and do not notice this chunking effect. In contrast, Expect is so fast that it is almost always waiting. Thus, it sees most output come as chunks rather than whole lines. With this in mind, suppose you wanted to find out the version of `ftp` that a host is using. By looking back at the output, you can see that it is contained in the greeting line that begins "220" and ends with "`ready.`". Naively, you could wait for that line as:

```
expect "220*"                       ;# dangerous
```

If you are lucky, you might get the entire line stored in `$expect_out(0,string)`. You might even get the next line in there as well. But more likely, you will only get a fragment, such as "220 f" or "220 ftp.UU.NE". Since the pattern 220* matches either of these, **expect** has no reason to wait further and will return. As I stated earlier, **expect** returns with whatever is the longest string that matches the pattern. The problem here is that the remainder of the line may not have shown up yet!

If you want to get the entire line, you must be more specific. The following pattern works:

```
"220*ready."
```

By specifying the text that ends the line, you force **expect** to wait for the entire line to arrive. The "`.`" is not actually needed just to find the version identifier. You could just make the pattern:

```
"220*re"
```

Leaving off the e would be too short. This would allow the pattern to match the `r` in `server` rather than `ready`. It is possible to make the overall pattern even shorter by looking for more unusual patterns. But quite often you trade off readability. There is an art to choosing patterns that are correct, yet not too long but still readable. A good guideline is to *give more priority to readability*. The pattern matching performed by Expect is very inexpensive.

More Glob Patterns

In all the examples so far using the * wildcard, it has matched an arbitrarily long string of characters. This kind of pattern specification is called *shell-style* since it is similar to the way filename matching works in the shell. The name of the program which did this matching for the Bourne shell was called glob. Hence such patterns are often called *glob-style* also. From now on, I will just call them *glob patterns*.

Tcl's "string match" command also uses glob patterns. Glob patterns support two other wildcards. They are "?" and "[]".

? matches any single character. For example, the pattern a?d would match abd but not abcd.

Ranges match any character specified between square brackets. For example, [abcdef0123456789] matches any hexadecimal digit. This pattern can also be expressed as [a-f0-9]. If you want to match a literal hyphen, make it the first or last character. For example, [-a-c] matches "-", "a", "b", or "c".

Unfortunately, brackets are also special to Tcl. Anything in brackets is evaluated immediately (unless it is deferred with braces). That means that an expect command using a pattern with a range must be written in one of two ways:

```
expect "\[a-f0-9]"     ;# strongly preferred
expect {[a-f0-9]}
```

In the first case, the backslash (\) allows the bracket to be passed literally to the expect command, where it is then interpreted as the start of a range. In the second case, the braces force everything inside to be read as their literal equivalents. I prefer the first style—because in the second case, sequences such as \n and $pat embedded in braces are not processed but are taken as literal character sequences of \ and n and $ and p and a and t. This is usually not what is intended.

You can prefix the right bracket with a backslash if it makes you feel good, but it is not necessary. Since there is no matching left-hand bracket to be matched within the double-quoted string, nothing special happens with the right-hand bracket. It stands for itself and is passed on to the expect command, where it is then interpreted as the end of the range.

Backslashes

Tcl makes various substitutions when you have backslashes, dollar signs, and brackets in command arguments. You should be familiar with these from Chapter 2 (p. 23). In this section, I am going to focus on backslashes.

Backslash translations are done by Tcl only when processing command arguments. For example, \n is translated to a linefeed, \ [is translated to a " [", and \\ is translated to a "\". Sequences that have no special translation are replaced by the character without the backslash. For example, \z is translated to a "z".

While pattern matching, Expect uses these translated values. For example:

```
expect "\n" ;# matches \n (linefeed character)
expect "\r" ;# matches \r (return character)
expect "\z" ;# matches z  (literal z)
expect "\{" ;# matches {  (literal left brace)
```

If any backslashes remain after Tcl's translation, the *pattern matcher* (i.e., pattern matching algorithm) then uses these remaining backslashes to force the following character into its literal equivalent. For example, the string "*" is translated by Tcl to "*". The pattern matcher then interprets the "*" as a request to match a literal "*".

```
expect "*"    ;# matches * and ? and X and abc
expect "\\*"  ;# matches * but not ? or X or abc
```

Similarly, backslashes prevent a ? from acting like a wildcard.

```
expect "?"    ;# matches * and ? and X but not abc
expect "\\?"  ;# matches ? but not * or X or abc
```

So that you can see the consistency here, I have written out some more examples. Do not try to memorize these. Just remember two rules:

1.   Tcl translates backslash sequences.

2.   The pattern matcher treats backslashed characters as literals.

These rules are executed in order and only once per command.

For example, in the second command below, Tcl translates the "\n" to a linefeed. The pattern matcher gets the linefeed and therefore tries to match a linefeed. In the third command, Tcl translates the "\\" to "\" so that the pattern matches sees the two characters "\n". By the second rule above, the pattern matcher interprets this as a literal n. In the fourth command, Tcl translates "\\" to "\" and "\n" to a linefeed. By the second rule, the pattern matcher strips off the backslash and matches a literal linefeed.

In summary, \n is replaced with a linefeed by Tcl but a literal n by the pattern matcher. Any character special to Tcl but *not* to the pattern matcher behaves similarly.

```
expect "n" ;# matches n
expect "\n" ;# matches \n (linefeed character)
expect "\\n" ;# matches n
expect "\\\n" ;# matches \n
expect "\\\\n" ;# matches sequence of \ and n
expect "\\\\\n" ;# matches sequence of \ and \n
```

```
expect "\\\\\\n" ;# matches sequence of \ and n
expect "\\\\\\\n" ;# matches sequence of \ and \n
expect "\\\\\\\\n" ;# matches sequence of \, \, and n
```

In the next set of examples, * is replaced with a literal * by Tcl *and* by the pattern matcher. Any character special to the pattern matcher but *not* Tcl behaves similarly.

```
expect "*" ;# matches anything
expect "\*" ;# matches anything
expect "\\*" ;# matches *
expect "\\\*" ;# matches *
expect "\\\\*" ;# matches \ followed by anything
expect "\\\\\*" ;# matches \ followed by anything
expect "\\\\\\*" ;# matches \ followed by *
```

The "[" is special to both Tcl and the pattern matcher so it is particularly messy. To match a literal "[", you have to backslash once from Tcl and then again so that it is not treated as a range during pattern matching. The first backslash, of course, has to be backslashed to prevent it from turning the next backslash into a literal backslash!

```
expect "\\\["    ;# matches literal [
```

This is quite a headache. In fact, if the rest of the pattern is sufficiently specific, you may prefer to improve readability by just using using a ? and accepting any character rather than explicitly forcing a check for the "[".

The next set of examples shows the behavior of "[" as a pattern preceded by differing numbers of backslashes. If the "[" is not prefixed by a backslash, Tcl interprets whatever follows as a command. For these examples, imagine that there is a procedure named XY that returns the string "n*w".

```
expect "[XY]" ;# matches n followed by anything
expect "\[XY]" ;# matches X or Y
expect "\\[XY]" ;# matches n followed by anything followed by w
expect "\\\[XY]" ;# matches [XY]
expect "\\\\[XY]" ;# matches \ followed by n followed ...
expect "\\\\\[XY]" ;# matches sequence of \ and X or Y
```

The \\[XY] case deserves close scrutiny. Tcl interprets the first backslash to mean that the second is a literal character. Tcl then produces "n*w" as the result of the XY command. The pattern matcher ultimately sees the four character string "\n*w". The pattern matcher interprets this in the usual way. The backslash indicates that the n is to be matched literally (which it would even without the backslash since the n is not special to the pattern matcher). Then as many characters as possible are matched so that a w can also be matched.

By now, you may be wondering why I write all patterns in double quotes in preference to using braces. It is true that braces shorten some of the patterns I have shown here.

However, braces do not allow patterns to be specified from variables, nor do they allow backslashed characters such as newlines. But such patterns occur so frequently that you have to be familiar with using double quotes anyway. Constantly thinking about whether to use braces or double quotes is unproductive. Learn how to use double quotes and do not think further about using braces for patterns. If you know Tcl very well and skipped Chapter 2 (p. 23), it may be helpful for you to now go back and read the beginning of it as well as the discussion of `eval` on page 56.

Handling Timeout

Much of the time, **expect** commands have only one argument—a pattern with no action—similar to the very first one in this chapter:

```
expect "hi"
```

All this does is wait for `hi` before continuing. You could also write this as:

```
expect "hi" {}
```

to show the empty action, but **expect** does not require it. Only the last action in an **expect** command can be omitted:

```
expect {
    "hi"      {send "You said hi\n"}
    "hello"   {send "Hello yourself\n"}
    "bye"
}
```

As a natural consequence of this, it is typical to write **expect** commands with the exception strings at the top and the likely string at the bottom. For example, you could add some error checking to the beginning of the anonymous `ftp` script from the previous chapter:

```
spawn ftp $argv
set timeout 10
expect {
    "connection refused" exit
    "unknown host" exit
    "Name"
}
send "anonymous\r"
```

If the script sees `Name` it will go on and send `anonymous\r`. But if it sees "unknown host" or "connection refused", the script will exit. Scripts written this way flow gracefully from top to bottom.

If, after 10 seconds, none of these patterns have been seen, **expect** will timeout and the next command in the script will be executed. I used this behavior in constructing the `timed_read` script in the previous chapter. Here, however, I only want to go to the next command if `Name` is successfully matched.

You can distinguish the successful case from the timeout by associating an action with the timeout. This is done by using the special pattern `timeout`. It looks like this:

```
expect {
    timeout {puts "timed out"; exit}
    "connection refused" exit
    "unknown host" exit
    "Name"
}
```

If none of the patterns match after ten seconds, the script will print "`timed out`" and exit. The result is that the script is more robust. It will only go on if it has been prompted to. And it cannot hang forever. You control how long it waits.

Although the `timeout` pattern is invaluable, it is not a replacement for all error handling. It is tempting to remove the patterns "`connection refused`" and "`unknown host`":

```
expect {
    timeout exit
    "Name"
}
```

Now suppose "`unknown host`" is seen. It does not match `Name` and nothing else arrives within the ten seconds. At the end of ten seconds, the command times out. While the script still works, it fails very slowly.

This is a common dilemma. By explicitly specifying all the possible errors, a script can handle them more quickly. But that takes work on your part while writing the script. And sometimes it is impossible to find out all the error messages that a program could produce.

In practice, it suffices to catch the common errors, and let `timeout` handle the obscure conditions. It is often possible to find a pattern with appropriate wildcards that match many errors. For example, once `ftp` is connected, it is always possible to distinguish errors. `ftp` prefaces all output with a three-digit number. If it begins with a 4 or 5, it is an error. Assuming `ftp`'s line is the only thing in `expect`'s input buffer, you can match errors using the range construct described on page 91:

```
expect {
    timeout {unexpected ...}
    "^\[45]" {error ...}
    "ftp>"
}
```

As I described in Chapter 3 (p. 73), the ^ serves to anchor the 4 or 5 to the beginning of the buffer. If there are previous lines in the buffer—as is more likely—you can use the pattern "\n\[45]". The linefeed (\n) matches the end of the carriage-return linefeed combination that appears at the end of any line intended to be output on a terminal.

When the `timeout` pattern is matched, the data that has arrived is *not* moved to `expect_out(buffer)`. (In Chapter 11 (p. 252), I will describe the rationale for this behavior.) If you need the data, you must match it with a pattern. You can use the `*` wildcard to do so:

```
expect *
```

As I noted earlier, this command is guaranteed to return immediately, and `expect_out(buffer)` will contain what had arrived when the previous timeout occurred.

By convention, the `timeout` pattern itself is not quoted. This serves as a reminder to the reader that `expect` is not waiting for the literal string "`timeout`". Putting quotes around it does not change `expect`'s treatment of it. It will still be interpreted as a special pattern. Quotes only protect strings from being broken up, such as by spaces. For that reason, you can actually write a subset of `expect` patterns without any quotes. Look at the following intentionally obfuscated examples:

```
expect "hi" there
expect  hi   there
expect "hi   there"
```

In the first and second commands, `hi` is the pattern, while "hi   there" is the pattern in the third command. For consistency, use quotes around all textual patterns, and leave them off the special pattern `timeout`. In Chapter 5 (p. 109), I will show how to wait for the literal string `timeout`.

Here is another example of the `timeout` pattern. You can use the `ping` command to test whether a host is up or not. Assume that host `elvis` is up and `houdini` is down. Not all versions of `ping` produce the same output, but here is how it looks when I run it:

```
% ping elvis
elvis is alive
% ping houdini
no answer from houdini
```

What `ping` actually does is to send a message to the host which the host should acknowledge. `ping` usually reports very quickly that the host is up, but it only says "`no answer`" after waiting quite a while—20 seconds is common.

If the host is on your local network, chances are that if the host does not respond within a second or two, it is not going to respond. If you are only looking for a host to farm out some background task, this heuristic works well. Realistically, it is exactly the same heuristic that `ping` uses—just a little less tolerant. Here is an Expect script that provides a `ping`-like response within 2 seconds.

```
spawn ping $host
set timeout 2
expect "alive" {exit 0} timeout {exit 1}
```

If the `expect` sees `alive` within two seconds, it returns 0 to the caller; otherwise it returns 1. When called from a `/bin/sh` script, you find the result by inspecting the status. This is stored in the shell variable `$?` (or `$status` in `csh`).

```
$ echo $?
0
```

Strictly speaking, the status must be an integer. This is good in many cases—integers are easier than strings to check anyway. However, it is possible to get the effect of returning a string simply by printing it out. Consider the following commands which print out the same messages as `ping`:

```
spawn ping $host
set timeout 2
expect "alive" {exit 0} timeout {
    puts "no answer from $host"
    exit 1
}
```

The `timeout` action prints the string "`no answer from ...`" because the script will abort `ping` before it gets a chance to print its own error message. The `alive` action does not have to do anything extra because `ping` already prints the string. Both strings are sent to the standard output. In Chapter 7 (p. 175), you will see how to prevent printing strings from the underlying process, and even substitute your own if desired.

Some versions of `ping` have a user-settable timeout. But the technique I have shown is still useful. Many other programs are completely inflexible, having long fixed timeouts or none at all.

`rsh` is a program for executing shell commands remotely.[†]   `rsh` is an example of a program that is very inflexible when it comes to timeouts. `rsh` waits for 75 seconds before deciding that a machine is down. And there is no way to change this time period. If `rsh` finds that the machine is up, `rsh` will then execute the command but without any ability to timeout at all. It would be nice if `rsh` and other commands all had the ability to timeout, but it is not necessary since you can achieve the same result with an Expect script.

---

† Some systems call it `remsh`.

Rather than writing separate scripts to control `rsh` and every other problem utility, you can write a parameterized script to timeout any program. The two parameters of interest are the program name and the timeout period. These can be passed as the first and second arguments. Assuming the script is called `maxtime`, it could be used from the shell to run a program `prog` for at most 20 seconds with the following:

```
% maxtime 20 prog
```

Here is the script:

```
#!/usr/local/bin/expect --
set timeout [lindex $argv 0]
spawn [lindex $argv 1]
expect
```

The script starts by setting the timeout from the first argument. Then the program named by the second argument is spawned. Finally, `expect` waits for output. Since there are no patterns specified, `expect` never matches using any of the output. And because there are no patterns to match, after enough time, `expect` times out. Because there is no `timeout` action, `expect` simply returns, and the script ends. Alternatively, if the program ends before the timeout, `expect` notices this and returns immediately. Again, the script ends.

Handling End Of File (eof)

In the previous example, the `expect` command waited for output for a specific period of time. If the program terminates, there can be no more output forthcoming. `expect` recognizes this. Specifically, `expect` recognizes the closing of the connection to the spawned process. This closing is referred to as *end of file* or more succinctly, *eof*.[†]

While it is not a rule, usually a process closes the connection just prior to exiting. By default, the `expect` command simply returns when it sees an eof (i.e., closing). In light of this, it is worth reviewing the `maxtime` script.

After the `maxtime` script spawned a process, `expect` waited. Since there were no patterns, the output could not match. If the process continued running up to the timeout period, `expect` would return and the script would return. If the process stopped running before the timeout period, the process would first close the connection. `expect` would see this as an eof. Again, `expect` would return and then the script would return.

---

† The terminology comes straight from UNIX, where all output sources can be viewed as files, including devices and processes.

Similarly to the way an action is associated with a timeout, it is possible to associate an action with an eof. The special pattern eof is used. For example, the maxtime script could use this to report whether the spawned program completed within the allotted time or ran over.

```
#!/usr/local/bin/expect --
set timeout [lindex $argv 0]
eval spawn [lrange $argv 1 end]
expect {
    timeout {puts "took too much time"}
    eof     {puts "finished in time"}
}
```

Here are some test cases called from the shell using the UNIX sleep command. The sleep command is the perfect program to test with since it waits for exactly the amount of time you request.

```
% maxtime 2 sleep 5
spawn sleep 5
took too much time
% maxtime 5 sleep 2
spawn sleep 2
finished in time
```

In the first case, sleeping for five seconds took longer than two, so the script reported that it "took too much time". In the second case, sleeping for two seconds is easily accomplished in five seconds, so the script said "finished in time".

Hints On The spawn Command

I made one other change to the script that is worth noting. The first script only accepted a single argument as a program name. But this new version of maxtime understands that additional arguments after the program name are arguments to the program. This is accomplished with the command:

```
eval spawn [lrange $argv 1 end]
```

The lrange extracts all but the first argument (the timeout) and returns a list where the first element is the program name and the remaining elements are the arguments to the program. Assuming lrange produces "sleep 5", eval joins that to spawn ending up with:

```
spawn sleep 5
```

eval executes this as if it were the original command line. Compare the eval command with the following:

```
spawn [lrange $argv 1 end]      ;# WRONG!
```

In this case, **spawn** takes the result of **lrange** as a program name and tries to run that program. Again, the result of **lrange** is "**sleep 5**", and this entire string is then used as the program name. Needless to say, there is no program by the name "**sleep 5**".

It is worth remembering the command "**eval spawn [lrange $argv ... end]**". It is handy for writing scripts that allow optional command-line arguments to be passed in to become the arguments to the spawned process. This command or a variation of it appears in many of the later examples in this book.

Here is the production version of the **maxtime** script:

```
#!/usr/local/bin/expect --
set timeout [lindex $argv 0]
eval spawn [lrange $argv 1 end]
expect
```

One other precautionary note about **spawn** should be observed for now. Do not use **spawn** from within a procedure. Just call **spawn** from outside procedures. In scripts that only run a single process, this is an easy guideline to follow. In Chapter 10 (p. 240), you will learn more about **spawn** and at that point, the restriction will be lifted.

Back To Eof

In the **ping** script on page 97, there was no specific handling of the eof. Here is that script again:

```
spawn ping $host
set timeout 2
expect "alive" {exit 0} timeout {exit 1}
```

If **expect** sees an eof, then **ping** terminates within the timeout but without producing output containing "**alive**". How is this possible? After all, a host is either up or incommunicado, right? In fact, there is a third case. **ping** also reports if the host does not exist— that is, if there is no computer with such a name. In this case, **ping** says "**unknown host**", closes the connection, and exits. **expect** sees an eof, but since there is no eof pattern and corresponding action, the **expect** command returns. There are no more commands so the script ends.

When the script ends by running out of commands, an implied "**exit 0**" is executed. This is typical for interpreters, and UNIX commands conventionally return 0 to indicate that a command is successful. But in this case, the script returns 0 when given a non-existent host. This is clearly the wrong behavior. Unfortunately, the right behavior is not as clear. You could return 1 and revise the definition of what that means from "failure due to timeout" to simply "failure". Or you could choose a different number, say, 2. Either can be justified depending on the use to which you want to put the script. **ping** returns 1 when the host is unknown so I will follow suit. Here is the revised script to handle the eof:

```
spawn ping $host
set timeout 2
expect "alive" {exit 0} timeout {exit 1} eof {exit 1}
```

In some ways this still does not handle the problem perfectly. For example, without looking directly at the source to `ping`, I do not know if there are other ways it could behave. For now, I am just lumping everything I do not know into an error.

But this may be sufficient. Indeed, one of the reasons for using Expect is that you may not be able to see the source in the first place. So taking a conservative approach of calling everything that is not expected an error, is a practical and common solution.

Timeout and eof are the only types of exception conditions possible. As in the `ping` example, both exceptions often deserve the same type of handling. For this reason, there is a special pattern called `default` that represents both conditions. The last line of the ping script could be rewritten to use `default` as:

```
expect "alive" {exit 0} default {exit 1}
```

Using `default` (or both `timeout` and `eof`) covers all possible conditions that an `expect` command can match. It is a good idea to account for all conditions in every `expect` command. This may seem like a lot of work, but it can pay off handsomely during debugging. In Chapter 11 (p. 259), I will describe how to use the `expect_before` and `expect_after` commands to catch all timeouts and eofs without specifying them on each `expect`. Those commands can greatly simplify your scripts.

The close Command

When a spawned process closes its connection to Expect, the `expect` command sees an eof.

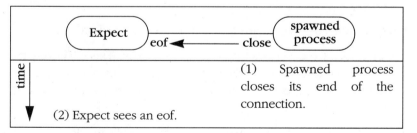

This scenario can also occur in the reverse direction. Expect can close the connection and the spawned process will see an eof.

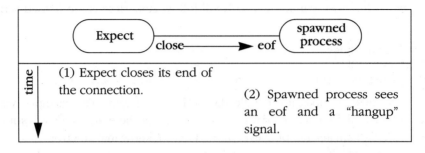

By closing the connection, Expect is telling the spawned process that it has nothing more to say to the process. Usually the process takes this as an indication to exit. This is similar to what occurs when you press ^D while manually interacting with a process. The process does not see the ^D. Rather, the system turns this into an eof. The process reads the eof and then responds by closing the connection and exiting.

There is one difference between how Expect and the spawned process treat a closed connection. When Expect closes the connection, the spawned process sees an additional indication in the form of a hangup signal. Most processes take this as an instruction to immediately exit. The net result is very similar to reading an eof. In either case, the process exits. Later in the book, I will go into more detail about what signals are and how you can ignore them or take advantage of them.

From Expect, the command to close the connection to a process is `close`. It is called as:

```
close
```

No matter which side—the Expect process or the spawned process—closes the connection first, the other side must also close the connection. That is, if the spawned process first closes the connection, then the Expect process must call `close`. And if the Expect process first calls `close`, the spawned process must then call `close`.

Fortunately, in many scripts it is not necessary to explicitly close the connection because it can occur implicitly. There are two situations when you do not have to use `close`:

- when the Expect process ends, or
- when the **expect** command reads an eof from the spawned process.

In both of these cases, Expect closes the connection for you. This effectively means that the only time you need to explicitly write `close` is when you want to close the connection before the spawned process is ready to *and* you are not ready to end the entire Expect script.

In all the examples so far it has not been necessary to explicitly close the connection. Either **expect** read an eof or the script exited, thereby sending an eof to the spawned process, which in turn closed its end of the connection. It is not necessary to wait for an eof after you have already closed the connection. Indeed, it is not even possible. When the connection is closed, you cannot read anything—data or eof. The connection no longer exists.

Here is an example of why you might want to call `close` explicitly. Imagine you are interacting with `ftp`. If you have an "ftp> " prompt, you can send the command `quit\r` and `ftp` will immediately exit, closing the connection from its end. But suppose `ftp` is in the middle of transferring a file and you need to close the connection immediately. You could interrupt `ftp`, wait for it to prompt, and then send the `quit\r` command. But it is simpler to just close the connection. `ftp` will abort the transfer and quit.

This may seem like a fairly rude way of doing things. After all, you do not have to abruptly close connections like this. You can always work through whatever scenario a program wants for it to initiate the close on its side. But it is important to understand this technique in order to handle things such as when you kill an Expect script, for example, by pressing ^C.

By default, ^C causes Expect to exit (i.e., "`exit 0`"). This in turn will close the connection to the spawned process, and the spawned process will die. If you want the spawned process to continue on after the Expect script exits, you have to make special arrangements. I will describe more about this later.

Programs That Ignore Eof

There is an exception to the scenario that I just described. Some interactive programs are rather cavalier when they encounter an eof and do not handle it correctly. However, if you are prepared for this situation, you can work around it easily enough. There are two kinds of common misbehavior:

- Some programs ignore eof.
- Some programs ignore data just before eof.

I will discuss the two cases separately.

Some programs ignore eof. Even if you close the connection (by calling `close`, exiting the script, or pressing ^C), they ignore the eof and continue waiting for more characters to arrive. This is characteristic of the ubiquitous `telnet` implementation and many other programs that run in raw mode. *Raw mode* means that no special interpretations are applied to input characters. For instance, ^C no longer serves as an interrupt, and ^D no longer acts as an eof. Since users cannot send an eof, these programs have no reason to expect it and thus do not look for it. The problem is, an eof is exactly what they get when the connection is closed.

Avoid explicitly closing programs like these before they are ready. Instead, force them to close the connection in the way they would when using them manually. For instance, `telnet` will close the connection on its own once you log out of the remote host. If you do not gracefully log out, thereby letting `telnet` shut down the connection, you will be left with a `telnet` process on your system talking to no one. Such a process must then be killed by hand using the UNIX `kill` command. (It is possible to do this from Expect, but I will not go into it until Chapter 13 (p. 296).)

Some programs detect eof but ignore any other data that comes along with it. An example is the following Expect script which runs `ftp`. Three files are requested but after the script has finished, only two of the files are found.

```
spawn ftp . . .
# assume username and password are accepted here
expect "ftp> " {send "get file1\r"}
expect "ftp> " {send "get file2\r"}
expect "ftp> " {send "get file3\r"}
```

After sending "`get file3\r`", Expect immediately closes the connection to `ftp` and exits. Then `ftp` reads the command but also finds the eof as well. Unlike `telnet` in the previous example, `ftp` checks for the eof but it mistakenly assumes that the eof also means there is no data to process. It simply does not check and therefore the "`get file3\r`" is never done.

In this example, the solution is to add a final `expect` command to wait for another prompt. An even simpler example is the following script which starts the `vi` editor and sends a command. The command inserts "`foo`" into a file which is then saved. The "`q`" tells `vi` to quit.

```
spawn vi file
send "ifoo\033:wq\r"
```

Because of the final quit command, there is no prompt for which to wait. Instead, it suffices to wait for an eof from `vi` itself. And since the eof has no action, the `eof` keyword can be omitted as well. Here is the corrected script:

```
spawn vi file
send "ifoo\033:wq\r"
expect
```

Spawned processes that exit on the hangup signal behave similarly to programs that ignore data just before an eof. The solution is the same. Wait for the spawned process itself to close the connection first.

The wait Command

After closing the connection, a spawned process can finish up and exit. Processes exit similarly to the way that Expect scripts do, with a number (for example, "`exit 0`"). The operating system conveniently saves this number and some other information about how the process died. This information is very useful for non-interactive commands but useless for interactive commands. Consequently, it is of little value to Expect. Nonetheless, Expect must deal with it.

Expect must retrieve this information—even if only to discard it. The act of retrieving the information frees various valuable resources (process slots) within the computer. Until the information is retrieved, the operating system maintains the information indefinitely. This can be seen from the output of `ps`. Assuming a spawned process has died and the connection has been closed, `ps` shows something like this:

```
PID   TT  STAT  TIME  COMMAND
4425  ?   Z     0:00  <defunct>
```

The Z stands for *zombie*—someone's attempt to humorously describe a process that is dead but still haunts the system in an almost useless way. Even the process name and arguments have been discarded—no matter what they were originally, they show up here as `<defunct>`.

To get rid of this zombie, use the `wait` command. It is called simply as:

```
wait
```

The `wait` command returns a list of elements including the spawn id and process id. These elements are further described in Chapter 14 (p. 313). For now, ignore the return value of `wait`.

Because a process will not disappear from the system until you give the `wait` command, it is common to speak of *waiting for* or *waiting on* a process. Some people also like to use the term *reap* as in "reaping a process".

Because `wait` follows `close`, it is very common to see people write "`close;wait`" on a single line. But if the connection is closed implicitly, the `wait` must appear by itself. Like `close`, the `wait` command can also occur implicitly. Unlike `close`, however, `wait` implicitly happens in only one case—when an Expect process (i.e., script) exits. On exit, all the spawned processes are waited for.

This means that Expect scripts that only spawn a single process and then exit, need not call `wait` since it will be done automatically. The example scripts so far have all taken advantage of this. Later on, I will show a script in which it is important to explicitly wait.

One last thing about `wait`: If you call it before a process has died, your Expect script will wait for the process to die—hence the name. It is possible to avoid the delay by using the -nowait flag.

```
wait -nowait
```

Exercises

1. Write a pattern to match hexadecimal numbers. Write a pattern to match Roman numbers.

2. Write a pattern to match the literal string `timeout`. Write a pattern to match the literal string `"timeout"` (with the double quotes).

3. Write a script that takes a string and produces a pattern that will match the string. Make the script prompt for the string to avoid any interpretation of it by the shell.

4. On page 101, I described what happens if the spawned process closes the connection first and what happens if the script closes the connection first. What happens if both the script and the spawned process close the connection simultaneously?

5. Write a script that automatically retrieves the latest release of Expect and installs it. In what ways can you generalize the script so that it can retrieve and install other software?

5

Regular Expressions

The previous chapter described glob patterns. You were probably familiar with them from the shell. Glob patterns are very simple and are sufficient for many purposes. Hence they are the default style of pattern matching in **expect** commands. However, their simplicity brings with it limitations.

For example, glob patterns cannot match any character *not* in a list of characters, nor can glob patterns match a choice of several different strings. Both of these turn out to be fairly common tasks. And while both can be simulated with a sequence of several other commands, Expect provides a much more powerful and concise mechanism: regular expressions.

Regular Expressions—A Quick Start

In order to jumpstart your knowledge of regular expressions (*regexp* for short), I will start out by noting the similarities. As the following table of examples shows, every glob pattern is representable by a regular expression. In contrast, some regular expressions cannot be represented as glob patterns.

For example, both the glob pattern `foo` and the regular expression `foo` match the literal string "foo". Backslash works in the usual way, turning the following character into its literal equivalent. "^" and "$" also work the same way as before. Regular expression ranges work as before, plus they can also be used to match any character *not* in the range by placing a "^" immediately after the left bracket. (I will show more detail on this later.) Besides this, the only significant differences in the table are the last two lines which describe how to match any single character and any number of any characters.

Except for ".*", each of the patterns in the table is called an *atom*. A * appended to an atom creates a pattern that matches any number (including zero) of the particular atom.

Table 5-1. Comparison of glob patterns and regular expressions.

glob	regexp	English
s	s	literal s
*	*	literal *
^	^	beginning of string
$	$	end of string
[a-z]	[a-z]	any character in the range a to z
	[^a-z]	any character *not* in the range a to z
?	.	any single character
*	.*	any number of characters

For example, the regular expression "a*" matches any string of a's, such as "a", "aa", "aaaaaaaaa" and "". That last string has no a's in it at all. This is considered a match of zero a's.

The pattern [0-9]* matches strings made up of integers such as "012" and "888". Notice that the atom does not have to match the same literal value each time. When matching "012", the range "[0-9]" first matches "0", then it matches "1", and finally matches "2".

You can uses ranges to construct more useful patterns. For example [1-9][0-9]* matches any positive integer. The first atom matches the first digit of the number, while the remaining digits are matched by the "[0-9]*".

C language identifiers can be matched with the pattern "[a-zA-Z_][a-zA-Z0-9_]*". This is similar to the previous pattern. In both cases the first character is restricted to a subset of the characters that can be used in the remaining part of the string.

In both cases the * only applies to the immediately preceding range. That is because the * only applies to the immediately preceding atom. One range is an atom; two ranges are not an atom.

Atoms by themselves and atoms with a * appended to them are called *pieces*. Pieces can also consist of atoms with a + or ? appended. An atom followed by + matches a sequence of one or more matches of the atom. An atom followed by ? matches the atom or the empty string. For example, "a+" matches "a" and "aa" but not "", while "a?" matches "a" and "" but not "aa". The pattern "0x[0-9a-fA-F]+" matches a hexadecimal number in the C language such as "0x0b2e" or "0xffff". The pattern "-?[1-9][0-9]*" matches positive or negative integers such as 1, 10, 1000, -1, and -1000. Notice how the [1-9] range prevents a zero from being the first digit, avoiding strings like -05 and 007.

"`-?[1-9][0-9]*`" is a sequence of three pieces. Any sequence of pieces is called a *branch*. Branches separated by a | match any of the branches. For example, you could extend the previous pattern to match any integer with the pattern "`-?[1-9][0-9]*|0`". The first branch matches any nonzero integer while the second branch matches zero itself.

Tcl integers can be written in decimal, hex, or octal. The following pattern uses three patterns to match such integers: "`-?[1-9][0-9]*|0x[0-9a-fA-F]+|0[0-7]*`". The first branch ("`-?[1-9][0-9]*`") matches any positive or negative decimal constant. The second branch matches any hex constant. The third branch matches any octal constant. A separate branch for zero is not needed, since it is matched by the octal branch already. Fortunately, zero in octal is equal to zero in decimal, so there is no problem interpreting it in a different way!

Identifying Regular Expressions And Glob Patterns

In order to actually use a regular expression, you must do two things. First, you must backslash any characters that are special to Tcl. For example, the regular expression to match a single digit is "`[0-9]`". To prevent Tcl from trying to evaluate 0-9 as a command, the leading bracket must be prefixed with a backslash so that it looks like this:

`\[0-9]`

See Chapter 4 (p. 91) for more information on using backslashes.

The second thing you must do is to tell **expect** that a pattern is a regular expression. By default, **expect** assumes patterns are glob patterns. Another line can be added to Table 5-1.

glob	regexp	English
-gl	-re	pattern type prefix

Patterns prefixed with −re are regular expressions. For example, the following command matches "a", "aa", and "aaaaa". It does not match "ab".

`expect -re "a*"   ;# regexp pattern`

Without the −re, the command matches "aa", "ab", and "ac" (among other things).

`expect "a*"      ;# glob pattern`

It is possible to have a mixture of glob patterns and regular expressions. In the following example, "a*" is a regular expression but "b*" is a glob pattern.

```
expect {
    -re "a*" {action1}
    "b*" {action2}
}
```

The `expect` command also accepts the `-gl` flag. The `-gl` flag tells `expect` that the pattern is a glob pattern. This is useful if the pattern looks like one of the keywords such as `timeout` or a flag such as `-re`.[†]

```
expect {
    eof {found_real_eof}
    -gl "timeout" {found_literal_timeout}
    -gl "-re" {found_real_dash_r_e}
}
```

You might also want to pass the pattern as a variable. In this case, the `-gl` flag also protects the pattern from matching a keyword or flag.

```
expect -gl $pattern
```

If you completely declare your pattern types, you can embed them inside of subroutines and pass patterns as arguments without worrying about them being misinterpreted. This is especially useful if you might reuse the subroutines in the future or allow users to pass arbitrary patterns in to a script. Users of your scripts should not have to care about the keywords inside of Expect.

Using Parentheses To Override Precedence

Once you understand how to build regular expressions, you need not worry about remembering the terms "atom", "piece", and "branch". The terms exist only to help you learn the precedence of the regular-expression operators. To avoid confusion, from now on I will generically refer to any *subpattern* of a complete pattern when it is unimportant whether it is an atom, piece, or branch.

Because operators such as `*` and `+` act only on atoms, they cannot be applied directly to pieces and branches. For example, the pattern `ab*` matches an `a` followed by any number of `b`'s. In order to treat any subpattern—atom, piece, or branch—as an atom, enclose it in parentheses. Thus, in order to match any number of `ab`'s, use the pattern "`(ab)*`".

Matching real numbers is a good exercise. Real numbers have a whole portion to the left of the decimal point and a fractional portion to the right. A direct rendering of this concept is "`-?[0-9]*\.?[0-9]*`". Notice the period is escaped by placing a

---

† Any non-keyword pattern beginning with a hyphen must be preceded with "-gl" (or some other pattern type). This permits the addition of future flags in Expect without breaking existing scripts.

backslash in front of it. This forces it to match a literal period rather than any character. The entire pattern matches things like "17.78", "-8", and "0.21". Unfortunately, it also accepts 0000.5, which does not seem quite right. You can reject leading zeros while still accepting a single zero the same way I did earlier—with a branch: "-?(0|[1-9][0-9]*)?\.?[0-9]*". This pattern accepts the earlier numbers but it rejects "0000.5". Unfortunately, it still matches "-0". You can fix this as an exercise but it is not worth worrying about that much. In Chapter 6 (p. 140), I will demonstrate how to handle this problem much more easily.

To use this regular expression in a command, any characters special to Tcl must also be escaped as I described in the previous section. Here is what the complete command might look like:

```
expect -re "-?(0|\[1-9]\[0-9]*)?\\.?\[0-9]*"
```

In practice, most patterns do not get very complex. It is almost always possible to get by using simple patterns. For example, you could use patterns that accept bad data (such as numbers with multiple leading zeros) if you know that the program never generates them anyway. Deciding how much effort to invest in writing patterns takes a little experience. But it will come with time.

Using Parentheses For Feedback

In the previous section, parentheses were used to group subpatterns together. Parentheses also play another role—a role that leads to much shorter scripts than would otherwise be possible. When a regular expression successfully matches a string in the input buffer, each part of the string that matches a parenthesized subpattern is saved in the array expect_out. The string that matches the first parenthesized subpattern is stored in "expect_out(1,string)". The string that matches the second is stored in "expect_out(2,string)". And so on, up to "expect_out(9,string)".

For example, suppose you want to know the characters that occur between two other characters. If the input buffer contains "junk   abcbcd" and I use the pattern "a(.*)c", this matches the input buffer and so expect makes the following assignment:

```
set expect_out(1,string) "bcb"
```

expect also stores the string that matches the entire pattern in the variable "expect_out(0,string)":

```
set expect_out(0,string) "abcbc"
```

Finally, expect stores the whole string that matches the entire pattern as well as everything that came before it in expect_out(buffer):

```
set expect_out(buffer) "junk abcbc"
```

The "d" in the input buffer was never matched, so it remains there.

The last two assignments (to expect_out(buffer) and expect_out(0,string)) occur with glob patterns as well.

The values of expect_out are never deleted but can be overwritten by new expect commands. Assuming that the input buffer holds "junk   abcbcd", the following sequence of commands both match:

```
expect -re "a(.*)c"
expect -re "d"
```

Earlier I showed the assignments that occur during the first command. When the second command executes, two other assignments take place:

```
set expect_out(buffer) "d"
set expect_out(0,string) "d"
```

expect_out(1,string) remains equal to "bcb" from the earlier expect command.

More On The timed-read Script

In Chapter 3 (p. 77), I defined an Expect script called timed-read. Called from the shell with the maximum number of seconds to wait, the script waits for a string to be entered, unless the given time is exceeded. Here it is again:

```
set timeout $argv
expect "\n" {
    send [string trimright "$expect_out(buffer)" "\n"]
}
```

In that earlier example I used "string trimright" to trim off the newline. It is possible for the expect command to do this in the pattern matching process, but not with glob patterns. I will use a regular expression to rewrite the script above without using the string command.

```
# timed read using a regular expression
set timeout $argv
expect -re "(.*)\n" {
    send $expect_out(1,string)
}
```

In the expect command, the -re flag declares the following pattern to be a regular expression instead of a glob pattern. As before, the pattern is quoted with double quotes. The pattern itself is:

```
(.*)\n
```

This matches any string of characters followed by a "\n". All the characters except for the \n get stored in expect_out(1,string). Since the pattern is successfully matched, the action is executed. The action is to send all the characters in $expect_out(1,string) to the standard output. Of course, these characters are exactly what was just typed without the terminating "\n".

Pattern Matching Strategy

At the beginning of the previous chapter was an example where the string "philosophic\n" was matched against the pattern "*hi*". This pattern can be rewritten as a regular expression:

```
expect -re ".*hi.*"
```

Adding parentheses around various pieces of the pattern makes it possible to see exactly how the string is matched. Here is a snapshot of Expect running interactively. First I entered the expect command to wait for a string. Then I entered philosophic and pressed return. Finally I printed the first four elements of expect_out surrounded by angle brackets.

```
expect1.1> expect -re "(.*)(hi)(.*)"
philosophic
expect1.2> puts "<$expect_out(0,string)>"
<philosophic
>
expect1.3> puts "<$expect_out(1,string)>"
<philosop>
expect1.4> puts "<$expect_out(2,string)>"
<hi>
expect1.5> puts "<$expect_out(3,string)>"
<c
>
expect1.6>
```

You can see that the entire string matched was "philosophic\n". The first ".*" matched "philosop" while the second ".*" matched "c\n". "hi", of course, matched "hi" but notice that it was the second "hi" in the string, not the first "hi". This is similar to the way the analogous glob pattern worked in the previous chapter.

But regular expressions are more complex than glob patterns. For instance, a subexpression may not necessarily match as many characters as possible if there is another interpretation that allows the regular expression to match earlier in the string. Consider the regular expression "a?b" and the string "ba". In this case, the pattern matches the substring "b" at the beginning of the string. The "a" at the end is left unmatched. This is the most important rule of regular expressions: *A regular expression matches at the earliest possible position in the string.*

The next rule is: *The left-most matching branch is used.* Consider the behavior of the regular expression "a|ab" on the string "ab". The first branch matches only the first character while the second branch matches the entire string. Following the rule, the first branch is used even though it matches fewer characters.[†]

The first rule is more important than the second (branching) rule. Imagine the string "acab" with the regular expression "a(b|c)". This matches "ac". The second branch is used because it allows the match to begin at an earlier character in the string than does the first branch.

Only after these two rules are observed is length of importance. The third rule is: *The longest match is used.* For example, the regular expression "a*" matches every character of the string "aaaa". And the expression ".*" always matches the entire string, no matter what it is!

The least important rule is: *Subexpressions are considered from left to right.*

These last two rules describe the behavior shown earlier with the pattern ".*hi.*" on the string "philosophic". As a simple case, consider the expression ".*.*". The fourth rules requires that the left-hand ".*" be considered first. By the third rule, it matches the entire string. The right-hand ".*" necessarily matches the empty string.

Does the pattern "a*(b*|(ab)*)" match the string "aabab"? The only way to satisfy all four rules is for the pattern to match the first three characters and leave the trailing "ab" unmatched. The "a*" matches the first two a's and the "b*" branch matches the first "b". Since only one branch is necessary for the entire pattern to match, the entire pattern is considered to have matched successfully.

It is possible to match *every* character in aabab by only matching one "a" with the pattern "a*" and then using the second branch to match "abab", but this violates the third and fourth rules. This matching can be forced by appending a "$" anchor to the expression. Then no other matches are possible. Another solution is just to reverse the branches.

It is useful to draw parallels between types of regular expressions and control structures. Often this can lead to simpler or more readable code. For instance two consecutive **expect** statements:

[†] The regular expressions described here differ slightly from POSIX.2 regular expressions. For example, POSIX regular expressions take the branch that matches the longest sequence of characters. As of May 1994, no plans have been formalized to introduce POSIX-style regular expressions. There are enough minor differences that, if POSIX regular expressions were added, they would likely be added as a new pattern type, rather than as a replacement for the existing regular expressions.

```
expect -re "a"
expect -re "b"
```

can often be combined:

```
expect -re "a.*b"
```

Similarly, branches are similar to writing the patterns entirely separately. For example, it might be helpful to write the pattern "c(d*)|d" as two separate patterns:

```
expect {
    -re "c(d*)" action
    -re "d"     action
}
```

In this example, the d at the end of the branch is hard to see, while the second version makes it very clear.

However, it is worth recognizing that both forms in these last two examples do not have precisely the same behavior. In the first example, the lone "b" will match the first "b" after the "a" while ".*b" will match the last "b" after the "a". In the second example, the second branch ("d") can match strings with the first branch ("c") present, while the rewrite with the two -re's will always match using the first regular expression. Both of these differences are because a regular expression matches at the earliest possible position in the string.

Nested Parentheses

The regular expression a*((ab)*|b*) has nested parentheses. How are the results stored in the expect_out array? They are determined by counting left parentheses: the subexpression which starts with the *N*th left parenthesis corresponds with expect_out(*N*,...). For example, the string that matches ((ab)*|b*) is stored in expect_out(1,string), and the string that matches (ab) is stored in expect_out(2,string). Of course, the only string that could possibly match "ab" is "ab". If you want to record the string of ab's that corresponds to (ab)* then you have to put another pair of parentheses around that, as in "((ab)*)".

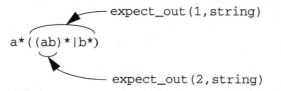

Strings that match parenthesized subpatterns are stored in the expect_out array.

The string matched by the whole pattern is stored in `expect_out(0,string)`. This makes sense if you imagine the whole pattern is wrapped in another set of parentheses. And you can also imagine the whole pattern prefaced by a `.*` pattern[†] and wrapped in yet another pair of parentheses to determine the value of `expect_out(buffer)`.

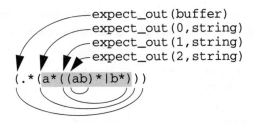

The original pattern is shaded. Text that matches the imaginary pattern (.*(...)) is stored in expect_out(0,string) and expect_out(buffer).

Always Count Parentheses, Even Inside Of Alternatives

To decide which element of `expect_out` to use, count the number of prior parenthesized expressions. The simplest way to do this is just to count the number of left parentheses. This works even if the parentheses occur in an alternative.

Consider the pattern "`(a)|(b)`". If the string is "a", then `expect_out(1,string)` will be set to "a". If the string is "b", `expect_out(2,string)` will be set to "b". In this way, it is possible that `expect_out(2,string)` can be defined but not `expect_out(1,string)`.

This behavior may seem to be a disadvantage—the limit of nine parentheses can be used up even when appearing in non-matching alternatives.[‡] But the advantage is that you can know ahead of time where in `expect_out` matching strings will be without worrying about whether other alternatives matched or not. For instance, the pattern `a*((ab)*|b*)(c*)` is similar to the pattern from the previous example but with `(c*)` appended. `expect_out(1,string)` and `expect_out(2,string)` are set as before. The string matching `(c*)` is stored in `expect_out(3,string)` whether or not `(ab)` is matched.

---

† Unlike the usual meaning of `.*` which matches as many characters as possible, this imaginary `.*` matches as few characters as possible while still allowing the match to succeed. Chapter 3 (p. 73) describes this in terms of anchoring.

‡ In reality, it is fairly unusual to use more than four or five pairs of parentheses. I have never run up to the limit of nine.

In cases like this one, it may not be immediately evident whether elements of expect_out were written by the current expect since the elements can retain values from prior expect commands. If you need to be certain, unset the variables before the expect command. Occasionally, it is convenient to set them to default values. The following example shows both ideas:

```
set expect_out(1,string) "ab"    ;# if no match, use this
unset expect_out(2,string)       ;# if no match, notice
expect -re "a*((ab)*|b*)(c*)"
if [info exists expect_out(2,string)] {
    # expect_out(2,string) has been assigned, so use it
}
```

Example—The Return Value From A Remote Shell

While I have shown some fairly complex patterns, real patterns are usually pretty simple. In fact, sometimes other issues can make the patterns seem like the easy part of writing scripts.

The rsh program executes a command on a remote host. For example, the following command executes the command "quack twice" on host duck.

% rsh duck quack twice

While quack is a mythical program, you can imagine it shares a trait common to many programs. Namely, quack reports its status by returning an exit value. If quack works correctly, it exits with the value 0 (which by convention means success). Otherwise it exits with the value 1 (failure). From the C-shell, the status of the last command is stored in the variable status. I can demonstrate a successful interactive invocation by interacting directly with the C-shell.

```
% quack twice
% echo $status
0
```

Unfortunately, if quack is executed via rsh, the same echo command will not provide the exit status of quack. In fact, rsh does not provide any way of returning the status of a command. Checking the value of status after running rsh tells you only whether rsh itself ran successfully. The status of rsh is not really that useful. It reports problems such as "unknown host" if you give it a bogus host. But if rsh locates the host and executes the command, that is considered a success and 0 is returned no matter what happens inside the command. In fact, the rsh is considered a success even if the command is not found on the remote host!

```
% rsh duck date
Wed Feb 17 21:04:17 EST 1993
% echo $status
0
% rsh duck daet
daet: Command not found.
% echo $status
0
% rsh duuck date
duuck: unknown host
% echo $status
1
```

There is no easy way to fix rsh without rewriting it. However, it is possible to write an Expect script that uses rlogin to do the job. Fortunately, rsh aims to provide an environment as close as possible to rlogin, so the hard part is done already. All that is left is to extract the *right* status. Here is an Expect script that does it—executing the command remotely and returning the remote status locally.

```
#!/usr/local/bin/expect --
eval spawn rlogin [lindex $argv 0]
expect "% "
send "[lrange $argv 1 end]\r"
expect "% "
send "echo \$status\r"
expect -re "\r\n(.*)\r\n"
exit $expect_out(1,string)
```

The second line spawns an rlogin process to the remote host. Next, the script waits for a prompt from the remote host. For simplicity here, the prompt is assumed to end with "% ". The lrange extracts the commands and any arguments from the original invocation of the script. A return character is appended, and the command is sent to the remote host. After reading another prompt, the status is read by having the shell echo it.

Notice that in the second send command, the $ is preceded by a backslash. This prevents Tcl from doing variable substitution on the variable status locally. The string "$status" has to be sent literally. (When using the Bourne shell, the Expect script would have to ask for $? instead of $status.)

The regular expression "\r\n(.*)\r\n" is used to pick out the status. To see why this particular pattern is used, it helps to consider what the process sends back after the script has sent the string "echo $status\r". The following figure shows the whole dialogue.

Upon logging in, the first thing to appear is the message of the day followed by the prompt ("% "). Then the command "quack twice" is sent with a return appended. This is echoed by the remote shell, and you can see that the return is echoed as a \r\n

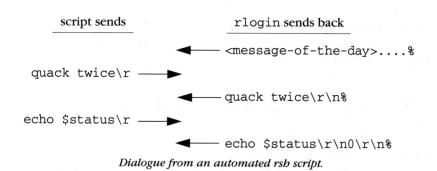

Dialogue from an automated rsb script.

sequence. Some time passes as the command runs. If it produces output, it would appear at this point. Finally another prompt appears after which the script requests that the status be echoed. The request itself is echoed followed by a "\r\n", the status itself, and yet another "\r\n". Another prompt appears, but the script has the information it wants in expect_out(1,string) already. So the script immediately terminates with the appropriate exit value.

It still may not be clear why the shell responds the way it does in this interaction. By default, a shell echoes everything that is sent to it. This is perfectly normal and is exactly what happens when you type directly to a shell. The shell arranges things so that when you press the **x** key, the letter **x** is echoed so that you can see it. Some translations also take place. For instance, when you press return, a return-linefeed sequence (\r\n) is echoed. Sure enough, that is just what can be seen from the remote shell. And it explains why the result of echo is seemingly surrounded by these characters. The first pair is the end of the echoed command, while the second is formatting from the echo command itself. (As I mentioned earlier, the echo command actually writes a newline (\n) and the terminal driver converts this to a return-linefeed sequence (\r\n).)

A few minor modifications can help the script. First, it is unlikely that you want any of the expect commands to time out, so the timeout should be disabled by saying "set timeout -1". Second, it is not necessary to send the two commands separately. Third, it is not necessary to explicitly write both characters in the return-newline sequence. You just need the characters that directly surround the status. Finally, I have wrapped the send with an eval to handle strings with embedded whitespace.

The rewritten script is:

```
#!/usr/local/bin/expect --
eval spawn rlogin [lindex $argv 0]
set timeout -1
expect -re "(%|#|\\\$) "
eval send "[lrange $argv 1 end];echo \$status\r"
expect -re "\n(.*)\r"
exit $expect_out(1,string)
```

Although it is a good start, even this new script is not yet a complete replacement for `rsh`. This script only works for remote commands that produce no output because the final `expect` command matches anything after the first line of output. Try fixing the script so that it works for commands that produce any amount of output.

Matching Customized Prompts

This new script (above) manages to find yet another excuse for a regular expression. The string it is capable of finding is either "% " or "$ " or "# ". This is a pretty good stab at recognizing common prompts since traditionally most C-shell users end prompts with "% ", most Bourne shell users end prompts with "$ ", and root prompts in any shell typically end with "# ". The $ has to be quoted because it is special to the pattern matcher. (More on this on page 125.)

Of course, users are free to customize prompts further, and some do, wildly so. There is no way to pick a pattern for the prompt that suffices for everyone. If you are just writing a script for yourself, you can always find a pattern that will match your prompt. But if you want a script that works for any user, this can be a challenge. Users are free to change their prompt at any time anyway and you cannot predict the future.

One reasonable solution is to have each user define a pattern that matches their own prompt. A good way to do this is to have users store their patterns in the environment variable `EXPECT_PROMPT`. As a reminder, this variable should be set immediately after the customization of the real prompt in their `.cshrc` or wherever they do set it. By keeping them together, when the user changes their prompt, they will naturally think to change their prompt pattern at the same time.

Here is Tcl code to read the environment variable `EXPECT_PROMPT`. The variable is retrieved from `env`, a predefined variable that holds all environment values. If the variable is not set, a default prompt pattern is used so that there is a good chance of still having a script function correctly.

```
set prompt "(%|#|\\\$) "           ;# default prompt
catch {set prompt $env(EXPECT_PROMPT)}
```

Once `prompt` is set, you can use it as follows:

```
expect -re $prompt
```

An extract of a `.cshrc` file that has a prompt specialized to contain the current directory followed by "> " might look like this:

```
setenv PROMPT "$cwd\!> "
setenv EXPECT_PROMPT "> "
```

There is another potential problem with trying to match shell prompts. Namely, the pattern may match something unexpected such as the message-of-the-day while logging in. In this case, the command will be sent before the prompt appears. When it does eventually appear, the prompt will be misinterpreted as a sign that the program has completed. This one-off error is a general problem that manifests itself when a pattern matches too early.

One way to defend against this problem is to end the pattern with "$".

```
set prompt "(%|#|\\\$) $"
```

A bare $ matches the end of the input, analogously to the way ^ matches the beginning of the input. If more data has arrived that cannot be matched, **expect** continues waiting. This is very similar to the way people distinguish prompts. If you see your prompt (or something that looks even close to a prompt) in the middle of the message-of-the-day, you will not be fooled because you will see the computer continuing to print more text.

On the other hand, Expect is much faster than you are. The computer may appear to have stopped typing, perhaps even in the middle of the message-of-the-day, only because the CPU is being shared among many tasks. This unintentional pause can make Expect think that all the input has arrived.

There is no perfect solution. You can start another **expect** command to wait for a few more seconds to see if any more input arrives. But there is no guarantee even this or any time limit is good enough. Even humans can be faked out by random system indigestion. When was the last time you thought your program was hung, so you started pressing ^C only to find out that the network or some other resource was just temporarily overloaded?[†]

While it is possible to take extra steps, there simply is no way to guarantee that something that looks like a prompt really is a prompt, considering that even humans can be fooled. But for most purposes, a $ helps substantially in the face of unknown data that could unintentionally cause a premature match.

---

† In *Computer Lib*, Ted Nelson described a system administrator who was plagued by continual computer crashes. The system administrator eventually decided to blame a miscreant with the initials RH after discovering that a program named RHBOMB was always running when the system crashed. Several months later, the same system administrator noticed a file called RHBOMB. Rather than immediately accuse RH of hacking again, the system administrator decided to first look at the file. He issued the command to print the file on the screen: PRINT RH-BOMB. All of a sudden, his terminal printed "TSS HAS GONE DOWN" and stopped. No prompt. Nothing else appeared. The system administrator thought to himself: "Incredible—a program so virulent that just *listing* it crashed the system!"

His fear was unjustified. The file turned out to be the string "TSS HAS GONE DOWN" followed by thousands of null characters, effectively not printing anything but delaying the system from printing the next prompt for a long time.

Fortunately, the specific problem of changing messages-of-the-day is moot. On most systems, the message-of-the-day no longer serves as a news distribution mechanism, having been replaced by superior interfaces such as Usenet news or other bulletin board-like systems. Instead, the message-of-the-day usually contains a message describing the revision level of the system, copyrights, or other information that rarely changes. In this case, users just need to choose patterns that avoid matching this characteristic information while still matching their prompts.

Example—A Smart Remote Login Script

In Chapter 3 (p. 83), I showed a script called `aftp`. This automated the initialization for an anonymous `ftp` session and then passed control from the script to the user. The same idea can be applied to many other programs.

Imagine the following scenario. You try to create a file only to find out that your computer has no permission to change the file system because it is mounted read-only from another computer, the file server.

```
% rm libc.a
rm: libc.a not removed: Read-only file system
```

All you have to do is log in to the server and then repeat the command:

```
% rlogin server
You are logged in to the server.  Please be careful.
% rm libc.a
rm: libc.a: No such file or directory
```

Oops. You are not in the right directory. `rlogin` does not propagate your current working directory. Now you have to find out what directory you were in, and enter the appropriate `cd` command. If the directory is long enough or if you do this kind of thing frequently, the procedure can become a nuisance.

Here is a script to automatically `rlogin` in such a way that you are automatically placed in the same directory on the remote host.

```
set cwd [pwd]
spawn rlogin $argv
expect "% "
send "cd $cwd\r"
expect "% "
interact
```

The scripts starts by running `pwd`, which returns the current directory. The result is saved in the variable `cwd`. Then `rlogin` is spawned. When the prompt arrives, the script sends the `cd` command and then waits for another prompt. Finally, `interact` is executed and control is returned to the keyboard.

When you run the script, the output appears just as if you had actually typed the cd command yourself.

```
mouse1% rloginwd duck
spawn rlogin duck
You are logged in to duck.  Quack!
duck1% cd /usr/don/expect/book/chapter4/scripts
duck2%
```

The script is purposely simplified for readability. But it can be simplified even further. Doing so illustrates several important points. When pwd is executed, it runs on the same machine on which the script is running. Even after rlogin is spawned, pwd is run on the original system. You can move the pwd right into the send command, thereby obviating the need for the variable cwd altogether. pwd will still refer to the original directory. Indeed, even if you send yet another rlogin command to the remote host, the script continues to run on the original host. Remember that commands started via exec, spawn, catch or otherwise evaluated by Tcl are run on the original host in the original process. Commands that are sent via send operate in whatever new context has been established in the spawned process.

Just before the interact command is an expect command to wait for the prompt. This is actually unnecessary. What happens without the expect? The interact command gets control immediately. But what happens then? interact waits for either the user to type or the system to print something. Of course, the user will wait for the prompt, and when it arrives, interact will echo it so that the user can see it.

The difference then is that with the explicit expect, expect does the waiting, while with no expect, interact waits. In theory, the user could type only during interact, but in reality, the user will wait for the prompt in either case, so there is no functional difference. Hence, the expect can be omitted. Here is the final script, with these minor changes and all the other good stuff added back.

```
#!/usr/local/bin/expect --
set timeout -1
eval spawn rlogin $argv
set prompt "(%|#|\\\$) $"              ;# default prompt
catch {set prompt $env(EXPECT_PROMPT)}
expect -re $prompt
send "cd [pwd]\r"
interact
```

The technique shown in this script can be used for all sorts of things besides setting the current working directory. For example, you could copy all the environment variables. On systems running the X window system, it is useful to initialize the environment variable DISPLAY with the display name of your local host. Then commands executed on the remote system will be displayed on your local screen. If you use the same script on the second host to remotely login to yet another host, the original host definitions will continue to be used. If the remote system has no access to the local file system, it might also be useful to copy the X authority file.

What I have shown here is just the tip of the iceberg. The `interact` command can do all sorts of other interesting things. These are described in Chapter 15 (p. 323) and Chapter 16 (p. 349).

One final note: This script assumes that `rlogin` does not prompt for a password. If it does, the script will fail. Explicitly waiting for passwords requires a little extra work. I will demonstrate how to do that in Chapter 8 (p. 199). In Chapter 15 (p. 340), I will demonstrate a simpler and more general approach to this kind of script that allows passwords and any other interactions to be handled automatically.

What Else Gets Stored In expect_out

In this chapter and the previous one I have shown how the `expect_out` array is used to store strings that match parenthesized subpatterns. The `expect` command can also set several other elements of `expect_out`.

If the pattern is preceded by the `-indices` flag, two other elements are stored for each element `expect_out(X, string)` where X is a digit. `expect_out(X, start)` is set to the starting position of the first character of the string in `expect_out(buffer)`. `expect_out(X, end)` is set to the ending position.

Here is a fragment of one of the earlier `rsh` scripts, just as it queries the remote shell for the status, but with the `-indices` flag added:

```
send "echo \$status\r"
expect -indices -re "\r\n(.*)\r\n"
```

The `-indices` flag precedes the pattern (including its type). In later chapters, you will learn about other `expect` flags. All of these flags follow this model—they precede the pattern.

With the `-indices` flag, the `expect` command implicitly makes the following assignments:

```
set expect_out(0,start) "12"
set expect_out(0,end) "16"
set expect_out(0,string) "\r\n0\r\n"
set expect_out(1,start) "14"
set expect_out(1,end) "14"
set expect_out(1,string) "0"
set expect_out(buffer) "echo \$status\r\n0\r\n"
```

These elements are set before an **expect** action begins executing. To be precise, the scope inside an **expect** action is exactly the same scope as that which contains the **expect** itself. In simple terms, as long as you are in a single procedure, a variable defined before the **expect** (or within it) can be referred to from inside an **expect** action. Similarly, a variable defined by **expect** or within an **expect** action can be accessed after the **expect** has completed. I will provide more detail about actions and scopes in Chapter 6 (p. 140).

Later in the book, I will describe yet additional elements of **expect_out**. However, these are the only ones that are important for now.

More On Anchoring

In the example on page 119, I defined a prompt as "(%|#|\\\$) $". An obvious question is: "Why do you need those backslashes? (Or perhaps, "Okay, I know I need backslashes, but why three? Why not seventeen or some other random number?!")

The answer is exactly the same reason as I described in Chapter 4 (p. 91). In this case, the dollar sign is special both to the pattern matcher and to Tcl. This is similar to the problem with the "[".

To restate, the dollar sign must be prefaced with a backslash to get the pattern matcher to use it as a literal character. Without the backslash, the pattern matcher will use the dollar sign to match the end of the string. However, both the backslash and the dollar sign are also special to Tcl. When Tcl parses command arguments, it will try to make substitutions whenever it sees backslashes and dollar signs.

To avoid losing the backslash, the backslash itself must be prefaced with a backslash. Similarly, the dollar sign must be prefaced with a backslash. The result is "\\" and "\$", or when combined, "\\\$".

As always, there is more to this sorry story. The dollar sign substitution made by Tcl only occurs when an alphanumeric character follows. That is, "$foo" is replaced by the value of the variable **foo**. Since "$" all by itself would imply a variable name of no characters—obviously meaningless—Tcl does not perform any substitution on the dollar sign in such cases. For this reason, you can write the original pattern with two or three backslashes. Both have the same effect.

```
expect -re "(%|#|\\$) $"     ;# RIGHT
expect -re "(%|#|\\\$) $"    ;# RIGHT
```

However, in the case where you are matching the literal "$a", you need three.

```
expect -re "(%|#|\\$a) $"    ;# WRONG
expect -re "(%|#|\\\$a) $"   ;# RIGHT
```

This non-substitution behavior occurs anywhere "$" is not followed by an alphanumeric character such as in the string "$+". It is good programming practice to always use three backslashes when trying to match a dollar sign. For example, if you unthinkingly change the "+" to an "x" one day, the script will continue to work if you had used three backslashes originally but not if you had used two.

Nonetheless, even if you always use three backslashes, you should be aware that two work in this case. Matching a dollar sign prompt is so common, you are likely to see this a lot in other people's scripts.

Earlier in this section, I mentioned that the $ is special to the pattern matcher. To be more specific, unless preceded by a backslash, the $ is special *no matter where in the string it appears*. The same holds for "^". At this point, you might be asking yourself: Why does the pattern matcher insist on interpreting a $ as the end of a string even when it is in the middle of the pattern? The reason is that there are patterns where this is exactly the behavior you want. Consider the following:

```
expect -re "% $|foo"
```

This commands waits for either a "% " prompt or the string foo to appear. Clearly, the $ is in the middle of the pattern and makes sense. More complex scenarios are possible. For example, the pattern above might be stored in a variable and substituted into the middle of another pattern. You would still want the $ to have the same effect.

In contrast, glob patterns are much simpler. They do not support concepts such as alternation. So attempting to anchor the middle of a glob pattern is pointless. For this reason, the glob pattern matcher only treats ^ as special if it appears as the first character in a pattern and a $ if it appears as the last character.

Exercises

1. Modify the timed-read script on page 112 so that it can take an optional default answer which will be returned if the timeout is exceeded.

2. Modify the rsh script on page 119 so that it returns the remote status of programs no matter how much output they produce.

3. Modify the rlogin script on page 122 so that it copies the X authority file. Modify the script so that it also supports telnet.

4. The dump program starts by printing an estimate such as:
   DUMP: estimated 1026958 blocks (501.44MB) on 0.28 tape(s).
   Write a script to print out how many tapes the next backup will take.

5. dump's knowledge of backup peripherals is often out of date. Assuming you are using a device much bigger than dump realizes, write a script so that dump never stops and asks for a new tape.

6. Enhance the script you wrote for the previous question so that it does a better job of asking for tapes. For example, if your tapes are ten times as big as dump thinks, then the script should ask only once for every ten times that dump asks.

In This Chapter:

- *Very Complex Patterns*
- *Executing Actions When Patterns Match*
- *Patterns Matching Plain Strings*
- *The Limits Of Pattern Matching*
- *Handling Parity And Nulls*

6

Patterns, Actions, And Limits

In this chapter, I will describe the limits of patterns, including what to do when you hit them. I will also cover the darker side of range patterns—matching anything *but* certain characters. In the second half of the chapter, I will go into more detail on pattern actions including flow control. Finally, I will cover some miscellaneous pattern matching issues that do not fit anywhere else.

Matching Anything But

As I said in Chapter 5 (p. 113), pattern pieces match as many characters as possible. This makes it a little tricky to match a single line, single word, or single anything. For example, the regular expression ".*\n" matches a single line, but it also matches two lines because two lines end with a "\n". Similarly, it matches three lines, four lines, and so on. If you want to read lines one at a time from another program, then you cannot use this kind of pattern. The solution is to use the "^".

In Chapter 3 (p. 73), I showed that the "^" matches the beginning of the input buffer. When ^ is the first character of a regular-expression range, it means *match anything but the given characters*. For example, the regular expression [^ab] matches any character except a or b. The pattern [^a-zA-Z] matches any character but a letter.[†]

A range can be used to build larger patterns. The pattern "[^]*" matches the longest string not including a blank. For example, if the input buffer contained "For example, if the input buffer contained ", the following expect command could be called repeatedly to match each word in the input.

---

† To match any character but a "^", use the pattern "[^^]". To match a "^" outside a range, quote it with a back-slash. To match a "^" inside a range, put it in any position of the range but the first. To match any character but a "]", use the pattern "[^]]".

```
expect -re "(\[^ ]*) "
```

The range matches each word and the result is stored in $expect_out(1,string). The space at the end of the word is matched explicitly. Without the explicit space, the input buffer is left beginning with a space (" cow jumped ...") and subsequent matches return the null string before the first space.

Remember that the length of the match is important, but only after the starting position is taken into account. Patterns match the longest string at the first possible position in the input. In this example, 0 characters at column 0 are successfully matched even though the pattern can also match 3 characters at column 1. Because column 0 is before column 1, the earlier match is used.

There is no explicit means to match later matches than earlier ones, but often it is possible to simply pick a more descriptive pattern. In this example, the space can be skipped over. Alternatively, the * can be replaced by a + to force the pattern to be at least one letter. This effectively skips over the space between the words without the need to explicitly match it.

```
expect -re "\[^ ]+"
```

Now the word is stored in "expect_out(0,string)". Because the pattern does not match whitespace, there is no need to select pieces of it, and the parentheses are no longer needed, simplifying the pattern further.

Here is the opening dialogue greeting from Uunet's SMTP server. SMTP is the mail protocol used by most Internet computers. The server is normally controlled by a mail program to transfer mail from one host to another, but you can telnet to it directly and type commands interactively. The telnet program adds the first three lines, and Uunet sends back the line that begins "220":

```
% telnet relay1.uu.net smtp
Trying 192.48.96.5 ...
Connected to relay1.uu.net.
Escape character is `^]'.
220 relay1.UU.NET Sendmail 5.61/UUNET-internet-primary ready at
    Mon, 22 Feb 93 23:13:56 -0500
```

In the last line (which wraps over two physical lines on the page), the remote hostname appears immediately after the "220". In order to match and extract the hostname, use the following command:

```
expect -re "\n220 (\[^ ]+) "
```

There are several subtle things about this command. First of all, the SMTP protocol dictates that responses are terminated by \r\n and that the initial response to the connection begins with the string 220 followed by the host or domain identification. Thus, you are guaranteed to see the string "220".

Unfortunately, the `telnet` program prints out the IP address of the remote host name in its "`Trying ...`" message. Since it is quite possible for part of the IP address to actually be "`220`", the pattern starts with \n to match the end of the previous line, effectively forcing the 220 to be the first thing on its own line. A space is skipped and then the familiar "`[^  ]+`" pattern matches the hostname.

Unlike the previous example, yet another space follows the "`[^  ]+`" pattern. Since the pattern explicitly forces the hostname to be non-null, why is space needed at the end of the name? As I described in Chapter 4 (p. 89), network or other delays might crop up at any time. For example, if the greeting line had only partially printed by the time the pattern matching had begun, the input buffer might contain just "`220  rela`". Without the explicit space after the hostname, the pattern would match "`rela`". With the explicit space, the pattern will match the full "`relay1.UU.NET`".

Matching the hostname from the SMTP dialogue is not an artificial example. This technique can be used to convert IP addresses to hostnames when the IP-to-hostname directory entries do not exist, a common fault in many domains. In practice, the likelihood of a host running an SMTP server is much higher than the likelihood that its domain name server is correctly configured with complete reverse mappings. The `gethostbyaddr` example script that comes with the Expect distribution resorts to this and a number of other techniques to convert host addresses to names.

The ability to automate `telnet` opens up worlds of possibilities. All sorts of useful data can be collected and manipulated through interfaces that were originally designed only for humans.

Much of this information is rather open-ended. There may be no standards describing it other than a particular implementation. However, by studying sufficient output, you can usually come up with Expect scripts to read it back in. And if you cannot write an Expect script to understand a program's output, chances are that humans cannot understand the output to begin with.

Really Complex Patterns

Writing scripts to understand natural language is not particularly difficult, but Expect does not give any particular assistance for the task. Regular expressions by themselves are certainly not sufficient to describe arbitrarily complex patterns. In some situations, it is even reasonable to avoid using complex patterns and instead match input algorithmically using Tcl commands.

Take the case of automating `ftp`. In Chapter 3 (p. 83), I showed that it was very easy to retrieve a file *if* the name was known in advance—either by the script or the user. If the name is not known, it is harder. For example, `ftp` does not support directory retrieval.

This can be simulated by retrieving every file in the directory individually. (You can automate this to some degree using `ftp`'s built-in wildcards, but that does not handle subdirectories so it is not a complete solution and I will ignore it for now.)

Further, imagine that you want to only retrieve files created after a certain date. This requires looking at a "long" directory listing. As an example, here is a listing of the directory /published/usenix on `ftp.uu.net`.

```
ftp> cd published/usenix
250 CWD command successful.
ftp> ls -lt
200 PORT command successful.
150 Opening ASCII mode data connection for /bin/ls.
total 41
drwxrwsr-x   3 3      2  512 Sep 26 14:58 conference
drwxr-sr-x 1695 3     21 39936 Jul 31  1992 faces
lrwxrwxrwx   1 3      21   32 Jul 31  1992 bibliography
    -> /archive/doc/literary/obi/USENIX
226 Transfer complete.
remote: -lt
245 bytes received in 0.065 seconds (3.7 Kbytes/s)
ftp>
```

It is easy to pick out the directory listing from this output. As before, you can see the protocol responses that each start with a three-digit number. These can be matched directly, but there is no way of separately matching all of the bits and pieces of information in the directory listing in a single pattern. There is just too much of it. And this is a short directory. Directories can contain arbitrarily many files.

Upon close examination, you can see that the directory lines use different formats. For example, the third file is a symbolic link and shows the link target. The second and third files show modification dates with the year while the first file shows the date with the time. And for a dash of confusion, the formatting is inconsistent—the columns do not line up in the same place from one entry to the next.

One way to deal with all of this is to match the fields in each line, one line at a time in a loop. The command to match a single line might start out like this:

```
expect -re "d(\[^ ]*) +(\[^ ]*) +(\[^ ]*) +(\[^ ]*) +(\ ...
```

The command is incomplete—the pattern does not even fit on the page, and it only describes directories (notice the "d" in the front). You would need similar patterns to match other file types. This complexity might suggest that this is the wrong approach.

An alternative is to use patterns only at a very superficial level. You can match the individual lines initially and then later break up the lines themselves. At this point, matching a single line should be no surprise. It is just a variation on what I have already shown in many different forms:

```
expect -re "(\[^\r]*)\r\n"
```

To get the individual pieces out, you can now use any of the plain old Tcl commands. You can treat $expect_out(1,string) as a simple list and index it. For example, to obtain the file name:

```
lindex $expect_out(1,string) 8
```

To obtain the month and day:

```
lrange $expect_out(1,string) 5 6
```

Using the following commands, you can get the file's type field (the first character on each line from "ls -l") and then process the files, directories, and symbolic links differently:

```
set type [string index $expect_out(1,string) 0]
switch -- $type \
    "-" {
        # file
    } "d" {
        # directory
    } "l" {
        # symbolic link
    } default {
        # unknown
    }
```

With no flags other than "--", the patterns in the switch command are a subset of the glob patterns (everything but ^ and $). This fragment of code actually comes out of the recursive ftp script (rftp) that comes with Expect as an example.

With actions, the whole command to switch on the file type is not much more complicated. There are two of them—one to "get" files and one to "put" files. Below is a procedure to put files. The procedure is called for each file in the directory listing. The first argument is the name of the file, and the second argument is the first character of the type field.

```
proc putentry {name type} {
    switch -- $type \
    "d" {
        # directory
        if {$name=="." || $name==".."} return
        putdirectory $name
    } "-" {
        # file
        putfile $name
```

```
    } "l" {
        # symlink, could be either file or directory
        # first assume it's a directory
        if [putdirectory $name] return
        putfile $name
    } default {
        puts "can't figure out what $name is, skipping\n"
    }
}
```

For each directory encountered, `putdirectory` is called, which changes directories both remotely and locally and then recursively lists the new directory, calling `putentry` again for each line in the list. The files "." (current directory) and ".." (parent directory) are skipped.

Regular files are transferred directly by sending a `put` command inside `putfile`. Symbolic links are trickier since they can point either to directories or plain files. There is no direct way to ask, so the script instead finds out by blindly attempting to transfer the link as a directory. Since the attempt starts by sending a "cd" command, the `putdirectory` procedure fails if the link is not a directory. Upon failure, the script then goes on to transfer it as a plain file. Upon success, the procedure returns.

Really Simple Patterns

Occasionally it is useful to prevent the pattern matcher from performing any special interpretation of characters. This can be done using the `-ex` flag, which causes *exact* matching. For example, the following command matches only an asterisk.

```
    expect -ex "*"
```

When using `-ex`, patterns are always unanchored. The ^ and $ match themselves literally even if they appear as the first or last characters in a pattern. So the following command matches the sequence of characters "^", "*", "\n", and "$". The usual Tcl interpretations apply. Hence, the \n is still interpreted as a single character.

```
    expect -ex "^*\n$"              ;# matches ^ * \n $
```

Consider another example:

```
    expect -ex "\\n"
```

Tcl interprets the \\n as the two-character string "\n" and the exact matching occurs with no further backslash processing. This statement matches a backslash followed by an n.

The results of exact matches are written to `expect_out(buffer)` and `expect_out(0,string)` as usual, although `expect_out(0,string)` is necessarily set to the original pattern.

Using `-ex` may seem like a way to simplify many patterns, but it is really only useful in special circumstances. Most patterns either require wildcards or anchors. And strings such as "foo" are so simple that they mean the same thing when specified via `-gl` in the first place. However, `-ex` is useful when patterns are computer-generated (or user-supplied). For example, suppose you are creating Expect patterns dynamically from a program that is producing SQL queries such as:

```
select * from tbl.col where col like 'name?'
```

To protect this from misinterpretation by `-gl` or `-re`, you would have to analyze the string and figure out where to insert backslashes. Instead, it is much simpler to pass the whole thing as a pattern using `-ex`. The following fragment reads a pattern from a file or process and then waits for it from the spawned process.

```
set pat [gets $patfile]
expect -ex $pat
```

If you are hand-entering SQL commands in your Expect scripts, then you have to go a step further and protect the commands from being interpreted by Tcl. You can use braces to do this. Here is an example, combined with the `-ex` flag.

```
expect -ex {select from * tbl.col where col like 'name?'}
```

I show this only to discourage you again from using braces around patterns. While it works in this example, it is not necessary since you can prevent the substitutions at the time you handcode it by adding backslashes appropriately. Chances are that you will want to make variable substitutions in these or else they would have been stored in a file anyway. And if you are using more than a few patterns like these, you probably will not have them embedded in your scripts, so you do not need to worry about the Tcl substitutions in the first place.

Matching One Line And Only One Line

Matching a single line is such a common task that it is worth getting very familiar with it. The one-line script on page 133 matches a single line and this same technique will show up in many more scripts so it is worth examining closely here.

Suppose you want to search for a file in the file system with the string "frob" at the beginning of the name. There may be many files named "frob" (well, maybe not). You are just interested to know if there is at least one. The obvious tool to use is `find`.

Unfortunately, `find` provides no control over the number of files it finds. You cannot tell it to quit after one. Here is an Expect script to do just that:

```
spawn find . -name "frob*" -print
set timeout -1
expect -re "\[^\r]*\r\n"
```

The script starts by spawning the `find` command. The timeout is disabled since this could be a very long running command. The `expect` pattern waits for one complete line to appear, and then the script exits. This works because the range waits for any character that is not a `\r` and the `*` waits for any number of them—that is, any number of characters that are not `\r`'s. The second `\r` both allows and forces a single `\r`. Finally the `\n` matches the linefeed in the carriage-return linefeed sequence. The only thing that can be matched is a single line.

Without Expect, it is possible to get `find` to kill itself by saving its process id in a file and then forking the `kill` command from an `-exec` clause in the `find`. However, doing this is fairly painful. And `find` is just a special case. Many other commands do not have the power of `find` yet share the same problem of lacking any sophisticated control. For example, `grep` does not have any way to execute arbitrary commands when it matches. There is no way to tell `grep` to print only the first match.

For this and other commands, here is an Expect script which I call `firstline`:

```
#!/usr/local/bin/expect --
eval spawn $argv
set timeout -1
expect -re "\[^\r]*\r\n"
```

Immediately after matching the first line of output, `firstline` exits. Note that if the underlying process produces output quickly enough, the script may actually print several lines of output. That does not mean the pattern is matching multiple lines. It is still only matching one. However, by default Expect prints out everything it sees whether or not it matches.

In Chapter 7 (p. 175), I will describe how to change this default so that you can write scripts that only print out what they match.

Tcl's string match Command

Having matched a single line, it is no longer possible to automatically break it up into pieces stored in the array `expect_out`. Tcl does, however, offer a standalone version of both the regular expression and glob pattern matchers.

Glob pattern matching is explicitly done using the "string match" command. The command follows the format:

```
string match pattern string
```

The string replaces the implicit reference to the input buffer in an **expect** command. The command returns 1 if there is a match or 0 if there is no match. For example:

```
if [string match "f*b*" "foobar"] {
    puts "match"
} else {
    puts "no match"
}
```

The switch command (demonstrated on page 133) is a little more like the **expect** command. It supports multiple patterns and actions, but like "string match", switch uses an explicit string. Neither switch nor "string match" support the ^ and $ anchors.

Tcl's regexp Command

Tcl's regexp command matches strings using regular expressions. The regexp command has the same internal pattern matcher that expect uses but the interface is different. The expect command provides the string implicitly while regexp requires that the string be an explicit argument.

The calling syntax is as follows:

```
regexp pattern string var0 var1 var2 var3 . . .
```

The first argument is a pattern. The second argument is the string from which to match. The remaining arguments are variables, set to the parts of the string that match the pattern. The variable *var0* is set to the substring that was matched by the whole pattern (analogous to expect_out(0,string)). The remaining variables are set to the substrings that matched the parenthesized parts of the pattern (analogous to expect_out(1,string) through expect_out(9,string)).

```
expect1.1> set addr "usenet@uunet.uu.net"
```

For example, the following command separates the Internet email address (above) into a user and host:

```
expect1.2> regexp (.*)@(.*) $addr ignore user host
1
expect1.3> set user
usenet
expect1.4> set host
uunet.uu.net
```

The first parenthesized pattern matches the user and is stored in the variable user. The @ matches the literal @ in the address, and the remaining parenthesized pattern matches the host. Whatever is matched by the entire pattern is stored in ignore, called this because it is not of interest here. This is analogous to the expect command where expect_out(0,string) is often ignored. The command returns 1 if the pattern matches or 0 if it does not.

The regexp command accepts the optional flag "-indices". When used, regexp stores a list of the starting and ending character positions in each output variable rather than the strings themselves. Here is the previous command with the -indices flag:

```
expect1.5> regexp -indices (.*)@(.*) $addr ignore user host
1
expect1.6> set user
0 5
expect1.7> set host
7 18
```

The expect command also supports an "-indices" flag (shown in Chapter 5 (p. 124)) but there are differences between the way expect and regexp support it. The expect command writes the indices into the expect_out array alongside the strings themselves so you do not have to repeat the expect command to get both strings and indices. Also, the elements are written separately so that it is possible to extract the start or ending index without having to break them apart.

Tcl's regsub Command

The regsub command makes substitutions in a string that matches a regular expression. For example, the following command substitutes like with love in the value of olddiet. The result in stored in the variable newdiet.

```
expect1.1> set olddiet "I like cheesecake!"
I like cheesecake!
expect1.2> regsub "like" $olddiet "love" newdiet
1
expect1.3> set newdiet
I love cheesecake!
```

If the expression does not match, no substitution is made and regsub returns 0 instead of 1. However, the string is still copied to the variable named by the last parameter.

Strings that match parenthesized expressions can be referred to inside the substituted string (the third parameter, love in this example). The string that matched the first parenthesized expression is referred to as "\1", the second as "\2", and so on up to "\9". The entire string that matched is referred to as "\0".

In the following example, cheesecake matches the parenthesized expression. It is first substituted for \1 in the fourth argument, and then *that* string replaces "cheesecake!" in the original value of olddiet. Notice that the backslash must be preceded by a second backslash in order to prevent Tcl itself from rewriting the string.

```
expect1.4> set substitute "the feel of \\1 in my nose."
the feel of \1 in my nose.
expect1.5> regsub "(c.*e)!" $olddiet $substitute odddiet
1
expect1.6> set odddiet
I like the feel of cheesecake in my nose.
```

If you find this a little confusing, do not worry. You can usually accomplish the same thing as regsub with a couple of other commands. The situations in which regsub can be used do not arise that often—indeed, regsub is used only one other place in this book (page 216). However, when the need arises, regsub is a real timesaver. To make it even more useful, the regsub command can be applied to every matching pattern in the string by using the -all flag.

Ignoring Case

The -nocase flag indicates that a match should occur as if any uppercase characters in the string were lowercase. The -nocase flag works for both regexp and expect. Like other expect flags, -nocase is applied separately to each pattern.

The -nocase flag can dramatically simplify patterns. Compare the following commands. All of them match the strings "hi there!", "Hi there!", "Hi There!", and "HI THERE!", but the last command is the shortest and most readable.

```
expect "\[Hh]\[Ii] \[Tt]\[Hh]\[Ee]\[Rr]\[Ee]!"
expect -re "(hi there|Hi there|Hi There|HI THERE)!"
expect -re "(hi|Hi|HI) (there|There|THERE)!"
expect -nocase "hi there!"
```

From the expect command, the -nocase flag can be used with glob patterns, regular expressions, and exact strings. Non-alphabetic characters are not affected by the -nocase flag.

Do not use -nocase with uppercase characters in the pattern. Uppercase characters in the pattern can never match.

```
expect -nocase "HI THERE!"    ;# WRONG, CAN NEVER MATCH!
expect -nocase "hi there"     ;# RIGHT!
```

All Those Other String Functions Are Handy, Too

There are numerous other string manipulation functions that can be used when working with patterns. For example, in Chapter 3 (p. 77), I used "string trimright" to remove all the newline characters from the end of a string.

Another function that is very handy is scan. The scan command interprets strings according to a format. scan is analogous to the C language scanf function. For the most part, scan is less powerful than regexp, but occasionally the built-in capabilities of scan provide exactly the right tool. For example, a regular expression to match a C-style real number is:

```
-?([0-9]+.?[0-9]*|[0-9]*.[0-9]+)([eE][-+]?[0-9]+)?
```

And that is before adding the backslashes in front of "[" and "."! A much better alternative is to use the scan command. This can match real numbers, plus you can constrain it for precision. All you have to do is feed it a string containing a number. You can have expect look for the end of the number (such as by seeing whitespace) and then call:

```
scan $expect_out(0,string) "%f" num
```

In this example, the number is stored in the variable num. The %f tells scan to extract a real number. Chapter 2 (p. 46) has more information on scan and other string manipulation commands.

Actions That Affect Control Flow

So far, all I have used in the way of expect actions are commands such as set or if/ then or lists of such commands. The following expect command illustrates both of these:

```
expect {
    a {set foo bar}
    b {
        if {$a == 1} {set c 4}
        set b 2
    }
}
```

It is possible to use commands that affect control flow. For example, the following while command executes someproc again and again until the variable a has the value 2. When a equals 2, the action break is executed. This stops the while loop and control passes to the next command after the while.

```
while 1 {
    if {$a == 2} break
    someproc
}
```

You can do similar things with `expect` commands. The following command reads from the output of the spawned process until either a 1 or 2 is found. Upon finding a 1, `someproc` is executed and the loop is repeated. If 2 is found, `break` is executed. This stops the `while` loop, and control passes to the next command after the `while`. This is analogous to the way `break` behaved in the `if` command earlier.

```
while 1 {
    expect {
        "2" break
        "1"
    }
    someproc
}
```

Example — rogue

This previous example is a very typical Expect fragment. It does not take much more to produce a useful script. As an example, the following script provides a small assist in playing the game of `rogue`. `rogue` is an adventure game which presents you with a player that has various physical attributes, such as strength. Most of the time, the strength rating is 16, but every so often—maybe one out of 20 games—you get an unusually good strength rating of 18. A lot of `rogue` players know this, but no one in their right mind restarts the game 20 times to find those really good configurations—it is too much typing. The following script does it automatically:

```
while 1 {
    spawn rogue
    expect {
        "Str: 18" break
        "Str: 16"
    }
    send "Q"
    expect "quit?"
    send "y"
    close
    wait
}
interact
```

Inside a loop, `rogue` is started and then the strength is checked to see if it is 18 or 16. If it is 16, the dialogue is terminated. Like `telnet` (see Chapter 4 (p. 103)), `rogue` does not watch for an eof either, so a simple close is not sufficient to end the dialogue. "Q" requests that rogue quit. The game asks for confirmation to which the script replies "y". At this point, both the script and rogue close the connection. Then the script executes wait. As I described in Chapter 4 (p. 105), wait tells the system that it can discard the final exit status of the rogue process.

When rogue exits, the loop is restarted and a new game of rogue is created to test. When a strength of 18 is found, the break action is executed. This breaks control out of the while loop and control drops down to the last line of the script. The interact command passes control to the user so that they can play this particular game.

If you run this script, you will see dozens of initial configurations fly across your screen in a few seconds, finally stopping with a great game for you to play. The only way to play rogue more easily is under the debugger!

Character Graphics

The output produced by rogue in the previous section contains explicit cursor positioning character sequences. This can potentially cause the screen to be drawn in such a way that patterns fail to match the visible output. For example, imagine a score of 1000 being updated to 2000. To make the screen reflect this change, the program need only position the cursor appropriately and then overwrite the 1 with a 2. Needless to say, this will not match the string 2000 because the 2 arrived after the 000.

This particular problem does not arise in the rogue example because the screen is being drawn from scratch. This idea can be used to provide a general solution. To read the screen as if it were printed from top to bottom, force the spawned program to redraw the screen from scratch. Typically, sending a ^L suffices.

Alas, redrawing the screen does not solve other problems. For instance, there is still no way to tell where the cursor is. This may be critical if you are testing, for example, a menu-application to make sure that the cursor moves correctly from one entry to the next.

In Chapter 19 (p. 458), I will describe a way to handle this and other related problems more directly by maintaining an explicit representation of the terminal screen.

More Actions That Affect Control Flow

Just as `break` was used in the `rogue` script, so can all of the other flow-control commands be used inside of `expect` commands. For example, a `return` command inside of an `expect` causes the current procedure to return:

```
proc foo {
    expect {
        "1" return
        "2"
    }
    someproc
}
```

The `continue` command causes control to resume at the beginning of the nearest enclosing `while` or `for` loop. `continue`, `break`, and `return` can be mixed in intuitive ways. In the following example, the patterns 1, 2, and 3 do not mean anything in particular. They are just placeholders. The actions are what is interesting.

```
proc foo {
    while 1 {
        expect {
            "1" {
                return          ;# return from foo
            }
            "2" {
                break           ;# break out of while
            }
            "3" {
                if {0==[func]} {
                    exit        ;# exit program
                } else {
                    continue    ;# restart while
                }
            }
        }
        someproc
    }
    some-other-proc
}
```

In Chapter 3 (p. 83), I showed a script that started an anonymous `ftp` session and let you interact after performing the login automatically. Using some of the things you have seen since, it is possible to write a more capable version of the anonymous `ftp` script, `aftp`. The one below retries the connection if the remote host refuses because it is down or there are too many users. A procedure called `connect` is defined and called repeatedly in a loop. Anonymous `ftp` administrators may not appreciate this approach, but it is sometimes the only way to get through to a site that is very popular. Once connected, the script sends the binary command to disable any data conversions. As with the earlier version, this script ends by dropping into an interact. Then you can interact as in the earlier script.

```
#!/usr/local/bin/expect --

proc connect {host} {
    expect "ftp>"
    send "open $host\r"
    expect {
        "Name*:" {
            send "anonymous\r"
            expect {
                "Password:" {
                    send "don@libes.com\r"
                    expect "login ok*ftp>"
                    return 0
                }
                "denied*ftp>" {
                    # too many users, probably
                    send "close\r"
                    return 1
                }
                "failed*ftp>" {
                    # some other reason?
                    send "close\r"
                    return 1
                }
            }
        }
        "timed out" {
            return 1
        }
    }
}

set timeout -1

spawn ftp -i
while {[connect $argv]} {}
send "binary\r"
interact
```

Matching Multiple Times

Many tasks require an `expect` to be repeated some number of times. Reading files from a list is an example of this. In the example on page 133, I matched a single line with the command:

```
expect -re "(\[^\r]*)\r\n"
```

This can be wrapped in a loop to read multiple lines and break when a prompt appears:

```
while 1 {
    expect {
        -re "(\[^\r]*)\r\n"    process_line
        $prompt    break
    }
}
```

This version has additional patterns upon which to break out of the loop:

```
while 1 {
    expect {
        -re "(\[^\r]*)\r\n" process_line
        eof {
            handle_eof
            break
        }
        timeout {
            handle_timeout
            break
        }
        $prompt break
    }
}
```

Here, `handle_eof` and `handle_timeout` are imaginary procedures that perform some processing appropriate to the condition. More importantly, notice that all of the patterns but one terminate by breaking out of the loop. It is possible to simplify this by using the `exp_continue` command.

When executed as an `expect` action, the command `exp_continue` causes control to be continued inside the current `expect` command. `expect` continues trying to match the pattern, but from where it left off after the previous match. `expect` effectively repeats its search *as if* it had been invoked again.

Since `expect` does not have to be explicitly reinvoked, the `while` command is not necessary. The previous example can thus be rewritten as:

```
expect {
    -re "(\[^\r]*)\r" {
```

```
        process_line
        exp_continue
    }
    eof handle_eof
    timeout handle_timeout
    $prompt
}
```

In this example, each line is matched and then processed via `process_line`. `expect` then continues to search for new lines, processing them in turn.

Compare this version with the previous one which was written with an explicit loop. The rewrite is a lot shorter because it does not need all the explicit `break` commands. There is no hard and fast rule for when to use an explicit loop instead of `exp_continue`, but a simple guideline is to use `exp_continue` when there are fewer actions that repeat the loop than those that break out of the loop. In other words, explicit loops make actions that repeat the `expect` shorter. `exp_continue` makes actions that break out of the loop shorter.

When the `exp_continue` action is executed, the `timeout` variable is reread and `expect`'s internal timer is reset. This is usually what is desired since it is exactly what would happen with an `expect` in an explicit `while` or `for` loop. For example, if `timeout` is set to ten seconds and input lines arrive every second, the `expect` command will continue to run even after ten lines have arrived. Each time `exp_continue` is executed, `expect` then waits up to ten more seconds.

To avoid resetting the timer, call `exp_continue` with the `-continue_timer` flag.

```
    exp_continue -continue_timer
```

With a very small timeout, `exp_continue` offers a convenient way to discard additional characters that arrive soon after a match.

```
    set timeout 1
    expect -re ".+" exp_continue
```

In the command above, characters are ignored as long as they keep arriving within `$timeout` seconds of one another. When the output finally settles down, the `expect` command completes and control passes to the next command in the script.

Here is a variation on the same idea. The following fragment recognizes the string "ok" if it arrives in output, each character of which arrives within `$timeout` seconds of one another.

```
    set buf ""
    expect -re ".+" {
        append buf $expect_out(buffer)
    }
```

```
if [regexp "ok" $buf] {
    . . .
```

In Chapter 15 (p. 344), I will show how to do the same thing but without the explicit buffering in the action.

Recognizing Prompts (Yet Again)

In Chapter 5 (p. 120), I described how to match a variety of different prompts and potentially any prompt that a user might choose. A problem I did not address is that programs can require interaction even before the first prompt. One such program is tset, which is used to set the terminal type.

tset is fairly clever, but if it cannot figure out the terminal type, tset prompts the user. The tset prompt is well defined. The prompt starts with a fixed string and then has a default terminal type in parentheses, such as:

```
TERM = (xterm)
```

At this point, the user can either enter the terminal type or simply press return, in which case the type is set to the default. In most scripts, the default is fine.

The following fragment handles this interaction:

```
expect {
    "TERM = *) " {
        send "\r"
        exp_continue
    } -re $prompt
}
```

Both the prompt from tset and the shell are expected. If the shell prompt shows up first, the expect is satisfied and the script continues. If the tset prompt appears, the script acknowledges it and uses exp_continue to repeat and look for the shell prompt.

The fragment does a little more work than it needs. If it finds the tset prompt once, it looks for it again even though it will not appear. To avoid this, the loop would have to be unrolled—but it would have no substantive benefit. It is easier to write and more readable as it is.

Fortunately, tset is the only interactive program that is commonly encountered while logging in. If you have need to handle anything else, it is likely unique to a user or situation. If need be, a hook can be provided for users that invoke other interactive programs while logging in.

Similarly to the way users can define their own EXPECT_PROMPT environment variable, users can also write their own Expect fragments to automate a login interaction. For example, suppose a user's .login always prompts "read news (y|n):" upon logging in. To handle this, have the user create a file called ".login.exp". Inside it would be just the fragment to automate their personal interaction:

```
expect "read news (y|n):"
send "n\r"
```

Application scripts can then handle the interaction by detecting the presence of the file and using it just prior to looking for the shell prompt.

```
if [file readable ~/.login.exp] {
    source ~/.login.exp
}
expect -re $prompt
```

Speed Is On Your Side

Another use of exp_continue appears in the robohunt script that comes with Expect as an example. robohunt automates the game of hunt. Unlike the rogue script mentioned earlier, robohunt plays the whole game for you. hunt is a character graphics game that lets you navigate through a maze. You attack other players or crash through walls simply by moving into them. Certain walls cannot be broken through. If you try to do so, the game responds by ringing the bell, done by sending a ^G.

The other details of the game or script are not important except for one aspect. The script works by precalculating a number of moves and sending each batch of moves out at once. The script uses a crude heuristic for deciding which way to move, so it occasionally runs into a wall and keeps running into a wall for the rest of the batch of moves. This causes the game to send back a whole slew of ^G's. The script handles it with the following command:

```
set bell "\007"
expect {
    -re "^$bell+" exp_continue
    -re "again\\? " {send y}
    -re ".+"
}
```

The first pattern checks if the output starts out with a sequence of ^G's (here denoted by "\007"). If the ^G's are found, they are matched and effectively discarded as the action simply restarts the expect command.

If the script's player is killed, the game stops and asks "Do you want to play again? ". It suffices to check for the final question mark and space, but this would leave the script with a fairly cryptic pattern. Adding "`again`" to the pattern makes it more readable with no significant impact on performance.

The third pattern checks for anything else. The only reason why anything else might appear is that the game is printing out its usual display of the screen which in turn means that it is waiting for new moves. So the `expect` command completes and control passes to another part of the script that computes and sends a new move.

The `robohunt` script may seem rather lacking in sophisticated logic and in many ways just plain stupid. It is. But it can overwhelm a human opponent by sheer speed despite constant blunders and an obvious lack of any deep understanding of its task. Nonetheless, it is not to be scoffed at. This is precisely the idea used by many computer algorithms that accomplish seemingly difficult tasks.

The `robohunt` script is virtually impossible for a human player to play against simply because the script is so fast. While this technique is not the usual reason Expect scripts are useful, it is certainly a technique worth remembering.

Controlling The Limits Of Pattern Matching Input

Expect is usually much faster than any human. However, certain behavior can force Expect to be slower than it could be or even worse, to fail altogether.

Some programs produce an astounding amount of output. Graphics programs are one example, but even programs that simply list files can produce a flood of output. The rate is not a problem. Expect can consume it and make way for more very quickly. But Expect has a finite amount of memory for remembering program output. By default, the limit is enough to guarantee that patterns can match up to the last 2000 bytes of output.[†]

This is just the number of characters that can fit on a 25 row 80 column screen. When a human is viewing a program producing a lot of output, everything but the last 2000 or so characters scroll off the screen. If a decision has to be made, the human must do it based only on those last 2000 characters. Following the philosophy that Expect does what a human does, Expect effectively defaults to doing the same thing: throwing away everything but the last 2000 characters.

This may sound like a lot of information can be missed, but there are some ameliorating factors. In particular, if an interactive program produces a lot of output (more than a screenful) and wants to make sure that everything is seen, it will present the user with a prompt (e.g., "`more?`"). Expect can recognize this too.

---

† This is not exactly the same thing as simply saying "the limit is 2000 bytes" for reasons I will get to shortly.

The behavior of Expect to forget (i.e., throw things away) does not mean that Expect will not attempt to match output against the current patterns. Output actually arrives in small groups of characters—typically no more than 80 characters (i.e., a line) maximum. Faster programs produce these chunks faster rather than producing larger chunks. As I described in Chapter 4 (p. 89), as each chunk arrives, Expect attempts to match against it with whatever is remembered from the previous output. No matter how big the chunks used, Expect attempts to match every character in the output at least once after 1999 additional characters have arrived.

Much of the time, this works quite well. However, it does not always make sense to force Expect into literally following human behavior. A human, for example, might want to see a large directory listing. Since it will immediately scroll off the screen, the choice is to pipe it through a program like `more`, redirect it into a file, or perhaps run the session inside of a scrollable shell provided by an `emacs` or `xterm` window. This is not necessary with Expect. It is a computer program after all, and can remember as much information as it is told.

The maximum size of matches that Expect guarantees it can make is controlled with the `match_max` command. As an example, the following command ensures that Expect can match program output of up to 10000 characters.

```
match_max 10000
```

The figure given to `match_max` is *not* the maximum number of characters that can match. Rather, it is a *minimum* of the maximum numbers of characters that can be matched. Or put another way, it is possible to match more than the current value but larger matches are not guaranteed.[†]

The limit to how high you can set `match_max` is governed by your particular operating system. Some systems add additional limits (such as by your system administrator or the shell's `limit` command), but these are usually arbitrary and can be increased. In any implementation, you can count on being able to set the limit to a megabyte or more, so you probably do not have to worry about this limit when designing Expect algorithms.

To change the default buffer size of all future programs that will be spawned in the current script, use the `-d` flag. The "d" stands for "default". This does not change the size for the currently spawned process.

```
match_max -d 10000
```

---

† The peculiar definition of `match_max` is a concession to performance. In order to efficiently carry out the process of reading and matching new characters along with old ones, during the matching process Expect uses up to double the space declared by `match_max`. Thus, it is possible to match up to twice as much as `match_max` guarantees.

With no arguments, `match_max` returns the value for the currently spawned process. With a `-d` flag and no numeric argument, `match_max` returns the default value.

Setting the buffer size sufficiently large can slow down your script, but only if you let the input go unmatched. As characters arrive, the pattern matcher has to retry the patterns over successively longer and longer amounts of input. So it is a good idea to keep the buffer size no larger than you really need.

As soon as a pattern matches, the input that matches and anything before it in the buffer is removed. You can use this to speed up pattern matching. Just remove any unnecessary input by matching it. For example, imagine you want to collect the body of a mail message. Unfortunately, the mail program starts off by displaying several thousand bytes worth of headers before it gets to the body of the message. You are not interested in the headers—they only slow down the pattern matching.

Rather than just matching everything (or the prompt at the end), it is quicker to match the headers, throw them away, and then return to searching for the prompt. This could be done conveniently using `exp_continue`. If you need the headers, too, consider matching for them separately. While you have to write two **expect** commands, the result also speeds up the overall matching process. You can speed up the matching even further by matching each line individually. If the line containing the prompt arrives, you are done. If any other line arrives, append the line to a buffer and repeat the **expect** command as before. In this way, the pattern matcher never has to rematch more than a line's worth of data. This technique can produce a significantly faster response if you are waiting for the prompt at the end of a 100K mail message!

For most tasks, the speed of pattern matching is not a concern. It usually happens so quickly that you never notice a delay. But enormous amounts of unmatched input combined with sufficiently complex patterns can take several seconds or more, causing noticeable delays in processing. In such cases, if you cannot simplify your patterns, it may pay to change your strategy from trying to match a large amount of data with a single pattern to iteratively matching characters or lines or whatever chunks are convenient as they arrive and storing them for later processing.

The full_buffer Keyword

On page 149, I described how **expect** discards input when its internal buffer is exceeded. The special pattern `full_buffer` matches when no other patterns match and **expect** would otherwise throw away part of the input to make room for more.[†]

---

† There is a way to obtain the discarded input without explicitly matching `full_buffer` or any other action. However, I will not introduce the tools to accomplish this until Chapter 18 (p. 407).

When `full_buffer` matches, all of the unmatched input is moved to `expect_out(buffer)`.

As with other special patterns, such as `eof` and `timeout`, `full_buffer` is only recognized when none of the `-gl`, `-re`, or `-ex` flags has been used.

The following fragment was written for someone who needed a program that would "spool up" a relatively slow stream from the standard input and send it to a `telnet` process every 3 seconds. They wanted to feed `telnet` with a few big chunks of data rather than lots of tiny ones because they were running on a slow network that could not afford the overhead.

```
set timeout 3
while 1 {
    expect_user {
        eof exit
        timeout {
            expect_user "*"
            send $expect_out(buffer)
        }
        full_buffer {send $expect_out(buffer)}
    }
}
```

The program works by sitting in a loop which waits for three seconds or a full buffer, whichever comes first. If the buffer fills, it is sent out immediately. If three seconds pass, another `expect` command is executed to retrieve whatever data has arrived, and that data is sent to the remote side.

The `expect_user` command is a special version of the `expect` command that reads from the standard input. I will describe this command in detail in Chapter 8 (p. 192).

Double Buffering

When a spawned process produces a line of output, it does not immediately go into Expect's buffer. In Chapter 4 (p. 89), I described how the UNIX kernel processes characters in chunks. The kernel, in a sense, contains its own buffer from which it doles out these chunks when `expect` asks for more.

This kernel buffer is separate from `expect`'s buffer. The kernel's buffer is only checked when `expect` cannot find a match using the data already in its own buffer. This *double buffering* rarely has any impact on the way scripts behave. However, there are some cases in which the buffering does make a difference. For instance, imagine that you have a shell script named `greet` that prints `hello`, sleeps five seconds, and then prints `goodbye`.

```
echo hello
sleep 5
echo goodbye
```

Now, consider the following Expect script:

```
spawn /bin/sh greet
expect "h"
exec sleep 10
expect -re ".*o"
```

This script finds the h from `hello` and then sleeps for 10 seconds. During that time, the shell script prints `goodbye`. This string is handed to the kernel which buffers it until Expect asks for it.

When Expect awakens, `expect` searches its input buffer for anything with an o at the end. This is satisfied by `ello` and `expect` returns. The string `goodbye` is not tested because it is never read by `expect`.

A more realistic situation arises when using the simple "`*`" pattern. This always matches everything in `expect`'s internal buffer and returns immediately. It never causes `expect` to ask the kernel for more input, even if there is no data waiting.

So "`expect  "*"`" clears `expect`'s internal buffer but not the kernel's buffer. How can the kernel's buffer be cleared? Intuitively, you need to read everything that is waiting. But how do you know what "everything" is? `expect` can only ask for the amount of data described by the `match_max` command. If you can guarantee how much the spawned process has written, you can do this:

```
expect "*"          ;# clear Expect's internal buffer
match_max $big      ;# get ready for everything waiting
expect -re ".+"     ;# read it, match it, discard it
```

If you are not prepared to declare how much could have been written, you cannot have `expect` read in a loop. The spawned process may be writing at the same time that you are reading in which case you can start throwing away more than what was "old".

Realistically, system indigestion can throw off any timing that you are hoping to rely on to decide when it is time to flush buffers. The best solution is still to explicitly provide patterns to match old output and then have the script throw the buffer away.

In general, asking for `expect` to flush kernel buffers usually indicates that something is poorly designed—either the Expect script or the application. In Chapter 8 (p. 192), I will describe an application where these kinds of problems have to be dealt with.

Perpetual Buffering

The -notransfer flag prevents expect from removing matching characters from the internal buffer. The characters can be matched repeatedly as long as the -notransfer flag is associated with the pattern.

```
expect -notransfer pat
```

The -notransfer flag is particularly useful for experimenting with patterns. You can drive a program up to a point where it loads up the internal buffer and then try various patterns against it again and again. For convenience, the -notransfer flag can be abbreviated "-n" when Expect is running interactively.

In the next chapter, I will show some additional debugging aids that can be usefully combined with the -notransfer flag.

The Politics Of Patterns

Creating a pattern that matches a string is not always an easy task. A common dilemma is whether to use a very conservative pattern or a more liberal pattern.

Conservative patterns typically have few or no wildcards and only match a limited number of strings. While easy to read, they carry the potential risk of not being able to match a string that deviates from the expected.

Liberal patterns are more forgiving with the ability to match any string that could conceivably appear. However, these patterns underspecify the requirements of a string and therefore risk matching strings that were not intended to be matched.

For example, automating a login requires that the initial prompt be accepted. There is surprising nonconformity even at this level. For instance, UNIX systems commonly prompt with "login:" while VMS systems prompt with "Username:". One way to automate this might be:

```
expect -re "(login|Username): "
```

But if you run into a system someday that just prompts "User", it will not be accepted. This string and others can be added to the command, but eventually you may end up just accepting anything that ends with a colon and a space:

```
expect -re ".*: $"
```

The $ lowers the risk of the string appearing in the middle of some other output.

Incidentally, handling VMS and UNIX systems in a single script may seem hard to believe. However, the passmass script that comes with Expect as an example does just this. passmass sets your password on any number of hosts. The idea is that you want to keep your password the same on all the computers that you use, but when it comes time to change it, you only want to do it once. `passmass` does this—it logs into each machine and changes your password for you.

The actual password-changing dialogue is fairly similar from one operating system to another. Of course, the prompts are wildly different. So are the diagnostics reporting, for example, that your new password is not acceptable.

Here is an excerpt from `passmass`, where it sends the new password and then resends it as a verification. The `badhost` function records the hosts that fail so that it is easy to see afterwards which ones require manual assistance.

```
send "$newpassword\r"
expect -re "not changed|unchanged" {
    badhost $host "new password is bad?"
    continue
} -re "(password|Verification|Verify):.*"
send "$newpassword\r"
expect -re "(not changed|incorrect|choose new).*" {
    badhost $host "password is bad?"
    continue
} $prompt
```

Expecting A Null Character

The *null* character is another name for a zero-valued byte.[†] Tcl provides no way to represent nulls in strings. Indeed, internally Tcl reserves null to delimit strings—so even if you could get a null in a string, you cannot do anything useful with the result. Fortunately, this is not a problem.

Nulls are almost never generated by interactive processes. Since they have no printing representation, users cannot see them and so there is little point in sending nulls to users. Nonetheless, nulls have valid uses. The most common use for nulls is to control screen graphics. The nulls are used either to delay character arrival on slow screens or as parameters to screen formatting operations. Both of these operations work correctly in Expect. Expect passes nulls to the standard output just like any other character.

By default, Expect removes any nulls before doing pattern matching. This is done for efficiency—it allows the pattern matcher to use the same internal representation of strings that Tcl uses.

Removal of nulls can be disabled with the `remove_nulls` command. The nulls can then be matched explicitly using the `null` keyword. To prevent nulls being removed

---

† Pedants insist that the correct term is NUL and that "null character" is meaningless. However, both Standard C and POSIX define "null character" so I believe this term to be accepted and understood by most people.

from the output of the currently spawned process, use the command `remove_nulls` with an argument of 0. The following fragment calls `remove_nulls` and then looks for a null in the output.

```
remove_nulls 0          ;# disable null removal
expect null             ;# match a null
```

An argument of 1 causes nulls to be removed. The `remove_nulls` command handles its arguments similarly to the `match_max` command. With no arguments, the value for the currently spawned process is returned. With a `-d`, the default value is returned. A new default is set by using `-d` followed by 0 or 1.

You cannot directly embed the `null` keyword inside of another pattern. Nulls can only be matched by themselves. Null matching is unanchored. Hence, when `expect` looks for a null it skips over any other characters to find it. Any characters that are skipped can be found, as usual, in `expect_out(buffer)`. Since nulls are internally used to terminate strings, unanchored patterns cannot be matched into the buffer past a null. Fortunately, this is not a problem since the `null` pattern can always be listed (and searched for) last. I will show an example of this shortly.

If nulls are being used to pad data, it is just a matter of waiting for the correct number of nulls. For example, to wait for two nulls:

```
expect null
expect null
```

The more typical use is when receiving binary data. For example, suppose you expect an equal sign followed by an integer represented as four bytes, most significant byte first. This task is best separated into two parts, illustrated by the two commands in the following fragment:

```
expect "="
set result [expect_four_byte_int]
```

The first command looks for the equals sign. The second is a procedure to collect a four byte integer that may contain binary zeros. This procedure is not predefined by Expect but here is an example of how you might write it:

```
proc expect_four_byte_int {} {
    set x 0
    for {set i 0} {$i<4} {incr i} {
        set x [expr $x*256]
        expect "?" {
            scan $expect_out(0,string) %c d
            incr x $d
        } null
    }
}
```

```
        return $x
}
```

The procedure works by expecting a single byte at a time. Null bytes are matched with the `null` keyword. Non-null bytes are matched with the "?". Each time through the loop, the previous subtotal is shifted up to make room for the new byte. The new byte value is added to the current subtotal. Since a null has a 0 byte value, no addition and hence no action is even necessary in that case. It just has to be matched.

This approach to handling null bytes may seem slow and awkward (and it is), but the reality is that Tcl is optimized as a user interface, and handling binary data in a user interface *almost* never happens. The tradeoff of allowing null to be handled differently is that it allows the rest of Tcl to be much simpler than it otherwise would be.

Parity

Parity refers to the process of error detection by modification and inspection of a single bit in each byte. There are two basic types of parity. Odd parity means that the number of 1 bits in the byte is odd. If a letter is not naturally represented by an odd number of 1 bits, the high-order bit is forced to be 1. Even parity is just the opposite.

Parity was never much good, being very susceptible to transmission noise. In this day and age, parity is totally useless. Nonetheless, some old computer peripherals generate it anyway. And worse, they provide no way of disabling it. Locally spawned processes do not add parity in the first place. You only have to worry about parity when communicating with other peripherals, such as modems or telecommunication switches.

By default, `expect` respects parity. `expect` passes characters with their parity on to the standard output (or log file) and also does pattern matching with the original parity. The reason this is useful, of course, is that many programs use all the bits in a byte to represent data. Eight-bit character sets (prevalent in Europe) do not work if one of the bits is used for parity.

Usually, parity is not a consideration. Indeed, if your Expect dialogues are working just fine, then you can skip this section. However, you may occasionally find that some of your characters are unreadable or just plain wrong. For example, suppose that you use `tip` to dial up another computer and the following gibberish appears instead of a prompt to login:

        lo¿i¿:¿

In this case, the ¿ represents a character that would have had an even number of bits but was modified to force odd parity. You may not see this particular symbol but similar garbage will definitely clue you in that there is a problem.

In many cases, you can just tell the remote side not to generate parity. If the equipment does not support any way of changing parity, you can use the `parity` command.

The `parity` command handles its arguments similarly to the `match_max` and `remove_nulls` commands. When called with an argument of 0, parity is stripped from the current process. If called with a nonzero argument, parity is not stripped. With no argument, the current value is returned. With the `-d` flag, the parity is set or examined for future processes.

```
parity 0    ;# strip parity
```

The `parity` command only affects how Expect treats parity. Your terminal parameters can affect it as well. For example, if your terminal is set to strip parity on input, any eight-bit characters you enter will arrive without the high-order bits. Output from spawned processes can also be affected because they have their own terminal settings. If your system does not have a "sane" idea of initial terminal parameters, you will have to correct or override it. I will describe how to do this in Chapter 13 (p. 300).

Length Limits

I have already mentioned that the number of parenthesized expressions in regular expressions is limited to 9. There are two other limits worth mentioning. While it is highly unlikely that you will run into them, describing them may help your peace of mind.

There is a limit on the length of regular expressions. The precise figure depends on the details of a particular regular expression, but 30,000 characters is a safe bet. The length of glob patterns and the strings against which either glob patterns or regular expressions match are limited only to the amount of available memory.

Comments In expect Commands

It is tempting to add comments after patterns and actions. However, it cannot be done arbitrarily. For example, the following example does not do what was intended.

```
expect {
    "orange" squeeze_proc    # happens every morning
    "banana" peel_proc
}
```

The problem in this code fragment is that the comment occurs in a place where the `expect` command is expecting patterns and actions. The `expect` command does not have any special way of handling comments. In this example, the `expect` command simply assumes that "#" is a pattern and `happens` is the associated action. `every` and `morning` are also interpreted as a pattern and action.

This particular comment is rather lucky. The pattern `banana` is still used as a pattern. However, if the comment had one more word in it, `banana` would be used as an action and `peel_proc` as a pattern!

Remember that comments behave a lot like commands.[†] They can only be used where commands can be used. If you want to associate a comment with an action, then use braces to create a list of commands and embed both the comment and the action within the list. In the following fragment, all of the comments are safe.

```
expect {
    "orange" {
        # comments can appear here safely, too
        squeeze_proc    ;# happens every morning
        # comments can appear here safely, too
    }
    "banana" peel_proc
}
```

Restrictions On expect Arguments

The `expect` command allows its arguments to be surrounded by a pair of braces. This behavior was described in Chapter 3 (p. 76) and is used heavily throughout the book. Bracing the argument list is a convenient feature. Without it, you would have to put backslashes at the ends of many lines to keep long `expect` commands together.

Consider these two forms:

```
expect \
    pat1 act1 \
    pat2 act2 \
    pat3 act3

expect {
    pat1 act1
    pat2 act2
    pat3 act3
}
```

Unfortunately, there is one pitfall with the second form. When the second form is used, there is a question whether the list is a list of patterns or just a single pattern. Although unlikely, it is possible that a pattern could really be "\npat1   act1\npat2

[†] The only significant difference between comments and commands is that arguments of a comment are not evaluated.

`act2\npat3 act3\n`". And while this pattern does not visually look like the multiline `expect` command above, internally the same representation is used for both.

The `expect` command uses a heuristic to decide whether the argument is a pattern or a list of patterns.[†] The heuristic is almost always correct, but can be fooled by very unusual patterns or indentation. For instance, the pattern in the previous paragraph is misinterpreted as a list of patterns. It simply looks too much like a list of patterns. Fortunately, situations like this almost never arise. Nonetheless, you may need to worry about it, particularly if you are machine-generating your Expect scripts.

In order to force a single argument to be treated as a pattern, use the `-gl` flag. (The pattern must be a glob pattern or else it would already have a `-re` or `-ex` flag which necessarily would mean there must already be two arguments.) For example:

```
expect -gl $pattern
```

The opposite problem can also occur. This is, Expect may mistake a list of patterns for a single pattern. The most likely reason for this to happen is if you provide the list all on the same line. Consider the following command:

```
expect {pat1 act1 pat2 act2}
```

The `expect` command will assume you are looking for the pattern "`pat1  act1 pat2 act2`". Here, `expect` is thrown off by the lack of newlines. After all, there is no point in using braces if you are just going to put all the patterns on the same physical line as the `expect` command. Leaving them off would be simpler (and take less space).

A newline after the opening brace is sufficient to clue `expect` in to the fact that the argument is intended as a list of patterns and actions. Alternatively, you can force a single argument to be treated as a list of patterns by using the `-brace` flag before the list. This allows you to have an `expect` command with multiple patterns—all of which fits on a single line.

```
expect -brace $arglist
```

In the next section, I will demonstrate another use for the `-brace` flag.

eval — Good, Bad, And Ugly

It is occasionally useful to dynamically generate `expect` commands. By that I mean that the commands themselves are not prewritten in a script but rather are generated while the script is running.

---

† Both the `expect` and `interact` commands use this same heuristic.

As an example, suppose you want to wait for a particular pattern ("pat1") and optionally look for another pattern ("pat2") depending on whether a variable ("v2") is 1 or 0.
An obvious rendering of this logic is as follows:

```
if {$v2} {
    expect pat1 act1 pat2 act2
} else {
    expect pat1 act1
}
```

This works. However, lengthy lists of patterns and actions can make this code difficult
to maintain. If you want to make a change to an **expect** command, you will have to
make it twice. The odds of a programming error are going to go up.

Even worse, this solution does not extend well if you add another pattern that is dependent on another variable. You will need to have four **expect** commands to cover all
the possibilities. Additional variables quickly cause this technique to become totally
unmanageable.

It is tempting to store the patterns and actions into variables which are later appended
to the remaining patterns; however, this must be done with care. Examine this *incorrect*
attempt:

```
if {$v2} {
    set v2pats "pat2 act2"
} else {
    set v2pats ""
}
if {$v3} {
    set v3pats "pat3 act3"
} else {
    set v3pats ""
}

expect pat1 act1 $v2pats $v3pats   ;# WRONG
```

In the **expect** command, the patterns in **v2pats** and **v3pats** are listed as separate
arguments. **expect** interprets **$v2pats** as a pattern and **$v3pats** as the associated
action. Obviously this is not what is intended.

A better and very efficient solution is to iteratively build up a list of the patterns and
actions, adding to it as appropriate. When ready, the list is passed to **expect**.

```
set patlist ""
if {$v2} {lappend patlist "pat2" act2}
if {$v3} {lappend patlist "pat3" act3}
expect -brace "pat1 act1 $patlist"
```

Each additional variable and pattern adds only one line. At the end is a single `expect` command. Notice the `-brace` argument which forces `expect` to interpret the argument as a list instead of a single pattern. This is one of the few situations where it is absolutely necessary to give `expect` a hint about its argument actually being a *set* of patterns.

One remaining drawback is that patterns and actions on the last line cannot use double quotes in the usual way (to surround the patterns) since the entire list is already double quoted. If `pat1` is a variable reference that expands to a string with embedded whitespace, `expect` sees this as two separate arguments. Using braces instead of either set of quotes (inner or outer) does not help because then the variable substitutions cannot occur.

The only way out of this dilemma is to use `eval`. The `eval` command appends all of its arguments together and then evaluates the resulting string as a new command. Here is the idea:

```
eval expect "$pat1" act1 $patlist    ;# almost right!
```

The `eval` command dynamically generates a new `expect` command with the remaining arguments. The `-brace` flag is no longer necessary since the arguments are now passed separately.

The `eval` command breaks apart any arguments that are also lists. This is just what you need to handle `patlist`, but it is not right for `$pat1` and `act1`. They must be protected if they include whitespace. The most general solution is to put `$pat1` and `act1` inside of a `list` command. This also protects patterns with special symbols like braces. Consider either of these:

```
eval expect [list "$pat1"] [list act1] $patlist
eval expect [list "$pat1" act1] $patlist
```

If `act1` is just a list of commands already in braces, a second set of braces suffices.

```
eval expect [list "$pat1"] {{
    cmd1
    cmd2
}} $patlist
```

This may look peculiar, but then most `eval` commands do. Fortunately, this kind of situation rarely arises, but if it does you have a general solution for it.

Exercises

1. Experiment with `telnet` by writing a script to try all of the different port numbers. Record what comes back.

2. In the `aftp` script on page 144, I hardcoded my own name and address. Modify the script so that it uses the name and address of whomever runs it.

3. Write the `putfile` and `putdirectory` procedures that are used by the excerpt from `rftp` on page 133.

4. Write a procedure to count the number of lines in a string. Do it without looping. Modify the procedure so that it counts the number of digits in a string. Where might this be useful?

5. Enhance the `maxtime` script from Chapter 4 (p. 98) so that it can exit after there is no output for the given amount of time. Provide a command-line option to select this behavior.

In This Chapter:

- *Figuring Out Why Patterns Do Not Match*
- *Suppressing Output From Processes*
- *Capturing Output From Processes*

7

Debugging Patterns And Controlling Output

In this chapter, I will discuss the generation and suppression of certain types of output, including normal and diagnostic output. Diagnostic output includes information helpful for debugging pattern matching problems. I will discuss debugging of script control flow and scripts as a whole in Chapter 18 (p. 403).

Pattern Debugging

In the last couple of chapters, I described how to write patterns. Clearly there are some tricky issues of which you have to be aware. Writing effective patterns is a challenging art for several reasons.

First, you have to know the rules for constructing patterns. Second, you have to understand the rules for expressing them in Tcl. Third, you have to know what characters are in the string you expect. Misunderstanding any one of these steps can cause you to write patterns that do not match.

When patterns do not match as intended, a common symptom is that the script executes very slowly. For example, the following is a fragment of a script to log in. It ought to execute quickly.

```
expect "Login: "
send "don\r"
expect "Password: "
send "swordfish\r"
```

However, on a typical system this fragment takes 20 seconds to execute instead of one or two seconds. There are two problems. The first is with the patterns. The first pattern says to expect "Login: " but on a typical UNIX system the prompt is "login: ".

Instead of matching, the script waits for more input for another 10 seconds (because that is the default timeout). After 10 seconds, expect times out. Since there is no timeout action, the user is not informed that the pattern failed to match. The expect simply returns and control passes to the next command in the script.

This kind of mistake is not uncommon. Part of the reason is that on a UNIX system, the default login prompt starts with a lowercase letter while the password prompt starts with an uppercase letter. This kind of inconsistency, rampant in many interactive interfaces, is ignored by most users and naturally shows up in scripts like these.

The second problem is due to another user-interface inconsistency. There is a space character at the end of the "Password: " pattern. But the actual prompt received is "Password:", which does not have a space at the end! This type of incorrect pattern is an easy mistake to make because most prompts include a trailing space—but not the one for the password. Repeating the earlier logic, the script waits for another 10 seconds.

Scripts with these kinds of errors may work, but with snail-like speed. One way to find out the problem is to ask Expect what it is doing internally.

The command "exp_internal 1" causes Expect to print diagnostics describing some of its internal operations. Among other things, this includes the comparisons that occur within the expect command. Here is the script using "exp_internal 1" along with a telnet command.

```
spawn telnet uunet.uu.net
exp_internal 1
expect "Login: "
send "don\r"
expect "Password: "
send "swordfish\r"
```

When run through the first expect-send sequence, the output starts out like this:

```
spawn telnet uunet.uu.net
expect: does "" (spawn_id 5) match glob pattern "Login: "? no
Trying
expect: does "Trying " (spawn_id 5) match glob pattern "Login: "?
    no
192.48.
expect: does "Trying 192.48." (spawn_id 5) match glob pattern
    "Login: "? no
96.2 ..
expect: does "Trying 192.48.96.2 .." (spawn_id 5) match glob
    pattern "Login: "? no
```

What you see is the normal output from Expect plus the diagnostic output describing exactly what is in the input buffer and what the current patterns are. Each line that begins with "expect: does" prefaces a comparison. The current input buffer follows, surrounded by double quotes, and then the pattern that is being used, also in double quotes. For instance, expect initially starts out with nothing in the input buffer and so you see:

```
expect: does "" (spawn_id 5) match glob pattern "Login: "? no
```

Then the string "Trying   " arrives. This is part of the string that telnet normally prints when it opens a connection. Expect adds this to the input buffer and retries the pattern:

```
expect: does "Trying " (spawn_id 5) match glob pattern "Login: "?
    no
```

After each test, expect prints the word "no" if the match was unsuccessful or "yes" if it was successful. The (spawn_id 5) is an indication of which spawned process was participating in this match. I will describe the particular meaning of this further in Chapter 10 (p. 233). For now, I assume there can only be one process, and I will omit the process identifier in the rest of this example.

Skipping ahead, you can eventually find Uunet's greeting message:

```
UUNET Communications Services (uunet)
expect: does "Trying 192.48.96.2 ...\r\nConnected to
    uunet.uu.net.\r\nEscape character is `^]'.\r\n\r\nUUNET
    Communications Services (uunet)\r\n\r\n\r\n\r" match glob pattern
    "Login: "? no
```

Notice how the input buffer has been converted to a kind of backslash-like representation. That is, carriage-returns are displayed as "\r" and linefeeds as "\n". This is very helpful if you need to match these explicitly.

Immediately after this, Uunet sends its login prompt—for which the script has been waiting.

```
login:
expect: does "Trying 192.48.96.2 ...\r\nConnected to
    uunet.uu.net.\r\nEscape character is '^]'.\r\n\r\nUUNET
    Communications Services (uunet)\r\n\r\n\r\n\r\nlogin: " match glob
    pattern "Login: "? no
```

Now you can see the login prompt, and it becomes obvious that the pattern will never match. Sure enough, expect sits for the remaining time and then finally reports that it timed out.

```
expect: timed out
send: sent "don\r"
```

The send command similarly produces messages describing what it has done. In this case, it has sent the string don\r back to the process.

Now that the script has sent the username, it immediately goes on to the next step—waiting to be prompted for the password:

```
expect: does "Trying 192.48.96.2 ...\r\nConnected to
    uunet.uu.net.\r\nEscape character is '^]'.\r\n\r\nUUNET
    Communications Services (uunet)\r\n\r\r\n\rlogin: " match glob
    pattern "Password: "? no
don

expect: does "Trying 192.48.96.2 ...\r\nConnected to
    uunet.uu.net.\r\nEscape character is '^]'.\r\n\r\nUUNET
    Communications Services (uunet)\r\n\r\r\n\rlogin: don\r\n"
    match glob pattern "Password: "? no
```

At this point, the password has not appeared. What has appeared, however, is the username that the script sent earlier. You see the username come back simply because the remote side is echoing it. This is normal and is the reason why you see most of your own keystrokes when you type them. By comparison, the password will not be echoed.

```
Password:
expect: does "Trying 192.48.96.2 ...\r\nConnected to
    uunet.uu.net.\r\nEscape character is '^]'.\r\n\r\nUUNET
    Communications Services (uunet)\r\n\r\r\n\rlogin:
    don\r\nPassword:" match glob pattern "Password: "? no
expect: timed out
send: sent "swordfish\r"
```

You can now see very clearly that the input buffer contains "Password:"—*without* a space—but the pattern is looking for "Password: "—*with* a space. The pattern fails to match of course. And if you look closely, you can even see that the login prompt is still in the input buffer. That is because it was never matched and so never got removed from the buffer either.

The current expect command eventually times out, and the script continues with the next line. If the rest of the script works, the errors at the beginning do not add up to much; however, they really should be fixed. At the very least, they unnecessarily slow down the script. At the very worst, the script could send things at times when it does not make sense, ending up with unpredictable behavior and an unreliable script. Remember this as you write scripts. If your script pauses for a significant amount of time, even though the prompt it is looking for has already come, there is almost certainly something going wrong that you should investigate.

Here is another version of the script. It is worth studying because it works quite differently than a straightline script where one expect command follows another rigidly. In this script, there is a `while` loop enclosing a single `expect` command in which all the patterns are listed together. The sole advantage to doing so here is that you need only write one `timeout` action rather than a `timeout` in every `expect` command. In some situations, this kind of processing is very useful toward simplifying the overall control while adding flexibility. But in Chapter 11 (p. 259) I will show better ways of economizing on the number of times you have to write `timeout`.

More importantly, the patterns are correct this time. The diagnostic output will show the two patterns being matched against the same input each time, and ultimately one pattern will always be matched. I have also added the `-indices` flag (see Chapter 5 (p. 124)) so that you can see its effect.

```
spawn telnet ftp.uu.net
exp_internal 1
set timeout 30
while 1 {
    expect {
        -indices "login: " {
            send "don\r"
        } -indices "Password:" {
            send "swordfish\r"
        } timeout {
            puts "warning: timed out"
        }
    }
}
```

The script starts the same way as before: by spawning a `telnet` process.

```
spawn telnet ftp.uu.net
expect: does "" match glob pattern "login: "? no
"Password:"? no
```

`expect` starts out by attempting to match both patterns against an empty buffer since nothing is received immediately. Here, they both fail. The string "`trying `" arrives and then some more input dribbles in. In each case, the patterns fail to match.

```
Trying
expect: does "Trying " match glob pattern "login: "? no
"Password:"? no
192.48.96.9 ...
expect: does "Trying 192.48.96.9 ...\r\n" match glob pattern
    "login: "? no
"Password:"? no
Connect
expect: does "Trying 192.48.96.9 ...\r\nConnect" match glob pattern
    "login: "? no
"Password:"? no
ed to f
```

```
expect: does "Trying 192.48.96.9 ...\r\nConnected to f" match glob
    pattern "login: "? no
"Password:"? no
tp.uu.net.
Escape character is '^]'.
expect: does "Trying 192.48.96.9 ...\r\nConnected to
    ftp.uu.net.\r\nEscape character is '^]'.\r\n" match glob
    pattern "login: "? no
"Password:"? no
```

Finally you can see Uunet's greeting message. The script is still looking for "`login:  `" (and "`Password:`" for that matter).

```
SunOS UNIX (ftp)
expect: does "Trying 192.48.96.9 ...\r\nConnected to
    ftp.uu.net.\r\nEscape character is '^]'.\r\n\r\n\r\nSunOS UNIX
    (ftp)\r\n\r\n\r\n\r" match glob pattern "login: "? no
"Password:"? no
login:
expect: does "Trying 192.48.96.9 ...\r\nConnected to
    ftp.uu.net.\r\nEscape character is '^]'.\r\n\r\n\r\nSunOS UNIX
    (ftp)\r\n\r\n\r\nrlogin: " match glob pattern "login: "? yes
```

Here is the first successful match. Expect prints out `yes` after the pattern that has been matched and then prints the internal assignments that are made before any actions are executed.

```
expect: set expect_out(0,start) "103"
expect: set expect_out(0,end) "109"
expect: set expect_out(0,string) "login: "
expect: set expect_out(buffer) "Trying 192.48.96.9 ...\r\nConnected
    to ftp.uu.net.\r\nEscape character is '^]'.\r\n\r\n\r\nSunOS
    UNIX (ftp)\r\n\r\n\r\nrlogin: "
```

Now the corresponding action is executed, sending the string `don\r` to the process.

```
send: sent "don\r"
expect: does "" match glob pattern "login: "? no
"Password:"? no
don
expect: does "don\r\n" match glob pattern "login: "? no
"Password:"? no
Password:
expect: does "don\r\nPassword:" match glob pattern "login: "? no
"Password:"? yes
expect: set expect_out(0,start) "7"
expect: set expect_out(0,end) "15"
expect: set expect_out(0,string) "Password:"
```

```
expect: set expect_out(buffer) "don\r\nPassword:"
send: sent "swordfish\r"
```

Uunet responds with a prompt for the password. This is immediately matched by the script and the password itself is sent back.

You may have noticed that the script does not do anything differently after sending the password. It is rather dumb—it just continues looking for "`login: `" or "`Password:`" whether it logs in successfully or not. Nonetheless, it suffices to show the kind of diagnostics you can get from the `exp_internal` command.

In Chapter 6 (p. 154), I described the –notransfer flag. Together, the –notransfer flag and the internal diagnostics should be very helpful for debugging most of the pattern matching problems you encounter.

Enabling Internal Diagnostics

In long scripts, it is convenient to be able to turn Expect's internal diagnostics off. You can do this with the command "`exp_internal 0`". You can use the `exp_internal` command to turn the diagnostics off and on as you like. For example, it is common to surround just a small group of commands or even one command with `exp_internal` commands as you narrow down where the problem lies in a script.

```
exp_internal 1
expect
exp_internal 0
```

You may also find it convenient to conditionalize the use of `exp_internal`. For example, you can set a global variable that controls whether all of the `exp_internal` commands are actually executed. The following code permits "`exp_internal 1`" commands in the code to execute only when the variable debug_enable is nonzero. The idea is that this variable is set once—which is much easier than adding or commenting in and out commands scattered throughout a script. (In Chapter 9 (p. 223), I will describe how to get this effect on a script-wide basis without changing the script at all.)

```
if $debug_enable {exp_internal 1}
expect . . .
exp_internal 0
send . . .
expect . . .
if $debug_enable {exp_internal 1}
send . . ..
expect . . .
exp_internal 0
```

The "exp_internal 0" commands do not have to be conditionalized. It is not an error to execute "exp_internal 0" even if diagnostics have not been enabled. In this case, "exp_internal 0" is just ignored.

An even more convenient way to control diagnostic output is to define procedures such as the following one:

```
proc debug_on {} {
    global debug_enable
    if {$debug_enable} {exp_internal 1}
}
```

Now the code would look slightly simpler. Here is just the beginning of the code above rewritten to use debug_on and a similar procedure debug_off.

```
debug_on
expect
debug_off
send . . .
expect . . .
debug_on
```

The advantage to this, besides being simpler to write, is that the variable debug_enable will also be accessible because of the global command in the procedure debug_on. With the earlier technique, global commands have to be added to every procedure containing the "if $debug_enable" test.

Enabling Expect's internal diagnostics can cause a tremendous amount of output to be produced since many of the internal actions and decisions that Expect makes are printed out. The process of producing diagnostic output does not change any of the external behavior of Expect except for what is shown at the terminal. Since Expect continues to display the output of whatever process it controls as well as the diagnostic output, the total effect can be very disorienting, sometimes making it difficult to figure out what is normal process output and what is diagnostic output. It is possible, however, to separate the two output streams so that they are readable.

It is important to understand that normal terminal output consists of two "streams of output". One is called *the standard output* and the other is called *the standard error.* Most program output gets written to the standard output but error messages get written to the standard error. The usual shell output redirection ("program > output-file") redirects only the standard output. This allows programs to print error messages to the user and not have them go down the pipe where they will not be seen. Try invoking grep, for example, on a non-existent file while redirecting the output. You will still see the error message.

Expect works the same way. Most output is sent to the standard output while the diagnostic output is sent to the standard error. These can be separated by shell redirection when the Expect program or script is started. For example, you might want to send the diagnostics to the file "`diag`". In the Bourne or Korn shell, you do this by starting your Expect script like this:

```
$ scriptname args 2> diag
```

Most people consider the C-shell syntax so peculiar that they find it easier to explicitly run one of the other shells in such situations and type the previous command. If you do need to stay in the C-shell for some reason, use the following command:

```
% (scriptname args > /dev/tty) >& diag
```

Once you have redirected the output, you can watch it from another window, in this case by executing the command "`tail -f diag`" which prints out any new diagnostics as they are written to the file. The command "`tail -f diag | more`" lets you read the diagnostics before they roll off the screen. If there are not that many diagnostics or if you do not need to save them in a file, you might consider writing them directly to another window. Get the name of the window where you want the output to appear by executing the `tty` command in that window. The response will be the name of a terminal device such as "`/dev/ttyp1`". Now start the script in the other window as:

```
$ scriptname args 2> /dev/ttyp1
```

Redirecting the standard error can introduce one tiny problem into your interaction with Expect. Namely, any real errors that occur in your script or session are also sent to wherever you have redirected the standard error. You cannot see them in the window from which you started Expect even if you normally see them there. Fortunately, this problem only arises when doing script development since production scripts should not produce any errors. Just remember to watch wherever you have the standard error redirected.

Logging Internal Diagnostics

It is possible to achieve all sorts of effects by playing games with redirection. One of the more useful things is to log both the standard output and standard error to a file. Expect provides this same capability in a more flexible way than can be achieved with redirection. This is done using the `exp_internal` command with the `-f` argument. An output file name must follow the `-f` along with a 0 or 1. The 0 or 1 disables or enables the generation of diagnostics just as before. However, the standard output and standard error is still logged to the file even if a 0 is supplied to `exp_internal`.

To summarize:

`exp_internal 0`	no diagnostics
`exp_internal 1`	send pattern diagnostics to standard error
`exp_internal -f` *file* `0`	copy standard output and pattern diagnostics to *file*
`exp_internal -f` *file* `1`	copy standard output and pattern diagnostics to *file* and send pattern diagnostics to standard error

The form "`exp_internal -f` *file* `0`" is particularly useful because Expect appears to act just as if no diagnostics were being generated, even though it is actually writing the usual output and diagnostics to a file at the same time. You can put this particular command in production scripts and users will not be affected by the command. If a user then reports a bug, you can check the file and see exactly what went wrong.

As before, `exp_internal` commands can be placed around pieces of code to limit the amount of diagnostics they produce. Each `exp_internal` command closes any previous file that was named by an `exp_internal` command. So you can log different parts of a script to different files. When the script ends, any open `exp_internal` file is closed.

Disabling Normal Program Output

In the previous section, I showed how to generate, control, and suppress diagnostics produced by Expect. *All* output produced by spawned programs, however, appears on Expect's standard output. It is possible to redirect or suppress this as well, but it is done in a different way.

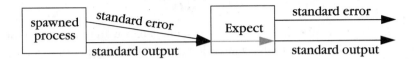

Inside of Expect, the standard output and standard error of a spawned process are joined together and ultimately appear as the standard output of Expect.

The standard error and standard output of a spawned process are joined together inside of Expect. This is done before pattern matching occurs so that patterns must account for both streams appearing simultaneously. The reason this is done is partly philosophical and partly practical.

Philosophically speaking, interactive programs always have the outputs merged together anyway—on the screen. It is impossible for users to visually distinguish between characters appearing on the standard output versus the standard error. Their minds make up for it by scanning the output, both for normal output and errors at the same time. If humans can do it, then so can scripts. This is the philosophy that Expect takes.

Practically speaking, few interactive programs send things to the standard error. What is the point? A user is watching the standard output anyway. The user sees the error whether it appears on one stream or the other. (When was the last time you ran ftp, for example, with either output stream redirected?) Ironically, Expect could be cited as a counterexample to this. It goes out of its way to send its errors to the standard error. However, it does this specifically to assist in the case when it is run non-interactively. In such a situation, the standard output could very understandably be redirected. But used interactively, the separation of standard error and standard input is not particularly useful.

I showed earlier how the standard error of Expect can be redirected. Similarly, so can the standard input. This is done using the traditional "<" notation. However, this kind of redirection is crude. It can only be done once, when starting Expect, and the redirection can never be changed after that.

The log_user Command

In Expect scripts, it is very useful to hide the underlying dialogue, perhaps substituting new output. Sometimes it is useful just to show parts of the dialogue. You can do this with the log_user command. "log_user 0" stops the output of the spawned process from appearing in the standard output of Expect. "log_user 1" restores it.

The following script verifies email destinations at remote hosts by exercising the vrfy command supported by SMTP, a mail transfer protocol commonly used on the Internet. The script takes an email address as an argument.

```
#!/usr/local/bin/expect --

regexp (.*)@(.*) $argv ignore user host
spawn telnet $host smtp
set timeout -1
expect -re "220.*\r\n"
send "vrfy $user\r"
expect -re "(250|550).*\r\n"
```

The first command in the script extracts the user and host names from the original argument. This is done using the very same regexp command that I used as an example in

Chapter 6 (p. 137). The remainder of the script performs the interaction with the remote host.

The script is named `vrfy`. When I run it, here is what appears:

```
% vrfy jobs@next.com
spawn telnet next.com smtp
Trying 129.18.1.2 ...
Connected to next.com.
Escape character is '^]'.
220 NeXT.COM Sendmail NX5.67d/NeXT0.5-Aleph-amm ($Revision: 1.4 $
    $State: Exp $) ready at Thu, 1 Apr 93 21:32:19 -0800
vrfy jobs
250 <jobs>
```

By adding "`log_user  0`" to the script and giving the final **expect** command an explicit action, the output is simplified dramatically. Here is the new version using `log_user`.

```
#!/usr/local/bin/expect --

log_user 0
regexp (.*)@(.*) $argv ignore user host
spawn telnet $host smtp
set timeout -1
expect -re "220.*\r\n"
send "vrfy $user\r"
expect "250" {puts "GOOD"} \
        "550" {puts "BAD"}
```

Here is what it looks like when I run it with a few test cases.

```
% vrfy jobs@next.com
GOOD
% vrfy jobs@apple.com
BAD
```

This new version is just as functional, and the output is much easier to read.

Output generated by the `puts` command still appears in Expect's standard output. The effect of "`log_user  0`" only disables output from the underlying spawned process.

`send` commands are not directly affected by `log_user`. The characters still go to the spawned process. However, the same characters normally show up eventually in the output of a spawned process because of echoing. While the echoing is still done by the spawned process, "`log_user  0`", as before, prevents the characters from being sent on to Expect's standard output. So it may seem that `log_user` has an effect on `send`, but this is true only indirectly.

As an example, suppose a connection to a remote host has been spawned and you want to get the remote date, but without seeing the date command itself echoed. A common error is to write:

```
log_user 0                      ;# WRONG
send "date\r"                   ;# WRONG
log_user 1                      ;# WRONG
expect -re .*\n                 ;# WRONG
```

When run, the log_user command has no effect because Expect does not read the echoed "date" until the expect command. The correct way to solve this problem is as follows:

```
send "date\r"
log_user 0
expect -re "\n(\[^\r]*)\r"     ;# match "date" cmd
                                ;# and actual date
log_user 1
puts "$expect_out(1,string)"   ;# print actual date only
```

In this rewrite, the expect command skips over the date command string by matching for the \n echoed back. The pattern also matches the next line, which is the actual date. The parentheses select just the information wanted (the date), which can then be printed with an explicit puts command. (If you are sending a lot of commands to a remote shell it may be more convenient to just disable all echoing in the first place. I will demonstrate this in Chapter 12 (p. 273).)

One other thing suppressed by "log_user 0" is the side-effect of spawn. The spawn command normally echoes itself to the standard output. This is disabled with "log_user 0".

Because output describing everything going on underneath can be surpressed, it is possible to write scripts that produce no output at all. Instead, a script can cause side-effects such as writing files or setting a final status value. The vrfy script can be rewritten to set a testable status value by changing the last line from:

```
expect "250" {puts "GOOD"} \
       "550" {puts "BAD"}
```

to:

```
expect "250" {exit 0} \
       "550" {exit 1}
```

Now `vrfy` can be used in a shell script without producing any output. For example, from a Bourne shell script, you can use the script as:

```
if vrfy jobs@apple.com; then
    . . . do something . . .
fi
```

Note that the shell considers an exit value of zero as true. Anything else is considered false. This differs from most languages (e.g., Tcl, C) where anything *but* zero is true.

I can now go back to some earlier scripts and modify them not only to be non-interactive but to suppress all output. Here is a modified version of the `ping` script from Chapter 4 (p. 97) which only waits two seconds to complete the `ping`.

```
#!/usr/local/bin/expect --
log_user 0
spawn ping $host
set timeout 2
expect "alive" {exit 0} timeout {exit 1}
```

Whether or not the `ping` succeeds, the script prints nothing. The final command sets the status value though, so that the script can be used easily from shell scripts.

Remember the `firstline` script from Chapter 6 (p. 136)? It ran an arbitrary program, stopping after matching the first line of output. As written, however, the script had the drawback that if input arrived quickly enough, several lines could appear in the output.

You can fix this script by using `log_user` and handling the output explicitly. Here is a new version that does just that.

```
#!/usr/local/bin/expect --
log_user 0
eval spawn $argv
set timeout -1
expect -re "(\[^\r]*)\r"
puts "$expect_out(1,string)"
```

Example — su2

Suppose you accidentally type a command that requires root access, but are not root at the time. If it is just one command, you can type "su root !!", but more commonly you need to enter several more commands that need root access. su provides no way to pass the old command in to the new root shell and then remain in the new root shell.

The usual solution is to invoke su, type the password, and then retype the command. If you have windows, you can start su and then copy and paste the command from one window to another. Either way, it is a bit of a hassle. The problem is that su provides no mechanism for going back in the history and bringing it to the new environment. If it did, you would not need to retype or copy and paste the old command—su would automatically know it.

Here is a script that addresses this problem. It starts su, gives it the command supplied as the script argument, and then passes control to the user. For simplicity, the password is taken from the command line. (In Chapter 8 (p. 201), I will show how to provide it in a much more secure way.) This version is called su2.

```
#!/usr/local/bin/expect --

set timeout -1
log_user 0
spawn su
expect "Password:"         ;# discard su's password prompt
send "[lindex $argv 0]\r"  ;# send password to su
expect "\r\n"
log_user 1
expect "Sorry" exit "# "
send "[lrange $argv 1 end]\r"
interact                   ;# let user type more cmds to root shell
```

The script temporarily suppresses the output from the su command when the password is prompted for and consumed. Here is how it appears when I use it. First I set up the scenario by typing a command that is rejected:

```
% touch /etc/passwd
touch: cannot touch /etc/passwd: no write permission
```

Now I call the Expect script with the root password and !! to refer to the previous command. This shell echoes it because it contains a history reference.

```
57% su2 xxj24k !!
su2 xxj24k touch /etc/passwd
1# touch /etc/passwd
2#
```

The script then kicks in and starts su. With "log_user 0", the script responds to the password prompt without displaying it, and then feeds the command to the root shell. Finally, the script passes control to the keyboard via the interact command, leaving me in the root shell.

The result is that I have typed no more than necessary. In fact, with a shell function, you can even have your shell provide the history reference for you. But passing an argument such as !! is a good way. This allows fast references to other commands in the history. And, if your shell supports command-line editing, you can back up to the previous command and just insert the "su2" in front of it.

In this example, "log_user 1" came after "log_user 0", but like "exp_internal 1" and "exp_internal 0", either "log_user 1" or "log_user 0" may be repeated without the other. For example, using "log_user 0" twice in a row is legitimate. It is not necessary to keep track of what has happened in the past.

Recording All Expect Output

It is possible to save in a file all the output that Expect produces. This includes not only the output from a spawned process, but anything that Expect itself generates such as diagnostics. Conceptually, this is akin to piping Expect's standard output and standard error through the tee program. However, tee is fairly inflexible in that its piping cannot be modified once Expect has started.

Expect has a programmatic means to start and stop recording (or *logging*). Given a file name argument, the log_file command opens the file and begins recording to it. If a log file is already open, the old file is closed first. Using the -open or -leaveopen flag, the log_file command can also record to a file opened by the open command. The use of these flags is identical to their use in the spawn command which I will describe in detail in Chapter 13 (p. 289).

Recording is done by appending to the file, so if anything has previously been stored in the file, it remains. To start over, use the -noappend flag (or simply remove the file first).

For example, the UNIX script command can be emulated with the following commands:

```
spawn $env(SHELL)
log_file -noappend typescript
interact
```

First a shell is started. Notice how the user's desired shell is determined by getting it from the environment where it is stored in the variable SHELL. This is much more polite than simply starting up, say, /bin/csh. The log_file command then opens the file typescript. The -noappend flag forces the log to start out empty. Finally, interact passes control to the user. Everything the program sends to the user is recorded. As before, user keystrokes are not recorded directly. The keystrokes are only recorded if they are echoed. Thus, if a user types a password, the password is not recorded.

In Chapter 15 (p. 334), I will show a modified version of this script that allows a user to turn recording on and off as desired.

log_file is very useful for debugging Expect scripts. It can be used to transparently record everything the user sees. Then, if a user reports a problem with the script, you can examine the log file to see exactly what the user was doing. If parity is being stripped, characters are saved to the log without parity. Nulls are recorded to the log even if they are being removed for the purposes of pattern matching.

You can save space by turning off logging when it is not necessary. This is accomplished by calling `log_file` with no arguments. For example, the following fragment starts recording, does some I/O, stops recording, does some more I/O, and then starts recording again.

```
expect . . . ; send . . .
# start recording
log_file telnetlog
expect . . . ; send . . .
# stop recording
log_file
expect . . . ; send . . .
# start recording
log_file telnetlog
expect . . . ; send . . .
```

By default, `log_file` records only what the user sees. If the `log_user` command has been invoked to suppress output from a spawned program, the suppressed output is not recorded by `log_file` since the user is not seeing it either. The `log_file` can record the suppressed output by using the -a flag (for "*all* output").

```
log_file -a log
```

As before, this logging can be disabled by issuing `log_file` with no arguments. To return to logging just what the user sees, invoke `log_file` without the -a.

```
log_file -a log
expect . . . ; send . . .
log_file log
```

The `log_file` command should not be viewed as the only way to log sessions. It is useful for many purposes, however it does not provide support for very sophisticated types of logging. Many of these can be achieved not with the `log_file` command but with a little straightforward coding. For example, I will describe how to log multiple process to separate files in Chapter 18 (p. 407) without using the `log_file` command.

Another deficiency of the `log_file` command is that it does not save the output of Tcl commands. Arbitrary Tcl commands provide their own output mechanism. Fortunately, this is not a real problem because there is only one Tcl command that ordinarily sends character to the standard output: `puts`. Expect provides a substitute for `puts`: `send_user`. For example, to send the string "`hello world\n`" to the standard output:

```
send_user "hello world\n"
```

`send_user` is a little different than `puts` in that `send_user` does not append a newline at the end of every string. `send_user` also supports some other behaviors that will be covered in Chapter 8 (p. 185) and Chapter 12 (p. 271). Most importantly though, send_user allows logging of output through log_file. So if your other choices are equal, use send_user instead of puts.

Sending Messages To The Log

The send_log command is similar to the send command; however, send_log writes to the log without writing to the standard output. It also writes to any file opened by exp_internal. The log_user command has no affect on send_log.

```
send_log "Beginning transaction at [exec date]\n"
```

About File Names

Both the exp_internal and log_file commands accept filename arguments that begin with a tilde ("~"). The tilde is interpreted as meaning "home directory" exactly the way it is defined by the C-shell. For example:

```
exp_internal -f ~fred/debuglog 0
```

This command saves diagnostic information to the file debuglog in fred's home directory.

No other interpretation is given to the file name. If you include a wildcard such as a "*", the file will be created with that name, exactly as you have specified. If you want wildcards expanded, use the glob command.

Log And Diagnostic State

The log and diagnostic states can be obtained by calling the original commands with the -info flag. The previous parameters are returned. This is commonly used to establish a temporary state.

For example, a subroutine that must be sure that output to the user is disabled should save and restore the state of log_user.

```
proc sub {} {
    set state [log_user -info]    ;# save old state
    log_user 0                     ;# set new state
    # your code goes here
    eval log_user $state           ;# restore old state
}
```

Notice the final call to restore the old state. It uses `eval` in order to support the possibility of a multi-element state. The list of elements will be split in such a way that the command sees them as separate arguments.

The `log_user` command is not currently defined to take multiple parameters; however, future expansion is likely so it is a good idea to handle it this way. The `log_file` and `exp_internal` commands take multiple arguments already.

Exercises

1. On page 172, I described a convenient but simplistic procedure for enabling diagnostics. Write a procedure that uses keywords to select subsets of information to be printed.

2. Write a procedure called `assert`, patterned after the one in the C language. The procedure should evaluate an expression given as its argument. If the expression is false, it should be printed with an appropriate diagnostic.

3. Modify the `script` implementation on page 180 so that it writes a welcome message (to the log as well) just like the real `script` command.

4. Your system administrators are paranoid. They are willing to give you the root password only if you send them a log of everything you do while using it. Write a non-set-uid script that provides root access and records all of your interactions.

In This Chapter:
- *Interacting With A User And Process In The Same Script*
- *Passwords And Other Security Issues*
- *Sleeping*
- *Setting Terminal Parameters*
- *Executing Programs With And Without Redirection*

8

Handling A Process And A User

In this chapter, I will describe how to use the **send** and **expect** commands to interact with the user and a process in the same script. For scripts that require passwords, a common approach is to interact with the user only to get the password and then to automate the remainder of the program. I will describe how to do this in a secure manner and I will also describe other topics related to passwords and security.

It is desirable to suppress character echoing while prompting for passwords. I will describe how to do this along with a broader discussion of terminal modes and how you can control them to achieve a variety of other effects.

The send_user Command

In Chapter 3 (p. 71), **send** was used to print strings to the the standard output. The first program in that chapter printed out "**hello world**" and was just one command:

```
send "hello world\n"
```

However, once a process has been spawned, the **send** command no longer prints to the standard output but instead sends strings to the spawned process. In the following script, the **send** command sends its argument to the spawned process, **ftp**:

```
spawn ftp ftp.uu.net
expect "Name"
send "anonymous\r"
```

The `expect` command works the same way. Initially, it reads from Expect's standard input but as soon as a process has been spawned, `expect` reads from the process.

If the process dies and a new process is spawned, `send` and `expect` refer to the new process. In Chapter 10 (p. 233), I will describe how to use `send` and `expect` to communicate with two processes simultaneously. Communicating with a process and a user is a special case of this. Because it is so common, it merits special commands in Expect.

The `send_user` command sends strings to the standard output just the way `send` does when Expect starts. Both can initially be used to send strings to the standard output. But after a process is spawned, `send` sends strings to the process while `send_user` continues to send strings to the standard output. The command `send_user` is so named because normally the standard output is immediately sent to the user. Of course, if the standard output is redirected, the `send_user` command sends strings according to that redirection.

A common use of `send_user` is to issue informative messages on the progress of an interaction with a spawned process. This is helpful when `log_user` has been invoked to suppress the normal output of a process. For example, here is the `ftp-rfc` script from Chapter 3 (p. 82). The `log_user` command has been added to suppress output from `ftp`, and a couple of `send_user` commands have been added.

```
#!/usr/local/bin/expect --
# retrieve an RFC (or the index) from uunet via anon ftp

if {[llength $argv] != 1} {
    send "usage: ftp-rfc {-index|#}\n"
    exit
}

set timeout -1
log_user 0

send "spawning ftp\n"
spawn ftp ftp.uu.net
expect "Name"

send_user "logging in as anonymous\n"
send "anonymous\r"
expect "Password:"
send "don@libes.com\r"
expect "ftp> "
send "cd inet/rfc\r"
expect "ftp> "
send "binary\r"
expect "ftp> "
```

```
send_user "retrieving file\n"
send "get rfc$argv.Z\r"
expect "ftp> "

send_user "uncompressing\n"
exec uncompress rfc$argv.Z

send_user "all done\n"
```

When this new script runs, none of the underlying interaction is seen. Instead what appears is:

```
% ftp-rfc -index
spawning ftp
logging in as anonymous
retrieving file
uncompressing
all done
```

The most immediate benefit of doing this is that it is much easier to immediately tell what the state of the process is. But a more likely use is that this script can now be run by someone who would not otherwise be able to handle the complexities of `ftp` or whatever process is being automated.

All sorts of sins can be covered up in this way. For example, a script can log into a remote computer and make it seem like the process is running locally. If you need a few more days to finish porting your software to a machine, you can make it look like it already works when pressed to give a demonstration before the work has been completed. Or suppose that your program has a bug that causes it to crash every so often. An Expect script could hide this pesky little detail by just restarting the program when it crashes but otherwise letting the normal output of the program appear. It is even possible to run programs under the debugger. The script could set breakpoints during buggy maneuvers, fix things up, and then let the program continue to run. In Chapter 15 (p. 323), I will show how the `interact` command makes these subtle translations even easier to write.

The send_error Command

A task related to printing information is that of printing error messages. It is a good idea to print error messages in such a way that they can be easily separated from the normal output of the program. In particular, error messages go to the standard error stream while normal output goes to the standard output stream.

The benefit of sending errors to a separate stream is that, once separated, the two streams can be easily sent to different places. Typically, the standard output is redirected to a file or piped to another process while the standard error remains undirected so that it can be seen at the terminal.[†] For example, the command "cat foo | wc" (to count the words in foo) will print "foo: no such file" if foo does not exist. You see the error message because the standard error is not redirected. If the diagnostic was sent along with the normal output of cat, wc would report that foo had four words only because that is how many are in the error message!

Expect scripts should be written the same way. Normal output that you might wish to redirect or pipe should be sent to the standard output. Error messages should be sent to the standard error. There are two ways of doing this: send_error and "puts stderr". send_error is similar to send_user and send whereas "puts stderr" is similar to puts.

I will show more differences later. To summarize the differences so far between variations on puts and the variations on send:

puts	automatically appends newline unless –newline flag given
send	is recorded by log_file

It is a good idea to add error checking to any script which might conceivably fail. It is almost always easier to fix problems if you have made some attempt at detecting them in the first place. And it is certainly easier for users to report problems if they see error messages that relate to them rather than the underlying application.

The ftp-rfc script can be beefed up with error detection and send_error in a number of places. For instance, the first command verifies that there is at least one argument. This could be rewritten to check that only –index or a number is provided. At the very least, the error message should be sent to the user via send_error.

If a lot of usage checking must be done, it is convenient to have a function to call that prints out the usage string and exits. Notice that usage calls send_error.

```
proc usage {} {
    send_error "usage: ftp-rfc {-index|#}\n"
    exit 1
}
```

Since functions must be defined before being used, a usage function like this should generally be the first thing in the script (besides comments). Having it at the top of the script also makes it convenient in the event that you or someone else lists out the script trying to figure out how to call it.

---

† It is occasionally useful to do the opposite—redirecting *only* the standard error. I showed how to do this in Chapter 7 (p. 173).

Multiple tests can now be made against the arguments—if any fail, usage can be invoked.

```
if {[llength $argv] != 1} usage
if {[string compare $argv "-index"] != 0} {
    if {[regexp "^\[0-9]+$" $argv] != 1} {
        usage
    }
}
```

The first check is the same as before. The argument is next checked against the string "-index". If this fails, the script attempts to interpret the argument as an integer. regexp will return 1 if the argument can be interpreted as a number. If that does not work, then the usage function is called and the script exits.

Using llength (or any of the list functions) can be dangerous here because the argument may not be a list. For example, if the argument has unmatched braces, llength will generate an error. It is better to use the non-list functions when you have no idea of what the input is like. An even better solution in this example is to skip the call to llength entirely—the test is actually redundant here. If the argument is a multiple-element list, then obviously it cannot be a number or the string "-index". The remaining operations can be further compressed into a single regexp. The result is:

```
if {[regexp "^(-index|\[0-9]+)$" $argv] != 1} usage
```

Each **expect** should check for any likely incorrect result as well as the correct result. Deciding what constitutes a "likely incorrect" result is often a difficult problem. This particular script disables the timeout, which removes the possibility of timeouts entirely. This simplifies the script. However, the script can now hang if all possibilities are not accounted for in the **expect** patterns. Deciding whether or not to work this way is a judgement call. There is no choice that is always right or wrong.

Certain parts of the ftp conversation are so likely to work that it is pointless to check them. For example, if ftp does not initially prompt for a user name, chances are that something so peculiar has happened that it is impossible to write a script that would correctly predict in advance how to recover from the situation anyway.[†]

The conversation becomes more interesting once the script begins interacting with the remote host. At this point, the remote host prefixes all textual responses with a three-digit code and follows the final response with the prompt "ftp> ".

The original script assumed that the string "ftp> " was a sign that the previous command had executed successfully. However, interactive programs that prompt

---

† One possible error that could be checked involves the operating system rather than the process. In particular, the operating system may not have sufficient resources (i.e., memory) to even start the process. I will cover this in Chapter 13 (p. 296).

virtually always reprompt whether the previous command was right or wrong. Not only does ftp work this way, but so do shells, debuggers, and even Expect itself.

Unfortunately, ftp has a large number of possible responses, even relying on the three-digit prefixes of each response. Generally, however, a successful response begins with the digit "2". For the purposes of this script, anything else is considered an error.

It is important to make sure that ftp has no more to say before sending new commands. ftp uses a convention that makes this condition easy to detect. A dash following the third digit of the three-digit prefix indicates that more responses follow. A blank space following the third digit indicates that no more responses follow. Responses are also defined so that they are terminated by a \r\n and have no other embedded \r\n within.

Based on all of this, a very reliable way to check for a successful command is:

```
expect {
    -re "\n2.. \[^\r]*\r\nftp> "   {}
    -re "\n... \[^\r]*\r\nftp> "   {
        send_error "failure"
        exit
    }
}
```

The first pattern looks for a line beginning with a "2" followed by two more characters, a space, and then a single line immediately followed by a new line containing only the prompt "ftp> ".

Notice that in the event of a successful response, the action is just an empty set of braces. This is a no-op. What happens is that after the match, the no-op is executed (or rather, nothing is executed), and control passes to the line following the expect.

The no-op cannot be omitted. Reversing the patterns in order to omit the no-op action is a mistake. Consider the following fragment:

```
expect {
    -re "\n... (\[^\r]*)\r\nftp> "   {      ;# WRONG!
        send_error "failed: $cmd\n"
        send_error "reason: $expect_out(1,string)\n"
        exit
    }
    -re "\n2.. \[^\r]*\r\nftp> "
}
```

In this example, the failure pattern would always match whenever the success pattern matches, and since the failure pattern is listed first, the success pattern can never match.

The original test used throughout the script was simply:

```
expect "ftp> "
```

The new command can now replace this. Here is a fragment of the resulting script:

```
send "cd inet/rfc\r"
expect {
    -re "\n2.. \[^\r]*\r\nftp> "   {}
    -re "\n... \[^\r]*\r\nftp> "   {
        send_error "cd failed"
        exit
    }
}
send "binary\r"
expect {
    -re "\n2.. \[^\r]*\r\nftp> "   {}
    -re "\n... \[^\r]*\r\nftp> "   {
        send_error "binary failed"
        exit
    }
}
```

Notice the repetition of the huge **expect** command. One way of avoiding this is to put the whole thing in a procedure:

```
proc sendexpect {cmd} {
    send "$cmd\r"
    expect
        -re "\n2.. \[^\r]*\r\nftp> "   {}
        -re "\n... \[^\r]*\r\nftp> "   {
            send_error "failed: $cmd\n"
            exit
        }
}
```

This section of the resulting script could then be simplified to look like this:

```
sendexpect "cd inet/rfc\r"
sendexpect "binary\r"
sendexpect "get rfc$argv.Z\r"
```

By passing the outgoing command through the procedure, the error messages can also be improved. If an error occurs, say in the **get** command, the script says:

```
failed: get rfc-2001.Z
```

Adding the error message from **ftp** is easy. Just modify the failure pattern to save the text string. It can then be retrieved from **expect_out(1, string)**.

```
-re "\n... (\[^\r]*)\r\nftp> "  {
        send_error "failed: $cmd\n"
        send_error "reason: $expect_out(1,string)\n"
        exit
}
```

If the file was not found, the output would look like this:

```
failed: get rfc-2001.Z
reason: rfc-2001.Z: No such file or directory
```

The expect_user Command

In Chapter 3 (p. 72), you saw how to read from the user (i.e., standard input of the Expect process) using the expect command. expect reads from the standard input until a program is spawned. After that, expect reads from the spawned process.

expect is analogous to send. Both communicate with the user until a process is spawned, after which, both commands communicate with the spawned process. It should be no surprise that a command called expect_user exists analogous to send_user. expect_user continues communicating with the user even after a process has been spawned.[†]

For example, the following fragment might appear in a script which has spawned ftp and is about to transfer a file.

```
expect "ftp> "
send_user "ftp is running.  Press return to transfer file:"
expect_user "\n"
send "get foo\r"
```

The first command waits for ftp's prompt. The user is then prompted to press return, and expect waits for it. As I mentioned in Chapter 3 (p. 72), the terminal driver translates the return to \n while using expect, and the same thing occurs with expect_user. Once expect_user is satisfied, the script sends a get command to ftp.

All of the expect flags and patterns work with expect_user. For example, the following code fragment queries the user for an RFC number. The fragment illustrates the use of regular expressions, timeout, and a break action.

---

† If the standard input has been redirected (by shell redirection when the script was started), expect_user will read from the standard input. It is possible to read directly from (and write directly to) the user nonetheless. I will cover this on page 210.

```
while 1 {
    send_user "Enter an RFC number: "
    expect_user {
        -re "(\[0-9]+)\n" break
        -re (.*)\n {
            send_error "$expect_out(1,string) is garbage!\n"
        }
        timeout {
            send_error "Sorry, I can't wait any longer!\n"
            exit 1
        }
    }
}
send_user "You asked for RFC $expect_out(1,string).\n"
```

When run, the interaction looks like this:

```
Enter an RFC number: aerasdf
aerasdf is garbage!
Enter an RFC number: 34
You asked for RFC 34.
```

And if the user does not respond within the timeout, the script prints a message and exits.

```
Sorry, I can't wait any longer!
```

Dealing With Programs That Reprompt

As a matter of style, it is bad form to reissue a prompt upon a timeout. It is even worse to issue a different prompt. The problem is that the user may have been in the middle of entering a response. Users will wonder if their previous keystrokes have been discarded and should be re-entered or changed. While terminal drivers usually offer a way to find out this information (typically by pressing ^R), an automated program such as an Expect script may not notice that a new prompt has been issued. If a new prompt is asking a different question than the script is answering, serious problems could result.

In the general sense, there is a race condition (unresolvable timing problem) raised by reprompting, and this can result in problems for humans as well as scripts. There are three strategies which I have outlined below. In each case, there is a gamble that can lose, described by the scenario following it. I will explain the steps in each scenario, italicizing the step at which things go awry.

1. The program does not discard its input buffer ever. This causes trouble if:

> The user begins to enter a response.
>
> The program decides the timeout has expired.

The user presses return.

The program prints a new prompt.

The program reads the user's old answer.

The user is left with a new prompt.

The user answers it.

The program reads the old answer at the next prompt (and the user again answers when the program is not listening) or the program flushes the buffer as in scenario 2 or 3.

2. The program discards its input buffer and then prints the new prompt. This causes trouble if:

    The program decides the timeout has expired and flushes the buffer.

    The user presses a key.

    The new prompt is printed.

    The program reads the keystroke entered after the buffer was flushed.

3. The program prints the new prompt and then discards its input buffer. This causes trouble if:

    The program decides the timeout has expired and reprompts.

    The user sees the new prompt and presses some keys.

    The program discards the buffer and the new keystrokes.

    The user does not realize the buffer has been flushed and presses more keystokes and presses return.

    The program reads the end of the user's response but misses the beginning of it.

Fortunately, reprompting is rarely done, in part because it just introduces problems, but also because it adds so much complexity to the program itself in order to flush buffers and interrupt reads. Expect happens to make this functionality very easy. But do not get carried away with enthusiasm. Reprompting is still a bad thing.

While there are no guaranteed ways to work with programs that reprompt, Expect scripts generally do not have a problem with them or can be made to work with them easily. An example program that follows strategy 1 is the UNIX dump program, which copies files to backup media. If dump reaches the end of a tape, dump prompts for a new tape to be mounted. Since tape drives have no way of automatically signalling that a new tape has been mounted, the operator must also press return on the terminal. If there is no response from the operator after several minutes, dump rings the terminal's bell several times and sends out the new prompt. The idea is that the operator's attention is probably on a nearby terminal. Since the terminal is only waiting for a return to be pressed rather than some long answer that might be partially entered, dump does not have to flush the buffer.

Expect scripts to automate dump do not run into any problems because of this. Typically, dump can be "faked out". For instance, if the system can automatically change tapes via a carousel or if the tapes are virtual, nothing physical has to take place. In either case, the Expect script responds to dump so quickly after dump's initial response that the problem is avoided entirely. In a similar way, Expect avoids problems with programs that use strategy 2 in prompting.

Another example program that does reprompting is rn, a popular program for reading Usenet news. The obvious script to drive rn fails. Here is a fragment:

```
expect "read now \\\[ynq] "
send "y"                        ;# WRONG
```

The problem is that rn uses strategy 3. It prompts and then flushes the input buffer. This is actually convenient for real users. People often scan through the prompts to read each newsgroup by simply holding down the n key to go from one to the next. If rn did not flush the buffer, the number of n's could get way ahead of the questions and when you saw a newsgroup you were interested in, rn would not stop until much later.

rn has a "-T" flag which allows it to run without this feature (which it calls *typeahead*), but many programs are not so considerate. A simple solution is to pause briefly. One way to do it is by invoking the UNIX sleep command:

```
exec sleep 1
```

A simpler way to achieve the same result is to just set the timeout to 1 and do an expect. You can put this in a procedure, thereby localizing the timeout so that it does not have to be reset afterwards. By declaring timeout as a formal parameter, an explicit set is unnecessary because timeout is initialized when the procedure is called. The resulting procedure definition is short!

```
proc sleep {timeout} {
    expect
}
```

The rewritten fragment to automate rn looks like this:

```
expect "read now \\\[ynq] "
sleep 1
send "y"
```

Of course, the sleep and send could be packaged up in a single procedure to make this look cleaner.

Dealing With Programs That Miss Input

A problem related to buffer flushing can happen when Expect is used to drive modems or other communications devices. Serial interfaces (i.e., UARTs) can go through states during which time they cannot accept input. For example, characters are ignored when the speed or some other characteristic of the interface is changed. This also occurs when making initial connections (via telnet, tip, kermit, etc.) to a new host, modem, or communications switch.

Consider the following fragment used to dial a Hayes-compatible modem:

```
spawn tip modem
expect "connected"
send "atd1234567\r"
expect "CONNECTED"
```

When run, tip says the modem is connected but yet it does not respond. Mysteriously, when you do the same interaction by hand, it works fine.

The problem is that the modem is not yet listening when you have sent the dial command to it. It may seem like the modem ought to be listening, but in fact all the "connected" message means is that the UART control lines (e.g., DTR) have been raised. The modem then has to initialize itself. If you do not allow time for the initialization, the modem will miss your command.

Unfortunately, Hayes-compatible modems do not prompt, so you cannot use a simple expect command to wait. Inserting a brief pause is a simple enough solution. However, the most reliable solution is to loop, sending AT commands and waiting for an OK in response before sending anything further.

Some systems exhibit even worse problems—due to a limited hardware input buffer, characters can be missed if they arrive too quickly after one another. I will describe how to handle this problem in Chapter 12 (p. 275).

Sleeping

In the previous section, I showed two ways to get Expect to sleep for a while. Either way is a little painful. Using exec to sleep for a second is a tad expensive. Because of the overhead in creating a new process—inherent in exec—the actual time slept can be significantly greater than one second. The second way requires the "borrowing" of a spawned process. Although this works, it is possible to imagine unintended consequences, such as missing an eof when the spawned process unexpectedly closes the connection while the script is sleeping. In Chapter 20 (p. 488), I will show that there is a time and place for this style of sleeping.

Expect provides a command called `sleep` that avoids all of the complications I just mentioned. `sleep` does not require an existing spawned process nor does it create a new process. It is called with a single argument describing how many seconds for which to sleep. For example, the following command sleeps two seconds:

```
sleep 2
```

Fractional seconds are also permitted. The following command sleeps for two and a half seconds.

```
sleep 2.5
```

Any nonnegative floating-point argument is acceptable. As with the UNIX `sleep` command, the time slept may be slightly longer than requested.

Line Versus Character-Oriented And Other Terminal Modes

In all of the examples of `expect_user` so far, the script does not actually get to see any user input until a return is pressed. This is a natural result of the terminal interface being line-oriented. By default, the terminal driver buffers all the keystrokes until a return is pressed. Only when the return is pressed are the characters delivered to the script. While characters are being buffered, the terminal driver performs some minimal processing of the keystrokes such as echoing them, and erasing them if you press backspace or delete. By doing this processing in the terminal driver, many programs are drastically simplified while still providing a minimally intelligent user-interface.

If the following fragment is used to get input, the user can fix corrections by erasing characters and retyping up until a return is pressed. The value of `expect_out` will not have any of the editing characters that were entered to fix typos.

```
send "Enter your name: "
expect_user "\n"
```

All the examples so far have ended patterns from the standard input with a "\n". In line-oriented mode, however, there is nothing else with which lines can end, so it is really just a formality. If the pattern has no "\n", `expect_user` will still wait for the return to be pressed before attempting any matches.

It is possible to put the terminal into a mode in which it is character-oriented. In this case, `expect_user` does not wait until a return has been pressed. `expect_user` attempts to match the input against the patterns immediately. In fact, since humans are so slow (relatively speaking), the pattern matcher will likely run after every keystroke.

The terminal modes are changed with the `stty` command. Expect's `stty` command takes arguments similarly to the way that the UNIX `stty` command does. For example:

```
stty raw
```

This command puts the terminal into *raw mode*, meaning that keystrokes are not inter-preted in any way by the terminal driver but are immediately passed on to the `expect_user` command. Raw mode is a specific type of character-oriented mode, but is almost always what is desired. The opposite of raw mode is *cooked mode*. It repre-sents the most common form of line-oriented modes.

Once the terminal is in raw mode, patterns without the \n can match without the user pressing return:

```
send "Continue?  Enter y or n: "
expect -re "y|n"
```

The return character itself is also handled differently. In line-oriented mode, the return is translated to a \n (often called "newline"). In raw mode, no such translation is performed. Thus, if you want to match when the user presses return, the \r must be used:

```
send "Enter your name: "
expect -re ".*\r"
```

All other control characters such as backspace, delete, control-C, etc. are also stored in `expect_out` rather than performing their normal function. For this reason, raw mode is not generally used when prompting users for names, files, passwords, etc. Users want the ability to edit these as they type. Raw mode is better for entering short confirmations or commands, such as one- or two-letter sequences inside a menu system or in a screen-oriented editor.

The terminal driver also performs output processing as well as input processing. While in cooked mode, the terminal driver translates \n to carriage-return linefeed sequences. The `send_user` command performs this same translation when in raw mode. To skip this translation, the `-raw` flag should be given to `send_user`.

```
send_user "A new\nline character\n"
stty raw
send_user -raw "A new\nline character\r\n"
send_user "A new\nline character\r\n"
```

When this script is run, it produces the following output:

```
A new
line character
A new
      line character
A new
line character
```

Notice that the second `send_user` was completely untranslated. The first `send_user` was translated by the terminal driver, while the third was translated by `send_user`.

The following command returns the terminal to line-oriented mode:

```
stty -raw
```

Bearing in mind the earlier discussion of the possibility of losing characters while switching modes, `stty` should be executed during times when the user is not typing, such as before a prompt rather than after.

```
stty raw           ;# Right time to invoke stty
send "Continue?  Enter y or n: "
stty raw           ;# Wrong time to invoke stty
```

Echoing

Another mode that is frequently changed is echoing. By default, the terminal driver echoes printable characters typed at the keyboard. If a script needs to query for, say, a password, the echoing should be disabled. The following two commands disable and re-enable echoing.

```
stty -echo         ;# disable echo
stty echo          ;# enable echo
```

Here is an archetypal procedure to query the user for a password:

```
proc getpass {} {
    set timeout -1
    stty -echo
    send_user "password: "
    expect_user -re "(.*)\n"
    send_user "\n"
    stty echo
    return $expect_out(1,string)
}
```

When called, `getpass` returns the password as its return value. Inside, you can see two `stty` commands surround the `expect_user` that waits for the password. Notice how the first `stty` is done before the prompt. This guarantees that user input cannot possibly be echoed no matter how fast it starts arriving after the prompt. (In Chapter Chapter 17 (p. 399), I will describe the opposite situation—when you are stuck automating a process that works this way.)

After `expect_user` returns, the cursor remains at the end of the prompt. Even though the user pressed return, nothing happens because echoing is disabled. It is important to give the user feedback that the line was accepted. Hence a \n is printed. This simulates the effect of echoing being disabled just for the bare password. This is not a problem specific to Expect. Any password reading routine has to do the same thing.

In Chapter 7 (p. 179), I presented a script called `su2` which spawned an `su` process to reexecute a command and then leave the user in a root shell. As I originally defined it, the password was entered as a parameter on the command line. That approach presents a security problem. The command line is viewable by someone reading over the user's shoulder. But even worse, the command line is accessible via commands such as `ps` to anyone logged in on the same system.

To avoid exposure, programs that require passwords must prompt for them interactively. Examples include `su`, `passwd`, `crypt`, and `rlogin`. Responding to this interactive prompting cannot be automated by the shell but can by Expect.

Here is the `su2` script modified to prompt the user for the password.

```
#!/usr/local/bin/expect --

stty -echo
send_user "password: "
expect_user {
    timeout {
        send_user "\nSorry\n"
        exit
    } -re "(.*)\n" {
        set password $expect_out(1,string)
    }
}

send_user "\n"
stty echo

set timeout -1
log_user 0
spawn su
expect "Password:"          ;# discard su's password prompt
send "$password\r"          ;# send password to su
expect "\r\n"
log_user 1
expect "Sorry" exit "# "
```

```
send "$argv\r"
interact                ;# let user type more cmds to root shell
```

The script starts off by querying the user for the root password. A `timeout` pattern has been added. Using the default timeout, the script prints `Sorry` and exits if nothing has been entered after 10 seconds.

The remainder of the script is almost exactly the same. The password is now retrieved from `expect_out` instead of `argv`, and there is no longer a need for the `lrange` command to extract the argument from `argv` since there is no password in the list.

Prompting For A Password On Behalf Of A Program

Reading passwords is the most frequent reason to use "`stty -echo`", and it comes up in many places and in many ways. Here is an excerpt from a script that logs in to another host. If the second host demands a password, the script turns around and asks the user. The script does not print the original prompt but instead manufactures a new prompt including the username and host so that the user understands exactly which password is expected, even though the user has seen no other dialogue (and may not even know what the script is doing).

```
expect {
    assword: {
        stty -echo
        send_user "password (for [exec whoami]) on $host:"
        set old_timeout $timeout; set timeout -1
        expect_user -re "(.*)\n"
        send_user "\n"
        set timeout $old_timeout
        send "$expect_out(1,string)\r"
        exp_continue
    } "incorrect" {
        send_user "invalid password or account\n"
        exit
    } timeout {
        send_user "connection to $host timed out\n"
        exit
    } eof {
        send_user "connection to host failed: "
        send_user "$expect_out(buffer)"
        exit
    } -re $prompt
}
```

The first `expect` looks for a password prompt, a shell prompt, and various failure conditions all at the same time. If no password is required, the final pattern matches and the script goes on to the next command. If the remote computer does prompt for a password, the user is requested to supply the password. The current timeout is saved in `old_timeout` and restored later. This is analogous to setting it as a local variable in a procedure.

Once the user has supplied the password, the script sends it on to the remote host, and `exp_continue` causes the `expect` command to go back and look for more output—hopefully the shell prompt.

The various failure conditions are all reported back to the user. If an eof is detected, any remaining output from the remote host is printed. The final output presumably contains the reason that the remote host closed the connection. There is no need to terminate it with a newline, since it invariably has one already, being originally formatted for human viewing.

Security And Insecurity

Quite often, it is possible to automate everything except reading the password. As I explained earlier, the password should not be passed as an argument to a script for security reasons. An alternative to prompting is to embed the password directly in the script. There are two ways to secure such files—by file protection or by host protection. I prefer host protection but I will cover file protection first—if only to make the merits of host protection more obvious.

Securing Scripts By File Protection

Scripts containing passwords should be unreadable to users with normal utilities such as `cat` and `vi`. However, such scripts must still be executable. Unfortunately, the UNIX file system has no direct way of creating scripts which are executable but unreadable. On systems which support setgid shell scripts, you may indirectly simulate this as follows:

Create the Expect script (that contains the password) as usual. Make its permissions be 750 (`-rwxr-x---`) and owned by a trusted group, i.e., a group which is allowed to read it. If necessary, create a new group for this purpose. Next, create a `/bin/sh` script with permissions 2751 (`-rwxr-s--x`) owned by the same group as before. The shell script should invoke both Expect and the script name by their absolute pathnames.

The resulting shell script can be run by anyone, and the shell script in turn has permission to run the Expect script which is otherwise unreadable to everyone.

This may seem a little kludgey. In fact, it is worse than that. Storing unencrypted passwords in files is almost always a disaster, and there are usually better ways of getting the same effect. Consider that when the password is stored in your head, it is much easier to update. But once a password is stored in a script, each script containing the password has to be found and changed. Even worse, the scripts are more susceptible (than your brain) to yielding their contents. Consider what might happen if you run out of your office for a bathroom emergency. Someone could walk in, sit down at your workstation, and immediately have complete access to your files including the ones containing passwords. If a hacker steals a backup tape or stumbles onto a root login, all the files on the system can be read along with any unencrypted passwords in scripts.

As if this is not bad enough, the implementation of setuid and setgid scripts is insecure on some UNIX systems. It is often possible to trick such scripts into running a completely different program than the script originally called for. To avoid this problem, you must write a C program that is setuid to invoke the Expect script. To avoid a total breech of security, it is best to avoid root-setuid shell scripts on such systems. The use of a non-root group in the technique described earlier is a reasonable compromise at medium security sites.

A very different problem is that of writing setuid or setgid Expect scripts in the first place. Setuid Expect scripts have many of the same problems as setuid shell scripts. Writing such scripts should be avoided except by very experienced programmers. Examples and explanations of such scripts are beyond the scope of this book. If you are interested in more information on this aspect of scripts, read the Computer Security FAQ frequently posted to the Usenet newsgroup `news.answers`.

Securing Scripts By Host Protection

As I described in the previous section, it is unwise to depend on the file system to protect passwords embedded in scripts. A better alternative is to depend on the protection of a secure host. Such a host must prevent users who should not read the script from even logging in. In this case, the file protections are irrelevant since the users cannot even get to the file system that holds the file. Ideally, the host should be physically secure as well. This means that random users cannot physically access it nor can they walk off with the backup tapes. The host should not even permit root access over the network. Of course, remote mounting should not be permitted. Indeed, all unnecessary daemons should be disabled.

Given a secure host, passwords may be embedded in scripts. If necessary, the scripts can begin by connecting to another host and then performing the desired interaction. Passwords will be available to a network sniffer, of course, but the risk is no greater than from a real person doing the same thing.

Such scripts may be run out of `cron`, allowing scripts to run programs that normally require passwords to run automatically and at times when no users are available. This is a common problem with databases that collect information that must be processed in the wee hours of the morning.

Scripts may also be run on demand at user request. Although users cannot log in to secure hosts, Expect scripts may be installed as `inetd` daemons allowing them to be started simply by running `telnet` with the specific port number or service name. I will describe this further in Chapter 17 (p. 392) with an example demonstrating how to allow users to interact with remote applications that require secret passwords.

Resetting The Terminal Upon Exit

When an Expect script ends, the terminal modes are automatically restored to those that were in effect when the Expect script began. For example, if the script put the terminal into raw mode, the terminal is taken out of raw mode when the script ends. This occurs whether the `exit` command is called explicitly or the script simply ends.

This makes error handling a little easier especially while debugging. During script development, it is not uncommon to have the script blow up as errors are encountered. By default, when an error occurs, Expect restores the terminal modes and exits. This makes it very easy to recover even from severe errors in the script.

More On The stty Command

Except for `stty`, all of the non-interactive UNIX programs executed so far have been run by the `exec` command. Compare:

```
exec kill -9 $pid
exec cat /etc/motd
exec touch foo
stty raw
```

It is possible to execute `stty` via `exec` on some systems but the required redirection is system dependent. Some `stty` implementations are sensitive to any redirection of standard error while other implementations require the standard error be redirected in order to catch errors. There is no way to call `stty` with `exec` that is both portable and reliable.

Expect addresses this problem by providing a built-in `stty` that uses the native UNIX `stty` command with redirection defined appropriately for your system. Additional redirection should be omitted if you want to affect the controlling terminal. For example, the following command disables echoing on the controlling terminal.

```
stty -echo
```

Because Expect's `stty` command in turn calls your native `stty` command, you can pass to Expect's `stty` any arguments already understood by your native `stty`. That means that vendor or site-dependent arguments can be used with Expect's `stty`. On the other hand, if you want your scripts to be portable, you should stick with the POSIX 1003.2 `stty` arguments or perhaps even those from the archaic-but-last-common-to-all-UNIX Version 7.

For a number of reasons, Expect's `stty` command recognizes several `stty` arguments. When the arguments are recognized, Expect's `stty` command changes the terminal modes without calling the native `stty`. While the time saved by not creating a process is minimal, mode changes often occur precisely when interacting with a user. Avoiding these extra processes allows Expect to respond more quickly to user interaction just when users are most likely to notice it. Knowledge of the current terminal setting also enables a few commands (e.g., `interact`) to take several shortcuts and run faster. Yet another reason Expect's `stty` recognizes certain arguments is to make up for the lack of support by the UNIX `stty` command for these arguments.

The arguments recognized by Expect's `stty` are:

`raw`	raw mode—do not process characters
`-raw`	cooked mode—process characters
`cooked`	same as `-raw`
`-cooked`	same as `raw`
`echo`	echo characters
`-echo`	do not echo characters
`rows`	return the number of rows
`rows #`	set the number of rows to #
`columns`	return the number of columns
`columns #`	set the number of columns to #
`< /dev/tty`*XX*	set the named terminal

If an argument which sets the terminal mode is recognized, `stty` returns the previous settings of raw and echo. For example, suppose Expect is running with the terminal set to `-raw` and echo. If I issue a command to put the terminal into raw mode and then back to cooked mode, the interaction looks like this:

```
expect1.3> stty raw
-raw echo
expect1.4> stty cooked
raw echo
expect1.5> stty raw
-raw echo
```

In the first command, `stty` recognized the argument. It put the terminal into raw mode and then returned the previous raw and echo settings.[†] Next, I put the terminal in cooked mode. Finally, I put it back into raw mode. Notice that `stty` reported the final terminal mode using `-raw` even though I used the argument `cooked`. They both mean the same thing but `raw` and `-raw` are the official names.

It is common to use `stty` inside a procedure where the terminal mode is immediately set and later restored just before the procedure returns. This can be done by saving the return value from `stty` and using it as the argument later. However, the `stty` command expects separate arguments. It is possible to extract the appropriate arguments using `lindex` but it is simpler to use `eval`. Based on this observation, the procedure to get a password that I showed on page 199 can be rewritten:

```
proc getpass {prompt} {
    set oldmode [stty -echo -raw]
    send_user "$prompt"
    set timeout -1
    expect_user -re "(.*)\n"
    send_user "\n"
    eval stty $oldmode
    return $expect_out(1,string)
}
```

The `getpass` procedure works no matter whether the terminal is already in cooked mode or raw mode. While in `getpass`, the terminal is put into cooked mode, and upon completion the previous mode is restored. Echoing is handled similarly.

If the terminal is already in cooked (or another recognized) mode, `stty` does nothing except return the current value of the mode. This means it is unnecessary for you to try to avoid calling `stty` in the interest of efficiency. The `stty` performs this test very quickly internally.

In the earlier `getpass` definition, the prompt was hardcoded. This new definition of `getpass` parameterizes the prompt. You might question why `getpass` does the prompting in the first place rather than having the calling procedure do it. After all, the caller could send a prompt and then call `getpass`, right? In theory, this is true. Unfortunately, in reality this opens a tiny window of vulnerability. When the `stty` command changes the terminal parameters, any characters being typed at that moment can be discarded by the terminal driver. To avoid any loss of characters, prompting should be done after the dangerous time when characters can be lost—in other words, *after* the `stty` command. Since `getpass` executes `stty` and `expect`, `getpass` also necessarily needs to know the prompt since it must be sent between the other two

---

† You might expect the output in this example to be improperly formatted in raw mode. This formatting problem does not occur because Expect specifically avoids this problem. I will describe this further in Chapter 9 (p. 226).

commands. This is similar to the problem with AT-style modems that I described on page 196.

The arguments to set and return the rows and columns are described and used in Chapter 14 (p. 316) and Chapter 16 (p. 364).

Any of the `stty` arguments can be applied to other terminals by ending the command with the input redirection symbol followed by the terminal name. For example:

```
stty raw < /dev/ttya
```

The terminal settings can also be queried in this way. I will show examples of this in Chapter 13 (p. 290), Chapter 14 (p. 316), and Chapter 16 (p. 364).

With no or unrecognized arguments, Expect's `stty` command returns system-specific output from the UNIX `stty` command. Shown below are several examples of how Expect's `stty` behaves on my own system. Note that while the parameters I have used are portable to all modern UNIX systems, the output is not and varies from system to system.

```
expect1.1> stty
speed 9600 baud;
-inpck -istrip imaxbel
iexten crt
expect1.2> stty -a
speed 9600 baud, 24 rows, 80 columns
-parenb -parodd cs8 -cstopb -hupcl cread -clocal -crtscts
-ignbrk -brkint -ignpar -parmrk -inpck -istrip -inlcr -igncr -icrnl
    -iuclc
-ixon -ixany -ixoff -imaxbel
-isig -iexten -icanon -xcase echo -echoe -echok -echonl -noflsh
    -tostop
-echoctl -echoprt -echoke
-opost -olcuc -onlcr -ocrnl -onocr -onlret -ofill -ofdel
min 1, time 0
erase  kill   werase rprnt  flush  lnext  susp   intr   quit stop
    eof
^?     ^U     ^W     ^R     ^O     ^V     ^Z/^Y  ^C     ^   ^S/^Q
```

The system Command

The `system` command is similar to the `exec` command. But unlike the `exec` command, `system` runs UNIX commands without redirecting either of the standard output or standard error.

In early releases of Tcl, there was no support for running programs without unredirected I/O. Now it is possible, yet the `system` command remains—partly for historical reasons and partly because the interface is simpler than exec for a few common problems.

For example, if the script needs to allow a program such as more to directly interact with a user, this is accomplished slightly more easily with system. Compare:

```
system more file
exec    more file >@ stdout 2>@ stderr
```

The system command is also much more efficient than exec. If you are executing many fast UNIX commands (e.g., renaming or removing lots of files via mv or rm), the system-based approach will operate more quickly. On the other hand, if you are executing long-running commands or just a few commands, the difference between exec and system is not likely to be important.

Another difference between system and exec is in the way arguments are handled. The exec command passes the original arguments to the program untouched. In contrast, the system command appends them together in the style of the concat command. Consider the following commands:

```
exec    Eprog a b "c d"
system  Sprog a b "c d"
system "Sprog a b  c d"
```

With exec, Eprog is called with three arguments ("a", "b", and "c d") while both invocations of Sprog called with system receive four arguments ("a", "b", "c", and "d").

This difference in argument handling was not designed capriciously. Rather, it reflects a difference in how exec and system work. Internally, exec duplicates much of the behavior of the shell: scanning, parsing, setting up redirection, and creating processes. The system command, on the other hand, gathers all the arguments into a single string and literally passes it to the shell itself (/bin/sh). If you want exact Bourne-shell semantics, the simplest way is to call system.

It is possible to make either command handle its arguments more like the other. With exec, the solution is to use eval. For instance, suppose you want to remove a number of files stored in a list. This can be done through either of the following commands:

```
eval exec rm $files
system "rm $files"
```

Alternatively, suppose you want to remove the file named "foo bar"—with a space in the middle of it. Ordinarily, the space would separate arguments in Tcl. Thus, the argument must be quoted:

```
exec rm "foo bar"
```

Passing this command to /bin/sh is a little trickier because Tcl tries to process the double quotes before /bin/sh gets to see them. Using single quotes works well in this example:

```
system "rm 'foo bar'"
```

Handling characters that are special to both Tcl and /bin/sh requires a little more work. For example, the following commands show how a dollar sign is treated using different styles of quotes. If you want to learn more about /bin/sh, read its documentation.

```
system "echo 'foo $PATH'"      ;# Tcl expands $PATH
system "echo \"foo $PATH\""    ;# Tcl expands $PATH
system "echo \"foo \$PATH\""   ;# shell expands $PATH
system {echo "foo $PATH"}      ;# shell expands $PATH
system {echo 'foo $PATH'}      ;# no one expands $PATH
system "echo 'foo \$PATH'"     ;# no one expands $PATH
system {echo "foo \$PATH"}     ;# no one expands $PATH
```

I will not describe /bin/sh any further here. There are many good books on it which describe its quoting conventions in detail.

Redirecting The Standard Input Or Output

Earlier I showed that the expect_user command reads from the standard input. By default, the standard input is the keyboard. However, like any program, Expect can have its standard input redirected. This is done using the usual shell redirection syntax.

```
% script < input-file
```

In the command above, the Expect script reads its standard input from input-file. Whenever an expect_user command occurs, input is also read from input-file. In this way, Expect can act as a filter. The same thing happens when Expect is called in these other ways:

```
% expect script < input-file
% cat input-file | expect script
% cat input-file | expect script | yet-another-script
```

In all of these commands, input comes from input-file, and the Expect script controls what happens.

The send_user command is analogous to expect_user. The send_user command sends output to the standard output. By default, the standard output is the screen. If the standard output is redirected, then send_user will send output to where the redirection indicates.

It is also possible to read commands (rather than data) from the standard input. I will describe this in Chapter 9 (p. 224).

The expect_tty Command

If you have redirected the standard input, it is still possible to read from the terminal. This is done by using the expect_tty command. It is called just like expect or expect_user. The following example waits for the string foo to be entered followed by a return.

```
expect_tty "foo\n"
```

If this command is embedded in a script and the script is invoked with the input redirected, Expect will wait until the user physically types the string on the keyboard.

expect_tty has its advantages and its disadvantages. An advantage is that by overriding shell redirection, very powerful effects can be produced that are not possible any other way. For instance, the more program, which pages through files, reads from the standard input and the keyboard at the same time. This allows more to read files in a pipeline and still be controlled from the keyboard as it runs. To build a script that behaves like more, use expect_tty to read from the keyboard while using expect_user to read from the standard input.

The disadvantage to using expect_tty is that it cannot be redirected from the shell. This may seem circular. After all, that is the very point of the command. However, there is always a time when you want to force commands to come from a file—for example, if you are testing the more command. Because more behaves this way, it cannot be automated from the shell (although more can be automated from Expect). So expect_tty should not be used capriciously. expect_tty generally produces programs that do not work well in pipelines, with the result that they cannot easily be used as building blocks in the UNIX style of a workbench of small synergistic tools.

The send_tty Command

send_tty is analogous to expect_tty. The send_tty command sends its output to the screen in such a way that it cannot be redirected by the shell. send_tty shares the very same advantages and disadvantages of expect_tty.

expect_tty and send_tty work by communicating through a special file called /dev/tty. Expect is one of a few programs that has the power to redirect communications with programs that communicate through /dev/tty. When programs are spawned by Expect, all of their inputs (/dev/tty and unredirected standard input) are merged into a single input to which the send command can write. Similarly, all of their outputs (/dev/tty and any unredirected standard output or standard error) are merged into a single output from which the **expect** command can read.

Thus, Expect reads and writes from processes with the same view that a real person has. In the same way a person can read all of the unredirected output or write all of the unredirected input, so can Expect. If a human can control a program, then the program can be controlled with Expect also. This is the power of Expect.

Exercises

1. It takes a long time for GNUS, the Emacs news reader, to start. Rather than watching the window out of the corner of your eye, write a script that starts an iconic window running GNUS. When it is ready to use, get the user's attention in some way such as by playing a sound or deiconifying the window.

2. On page 196, I described why it is a good idea to embed the sending of the first AT command to a modem inside a loop. Write the code for this.

3. The **getpass** script on page 199 uses the regular expression "(.*)\n" to wait for a password from the user. What might happen if the computer is really bogged down and the user enters several lines in advance? Think of at least two reasons why users will not do this. Modify the script anyway to avoid the problem.

4. The **newgrp** command has some peculiar characteristics. For instance, **newgrp** behaves differently when run from a terminal. And some shells (e.g., /bin/sh) recognize it and run it in such a way that the **newgrp** removes any traces of the original shell process. Write an Expect script to fix this behavior.

5. Use the −**nocase** flag from Chapter 6 (p. 139) to make the script on page 201 a little less vulgar.

6. On page 202, I described why it is dangerous to store passwords in scripts. Is it any safer if the scripts are encrypted?

7. Using **grep**, search through all the source code on your system. Find programs that directly talk to /dev/tty. Justify each program's use of /dev/tty.

8. After accidentally falling asleep and rolling your head on the keyboard, you need to delete the files "a sd^F", "−", and "−r *". How would you do this using **exec**? How would you do this using a spawned shell?

In This Chapter:
- *Running Expect*
  Scripts From Shells
- *Running Expect*
  Interactively
- *Expect's Command-*
  Line Arguments
- *Giving The User*
  Access To The
  Command-Line
  Interpreter
- *Changing Expect's*
  Prompt

9

The Expect Program

In this chapter, I will cover Expect's command-line arguments and describe more about how Expect scripts fit in with other UNIX utilities. I will also focus on the difference between running Expect interactively versus non-interactively.

Expect — Just Another Program

To the operating system, Expect is just another program. There is nothing special about it. For example, it has attributes similar to many other programs you are familiar with:

- Expect has standard input, standard output, and standard error. They can be read from and written to. They can be redirected.

- Expect can be run in the background from the command-line using & or from cron or at.

- Expect can be called from other programs, such as C programs, shell scripts, awk scripts, and even other Expect scripts.

Expect is also an interpreter, and it shares attributes of most other interpreters:

- Expect supports the #! convention.

- Expect can be run interactively, taking commands from the keyboard, or non-interactively, taking commands from scripts or standard input.

- Expect takes flags or can pass them on to scripts.

Like most interpreters, Expect takes a file name as an argument, and uses it as a source from which to read commands.

```
% expect script.exp
```

If you want to pass additional information to the script, you can do so just by putting it at the end of the command line.

```
% expect script.exp foo bar 17
```

Inside the script, this information can be found in the variable `argv`. The value of `argv` can be manipulated as a list. Here is a script called "`echo.exp`". It echoes each argument, prefaced with its index in `argv`.

```
#!/usr/local/bin/expect --
set argc [llength $argv]
for {set i 0} {$i<$argc} {incr i} {
        puts "arg $i: [lindex $argv $i]"
}
```

When I run this script from the command line with some random arguments, it looks like this:

```
% expect echo.exp foo bar "17 and a half"
arg 0: foo
arg 1: bar
arg 2: 17 and a half
```

The last argument was kept together by double quoting it. This is a shell mechanism. Without the double quotes, the shell breaks apart arguments that are separated by whitespace. If present, the double quotes are stripped off before passing the arguments to Expect. Notice that this is exactly the same way that Tcl uses double quotes.

The script name is not included in the argument list. The arguments are only those of the script, not of Expect. This is convenient in many scripts because the argument list can be directly used without stripping out the command name.

The script name is stored in the variable `argv0`. Adding the command "`puts "argv0: $argv0"`" as the first line of the example script causes it to print an additional line:

```
argv0: echo.exp
arg 0: foo
arg 1: bar
arg 2: 17 and a half
```

The `expect` from the original command line vanishes as if the script itself had been called without it. There is little reason to have the `expect` in there anyway. Obviously, the Expect script knows that it is an Expect script. But there is an even more important reason to get rid of it—so that a script sees the same arguments whether it is invoked as "`expect script`" or just "`script`". I will show later why this is so useful.

The echo.exp script explicitly calculates the length of argv according to llength. As a convenience, Expect sets argc to this value at the same time that argv and argv0 are set, so it is possible to omit the initialization of argc in echo.exp.

Invoking Scripts Without Saying "expect"

On all but the most ancient UNIX systems, it is not necessary to type "expect" to run an Expect script. Just the script name is necessary. Assuming the script is constructed properly, both of the following commands do the same thing:

```
% expect script
% script
```

In the first command, the operating system runs Expect which executes the script. In the second case, the operating system has to use some other means of deducing that the script wants to be executed by the Expect interpreter. The system figures this out by reading the first line of the script. The name of the interpreter must appear after the characters #! in the first line. You must specify the complete path for Expect (even if its directory is in your PATH). In this book, I have assumed that Expect is in /usr/local/bin/expect but that may not be true for your system.

```
#!/usr/local/bin/expect
```

If you mark the script as executable (using "chmod +x script"), you can run the script without typing "expect" in front of the script name each time.[†]

```
% script
```

This is shorthand for explicitly saying "expect script". I will occasionally explain the shorthand form in terms of the full "expect script" form to help describe how other arguments are handled.

The #! mechanism has one significant drawback. On many systems, the total length of the first line is limited to 32 characters. If you use more than 32 characters, the operating system will not pass them to Expect. Expect will not see them.

A simple way to verify this (or find out the limit on your system) is to invoke the following in a script using just the script name. Where your system truncates its arguments will be visually obvious from the output.

```
#!/bin/echo 12345678901234567890123456789012345678901234567890
```

The 32 character limit includes the #! and any arguments after the script name. As I will describe later, arguments are typically "--" or "-f". Subtracting five for "#!" and " --"

---

† The directory containing the script must be in the PATH environment variable. Some shells also require you to execute the rehash command in order to recognize brand new scripts as commands. Do this after the chmod.

leaves 27. As an example, `/usr/local/bin/expect` is 21 characters and so that path will work because 21 is not greater than 27.

If you keep programs in a common directory that has more than 27 characters in its name, create another directory with a shorter name. In the new directory, create a symbolic link to the true Expect executable.

For more information on the `#!` mechanism, read the **execve** man page on your own system. Some systems may be different than what I have described here.

Very old systems do not follow the `#!` convention at all, and instead use `/bin/sh` to execute all scripts. Inserting the following lines at the beginning of your script allows it to be portable between such systems and modern ones that do invoke the correct interpreter.[†]

```
#!/bin/sh
set kludge { ${1+"$@"}
shift
shift
exec expect -f $0 ${1+"$@"}
}
# rest of script follows
```

Rewriting The #! Line

If you need to move your scripts to another system which has Expect installed in a different place, you may need to rewrite the first line of many scripts. For instance, the Expect installation does this when installing the sample scripts that accompany it. The installation accomplishes this by running a script called `fixline1` on each Expect script. Here is `fixline1`:

```
#!/usr/local/bin/expect --
regsub "^#!(.*/)*(.*)" [gets stdin] "#!$argv/\\2" line1
puts -nonewline "$line1\n[read stdin]"
```

The script works by reading the first line and looking for `#!` followed by a slash. This is replaced with the new path and then the remainder of the file is rewritten as well. This rewrites scripts that have first lines such as the following:

```
#!expect
#!expect --
#!../expectk --
#!/usr/local/bin/expectk anyoldargs
```

---

† Thanks to Paul Mackerras, Dept. of Computer Science, Australian National University, for this gem.

The script is called (usually from a `Makefile`) as follows:

```
expect fixline1 newpath < oldscript > newscript
```

where *oldscript* is the original script and *newscript* is the new version with the path set to *newpath*. This script can be used to rewrite any file that uses the #! in the first line. Of course, the literal "expect" is needed only before `fixline1` has rewritten its own first line.

The .exp Extension

Expect script names need not end with ".exp" although this can serve as an easy way to distinguish Expect scripts from other files. Modern versions of the UNIX `file` command can also report that a file is an Expect script. They do this by looking at the #! in the first line. Thus, it is a good idea to use this line even if you always invoke Expect explicitly when using the script.

```
% file echo.exp
echo.exp:       executable /usr/local/bin/expect script
```

The - - And Other Flags

In Chapter 3 (p. 72), I mentioned the #! line with "--" at the end. I did not explain it at the time, but most of the scripts so far have used this line. I described the #! earlier in this chapter. Now I will explain "--". The "--" is a flag to Expect. It says not to interpret any of the script arguments but just to pass them on to the script. This is comparable to saying:

```
expect -- script args
```

Without the "--", Expect itself interprets arguments that *look like* flags. Arguments that look like flags begin with a "-" and appear before arguments that *do not look like* flags. What is important here is that after Expect finds an argument that does not look like a flag, then no other argument can be a flag. I will discuss this more later.

Flags that Expect knows about are:

-b	read the script a line at a time (i.e., unbuffered)
-c *cmd*	execute this command before any in the script
-f *file*	read commands from this file
-d	print internal (diagnostic) information
-D	enable the debugger
-i	run interactively

-n	do not source `~/.expect.rc`
-N	do not source `$expect_library/expect.rc`
-	read commands from the standard input
--	do not interpret remaining arguments

Some flags take arguments. These can be run together with the flag itself, but for consistency I always put a space between them. For the sake of accuracy, the term *flag* includes both the dash, letter, and any arguments.

In the following sections, I will describe each of these flags in detail.

The -c Flag

The `-c` flag provides a way of executing commands specified on the command line rather than in a script. This is handy when writing shell scripts, and you have a really short task for Expect that does not justify a separate script. For instance, the following shell command is similar to the `timed-read` command in Chapter 3 (p. 77).

```
expect -c 'expect "\n" {send $expect_out(buffer)}'
```

Since no timeout is specified, the command waits up to 10 seconds. If the user types a string and presses return within the allotted time, the user's string is returned, otherwise the empty string is returned. Notice that the entire argument to `-c` is quoted using single quotes. This tells the shell not to perform any variable expansion.

The `-c` flag can also be used to execute commands before a script takes control. For example, you can set the variable `debug` to 1 by invoking Expect from the shell as:

```
% expect -c "set debug 1" script
```

Inside the script, you can check the value of this variable:

```
if [info exists debug] {
    puts "debugging mode: on"
} else {
    set debug 0
}

# imagine more commands here

if $debug {puts "value of x = $x"}
```

When the script is run, it checks if `debug` is defined by evaluating "`info exists`", a Tcl command which returns 1 if the variable is defined or 0 if it is not. If it is defined, the script can then test it later to determine if it should print debugging information internal to the script. The `else` clause sets `debug` to 0 just so that later a simple "`if $debug`" test can be used.

There is nothing special about the variable "`debug`". Any command could be executed. Multiple commands can be executed either by separating them with semicolons or by using additional `-c` arguments. Multiple `-c` arguments are executed from left to right.

```
% expect -c "set debug 1; set foo bar" -c "puts hi" script
```

In Chapter 18 (p. 405), I will cover a command that enables command tracing so that you can easily follow the flow of control in a script. This command is almost always issued via "`-c`".

If you give the `-c` before the script name, it will not be included in the `argv` variable when the script ultimately gets control. Here is an example of this behavior using the `echo.exp` script from page 214, amended to also print `argv0`.

```
% expect -c "set foo 1" echo.exp foo bar 17
argv0: echo.exp
arg 0: foo
arg 1: bar
arg 2: 17
```

If you give the `-c` after the script name, it will not be interpreted but passed on to the script itself in the `argv` variable.

```
% expect echo.exp -c "set debug 1" foo bar 17
argv0: echo.exp
arg 0: -c
arg 1: set debug 1
arg 2: foo
arg 3: bar
arg 4: 17
```

The same thing happens if you invoke the script by its name without "`expect`":

```
% echo.exp -c "set debug 1" foo bar 17
argv0: echo.exp
arg 0: -c
arg 1: set debug 1
arg 2: foo
arg 3: bar
arg 4: 17
```

The behavior demonstrated here is not specific to `-c` but occurs with any Expect flag. It occurs because of the `--` in the first line of the script. As an example, this causes the previous invocation to be interpreted as:

```
% expect -- echo.exp -c "set debug 1" foo bar 17
```

The -- means "do not interpret the remaining arguments as flags", so that the -c is not interpreted as a flag but is passed on to the script. It is possible to change this behavior by removing the -- from the #! line in the script. Unfortunately, simply removing it leaves a line interpreted as if it had been typed:

```
% expect echo.exp -c "set debug 1" foo bar 17
```

The -c still appears after something that does not look like a flag—namely the script name. And anything that appears after something else that does not look like a flag, cannot itself be a flag. The script name, however, can be made to look like a flag by prefacing it with a "-f".

The -f Flag

The -f flag names a file from which to read commands, i.e., a script. Interactively, this may seem pointless. If you say "expect script", it is assumed that you meant "expect -f script" anyway. In fact, there is no reason to ever use -f from the command line. It is only provided so that it can be used from the #! line as:

```
#!/usr/local/bin/expect -f
```

Just as with "--", when a script starts out with this -f line and is invoked just by its name (without "expect"), it behaves as you had entered the following command:

```
% expect -f script args
```

Now you can use Expect flags such as -c and they will be correctly handled. Since the "-f script" looks like a flag, Expect continues looking and finds the -c and interprets this as a flag, too.

```
% echo.exp -c "set debug 1" foo bar 17
argv0: echo.exp
arg 0: foo
arg 1: bar
arg 2: 17
```

The drawback, of course, is that if you want to pass flags to your own script, you then have to also use "--". For example:

```
% echo.exp -- -e -ZZ -c
```

-e and -ZZ are not flags known to Expect, but you must still use the -- or else Expect will tell you that you have used an illegal flag.

```
% echo.exp -e -ZZ -c
expect: illegal option -- e
```

Writing The #! Line

Now that you have seen all the nitty gritty details, I will state two simple guidelines on how to write the #! line that should help you manage the other flags.

- During development, either invoke expect scripts as "`expect script`" or use the line "`#!path/expect -f`".

- Production scripts should be invoked by name and use the line "`#!path/expect --`".

Replace "*path*" (above) with whatever is appropriate for your system as I described on page 215.

The –i Flag

The `-i` flag makes Expect run interactively. Expect will read commands from the standard input (which usually means the keyboard). This is useful if you are using the `-c` flag, which otherwise would have Expect exit after it finishes executing the given command.

Normally, the first argument to Expect is taken as a script name, but if you provide a `-i` flag, the argument is just passed uninterpreted. Compare the following invocations where "1", "2", and "3" are not intended as filenames. This can be useful if you are feeding Expect commands from a pipe into Expect's standard input.

```
% expect 1 2 3
couldn't read file "1": No such file or directory
% expect -i 1 2 3
expect1.1> set argv
1 2 3
expect1.2>
```

In the simple case where there is no script name or `-c` flag, Expect runs interactively by default. So it is never necessary to say "`expect -i`" by itself. You could, but it is redundant.

The –n And –N Flags

By default, Expect reads and evaluates the commands in two files when it starts. It does this whether you run Expect interactively or from a script. Generically, the files are called *dot rc* or *.rc files*.

The first file Expect reads is `expect.rc` in the directory `$expect_library`. The variable `expect_library` is predefined by the person who installed Expect on your computer. It contains a directory for common Expect scripts and fragments that can be used from other scripts.

The file `expect.rc` can be used to customize Expect on a particular computer without changing the binary. This is very useful if Expect is shared among many computers because it is on a common file system. Rather than having multiple different copies of Expect, each host can modify `expect.rc`—presumably a very short file.

Next, the file `.expect.rc` is read. Expect looks for `.expect.rc` in the directory specified by the environment variables DOTDIR or HOME in that order. The `.expect.rc` file can be used to customize Expect on a personal basis. This would, for example, be an appropriate way to define your own personal prompts for Expect to use when it is interactively prompting for commands. Changing the prompt is shown in more detail on page 228.

Another common use for `.expect.rc` is to configure Expect applications that use the Tk extension to control the X Window System. For example, the `tk_strictMotif` flag can be used to disable Tk's default behavior of automatically highlighting buttons as the cursor crosses them. During demos, people who are not in control of the mouse must concentrate more closely on the cursor. If I have to move the mouse to the other side of the window, the buttons flashing in the middle of the window actually make it harder for the audience to find the cursor because it is so much smaller than most buttons. To avoid this distraction during demos, I add "`set tk_strictMotif 0`" to my `.expect.rc` file to disable this behavior in all my programs.

If the `.expect.rc` and `expect.rc` files do not exist, Expect just goes on. It is also possible to skip these files by using the −n and −N flags. The −n flag skips the `.expect.rc` file while the −N flag skips the `expect.rc` file.

Any commands that appear in −c flags are executed before the `expect.rc` and `.expect.rc` files.

You must be very careful when adding commands to these `.rc` files. They are used even when you run someone else's script, and it is therefore possible to affect the way any Expect scripts behaves. For example, if you define a variable in `expect.rc` that a script attempts to use as an array, the script will fail in an unexpected way.

On the other hand, the `.rc` files make it possible to create very powerful results. For instance, you can declare debugging functions that are activated only when a certain procedure is called or a certain variable is used, even if the Expect script is indirectly started from another Expect script. Without `.rc` files, there is no way to have this type of control short of editing the scripts.

This style of invoking `.rc` files *all* the time is different from most other Tcl applications which invoke the `.rc` files only when running interactively. In Expect, the script always has the potential to become interactive even if it is not interactive at the start. The `interpreter` command (see page 225) is an obvious example of this, but it is even possible for scripts that are running in the background disconnected from a terminal to become interactive. I will describe this further in Chapter 17 (p. 378).

More traditional Tcl applications set the variable `tcl_interactive` to 1 when Tcl is running interactively and to 0 otherwise. This is used, for instance, during Tcl's initialization to allow unknown commands to be evaluated as UNIX commands. Expect does its best to honor the spirit of this behavior difference by also setting `tcl_interactive` when Expect starts. However, `tcl_interactive` is not updated over time. This is no great loss since it is usually not referenced over time either. Expect scripts that care about the value of `tcl_interactive` are free to update it themselves.

The -d Flag

The -d flag causes diagnostics to be printed out that describe the internal operation of Expect. Do not read too much into this—the diagnostics are not a systematic means for debugging. Rather, it is an accumulation of tiny windows that have been carved into various places in Expect, enabling you to see what is going on without too much effort.

The -d flag does not change the behavior of Expect. Nonetheless, it can provide extremely enlightening information, especially with respect to pattern matching. This information is further described in Chapter 7 (p. 165).

The -D Flag

The -D flag enables a debugger that is described in more detail in Chapter 18 (p. 410), so I will just explain the flag very briefly here. "-D" takes a boolean argument describing whether to start the debugger or to just initialize it so that the debugger can be started at a later time (such as by a command or by pressing ^C).

Here is an example that starts the debugger so that you get interactive control before the first command in `script` is executed.

```
% expect -D 1 script
```

Arguments to the left of the -D are processed before starting the debugger. Arguments to the right are processed after starting the debugger. Consider the following command:

```
% expect -c "set a 1" -D 1 -c "set b 2"
1: set b 2
dbg1.1>
```

In this example, Expect evaluated "set a 1" and then started the debugger. The debugger shows that the next command to be executed is "set b 2" and then interactively prompts for a command.

The –b Flag

The –b flag forces the script file to be read one line at a time (i.e., unbuffered). This is not normally necessary, but could be useful if the script file has not been completely written by the time Expect begins executing it. In general, however, it is simpler just to feed commands to the standard input of Expect (see next section). This avoids the necessity of a temporary script file.

By default (i.e., without the –b flag), the entire script is read into memory before being executed. A benefit of this is that you can edit scripts while executing them, and you do not have to worry about Expect (or a user) getting confused by the script changing out from under them.

The – Flag

Normally, Expect reads commands from a script. And if no script is named on the command line (or the –i flag is used), Expect prompts to the standard output and reads commands from the standard input.

The "–" flag tells Expect to read commands from the standard input without prompting. Using "–", another program that is dynamically generating commands can redirect them to the standard input of Expect.

Strictly speaking, the "–" is not a flag but a reserved file name. (Using a "–" for this is a common UNIX convention.) Therefore, the "–" must appear separately and after all of the other command-line flags. If you actually have a script file called "–" (for some insane reason), you can invoke it as "expect ./–" to get Expect to understand that it really is the name of a script file.

Here are two example invocations of Expect from the shell:

```
% expect - < command-file
% command-generator | expect -
```

The first command reads the commands in command-file. The second command runs command-generator and feeds its output to Expect.

Reading commands and data from the same file is not supported. For example, if Expect is reading commands from the standard input, the expect_user command should not be one of the commands read.

The interpreter Command

When Expect runs interactively, it prompts for a command. The command is evaluated and Expect prompts for another command. This continues, typically, until you press ^D or enter the `exit` command. It is possible to kill Expect in a myriad of other ways, such as by sending it a kill signal or closing the standard input but I will not describe these further here.

When Expect is interactively prompting for commands, it is actually running a command called `interpreter`. The `interpreter` command can be invoked just like any command. It takes no arguments and is invoked simply as:

```
interpreter
```

The `interpreter` command is often used just for experimenting with Expect. For example, you might write a dozen or so lines of code at a time and then want to test them out even though the script is not complete. Rather than just having the script exit, you can stick in an `interpreter` command at the end. When the script is executed, you will get control so that you can see what has been accomplished and can play around a little more.

With a small modification to any script, you can use `interpreter` as part of a general strategy for catching any errors. Just nest any executable commands at the top level inside a `catch` command. This technique is ideal once you have a complete script but are still running across occasional errors. Make your script look like this:

```
# define all procedures
proc first { . . .
proc second { . . .
proc third { . . .

# call first procedure that starts things rolling
if [catch first msg] {
    puts $msg
    interpreter
}
```

If no uncaught error occurs, the script runs to completion. If an error is not caught, a message describing the error is printed and `interpreter` is run so that you can poke around.

In Chapter 17 (p. 371), I will describe how to extend this technique to handle two other cases—when other users are running your script and when the script is running in the background.

The Terminal Mode During The interpreter Command

If the terminal is not in cooked mode, the `interpreter` command temporarily switches the terminal back to cooked mode while prompting the user for a command. This is helpful if the terminal is in raw or no-echo mode. Users can see and edit commands in the way they are used to. Once the command is entered, the terminal is restored to its prior mode for execution of the command itself.

Output is handled similarly to the way input is handled. The `interpreter` command prints the return value of each command on the standard output. This is performed in cooked mode so that it is formatted appropriately. Output produced explicitly (i.e., `puts`, `send`) is not affected since that output is produced while the command is in execution and the terminal is in the original mode.

The interpreter Prompt

By default, the interpreter prompts with a string like "`expect1.1>` ". After each command, the number on the right advances by one. That number is the *history event* number. The following example shows the first command being reexecuted using its history event number.

```
expect1.1> puts "hello"
hello
expect1.2> expr 2*100
200
expect1.3> history redo 1
hello
expect1.4>
```

Notice how the first prompt contains "`1.1`", the second "`1.2`", and the third "`1.3`". The third command reinvokes the first command by using Tcl's `history` command. While this example is not terribly impressive, the different subcommands of Tcl's `history` command might be worth learning if you spend a lot of time experimenting interactively.[†] I will not describe the `history` command further in this book. See the Tcl reference material for more information.

---

† The default definition of unknown provides a csh-like interface which supports ! and ^ style history. There are several alternatives to this that provide a friendlier user interface. However, you have to obtain and install them yourself. One is to use an emacs shell which has multi-line editing and recall ability built in. I find this sufficient for my needs as I do not spend a lot of time interactively typing to Expect. Another alternative is GNU's readline. This provides more limited functionality but is easier to use than emacs. readline is linked to Expect during compilation. A third alternative is ile (Interactive Line Editor), written by Bob Pendleton. ile is similar to GNU's readline, although ile works in an entirely different way. Much like Expect, ile sits on top of a program and requires no changes to the program itself.

The first number in the prompt is the number of pending calls to `Tcl_Eval`. (`Tcl_Eval` is the function inside of Tcl that evaluates commands.) For instance, if I type "`interpreter`", `Tcl_Eval` runs the interpreter. While the interpreter is running, `Tcl_Eval` is suspended so the number of pending calls to `Tcl_Eval` is one more than before.

```
expect1.4> interpreter
expect2.5>
```

The second number is incremented as usual. The depth of `Tcl_Eval` calls are irrelevant to the history event number. For example, it is possible to refer to a history event from a different call to `Tcl_Eval`. The following reinvokes the `puts` command entered from the earlier level.

```
expect2.5> history redo 1
hello
expect2.6>
```

You can return from the interpreter with the `return` command.

```
expect2.6> return
expect1.7>
```

You cannot return beyond the first level. Conceivably, a `return` from this level could exit Expect but since you can type `exit` to do that, Expect assumes that returns from this level are an accident and discards them.

Any command that can, in turn, call the `interpreter` command can increment the number of `Tcl_Eval` calls. For instance, here is a `while` loop that calls the `interpreter`.

```
expect1.7> while 1 interpreter
expect3.8>
```

`Tcl_Eval` was invoked once to process the `while` and again to process the `interpreter`, so the number of `Tcl_Eval` calls in the prompt is raised by two. What happens when you return from this?

```
expect3.8> return
expect3.9>
```

The number of calls to `Tcl_Eval` remains the same indicating that the `interpreter` command is still running. Actually, it returned to the `while` loop which simply recalled the `interpreter` command again. Later, I will show how to get out of this kind of loop.

Changing The Prompt—prompt1 And prompt2

The prompt can be changed by defining your own procedure called `prompt1`.

```
expect1.1> proc prompt1 {} {send_user "yes master? "}
yes master? puts hello
hello
yes master?
```

The definition of the default prompt is:

```
proc prompt1 {} {
    send_user "expect[expr 1+[info level]]."
    send_user "[history nextid]> "
}
```

You can build all sorts of interesting prompts this way. Here is one that displays the current directory followed by the history event number:

```
yes master? proc prompt1 {} {
+> send_user "[pwd][history nextid]> "
+> }
/usr/libes4> cd /tmp
/tmp5> puts hello
hello
/tmp6>
```

If you type an incomplete command, a different prompt is used. By default, the prompt is "`+> `". You can see it in the previous example where I redefined `prompt1` to contain the current directory. In general, leaving a brace, bracket, or double quote unmatched prevents the command from being evaluated.

This second type of prompt can be redefined by changing the function `prompt2`. The default definition is:

```
proc prompt2 {} {
    send_user "+> "
}
```

Causing The interpreter Command To Return

In general, the `interpreter` command executes its commands and continues prompting for more commands. If there is an error, `interpreter` simply reprompts. It is expected that lots of commands will have errors since the `interpreter` is specifically designed for experimenting.

The `break`, `continue`, and `return` commands are treated differently, however. The `break` and `continue` commands cause `interpreter` to generate a `break` or `return` in its caller.

```
while {1} {
    interpreter
}
```

In the example above, a break command would cause the loop to break, and a continue command would cause it to continue. Here is what happens when I interactively enter them to an Expect process. I have added a puts before and after the interpreter command so that it is more obvious which commands are being evaluated.

```
expect1.1> while {1} {
+> puts "x"
+> interpreter
+> puts "y"
+> }; puts "z"
x
expect3.2> continue
x
expect3.3> break
z
expect1.4>
```

After entering continue, the interpreter command returned and the loop continued. After entering break, the interpreter command returned and the loop ended, passing control to the following command (puts "z").

The interpreter command handles return differently than break or continue. Instead, return causes the interpreter command to return to its caller and proceed with the next command.

Examine the following commands in which I define a procedure p, immediately invoke it, and then return:

```
expect1.1> proc p {} {
+> interpreter
+> puts "x"
+> }
expect1.2> p
expect3.3> return
x
expect1.4>
```

The interpreter command returned and the command immediately after it was called next.

It is also possible to cause interpreter's caller to return. To do this, use the command inter_return. Here is another execution of the procedure p terminating with inter_return. Notice that an x is not printed this time, indicating that p returned immediately after interpreter did.

```
expect1.4> p
expect3.5> inter_return
expect1.6>
```

The handling of `return` may seem to be artificially different than the handling of `break` and `continue`. But this is for good reason. Almost always, you want the behavior offered by `return` rather than `inter_return`. Also, your scripts may allow users to use `interpreter`. In this case, it is much easier to tell them to "type `"return"` to return to your session" than the alternative.

I just mentioned that `inter_return` is rarely used with `interpreter`. In fact, `break` and `continue` are hardly ever used with `interpreter` either. However, these same behaviors of `continue`, `break`, `return`, and `inter_return` will arise much more usefully in the context of the `interact` command in Chapter 15 (p. 339).

^D

Earlier I mentioned that the `interpreter` command is sensitive to ^D. Like many UNIX programs, the `interpreter` command understands ^D to mean eof. When you press ^D, the `interpreter` command returns in such a way that Expect is also forced to exit as if you had typed `exit`.

If you just want the `interpreter` command to return so that more commands are executed, use the `return` command as I described earlier. If you want to be able to make sure some code is executed no matter whether you exit by ^D or by typing `exit` or `return`, use an exit handler (see Chapter 14 (p. 321)). This is useful if you are just playing around and want to kill the script as quickly as possible while still letting it clean itself up.

Using interpreter In Production Scripts

While I have mentioned that the `interpreter` command is very useful while experimenting, it can also be used in production scripts. Indeed, this is one of the reasons it is so useful to be able to change the prompt. With only a little work you can produce a customized interaction.

For example, if you press `telnet`'s escape character, you are placed into a little interaction where you can do things like query and set variables. By using the `interpreter` command, you do not have to write a lot of new commands because the basic Tcl commands are sufficient for so many things.

Here is the `escape` procedure from `dislocate`, a script that moves processes into and out of the background.

```
proc escape {} {
    puts "\nto disconnect, enter: exit (or ^D)"
    puts "to suspend, press appropriate job control char"
    puts "to return to process, enter: return"
    interpreter
    puts "returning..."
}
```

If you press the escape sequence while interacting with your process, this is what you see. Here, I am interacting with lpc. (The escape character does not actually appear even though I typed it.)

```
lpc>
to disconnect, enter: exit (or ^D)
to suspend, press appropriate job control char
to return to process, enter: return
dislocate> return
returning...
lpc>
```

You can choose to throw out whatever messages you like. In this example, I wanted to remind users how to do disconnection, suspension, and resumption. But if setting variables are important, then remind them of that. Consider defining a help procedure and then saying "to get more information, enter: help".

Allowing users total access to Tcl can be a great idea. Users can use your scripts in new ways that you never thought of. Because they can write loops and procedures, they can automate things that are of interest only to themselves, and so you do not have to do a lot of special case coding for each one.

On the other hand, your users may not be technically competent enough to handle this responsibility. With complete access to the internals of your script, they can set variables that they should not and thus can potentially cause any kind of disaster. If you do not trust your users to follow directions, or if you just want a bulletproof script, then do not use interpreter. Instead, write your own command loop and parse commands yourself. This is pretty easy to do, depending on what you need. If you only want to provide a couple of commands, a switch inside of a while loop is often sufficient.

For example, here is a fragment that allows users to enter just a few predeclared commands. If a user enters "read foo" for example, "user_read foo" is executed. Also, the commands help or ? both call user_help. And anything that is not in the list calls user_badcmd.

```
while 1 {
    if {[gets stdin buf] == -1} break
    set cmd [lindex $buf 0]
    if {[string compare $cmd ""] == 0} continue
    set args [lrange $buf 1 end]
```

```
    switch -- $cmd \
    "read" {
        user_read $args
    } "write" {
        user_write $args
    } "save" {
        user_save $args
    } "help" {
        user_help
    } "?" {
        user_help
    } default {
        user_badcmd $cmd
    }
}
```

Exercises

1. Use the `-c` flag to implement the `maxtime` script from Chapter 4 (p. 100) but without using a file to store the script.

2. Figure out how the script on page 216 works.

3. Redefine your Expect prompt so that it shows the host name, the last two elements in your current working directory, and the history event number. Save this in your `.expect.rc` file.

4. Rewrite the script on page 231 so that the references to the user_*XXX* commands are dynamically generated. Wrap the result in a procedure called `app_interpreter`.

5. Using the `aftp` script in Chapter 6 (p. 144), create aliases in your shell's `.rc` file for your favorite hosts so that you can type the host name as the command rather than having to type `aftp` first.

6. The `rup` program shows the status of machines on the local network. Unfortunately, `rup` can wait a significant amount of time for responses before timing out, and it provides no flags to modify this behavior. Write a `rup` script that understands a `-timeout` flag.

7. The command loop on page 231 can blow up if the user feeds it strings that are not valid lists. Fix the script so that it cannot blow up.

In This Chapter:
- *Multiple Processes*
- *What Is A Spawn Id?*
- *Interacting With Multiple Processes*
- *Scopes*
- *Job Control*

10

Handling Multiple Processes

In this chapter, I will describe how to build scripts that communicate with multiple processes. Using multiple processes, you can build scripts that do much more than simple automation. For instance, you can connect programs together or borrow the facilities of one to enhance those of another. You can also do it transparently so that it seems like a single program to anyone running the script.

The spawn_id Variable

In the following script, two processes are spawned. The first is bc, an arbitrary precision arithmetic interpreter. The second is a shell. By default, send and expect communicate with the most recently spawned process. In this case, the following expect reads from the shell because it was spawned after bc.

```
spawn bc

spawn /bin/sh
expect $prompt                ;# communicate with /bin/sh
```

Why is this? When a spawn command is executed, the variable spawn_id is set to an identifier that refers to the process. The spawn_id variable is examined each time send and expect are called. send and expect know how to access the process by using the value in spawn_id.

If another process is spawned, spawn_id is automatically set to an identifier referring to the new process. At this point, send and expect then communicate with the new process. In this example, "spawn bc" stored an identifier into spawn_id, but "spawn /bin/sh" replaced that with a new identifier to the shell process. The following expect command therefore communicates with the shell.

It is possible to communicate with the old process by setting `spawn_id` back to the identifier for that process. `spawn_id` is not special in this regard. It is read or written using the same commands that access other variables. For example:

```
spawn bc
set bc_spawn_id $spawn_id       ;# save bc's spawn id

spawn /bin/sh
set shell_spawn_id $spawn_id    ;# save shell's spawn id

set spawn_id $bc_spawn_id       ;# talk to bc
send "scale=50\r"
```

Clearly, the value of `spawn_id` is very important. Indeed, the process whose identifier is stored in `spawn_id` is known as the *currently spawned process*. In the script above, bc is initially the currently spawned process, and then /bin/sh becomes the currently spawned process. When `spawn_id` is reset by an explicit `set` command, bc once again becomes the currently spawned process.

While not the only ones, the UNIX program bc and the related program dc are very useful to have spawned while other programs are running. Both bc and dc are capable of arbitrary precision mathematics. For example, suppose you are interacting with a process which requires you to multiply some very large number together but does not provide support itself to do it. Just change to the spawn id from bc and get the answer through an interaction like this:

```
send "1234567897293847923*23422938431840129833423874\r"
expect -re "\n(.*)\r\n
```

Here is an interaction with dc to change a decimal number to the oddball base of 6.

```
send "1928379182379871\r6op\r"
expect -re "\n.*\n(.*)\r\n"
```

Both of these leave the result in `expect_out(1,string)`.

Example — chess Versus chess

Very useful results can be produced by communicating with multiple processes. A simple but amusing example is the problem of having one chess process play a second chess process. In order to accomplish this, the standard output of one process must be fed to the standard input of another, and vice versa.

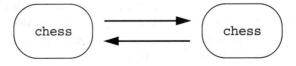

As an Expect script, the basic idea might be implemented this way:

```
set timeout -1

spawn chess      ;# start player one
set chess1 $spawn_id

spawn chess      ;# start player two
set chess2 $spawn_id

while 1 {
    expect "(.*)\n"             ;# read move
    set spawn_id $chess1
    send $expect_out(1,string)  ;# send move to other
                                ;# player

    expect "(.*)\n"             ;# read response
    set spawn_id $chess2
    send $expect_out(1,string)  ;# send back
}
```

The first four lines start two chess processes and save the respective spawn ids. Then the script loops. The loop starts by reading a move from the first process. spawn_id is changed to the second process, and the move is sent there. The response is collected, spawn_id is set back to the original chess process, and the response is sent back to the first process. The loop repeats, allowing moves to go back and forth.

Alas, the UNIX chess program was not intended to read its own output, so the output has to be massaged a little before being used as input.[†] Oddly, the program prints out moves differently depending on if it goes first or second. If the program goes first, its own moves look like this:

```
1. n/kn1-kb3
```

But if the program goes second, its own moves have an extra "..." in them and look like this:

```
1. ... n/kn1-kb3
```

Pairs of moves are numbered from 1 on up. The "1." is the move number and has to be ignored. The program also echoes the opponent's moves. Indeed, they are echoed twice—once when they are entered, and then once again prefixed by a move number. Here is what this looks like to the person who moves first:

p/k2-k4	*echo as first player types move*
1. p/k2-k4	chess *program reprints it*
1. ... p/qb2-qb3	chess *program prints new move*

---

† Ken Thompson wrote this chess program which continues to be distributed with most versions of UNIX.

Following is a command that matches the new move, leaving it in expect_out(1,string). Notice that the literal periods are prefaced with backslashes since they would otherwise match any character:

```
expect -re "\\.\\.\\. (.*)\n"
```

To the person who moves second, the interaction looks like this:

p/k2-k4	*echo as second player types move*
1. ... p/k2-k4	chess *process reprints it*
2. p/q2-q4	chess *process prints new move*

In this case, the new move is matched slightly differently:

```
expect -re "\\.\\.\\. .*\\. (.*)\n"
```

The patterns themselves are straightforward; however, the chess processes themselves must be started differently so that one moves first while the other waits to hear a move first. The script sends the string first\r to one of the processes to get it to move first. Of course, before doing this the script waits until the process acknowledges that it is listening. The process does this by printing "Chess\r\n". Here is what that looks like:

Chess	chess *process says it is ready*
first	*type this to get process to move first*
1. p/k2-k4	chess *process prints first move*

Once the first move has been read, it is possible to loop, handling moves the same way each time. Here is the code to start both processes. The first process is told to move first. The second process moves second.

```
set timeout -1

spawn chess                    ;# start player one
set id1 $spawn_id
expect "Chess\r\n"
send "first\r"                 ;# force it to go first
expect -re "1\\. (.*)\n"       ;# read first move

spawn chess                    ;# start player two
set id2 $spawn_id
expect "Chess\r\n"
```

Now the loop can be expressed more parametrically:

```
while 1 {
    send $expect_out(1,string)
    expect -re "\\.\\. (.*)\n"
    set spawn_id $id1

    send $expect_out(1,string)
    expect -re "\\.\\. .*\\. (.*)\n"
```

```
      set spawn_id $id2
}
```

One tiny simplification has been made that deserves elaboration. In the patterns, it is only necessary to match two periods even though three are printed, since nothing else in the output could possibly match the two periods. One period would not be sufficient—that could match the period in the move number. The space following the two periods serves to enforce that they are the second and third periods rather than the first and second.

The script could use one other improvement. Currently there is no check for the end of the game. The game ends by either player resigning. Resignation is actually trivial to check. The program prints a little message and then exits. Since the program does not print a new move, Expect will read an eof. Adding "eof exit" to the two **expect** commands in the loop will thus allow the script to cleanly exit.

Example—Automating The write Command

Scripts are not limited to interactions with two processes. Large numbers of processes can be spawned from a single script. As an example, imagine a script that runs several write processes simultaneously. Why would this be useful? The UNIX write program allows a person to type messages on one other person's terminal. The wall program allows messages to be typed on everyone's terminal, but there is nothing in between—a program that types to a subset of terminals.

Using Expect, it is possible to write a script that writes messages to any set of users simultaneously. Here is the first half of such a script.

```
#!/usr/local/bin/expect --
set ulist {}
foreach user $argv {
    spawn write $user
    lappend ulist $spawn_id
}
```

The script reads the user names from the argument list. Each spawn id is appended to the list ulist. ulist is not a special variable. It could have been called anything. Notice that ulist is initialized to an empty list and then lappend is used to append to it. This is a common idiom for adding elements to lists. As an aside, lappend permits the initialization ("set ulist {}") to be omitted. But making it explicit protects you if the code is later moved to a place where ulist might have a previous value.

Once all the spawn ids have been created, text can be sent to each process. In the second half of the script, text is read from the user via **expect_user**. Each time the user presses return, the line is sent to each spawned process.

```
set timeout -1
while 1 {
    expect_user {
        -re "\n" {}
        eof break
    }

    foreach spawn_id $ulist {
        send $expect_out(buffer)
    }
}
```

Each time through the `foreach` loop, `spawn_id` is assigned an element from `ulist`. This conveniently changes the currently spawned process so that the `send` command sends the text to each spawned process.

If the user presses ^D, `expect_user` reads an eof, the loop breaks, and the script exits. The connection to each `write` process is closed, and each process exits.

How exp_continue Affects spawn_id

Earlier I noted that the `expect` command decides which process to communicate with based on the value of `spawn_id`. The `expect` command checks the value of `spawn_id` at two times: when it starts and after every `exp_continue` command. This means that with an appropriate action in an `expect` command, you can change the currently spawned process while the `expect` command is running.

The Value Of spawn_id Affects Many Commands

The `chess` and `write` scripts are good examples of how `spawn_id` affects both the `send` and `expect` commands. To recap, `send` and `expect` communicate with the currently spawned process—that is, the process whose spawn id is stored in the variable `spawn_id`. Other commands that are affected by `spawn_id` include `interact`, `close`, `wait`, `match_max`, `parity`, and `remove_nulls`. In later chapters, I will describe still more commands that are affected by `spawn_id`.

As an example, here is a code fragment to `close` and `wait` on a list of spawn ids.

```
foreach spawn_id $spawn_ids {
    close
    wait
}
```

This loop could have been added to the earlier `write` script—except that the script effectively does the `close` and `wait` upon exit anyway. However, remember from Chapter 4 (p. 103) that programs that run in raw mode (such as `telnet`) often need explicit code to force them to exit. That code might be appropriate in such a loop.

Imagine writing a script that `telnets` to several hosts and simultaneously sends the same keystrokes to each of them. This script could be used, for example, to reboot a set of machines, change passwords, test functionality, or any number of things that have to be performed directly on each machine.

Symbolic Spawn Ids

For efficiency, Expect uses integers to represent spawn ids. For instance, if you examine the value of `spawn_id`, you will find it is an integer. However, you should avoid relying on this knowledge—it could change in the future.

One thing you can rely on is that a spawn id can be used as an array index. You can use this fact to associate information with the spawn ids. For example, if you have spawned several `telnet` sessions, you can retrieve the original hostname if you save it immediately after the `spawn`.

```
spawn telnet potpie
set hostname($spawn_id) potpie
```

Once saved, the hostname can be retrieved just from the raw spawn id alone. This technique can be used inside a procedure. With only the spawn id passed as an argument, the hostname is available to the procedure.

```
proc wrapup {who} {
    global hostname
    set spawn_id $who
    send "exit\r"
    puts "sent exit command to $hostname($spawn_id)"
}
```

Similar associations can be made in the reverse direction. It is also possible to associate several pieces of information with a spawn id. Consider these assignments.

```
spawn $cmdname $cmdarg
set proc($spawn_id,cmdname) $cmdname
set proc($spawn_id,cmdarg) $cmdarg
set proc($cmdname,spawn_id) $spawn_id
```

These assignments could be wrapped up in a procedure so that they occur every time you spawn a process.

Job Control

Changing `spawn_id` can be viewed as job control, similar to that performed by a user in the shell when pressing ^Z and using `fg` and `bg`. In each case, the user chooses which of several processes with which to interact. After making the choice, the process appears to be the only one present—until the user is ready to switch to interacting with another process.

Shell-style job control, however, cannot be automated in a shell script. It is tied to the idea of a controlling terminal, and without one, job control makes no sense. You cannot embed commands such as `fg` or `bg` in a shell script. Shell-style job control is oriented towards keyboard convenience. Jobs are switched with a minimum of keystrokes. Expect's job control—`spawn_id`—is not intended for interactive use. By comparison with the shell, Expect's job control is verbose. But it is quite appropriate for a programming language. In later chapters, I will show an alternative form of job control that is less verbose, plus I will demonstrate how to imitate C-shell job control. For now, though, I will stick with this verbose form.

In a programming language, you can embed the repetitive things inside of procedures. This is the right way to use Expect as well. If you find yourself frequently writing "`set spawn_id . . .`", consider defining a procedure to automate these commands.

For example, suppose you have a script that automates an `ftp` process. As the `ftp` process runs, it writes status messages to a user via `write`. In this case, you need two spawn ids, one for `write` and one for `ftp`.

```
spawn write; set write $spawn_id
spawn ftp  ; set ftp   $spawn_id
```

To send a status message, `spawn_id` is changed from `$ftp` to `$write` and then the `send` command is called. Finally, `spawn_id` is set back so that the `ftp` interaction can continue.

```
send "get $file1\r";   expect "220*ftp> "

set spawn_id $write
send "successfully retrieved file\r"

set spawn_id $ftp
send "get $file2\r";   expect "220*ftp> "
```

This example can be simplified by writing a procedure called, say, `report`.

```
proc report {message} {
    global write

    set spawn_id $write
    send $message
}
```

In the `report` procedure, the message is passed as an argument. It is called as:

```
report "successfully retrieved file\r"
```

The spawn id of the `write` process is retrieved from the global environment by declaring `write` as a global variable. `spawn_id` is then set to this value. As before, `send` uses `spawn_id` to determine which process to communicate with.

This `spawn_id` variable is local to the procedure. It is only visible to commands (such as `send`) inside the procedure, and it goes away when the procedure returns. This greatly simplifies the caller. It is no longer necessary to reset `spawn_id` to `ftp` because it is done implicitly by the procedure return. Here is what the caller code would now look like:

```
send "get $file1\r";    expect "220*ftp> "
report "successfully retrieved file\r"
send "get $file2\r";    expect "220*ftp> "
```

This is much cleaner than without the procedure call. Using procedures in this fashion greatly simplifies code.

Procedures Introduce New Scopes

A procedure introduces a new scope. This normally hides variables unless the `global` command (or `upvar` or `uplevel`) is used. Because Expect depends so much on implicit variables (`spawn_id`, `timeout`, etc.), Expect commands have a special behavior when it comes to reading variables.

* When reading a variable, if a `global` command has declared the variable, the variable is looked up in the global scope. If undeclared, the variable is first looked up in the current scope, *and if not found, it is then looked up in the global scope.*

The italicized phrase emphasizes how Expect differs from the usual Tcl scoping mechanism. To say this a different way, while reading variables, Expect commands search the global scope for variables if they are not found in the local scope.

In the `report` procedure defined above, `spawn_id` was defined locally. By the rule just stated, `spawn_id` would be found in the local scope. Without the `set` command in `report`, `spawn_id` would be found in the global scope.

This rule can be used to simplify scripts. In the `ftp` example on page 241, each time a command was sent to `ftp`, it was immediately followed by an `expect` to check that the command succeeded.

```
send "get $file2\r";   expect "220*ftp> "
```

You can wrap this sequence into a procedure so that each time a command is sent, the response is checked:

```
proc ftpcmd {cmd} {
    send "$cmd\r"
    expect "220*ftp> "
}
```

In this procedure, again, `spawn_id` is not defined locally, nor is it mentioned in a `global` command. Thus, both the `send` and `expect` commands look it up from the global scope.

The `expect` command also does the same thing with the `timeout` variable. Because none is defined in the procedure, the global `timeout` is used. Compare this new definition of `ftpcmd`:

```
proc ftpcmd {cmd} {
    set timeout 20
    send "$cmd\r"
    expect "220*ftp> "
}
```

Here, the `set` command explicitly sets `timeout` to `20`. This instance of `timeout` is local to the procedure scope. It is used by `expect`, but when `ftpcmd` returns, this local `timeout` disappears.

Here is yet another definition of `ftpcmd`. In it, a `global` command makes `timeout` refer to the global version. The `set` command changes the global `timeout`, and `send` and `expect` refer to the global `timeout`.

```
proc ftpcmd {cmd} {
    global timeout
    set timeout 20
    send "$cmd\r"
    expect "220*ftp> "
}
```

Before leaving this example, it is worth noting that tiny procedures like this one can be very helpful. They simplify the calling code—in this example, you no longer have to remember to write the expect command after every send command. If sophisticated actions are required in expect commands to handle error checking, then you need edit only a single procedure. Without a procedure, you need to add the error checking to every expect command. And if the expect command ever changes, by isolating the code in one place, it only has to be changed once.

How Expect Writes Variables In Different Scopes

Although Expect commands look in two scopes when reading variables, only one scope is used when writing variables.

- When writing a variable, the variable is written in the current scope unless a global command has declared the variable, in which case, the variable is written in the global scope.

This is the usual Tcl behavior, but since it differs from the previous rule, I will describe it in more detail.

In the previous definition of ftpcmd, the expect command looks for ftp to return "220*ftp>   ". The expect command, as usual, writes what it finds into expect_out(buffer). However, expect writes the variable into the local scope. That means that the caller does not see the updated expect_out. In the following code, the caller assumes expect_out is not overwritten by ftpcmd.

```
expect $shellprompt
ftpcmd "get file"
send_user "found shell prompt: $expect_out(buffer)\n"
```

If you need a procedure to write into the global version of expect_out, then a global command must be used in the procedure. Here is a definition for ftpcmd which does that.

```
proc ftpcmd {cmd} {
    global expect_out

    send "$cmd\r"
    expect "220*ftp> "
}
```

The rules just described for expect_out hold for spawn_id as well. You need a global command if you want to write the value of spawn_id outside the current procedure. Without a global command, the spawn command writes spawn_id into the local scope. As soon as the procedure returns, spawn_id reverts back to its old definition. In Chapter 4 (p. 100), I suggested that you should not invoke spawn from a procedure—until after reading this chapter. Now you can see the reason why: Without knowing about the spawn_id variable and how it is scoped, it is impossible to use spawn from a procedure and be able to interact with the spawned process after the procedure returns.

A procedure that spawns a process to be used later should provide some means for returning the spawn id. One way is to use a `global` command.

```
proc spawn_ftp {host} {
    global spawn_id

    spawn ftp $host
}
```

It is possible to return the information in other ways, such as by explicitly returning it or by writing it into some other variable in an another scope. Here is the same procedure written to return the spawn id. Notice that it does not use a `global` command.

```
proc spawn_ftp {host} {
    spawn ftp $host
    return $spawn_id
}
```

And here is a procedure that returns it to the caller by using the `upvar` command. If the caller is another procedure, `spawn_id` will be local to *that* procedure—unless, of course, one of the techniques illustrated here is used.

```
proc spawn_ftp {host} {
    upvar spawn_id spawn_id
    spawn ftp $host
}
```

The `upvar` command requires `spawn_id` to be mentioned twice. The first mention is the name in the calling scope. The second is the name in the current scope. After the `upvar`, every use of `spawn_id` in `spawn_ftp` references the spawn id in the caller. For example, in the earlier script the variable `ftp` was set to the spawn id of an `ftp` process. To do this in a script, the `upvar` command would be:

```
upvar ftp spawn_id
```

The `upvar` command is commonly used when passing parameters by reference. For example, it is possible to have the caller decide the name of the variable in which to save the spawn id. The name of the variable is passed as an additional variable and then dereferenced inside of `spawn_ftp`.

```
proc spawn_ftp {host spawn_id_var} {
    upvar $spawn_id_var spawn_id
    spawn ftp $host
}
```

```
proc work {
    spawn_ftp uunet.uu.net uunet_id
    # uunet_id is valid in here
    . . .
}

work
# uunet_id is no longer valid out here
```

After execution of `spawn_ftp` in the procedure `work`, the variable `uunet_id` will have the spawn id of an `ftp` process to `uunet.uu.net`. After `work` returns, `uunet_id` will no longer be set (presuming it was not set to begin with).

Predefined Spawn Ids

Three variables contain spawn ids predefined by Expect. These do not correspond to actual processes, but can be logically used as if they do. They are:

`user_spawn_id`	standard input and standard output
`error_spawn_id`	standard error
`tty_spawn_id`	controlling terminal (i.e., `/dev/tty`)

`user_spawn_id` contains a spawn id associated with the standard input and standard output. When `spawn_id` is set to the value of `user_spawn_id`, expect reads from the standard input, and `send` writes to the standard output. This is exactly what happens when Expect is started, before any processes have been spawned.

```
set spawn_id $user_spawn_id
expect -re "(.*)\n"       ;# read from standard input
```

`tty_spawn_id` contains a spawn id associated with the controlling terminal. Even if the standard input, standard output, or standard error is redirected, the spawn id in `tty_spawn_id` still refers to the terminal.

```
set spawn_id $tty_spawn_id
expect -re "(.*)\n"       ;# read from /dev/tty
```

With these spawn ids, you can view the user running the Expect script as a process. The user can be sent input and can provide output to the Expect script, just like a process. While users are less reliable (usually), they can effectively be treated just like a process when it comes to interacting with them from Expect. Viewing processes as users and vice versa works well and can be quite handy. Because of this, algorithms do not have to be rewritten depending on from where input comes or output goes.

In the case that input and output are *always* associated with a human, scripts can use `send_user`, `send_tty`, `expect_user`, and `expect_tty`. These produce the same result as setting `spawn_id` to the values in `user_spawn_id` or `tty_spawn_id` and then calling `send` or `expect`.

Exercises

1. Write a procedure called `bc` which evaluates an arbitrary precision arithmetic expression (see page 233). The procedure should pass the expression to a `bc` process that has already been spawned and return the result so that it can used with other Tcl commands. For example:

   ```
   set foo [bc 9487294387234/sqrt(394872394879847293847)]
   ```

2. Modify the `chess` script so that it keeps track of the time spent by each player and optionally halts the game if either player exceeds a time limit.

3. Named pipes allow unrelated processes to communicate. Write a script that creates a named pipe and writes a chess move to it. Write another script that opens the other end of the pipe and reads a chess move from it. Create another pipe so the scripts can communicate in the other direction as well.

In This Chapter:

- *Waiting For Output From Multiple Processes At The Same Time*
- *Simplifying Scripts That Frequently Use The Same Patterns*

11

Handling Multiple Processes Simultaneously

In the previous chapter, I introduced the concept of a spawn id and how the `spawn_id` variable could be used to change the attention of Expect commands between multiple processes. In this chapter, I will demonstrate a mechanism that provides a more explicit way of denoting the current spawn id. Explicitly naming spawn ids makes it possible to handle multiple spawn ids in the same command.

I will also cover the `expect_before` and `expect_after` commands, which can greatly simplify scripts by performing common tests (such as for `eof` and `timeout`) in only a single command of the script.

Implicit Versus Explicit Spawn Ids

The previous chapter demonstrated various ways of interacting with two processes, an `ftp` process and a `write` process. By setting the variable `spawn_id`, the `send` and `expect` commands can communicate with either process. Here is an example of that from the previous chapter:

```
set spawn_id $ftp
send "get $file1\r";    expect "220*ftp> "

set spawn_id $write
send "successfully retrieved file\r"

set spawn_id $ftp
send "get $file2\r";    expect "220*ftp> "
```

It is also possible to supply `send` and `expect` with an explicit parameter representing a spawn id. In this case, the commands do not use the `spawn_id` variable. Instead the spawn id is passed as an argument following the flag "`-i`". For example:

```
send -i $write "successfully retrieved file\r"
```

This command sends the string to the `write` process. The value of `spawn_id` is irrelevant, as `send` uses the value following the `-i` flag. The value of `spawn_id` remains what it was before the command.

Using this line, you can rewrite the earlier fragment as:

```
set spawn_id $ftp
send "get $file1\r";    expect "220*ftp> "

send -i $write "successfully retrieved file\r"

send "get $file2\r";    expect "220*ftp> "
```

The "`send -i`" sends the string to the `write` process while all the other commands communicate with the `ftp` process.

Using `-i` is convenient when the script only has to send one thing to another process while a lot of interaction is occurring with the currently spawned process.

The `-i` flag is also supported by the `expect` command. The `expect` commands in the previous example could have been written:

```
expect -i $ftp "220*ftp> "
```

If multiple patterns are used, they are all tested against the output from the spawn id following the `-i` flag. In the following example, `expect` executes `action` if either of the 220 or 550 codes are returned by the `ftp` process.

```
expect {
    -i $ftp
    "220*ftp> "          action
    "550*ftp> "          action
}
```

Notice how the braces enclose all of the arguments including the `-i` flag. Patterns can be specified on the same line as the `-i` flag. Do whatever you think is most readable. Here is another rendition of the command. It looks different but does the same thing.

```
expect {
    -i $ftp "220*ftp> "   action
    "550*ftp> "           action
}
```

All of the other `expect` flags and keywords work with the `-i` flag as well. The following example shows two regular expressions, the `timeout` keyword, and the `exp_continue` action.

```
expect {
    -i $ftp -re "2(5|0) .*ftp> "     {action1}
    -re "220-.*ftp>" {
            exp_continue
    }
    timeout
}
```

Many of the commands in Expect support the `-i` flag in the same way as `send` and `expect`. Other commands supporting `-i` include `close`, `interact`, `match_max`, `parity`, `remove_nulls`, and `wait`.

Waiting From Multiple Processes Simultaneously

By using multiple `-i` flags in a single `expect` command, it is possible to wait for different processes simultaneously. The following fragment executes `ftp_action` if an `ftp` process sends its prompt, or it executes the shell action if the shell sends its prompt.

```
expect {
    -i $ftp "ftp> " {ftp_action}
    -i $shell $prompt {shell_action}
}
```

At most one of the actions can be executed. After the action, control passes to the next line in the script. This is very similar to prior `expect` commands.

There is an input buffer associated with each spawn id. So any output from `ftp` is kept separate from that of the shell. Of course, when the output(s) appear on the terminal, they are mixed together, but that is just what you would see at the terminal yourself while running multiple processes simultaneously. Usually, this is not a problem. But if you do not want to see the outputs mixed together, `expect` one spawn id at a time. Alternatively, use `log_user` 0 to disable the normal output, and then explicitly write the output by calling "`send_user $expect_out(buffer)`" when convenient.

If some but not all of the `ftp` prompt appears and the entire shell prompt appears, `shell_action` will execute. The beginning of the `ftp` prompt will remain in the input buffer for the next `expect` command.

Patterns corresponding to a single -i flag are matched sequentially as before. Because multiple processes are never active simultaneously, patterns with different -i flags are not ordered. Consider the next example:

```
expect {
    -i $proc1 "pat1x"  act1x
              "pat1y"  act1y
    -i $proc2 "pat2x"  act2x
}
```

In this command, there are two patterns for proc1 and one for proc2. While the expect command is waiting, if proc1 produces output, it is examined first for pat1x and then for pat1y. If proc2 produces output, it is examined for pat2x. Whichever process produces output first determines which of the sets of patterns is tested first.

Example — Answerback

At login time, some systems attempt to figure out the type of terminal being used. This is done by a technique called *answerback*. The system queries the terminal by sending it a special escape sequence.[†] Instead of printing the escape sequence on the screen, the terminal responds by returning an identification code describing what type of terminal it is.

The fragment below telnets to a host, logs in, and then begins interacting with a program. What happens if the systems asks the terminal to identify itself?

```
spawn telnet hostname
expect "name: " {send "$username\r"}
expect "word: " {send "$password\r"}

# possible answerback occurs here

expect $prompt {send "$program\n"}
. . .
```

After the password, the script waits for the prompt. Instead, the system sends the request for identification sequence. Expect handles this just like any other output from the process—it echoes the request to the standard output and continues looking for the prompt. Now the terminal intercepts the escape sequence and responds with its identification code. The identification code appears to Expect on the standard input, just as if the user had typed it. Unfortunately, the Expect script is not watching the standard input. So the script continues to wait, the system also waits, and the user fumes.

---

† Many programs do similar things. For instance, X11's resize program queries for the terminal size rather than the type. resize can be handled with the same approach as I describe here for handling terminal type queries.

Here is a better version:

```
spawn telnet hostname
expect "name: " {send "$username\r"}
expect "word: " {send "$password\r"}

# handle possible answerback here

stty raw -echo
expect {
    "$prompt" {send $program\r}
    -i $user_spawn_id -re ".+" {
        send $expect_out(buffer)
        exp_continue
    }
}
stty -raw echo
. . .
```

This script starts out the same way, but while looking for the prompt, the script also watches for characters coming from the standard input. There is no need to recognize the precise response (or request for that matter). Whatever characters are sent back *must* be the response, so the regular expression ".+" (which matches any sequence of one or more characters) is sufficient. `exp_continue` forces the `expect` to repeat. If more characters appear from the standard input, they are also sent back. Eventually the prompt appears and control passes to the next command in the script.

If the system stops requesting the terminal identification or (more likely) the same script is used on a system where no identification is required, the script still works. It is even conceivable that the system interacts in a very complex way with the terminal, perhaps responding to the terminal identification by asking for further information. It would not be possible to write the script while only listening to one source of information at a time.

The `expect` is surrounded by two `stty` commands. The first `stty` command has the arguments `raw` and `-echo`. Without the `raw` argument, the terminal would have to end its response with a carriage-return—which it almost certainly does not do. The `-echo` disables echoing so that the response is not echoed back to the terminal. The second `stty` simply undoes the effect of the first `stty`. In Chapter 15 (p. 340), I will describe a shorter way of writing this same script.

Here is the main body of the `chess` script from the previous chapter, rewritten to accept input from either source at any time. While the real game of `chess` does not benefit from this rewrite, it demonstrates that the script can be written without regard to whether moves alternate strictly or not:

```
while 1 {
    expect {
```

```
        -i $id2 -re "\\.\\. (.*)\n" {
            send -i $id1 $expect_out(1,string)
        }
        -i $id1 -re "\\.\\. .*\\. (.*)\n" {
            send -i $id2 $expect_out(1,string)
        }
    }
}
```

Which Pattern Goes With Which Spawn Id

In the chess script on page 251, it is very clear which pattern associates with which spawn id—any pattern immediately preceded by a "-i" flag is associated with the spawn id that follows. If additional patterns are specified before another "-i" flag, the additional patterns are associated with the most recently specified spawn id. Here is an example:

```
expect {
    -i $id1
    "patternX"    actionX
    "patternY"    actionY
    -i $id 2
    "patternZ"    actionZ
}
```

In the fragment above, expect waits for either patternX or patternY from spawn id id1, or patternZ from id2.

Patterns that appear before any -i flags are associated with the currently spawned process, described by the contents of the spawn_id variable. This is exactly what was done earlier in the second telnet example on page 250.

The keyword pattern eof works just like any other pattern associated with the most recent spawn id. Here is the chess script augmented with eof patterns.

```
while 1 {
    expect {
        -i $id2 -re "\.\. (.*)\n" {
            send -i $id1 $expect_out(1,string)
        }
        eof exit
        -i $id1 -re "\.\. .*\. (.*)\n" {
            send -i $id2 $expect_out(1,string)
        }
        eof exit
    }
}
```

In this example, the first "eof exit" is associated with id2 and second "eof exit" with id1. It is possible to associate the same pattern with multiple spawn ids. I will show how to do that shortly.

The timeout keyword works as before; however, it is worth pointing out that the timeout does not associate with any particular spawn id. So it does not matter where you put the timeout keyword (or even if you leave it off entirely). Here is a previous fragment written with a timeout pattern.

```
set timeout 15
expect {
    timeout timeout_action
    -i $id1
    "patternX" actionX
    "patternY" actionY
    -i $id 2
    "patternZ" actionZ
}
```

This fragment times out after 15 seconds if none of the patterns match from either spawn id id1 or id2. Even though there is no -i flag preceding timeout, the pattern does not associate with the currently spawned process. Timeouts do not associate with processes.

For the same reason, it does not make sense to have two different timeouts. The shortest one will always win, after all. However, there are certainly algorithms for which it does make sense to wait different amounts of times for input from different sources. I will address this situation in Chapter 15 (p. 343).

Which Spawn Id Matched

Except for timeout, patterns are always associated with a particular spawn id. You have already seen cases where actions are completely different. A common technique is to pass the spawn id itself to each action as a parameter, reusing the same action.

The following fragment runs a command on the fastest of three systems.

```
spawn rlogin $host1; set spawn_id1 $spawn_id
spawn rlogin $host2; set spawn_id2 $spawn_id
spawn rlogin $host3; set spawn_id3 $spawn_id
expect {
    -i $spawn_id1 $prompt {work $host1}
    -i $spawn_id2 $prompt {work $host2}
    -i $spawn_id3 $prompt {work $host3}
}
```

There is no explicit comparison to find which is fastest. Rather, it is implicitly derived just by virtue of it being the first to complete the rlogin sequence and return a prompt.

When the first of the three systems returns the prompt, the "winning" spawn id is passed to the procedure work which does the actual interacting. The remaining spawn ids are simply ignored.

The technique demonstrated here can certainly be refined. For example, the systems could all have their load average checked, memory usage checked, etc., but the general idea extends to other applications involving multiple processes being controlled. As an aside, the simplistic use of rlogin as a test for speed is in many cases quite accurate. Both the initial network connection and login sequences themselves are fairly high-overhead operations, and serve as good indicators of subsequent response time for many interactive programs.

This example can be simplified. The **expect** command records the matching spawn id in expect_out(spawn_id) before executing an action. This value can be stored into spawn_id itself or used as the argument to a -i flag. The following fragment passes the spawn id as an argument to another procedure. This version of the work procedure is especially designed to expect the spawn id as a parameter.

```
expect {
    -i $host1 $prompt {}
    -i $host2 $prompt {}
    -i $host3 $prompt {}
}
work $expect_out(spawn_id)
```

This method avoids having to write a different action for each spawn id. Conceivably, the work procedure could even refer (perhaps by upvar or global) to expect_out so that a parameter is not even necessary. In the next section, I will show how to simplify this even further.

Spawn Id Lists

It is possible to associate a single action with the multiple spawn ids simultaneously. This is accomplished by using a list of spawn ids as an argument to the -i flag. The previous expect command could be written:

```
expect {
    -i "$host1 $host2 $host3" $prompt {
        work $expect_out(spawn_id)
    }
}
```

This syntax is just a generalization of the earlier syntax. For example, additional patterns can be added, in which case they also refer to the three processes. The following adds on a test that catches an eof from any of the processes.

```
expect {
    -i "$host1 $host2 $host3" $prompt {
        work $expect_out(spawn_id)
    }
    eof exit
}
```

More `-i` flags can be used as before. For example, if you wanted to look for the prompt from the three processes and also the possibility of a special pattern from just `host1`, you could write that as:

```
expect {
    -i "$host1 $host2 $host3" $prompt {
        work $expect_out(spawn_id)
    }
    eof exit
    -i $host1 another-pattern {host1-action}
}
```

If you want, you can put all `-i` arguments in double quotes when using a single spawn id. The quotes are only absolutely necessary when using lists. Do not use braces since they force the $ to be interpreted literally.

```
expect -i "$host1 $host" pattern    ;# OK
expect -i "$host1" pattern          ;# OK
expect -i $host1 pattern            ;# OK
expect -i {$host1} pattern          ;# WRONG!
```

Example — Connecting Together Two Users To An Application

The following fragment is one possible way of writing the kernel of `kibitz`, an Expect script that connects together two users and an application (such as a shell). Both users can type to the application, and both users see the results. This is very useful for consulting or group editing.

Here, `app` is the spawned process shared between the users. One user is connected to the standard input and the other user is referred to by the spawn id `user2`.

```
expect {
    -i "$user_spawn_id $user2" -re ".+" {
        send -i $app $expect_out(buffer)
        exp_continue
    }
    -i $app -re ".+" {
        send_user -raw $expect_out(buffer)
        send -i $user1 $expect_out(buffer)
        exp_continue
    }
}
```

The script waits for input from both users and the application, all at the same time. The
.+ pattern in each case allows the script to process as many characters as arrive. Actual
processing is simple. Characters from either user are sent to the application. Characters
from the application are sent to both users.

No code is necessary to send the keystrokes of one user to the other for echoing
purposes. The application takes care of all the echoing automatically. For example, a
program such as a shell normally echos typed characters back to the user. In this case,
the script ends up sending them to both users. So both users see what each other types.

Each action ends by executing exp_continue. This is more verbose than wrapping
the entire expect in a while loop, but it is more efficient. By remaining in the
expect after each action, no time is spent reparsing the expect command each time.
The parsing time is insignificant in all but the most CPU-intensive applications.

In Chapter 16 (p. 355), I will show how to rewrite the kibitz loop in an even more
compact and efficient form.

Example — Timing All Commands

In Chapter 7 (p. 180), I showed how to emulate the UNIX script command which
records all input and output in an interactive session. Suppose you want a record of just
the lines input by the user along with a timestamp showing when each was entered.
That can be done with the following script called timeallcmds. It is split into two
parts: an initialization and a loop. Here is the initialization:

```
log_user 0
spawn $env(SHELL)
stty raw -echo
set timeout -1
set fp [open typescript w]
```

Logging is turned off and the terminal is put into no-echo mode. This allows the script
complete control over all output that the user sees. The terminal is also put into raw

mode. Then the timeout is disabled. Finally, a log file is created. It is called `type-script` just as in the UNIX `script` command.

Once the initialization is complete, the script loops executing an **expect** command repeatedly. The **expect** command waits for characters from either the user or the process. Characters from the process get sent to the user so that they can be immediately seen. Characters from the user are logged and sent on to the process.

```
expect {
    -re ".+" {
        send -i $user_spawn_id $expect_out(buffer)
        exp_continue
    }
    eof exit
    -i $user_spawn_id -re "(.*)\r" {
        send -i $spawn_id $expect_out(buffer)
        puts $fp $expect_out(1,string)
        puts $fp [exec date]
        exp_continue
    }
    -re ".+" {
        send -i $spawn_id $expect_out(buffer)
        puts -nonewline $fp $expect_out(buffer)
        exp_continue
    }
}
```

Two patterns are used to wait for characters from the user. One accepts strings terminated with a return. In both cases, the characters are logged and sent to the process. But if the user presses return, a timestamp is also sent to the log.[†]

Also notice that the `\r` from the user is matched but not sent to the log. This lets the log look a little cleaner in most editors since the log does not have `\r\n` sequences at the end of each line. Instead, only newlines remain.

If I took a photo of the screen after I finished running it, it might look like this:

```
56% timeallcmds
1% date
Thu Dec 23 22:57:44 EST 1993
2% echo foo
foo
3% qwertyuiop
command not found: qwertyuiop
3% vi /tmp/foo.c
```

---

† In Chapter 23 (p. 528), I will show a much more efficient and flexible way of generating timestamps.

```
4%
57%
```

The `transcript` file ends up with the following:

```
date
Thu Dec 23 22:57:44 EST 1993
echo foo
Thu Dec 23 22:57:45 EST 1993
qwertyuiop
Thu Dec 23 22:57:47 EST 1993
vi foo.c^?^?^?^?^?/tmp/foo.c
Thu Dec 23 23:06:31 EST 1993
ihello there
Thu Dec 23 23:06:37 EST 1993
this is line 2
Thu Dec 23 23:06:41 EST 1993
^[:wq
Thu Dec 23 23:06:42 1993
^D
```

After each line of input is the timestamp when I pressed the return key. While it is not apparent from the scenario above, the transcript shows where I changed my mind and deleted characters. At one point I typed "`vi foo.c`" but then I changed my mind and replaced the file name with `/tmp/foo.c`.

After the invocation of `vi`, you can see where I typed some `vi` commands. The idea of logging `vi` may need more care then I have given here. But it is interesting to see that everything has indeed been logged.

The script ended after I typed the `vi` exit sequence and then a ^D which exited the shell. You can strip any of this out, of course. You can add another line to send the output from the shell to the log as well. There are many other possibilities.

Unfortunately, it is difficult to extend this script in some ways. In particular, it is not possible to wait for a two character sequence simply by changing the `\r` to, say, `\r\r`. Here are just the two patterns that are read from the user with the new `\r\r` pattern.

```
-i $user_spawn_id
    -re "(.*)\r\r" { . . .
    -re ".+" { . . .
```

With this new addition, the first pattern will never match. Well, it will *try* to match but humans type so slowly that both patterns will be tested before the second return arrives. Since the second pattern always matches any character, the likelihood of two returns matching the first pattern is almost non-existent. Humans simply cannot type fast enough.

In Chapter 15 (p. 334), I will show how to use the interact command to solve this problem, and I will show how to emulate the UNIX script command with yet more features.

Matching Any Spawn Id Already Listed

Frequently, different spawn ids may be watched for different patterns as well as a common pattern. For example, suppose you are waiting for pattern X from hostA or hostB, and pattern Y from hostC, or pattern Z from any of the three hosts. You might write:

```
expect {
    -i "$hostA $hostB" X
    -i "$hostC" Y
    -i "$hostA $hostB $hostC" Z
}
```

The global variable any_spawn_id contains a predefined value that matches any spawn id named in the current expect command. It can be used to simplify the previous command to:

```
expect {
    -i "$hostA $hostB" X
    -i "$hostC" Y
    -i "$any_spawn_id" Z
}
```

any_spawn_id can be used in a list as well. Suppose, you also want to watch one other process (hostD) but only for the common pattern Z. It could be done this way:

```
expect {
    -i "$hostA $hostB" X
    -i "$hostC" Y
    -i "$any_spawn_id $hostD" Z
}
```

The expect_before And expect_after Commands

One of the most common uses for any_spawn_id is to check for an eof. Even if an eof is not expected, it is a good idea to test for it. That way the script can gracefully shut down even if something unexpected happens.

Unfortunately, adding eof patterns to all expect commands can make for a lot of extra typing. It is possible to create and call a new procedure that automatically tacks on the eof patterns, but Expect provides a more direct solution.

The commands `expect_before` and `expect_after` declare patterns that are used automatically by subsequent `expect` commands. As an example, consider the following commands. Each one explicitly checks for an eof as well as the pattern. If the pattern is found, the next command is executed. If an eof occurs, the fictitious command `eofproc` is called.

```
expect {
    "login:" {send "$user\r"}
    eof eofproc
}
expect {
    "password:" {send "$password\r"}
    eof eofproc
}
expect {
    "$prompt" {send "$command\r"}
    eof eofproc
}
```

Because the "eof eofproc" is the same in each, it is possible to declare it once using `expect_after`. The following code behaves identically to the earlier code.

```
expect_after eof eofproc
expect "login:"    {send "$user\r"}
expect "password:" {send "$password\r"}
expect "$prompt"   {send "$command\r"}
```

As you can see, the code is much shorter than before. You can drastically simplify a lot of code this way and at the same time make it much more robust.

The difference between `expect_before` and `expect_after` is the order in which the patterns are applied. Patterns declared using `expect_before` are tested first—*before* any patterns in the `expect` command. Patterns declared with `expect_after` are tested last—*after* any patterns in the `expect` command.

This means that you can use the same patterns in the `expect_after` or `expect_before` commands as in the `expect` command. Only one pattern will be matched. For instance, it probably makes sense to treat the eof in a different way when the spawned process exits normally. Consider the following script:

```
spawn $program
expect_after {
    eof "$program died unexpectedly?"
    exit 1
}
expect $prompt {send $cmd1}
expect $prompt {send $cmd2}
expect $prompt {send $cmd3}
```

```
expect $prompt {send $exit-cmd}
expect eof {puts "program completed normally"}
```

This script performs several interactions before telling the program to exit. In the first four expect commands, an eof is unexpected but will be matched by the pattern in the expect_after command. In the last expect, the eof is matched by the explicit pattern in the command itself. Because expect_after patterns are matched after expect patterns, the expect_after action will not be executed. Instead, when the program exits normally, the script will print:

```
program completed normally
```

Suppose a script needs to know if the operator is about to take down the system. For example it could cleanly wrap up what it is doing rather than having the system die in the middle of its work. An expect_before command could declare a pattern and action to do this:

```
expect_before "system going down" wrapup
```

The procedure wrapup would be called if "system going down" is ever seen. Since expect_before is used, the pattern will be checked before any patterns in the expect command.

When an expect_before or expect_after action is triggered, it evaluates as if it originally appeared in the current expect command. For example, variable references in the action are evaluated in the context of the scope of the expect command. And actions such as break and continue affect the loop enclosing the expect.

expect_before and expect_after take the very same arguments as the expect command. For example, multiple patterns can be declared. Even the -i flag can be used. The chess script shown earlier can benefit from the following expect_before command, which terminates the script if either chess program resigns.

```
expect_before {
    -i $any_spawn_id eof {
        send_user "player resigned!\n"
        exit
    }
}
```

As I mentioned on page 259, the spawn id any_spawn_id matches any spawn id used in the expect command. This works as well with expect_before and expect_after. Similarly, any_spawn_id matches all spawn ids used in any expect_before or expect_after commands whether any_spawn_id is used from expect, expect_before, or expect_after.

As before, if an action needs to know from which spawn id the pattern was matched, it can check expect_out(spawn_id).

As the previous example shows, being able to use `any_spawn_id` from `expect_before` is very useful.[†] It avoids the burden of having to change the arguments of `expect_before` each time the spawn ids in the `expect` command change. If you need to call `expect_before` before every `expect`, then there is no benefit to using `expect_before`.

When using this technique, `expect_before` relies on `expect` for the spawn ids. In all the examples so far, the `-i` flag and spawn id have preceded a pattern. A pattern is not necessary, however. The mere use of the `-i` flag alone associates the following spawn id with `any_spawn_id`.

Using the `chess` script, you can wait for an eof from both players while only waiting for a pattern from one. This is done using the same `expect_before` command as above. But in the `expect` command itself, the first `-i` flag has no pattern.

```
expect_before {
    -i $any_spawn_id eof {
        puts "player resigned!"
        exit
    }
}
expect {
    -i $id1 -i $id2 -re "\.\. (.*)\n" {
        send -i $id1 $expect_out(1,string)
    }
}
```

Contrast the `expect` command to the following:

```
expect {
    -i "$id1 $id2" -re "\.\. (.*)\n" {
        send -i $id1 $expect_out(1,string)
    }
}
```

In the first version, the pattern is only expected from spawn id `id2`. In the second version, the pattern is expected from either spawn id.

How Long Are expect_before And expect_after In Effect?

All the examples so far have used a single `expect_before` in the script. It is possible to use multiple `expect_before` commands. The effect of multiple `expect_before` commands either augment or modify the effect of previous `expect_before` commands.

---

† Unless I am talking about the order in which patterns are matched or I explicitly mention an exception, everything I say about `expect_before` also holds true for `expect_after`.

By default, the patterns named by `expect_before` remain in effect until another `expect_before`. (Similarly with `expect_after`.) Consider the following commands:

```
expect_before "bpat1" bact1
expect "p1"
expect "p2"
expect_before "bpat2" bact2 "bpat3" bact3
expect "p3"
```

When `expect` is waiting for p1, it also waits for `bpat1` (from the `expect_before`). At the next command, `expect` waits for p2 and `bpat1`. However the last `expect` command waits for p3, `bpat2`, and `bpat3`. The `bpat1` pattern is no longer waited for. The effect of the second `expect_before` is to replace the patterns and actions of the first `expect_before`.

As long as you are working with the same spawn id, an `expect_before` replaces the patterns and actions of the previous `expect_before`.

If you change spawn ids either by using the `spawn_id` variable or by using an explicit `-i` flag, the new `expect_before` does not affect the previous `expect_before`. Consider the following:

```
expect_before -i $proc1 "bpat1"
expect_before -i $proc2 "bpat2"
```

After execution of these two commands, subsequent `expect` commands wait for both `bpat1` from `proc1` and `bpat2` from `proc2`. This behavior is convenient. As you spawn new processes, old ones continue to be watched and are unaffected by new processes being created.

Here is a more complex example:

```
spawn program; set proc1 $spawn_id
spawn program; set proc2 $spawn_id
spawn program; set proc3 $spawn_id
spawn program; set proc4 $spawn_id
spawn program; set proc5 $spawn_id

expect_before -i $proc1 "bpat1"
expect
expect_before -i "$proc1 $proc2" "bpat2"
expect
expect_before -i "$proc2 $proc3" "bpat3" act3 "bpat4"
expect
set spawn_id $proc1
expect
expect_before "bpat5"
expect
```

After the first `expect_before`, the `expect` command waits for `bpat1` from `proc1`. It also returns if an eof is received from either the currently spawned process (`proc5`) or `proc1`.

The second `expect` command waits for the pattern `bpat2` from either `proc1` or `proc2` and an eof from either of them or the currently spawned process. The pattern `bpat1` is forgotten because `proc1` was specified with a different pattern in the second `expect_before` command.

The third `expect` command waits for the patterns `bpat3` and `bpat4` from `proc2` and `proc3`. `proc1` is still monitored for `bpat2`. All of these processes including the currently spawned process are monitored for an eof.

The next `expect` comes immediately after `spawn_id` is changed. This `expect` command waits for the patterns `bpat3` and `bpat4` from `proc2` and `proc3`, `bpat2` from `proc1`, and an eof from `proc1`, `proc2`, and `proc3`. `proc4` and `proc5` are not checked for anything.

The final `expect_before` changes the patterns associated with the current process which is now `proc1`. So the final `expect` command waits for the patterns `bpat3` and `bpat4` from `proc2` and `proc3`, `bpat5` from `proc1`, and an eof from `proc1`, `proc2`, and `proc3`. As before, `proc4` and `proc5` are not checked for anything.

The patterns remembered by `expect_before` are completely separate from those of `expect_after`. In the following fragment, the `expect` command looks for both pattern X and pattern Y from the currently spawned process.

```
expect_before "X"
expect_after "Y"
expect
```

Using expect_before And expect_after With The Currently Spawned Process — DANGER

When an `expect_before` command is used with patterns that have no explicit spawn id, the patterns are associated with the currently spawned process *at the time of the expect_before command* rather than at the time of the `expect` command.

Consider the following:

```
spawn proc1
expect_before "pat1" action1
spawn proc2
expect pat2 action2
```

The `expect_before` associates the pattern `pat1` with `proc1`. Later, the `expect` command will wait for `pat2` from the spawned process `proc2`. The pattern `pat1` will be ignored if it comes from `proc2`. Action `action1` will only be executed if `pat1` is seen coming from `proc1`.

This behavior is consistent, but nonetheless, may seem a little non-intuitive in certain contexts. Consider the following:

```
expect_before "pat1" action1
spawn proc2
expect "pat2" action2
```

This script is the same as before, except that no process has been spawned before the `expect_before`. Thus, `pat1` will be expected from the standard input since that is the default "process" at that point.

It is a common error to use `expect_before` before the appropriate spawn id has been defined. The solution is either to use an explicit `-i` flag or to delay use of the `expect_before` until after the spawn id has been correctly set. In this example, reversing the order of the first and second lines suffices.

```
spawn proc2
expect_before "pat1" action1
expect "pat2" action2
```

Undoing The Effects Of expect_before And expect_after

If a spawn id is closed, the patterns from `expect_before` and `expect_after` associated with the spawn id are removed. It is also possible to explicitly remove the patterns associated with a particular spawn id. This is done by issuing the `expect_before` command with the spawn id but no patterns. For example, to remove the patterns associated with `proc`:

```
expect_before -i $proc
```

This form of `expect_before` supports all the same syntax as the other forms. For example, multiple spawn ids can be given either separately or together:

```
expect_before -i $proc1 -i $proc2
expect_before -i "$proc1 $proc2"
```

New patterns and spawn ids can be named at the same time. The following command removes any "before" patterns associated with `proc1` and associates the pattern `pat` with `proc2`.

```
expect_before -i $proc1 -i $proc2 "pat" action
```

A spawn id with no patterns is one place where the meaning between **expect** and expect_before differ. Consider the following two commands:

```
expect
expect_before
```

The **expect** command waits for an eof from the currently spawned process (or it times out). The expect_before command merely removes any patterns for the current spawn id established by a previous expect_before. In order to establish the eof pattern, the expect_before command must explicitly mention it.

```
expect_before eof
```

Information On The Current expect_before And expect_after Patterns

Both expect_before and expect_after can be queried for the patterns with which they are currently associated. Use "-info" as the first argument to **expect_before** or expect_after.

```
expect_before -info
```

By default, information about the current spawn id is returned. Here is a simple example of using expect_before and then verifying it.

```
expect1.1> expect_before {
+> pat act
+> eof eofact
+> -re repat
+> }
expect1.2> expect_before -info
-gl pat1 act1 eof eofact -re repat {}
```

The output of "expect_before -info" may not immediately look recognizable, but it is functionally identical to the original specification. The "-gl" signifies that the first pattern is a glob pattern. A pair of braces signifies that there is no action associated with the last pattern.

The output of "expect_before -info" may be used as an argument to expect_before again. This could be useful if you want to temporarily change expect_before and then reset it. To do this, first query and save the settings in a variable. Later, reset them by calling expect_before with the old settings.

While "expect_before -info" looks like (and indeed is) a list, it is also a string. To prevent expect_before from treating the entire string as a simple pattern, use the -brace argument (or the eval command). It looks like this:

```
set oldpats [expect_before -info]
# modify expect_before patterns here
  . . .
# now reset them
expect_before -brace $oldpats
```

With an optional spawn id, information about the named spawn id is returned.

```
expect_before -info -i $proc
```

Only one spawn id can be explicitly named at a time. However, the flag -all may be used to get the information on all the spawn ids simultaneously. In this case, -i flags are also produced in the output.

```
expect1.3> expect_before -info -all
-i 0 -gl pat1 act1 eof eofact -re repat {}
```

Notice that the -i flag is a zero—the actual value of the current spawn id. The "-info" flag always returns the real values of spawn ids. It has to, even if the original spawn id was provided using an expression such as $proc because the original expect_before never saw the string "$proc". Tcl replaces it with the value before expect_before ever gets a hold of the arguments. For the same reason, if you specify a pattern by using brackets or the form $variable, the patterns will be returned in their literal form. Any special characters are appropriately quoted so that they can be reused as arguments without damage. However, the representation may not match your original form, again for the same reason—expect_before will not see the arguments until they have been massaged by Tcl.

Here is an example:

```
expect1.1> expect_before "\\*"
expect1.2> expect_before -info
-gl {\*} {}
```

Although I entered ""*"", "expect_before -info" returned "{*}". However, they are functionally identical.

expect_before And expect_after Actions

Actions from the expect_before command are executed using the scope of the current expect command. Consider the fragment below. If an X is found in the output of the currently spawned process, the "puts $a" action is executed. The value of a is found from the scope of the exp procedure. Hence local is printed.

```
proc exp {} {
    set a "local"
    expect
}
set a "global"
expect_before X {puts $a}
exp
```

Similarly, control commands such as break, continue, and procedure calls also execute in the context of the current expect command. For example, if an exp_continue action is executed due to a pattern from an expect_before, the current expect is restarted.

Indirect Spawn Ids

Earlier, I showed how to store a list of spawn ids in a variable and pass that to the expect command. In this case, the argument to the −i flag is called a *direct spawn id.*

```
set list "$spawn_id1 $spawn_id2 $spawn_id3"
expect -i $list pattern {
    command
    exp_continue
}
```

Instead of passing a list directly, it is occasionally useful to pass the name of a global variable that contains the list of direct spawn ids. This is known as an *indirect spawn id.* For example:

```
set list "$spawn_id1 $spawn_id2 $spawn_id3"
expect -i list pattern {    ;# DIFFERENT!  No "$"!!
    command
    exp_continue
}
```

This example is identical to the previous example except that the list variable following the −i flag is passed without the $ preceding it. When the expect command begins, it reads the variable and uses the spawn ids in the list as if they had been specified directly. If the variable is changed while the expect command is in progress, the expect command accordingly modifies what processes are watched for patterns.

The following example shows how new spawn ids could be added to an expect in progress. Each time the add command is read, its argument is appended to the spawn id list stored in list.

```
expect -i list "add (.*)\n" {
    lappend list $expect_out(1,string)
    exp_continue
}
```

Indirect spawn ids can also be used with `expect_before` and `expect_after`. For example, the following command removes closed spawn ids from the list, terminating the `expect` command when the list is empty and continuing it otherwise. It is possible to determine which spawn id to remove from the list by examining the `expect_out(spawn_id)` variable.

```
expect_before -i list eof {
    set index [lsearch $list $expect_out(spawn_id)]
    set list [lreplace $list $index $index]
    if [llength $list] exp_continue
}
```

The first command in the action locates where the spawn id is in the list. The next command removes the spawn id. After the `exp_continue`, the list is reread and the `expect` command continues.

The previous example explicitly tested the list to see if it was empty. In the context of that example, it does not make sense to have an empty list. The `expect` command would not have any process to listen to.

There is no restriction in `expect` itself that requires lists to be non-empty. Indeed, it is not even necessary for the variable containing the list to exist. `expect` ignores patterns for which it has no spawn ids. If the `expect` command has no valid spawn ids at all, it will just wait. In Chapter 14 (p. 307), you will see that asynchronous events can provide a way of coming out of a spawn id-less `expect`.

As with direct spawn ids, the `-info` and `-i` flags can be used to retrieve information on indirect spawn ids. For example, the following command retrieves information about the patterns associated with the indirect spawn id list `ping`:

```
expect_before -info -i ping
```

If you retrieve the patterns using a direct spawn id, `expect_before` returns all the patterns associated with the spawn id, irrespective of whether the patterns were originally specified by the direct or indirect form of the spawn id. The patterns associated with the indirect form can be suppressed by using the `-noindirect` flag.

```
expect_before -info -i $id -noindirect
```

There is no `-nodirect` flag since the patterns associated only with the indirect form are returned by using `-i` with the indirect spawn id.

Indirect Spawn Ids—Are They Really That Useful?

Indirect spawn ids are most useful with long-lived `expect` commands. They are useful if you are looping inside of `expect` with `exp_continue`. But they are even more useful with `expect_before` and `expect_after`. You can avoid reissuing these commands every time a process is created or dies by using indirect spawn ids.

This idea can be simulated by writing a procedure that calls, say, `expect_before` for you each time a process is created. So the indirect spawn ids can still be considered a mere convenience at this point.

Later in the book, you will learn about the `expect_background` command (see Chapter 19 (p. 429)) which runs in the background and the `interact` command (see Chapter 16 (p. 359), both of which are generally very long-lived. Indirect spawn ids are particularly useful with these commands.

Exercises

1. Write an `ftp` mirror script—which copies a file hierarchy from one anonymous `ftp` site to another. Do it using a single spawn id. Do it again, but use two spawned `ftp` processes—one to retrieve the listings and one to do the I/O. What are the advantages and disadvantages of these two approaches.

2. Extend one of the scripts from the previous exercise to update multiple `ftp` sites simultaneously.

3. Write a script that watches a user interacting with a process and produces a new Expect script that automates the session.

In This Chapter:
- *Sending To Multiple Processes*
- *Sending Without Echo*
- *Sending Slowly*
- *Sending Erratically*
- *Sending Versus Putting*

12

Send

In this chapter, I will provide more detail about the `send` command, including its ability to send strings with special timings between the letters of a string. I will revisit the concepts from the previous two chapters—dealing with multiple processes—in the context of `send`. Finally, I will describe some interactions between `send` and other parts of Expect such as how to `send` without echoing.

The descriptions in this chapter will explicitly refer to the `send` command, but most of them apply to the related commands `send_user`, `send_error`, and `send_tty`.

Implicit Versus Explicit Spawn Ids

The previous chapter showed the differences between controlling `expect` with `spawn_id` versus using the `-i` flag. The `send` command can be controlled in the same way. For example, the two lines are equivalent—both send the string `foo` to the process corresponding to the spawn id in the `proc` variable.

```
set spawn_id $proc; send "foo"
send -i $proc "foo"
```

While the first line is longer, setting the spawn id is simpler if a single process is the focus of interaction for a group of commands. For example, if a login is performed, the implicit method (using `spawn_id`) looks like this:

```
set spawn_id $proc
expect "login:"
send "$name\r"
expect "Password:"
send "$password\r"
expect "$prompt"
```

Using explicit `-i` parameters requires more characters and is more difficult to read:

```
expect -i $proc "login:"
send -i $proc "$name\r"
expect -i $proc "Password:"
send -i $proc "$password\r"
expect -i $proc "$prompt"
```

Setting `spawn_id` makes it possible to easily localize which process is being interacted with. If the process has to be changed to a different one, only the **set** command has to change.

Procedures are excellent ways of localizing variables, thereby reducing complexity. For example, the following procedure takes a spawn id as an argument and performs a login interaction.

```
proc login {id} {
    set spawn_id $id

    expect "login:"
    send "$name\r"
    expect "Password:"
    send "$password\r"
    expect "$prompt"
}
```

If only a single process is being controlled, it is convenient to name the formal parameter `spawn_id`. Then, no explicit **set** is needed. It occurs implicitly at the time the procedure is called. Here is the same procedure definition rewritten using this technique:

```
proc login {spawn_id} {
    expect "login:"
    send "$name\r"
    expect "Password:"
    send "$password\r"
    expect "$prompt"
}
```

Sending To Multiple Processes

Unlike the `expect` command, the `send` command has no built-in support for sending to multiple processes simultaneously. The support is not necessary, since it is possible to achieve the same effect by writing a group of `send` commands or by writing one in a loop or procedure. For example, a string can be sent to a list of processes with the following command:

```
foreach spawn_id $procs {
    send $string
}
```

Notice that `spawn_id` is implicitly set by the `foreach` command. This is analogous to a formal parameter except that `spawn_id` retains the last value after the `foreach` finishes. This could be avoided by using a different variable and then passing it explicitly with `-i`, or alternatively by placing the entire command in a procedure.

In comparison, waiting for output from multiple processes cannot be simulated easily, hence it is built in. A number of other options are built into the `send` command because they are inherently difficult to achieve. These will be covered in the remainder of this chapter.

Sending Without Echoing

Many programs echo their input. For example, if you send the `date` command to the shell, you will see the string `date` followed by a date. More precisely, you will see everything that you would ordinarily see at a terminal. This includes formatting, too.

```
send "date\r"
expect -re $prompt
```

The command above ends with `expect_out(buffer)` set to "date\r\nSun Jun 13 18:54:11 EDT 1993\r\n%2 " (your date or prompt may be different). The `%2` at the end is a typical prompt. More importantly, the string `date` has been echoed. Also, each line ends with a `\r\n`, including the one you sent with a `\r`.

The echoing of `date` has nothing to do with the `send` command. To put this another way, there is no way to send the string and have `send` not echo it because `send` is not echoing it in the first place. The spawned process is.

In many cases, the spawned process actually delegates the task of echoing to the terminal driver, but the result is the same—you see your input to the process as output from the process.

Often, echoed input can be handled by accounting for it in patterns. Chapter 7 (p. 177) demonstrated a simple example of this. In general, when dealing with the shell, you can just search for the prompt, and you need not worry about anything that comes before it. One unfortunate possibility is that your command looks like a prompt. In this case, you have to adjust your pattern or take some other action. Another possibility is to change your prompt to something that will never resemble your input. This is often much easier than selecting a new pattern.

Yet another possibility is to turn off the echoing entirely. Few programs let you do this, but fortunately all shells do, and shells can be used to start any other programs. This provides a general solution. For example, you can spawn a shell and then send the command "`stty -echo`", after which your commands will no longer be echoed. "`stty echo`" reenables echoing.

After sending `stty` to a spawned shell, other commands started by the shell are similarly affected. Imagine starting a `cat` process from within the shell and then sending characters to it. Normally these characters would be echoed (no matter what `cat`'s destination). By preceding it with "`stty -echo`", no characters will be echoed.

Disabling the echo can greatly simplify scripts. For example, `cat` never prompts. But because of the default echoing, its output accumulates waiting to be read with the `expect` command. If you do not use `expect`, the operating system will eventually block `cat` from further execution because there is no more space for its output. The solution is either to do an `expect` every so often to flush output of `cat`, or to turn off echoing entirely. By turning off the echoing, you avoid having to use `expect` while sending to `cat`. I will show an example of this in Chapter 20 (p. 467).

Sending To Programs In Cooked Mode

When dealing with programs that run in cooked mode, you must observe certain precautions. In particular, the terminal driver has a big impact on how characters are understood by the program. The terminal driver makes all the translations that it normally does when you are typing by hand. For instance, the return character is translated to a \n, and the line kill character (typically ^U) removes all the characters typed so far in the current line.

Some characters generate signals. For instance, ^C and ^Z are usually tied to signals that interrupt and suspend a process. For example, in cooked mode a process never reads a ^Z. Rather, the terminal driver turns it into a signal which stops the process. When sending a ^Z by hand, control returns to a shell automatically. However, if the process was created directly by `spawn`, there is no shell to which to return, so once the process stops, it will not say "`suspended`" or anything else. The process is really stopped and will remain so until it receives a continue signal. Unless you are explicitly testing how a process reacts to a signal, there is no point in sending it characters like these. (Expect does not need to suspend processes anyway. To do job control, Expect scripts merely change `spawn_id` or use a `-i` flag.)

Another problem that arises in cooked mode is limitations in the device driver itself. For instance, you must avoid sending "too many" characters in a row without a return. Most UNIX systems do not allow you to send more than 256 characters while in cooked mode. Some allow as many as 1000 characters, but there is always a limit and it is always surprisingly low. These low limits may sound hard to believe, but systems can get away with them because people never type commands longer than this. Indeed, people rarely type commands longer than 80 characters.

These limits occur even on window systems. If you paste a large hunk of text into a shell window, the shell may lock up, beep, or perform some other distasteful behavior.

Don't confuse these limits with the length of a command that can be fed to the shell. That limit is typically 10K on older systems and a megabyte or more on modern systems. Stemming from the kernel, that limit holds for arguments to any program invocation (including the spawn and exec commands within Expect). The cooked mode limits, however, are due to the terminal drivers and occur only in interactive use.

Generally, these limits are easy to avoid. Write scripts so that they run programs just like a real human does. Send a command, read a response, send a command, read a response. Don't send multiple commands at once—unless that is what a real user would do.

I used the following script to test the number of characters that could be entered on a system that sent a ^G when the limit was exceeded.

```
spawn /bin/sh
expect "\\$ "               ;# match literal $ in shell prompt
for {set i 0} 1 {incr i} {
    send "/"
    expect "\007"  break  \
            "/"
}
puts "terminal driver accepted $i characters"
```

In raw mode, this problem does not exist. Any number of characters can be entered without pressing return.

Sending Slowly

It is often useful to send large quantities of information. A common scenario in which this arises is when sending mail via a commercial mail system such as GEnie or CompuServe. To reduce costs, you create and edit mail messages offline. Once the messages are prepared, you can then log in, start up the mailer, and feed the messages to it. This allows you to use your own editor as well as lower your costs for connect time.

The fragment of the script that sends the message from your system to the remote system can be very simple. For example, if the message is already stored in the variable message, one send command is sufficient:

```
send $message
```

The size of things that can be sent this way is limited only by the amount of memory that can be dynamically allocated on your system. On modern computers, this limit is well above a megabyte, and a 32-bit computer should have no problem with 50Mb or even 100Mb.

Before sending very large files, it is wise to ensure that the remote side is not echoing (as described earlier). If the echoing cannot be disabled, the process output must be consumed, such as by an **expect** command. Otherwise, your operating system has to store all these characters in memory. Most systems limit unread characters to 10K or even less. If more characters arrive, the operating system temporarily stops the spawned process until the Expect process can read them into its own buffers. Expect's own buffers are limited only by the amount of virtual memory on the computer.

This behavior of the operating system works in reverse as well. Expect can easily write output faster than a spawned process can read it. Most programs simply do not read data as quickly as another program can write it. Again, the operating system has to buffer the input, and if too much arrives, the Expect process itself will be temporarily stopped until the reading processing has consumed sufficient output so as to make room for more. The temporary halt is transparent to Expect itself. It may just seem like the send command has taken a long time to execute.

Some operating systems do not buffer interactive input well. Upon receiving more characters than they have space for, they might ignore new characters, respond with error messages, or other anomalous behavior. Many serial devices (e.g., modems, terminal drivers) behave similarly.

One solution is to break the outgoing string into pieces, sending a piece at a time separated by a delay. Here is a procedure that prints out 10 characters at a time, pausing one second between each group.

```
proc ten_chars_per_sec {s} {
    while {[string length $s] > 10} {
        send [string range $s 0 9]
        set s [string range $s 10 end]
        sleep 1
    }
    send $s
}
```

ten_chars_per_sec loops over a string, sending the first ten characters, recreating the string without the first ten characters, and delaying for one second before looping.

When there are less than ten characters remaining, the loop exits, and the remaining characters are sent out by the final command. If s happens to be empty (because the original length was perfectly divisible by 10), the command "send $s" has no effect at all.

The delay is achieved by executing a sleep command. Although the sleep command is efficient, the string manipulation might not be. If the string was large enough, constantly shifting the string could be fairly expensive. While the ten_chars_per_sec procedure can be rewritten more efficiently, Expect addresses the problem directly by providing explicit support for this common operation. The send command has a -s flag which causes the operation to occur *slowly*.

The slowness is controlled by the variable send_slow. The variable is a list of two numbers. The first is the number of characters to send at a time. The second number is a time to pause after each group of characters is sent. Here is an example:

```
set send_slow {2 .001}
send -s "Now is the time"
```

The fragment above sends the string "Now is the time" two characters at a time. Each pair of characters is separated by .001 seconds (i.e., one millisecond). This might be appropriate for a system that has a hardware serial interface that can accept two characters at a time before overflowing—a very common situation.

Arbitrarily large groups of characters and pauses can be used as well. This is useful when dealing with logical interfaces. They may allocate huge buffers, but without flow control, even the largest buffers can overflow. For example, to send 1000 characters with one second between each group of characters, you would say:

```
set send_slow {1000 1}
send -s $text
```

The first number, the number of characters, is always integral. The second number, the timeout, may be either integral or real (scientific notation is acceptable).

The following script may be used as a filter. It copies the standard input to the standard output at the rate of one hundred characters per second—a very slow rate.

```
#!/usr/local/bin/expect --
set send_slow {1 .01}        ;# send 1 character every .01 seconds
while {1} {
    expect_user eof exit -re ".+"
    send_user -s $expect_out(buffer)
}
```

Sending Humanly

With the –h flag, the send command sends characters in a way that resembles a human typing. Unlike "send –s", "send –h" enables variability and randomness. The time periods between every character can be different from one character to the next.

A varying sending speed is quite useful when trying to simulate the effect of interactive loads. For example, suppose you are testing a computer to see if it can handle a particular mix of CPU-intensive background processes and some interactive processes. Processing human interaction usually requires only a tiny fraction of the CPU. But by default, Expect scripts skip all the delays that real humans produce. Such scripts produce a very inaccurate simulation of interactive performance since the scheduler handles Expect processes as if they were just CPU-intensive processes.

The algorithm Expect uses to produce output at varying speeds is based upon a Weibull distribution, a common statistical tool for generating pseudo-random inter-arrival times. A few modifications have been made to suit its use in Expect. The output is controlled by the value of the send_human variable which takes a five-element list. The first two elements are average interarrival times of characters in seconds. The first is used by default. The second is used at word endings, to simulate the subtle pauses that occasionally occur at such transitions. The third parameter (the *shape*) is a measure of variability where 0.1 is quite variable, 1 is reasonably variable, and 10 is almost invariable. The whole range is from 0 to infinity.[†] The last two parameters are, respectively, a minimum and maximum interarrival time.

Intuitively, the elements are used from left to right. First, one of the two average arrival times is chosen. Then, it is shaped according to the variability and a pseudo-random factor. Finally, the result is clipped according to the minimum and maximum elements. The ultimate average can be quite different from the stated average if enough times are clipped by the minimum and maximum values.

As an example, the following command produces characters like a fast and consistent typist:

```
set send_human {.1 .3 1 .05 2}
send -h "I'm hungry.  Let's do lunch."
```

Characters are output at an average of one every .1 seconds, except for word endings where they average one every .3 seconds. (Word ending are transitions from an alphanumeric character to anything but an alphanumeric character.) The minimum time between characters is .05 seconds and the maximum time is 2 seconds. The shape parameter will be described further later.

---

† Expect has no concept of infinity, but numbers over 1000 are sufficiently close for the purposes of this algorithm.

The following might be more suitable after a hangover:

```
set send_human {.4 .4 .2 .5 100}
send -h "Goodd party lash night!"
```

Errors are not simulated. It is impossible for Expect to know what a "reasonable error" is or how to correct it—this depends on the particular spawned program. You can set up error correction situations yourself by embedding or programmatically generating mistakes and corrections in a send argument. For example, if the spawned process understands that a backspace removes earlier characters, the previous example can be "fixed" as follows:

```
send -h "Goodd\b party lash\bt night!"
```

The shape parameter controls the variability. The term *shape* refers to the control that the parameter has over a bell-like curve in which the time is likely to appear. The various curves are not particularly intuitive. However, you can examine several runs I made printing out the characters 0123456789 with an average time between characters of .1 seconds, and a minimum time of .05 seconds and maximum of 2 seconds.

The following graphs show the times between characters with the shape ranging from .125 to 16. The left-hand axis is the time in seconds that passed before the particular character was sent. Each character is shown in the axis at the bottom of the graph.

16 is almost large enough that no variation is seen. The line is essentially straight. Each character was sent almost exactly .1 seconds after the previous one. The graph showing the shape of 8 has a slight bend in the middle, but you probably would not notice the differences if you were watching the characters print. A scheduler might not either.

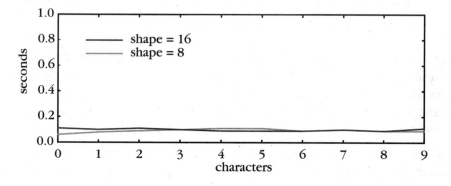

A shape of 4 allows a little bit more variability. You would probably not notice the difference however. The extremes are still within .07 seconds of one another.

A shape of 2 allows enough variability that the minimum time bound is reached. All times below .05 seconds are truncated back up to .05 seconds. The maximum time is .06 seconds above the maximum time when the shape was 4.

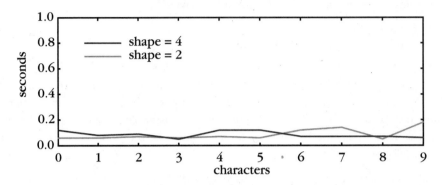

A shape of 1 shows significant inconsistencies, yet the values are still within .16 seconds of one another. A shape of between 1 to 2 probably represents a good typist.

A shape of .5 is the lowest in this sequence that could still be considered consistent. Several values have hit the minimum time. Without this bound, there would be a spread of a half of a second.

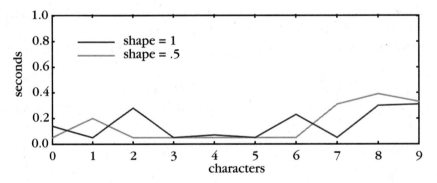

A shape of .25 shows significant inconsistencies. The maximum bound of 2 seconds has been reached. (The graph has been extended to show this behavior, but the scale remains the same.) Only three of the characters have times that are not truncated by the minimum or maximum bounds. This is probably a fair simulation of someone using the hunt-and-peck technique.

A shape of .125 is extremely variable. All but one of the inter-character times have been truncated. This probably does not describe the typing of any human. Nonetheless, it could conceivably be used to test some facet of the scheduler.

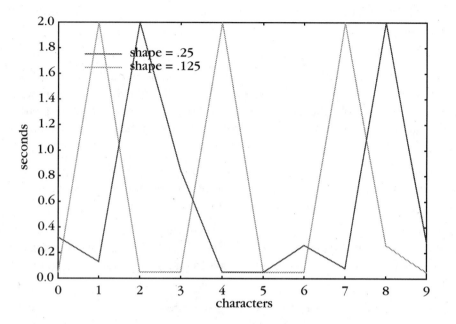

One final note—the timeouts described by send_slow and send_human have no interaction with the expect command and its timeouts. They are completely separate.

Sending Nulls

In Chapter 6 (p. 155), I described how to detect a null character. A null can be sent by calling send with the -null flag. By default, one null is sent to the currently spawned process.

```
send -null
```

An optional integer may be used to send several nulls. For example, the following command sends three nulls.

```
send -null 3
```

send uses the pattern "-null" while expect uses "null". The absence of a hyphen is historical—all of the special patterns lack a hyphen.

Sending Breaks

A break is a special condition of a serial communications line. It does not correspond to a particular ASCII character sequence, so it requires special handling in order to produce it using `send`. A break condition is generated by calling `send` with the `-break` flag.

```
send -break
```

The spawned program to which you are sending must understand and expect the break. Most programs do not understand a break as input even if they can generate it on output. For example, the `tip` program translates the input character sequence `\r~#` into an output break condition. `tip` itself does not accept the break condition from the user.

Historically, keyboards contained special keys to generate break conditions. However, such keyboards are rare today. Hence, most modern programs are like `tip`, accepting some combination of keystrokes to signify a break.

The only situation in which you are likely to generate a break directly by using "`send -break`" is when the spawned process is not an actual process but is instead a serial device. I have not yet described how to make such a connection, but I will in Chapter 13 (p. 290).

A break condition cannot be detected using the `expect` command. However, breaks can be turned into signals. This is similar to how a ^C in cooked mode is interpreted as an interrupt. I will discuss signals and how to detect them in Chapter 14 (p. 307). See your local `stty` documentation for more information on the break condition.

Sending Strings That Look Like Flags

Because the `send` command looks for special arguments such as `-s` and `-h`, you cannot send strings like these without taking some special action. An argument of "`--`" (two hyphens) forces `send` to interpret the following argument literally.[†] So if you want to send `-h`, you can say:

```
send -- "-h"
```

The "`--`" does not affect strings that do not otherwise have a special meaning to send. Thus you can preface any string with it. For example, the following two commands both do exactly the same thing—they send the string `foo`.

```
send -- "foo"
send "foo"
```

This behavior is particularly useful if you are sending the contents of a variable that can have any value.

---

† In contrast, the `expect` command does not provide "`--`" because the pattern-type flags (e.g., `-gl`) already provide a mechanism for preventing a flag-like interpretation of the following argument.

```
send $unknown           ;# DANGEROUS
send -- $unknown        ;# SAFE
```

Without the "--", it is possible that the unknown variable might contain something that looks like one of send's special flags. Using the "--" guarantees that the command is interpreted correctly.

You might also use the "--" with literals when you are generating Expect commands from another program rather than writing them by hand. For example, imagine that you are writing a C program which in turn spits out Expect commands. Your code might look like this:

```
printf("send \"%s\"",unknown);        /* DANGEROUS */
printf("send -- \"%s\"",unknown);     /* SAFE */
```

While the resulting Expect script supplies the send command with literal values, the same problem arises. The C program is not checking to make sure that the value it is supplying to the send command does not look like one of the send flags. The solution, again, is to use the "--".

Sending Character Graphics

In Chapter 6 (p. 142), I described how to handle spawned programs that generate character graphics. It is occasionally useful to generate character graphics from the script itself. Expect provides no built-in support for doing this. It is not necessary because you can call external programs such as tput.[†] For example, the cup operation moves the cursor. The following command moves it to row 23, column 4:

```
send_user -raw [exec tput cup 23 4]
```

Executing many calls to tput can be slow because it is a separate program. However, its different outputs can be saved in variables and reused, thereby avoiding excessive calls of exec. More sophisticated handling is possible with Curses extensions to Tcl. These are listed in the Tcl FAQ.

Comparing send To puts

Both the send command and the puts command cause characters to be output. However, they have differences which should already be apparent. But I will compare and contrast them here just to make things clear. Note that all of the variations on send

---

† Probably a more significant reason that Tcl scripts do not perform character graphics is because of Tk, a Tcl extension for the X Window System. Tk is so easy to use that it is hard to justify spending time writing character-graphic interfaces when the same amount of time can produce a much better interface in X. I will describe the use of Tk with Expect in Chapter 19 (p. 432).

follow the style of the `send` command itself. For example, it is possible to call `send_user` with the -h flag or `send_tty` with the -- flag.

The primary difference between `send` and `puts` is that `send` works with processes started by `spawn`, whereas `puts` works with files opened by Tcl's `open` command. For example, to write an AT-style reset command (the characters "ATZ\r") to a modem with a serial interface, `puts` could be used as follows:

```
set file [open "/dev/modem" "w"]
puts -nonewline $file "ATZ\r"
```

Doing the same thing with `send` requires a spawned process instead of an open file.

```
spawn tip modem
send -i $spawn_id "ATZ\r"
```

In this example, the "-i $spawn_id" is not needed. It is just here to contrast it with the $file argument in the `puts`. Without the -i specification, `send` writes to the `tip` process anyway because `spawn` automatically sets `spawn_id`. In contrast, with no file specification, `puts` writes to the standard output. The previous `open` has no effect on the default destination of `puts`.

```
puts "ATZ\r"     ;# write to standard output
send "ATZ\r"     ;# write to currently spawned process
```

In UNIX, processes can be viewed as files (to a degree). The `puts` command, thus, can write to processes as well—but only those opened by `open`. The `open` command starts processes (and process pipelines if a "|" prefaces the command). For example, the following fragment starts the word-count program, `wc`, and then sends it a list of words to count. The result of that is sent to `lpr`, which prints the word count out on a hard-copy printer.

```
set file [open "| wc | lpr" "w"]
puts $wordlist
```

By using the flag "w+" with `open`, it is possible to use both `gets` and `puts`.

```
set file [open "| tip modem" "w+"]
puts "ATZ\r"
```

Unfortunately, some (but not all) interactive programs do rather peculiar things with their standard input. For example, `tip` expects to read its input from a terminal interface and it tries to put this interface into raw mode. In this case, there is no terminal interface so `tip` will fail.

Some programs are not so demanding, but many are. Expect is the best way of dealing with these programs. In general then, `puts` is used for communicating with files and `send` is used for communicating with processes.

send and `puts` do not work with each other's identifiers. You cannot take a file created by open and use it with send. Nor can you take a spawn id and give it to `puts`.

```
puts $spawn_id "ATZ\r"      ;# WRONG
send -i $file "ATZ\r"       ;# WRONG
```

This does not mean, however, that `puts` and send cannot be usefully used together. Because they both deal with strings, they can be called with the same input. For example, upon receiving input (either from expect or gets), the output can be sent to both files and processes.

```
expect -re ".+" {
    send -i $id1 $expect_out(buffer)
    puts $file1 $expect_out(buffer)
}
```

Waiting for input from both processes and files is a little trickier and will be described further in Chapter 13 (p. 289).

This chapter has already covered the major features of the send command. send has several other features which were mentioned in earlier chapters. In particular, -raw is useful in raw mode (see Chapter 8 (p. 197)). The send command is also controlled indirectly by log_user (see Chapter 7 (p. 175)).

In contrast, the puts command is unaffected by log_user. Similarly, puts has no analog to -raw. The puts command provides no automatic translation mechanisms to deal with cooked or raw mode.

One final difference between puts and send is that puts terminates lines with a newline (unless you use the -nonewline flag). This is convenient when it comes to writing text files but not when controlling interactive programs that rarely want newlines. Most interactive programs either read characters one at a time or look for commands to end with a \r. The send command has no preference one way or the other and instead makes this explicit in every command. If you prefer, embed your send commands in a procedure that always tacks on the line terminator of your choice.

Exercises

1. Parameterize the `send_slow` script on page 277.

2. Write a script which runs a shell such that all of the output written to the standard output and standard error is written humanly.

3. Write a procedure that takes a 32-bit integer and sends it encoded as four bytes, each byte representing 8 bits worth. It should be analogous to the procedure `expect_four_byte_int` in Chapter 6 (p. 156).

4. Run the script on page 275 to find out the size of your system's canonical input buffer. Modify it if necessary to account for your system's behavior when the limit is reached. Is this behavior documented anywhere? Is the limit documented anywhere? Try the script on other systems.

5. Write statements that simulate the sending of the Up, Down, Left, and Right arrow keys on your keyboard.

6. Solve the previous exercise in a terminal-independent way by using information from the `termcap` file or `terminfo` database.

13

Spawn

Besides starting processes, spawn can be used to begin interactions with files and pipelines. In this chapter, I will go into detail on the spawn command. I will also cover ptys—what they are, how to control them, and their features and pitfalls.

The Search Path

The spawn command follows the "usual" rules in finding programs to invoke. Both relative and absolute filenames are acceptable. If a filename is specified with no directory at all, the value of the environment variable PATH is treated as a list of directories and each directory is searched until the given file is found. This searching is performed by the operating system and behaves identically to the way that programs are found from shells such as the Bourne shell and the C shell.

```
spawn /bin/passwd        ;# absolute
spawn passwd             ;# relative
```

In some cases, naming programs absolutely is a good idea. In other cases, relative names make more sense. If you do use relative names, it is a good idea to set PATH explicitly. For example:

```
set env(PATH) "/bin:/usr/bin"
```

Setting the path avoids the possibility of picking up local versions of utilities that users might otherwise have on their paths. Users at other sites may need to change the path, but the single definition at the top of a script makes the path easy to change.

While resetting the path is easy enough, there are circumstances when it makes more sense to refer to programs absolutely. For example, your system may have several versions of a utility (e.g., BSD, SV, POSIX, GNU). Naming a utility absolutely may be safer than using the path.

Rather than embedding a name literally, use variables so that all the references in a script can be changed easily if necessary. For example, you might localize a particular telnet as:

```
set telnet /usr/ucb/telnet
```

Later in the script, telnet would then be started this way:

```
spawn $telnet
```

Sets of programs that live in different subdirectories under a common directory could be localized with separate variables such as in this example:

```
set root "/usr/kidney"
set bindir "$root/bin"
set testdir "$root/test/bin"
set demoprog "$bindir/nephron-demo"
```

Scripts that use these initializations would have **spawn** commands such as:

```
spawn $bindir/control
spawn $testdir/simulate
spawn $demoprog
```

If you have a number of scripts using these definitions, they can be stored in a common file that is sourced by the scripts at start-up.

Like Tcl's **exec** command and the C-shell, **spawn** also supports the tilde notation. A tilde preceeding the first component of a filename is understood to mean the home directory corresponding to the user named by that component. For example, the following command spawns the pike program from the files of a user named shaney:

```
spawn ~shaney/bin/pike
```

Philosophy — Processes Are Smart

The previous chapter demonstrated how to open files or devices and send commands to them with puts. This technique calls upon another program to do the handling of the device. At first glance, you might consider this inefficient. Why run two programs when one will do? Consider that reusing another program allows you to isolate all the device-specific problems in one place. If the tip program already knows about serial devices and how, for example, to choose among baud rates, why burden other programs with the same knowledge?

Ideally, if you just had one program that knew everything about, say, your serial devices, you would not need any others. Or perhaps, other programs could call upon your serial device program when they needed to access a serial device. This is analogous to the concept of device drivers. Unfortunately, real device drivers are not high-level enough to isolate out the device dependencies for our purposes.

It is all too common to have numerous programs (`kermit`, `procomm`, `tip`, `cu`, etc.) that all do the same thing. The reason for having multiple programs to do the same thing is that one has features that another does not have and vice versa. So you keep them all around. Not only is this a problem when you require both features at the same time, but it is a problem when you upgrade or modify your serial device. For example, if you change some phone numbers in your `kermit` scripts, you also have to change them in any `procomm` scripts. Some of these programs use a database but none use the same one, so you have to change multiple databases, too.

Expect tries to avoid this quagmire by reusing programs and their knowledge. Expect does not have to be told any device-specific information—it relies entirely upon the device-specific program. If you want to communicate with a serial device, Expect can spawn `tip` (or `kermit`, etc.). To communicate with sockets, Expect can spawn `telnet`. And so on. This works because each of these devices is controlled by interactive programs which in turn can be controlled by Expect.

If you have a device unique to your machine with its own interactive interface, Expect can use it. By unburdening Expect from a lot of device specific information, it is simpler to use, plus you get to use the interface with which you are already familiar.

Treating Files As Spawned Processes

In UNIX, devices are files. Or at least, it is convenient to think that they are. Devices appear in the file system, and file-like operations can be performed on them. Expect uses these beliefs to support operations like `expect` and `send`.

In fact, these can be applied to files as well. In the previous chapter, I described how you can make any file look like a spawned process—for example, by spawning a process to read it with `cat`. A more direct way is possible.

Tcl's `open` command is capable of opening files. The `open` command returns a file identifier which can be used as an argument to `gets`, `puts`, etc. Using the `-open` argument of `spawn`, the file id can be turned into a spawn id.

```
set file [open "/etc/passwd" r]
spawn -open $file
expect . . .
```

This example opens the `/etc/passwd` file and searches through it until the given pattern appears. After the `spawn`, the file behaves exactly like a process. While there is no real process, for consistency, the file must be waited for after being closed. The value returned by `wait` always indicates a normal exit and can be ignored. This allows you to write code in which it does not matter whether a real process was spawned or not.

The first two commands in the fragment above can be condensed to one:

```
spawn -open [open "/etc/passwd" r]
```

Once the file has been passed to spawn, it should not be accessed by gets, puts, or any other Tcl function. Expect and Tcl do not share buffers internally, so joint access should generally be avoided. The file will be closed automatically when the spawn id is closed. If the file must be left open after the spawn id is closed, use -leaveopen instead of -open.

The spawn id in this example cannot be written to (with send) because open only opened the file for reading. To open for writing, the w flag should be used. "w+" allows reading *and* writing. Several variations on this exist. Read Tcl's open documentation for the complete details.

While the spawn command can convert a Tcl file to a spawn id, it is also possible to do the opposite. On page 304, I will describe how to convert a spawn id to a Tcl file identifier.

Opening Ttys

Normally, Expect calls upon tty-aware programs such as tip or cu to interact with ttys. However, using the technique described in the previous section, it is possible to open ttys or other devices directly. For example, if you have a tty port named /dev/ttya, you can open it as follows:

```
spawn -open [open /dev/ttya w+]
```

Unfortunately, that is not the whole story. Tty devices must be initialized. This is something that a program such as tip would do for you. Without such a program, you must do it yourself. In the interest of generality, Expect performs no special handling depending upon the type of file it has been handed. That is up to you.

You can initialize a tty using stty with the appropriate arguments. The only hard part is figuring out the arguments. There is no standard, and the parameters can vary depending on your task.

For most tasks, you want to disable special character processing. You also want to disable echo. These are accomplished as follows:

```
stty raw -echo < /dev/ttya
```

Flags such as -echo apply to the tty input. Unlike a traditional tty to which you log in, this tty is being used to "go out". So the tty's input (in the sense that stty cares) is provided by the remote side. For example, if you use the tty to connect to another serial port, then the output of that serial port is the input of this one.

If the serial port generates parity, you may need to handle that either by disabling it or telling stty to ignore it. Another stty command suffices:

```
stty istrip < /dev/ttya
```

The istrip flag strips off the parity bit. If you need an eight-bit connection, you can modify the terminal modes of both the tty and the remote serial port after you are logged in.

Note that raw is a conglomeration of other stty modes. This includes parity on some systems, so you may have to issue the stty commands separately as I have shown here.

The dozens of flags supported by stty vary from system to system. If the stty man page is unenlightening, examine your tty modes while your are using tip (or whatever program you are trying to simulate). This will tell you what the correct configuration should be.

Bugs And Workarounds

On some systems, bugs in the operating system prevent correct operation of "spawn -open [open . . .]" on some special files. For example, on SunOS, Expect cannot detect an eof from a fifo. Yet another operating system bug prevents AIX 3.2 from detecting input from physical tty devices.[†]

Fortunately, OS bugs like these are infrequent but Expect does a number of unusual things and you must gird yourself to work around such bugs. In the next section, I will describe a workaround for the fifo problem. A similar workaround can be applied to the other problem.

Process Pipelines And Ptys

The spawn command does not provide any facility for redirection or pipelines because the need for it is almost non-existent. Automating interactive programs virtually always require much more sophisticated handling of input and output, such as looking at the output before deciding on the next input.

Rather than burden the spawn command with features that are almost never used, it is easier to call upon existing programs in those rare occasions. There are a variety of

---

† The effect of this particular bug also shows up in the failure of expect_user to read input. A patch is available from the vendor.

programs that support redirection including Tcl's open command. Tcl's open command is also capable of building pipelines.

In the previous section, I noted that fifos cannot be handled with spawn on some operating systems. The following command interposes a cat process. The "|" indicates that the following file should be started as a process rather than a file that is simply read or written.

```
spawn -open [open "|cat -u $fifo" r]
```

While seemingly redundant, the fifo eof is now handled by cat which converts this to an eof that is detectable by Expect.[†] The same solution works with other devices that are not supported by select or poll.[‡]

Additional processes can be strung together in the first argument to open by separating them with "|" symbols. Bidirectional processes and process pipelines can be generated. They require the w+ flag to indicate that they will be both read and written.

All of the files, processes, and pipelines opened by open are opened without a terminal interface. For many programs, this is a problem. They expect to be dealing with a terminal. For example, they may want to change the terminal modes. This will fail if there is no terminal involved.

In contrast, each spawned process has a terminal interface associated with it. To programs, the interface "feels" like a real tty is behind it. The program can tell the tty to echo or not echo, for example. But the tty does not physically exist. Rather, it is simulated, and for this reason is known as a *pseudoterminal* or *pty* (pronounced "pity") for short. With a pty, interactive programs work properly.

When spawn is called with -open, no pty is provided. In the rare cases that a pty is needed along with a process pipeline or redirection, /bin/sh can be spawned before invoking whatever is needed. For example, in Chapter 7 (p. 174), I described how spawn normally combines the standard output and standard error. In contrast, the following command separates the standard error of a process so that it is written to a file.

```
spawn /bin/sh -c "exec 2> error.out; exec prog"
```

It works as follows: /bin/sh is spawned. The -c flag tells /bin/sh to execute the following argument as a command. The argument is composed of two commands that will be executed sequentially.

---

† On some systems, the −u flag to cat has a negative impact on performance. Chapter 23 (p. 526) shows a fast and simple way to test for this.

‡ Deficient select or poll support is such a severe defect that it is usually documented in the brief cover notes that accompany the operating system. For this reason, it is not necessary to understand further details about select and poll, so I will not provide any.

The first command is "exec 2> error.out". This command directs the shell to associate file descriptor 2 (i.e., the standard error) with the file error.out.

The next command is "exec prog". This command runs prog. Its input and output are still associated with the input and output of the shell (from /bin/sh) which in turn are associated with the spawn id. But the standard error remains tied to the file error.out. The exec in front of prog tells the shell that prog can take over the process resources of the shell. In effect, the shell exits leaving prog in its place.

While initially this may look rather confusing and complex, the result effectively leaves only the intended process running. The shell goes away after setting up the indirection. More complex redirection and pipelines can be constructed but they usually share the same underlying ideas.

Automating xterm

Expect normally works with programs that read either from the standard input or /dev/tty. Some programs do not read their input in this way. A good example is the xterm program. xterm is an X Window System client that provides a shell in a terminal emulator. In this section, I will describe three different ways to control xterm.

The xterm program reads user input from a network socket. The standard input and /dev/tty are both ignored. Hence, spawning xterm in the usual way is fruitless.

```
    spawn xterm                        ;# WRONG
```

Interacting in this way—with no special knowledge of xterm—requires a program that can drive X applications the way Expect drives character-oriented programs. Such programs exist. However, discussion of them is beyond the scope of this book.

Instead of attempting to control an xterm, it often suffices to have an xterm execute an Expect script. For example, suppose you want to be able to pop up a window that automatically runs the chess script defined in Chapter 10 (p. 234). The following command would suffice:

```
    xterm -e chess.exp
```

The xterm continues to take input in the usual way. Therefore it is even possible to have scripts that accept user input. For example, the auto-ftp script defined in Chapter 3 (p. 83) could be started up with the following command. Once running, it is controllable from the keyboard just the way an xterm normally is.

```
    xterm -e aftp.exp
```

Both of these examples give up the possibility of controlling the xterm from another script. It is possible to do this by having xterm run an open-ended script such as kibitz. I will present an example of this in Chapter 16 (p. 355).

A third way to control xterm is to spawn it so that the script replaces the process that xterm normally spawns internally. When xterm starts, it no longer starts a new process but talks to Expect. Expect reads what the user types and tells the xterm what to display.

This is a little more complicated, but it allows a script the ability to start multiple xterms and interact with them. Rather than the xterm driving Expect, Expect drives the xterm.

In order to talk to an xterm in this way, Expect must obtain a pty and pass it to the xterm. Expect will communicate using one end of it (the *master*), and the xterm will communicate using the other end (the *slave*).

When a process is spawned, Expect allocates the pty, creates the process, and arranges for the process to use the pty for its standard input among other things. However, as I mentioned earlier, xterm does not read its standard input. xterm normally spawns its own process. It is possible to start xterm so that it does not spawn a process but instead interacts with an existing one.

To do this, xterm requires that the pty name and file descriptor be passed to it when it is invoked. Expect normally allocates the pty as the process is created, but this is too late for xterm. xterm wants the pty name on the command line. The -pty flag causes the spawn command to generate a pty with no new process.

```
spawn -pty
```

During the spawn command, the name of the slave end of the pty is written to the variable spawn_out(slave,name). This occurs whenever a process is spawned, whether or not the -pty flag is present. (In Chapter 14 (p. 315), I will show another use for this variable.)

The pty must be initialized to raw mode and have echoing disabled.

```
stty raw -echo < $spawn_out(slave,name)
```

In X11R5 and earlier versions, the flag to run xterm in slave mode is rather peculiar. The flag is -S. It is followed by two characters denoting the suffix of the pty name and an integer representing the file descriptor. For example, if the slave is named /dev/ttyp0 and the file descriptor is 6, xterm is started with the flag "-Sp06".

The two-character format does not support all pty names and because of this, many vendors have modified xterm. For example, some versions of xterm use a 0 to pad suffixes that would otherwise be one character. The following code generates the two-character suffix, padding if necessary:

```
regexp ".*(.)(.)" $spawn_out(slave,name) dummy c1 c2
if {[string compare $c1 "/"] == 0} {
    set c1 "0"
}
```

There is no backward-compatible solution for ptys that use more than three characters for identification. However, as of X11R5, xterm does not actually use the information. So the code above suffices (unless your vendor has made radical changes).[†]

xterm also requires the open file descriptor corresponding to the slave. This information is written to the variable spawn_out(slave,fd) by the spawn command.

Now the xterm can be started. It is not necessary to use spawn since the pty has already been allocated. The exec command is appropriate. An ampersand forces it to run in the background so the script can go on to do other things.

```
exec xterm -S$c1$c2$spawn_out(slave,fd) &
```

Like spawn, the exec command returns the process id of the xterm.

Once the xterm is running, Expect should close its copy of the slave file descriptor. This is done by invoking the close command with the -slave argument.

```
close -slave
```

When xterm starts this way, it immediately sends back an X window id on a line by itself. Extensions such as TkSteal can use the X window id to provide reparenting, allowing an xterm to appear in a Tk widget hierarchy. If you do not want the X window id, just discard it.

```
expect "\n"          ;# match and discard X window id
```

At this point, the xterm can now be controlled. The send command will print strings on the xterm display. The expect command will read input from the user (including insertions made using the mouse).

For example, the following code spawns a shell and lets the user interact in the xterm until X is pressed. Then the user is prompted for a return, after which the xterm is killed and the script exits. (The "interact   -u" ties the xterm and the shell together—this will be explained further in Chapter 16 (p. 350).)

---

† As this book is being written, an initial release of R6 has appeared in which the relevant flag to xterm is identical to R5. So it is likely that the description of xterm in this section will continue to be valid. I have recommended to the X Consortium that xterm be modified so that it takes complete pty names. Then, xterm would not have to make any assumptions about the structure of the names. As of this writing, the code shown here is the most portable that can be written.

```
# assume xterm is initialized, spawn id is in $xterm,
# and xterm pid is in $xterm_pid

spawn $env(SHELL)

interact -u $xterm "X" {
    send -i $xterm "Press return to go away: "
    set timeout -1
    expect -i $xterm "\r" {
        send -i $xterm "Thanks!\r\n"
        exec kill $xterm_pid
        exit
    }
}
```

A real example that is more sophisticated than this one will be shown in Chapter 16 (p. 361).

Checking For Errors From *spawn*

All of the examples so far have assumed that spawn always succeeds. The bad news is that spawn does not always succeed. The good news is that it only fails in peculiar environments or in peculiar situations. In this section, I will describe the meaning of "peculiar" and how to check whether spawn succeeded or not.

The spawn command normally returns the process id of the newly spawned process.[†] This is generally of little value since spawned processes are more easily manipulable by their spawn ids. However, it is occasionally useful to be able to kill a process using its process id rather than going through some long interaction.

```
set pid [spawn program]
. . .
# some time later
exec kill $pid
```

Once killed, the process connection should be recycled by calling close and wait.

Running out of various system resources can cause spawn to fail. For example, spawn allocates dynamic memory as well as a logical terminal interface. Failures like this can be caught using Tcl's catch command:

```
if [catch "spawn program" reason] {
    send_user "failed to spawn program: $reason\n"
    exit 1
}
```

---

† "spawn -open" returns a process id of 0 to indicate no process was spawned. There is no process to kill.

Even if spawn does not return an error, that is not a guarantee that it was entirely successful. To understand why, it is necessary to explain a little of how spawn is implemented.

The spawn command follows the traditional UNIX paradigm for running a new program. First, Expect forks. Forking is the UNIX way of generating a new process. Initially, the new process is still running Expect code. This allows Expect to prepare the environment appropriately for the new program. The last step is for Expect (in the new process) to overlay itself with the new program. At this point, the original Expect process is still running, and the new process is running the requested program.

This last step of loading the program can fail if, for example, the program does not exist. If it does not exist, the new process must communicate this back to the Expect process. Ironically, the failure of the program to be found can be communicated but not its success. The reason is that the very act of successfully running the program removes any functionality of the earlier program (i.e., Expect). Thus, the new program has no idea how to signal success or even that it should.

Because of this, the original Expect process cannot wait around for a possible failure. The spawn command returns immediately. If the process does fail however, the new process sends back an error report in such a way that the Expect process hears it at the next convenient moment—the first expect command.

Here is an example of interactively running Expect and attempting to spawn a non-existent program:

```
% expect
expect1.1> spawn noprog
spawn noprog
18961
expect1.2> expect -re .+
noprog: No such file or directory
expect1.3> puts "expect_out = <$expect_out(buffer)>\n"
expect_out = <noprog: No such file or directory>
```

The error message is returned exactly the way any other output from the spawned process is—via expect_out. Differentiating between an error from the shell and real program output from the process may be difficult, if not impossible. The recognition problem is identical to what a real human faces when using interactively starting programs from the shell. How one differentiates between an error message and real program output is left to the user.

The format of the error message is as shown above. It is the program name, followed by a colon and space, followed by your particular system's standard error message. Other messages are possible in other scenarios, such as if the file exists but is not executable.

Checking the return value of spawn (as shown above with catch) is a good idea if you want your code to be bulletproof. These kinds of errors are often due to transient conditions that may go away if the operation is retried, such as a lack of memory.

On the other hand, checking spawn's success via the first expect is less valuable. For example, if a standard utility such as /bin/sh is being spawned, there is little point in checking if it succeeded. If it did not, the computer has such severe problems that few programs will be able to continue to run.

The primary circumstance in which to check the first expect after a spawn is when the program is unknown at the time the script is written. For example, if a user can type in arbitrary command names dynamically, these names should be checked. Note that using "file executable" is a reasonable test but it is not guaranteed since there is a window between the time the file can be tested and the time it is executed, during which the file can change.

spawn -noecho

In the previous example, all of the commands were entered interactively. When this is done, the return values of all commands are automatically printed by Expect. In the case of the spawn command, the return value was the process id. In that example, the process id was 18961. The command also echoed itself as a side effect. This is not the return value. If a spawn command appears in a script, the process id will no longer be printed to the standard output, but the command itself still echoes.

This echoing is intended as a convenience for simple scripts, much as the echoing performed by the expect command itself is. Both of these can be disabled with the log_user command. However, the log_user command disables all of the spawned program's output. To disable just the echoing produced by the spawn command, use the -noecho flag. This flag affects nothing else. Here is the previous example repeated using that flag.

```
% expect
expect1.1> spawn -noecho noprog
18961
expect1.2> expect -re .+
noprog: No such file or directory
expect1.3> puts "expect_out = <$expect_out(buffer)>\n"
expect_out = <noprog: No such file or directory>
```

Here is the same example, but using "log_user 0" instead of -noecho. Notice that both spawn and expect no longer echo anything.

```
% expect
expect1.1> log_user 0
```

```
expect1.2> spawn noprog
18961
expect1.3> expect -re .+
expect1.4> puts "expect_out = <$expect_out(buffer)>\n"
expect_out = <noprog: No such file or directory>
```

In all cases, spawn still produces a return value. This and all other return values disappear if run from a script.

Example — unbuffer

Most non-interactive programs behave differently depending on whether their output goes to the terminal or is redirected. In particular, output to a terminal normally appears as soon as a full line is produced. In contrast, output that is redirected to a file or a process is buffered by much larger amounts in the name of efficiency. This difference in buffering is automatically chosen by the UNIX stdio system.

Unfortunately, this means that some simple UNIX commands do not work as nicely as you might expect. For example, suppose a slow source is sending output to a fifo called /tmp/fifo and you want to read it using od and then pipe it into a pager such as more. The obvious shell command to do this is:

```
od -c /tmp/fifo | more
```

Alas, the stdio system compiled into od sees that its output is a pipe so the output is automatically buffered. Even if od receives a complete line, od does not send anything down the pipe until the buffer has been filled.

There is no way to fix od short of modifying and recompiling it. However, by using Expect, it is possible to make od think that its output is destined for a terminal. Since Expect connects processes to a pty, this is sufficient to satisfy the stdio system, and it changes to line-buffered I/O.

A script to do this is simple. All it has to do is spawn the process and wait for it to finish. Here is a script which does this, called unbuffer:

```
#/usr/local/bin/expect --
# Name: unbuffer
# Description: unbuffer stdout of a program

eval spawn -noecho $argv
set timeout -1
expect
```

The original command can now be rewritten to use unbuffer:

```
unbuffer od -c /tmp/fifo | more
```

Most other non-interactive UNIX utilities share the problem exhibited here by od. Dealing with the stdio system is one of the few times where it makes sense to run Expect on non-interactive processes.

Obtaining Console Output

Historically, the console was a dedicated terminal to which critical messages were sent concerning the status of the computer. The idea was that a person would be watching at all times and could take immediate action if necessary. With modern workstations, there is no physical console with a dedicated operator. Instead, the console is simulated with a dedicated window. For example, in the X window system, the command "xterm -C" starts an xterm window and tells the operating system to send all console messages to it.

Expect can do the same thing with the spawn command. The -console flag redirects all console messages so that they appear to be generated from a spawned process. It is sufficient to spawn any process. Even cat will do.

```
spawn -console cat
```

A simple use for this flag is to watch for errors from device drivers. For example, when performing backups, errors writing to the backup media may be sent to the console rather than the backup program. This is a consequence of the way certain drivers are written and is surprisingly common.

By spawning the backup program using the -console flag, it is possible to catch problems with the backup that might not otherwise be reported. In Chapter 17 (p. 380), I will describe how to make an Expect script actively look for a skilled user to fix any problems encountered, and initiate a session for the user connected to the spawned process automatically.

The -console feature can only be used by one program at a time. It is also a relatively recent addition to UNIX. Therefore, it is not yet supported by all systems. The -console flag is ignored on systems that do not support the ability to redirect console output.

Setting Pty Modes From spawn

Pty modes can have a big effect on scripts. For example, if a script is written to look for echoing, it will misbehave if echoing is turned off. Suppose a script is driving a shell that prompts with a bare "% ". If the script sends the command "whoami\r", the shell might return "whoami\r\ndon\r\n% ". In this case, the response could be matched with:

```
expect -re "\r\n(.*)\r\n% "
```

If the shell did not echo its input, the shell would return "don\r\n% ". But the expect command just shown fails to match this output.

For this reason, Expect forces "sane" pty modes by default. In fact, the sane flag is known to stty, the program which configures ttys and ptys. The particulars of sane differ from system to system; however, sanity typically implies characteristics as echoing, and recognition of erase and kill characters. Expect invokes stty to set the pty, so you can be assured that Expect's version of sanity is just what your local stty thinks. If for some reason you believe stty's understanding of sane is flawed and you are not in the position to change it (i.e., you do not have the source), you can redefine it when installing Expect on your system. This is covered in the installation procedure.

Unfortunately, one program's sanity is another program's gibberish. Some programs have special demands. As an example, it is possible to interact with a shell from inside of the Emacs editor (this has nothing to do with Expect so far). The shell session appears as a normal file (or "buffer" in Emacs-speak) except that when you press return, the current line is sent as a command to the shell and the results are appended to the end of the buffer. This has many benefits. For example, with an Emacs shell session, you can use Emacs commands to directly edit the input and output.

To make the Emacs shell-session work similarly to a session outside Emacs, Emacs changes the pty modes. For example, echoing is disabled so that you can edit the command line before passing it to the shell. Also, newlines produced by programs are no longer translated to carriage-return linefeed sequences. Instead, newlines remain as newlines.

Expect scripts written for the "normal" pty modes could fail if they were to only use Emacs' idea of pty modes. To avoid this, Expect performs a three-step pty initialization which leaves the pty with a suitable mixture of Emacs and user pty characteristics.

The first step initializes the pty so that it is configured just like the user's terminal. Next, the pty is forced into a sane state (as I described earlier). In most cases, this changes nothing; however, anything too unusual is reset. This is also important when the process is running from cron where there is no terminal from which to copy attributes in the first place. Finally, any other pty modes are changed according to the requirements of the script.

Each of these steps is controllable. The first step, copying the user's terminal modes, is done unless spawn is invoked with the -nottycopy flag. The second step, forcing the pty into a sane state, is done unless spawn is invoked with the -nottyinit flag. The third step is only done if the stty_init variable is defined, in which case it is passed as arguments to the stty program.

The order that the flags are given to `spawn` is irrelevant, but they must appear before the program name. Here are several examples. In each case, *prog* stands for a program to be spawned.

```
spawn -nottyinit prog
spawn -nottyinit -nottycopy prog
set stty_init "kill ! susp ?"
spawn prog
```

The last example sets the kill character to "!" and the suspend character to "?". Conceivably, this could be useful or necessary for running or testing a particular program. The `spawn` command does not enforce any kind of pty initialization. It is possible to use `-nottycopy` and `-nottyinit` and not define `stty_init` but this is not a good idea. Ptys are not otherwise initialized by most systems.

These options may seem complex, but in most cases they are not necessary. Going back to Emacs for a moment, the default behavior of `spawn` allows the correct functioning of Expect scripts. Expect scripts may "look funny" inside of Emacs with respect to character echoing, but then, so do commands such as `telnet` and `rlogin`. If you absolutely have to have Emacs look correct, use the `-nottyinit` flag. However, you must then go to extra effort to make your scripts avoid any dependencies on echoing, line termination characters, and anything else that the Emacs terminal modes affect.

Another example of how `stty` can introduce unexpected results is with the line kill character. On some UNIX implementations, `stty` believes the @ is the default line kill character (i.e., pressing it removes all previous characters typed on the line). The @ was a popular convention many years ago. Now, it is just archaic and ^U is much more common. On such archaic systems, sending strings such as "`user@hostname\r`" ends up sending only "`hostname\r`".

Yet another problem that occasionally crops up is what to do with parity. On some UNIX implementations, `stty` believes that parity should be disabled. This confuses programs that work with 8-bit character sets. If you can not fix your local `stty`, work around the problem by using the `-nosttyinit` flag or by setting `stty_init` to `-istrip`.

Hung Ptys

Historically, UNIX systems have provided a fixed number of ptys, pre-allocating filenames in the file system for each one. Most versions of UNIX no longer do this, but there are still some that do. With a static set of ptys, it is necessary to search through the list of files. Expect performs several tests on each pty before using it. These tests ensure that no other process is still using the pty.

Usually these tests are very quick, but programs that have misbehaved and are sloppy in their pty allocation and deallocation can force Expect to take up to ten seconds, waiting for a response from a pty that is still in use.[†] Normally, Expect goes on and continues trying other ptys until it finds one that can be allocated; however, such ptys can cause problems for most other programs. For example, programs that use ptys, such as xterm and Emacs, simply give up when encountering such a pty. If you see this happening, you can try spawning a process with Expect's diagnostic mode enabled. Expect will then report the ptys it is ignoring and you can verify that each one is in use by a functioning program. In some cases, the program may have exited but left the pty in a bizarre state. Expect's thorough pty-initialization procedure will reset the pty so that other processes can use it.

You can take advantage of Expect's ability to fix ptys with the following script called ptyfix.

```
#!/usr/local/bin/expect --
spawn cat
```

Or even simpler, just put the following shell command in an alias or menu:

```
expect -c "spawn cat"
```

Restrictions On Spawning Multiple Processes

There is no explicit restriction on spawning multiple processes—any number of processes may be running under control of Expect. However, some old—perhaps *archaic* is a better word—systems do not provide a facility for listening from multiple processes simultaneously. When Expect is installed, it looks for the presence of the select or poll system call. Either of these usually indicates that Expect can listen to multiple processes simultaneously.

Some systems provide select or poll but do not allow them to be used the way Expect needs. In this case, Expect simulates this functionality using the read system call with alarms. When using read, Expect has one major restriction. Only one process can be listened to (with either expect or interact) at a time.

Fortunately, such systems are rare and growing rarer.[‡] Although you cannot run Expect with all of its power on them, you can still get useful work done even by automating one application at a time.

---

† Expect leaves a timestamp in the form of a file in /tmp recording such ptys so that later attempts do not bother waiting. The file is left even after Expect exits, allowing later Expect processes to take advantage of this information. After an hour, the next Expect deletes the file and retests the pty.
‡ Expect detects and reports at installation time if your system cannot spawn multiple processes simultaneously.

Getting The Process Id From A Spawn Id

While the spawn command returns a process id, Expect can provide this information at any time by using the exp_pid command. With no arguments, exp_pid returns the process id of the currently spawned process. The process id of a particular spawn id can be returned by using a -i flag. For example:

```
expect1.1> exp_pid -i $shell
20004
```

Do not confuse this command with pid. The pid command is a built-in Tcl command that returns the process id of the Expect process itself.

Using File I/O Commands On Spawned Processes

You cannot directly read from or write to spawned processes with puts and gets. In general, there is little need for it because you can emulate the behavior with suitable send and expect commands. Nonetheless, it may be convenient to do so at times.

Earlier, I showed how the -open flag of the spawn command converts a file identifier to a spawn id. The exp_open command does the opposite. It converts a spawn id to a file identifier that may be used with gets and puts. The file identifier will be open for both reading and writing. If exp_open is called with no arguments, it converts the spawn id of the currently spawned process. If called with a -i argument, exp_open converts the given spawn id.

By default, after calling exp_open, the spawn id can no longer be accessed using send and expect. It becomes owned entirely by Tcl and should eventually be closed in the Tcl style and without doing a wait. On some systems, processes return spurious error indications during a close operation. Expect knows to ignore these errors; however, you may have to explicitly catch them from Tcl.

```
spawn /bin/csh
set file [exp_open]
catch {close $file}
```

You may have to call flush explicitly after I/O operations because the file commands normally buffer internally. Process output that does not terminate with a newline may be impossible to read unless you disable buffering or read it explicitly with read. In the following example, the first output from telnet is read using read since it does not end with a newline.

```
% expect
expect1.1> spawn -noecho telnet
```

```
4484
expect1.2> exp_open
file5
expect1.3> read file5 7
telnet>
```

The spawn id can be left open by calling `exp_open` with the `-leaveopen` flag. In this case, both the file and the spawn id must be closed explicitly. A `wait` must be executed. As with the `-leaveopen` flag in the `spawn` command, alternation of Tcl and Expect commands is best avoided because Tcl and Expect do not share buffers internally.

Exercises

1. On page 146 of *Advanced UNIX Programming* (Prentice Hall), Marc Rochkind describes how deadlock can occur when using pipes for bidirectional communication. Why does this *not* apply to Expect?

2. Modify the `firstline` script (page 178) to make it check that the `spawn` command succeeds and that the program is successfully executed. Upon failure, send any diagnostics to the standard error and return a nonzero status.

3. On page 292, there are two commands in the string passed to `/bin/sh`. Simplify the string.

4. Write a script that starts two `xterms`, each of which use a separate shell (as usual). Make the script create a transcript of both `xterms` in a single file. Provide a parameter that switches from logging by line to logging by individual character.

5. It is possible to write a better version of `ptyfix` (page 303) using the diagnostic output from Expect. Modify the script so that when Expect reports that a pty is hung, the new version finds the process that is responsible and kills it.

In This Chapter:
- *Handling ^C*
- *Generating And Taking Actions On Signals*
- *The wait Command*
- *Taking Action When The Script Ends*

14

Signals

If at all possible, avoid signals. They are tricky to use correctly, and signal-handling code is perhaps the most difficult to debug. Despite these warnings, there are situations in which signals are the only solution. In this chapter, I will describe the reasons why you may have to deal with signals and how to handle them. I will also present related details of the `wait` and `exit` commands.

Signals

Signals are software interrupts. They can be generated for a variety of reasons such as the pressing of certain keystrokes. In cooked mode, pressing control-C usually generates an interrupt signal in the foreground process. Processes can also generate signals in other processes—or even in themselves. This is commonly referred to as *sending* or *raising* or *generating* a signal. Finally, the operating system can generate signals for a number of reasons, such as if a power failure is imminent and the system is about to halt. For more in-depth information on signals, read your local man pages.

Specific signals are commonly referred to in several ways. For example, signal number 9 is usually written as SIGKILL in C programs. However, many utilities (e.g., kill) only accept 9 or KILL (without the SIG prefix). Expect accepts all three forms (9, KILL, or SIGKILL). For clarity in this book, I like to use the C-style although I will give examples of why the other two forms are occasionally useful.

The exact list of signals varies from one system to another but modern systems include those shown in the following table. There are others but the signals shown here are the ones you are most likely to deal with in an Expect script.

Name	Description
SIGHUP	hangup
SIGINT	interrupt
SIGQUIT	quit
SIGKILL	kill
SIGPIPE	pipe write failure
SIGTERM	software termination
SIGSTOP	stop (really "suspend")
SIGTSTP	keyboard stop
SIGCONT	continue
SIGCHLD	child termination
SIGWINCH	window size change
SIGUSR1	user-defined
SIGUSR2	user-defined

Assuming you have permission, these signals can be generated by using the `kill` command from a shell script or "`exec kill`" from an Expect script. For example, from an Expect script the following command sends an interrupt signal to process 1389.

```
exec kill -INT 1389
```

Expect processes can receive as well as generate signals. In the example above, if process 1389 is an Expect process, upon receiving a signal, the process looks for a command that is associated with the signal. An associated command is known as a signal *handler* or *trap*. If there is a handler, it is evaluated. When the handler has completed execution, the script (usually) returns to what it was doing before the signal arrived.

The association between a signal and its handler is created by the `trap` command. Only one handler can be associated with a signal at a time. If you make the association from within a procedure, the association remains in effect even after the procedure returns. Each association replaces the previous one for the signal of the same name.

For example, the following command causes a script to print "bye bye" and then to exit if an interrupt signal (`SIGINT`) is received.

```
trap {send_user "bye bye"; exit} SIGINT
```

The first argument of the `trap` command is the handler. A handler can be as simple as a procedure name or as complex as a long list of commands. Here are more examples:

```
trap intproc SIGINT
trap {
    send_user "bye bye"
    exit
} SIGINT
```

A handler can also return in the middle as if it were a procedure. Any return value is discarded.

```
trap {
    if [expr $test] return
    morestuff
} SIGINT
```

Multiple signals can be associated with the same command by enclosing them in a list. The following command associates the procedure `sigproc` with the signals `SIGINT`, `SIGUSR1`, and `SIGUSR2`. Using the "SIG" prefix in a long list of signals is tiresome, so I do not specify it in such cases.

```
trap sigproc {INT USR1 USR2}
```

If you associate a common procedure with multiple signals, you can use `trap` with the –name or –number flag to find out what signal is being processed.

```
trap {
    puts "got signal named [trap -name]"
    puts "got signal numbered [trap -number]"
} {INT USR1 USR2}
```

The command "`trap -name`" returns the name without the "SIG" prefix. If you want the name with the "SIG" prefix, just prepend "SIG" to the result.

```
trap {
    puts "got signal named SIG[trap -name]"
} {INT USR1 USR2}
```

You can redefine a signal while its handler is being evaluated. The change does not take effect until the next evaluation of the handler.

Signals may be ignored by using the keyword `SIG_IGN` as the first argument of the trap command. The "SIG" and underscore are *not* optional.

```
trap SIG_IGN {INT USR1 USR2}
```

By default, most signals cause Expect to terminate ungracefully. So if you intend to send signals to Expect, you should trap them. Scripts that terminate ungracefully do not have their exit handlers run and can also leave the terminal in raw mode.

You can reset the default behavior of a signal to that defined by the operating system by using the keyword SIG_DFL. If Expect's default behavior is different than SIG_DFL, I will mention it when describing the details of each signal (later). Otherwise, you can assume Expect's default behavior is precisely SIG_DFL.

As with "SIG_IGN", the "SIG_" prefix is required in "SIG_DFL".

```
trap SIG_DFL {INT USR1 USR2}
```

Signals In Spawned Processes

Most of this chapter covers signals occurring in the Expect process itself. But signals are also of concern to spawned processes. Unfortunately, there is little Expect can do to control the signal activity of a spawned process. In particular, there is no analog to the expect command for signals.

Signals can, however, be sent. As I mentioned on page 308, the UNIX kill command can be used to send arbitrary signals to a process.

Signals in spawned processes start out with the default behavior—corresponding to SIG_DFL. Processes override this for signals that they expect and care about. However, some unexpected signals may be delivered and the Expect programmer can control this to some extent.

As an example, recall that I mentioned in Chapter 4 (p. 101) that SIGHUP is delivered to a process when the Expect process closes its side of the connection. The default behavior of SIGHUP forces the spawned process to exit. Therefore, if you want the spawned process to continue after closing the connection, you must arrange for the signal to be ignored.

A signal is initially ignored in a spawned process by using spawn with the -ignore flag followed by a signal name. The -ignore flag understands the same style of signal names as the trap command; however, the signal names must be separated, one per flag. For example, the following command creates a sleep process immune to SIGHUP and SIGPIPE.

```
spawn -ignore SIGHUP -ignore SIGPIPE sleep 1000
```

Unless the spawned process overrides this signal handling, ignored signals are also initially ignored by children of the spawned process (and so on for children related in any way to the spawned process). This is particularly important in the case of SIGHUP because hangup signals are sent to the children of a spawned process when the spawned process dies. This is analogous to the behavior of most shells where the nohup command prevents processes from receiving a SIGHUP when the shell exits.

An explanation of the rationale for this is beyond the scope of this book, but it is related to job control. Job control-aware processes such as shells do not have problems with signals since they are generally carefully written with respect to signals, and they always reset all of their signals upon initialization.

Notes On Specific Signals

Signals are highly nonportable. Their behavior varies quite a bit from one system to another. Nonetheless, it is possible to state some generalizations about each one.

SIGINT — Software Interrupt Signal

SIGINT is an interrupt signal. It is usually generated by pressing ^C from the keyboard. The specific key can be changed using stty. The signal can, of course, also be generated via the kill command. If the SIGINT handler is set to SIG_DFL, a SIGINT will cause Expect to die without evaluating exit.

By default, Expect traps SIGINT and defines it to call exit. This association is defined with the command "trap exit SIGINT", which is evaluated when Expect starts. If you redefine the exit procedure, the trap will invoke your exit.[†]

If Expect is in raw mode, the ^C will not automatically generate a SIGINT but will instead be handled like any other character. For example, interact implicitly puts the terminal in raw mode so that a ^C is sent to the spawned process. You can define a pattern to match ^C and generate a SIGINT using kill, but that is not common practice and would be confusing to users.

In Chapter 9 (p. 223), I described how the debugger is enabled if Expect is started with the –D flag. Part of what –D does is to redefine the behavior of SIGINT as follows:

```
trap {exp_debug 1} SIGINT
```

Pressing ^C will then invoke the debugger rather than causing Expect to exit. If you want to redefine SIGINT so that it performs some other action (and does not exit), you can have the best of both worlds by defining it only if the debugger is not active:

```
if ![exp_debug] {trap myproc SIGINT}
```

The procedure myproc will only be called when the debugger is not active. If the debugger is active, ^C will invoke the debugger.

[†] The exp_exit command is an alias for Expect's exit. You should either invoke exp_exit from your exit or you should change the trap to invoke exp_exit. This will make sure that the terminal modes are reset correctly. I will describe the "exp_" aliases in more detail in Chapter 22 (p. 515)

There is nothing special about using SIGINT to invoke the debugger. This is just common practice. You can associate the debugger with no interrupts, a different interrupt, or several different interrupts. For example, to associate the debugger with both SIGUSR1 and SIGUSR2:

```
trap {exp_debug 1} {SIGUSR1 SIGUSR2}
```

While Expect comes with a debugger, you are free to use a different one, arranging it so that -D calls another routine on SIGINT. To do this, define the environment variable EXPECT_DEBUG_INIT. If this variable is defined, it is evaluated instead of the default trap definition for SIGINT. In fact, you are not limited to defining a handler for SIGINT. You can define it to be any command you want.

SIGTERM — Software Termination Signal

SIGTERM is similar to SIGINT except that SIGTERM usually implies that the process should clean itself up and exit. Expect defines SIGINT to do this initially, but SIGINT is frequently redefined to do other things that allow the process to continue.

Expect's default definition of SIGTERM is:

```
trap exit SIGTERM
```

If the SIGTERM handler is set to SIG_DFL, SIGTERM will cause Expect to die without evaluating exit.

SIGQUIT — Quit Signal

SIGQUIT is similar to SIGTERM; however, SIGQUIT is not usually caught. Instead, SIGQUIT provides a simple and reliable way to kill an Expect process. This is very useful if the script (or perhaps even Expect) has a bug and you want to stop the process as soon as possible. When the Expect process dies, a file called **core** is written to the current directory. The core file provides a representation of what was in memory when the SIGQUIT was received. With a C debugger, it is possible to look at this and see what was going on.

When in cooked mode, SIGQUIT is usually generated by ^\.

SIGKILL — Kill Signal

SIGKILL cannot be caught. It provides the surest way of killing an Expect process (short of rebooting). Do not worry about the fact that you cannot catch SIGKILL. It should only be used in the event that the process has already made some obvious error or is wildly out of control. There is no point in trying to clean up gracefully as if the process actually knew what it was doing. If it did, it would not be getting a SIGKILL in the first place.

SIGCHLD—Child Termination Signal

SIGCHLD is generated on the death of a child process. By default, the signal has no effect on an Expect process. That means you do not have to define a SIGCHLD handler. However, a SIGCHLD handler is useful if you want to get the exit status but do not want to block the script while waiting for the spawned process.

Some systems claim SIGCHLD is spelled SIGCLD but Expect insists that it be spelled SIGCHLD (as per POSIX) for portability. Take this as an omen. Expect goes to great lengths to make SIGCHLD work the same on all systems, but it is still a good idea to avoid trapping or ignoring SIGCHLD to avoid portability problems.

A signal handler for SIGCHLD must call wait within the signal handler. The wait command will fail if no child is waiting, if another signal handler fails during its execution, or if other reasons not having to do with a particular process occur. Otherwise, wait returns a list describing a process that was waited upon.

The list contains the process id, spawn id, and a 0 or -1. A 0 indicates that the process was waited upon successfully. In this case, the next value is the status.

```
expect1.3> wait
13866 4 0 7
```

In this sample output, the process id was 13866 and the spawn id was 4. The 0 indicates the process was waited upon successfully and that the next value (7 in this example) was the status returned by the program.

If the spawned process ends due to a signal, three additional elements appear in the return value. The first is the string CHILDKILLED, the second is the C-style signal name, and the last is a short textual description. For example:

```
expect1.1> spawn cat
spawn cat
2462
expect1.2> exec kill -ILL 2462
expect1.3> expect; wait
2462 4 0 0 CHILDKILLED SIGILL {illegal instruction}
```

If the third element returned by wait is -1, then an error occurred and the fourth element is a numeric error code describing the error further. Additional elements appear in the return value following the style of Tcl's errorCode variable. For example, if a system error occurred, three additional elements appear. The first element is the string "POSIX". The second element is the symbolic name of the errno error code. The third element is a short textual description of it.

SIGCHLD is unusual among signals in that a SIGCHLD is guaranteed to be delivered for each child termination. (In comparison, if you press ∧C three times in a row, you are guaranteed only that at least one SIGINT will be delivered.) Therefore, the SIGCHLD handler need not call wait more than once—the handler will be recalled as necessary.

No assumption can be made about the ordering of processes to be waited on. In order to wait on any spawned process, use the flags "-i -1". Since SIGCHLD can be generated for any child (not just spawned processes), such a wait should be embedded in a catch so that other deaths can be ignored.

Here is a sample SIGCHLD handler.

```
trap {
    if [catch {wait -i -1} output] return
    puts "caught SIGCHLD"
    puts "pid is [lindex $output 0]"
    puts "status is [lindex $output 3]"
} SIGCHLD
```

Here is an example using the handler above to catch the completion of the date command. Notice that the output begins where the next command is about to be typed.

```
expect2.2> spawn date
spawn date
5945
expect2.3> caught SIGCHLD
pid is 5945
status is 0
```

SIGHUP—Hangup Signal

SIGHUP is named after "hang up" to denote the historical action of hanging up the phone line connecting a user to a computer. Most shells preserve this ritual by sending a SIGHUP to each process started by the shell just before the shell itself exits.

Thus, if a user logs in, starts an Expect process in the background, and then logs out, SIGHUP will be sent to the Expect process.

By default, SIGHUP causes the Expect process to die without executing exit. If you want the Expect process to continue running, ignore SIGHUP:

```
trap SIG_IGN SIGHUP
```

For analogous reasons, Expect sends a SIGHUP to each spawned process when Expect closes the connection to the process. Normally, this is desirable. It means that when you call `close`, the spawned process gets a signal and exits. If you want the process to continue running, add the flag "`-ignore HUP`" to the `spawn` command. If the process does not reset the signal handler, then the `SIGHUP` will be ignored.

SIGPIPE—Broken Pipe Signal

`SIGPIPE` is generated by writing to a pipe after the process at the other end has died. This can happen in pipelines started by Tcl's `open` command, and for this reason `SIGPIPE` is ignored (`SIG_IGN`) by default. If the handler is set to `SIG_DFL`, the Expect process will die without executing `exit`.

SIGWINCH—Window Size Change Signal

A `SIGWINCH` signal can be generated when the window in which Expect is running changes size. For example, if you are using X and you interactively resize the `xterm` within which an Expect script is running, the Expect process can receive a `SIGWINCH`. By default, Expect ignores `SIGWINCH`. The `SIG_DFL` and `SIG_IGN` handlers both cause `SIGWINCH` to be ignored.

Some spawned processes are not interested in the size of a window. But some processes are. For example, editors need this information in order to know how much information can fit in the window.

Initially, a spawned process inherits its window size by copying that of the Expect process. (If the Expect process has no associated window, the window size is set to zero rows and zero columns.) This suffices for many applications; however, if you wish to resize the window, you have to provide a `SIGWINCH` handler.

In some cases, it is possible to send a command to the spawned process to inform it of the window size change. For example, if the spawned process is an `rlogin` that in turn is speaking to a shell, you can send it a `stty` command. In practice, however, the spawned process is almost certainly going to be something that does not provide any direct interface (or even an escape) to the shell. Fortunately, a simpler and more portable solution is possible.

All that is necessary is to change the window size of the spawned process. The following command establishes such a handler.

```
trap {
    set rows [stty rows]
    set cols [stty columns]
    stty rows $rows columns $cols < $spawn_out(slave,name)
} WINCH
```

The "stty   rows" returns the number of rows of the local window, and "stty columns" returns the number of columns. (The assignments are not necessary, of course, but the resulting code is a little more readable.) The final stty command changes the window size of the spawned process. When stty changes the window size, a SIGWINCH is automatically generated and given to the spawned process. It is then up to the spawned process to react appropriately. For example, in the case of rlogin, the spawned process (the rlogin client) will fetch the new window size and send a message to rlogind (the rlogin server), informing it of the new size. The rlogind process, in turn, will set its window size, thereby generating a SIGWINCH which can then be detected by any application running in the remote session.

This SIGWINCH handler must have the true name of the pty of the spawned process. As written, the example handler assumes the pty name has been left in spawn_out(slave,name). However, this variable is reset by every spawn command, so you probably want to save a copy in another variable and refer to the other variable in the handler.

SIGTSTP — Terminal-Generated Stop Signal
SIGSTOP — Kernel-Generated Stop Signal
SIGCONT — Continue Signal

By default, if the suspend character (normally ^Z) is pressed while Expect is in cooked mode, Expect stops (some people say "suspends"). If a shell that understands job control invoked Expect, the shell will prompt.

```
1% expect
expect1.1> ^Z
Stopped
2%
```

Expect is oblivious to its suspension (although when it is restarted, it may notice that significant time has passed).

If you want to perform some activity just before Expect stops, associate a handler with SIGTSTP. The final command in the handler should send a SIGSTOP. SIGSTOP cannot be trapped and necessarily forces Expect to stop. Expect does not allow you to define a trap for SIGSTOP.

For example, if a script has turned echo off, the following handler changes it back before stopping.

```
trap {
    puts "I'm stopping now"
    stty echo
```

```
      exec kill -STOP [pid]
} SIGTSTP
```

When `interact` is executing, `SIGTSTP` cannot be generated from the keyboard by default. Instead, a ^Z is given to the spawned process. However, it is possible to get the effect of suspending Expect when pressing ^Z. The following command does this by having the Expect process send a stop signal back to itself. It is triggered by pressing a tilde followed by a ^Z. (I will describe these features of `interact` in Chapter 15 (p. 344).) Although the tilde is not necessary, it allows a bare ^Z to still be sent to the spawned process conveniently.

```
interact -reset ~\032 {
    exec kill -STOP [pid]
}
```

The `-reset` action automatically restores the terminal modes to those which were in effect before the `interact`. If the modes were not cooked and echo, you will have to explicitly set them with another command before stopping. I will describe this in more detail in Chapter 15 (p. 333).

When Expect is stopped, it can be restarted by typing `fg` from the shell or by sending a `SIGCONT`. Common reasons to catch `SIGCONT` are to restore the terminal modes or to redraw the screen. If `SIGCONT` is not caught, it has no other effect than to continue the process.

If Expect was stopped from an action using the `-reset` flag within `interact`, the terminal modes are restored automatically. In all other cases, you must restore them explicitly.

SIGUSR1 And SIGUSR2 — User-Defined Signals

`SIGUSR1` and `SIGUSR2` are signals that have no special meaning attached to them by the operating system. Therefore, you can use them for your own purposes.

Of course, your purposes must still fit within the capabilities of signals. For example, you must not assume that signals can be counted. After a signal is generated but before it is processed by Expect, further signals of the same type are discarded. For example, pressing ^C (and generating `SIGINT`) twice in a row is not guaranteed to do any more or less than pressing it once. `SIGUSR1` and `SIGUSR2` work the same way. Once the signal handler has run, additional signals of the same type can again be received.

The `SIGUSR1` and `SIGUSR2` signals by themselves carry no other information other than the fact that they have occurred. If you generate one of these two signals for different reasons at different times, you also need some mechanism for allowing the receiving process to know what the reason is, such as by reading it from a file.

With this lack of ability to communicate extra information, it is rather mysterious that only two such user-defined signals exist. It is similarly mysterious that more than one exists. Chalk it up to the wonders of UNIX.

By default, SIGUSR1 and SIGUSR2 cause Expect to die.

Other Signals

Many other signals exist but it is generally not useful to catch them within an Expect script for their intended purposes. You might consider using other signals as additional user-defined signals, but the details are beyond the scope of this text.

One signal specifically worth mentioning is SIGALRM. SIGALRM is reserved to Expect and must not be sent or generated artificially. Expect does not allow it to be trapped.

While not shown here, other signals are all named in the same fashion. See your /usr/ include/signal.h file for more information.

The signal.h file also defines the mapping between names and signal numbers (see page 307). The minimum signal number is 1. The -max flag causes the trap command to return the highest signal number. Identifying the signals by number is particularly convenient for trapping all signals. The trap command is nested in a catch since some of the signals (i.e., SIGSTOP) cannot be caught.

```
for {set i 1} {$i<=[trap -max]} {incr i} {
    catch {trap $handler $i}
}
```

After executing this loop, selected signals can be redefined appropriately.

When And Where Signals Are Evaluated

Signal handlers are evaluated in the global scope. Global variables are directly accessible. Local variables in current procedures are inaccessible.

Ideally, handlers are evaluated immediately after the signals are received. However, in reality there may be a delay before evaluating handlers in order to preserve the consistency of the internal data structures of Expect.

Generally, you can count on signal handlers being evaluated before each Tcl command. Consider the following command:

```
set a [expr $b*4]
```

A signal that arrives just prior to this line in a script has its handler evaluated immediately. If a signal arrives while expr is executing, expr completes, the signal handler is run, and then the set command is executed. If a signal arrives while set is executing, the handler is deferred until just before the next command in the script.

Signal handlers are also evaluated during most time-consuming operations such as I/O. For example, if an expect command is waiting for a process to produce output, signal handlers can be executed.

Because signals are handled between each command and in the middle of long-running commands, delays in handling signals should not be significant and you should not be able to notice them even when using Expect interactively. There is one exception however. If a signal handler is in the process of being evaluated, no other signal handlers can be evaluated. For example, the following fragment prints acb after a ^C is pressed.

```
trap {
    send_user "b"
} SIGUSR1

trap {
    send_user "a"
    exec kill -USR1 [pid]
    sleep 10
    send_user "c"
} SIGINT
```

The reason this fragment behaves the way it does is as follows: A ^C generates a SIGINT. The first line prints a. Then kill generates a SIGUSR1 signal back to the Expect process. But because a signal is currently being processed, the SIGUSR1 is not processed. Instead, Expect continues with the sleep command, causing the script to sleep for 10 seconds. Then c is printed. When the trap finishes, Expect processes the SIGUSR1 trap. This simply prints out b and returns. Thus, the total effect is to print acb.

Keep signal handlers short (in duration) to avoid these kinds of surprises. Even better, do not depend on the ordering of signals. If you find yourself thinking very hard about how a script is going to react to a number of signals that arrive very close to one another, you probably should be using some other communications mechanism instead of signals in the first place.

If you are just using Expect as an extension, it is possible that signals may be evaluated in a different way than described here. See Chapter 22 (p. 515) for further information.

Avoiding Problems Caused By Signal Handlers

When designing signal handlers, consider the consequences of evaluating them between any commands in your program. For example, if you manipulate a data structure from within a signal handler while the data structure is simultaneously being manipulated outside of the handler, your data structure may end up partly with new values and partly with old values.

To avoid this kind of problem, stick to simple commands set as "set sigint 1", indicating that the signal handler has been run. Outside of the signal handler, check the sigint variable when it is safe to do so and take the relevant action at that time.

Another type of problem caused by signal handlers is that they can disturb time-sensitive operations. For example, a signal handler can cause an expect command to timeout if the handler takes sufficiently long to execute.

These are just a sampling of the difficulties of using signals. Further discussion of these tricky problems is beyond the scope of this book but may be found in most advanced UNIX programming texts.

Overriding The Original Return Value

If Expect is evaluating a Tcl or Expect procedure or command when a signal occurs, it is possible to change the return code that would otherwise be returned. Given a -code flag, the trap command substitutes the return code of the trap handler for the return code that would have been returned. For example, a break command in the handler causes the interrupted loop to break. A return command causes the interrupted procedure to return. And a normal return causes a command that is failing to succeed.

Clearly, this can be very confusing and disruptive to normal script flow, so you should avoid using it if possible. However, there are valid uses. For example, you can force an interpreter command to stop what it is doing and reprompt. This can be done on ^C using the following command:

```
trap -code {
    error unwound -nostack
} SIGINT
```

The error command generates an error and the -code flag forces the error to override whatever code would have been returned. The precise handling of error in this context is further described in Chapter 9 (p. 228).

If no command is in execution when the signal occurs, the return code is thrown away. In vanilla Expect (with no change from the way it is distributed), a command is always in execution, but when using Expect with Tk for example, there can be times when no command is in execution.

Using A Different Interpreter To Process Signals

This section is only useful if you have multiple interpreters in a single process. If you are using vanilla Expect, then you can skip this section.

By default, the signal handler is evaluated in the interpreter in which the `trap` command was evaluated. It is possible to evaluate the handler in the interpreter active at the time the signal occurred by using the `-interp` flag.

For example, if you are running several simulations whose speeds are controlled by the variables `speed` (one per interpreter), you could reverse the speed by pressing ^C with the following definition in effect:

```
trap -interp {
    set speed [expr -$speed]
} SIGINT
```

Exit Handling

It is often useful to execute commands when a script is about to exit. For example, you might want to make sure all temporary files are deleted before exiting. A list of commands can be declared in such a way that it is automatically executed when the script exits. Such a list is called an *exit handler.*

To declare an exit handler, invoke the `exit` command with the `-onexit` flag followed by the commands to execute. The commands are saved and will be invoked later when the script is about to exit.

```
exit -onexit {
    exec rm $tmpfile
    puts "bye bye!"
}
```

The exit handler runs whether a script exits by an explicit `exit` command or by running out of commands in a script. Signals which normally call `exit`, in turn run the exit handler. Thus, if you press ^C and have not changed the default action for `SIGINT`, the exit handler will be called. Signals that cause an ungraceful exit (i.e., core dump) do not execute the signal handler.

There are a few things which do not make sense inside an exit handler. Redefining the exit handler inside the exit handler does not cause the new exit handler to execute. No attempt is made to execute the exit handler twice. If an error (without a `catch`) occurs in the exit handler, there can be no recovery.

The exit handler can be removed and queried in the same way as signals. An empty command removes the exit handler. If the -onexit flag is given with no handler at all, the current handler is returned.

```
expect1.1> exit -onexit foo     ;# set
expect1.2> exit -onexit         ;# query
foo
expect1.3> exit -onexit {}      ;# unset
expect1.4> exit -onexit         ;# query
expect1.5>
```

Exercises

1. Write a procedure that defines reasonable default handlers for all signals.

2. Write a script that sends signals back to itself. Do the signals arrive while the kill command is still executing? After? Long after? What happens when the system is heavily loaded?

3. On page 319, I described several problems that signals can cause even when they are caught and handled. Do these problems apply to any example scripts in this book?

4. Write a script without using signals. Reread the first sentence in this chapter.

In This Chapter:
- *Typing Shortcuts*
- *Controlling Interactions*
- *Patterns and Actions*

15

Interact

In earlier chapters, `interact` was used in a very simple way. In reality, the `interact` command simplifies many tasks and opens up a world of new problems that can be solved. In this chapter, I will describe the more common uses for `interact`. In the next chapter, I will focus on using `interact` with multiple processes.

The interact Command

In Chapter 3 (p. 82), I introduced the `interact` command in the context of a script to automate `ftp`. The script carried out the initial part of the procedure—entering the user name and password—and then returned control to the user by calling `interact`.

The `interact` command is much more flexible than that example demonstrated. `interact` can also:

- execute actions when patterns are seen from either a user or a spawned process

- allow the user to take control of a spawned process, and return control to the script for further automated interaction, any number of times

- suppress parts or all of an interaction

- connect two or more spawned processes together, pairwise or in other combinations

Many of the things `interact` does can also be done by `expect`, but `interact` can do them more easily and efficiently. In this sense, `interact` is a higher-level command than `expect`. In other ways, `expect` and `interact` are duals. They do the same thing but have a very different way of looking at the world. As I explain `interact`, I will frequently bring up `expect` to compare the similarities and contrast the differences between the two.

In its simplest form, the `interact` command sets up a connection between the user and the currently spawned process. The user's terminal is put into raw mode so that the connection is transparent. It really feels like the user is typing to the process.

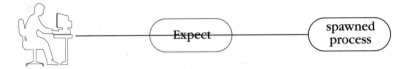

In its basic form, the interact command connects a user and spawned process.

If the spawned process exits, the `interact` command returns and the next line of the script is executed. In a simple script such as the anonymous `ftp` script (`aftp`), the `interact` command is the last line in the script, so the script simply exits when `interact` does.

Simple Patterns

Like the `expect` command, the `interact` command can execute actions upon detecting patterns. However, `interact` and `expect` behave very differently in many respects.

The syntax for specifying patterns and actions is similar to `expect`. Patterns and actions are listed as pairs of arguments. For example, the following `interact` command causes the date to be printed if ~d is typed by the user.

```
interact "~d" {puts [exec date]}
```

By default, a matched pattern is not sent on to the process. (Later, I will show how to change this behavior.) Thus, in this example, the process never sees the ~d.

Unlike the `expect` command, `interact` continues after matching a pattern and executing an action. `interact` continues shuttling characters back and forth between the user and process. It also continues matching patterns. In the example above, the ~d pattern can be matched again and again. Each time, the action will execute.

As with the `expect` command, additional pattern-action pairs may be listed. Also, all the arguments may be surrounded by a pair of braces, provided they do not all appear on the same line as the command. The `-brace` convention from the `expect` command is also supported. Here are two ways of expressing the same command:

```
interact "~d" {exec date} "~e" {eproc}

interact {
    "~d"    {exec date}
    "~e"    {eproc}
}
```

There are all sorts of useful effects that can be accomplished with these patterns. A very simple one is translating characters. For example, one of the problems with the UNIX terminal driver is that you can have only one erase character. Yet, it is often convenient to have both the backspace key and and the delete key generate erase characters—especially if you frequently switch from using one badly-designed keyboard to another. Assuming that you have defined delete as the erase character already (using `stty`), the following script translates the backspace character to a delete character. This effectively provides you with two erase characters.

```
interact "\b" {send "\177"}
```

This technique is often useful when you have to connect (e.g., `telnet`) to another computer that does not support remapping of keys at all. If you are used to pressing delete but the remote system wants to see backspace, just reverse the above script:

```
interact "\177" {send "\b"}
```

Single character translations are not the only possibility. For example, the following `interact` command maps all the lowercase keys to their Dvorak equivalents. There is no algorithmic mapping so each translation is explicitly spelled out.

```
interact {
    "q" {send "'"}    "w" {send ","}    "e" {send "."}
    "r" {send "p"}    "t" {send "y"}    "y" {send "f"}
    "u" {send "g"}    "i" {send "c"}    "o" {send "r"}
    "p" {send "l"}    "s" {send "o"}    "d" {send "e"}
    "f" {send "u"}    "g" {send "i"}    "h" {send "d"}
    "j" {send "h"}    "k" {send "t"}    "l" {send "n"}
    ";" {send "s"}    "z" {send ";"}    "x" {send "q"}
    "c" {send "j"}    "v" {send "k"}    "b" {send "x"}
    "n" {send "b"}    "," {send "w"}    "." {send "v"}
    "/" {send "z"}
}
```

Patterns can differ in length. For example, you can make abbreviations that automatically expand to their longer forms. Imagine that you are a physiologist writing a report on "glomerular nephritis". Rather than typing this phrase literally each time, you can define a few keystrokes which will expand into the full phrase.

```
interact {
    "~gn"      {send "glomerular nephritis"}
    "~scal"    {send "supercalifragalisticexpealidocious"}
    "~adm"     {send "antidisestablishmentarianism"}
    "relief"   {send "rolaids"}
}
```

The effect of this is very similar to that offered by editors such as vi's autoabbreviation mode. However, unlike these programs, interact's abbreviations work inside of any program that is running underneath Expect. If you spawn a shell and then interact with it, any program started from that shell is able to use these abbreviations.

Incidentally, I often start interact patterns with some unusual character such as a tilde (~). It is a good idea to use a special character like this. It protects you from unthinkingly entering a sequence for which interact is watching. Characters or sequences like these are knowns as escapes. Unfortunately, there is no best escape character or sequence. Tilde, for example, is often used in specifying home directories. If ~gn was someone's home directory, for instance, I would not be able to type it using the interact command above. It would always be intercepted and translated to glomerular nephritis.

One solution is to "double up" the escape to generate the same literal escape. Adding the following line to the example above guarantees that you can always be able to send a tilde followed by anything else by just typing an extra tilde first.

```
    "~~"    {send "~"}
```

With this addition, you can send ~gn by entering ~~gn even though ~gn is a pattern itself.

If you cannot give up a single character, sometimes two or even more characters work better. It is also possible to mix escapes. For example, some can start with one tilde, others with two tildes. And it is not necessary that all escapes be the same. For instance, some can start with % or ~, and yet others can have none at all as in the Dvorak script.

Actually, interact does not know anything about escapes. To it, characters are just characters. While I have been using the term "patterns", interact's default patterns have no wildcard matching at all and work in the style of the exact strings supported by the -ex flag in the expect command. For example, the following command runs starproc only when an asterisk is typed. No other character matches the "*".

```
    interact "*" starproc
```

Backslash is still interpreted directly by Tcl and therefore retains its special properties. For example, \r matches a return, \b matches a backspace, and \ followed by one to three octal digits matches a character specified by its octal value. A backslash itself can be matched by two backslashes or enclosing it in braces. Here are some examples:

```
interact "\\" proc       ;# match backslash
interact "\r" proc       ;# match return
interact "\\r" proc      ;# match backslash and r character
interact "\\\r" proc     ;# match backslash and return
```

With these `interact` patterns, there is no feedback analogous to `expect_out` to record what matched. The reason is that you can always tell what matched. The characters only match themselves, so the patterns automatically define the resulting match.

Much like the `expect` command, the `interact` command also supports regular expressions. These do provide feedback to the application; however, regular expressions are generally overkill for reading user input. More importantly, matching complicated user input in raw mode is very hard; users expect to be able to edit their input but `interact` simply passes the editing keystrokes on to the pattern matcher. For this reason, it usually makes more sense to detect these situations before they happen—by disabling raw mode temporarily and using `expect_user`. I will provide examples of this later on.

Exact Matching

This style of matching that I have used so far is called *exact* matching. It is simple to use, but you must take precaution that your patterns do not look like any of `interact`'s flags. Rather than memorizing them, the simplest way to prevent this from happening is to use the `-ex` flag. This is especially useful when patterns are stored in a variable.

```
interact {
    -ex $var action1
    -ex "-ex" action2
}
```

The first pattern above matches whatever is stored in the variable `var`. The second pattern matches the string `-ex` itself. Without the `-ex` flag, `interact` would look for `action2`.

Most of the time, you will not need to use `-ex` and you should not feel obliged to use it. The `-ex` flag is only necessary to match patterns that would otherwise be accepted as a keyword (e.g., `eof`, `timeout`) or a flag (any argument starting with a hyphen).

Matching Patterns From The Spawned Process

Output from the spawned process can be matched by using the -o flag. (Think of the "o" as standing for the "opposite" or "other direction".) The following command translates unix into eunuchs, vms into vmess, and dos into dog.

```
interact {
    -o
    "unix" {send_user "eunuchs"}
    "vms"  {send_user "vmess"}
    "dos"  {send_user "dog"}
}
```

All the patterns before the -o apply to the user keystrokes. All the patterns after the -o apply to the spawned process. For example, the following command is similar to the previous one except that if the user accidentally types one of the humorous nicknames, it is translated back to the correct name. Notice that the first three actions use send to send to the spawned process. The latter three actions use send_user to send to the user.

```
interact {
    "eunuchs" {send "unix"}
    "vmess"   {send "vms"}
    "dog"     {send "dos"}
    -o
    "unix" {send_user "eunuchs"}
    "vms"  {send_user "vmess"}
    "dos"  {send_user "dog"}
}
```

This example is artificial and may not seem to make a convincing case for using -o. In practice, matching output from a spawned process almost always requires using regular expressions, in part because process output can be very verbose.

Earlier I said that regular expressions are hard to use from interact. That is only true when reading keystrokes from users. Spawned processes, on the other hand, never do editing so the associated complexities disappear. Regular expressions are an extremely convenient way of matching output from spawned processes. I will describe regular expressions in the next section.

Regular Expressions

The interact command provides the ability to match regular expressions just like the expect command. The syntax is identical. The pattern is preceded by the -re flag.

For example, the following sends an X each time the user presses a tilde followed by any other character.

```
interact -re "~." {send "X"}
```

The tilde matches a tilde while the period matches any other character. Other special characters work as before.

When using regular expressions, it is possible to find out what characters were typed. Similar to the expect command, the interact command writes its matches to the array interact_out. If the characters ~abc were entered in the previous example, interact_out(0,string) would be set to ~a. The bc would be sent on to the spawned process and would not be saved anywhere.

As before, the -indices flag causes indices to be saved as well. Using this flag, the complete set of assignments would be:

```
set interact_out(0,start)   "0"
set interact_out(0,end)     "1"
set interact_out(0,string)  "~a"
```

The number 0 plays the same role that it did in the expect command. Parentheses can be used to pick out submatches. Matching strings are stored in interact_out using the indices 1 through 9.

There is no buffer element in interact_out as there is in expect_out. The reason for this is that the interact command processes unmatched characters as they arrive. So by the time a match occurs, unmatched characters are no longer present. Hence, matches *always* start with the first character remaining in the output buffer. I will revisit this concept shortly (page 331). For now, just remember that the buffer element of interact_out is never written. In theory, it would always have the same value as the "0,string" element so the buffer element is redundant and omitted for efficiency.

A simple use for interact_out is shown in the next script, written to aid a person who was unable to press two keys at the same time. Uppercase letters were not a problem—the user could press the shift-lock key, then the letter, then the shift-lock again to go back to lower case. But control characters could not be entered in a similar fashion because there was no way to lock the control key down.

I used a two character escape—after entering a / and \, the next character would be turned into its control equivalent. This worked out well. I did not want to reserve a single character as an escape mechanism—all the single characters might have to be entered, and it was very intuitive to remember since the sequence /\X graphically looks like ^X, a common way of writing "control-X" in text.

```
spawn $env(SHELL)
interact -re "/\\\\(.)" {                ;# match /\char
    scan $interact_out(1,string) %c i
    send [format %c [expr $i-96]]
}
```

The first command spawns the user's requested shell. The second command performs the interaction with the appropriate regular expression. The pattern /\\\\(.) matches the three character sequences beginning with / and \. The four backslashes are required to match a literal backslash because inside double-quotes, Tcl represents a backslash by two backslashes and the regular-expression pattern matcher does the same thing. (See Chapter 4 (p. 91) for a complete explanation of this.)

The remaining commands are executed if there is a match. The variable interact_out(1,string) contains the character itself. Tcl's scan command converts the character to its integer equivalent in ASCII. Subtracting 96 converts a lower-case value to a control value, and then format converts the integer value back to an ASCII character. Finally, the send command sends it on to the spawned process.

This all looks complicated but it works nicely and executes quickly. The script was a very short solution for the problem. This technique can be applied to many other problems. As an exercise, rewrite the Dvorak script (shown earlier) so that it uses a single action instead of one for each possible character.

As I mentioned earlier, regular expressions are used more often to match output from a spawned process than from a user. A simple but common use is to detect and deal with system inactivity monitors. For example, a VMS system used by a colleague of mine logs users out after 15 minutes of inactivity in the top-level shell (called "DCL"). DCL starts warning after 10 minutes of inactivity. The warnings look like this:

```
%DCL-W-INACT, session inactive for more than 10 minutes - you will
    be logged out in 5 minutes.
```

There is no way of disabling this behavior or message from VMS. To avoid the messages, they use the following interact command:

```
interact -o -re "%DCL-W-INACT.*\r\n" {
    send "show time\r"
}
```

The regular expression matches the warning message whenever it appears. The matched characters themselves are discarded. The .*\r\n near the end allows it to absorb all of the error message without specifying the entire text. Next, a very simple command (show time) is sent which resets the inactivity timer.

The result is that users see timestamps every 10 minutes when they are idle. But they see no irritating messages, and more importantly, they are not logged out automatically.

With one additional **expect** command in the action (expect -re ".*$prompt"), the timestamp and following prompt could be absorbed as well. This might be useful if you are trying to build a seamless application for users who should not have to know what is going on behind the scenes.

The **talk** program sends messages to the console window describing the user requesting the connection. A typical message looks like this:

```
Message from Talk_Daemon@lobotomy at 0:55 ...
talk: connection requested by bimmler@research.
talk: respond with:  talk bimmler@research
```

This message can be captured using the -console flag described in Chapter 13 (p. 300). The following script uses this flag and the resulting message to automatically start an xterm that runs a talk session back to the original user.

```
spawn -console $env(SHELL)
interact -o -re "talk: respond with:  talk (\[^ \r]*)\[ \r]" {
      exec xterm -e talk $interact_out(1,string) &
   }
```

The pattern is not quite trivial. What is not apparent when looking at the message is that talk may pad the username with spaces. Hence, the pattern has to go to some effort to allow the username to terminate at either a space or return character. Can you think of a better pattern for this?

What Happens To Things That Do Not Match

As characters are entered, they are compared to the patterns. Characters that do not match any of the patterns are sent to the spawned process. This includes characters before and after any matches. Any characters involved in a match are not sent to the spawned process. Consider the following interact command, which sends "hugs and kisses" if it sees XOX.

```
interact "XOX" {send "hugs and kisses"}
```

If the user types AXOXB, the spawned program receives "Ahugs and kissesB". The A does not match so it is sent literally. The XOX is replaced by the phrase "hugs and kisses". And the trailing B does not match so it is sent literally.

If the user types AXOYB, the spawned program receives AXOYB. The pattern XOX cannot match any part of what was entered, so it is all sent on.

If the user types XOXO, the spawned program receives "hugs and kissesO". The first XOX matches so it is translated and sent on, but the O that remains cannot possibly match XOX so it is sent literally.

If the user types XOXOX, the spawned program receives "hugs and kissesO" following the logic of the previous case. The trailing X can match the pattern XOX if another OX is entered so the interact command waits for more characters to be entered before deciding whether to send on the X or not. Suppose the user instead enters Z. In this case, the X can no longer match so interact sends the string XZ to the spawned process. What would have happened if the user entered another X rather than a Z? The new X would be eligible to match but the previous could no longer match so the previous X would be sent to the spawned process. The user will have typed XOXOXX and the spawned process will have received "hugs and kissesOX". The last X remains with interact waiting for more characters.

To summarize, the interact command buffers input until it can decide whether characters can or cannot match. If they cannot match, they are removed from the buffer and sent to the spawned process. If they match, their associated action is executed and the characters are removed from the buffer. And if they might match if more characters arrive, nothing at all happens—the characters simply remain buffered. This buffering behavior allows interact to do "the right thing" no matter how slowly or quickly characters are entered.

More Detail On Matching

If two or more patterns can match the same output, only one action will be executed. The action corresponds to the pattern that appears first in the command. This is just the way the expect command works. Here is an example that has both an exact pattern and a regular expression. When abc is entered, action1 is executed while action2 is executed if axc is entered. If the patterns were reversed, the exact pattern would never match since the regular expression would always match first.

```
interact {
    "abc" action1
    -re "a.c" action2
}
```

Pattern matching works differently in one respect between expect and interact. The expect command attempts to match a pattern beginning at every place in the input. Only after failing to match anywhere will expect try another pattern. In contrast, if interact fails to match a pattern starting from a particular place in the input, it then tries the next pattern beginning at the same place in the input.

The difference is only noticeable in a situation where two or more patterns can match in the input. This does not normally occur in user input but can be common when making substitutions in spawned process output, such as when using -o. Earlier I showed an example of -o. Here it is again:

```
interact {
    -o
    "unix" {send_user "eunuchs"}
    "vms"  {send_user "vmess"}
    "dos"  {send_user "dog"}
}
```

Now consider what happens when a spawned process produces the following output:

```
This software runs on both vms and unix.
```

Both unix and vms appear in the output so both can potentially match. Although unix is the first pattern listed, it appears later in the output so it does not match at first. Instead, vms matches and its action is executed. The input from "This software" up to "vms" is removed from the output and interact continues running. It then matches unix and the corresponding action is executed. The resulting output looks like this:

```
This software runs on both vmess and eunuchs.
```

With the expect matching algorithm, vms would not have been matched. Reversing the order of the patterns would change this behavior—allowing expect to match vms. But then, expect would misbehave if the order of vms and unix were reversed in the output.

There is no way to make expect work precisely as interact does and vice versa— which is partly why there are two different commands. Generally though, expect and interact are used for very different types of interaction, and their algorithms are well suited to their purpose. The expect command is primarily used to look for responses or prompts where it is important not to be distracted by things in the middle that may otherwise resemble patterns. In contrast, the interact command is not normally used for recognizing prompts but instead makes substitutions wherever they appear.

Echoing

Normally, the interact command depends on the spawned process to echo characters. For example, when you have spawned a shell and are interacting with it through the interact command, all the printable characters that you type are echoed by the shell. Nonprintable characters are not usually echoed back but instead invoke special actions such as erasing previous characters or generating signals. As with echoing, this special processing of nonprintables is also handled by the shell. The interact command does no special processing. It just shuttles characters back and forth.

The `interact` command works the same way when matching patterns. That is, no special action is taken to echo characters. However, because the characters are being buffered and not sent on to the spawned process, you will not see them appear on your screen. This is similar to the way the `tip` program works. `tip` does not echo its escape character unless additional characters are entered that force the escape not to match any known sequence.

For patterns that match short character sequences, the lack of echoing is rarely a problem. In most cases, users do not need to see a single character being echoed before they enter the next one. But patterns that are *long enough* (however you choose to define this) can use some sort of feedback. A simple strategy is to echo the typed characters.

By preceding a pattern with the `-echo` flag, `interact` echoes characters that match a pattern. Partial matches are also echoed. This echoing is most useful with actions that cause a local effect, such as modifying the behavior of a script. In this case, the user might not otherwise get any feedback.

The following script behaves similarly to the UNIX `script` command, which records all input and output in a file called `typescript`. However, this script also allows the user to turn recording on and off by typing ~r (to record) or ~s (to stop recording). This can be used to avoid recording things such as `vi` or `emacs` editor interactions in the middle of a longer shell session. The script starts with recording disabled.[†]

```
spawn $env(SHELL)
catch {exec rm typescript}
interact {
    "~s" {log_file}
    "~r" {log_file typescript}
}
```

As is, the script gives no feedback when the user types ~s or ~r, nor when the actions are executed. Adding `-echo` allows the escapes to echo.

```
interact {
    -echo "~s" {log_file}     .
    -echo "~r" {log_file typescript}
}
```

Once patterns are completely matched, you can add any kind of additional feedback you like. For example:

```
interact {
    -echo "~s" {
```

---

† The `catch` around the `exec` catches systems on which `rm` complains if no file is present. POSIX standardizes the `-f` flag to prevent such a diagnostic, but some systems complain anyway. Use `catch` to be maximally portable.

```
            send_user "\n stopped recording\n"
            log_file
        }
        -echo "~r" {
            send_user "\n recording\n"
            log_file typescript
        }
    }
```

The \n at the beginning of each send_user puts the message on another line, but you can take advantage of what is already on the screen to accomplish interesting effects. For example, you can incorporate the echoed keystrokes into new messages by writing the send_user commands as follows:

```
send_user "topped recording\n"   ;# prefaced by "s"
send_user "ecording\n"           ;# prefaced by "r"
```

This kind of thing can be very cute but generally leads to torturous code, so I only recommend it in very simple cases.

Avoiding Echoing

A problem with -echo is that a user may start entering a pattern that echoes but then go on to enter other characters that do not match the remainder of the pattern. The buffered characters plus the new ones will be sent to the spawned process. Assuming that the spawned process echoes them, if a pattern using -echo was causing them to echo already, the user will see characters echoed twice.

For example, in the recording script above, suppose the user enters ~q. The tilde matches and is echoed by Expect. The q does not match, so the tilde and q are sent to the spawned process and are likely echoed by the spawned process. Unfortunately, there is no trivial way to "unecho" a character without getting involved in knowing how to erase characters on the screen as well as what was on the screen in the first place. So the user ends up seeing "~~q"—one tilde too many.

There is no perfect solution for this problem except to avoid it to begin with (perhaps by not using -echo at all). But the next best possibility is to choose patterns that are less likely to match at any point unless the user is definitely entering a pattern.

Giving Feedback Without -echo

In practice I rarely use -echo. If the user really needs feedback, I give it immediately after recognizing that a pattern is being entered. There is no special support for this. Instead, simply use the escape prefix itself as the sole pattern and then pass control to another procedure that carries out the rest of the recognition. Here is an example from a script which uses ~~ to start commands.

```
interact "~~" cmd
```

In the cmd procedure, the user can now be directly prompted for commands:

```
proc cmd {} {
    send_user "command (g, p, ? for more): "
    expect_user {
        "g"     get_cmd
        "p"     put_cmd
        "?"     help_cmd
        "~"     {send "~~"}
        ... and so on
    }
}
```

The user now clearly knows what they are dealing with because the prompting is very explicit. There is no way for the user to be confused about echoing because the two-tilde sequence always invokes the cmd procedure, which in turn entirely suspends the interact until the procedure returns.

Note that if the user really intended to enter two tildes and not have them interpreted as a command, another tilde has to be entered. This is a fairly standard and customary inconvenience with interactions that suspend interact commands. This style is identical to that used by the UNIX telnet command when its escape is entered.

Telling The User About New Features

In the examples so far, the escape sequences were layered on top of the spawned process. In each case, the user must be informed of these new commands in order to take advantage of them. Indeed, the more obvious the underlying spawned process is, the more likely the user is to forget that there are extra commands available.

Printing out documentation while the program is running can be very helpful and is easy to do. The previous script showed one such example—printing out a list of choices when an escape prefix is entered. Here are some others.

The following extract is from a script that layers several commands on top of the traditional ftp client to enable it to perform recursive ftp. (Called rftp, this script comes with Expect as an example.) These new commands are entered as ~g (get recursively), ~p (put recursively), and ~l (list recursively).

```
puts "Once logged in, cd to the directory to be transferred and\
              press:\n"
puts "~p to put the current directory from the local to the remote\
              host\n"
puts "~g to get the current directory from the remote host to the\
              local host\n"
puts "~l to list the current directory from the remote host\n"
if {[llength $argv] == 1} {
   spawn ftp
} else {
   spawn ftp [lindex $argv 1]
}
```

When the script starts up, it prints the messages above, which describe the new commands. Then the script drops into an `interact` so that `ftp` can enter its usual dialogue. The tilde escape works well, because `ftp` does not use tilde for anything anyway.

Below is the complete version of the script to emulate the UNIX `script` command. A couple of things have been added to make it more like the original, but most important is the message that tells the user about the new commands. This message prints out immediately when the script starts. The first shell prompt then follows on a new line.

```
log_file typescript
spawn -noecho $env(SHELL)
send_user "recording to file typescript\n"
send_user "~s to stop recording, ~r to record\n"
interact "~s" {log_file} "~r" {log_file typescript}
send_user "recording to file typescript complete\n"
```

Here is how it looks to the user when run:

```
28% newscript
recording to file typescript
~s to stop recording, ~r to record
1%
```

Sending Characters While Pattern Matching

By default, characters are not sent to the spawned process until either a match is made or no match is possible. Characters that may potentially match are buffered. It is occasionally useful to disable this buffering.

The buffering is disabled using the `-nobuffer` flag. Using this flag, all characters are sent to the spawned process whether or not they match, do not match, or might match in the future.

For example, a site had a modem that was available to all users. The site administrators wanted to monitor the phone numbers being dialed. Using `tip` or some other interactive program, there was no way of recording the numbers. They used the following fragment in a script that ran on top of `tip`.

```
proc lognumber {} {
    interact -nobuffer -re "(.*)\r" return
    puts $log "[exec date]: dialed $interact_out(1,string)"
}
interact -nobuffer "\ratd" lognumber
```

The `interact` command (see last line) passes all characters to the spawned process. If the user presses return followed by `atd`, the `lognumber` procedure is invoked. The return forces the command to be entered at the beginning of a line—just one more safeguard against detecting the pattern at the wrong time.

Unlike the example on page 336, `lognumber` records everything until another return is pressed. The characters between the first `\ratd` and the next `\r` are the phone number. Because of the `-nobuffer` on the second `interact` command, the phone number is sent to the spawned process and echoed normally. The user cannot tell that the number is being recorded.

When the final return is pressed, the pattern matches and the `return` action is executed. The `return` action simply forces the `interact` to return to its caller (more on this in the next section), and the next command, `puts`, executes. The `puts` records the date and the phone number in a log file.

The log file will eventually look something like this:

```
Wed Aug 25 21:16:28 EDT 1993: dialed 2021234567
Wed Aug 25 23:00:43 EDT 1993: dialed 3013594830
```

The phone numbers in the log file will also contain things like backspaces or whatever erase characters the user might press to delete characters and fix errors. You could, of course, write a procedure to interpret these and strip them out after they are matched but before they are put in the log.

```
interact -nobuffer -re "(.*)\r" return
set number [cleanup $interact_out(1,string)]
puts $log "[exec date]: dialed $number"
```

A much easier solution is just to change to cooked mode temporarily and call **expect** to read the number. However, this approach also has a drawback in this example—users could conceivably press `\ratd` in some other context besides dialing a modem. In that case, you may well get a "number" that turns out not to be a number at all. In this example, the likelihood is pretty low—`\ratd` is a very unusual character sequence. In the general case, more heuristics could be added but there is no sure-fire way to know. For example, the user could be writing a manual on how to dial a modem. Obviously, making this look like a number was being dialed could be crucial to the task!

The continue And break Actions

Like the `expect` command, it is possible to have the `interact` command cause its caller to `break` or `continue`. Each of these can be used as an action. For example, in the following loop, if a user presses "+", `interact` returns and the `while` loop breaks.

```
while {1} {
    interact "+" break
}
```

The `continue` command works similarly. In the following loop, if a user presses "+", the `interact` returns and the loop breaks. If the "-" is pressed, the `interact` returns, and the `while` loop continues.

```
while {1} {
    interact "+" break "-" continue
}
```

The return Action

By default, the `return` command does not behave in a way analogous to `break` or `continue`. The `return` command does *not* cause the caller to return. Instead, when used as an action, `return` causes `interact` itself to return.

For example, consider the following commands:

```
interact "X" return
puts "interact done"
```

If the user presses X, the `interact` command returns and the `puts` command executes.

This behavior is very useful when you have a problem that is *almost* automated but has sections that require attention. The script will do most of the work, but you can grab control when necessary. You can interact and then return control to the script.

For example, `fsck`, the file system checker, looks for discrepancies in the file system. `fsck` describes the problems it encounters and interactively asks whether it should fix the problem. `fsck` waits for a y or n as an answer. The following script automatically answers one type of question yes and another type no. Everything else causes control to be turned over to the user via the `interact` command.

```
while 1 {
    expect {
        eof                      break
        "UNREF FILE*CLEAR\\?"    {send "y\r"}
        "BAD INODE*FIX\\?"       {send "n\r"}
        "\\? "                   {interact + return}
    }
}
```

When the user is through interacting, a plus causes `interact` to return, after which the script resumes control and continues answering questions.

In this example, control is completely turned over to the user. This is especially useful when the situation is very complicated and the user might need to explore things a lot. In more controlled situations—for example, when you do not trust the user or when the user does not understand what is happening behind the scene—the script should stick with `expect_user` and `send_user` commands.

It is also possible to have `interact` cause a `return` in its caller. This is more like what the `expect` command does with a `return` action. This behavior is useful if you call `interact` from within a procedure. The caller will return if `interact` executes the `inter_return` command. For example, the procedure below returns if a plus is pressed. If a minus is pressed, the `interact` command ends, but the procedure continues executing the next command after `interact`.

```
proc x {} {
    interact {
        "+" {inter_return}
        "-" {return}
    }
    send ". . ."
    expect ". . ."
```

In Chapter 11 (p. 250), I presented a script that used `expect` commands to handle answerback at login. Answerback requires communications to flow in both directions, and this should make you think of `interact`. The earlier script required nine lines to solve the problem. Using `interact`, it is possible to handle answerback using only one line:

```
interact -o -nobuffer $prompt return
```

This command permits the spawned process to interact with the terminal. When the prompt appears, `return` is executed which causes `interact` itself to return. The `-nobuffer` flag allows the prompt to appear in the output even though it has been matched.

This same idea can be used to convert the `rlogin` script in Chapter 5 (p. 122) into a `telnet` script. Remember that the script provided an interactive `rlogin` session with the same directory as the one on the local host. The script assumed that rlogin does not prompt for either account or password. In comparison, telnet is guaranteed to prompt. The solution is to substitute the code above in place of the wait for the prompt done by an **expect** command.

Here is the resulting script using telnet:

```
#!/usr/local/bin/expect --
# telnet-cwd - telnet but with same directory

eval spawn telnet $argv
if [info exists env(EXPECT_PROMPT)] {
    set prompt $env(EXPECT_PROMPT)
} else {
    set prompt "(%|#|\\\$) $"              ;# default prompt
}
interact -o -nobuffer -re $prompt return
send "cd [pwd]\r"
interact
```

The Default Action

The interpreter command lets you interactively give commands to Expect and is described further in Chapter 9 (p. 225). The interpreter command is very useful when debugging scripts or avoiding having to hardcode commands beyond some point where the interactions are stable enough. Just call interpreter with no arguments.

```
interpreter
```

The last action in an interact may be omitted in which case it defaults to inter-preter. The following two commands are equivalent:

```
interact X
interact X interpreter
```

The first form is simply a shorthand. There is no other inherent value to omitting the action. Note that this shorthand can only be used with the final pattern—with any other pattern, the subsequent pattern would be misinterpreted as the action to the previous pattern. Consider the following two commands. If X is pressed, the first command invokes interpreter while the second mistakenly invokes pattern.

```
interact X interpreter pattern action
interact X pattern action                  ;# OOPS!
```

It is common to write scripts that end by leaving the user in an interact command, interacting with a process in raw mode. The interpreter command provides a way to get back out to Expect before the script terminates. The environment can then be explored or manipulated while the script is still running.

While I just said that omitting the action is only a shorthand, it is intended to be a compellingly convenient shorthand. Indeed, it should be so compelling that you should never use `interact` without some sort of escape unless you have intentionally considered all the implications. When prototyping, get used to writing "`interact   X`" (or whatever your favorite escape character is) rather than just `interact`. It will save you in lots of situations such as when the spawned process hangs.

Detecting End-Of-File

Normally, a spawned process generates an eof when it exits. This can be detected by using the special pattern `eof`. When an eof occurs, the following action is executed. The syntax is identical to `expect`. For example, the following command prints out a message when an eof occurs. The `return` causes `interact` to return to its caller.

```
interact -o eof {
    puts "detected end-of-file"
    return
}
```

If an eof occurs but no `eof` pattern is given, the `return` action is executed by default. So you could write the fragment above more simply as just:

```
interact
puts "detected end-of-file"
```

You usually want to end an action for the `eof` pattern with `return`. It rarely makes sense to continue the interaction if the spawned process has exited. However, the next chapter has examples where it is meaningful to continue the interaction.

When `interact` detects an eof, it automatically closes the connection to the spawned process so that there is no need to call `close` explicitly. This is identical to the behavior of `expect` when it detects an eof. One tiny difference between `expect` and `interact` is that `interact` can never detect an eof from the user. Because `interact` puts the terminal into raw mode, the user has no way of generating an end-of-file. In `expect`, a ^D closes the input, but in `interact` a ^D is just sent on to the spawned process.

Matching A Null Character

The interact command can match a null character using the null pattern. This pattern works the same way as in the expect command. See Chapter 6 (p. 155) for more information.

Timing Out

The special timeout pattern matches after a given amount of time. Unlike the expect command, the timeout pattern does not depend on the timeout variable. Instead, the timeout is given after the keyword itself. The timeout is specified in seconds. The action follows the number of seconds. For example, the action in the interact command below is executed if the user presses no keys for more than an hour.

```
interact timeout 3600 {
    send_user "Idle for 1 hour - you are being logged out"
    return
}
```

In this example, the output of the spawned process is not timed. This is useful in preventing irrelevant system messages ("System going down at midnight.") from making the session seem active.

The interact command uses explicitly specified timeouts so that you can use different timers simultaneously. For instance, the following fragment times out the user after 10 seconds and the spawned process after 600 seconds.

```
interact {
    timeout 10 {
        send_user "Keep typing—we pay you by the character!"
    }
    -o
    timeout 600 {
        send_user "It's been ten minutes with no response.\
                I recommend you go to lunch!"
    }
}
```

On many systems, the following script can be used to fake out shells that automatically exit after periods of inactivity. The script works by detecting the inactivity and sending a space and immediately removing it.

```
spawn $env(SHELL)
interact timeout 3000 {send " \177"}
```

As shown here, the script waits for a little less than an hour under the assumption that the spawned program's timeout is exactly an hour. You can modify or parameterize the timeout. Some programs will need different keystroke fakes. For example, editors such as `emacs` and `vi` are more appropriately faked by sending ^G and escape respectively. In contrast, `ftp` would need a simple but real command such as "`binary\r`" to force the client to actually send something to the server since it is the `ftp` server that times out, not the client.

The following code achieves an effects similar to the fragment in Chapter 6 (p. 146). Both watch for output containing a pattern where each character is not separated from the next by more than $timeout seconds.

```
set status bad
interact {
    -o
    timeout $timeout inter_return
    $pattern {set status ok}
}
```

This code works differently but ultimately does much the same thing. The `-o` flag makes the subsequent patterns apply to the output of the spawned process. If too much time occurs between characters, the `inter_return` action causes the `interact` to complete. If `$pattern` appears in the output, a status variable is set and the `interact` command continues waiting for more characters to arrive (or the timeout to occur). The only significant difference in the code is that the buffering is done internally by `interact` rather than explicitly in the user-supplied actions.

A timeout value of -1 is equivalent to infinity. The associated action can never be executed. This is useful when the need for a timeout is not known in advance. Rather than rewriting the `interact` command dynamically, the timeout can be suppressed just by an appropriate variable assignment.

Compare:

```
interact timeout $timeout $action
```

with:

```
if {$need_timeout > 0} {
    interact timeout 100 $action
} else {
    interact
}
```

More On Terminal Modes (Or The -reset Flag)

The `interact` command puts the terminal into raw mode so that all characters can pass uninterpreted to the spawned process. When a pattern matches, actions are executed in raw mode as well. Usually this works well. Most actions do not depend on the terminal mode. For example, the following commands are all terminal-mode independent:

```
set a [expr 8*$a]
send "k\r"
send_user "hello\n"
```

You may be surprised that the last command works correctly since it includes a newline. Normally, newlines become linefeeds in raw mode. However, the `send_user` command automatically translates newlines to carriage-return linefeed sequences when the terminal is in raw mode. (See Chapter 8 (p. 197) if you want to disable this.) Thus, you can write such commands and not worry about the mode.

Some commands are mode dependent. Here are three example commands, each of which is mode dependent.

```
system cat file
exec kill -STOP [pid]
expect -re "(.*)\n"
```

The first command ("`system cat ...`") executes a program that writes directly to the standard input and output. The program assumes the terminal is in cooked mode and will misbehave if it is not. A common symptom of this misbehavior is displayed in the following output:

```
this is line one
                this is line two
                                this is line three
                                                and so on
```

The next command (`exec kill ...`) suspends the Expect process, placing the user back in the original shell. Shells that do not force cooked mode will behave incorrectly, leaving processes to run in raw mode when they expect cooked mode.

The last command (`expect ...`) is intended to read a single line in cooked mode. (This is similar to "`gets stdin`".) Not all `expect` commands require cooked mode. In fact, the example on page 336 was specifically intended to work in raw mode. However, when accepting long strings via `expect_user`, it is helpful to be in cooked mode to allow the user to edit the strings.

The `expect` command above checks for the newline character explicitly. This could be changed to look for either the linefeed or return character, but the cooked mode editing would still be lacking. The only way to obtain that is to go to cooked mode.

The simplest solution to fix all of these is to use the -reset flag when defining the action. For example, to define that ^Z (ASCII 32 in octal) suspends the Expect process, you can write the following:

```
interact -reset "\032" {exec kill -STOP [pid]}
```

The other actions could be written similarly. When the actions return, the mode is reset in the other direction—back to raw.

The -reset flag does not specifically force the terminal into cooked mode. Rather, it forces the terminal into whatever mode was set just before the interact command was executed. This allows you to set up your own (however bizarre) definition of a "normal" mode and flip between it and raw mode inside of interact and actions.

Unfortunately, this ability to set the "normal" mode means that -reset may not have the desired effect inside of an interact command that was in turn invoked from another interact. If you want cooked mode in such cases, you have to explicitly set it using stty in the action. Fortunately, this kind of situation is extremely uncommon.

If you do explicitly set the terminal mode inside an action without using -reset, reset the mode before returning to the interact. If you do not reset it, interact will continue running with your new terminal modes.

In Chapter 8 (p. 206), I mentioned that characters can be lost when terminal parameters are modified. This problem carries over to using -reset as well, since -reset potentially modifies terminal parameters. Fortunately, users do not type very quickly so this is rarely a problem; conceivably, however, this problem could arise if interact were used as a noninteractive filter. If you need absolute assurance that characters will not be lost, do not use the -reset flag.

Example — Preventing Bad Commands

The following fragment demonstrates how -reset could be used to prevent a user from entering certain commands. For example, suppose you want to provide an interface to another program that allows two commands that you would rather people not enter. You want to allow any others, just not these two.

Consider the following reasonable-looking but incorrect approach:

```
set badcmds "badcmd1|badcmd2"          ;# WRONG
interact -re "$badcmds.*\r" {           ;# WRONG
    put "command not allowed\r"         ;# WRONG
}                                        ;# WRONG
```

But as with the earlier modem monitor script, users can enter command-line editing characters to force the pattern to fail. For example, "ba<backspace>adcmd1" does not match the `interact` pattern and will be accepted by the spawned process.

One solution is to recognize the program prompt and shift into cooked mode while the user enters a command. Any command not in `badcmds` will be allowed. This algorithm could also be reversed to allow only a set of good commands.

```
set badcmds "badcmd1|badcmd2"
interact {
    -o -reset -nobuffer -re $prompt {
        expect_user {
            -re "^$badcmds.*\n" {
                puts "Command not allowed\n"
            }
            -re "(.*)\n" {
                send "$expect_out(1,string)\r"
            }
        }
    }
}
```

This script can also be written as an `expect` loop with an `interact` inside of it—similar to the one above but "inside out". How you structure the script is not that important. What is important is that you use cooked mode to read the results of potentially edited input. In general, if the spawned process is using cooked mode, then your script should too. Conversely, if the spawned process is using raw mode, your script should also.

There are some programs that provide much more sophisticated interfaces than what can be supported in cooked mode. In general, trying to follow what they are doing can require a lot of work. This is unfortunate but understandable—they are internally complicated and any script that attempts to track them will be also.

Exercises

1. Modify the Dvorak keyboard script (page 325) to so that it uses a single **send** command. Use an array to provide the mapping between input and output. Can you tell any difference in speed between the two implementations?

2. On page 330, I showed a script that responded to an inactivity message. However, some systems do not print a warning message. Rewrite the script so that it does not require a warning message. Experiment with resetting the timer by sending a null or a ^Q or a space-delete sequence.

3. Modify the `script` script (on page 334) so that it strips out carriage returns. Does "`stty -ocrnl`" help? How about "`tr -d '\015'`"?

4. Write a script to boot and simultaneously allow interaction with an auxiliary processor such as a vxWorks board. Make the script respond appropriately if the board hangs for more than one minute or if the board is power-cycled behind Expect's back.

5. Write a script that allows you to repeat a command in the shell (or any program) by pressing a single function-key. Write a second version that suspends this behavior when the shell is not prompting.

6. Write a script that provides "hotkey" service in the style of a DOS TSR, which will temporarily bring a background process to the foreground. Allow triggering either by keypresses or specific times.

In This Chapter:
- *Shuffling Input And Output Of Processes Every Which Way*
- *Connecting Multiple Processes Together*
- *kibitz And xkibitz*

16

Interacting With Multiple Processes

The previous chapter had numerous examples, all showing how to create a connection between a user and the currently spawned process. The interact command does this by default, but it is possible to create connections in other ways. In this chapter, I will cover how to use the interact command with a process other than the user and currently spawned process, or with multiple processes.

Connecting To A Process Other Than The Currently Spawned Process

Like many of the other commands in Expect, the interact command accepts the -i flag to indicate a spawn id to be used in place of the currently spawned process. For example:

```
spawn telnet
set telnet $spawn_id
spawn ftp
interact -i $telnet
```

In this example, interact connects the user to the telnet process. Without the "-i $telnet", the ftp process is connected.

Output from the process is tested against any patterns appearing after the -i flag. In other words, the -i behaves as if a -o flag had also appeared.

Connecting To A Process Instead Of The User

Just as the -i flag allows substitution of one side of the connection created by interact, the -u flag allows substitution of the other side. Specifically, the -u flag identifies a process to be used instead of the user.

```
spawn proc1
set proc1 $spawn_id
spawn proc2
interact -u $proc1
```

The interact command above connects the input of proc1 to the output of proc2 and vice versa. The processes interact as shown in the following figure.

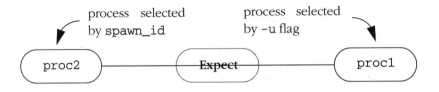

With the -u flag, the interact command connects two spawned processes together.

In the figure, there is no user involved. The user is still present but does not participate in the interact connection. The user keystrokes are not read nor is there any output to the user.

In Chapter 11 (p. 251), I showed how to have two chess processes communicate using expect commands in a loop. This could be rewritten using "interact -u" with the second chess process replacing the user. The original script was an expect command wrapped in a while loop, but the interact command loops internally. So using interact would avoid the extra command, making the script slightly shorter.

The chess problem is a familiar example but contrived—there is no real reason to use interact since the moves are synchronized. But in real uses, "interact -u" leads to much shorter programs.

Here is a script fragment to perform *dialback*, the act of having a computer dial a modem and connect to a user. This is useful in situations where the user cannot or does not want to be responsible for the connection. For example, dialback allows the phone charges to be billed to the computer rather than the user.

```
spawn login
set login $spawn_id
spawn tip modem
dial $argv              ;# you supply this procedure
interact -u $login
```

The script starts by spawning a `login` process. A `tip` process is spawned so that it can talk to a modem. A `dial` procedure dials the remote modem where the user is waiting. Finally, the `interact` command connects the modem to the `login` process, thereby establishing a complete connection.

The user may initially have to start this script, but can then immediately log out to let the computer call back. The cost to connect long enough to run the script is minimal. The computer picks up the remaining costs.

Another use for dialback is to improve security. Without dialback, anyone who can steal or guess a password can dial up and login. If dialback is enforced, the rogue can request a connection, but the computer can refuse if the number to be called back is not on a pre-approved list.

The `dial` procedure can be as simple as just "`send "ATDT...\r"`". With retry, security, logging, etc., a couple of dozen lines might be necessary.

It is worth comparing this dialback script with the one in Chapter 1 (p. 4). The earlier one takes advantage of modems that are directly connected to serial ports. And the serial ports must allow connections to be established in either direction. Some systems do not provide these capabilities. For example, you may have to `telnet` to another computer to get to a pool of modems shared by many hosts. In this case, only the script shown here will work.

In the first dialback script, Expect disappeared after the connection was made. The script shown here requires that Expect stick around to perform the `interact`. This can be an advantage because `interact` can still execute actions based on the characters that pass through it.

Patterns listed after the `-u` apply to the named process. To apply patterns to the other side of the connection, precede them with a `-o` or `-i` flag.

Example—rz And sz Over rlogin

`rz` and `sz` are popular programs that perform XMODEM, YMODEM, and ZMODEM transfers with the controlling terminal. `sz` sends a file to the controlling terminal and `rz` reads a file from the controlling terminal. Used together, they can transfer files between two hosts. The following script uses `rz` and `sz` to transfer a file across a connection created by `rlogin`. This is handy if security restrictions do not permit the use of `rcp`.

```
spawn rlogin $host; set rz $spawn_id
expect "% "
send "stty -echo\r"
expect "% "
send "rz -v\r"

spawn sz $file
interact -u $rz "\r~" {
    send -i $rz "\r~~"
}
```

After starting `rlogin`, the script turns off echoing. This prevents the `rz` command itself from being echoed by the shell and simplifies starting `sz`. `rz` is started with the `-v` flag which inhibits printing of the message "`rz ready.  Type "sz file ..." to your modem program`". Once `rz` is ready, `sz` is started and the two are connected together using "`interact -u`".

By default, `rlogin` provides an almost seamless connection. Unfortunately, there is no way to disable its escape character. The script works around this by watching for the character. The default escape is "~" but it is only detected by `rlogin` after a "\r". The script watches for this sequence and sends an extra "~" to force `rz` to receive both the "\r" and "~".

Most communication programs, `rlogin` included, provide an 8-bit connection. Alas, not all communication programs are so clean. Some implementations of `telnet`, for instance, strip the high-order bit of each character. Because of this, you cannot use `rz` and `sz` with those versions of `telnet`. If you are forced to use a 7-bit connection, then you must use a 7-bit protocol. In Chapter 20 (p. 467), I will present a script that sends files across a link that passes only 7 bits (e.g., `telnet`). That script also starts with the user interacting with the remote system. If you want to interactively decide which files to transfer, you will find that script more convenient than the example shown here, which is oriented toward being run non-interactively.

Chapter 17 (p. 378) will show another example of `-u` that allows a user to interact with background processes as if they were foreground processes. This is useful for debugging, for example, processes running under `cron`.

That chapter also describes how to make the script detach itself from the terminal. This is desirable with a script like `dialback`. You want to initially see any diagnostics (modem is busy, phone number is illegal, etc.) before logging out and waiting for the call back.

Redirecting Input And Output

The -i and -u flags each connect both the input and output of a process. It is possible to connect just the input or just the output using the -input and -output flags.

The -input flag identifies a spawn id from which input should be read. The -output flag identifies a spawn id to which output should be written. The general syntax for specifying connections is that a -output flag applies to the most recent -input flag. For example, the following flags indicate that input from spawn id i is written to spawn id o.

```
-input $i -output $o
```

The following fragment connects three processes together. Input from id1 is sent to id2 and id3. Input from id2 is sent to id1. Input from id3 is discarded.

```
interact {
    -input $id1 -output $id2 -output $id3
    -input $id2 -output $id1
    -input $id3
}
```

If id3 does not produce any output, it does not need to be listed. However, if a process is producing unwanted data, it must be discarded or else the operating system will eventually stop the process when its internal buffers fill up. Listing it without an associated -output flag as I have done here effectively causes the output to be discarded.

Patterns may be applied to spawned processes identified with -input flags. As with the -i and -u flags, patterns immediately follow the spawn id specifications to which they apply. For example, to execute the procedure doX whenever the character X is generated by id2, the pattern is listed immediately after the -input flag for id2.

```
interact {
    -input $id1 -output $id2 -output $id3
    -input $id2 "X" doX -output $id1
    -input $id3
}
```

The timeout and eof patterns behave just like other patterns with respect to -input (and -i and -u). For example, timeout follows the spawn id specification to which it applies.

Patterns cannot apply to a -output except in one case. The eof pattern following a -output may be matched if the output spawn id is closed. The eof pattern following a -input similarly matches if the input spawn id is closed.

Default Input And Output

When the `interact` command is given with no arguments, it is equivalent to:

```
interact {
    -input $user_spawn_id -output $spawn_id
    -input $spawn_id -output $user_spawn_id
}
```

Besides omitting all of the arguments, it is possible to omit just some of them and still get reasonable defaults. There are defaults for the first two processes since an interaction invariably involves at least two processes.

If the first `-input` is omitted, `user_spawn_id` is used. If the first `-output` is omitted, `spawn_id` is used. If the `-output` after the second `-input` is omitted, `user_spawn_id` is used. These can also be affected by the `-u` and `-i` flags. For example, if the `-u` flag appears, the new spawn id is used in place of the first `-input` and the second `-output`.

As an example, the following command establishes a connection between the user and an external process (not started by Expect). The external process provides two fifos for communication, one for input and one for output.

```
interact -output $out -input $in
```

The first input is implicit and is therefore `user_spawn_id`. User keystrokes are sent to `out`. Input from `in` is sent back to `user_spawn_id` so that the user can read it. The following figure shows the Expect process with the `interact` in progress.

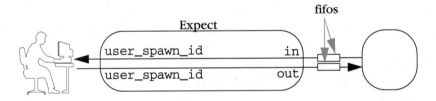

The external process could be a C program, but it is also expressible as another Expect script with an `interact` of its own. For example, the second script might connect a spawned process to the fifos with the following command:

```
interact -u $proc -output $out -input $in
```

The command looks exactly the same as the previous `interact` except that the spawned process has been substituted for the user with the `-u` flag. The spawned process will become the implicit output of the input from `in`.

Both of these commands actually appear in the `dislocate` script that comes with Expect. (The `dislocate` script is described in more detail on page 384.) The user-side `interact` command uses one pattern to provide the user with an escape character. The following fragment invokes the `interact` with an escape, preceded by a message to explain it:

```
puts "Escape sequence is $escape"
interact {
    -reset $escape escape
    -output $out
    -input $in
}
```

The escape is preceded by a `-reset` flag so that the messages in the `escape` procedure itself do not have to worry about the end-of-line formatting while in raw mode.

Controlling Multiple Processes — kibitz

It is possible to connect more than two processes simply by identifying more than two spawn ids with the `-input` or `-output` flags. The `kibitz` script that comes with Expect does this. First, I will describe `kibitz` from the user's point of view.

By default, `kibitz` runs a shell and connects both the original user and another user to it. The keystrokes of both users are sent to the shell and both users see the results. `kibitz` is ideal for allowing two people to see what one another is doing. For example, a novice user who is having a problem can use `kibitz` to let an expert see in real time what is going awry. The expert can begin typing at any time, showing the user the correct way to do something.

Lots of other uses are possible. For example, by running a full-screen editor, two people may carry out a conversation, and have the ability to scroll backwards, save the entire conversation, or even edit it while in progress. People can team up on games, document editing, or other cooperative tasks where each person has strengths and weaknesses that complement one another.

`kibitz` is started by the first user typing "`kibitz`" followed by the user name.

```
% kibitz debtron
```

This causes the second user (`debtron`) to be prompted to run `kibitz`. A message appears in their console asking them to run `kibitz`. The user sees:

```
Can we talk?  Run: kibitz -20899
```

The request includes a special argument that allows `kibitz` to uniquely distinguish one out of any number of other `kibitz` sessions in progress on the same host. So the second user types:

```
% kibitz -20899
```

Both users then see a shell prompt. As one user types characters, they are echoed to both users' screens. Any output from the shell goes to both users. `kibitz` continues in this way until either of the users makes the shell exit.

How kibitz Works

On page 354, I mentioned that `interact` could be used to connect fifos. This is exactly what `kibitz` does. The first `kibitz` spawns a shell and creates two fifos. The second `kibitz` opens the same fifos and then lets the user interact with the fifos. The first `kibitz` uses `interact` to tie the user, shell, and fifos together. The fifos are chosen by the first `kibitz` and presented to the second user as the argument to `kibitz`. In the example above, the 20899 from the argument is the unique part of the fifo name.

In the script, the user who started `kibitz` initially is accessed via `user_spawn_id`. Another user is connected by fifos, known as `userin` and `userout`. Lastly, the process is referred to as `process`.

The script executes a command similar to the following one to connect all three together. I have lined all the `-output` flags up to make them easier to see but that is not necessary.

```
interact {
    -input $user_spawn_id -output $process
    -input $userin         -output $process
    -input $process        -output $user_spawn_id
                           -output $userout
}
```

The interaction established is shown graphically in the figure below. The second user, communicating through the fifos, uses a second `kibitz` process to send keystrokes through the fifos to the shared process and similarly read the output produced by the shared process.

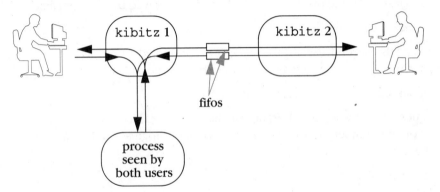

In Chapter 11 (p. 255), I showed how `kibitz` could be rendered with just `expect` commands. Compare this to the version using `interact`. The version using `expect` commands is more verbose because the looping (via `exp_continue`) is explicit as are the patterns (`-re  ".+"`) and `send` actions. All of that is implicit when using `interact`.

A number of things fall out of the `kibitz` design serendipitously. For example, while `kibitz` spawns a shell by default, it can just as easily spawn any process. For example, to spawn a different program, the program name and optional arguments are appended to the `kibitz` command line. Here is how one user might share an `emacs` process with another user.

```
% kibitz debtron emacs
```

Of course, you can run any program from the shell anyway. But the shell is totally unnecessary in some cases.

`kibitz` does not have any special code for handling more than two people. While such code could be added, it is easy enough just to have `kibitz` invoke another `kibitz`. For example, a user that wants to share a `vi` process with two users (`debtron` and `jim`) could say:

```
% kibitz debtron kibitz jim vi
```

`kibitz` goes to some effort to make things work as gracefully as possible. For example, `kibitz` understands hostname references in user names.

```
% kibitz jim@titan
```

Hostname references are implemented by having `kibitz` `rlogin` to the remote host and run `kibitz` there. As long as a password is not required, this is entirely transparent to the user. If a password is required, `kibitz` asks the user for it and then continues. A proxy account can be set up to allow users without accounts to `kibitz` into a host.

All of these approaches avoid having to install a special network daemon just for `kibitz`. In fact, `kibitz` avoids having to worry about all of the programming hassles having to do with machine portability, networking, and security. `kibitz` just uses whatever tools are already available on a host.

One last technical aspect of the internetwork `kibitz` implementation is worth mentioning because it can be applied to many other programs. Normally, characters are passed uninterpreted between `kibitz` processes. However, it is possible for the remote `kibitz` to need to report problems during initialization (e.g., "no such user exists by that name"). It would be inappropriate for the remote `kibitz` to pass such error messages back to the local `kibitz` only to have them sent to the shared process. Rather, the local `kibitz` should send them only to the user who originally invoked `kibitz`.

To deal with this, a tiny in-band protocol is used between the first two kibitz processes. Once the remote kibitz is running, it sends the string KRUN. This tells the local kibitz that the remote kibitz has begun running. Whatever the remote kibitz sends now (presumably diagnostics) is sent directly back to the user by the local kibitz. If the local kibitz fails to establish the connection, KABORT is sent to the local kibitz that, having already passed on any diagnostics to the user, exits as does the remote kibitz. If the remote kibitz successfully establishes the connection, it sends back KDATA meaning that anything after this is user data and should be sent back to the shared process.

The local kibitz implements all of this in two expect commands. The first waits for KRUN. The second (shown below) waits for KABORT or KDATA. The default pattern covers the case when the remote kibitz cannot even be started.

```
expect {
    -re ".*\n" {
        # pass back diagnostics to user
        send_user $expect_out(buffer)
        exp_continue
    }
    default exit
    KABORT exit
    KDATA
}
```

Combining Multiple Inputs Or Outputs

It is possible to combine multiple spawn ids in a single -input or -output. This uses the same syntax as the expect command uses to combine multiple spawn ids in a -i flag. Both of the following interact commands have the same result.

```
interact -input $i -output $o1 -output $o2
interact -input $i -output "$o1 $o2"
```

The second form is preferred unless the two output spawn ids have different eof actions. For example, in the following command, the action for an end-of-file on o1 is return, while the action for an end-of-file on o2 is "close $i".

```
interact -input $i -output $o1 -output $o2 eof {
    close $i
}
```

Input spawn ids can be combined similarly. The following command takes the input from i1 and i2 and sends it to o1.

```
interact -input "$i1 $i2" -output $o1
```

Note that writing two `-input` flags in a row with no `-output` in between causes the first input source to be discarded. This can be quite useful for the same reasons that it is occasionally handy to redirect output to `/dev/null` in the shell.

Using these shorthands, it is possible to write the `interact` in `kibitz` more succinctly:

```
interact {
    -input "$user_spawn_id $userin" -output $process
    -input $process -output "$user_spawn_id $userout"
}
```

Which Spawn Id Matched

The `expect` command always sets `expect_out(spawn_id)` to the spawn id associated with the matching output. This allows a single action parameterized on its spawn id to be shared between a number of spawn ids. For efficiency reasons, the `interact` command does not automatically do a similar assignment. Instead, the `-iwrite` flag controls whether the spawn id is recorded, in this case, to `interact_out(spawn_id)`.

The `-iwrite` flag should appear before each pattern to which it applies. For example, in the following fragment, `action1` and `action3` can access the value of `interact_out(spawn_id)` but `action2` cannot.

```
interact {
    -input "$user_spawn_id $userin"
    -iwrite "foo" {action1}
            "bar" {action2}
    -iwrite "baz" {action3}
}
```

See Chapter 11 (p. 253) for more examples of the `spawn_id` element.

Indirect Spawn Ids

Indirect spawn ids are lists of direct spawn ids that are stored in global variables; the variables are in turn passed by name. Commands using these variables as indirect spawn ids detect when they are modified. (This is described in more detail in Chapter 11 (p. 268).) Indirect spawn ids may be used in the `interact` command, similarly to the way they are used in the `expect` command. However, they are much more useful in the `interact` command, simply because `interact` commands are usually long-lived.

Indirect spawn ids may appear anywhere that explicit spawn id lists can. In the `expect` command, spawn id lists appear only as arguments to `-i` flags. In the `interact` command, spawn id lists appear as arguments to `-i`, `-u`, `-input`, and `-output` flags.

The following script connects to two hosts and allows you to `interact` with either one. Pressing ^A causes further interaction to occur with `hostA`. Pressing ^B causes further interaction to occur with `hostB`.

```
spawn telnet hostA; set A $spawn_id
spawn telnet hostB; set B $spawn_id
set proc $A

interact {
    "\1" {set proc $A}
    "\2" {set proc $B}
    -i proc
}
```

The variable `proc` is used to contain the indirect spawn id, but any variable can be used, even `spawn_id`. While `spawn_id` is the default, `interact` is not sensitive to changes in `spawn_id` unless it is explicitly named as an indirect spawn id.

Here is a different way to control the same scenario. In this case, ^A is used to toggle between the two processes.

```
spawn telnet hostA
set old $spawn_id
spawn telnet hostB

interact {
    "\1" {
        set tmp $spawn_id
        set spawn_id $old
        set old $tmp
    }
    -i spawn_id
}
```

Both of these examples could be said to implement shell-style job control. Unlike csh-style job control, however, you can customize these to your application. For example, you can choose the character sequences to switch on, and they can be any number of characters. You can control whether they toggle or flip or whatever. These techniques are not difficult to extend. For example, if you wanted to bounce around a ring of processes, you could create a list containing all of the spawn ids and then use the following action:

```
set spawn_id [lindex $list 0]
set list "[lrange $list 1 end] $spawn_id"
```

The following command connects a set of users to a single process so that their keystrokes go to the process and any results are returned to all of them. When the last user's connection closes, the `interact` returns.

```
interact {
    -input inputs -iwrite eof {
        set index [lsearch $inputs $interact_out(spawn_id)]
        set inputs [lreplace $inputs $index $index]
        set outputs [lreplace $outputs $index $index]
        if {[llength $inputs]==0} return
    } -output $process
    -input $process -output outputs
}
```

The users' spawn ids are stored in two lists. This gives users the flexibility to read their input from one place and write it to another, as is the case with fifos. Users represented by a single spawn id can have the same spawn id placed in both lists.

The input list is named by the `-input` flag. Input goes from there to the process named by the following `-output` flag. The `-iwrite` flag forces the `spawn_id` element of `interact_out` to be written so that any spawn id that is closed can be detected and removed from both lists. Only the input list is searched for the spawn id, so the spawn ids in the output list are assumed to be stored in the same order as those in the input list.

The length of the input list is checked to see if any spawn ids remain. If this check is not made, the `interact` will continue the connection. However, with only the process (in `process`) participating, all that will happen is that the output of it will be discarded. This could conceivably be useful if, for example, there was a mechanism by which spawn ids could be added to the list (perhaps through another pattern).

When inputs and outputs are modified, `interact` modifies its behavior to reflect the new values on the lists.

An Extended Example — xkibitz

This section covers an extended example: `xkibitz`. `xkibitz` is similar in effect to `kibitz` but works in a very different way. This script uses indirect spawn ids to be added and dropped dynamically. The script also draws together a number of other concepts including interacting with an `xterm` and handling a `SIGWINCH`.

`xkibitz` uses `xterms` to give multiple users the same view of a shell (or any application). The `xterms` provide a vehicle for easy interhost communication. `xkibitz` does I/O with remote hosts by spawning an `xterm` with the display set appropriately. By doing so, the script avoids having to deal with passwords, remote logins, or proxy servers. Interhost communication comes free because X provides it along with an authentication mechanism. This will become more meaningful as I walk through the script.

The script starts by defining a `help` procedure which just prints a message. The message lists the commands that can be used once the program starts. The "+" command adds a display. The "−" drops a display. The "=" lists the displays. And "return" returns `xkibitz` to the usual user-application interaction.

When a display is added, it is given a *tag*—a small integer that allows the user an easier means of identifying a display than the display name itself which can be very long.

```
#!/usr/local/bin/expect --

proc help {} {
    puts "commands          meaning"
    puts "--------          -------"
    puts "return            return to program"
    puts "=                 list"
    puts "+ <display>       add"
    puts "- <tag>           drop"
    puts "where <display> is an X display name such as"
    puts "nist.gov or nist.gov:0.0"
    puts "and <tag> is a tag from the = command."
}
```

Rather than reading commands directly, the script calls the Expect interpreter and lets that prompt the user for commands. The prompt is modified appropriately.

```
proc prompt1 {} {
    return "xkibitz> "
}
```

A couple of aliases for the `help` procedure are defined so that the user is more likely to get help when they need it. Also, the `unknown` procedure is redefined so that invalid commands can be handled with a hint to the user about what is expected.

```
proc h {} help
proc ? {} help
proc unknown {args} {
    puts "$args: invalid command"
    help
}
```

`xkibitz` keeps track of what it is doing by means of several global arrays. They are as follows:

`tag2pid`	Process id associated with a tag
`pid2tty`	Tty name associated with a process id
`pid2display`	Display name associated with a process id

`pid2tag`	Tag associated with a process id
`pid2sid`	Spawn id associated with a process id

These arrays make it easy to find out any information based on the tag or the process id. For example, the spawn id associated with $pid is $pid2sid($pid). To get the spawn id from the tag requires knowing the process id. That is just $tag2pid($tag). This can then be used as an index into `pid2sid` to get the spawn id.

An initial entry is made in the tables for the current process. Entries in all of the tables are not necessary for this process since it will never be deleted. The 0 tag is associated with this process. The integer variable, `maxtag`, always stores the highest active tag. This will be used to make sure that new displays get new tags.

```
set tag2pid(0)          [pid]
set pid2tty([pid])      "/dev/tty"
if [info exists env(DISPLAY)] {
    set pid2display([pid]) $env(DISPLAY)
} else {
    set pid2display([pid])  ""
}

# small int allowing user to more easily identify display
# maxtag always points at highest in use
set maxtag 0
```

Next, user commands are defined. "+" is defined as a Tcl procedure. It may look funny because there are no alphabetic characters but it is legal, convenient, and mnemonic. And Tcl provides a reasonable message if the wrong number of arguments are provided. `unknown` handles things that make no sense at all.

Letting the user interact with the Tcl interpreter directly is not always the best idea. But in this case, it simplifies the script a bit.

The code to add a display starts by spawning an `xterm` so that the script can read user keystrokes and write the screen display. This was described in detail in Chapter 13 (p. 293). The geometry is set to that of the controlling terminal of the script itself so that each `xterm` is the same size.

The new spawn id is appended to the variable `ids`. This variable will later be used as the indirect spawn id list. Appropriate entries are made in all the tables. The `maxtag` variable is incremented to get a new tag.

A bare `return` is used to make the procedure return silently. Without the `return`, the procedure would return the value of the previous `set` command—which is not something that the user cares about in the dialogue and might otherwise find confusing.

```
proc + {display} {
    global ids pid2display pid2tag tag2pid maxtag pid2sid
    global pid2tty

    if ![string match *:* $display] {
        append display :0.0
    }

    spawn -pty -noecho

    stty raw -echo < $spawn_out(slave,name)
    regexp ".*(.)(.)" $spawn_out(slave,name) dummy c1 c2
    if {[string compare $c1 "/"] == 0} {
        set c1 "0"
    }
    set pid [exec xterm \
            -display $display \
            -geometry [stty columns]x[stty rows] \
            -S$c1$c2$spawn_out(slave,fd) &]
    close -slave

    # xterm first sends back window id, discard
    log_user 0
    expect {
        eof {wait;return}
        -re (.*)\n
    }
    log_user 1

    lappend ids $spawn_id
    set pid2display($pid) $display
    incr maxtag
    set tag2pid($maxtag) $pid
    set pid2tag($pid) $maxtag
    set pid2sid($pid) $spawn_id
    set pid2tty($pid) $spawn_out(slave,name)
    return
}
```

All users added by the "+" procedure are directly controlled by the same `xkibitz` process. Here is a picture of the single process letting three users communicate with a shell. Compare this with the figure on page 356.

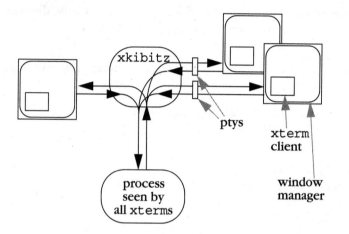

The "=" is another user command defined with a Tcl procedure. It examines each tag known to the script and prints out a little table based on the information. Here is an example of the output while three displays are active:

```
xkibitz> =
Tag  Size Display
  0 80x14 unix:0.0
  1 80x14 calvin:0.0
  2 80x14 hobbes:0.0
```

Some of the information—such as the display name—is extracted from other tables. Some information—such as the logical tty size—is fetched from the operating system itself.

```
proc = {} {
    global pid2display tag2pid pid2tty

    puts "Tag  Size Display"
    foreach tag [lsort -integer [array names tag2pid]] {
        set pid $tag2pid($tag)
        set tty $pid2tty($pid)

        puts [format "%3d [stty columns < $tty]x[stty \
                rows < $tty] $pid2display($pid)" $tag]
    }
}
```

The "-" commands drops a display. After checking the validity of the tag, it undoes everything that the "+" command did. First it removes the spawn id from the indirect spawn id list. Then it kills the xterm process. (Closing the spawn id is not enough since xterm does not listen for an eof. Instead xterm waits for a SIGCHLD. However, xterm will never get one because it did not create a process!)

The appropriate entries are then removed from the tables. Lastly, the maxtag variable is lowered until it once again describes the highest tag in use.

```
proc - {tag} {
    global tag2pid pid2tag pid2display maxtag ids pid2sid
    global pid2tty

    if ![info exists tag2pid($tag)] {
        puts "no such tag"
        return
    }
    if {$tag == 0} {
        puts "cannot drop self"
        return
    }

    set pid $tag2pid($tag)

    # close and remove spawn_id from list
    set spawn_id $pid2sid($pid)
    set index [lsearch $ids $spawn_id]
    set ids [lreplace $ids $index $index]

    exec kill $pid
    close
    wait

    unset tag2pid($tag)
    unset pid2tag($pid)
    unset pid2display($pid)
    unset pid2sid($pid)
    unset pid2tty($pid)

    # lower maxtag if possible
    while {![info exists tag2pid($maxtag)]} {
        incr maxtag -1
    }
}
```

As I mentioned above, the xterm program does not test its input for end of file. Hence if the script exits, xterms will be left around. To prevent this, an exit handler is established to kill the orphaned xterms. To avoid killing the script, its entry is immediately removed in the first command of the exit handler.

```
exit -onexit {
    unset pid2display([pid])          ;# avoid killing self

    foreach pid [array names pid2display] {
        catch {exec kill $pid}
    }
}
```

A handler for the WINCH signal is defined so that the window size of the first user is propagated to all the other ptys. First, the terminal is queried. Then the terminal size of the application is changed. Finally, in a loop the other ptys are set. The name of the terminal is saved (in the variable app_tty) later in the code immediately after the application is started.

As of X11R5, xterm lacks several hooks to make a more useful WINCH handler, but these may be added in the future. For instance, it should be possible to resize the window rather than just the pty. The operating system itself could also be more helpful. Alas, POSIX.1 only delivers WINCH when the size of the controlling terminal changes. In this script, all the ptys associated with xterms are not controlling terminals so there is no way to have WINCHs generated when these windows are updated. xterm could make up for this deficiency; however, xterm provides no way to be told of a pid to which signals should be sent upon resize events.

```
trap {
    set r [stty rows]
    set c [stty columns]
    stty rows $r columns $c < $app_tty
    foreach pid [array names pid2tty] {
        if {$pid == [pid]} continue
        stty rows $r columns $c < $pid2tty($pid)
    }
} WINCH
```

Near the end of the script is the code that handles the arguments to the script itself. This code appears here rather than earlier because the -display argument calls "+" and this procedure has to be defined and all of the data structures have to be initialized first.

Given an -escape flag, the user can change the escape string. By default, it is a control-right-bracket, which does not normally show upon being printed, so the variable escape_printable is set to something that "looks right". If the user changes the escape, then escape_printable is changed to the same thing. No conversion is made to a printable representation, but presumably the user does not need one since they just overrode the default.

After the arguments are parsed, the shell or application is spawned.

```
set escape \035     ;# control-right-bracket
set escape_printable "^\]"

while [llength $argv]>0 {
    set flag [lindex $argv 0]
    switch -- $flag \
    "-escape" {
        set escape [lindex $argv 1]
        set escape_printable $escape
        set argv [lrange $argv 2 end]
    } "-display" {
        + [lindex $argv 1]
        set argv [lrange $argv 2 end]
    } default {
        break
    }
}

if [llength $argv]>0 {
    eval spawn -noecho $argv
} else {
    spawn -noecho $env(SHELL)
}
set prog $spawn_id
set app_tty $spawn_out(slave,name)

puts "Escape sequence is $escape_printable"
```

Once everything has been set up, the user is dropped into an `interact` command that connects everything together. The user's keystrokes go to the application. So do all the keystrokes from the `xterms`. The output from the application goes to the user and the `xterms`.

If the user running the script enters the escape, an informative message is printed and then `interpreter` is started so that commands can be issued directly. When a `return` command is entered, `interpreter` returns and the interaction between the application and the ptys resume.

If the user quits the script or the application exits, `interact` returns. In this case, the exit handler is invoked to kill all the `xterms`, and the script exits.

```
interact {
    -input $user_spawn_id -reset $escape {
        puts "\nfor help enter: ? or h or help"
        interpreter
    } -output $prog
```

```
        -input ids -output $prog
        -input $prog -output $user_spawn_id -output ids
}
```

Exercises

1. Modify xkibitz so that it is not necessary to use whitespace to separate the interactive commands from the arguments.

2. Write the missing dial procedure (page 351).

3. Modify the dialback script (page 351) so that when the computer calls back, it provides a shell immediately instead of a login prompt.

4. Modify the rz-sz script (page 352) so that it transfers files in the other direction.

In This Chapter:
- *Running Scripts In The Background*
- *Disconnecting Script From The Foreground*
- *Communicating With Scripts In The Background*
- *A Manager For Disconnected Processes*
- *Expect Daemons For Gopher And Mosaic*

17

Background Processing

It is useful to run scripts in the background when they are totally automated. Then your terminal is not tied up and you can work on other things. In this chapter, I will describe some of the subtle points of background processing.

As an example, imagine a script that is *supposedly* automated but prompts for a password anyway or demands interactive attention for some other reason. This type of problem can be handled with Expect. In this chapter, I will discuss several techniques for getting information to and from background processes in a convenient manner.

I will also describe how to build a `telnet` daemon in Expect that can be run from `inetd`. While rewriting a `telnet` daemon is of little value for its own sake, with a few customizations such a daemon can be used to solve a wide variety of problems.

Putting Expect In The Background

You can have Expect run in the background in several ways. You can explicitly start it asynchronously by appending & to the command line. You can start Expect and then press ^Z and enter `bg`. Or you can run Expect from `cron` or `at`. Some systems have a third interface called `batch`.[†] Expect can also put itself into the background using the `fork` and `disconnect` commands.

[†] `cron`, `at`, and `batch` all provide different twists on the same idea; however, Expect works equally well with each so I am going to say "`cron`" whenever I mean any of `cron`, `at`, or `batch`. You can read about these in your own man pages.

The definition of *background* is not precisely defined. However, a background process usually means one that cannot read from the terminal. The word *terminal* is a historic term referring to the keyboard on which you are typing and the screen showing your output.

Expect normally reads from the terminal by using `expect_user`, "gets stdin", etc. Writing to the terminal is analogous.

If Expect has been started asynchronously (with an & appended) or suspended and continued in the background (via `bg`) from a job control shell, `expect_user` will not be able to read anything. Instead, what the user types will be read by the shell. Only one process can read from the terminal at a time. Inversely, the terminal is said to be controlling one process. The terminal is known as the *controlling terminal* for all processes that have been started from it.

If Expect is brought into the foreground (by `fg`), `expect_user` will then be able to read from the terminal.

It is also possible to run Expect in the background but without a controlling terminal. For example, `cron` does this. Without redirection, `expect_user` cannot be used at all when Expect lacks a controlling terminal.

Depending upon how you have put Expect into the background, a controlling terminal may or may not be present. The simplest way to test if a controlling terminal is present is to use the `stty` command. If `stty` succeeds, a controlling terminal exists.

```
if [catch stty] {
    # controlling terminal does not exist
} else {
    # controlling terminal exists
}
```

If a controlling terminal existed at one time, the global variable `tty_spawn_id` refers to it. How can a controlling terminal exist at one time and then no longer exist? Imagine starting Expect in the background (using "&"). At this point, Expect has a controlling terminal. If you log out, the controlling terminal is lost.

For the remainder of this chapter, the term *background* will also imply that the process lacks a controlling terminal.

Running Expect Without A Controlling Terminal

When Expect has no controlling terminal, you must avoid using `tty_spawn_id`. And if the standard input, standard output, and standard error have not been redirected, `expect_user`, `send_user`, and `send_error` will not work. Lastly, a `stty` command without redirection will always fail.

If the process has been started from `cron`, there are yet more caveats. By default, `cron` does not use your environment, so you may need to force `cron` to use it or perhaps explicitly initialize parts of your environment. For example, the default path supplied by `cron` usually includes only `/bin` and `/usr/bin`. This is almost always insufficient.

Be prepared for all sorts of strange things to happen in the default `cron` environment. For example, many programs (e.g., `rn`, `telnet`) crash or hang if the TERM environment variable is not set. This is a problem under `cron` which does not define TERM. Thus, you must set it explicitly—to what type is usually irrelevant. It just has to be set to something!

Environment variables can be filled in by appropriate assignments to the global array `env`. Here is an assignment of TERM to a terminal type that should be understood at any site.

```
set env(TERM) vt100
```

Later, I will describe how to debug problems that arise due to the unusual environment in `cron`.

Disconnecting The Controlling Terminal

It is possible to start a script in the foreground but later have it move itself into the background and disconnect itself from the controlling terminal. This is useful when there is some point in the script after which no further interaction is required.

For example, suppose you want to automate a command that requires you to type in a password but it is inconvenient for you to enter the password when it is needed (e.g., you plan to be asleep later).

You could embed the password in the script or pass the password as an argument to it, but those are pretty risky ideas. A more secure way is to have the script interactively prompt for the password and remember it until it is needed later. The password will not be available in any public place—just in the memory of the Expect process.

In order to read the password in the first place, Expect needs a controlling terminal. After the password is read, Expect will still tie up the terminal—until you log out. To avoid the inconvenience of tying up the controlling terminal (or making you log out and back in again), Expect provides the `fork` and `disconnect` commands.

The fork Command

The `fork` command creates a new process. The new process is an exact copy of the current Expect process except for one difference. In the new (child) process, the `fork` command returns 0. In the original Expect process, `fork` returns the process id of child process.

```
if [fork] {
    # code to be executed by parent
} else {
    # code to be executed by child
}
```

If you save the results of the `fork` command in, say, the variable `child_pid`, you will have two processes, identical except for the variable `child_pid`. In the parent process, `child_pid` will contain the process id of the child. In the child process, `child_pid` will contain 0. If the child wants its own process id, it can use the `pid` command. (If the child needs the parent's process id, the child can call the `pid` command before the `fork` and save the result in a variable. The variable will be accessible after the `fork`.)

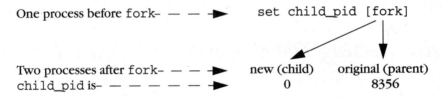

One process before fork- — — ➤   `set child_pid [fork]`

Two processes after fork- — — ➤   new (child)   original (parent)
child_pid is- — — — — — ➤   0   8356

If your system is low on memory, swap space, etc., the `fork` command can fail and no child process will be created. You can use `catch` to prevent the failure from propagating. For example, the following fragment causes the `fork` to be retried every minute until it succeeds:

```
while {1}
    if {[catch fork child_pid] == 0} break
    sleep 60
}
```

Forked processes exit via the `exit` command, just like the original process. Forked processes are allowed to write to the log files. However, if you do not disable debugging or logging in most of the processes, the results can be confusing.

Certain side-effects of `fork` may be non-intuitive. For example, a parent that forks while a file is open will share the read-write pointer with the child. If the child moves it, the parent will be affected. This behavior is not governed by Expect, but is a consequence of UNIX and POSIX. Read your local documentation on `fork` for more information.

The disconnect Command

The `disconnect` command disconnects the Expect process from its controlling terminal. To prevent the terminal from ending up not talking to anything, you must `fork` before calling `disconnect`. After forking, the terminal is shared by both the original Expect process and the new child process. After disconnecting, the child process can go on its merry way in the background. Meanwhile, the original Expect process can exit, gracefully returning the terminal to the invoking shell.

This seemingly artificial and arcane dance is the UNIX way of doing things. Thankfully, it is much easier to write using Expect than to describe using English. Here is how it looks when rendered in an Expect script:

```
if {[fork] != 0} exit
disconnect
# remainder of script is executed in background
```

A few technical notes are in order. The disconnected process is given its own process group (if possible). Any unredirected standard I/O descriptors (e.g., standard input, standard output, standard error) are redirected to `/dev/null`. The variable `tty_spawn_id` is unset.

The ability to disconnect is extremely useful. If a script will need a password later, the script can prompt for the password immediately and then wait in the background. This avoids tying up the terminal, and also avoids storing the password in a script or passing it as an argument. Here is how this idea is implemented:

```
stty -echo
send_user "password? "
expect_user -re "(.*)\n"
send_user "\n"
set password $expect_out(1,string)

# got the password, now go into the background
if {[fork] != 0} exit
disconnect

# now in background, sleep (or wait for event, etc)
sleep 3600

# now do something requiring the password
spawn rlogin $host
```

```
expect "password:"
send "$password\r"
```

This technique works well with security systems such as MIT's Kerberos. In order to run a process authenticated by Kerberos, all that is necessary is to spawn `kinit` to get a ticket, and similarly `kdestroy` when the ticket is no longer needed.

Scripts can reuse passwords multiple times. For example, the following script reads a password and then runs a program every hour that demands a password each time it is run. The script supplies the password to the program so that you only have to type it once.

```
stty -echo
send_user "password? "
expect_user -re "(.*)\n"
set password $expect_out(1,string)
send_user "\n"
while 1 {
    if {[fork] != 0} {
        sleep 3600
        continue
    }
    disconnect
    spawn priv_prog
    expect "password:"
    send "$password\r"
    . . .
    exit
}
```

This script does the forking and disconnecting quite differently than the previous one. Notice that the parent process sleeps in the foreground. That is to say, the parent remains connected to the controlling terminal, forking child processes as necessary. The child processes disconnect, but the parent continues running. This is the kind of processing that occurs with some mail programs; they fork a child process to dispatch outgoing mail while you remain in the foreground and continue to create new mail.

It might be necessary to ask the user for several passwords in advance before disconnecting. Just ask and be specific. It may be helpful to explain why the password is needed, or that it is needed for later.

Consider the following prompts:

```
send_user "password for $user1 on $host1: "
send_user "password for $user2 on $host2: "
send_user "password for root on hobbes: "
send_user "encryption key for $user3: "
send_user "sendmail wizard password: "
```

It is a good idea to force the user to enter the password twice. It may not be possible to authenticate it immediately (for example, the machine it is for may not be up at the moment), but at least the user can lower the probability of the script failing later due to a mistyped password.

```
stty -echo
send_user "root password: "
expect_user -re "(.*)\n"
send_user "\n"
set passwd $expect_out(1,string)
send_user "Again:"
expect_user -re "(.*)\n"
send_user "\n"
if {0 !=[string compare $passwd $expect_out(1,string)]} {
    send_user "mistyped password?"
    exit
}
```

You can even offer to display the password just typed. This is not a security risk as long as the user can decline the offer or can display the password in privacy. Remember that the alternative of passing it as an argument allows anyone to see it if they run **ps** at the right moment.

Another advantage to using the `disconnect` command over the shell asynchronous process feature (&) is that Expect can save the terminal parameters prior to disconnection. When started in the foreground, Expect automatically saves the terminal parameters of the controlling terminal. These are used later by **spawn** when creating new processes and their controlling terminals.

On the other hand, when started asynchronously (using &), Expect does not have a chance to read the terminal's parameters since the terminal is already disconnected by the time Expect receives control. In this case, the terminal is initialized purely by setting it with "stty sane". But this loses information such as the number of rows and columns. While rows and columns may not be particularly valuable to disconnected programs, some programs may want a value—any value, as long as it is nonzero.

Debugging disconnected processes can be challenging. Expect's debugger does not work in a disconnected program because the debugger reads from the standard input which is closed in a disconnected process. For simple problems, it may suffice to direct the log or diagnostic messages to a file or another window on your screen. Then you can use `send_log` to tell you what the child is doing. Some systems support programs such as `syslog` or `logger`. These programs provide a more controllable way of having disconnected processes report what they are doing. See your system's documentation for more information.

These are all one-way solutions providing no way to get information back to the process. I will describe a more general two-way solution in the next section.

Reconnecting

Unfortunately, there is no general way to reconnect a controlling terminal to a disconnected process. But with a little work, it is possible to emulate this behavior. This is useful for all sorts of reasons. For example, a script may discover that it needs (yet more) passwords. Or a backup program may need to get someone's attention to change a tape. Or you may want to interactively debug a script.

To restate: You have two processes (your shell and a disconnected Expect processes) that need to communicate. However they are unrelated. The simplest way to have unrelated processes communicate is through fifos. It is necessary to use a pair since communication must flow in both directions. Both processes thus have to open the fifos.

The disconnected script executes the following code to open the fifos. `infifo` contains the name of the fifo that will contain the user's input (i.e., keystrokes). `outfifo` contains the name of the fifo that will be used to send data back to the user. This form of `open` is described further in Chapter 13 (p. 291).

```
spawn -open [open "|cat $catflags < $infifo" "r"]
set userin $spawn_id

spawn -open [open $outfifo w]
set userout $spawn_id
```

The two `open`s hang until the other ends are opened (by the user process). Once both fifos are opened, an `interact` command passes all input to the spawned process and the output is returned.

```
interact -u $spawn_id -input $userin -output $userout
```

The `-u` flag declares the spawned process as one side of the `interact` and the fifos become the other side, thanks to the `-input` and `-output` flags.

What has been accomplished so far looks like this:

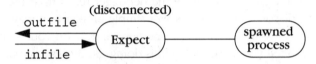

The real user must now read and write from the same two fifos. This is accomplished with another Expect script. The script reads very similarly to that used by the disconnected process—however the fifos are reversed. The one read by the process is written by the user. Similarly, the one written by the process is read by the user.

```
spawn -open [open $infifo w]
set out $spawn_id

spawn -open [open "|cat $catflags < $outfifo" "r"]
set in $spawn_id
```

The code is reversed from that used by the disconnected process. However, the fifos are actually opened in the same order. Otherwise, both processes will block waiting to open a different fifo.

The user's `interact` is also similar:

```
interact -output $out -input $in -output $user_spawn_id
```

The resulting processes look like this:

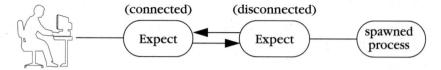

In this example, the Expect processes are transparent. The user is effectively joined to the spawned process.

More sophisticated uses are possible. For example, the user may want to communicate with a *set* of spawned processes. The disconnected Expect may serve as a process manager, negotiating access to the different processes. One of the queries that the disconnected Expect can support is *disconnect.* In this case, *disconnect* means breaking the fifo connection. The manager closes the fifos and proceeds to its next command. If the manager just wants to wait for the user, it immediately tries to reopen the fifos and waits until the user returns. (Complete code for such a manager is shown beginning on page 384.)

The manager may also wish to prompt for a password or even encrypt the fifo traffic to prevent other processes from connecting to it.

One of the complications that I have ignored is that the user and manager must know ahead of time (before reconnection) what the fifo names are. The manager cannot simply wait until it needs the information and then ask the user because doing that requires that the manager already be in communication with the user!

A simple solution is to store the fifo names in a file, say, in the home directory or /tmp. The manager can create the names when it starts and store the names in the file. The user-side Expect script can then retrieve the information from there. This is not sophisticated enough to allow the user to run multiple managers, but that seems an unlikely requirement. In any case, more sophisticated means can be used.

Using kibitz From Other Expect Scripts

In the previous chapter, I described kibitz, a script that allows two users to control a common process. kibitz has a -noproc flag, which skips starting a common process and instead connects together the inputs and outputs of both users. The second user will receive what the first user sends and vice versa.

By using -noproc, a disconnected script can use kibitz to communicate with a user. This may seem peculiar, but it is quite useful and works well. The disconnected script plays the part of one of the users and requires only a few lines of code to do the work.

Imagine that a disconnected script has reached a point where it needs to contact the user. You can envision requests such as "*I need a password to continue*" or "*The 3rd backup tape is bad, replace it and tell me when I can go on*".

To accomplish this, the script simply spawns a kibitz process to the appropriate user. kibitz does all the work of establishing the connection.

```
spawn kibitz -noproc $user
```

Once connected, the user can interact with the Expect process or can take direct control of one of the spawned processes. The following Expect fragment, run from cron, implements the latter possibility. The variable proc is initialized with the spawn id of the errant process while kibitz is the currently spawned process. The tilde is used to return control to the script.

```
spawn some-process; set proc $spawn_id
.  .  .
.  .  .
# script now has question or problem so it contacts user
spawn kibitz -noproc some-user
interact -u $proc -o ~ {
    close
    wait
    return
}
```

If proc refers to a shell, then you can use it to run any UNIX command. You can examine and set the environment variables interactively. You can run your process inside the debugger or while tracing system calls (i.e., under trace or truss). And this will all be under cron. This is an ideal way of debugging programs that work in the normal environment but fail under cron. The following figure shows the process relationship created by this bit of scripting.

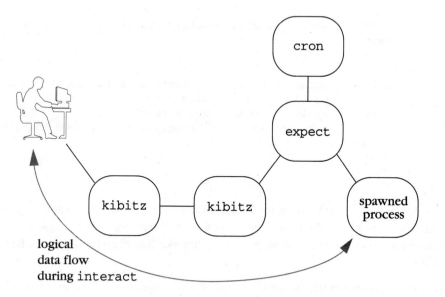

Those half-dozen lines (just shown) are a complete, albeit simple, solution. A more professional touch might describe to the user what is going on. For example, after connecting, the script could do this:

```
send "The Frisbee ZQ30 being controlled by process $pid\
    refuses to reset and I don't know what else to do. \
    Should I let you interact (i), kill me (k), or\
    execute the dangerous gorp command (g)? "
```

The script describes the problem and offers the user a choice of possibilities. The script even offers to execute a command (gorp) it knows about but will not do by itself.

Responding to these is just like interacting with a user except that the user is in raw mode, so all lines should be terminated with a carriage-return linefeed. (Sending these with "send -h" can lend a rather amusing touch.)

Here is how the response might be handled:

```
expect {
    g {
        send "\r\nok, I'll do a gorp\r\n"
        gorp
        send "Hmm.  A gorp didn't seem to fix anything. \
                        Now what (kgi)? "
        exp_continue
    }
```

```
    k {
        send "\r\nok, I'll kill myself...thanks\r\n"
        exit
    }
    i {
        send "\r\npress X to give up control, A to abort\
                            everything\r\n"
        interact -u $proc -o X return A exit
        send "\r\nok, thanks for helping...I'm on my own now\r\n"
        close
        wait
    }
}
```

Numerous strategies can be used for initially contacting the user. For example, the script can give up waiting for the user after some time and try someone else. Or it could try contacting multiple users at the same time much like the `rlogin` script in Chapter 11 (p. 253).

The following fragment tries to make contact with a single user. If the user is not logged in, `kibitz` returns immediately and the script waits for 5 minutes. If the user is logged in but does not respond, the script waits an hour. It then retries the `kibitz`, just in case the user missed the earlier messages. After `maxtries` attempts, it gives up and calls `giveup`. This could be a procedure that takes some last resort action, such as sending mail about the problem and then exiting.

```
set maxtries 30
set count 0
set timeout 3600   ;# wait an hour for user to respond

while 1 {
    spawn kibitz -noproc $env(USER)
    set kib $spawn_id
    expect eof {
            sleep 600
            incr count
            if {$count > $maxtries} giveup
            continue
        } -re "Escape sequence is.*" {
            break
        } timeout {
            close; wait
        }
}
```

If the user does respond to the `kibitz`, both sides will see the message from `kibitz` describing the escape sequence. When the script sees this, it breaks out of the loop and begins communicating with the user.

Mailing From Expect

In the previous section, I suggested using mail as a last ditch attempt to contact the user or perhaps just a way of letting someone know what happened. Most versions of cron automatically mail logs back to users by default, so it seems appropriate to cover mail here. Sending mail from a background process is not the most flexible way of communicating with a user, but it is clean, easy, and convenient.

People usually send mail interactively, but most mail programs do not need to be run with spawn. For example, /bin/mail can be run using exec with a string containing the message. The lines of the message should be separated by newlines. The variable to names the recipient in this example:

```
exec /bin/mail $to << "this is a message\nof two lines\n"
```

There are no mandatory headers, but a few basic ones are customary. Using variables and physical newlines makes the next example easier to read:

```
exec /bin/mail $to << "From: $from
To: $to
From: $from
Subject: $subject
$body"
```

To send a file instead of a string, use the < redirection.

You can also create a mail process and write to it:

```
set mailfile [open "|/bin/mail $to" w]
puts $mailfile "To: $to"
puts $mailfile "From: $from"
puts $mailfile "Subject: $subject"
```

This approach is useful when you are generating lines one at a time, such as in a loop:

```
while {....} {
    ...    ;# compute line
    puts $mailfile "computed another line: $line"
}
```

To send the message, just close the file.

```
close $mailfile
```

A Manager For Disconnected Processes— dislocate

Earlier in the chapter, I suggested that a disconnected background process could be used as a process manager. This section presents a script which is a variation on that earlier idea. Called `dislocate`, this script lets you start a process, interact with it for a while, and then disconnect from it. Multiple disconnected processes live in the background waiting for you to reconnect. This could be useful in a number of situations. For example, a `telnet` connection to a remote site might be impossible to start during the day. Instead you could start it in the evening the day before, disconnect, and reconnect to it later the next morning.

A process is started by prefacing any UNIX command with `dislocate`, as in:

```
% dislocate rlogin io.jupiter.cosmos
Escape sequence is '^]'.
io.jupiter.cosmos:~1%
```

Once the processing is running, the escape sequence is used to disconnect. To reconnect, `dislocate` is run with no arguments. Later, I will describe this further, including what happens when multiple processes are disconnected.

The script starts similarly to `xkibitz` in Chapter 16 (p. 361)—by defining the escape character and several other global variables. The file `~/.dislocate` is used to keep track of all of the disconnected processes of a single user. "`disc`" provides an application-specific prefix to files that are created in `/tmp`.

```
#!/usr/local/bin/expect --
set escape \035                ;# control-right-bracket
set escape_printable "^\]"

set pidfile "~/.dislocate"
set prefix "disc"
set timeout -1

while {$argc} {
    set flag [lindex $argv 0]
    switch -- $flag \
    "-escape" {
        set escape [lindex $argv 1]
        set escape_printable $escape
        set argv [lrange $argv 2 end]
        incr argc -2
    } default {
        break
    }
}
```

Next come several definitions and procedures for fifo manipulation. The `mkfifo` procedure creates a single fifo. Creating a fifo on a non-POSIX system is surprisingly non-portable—mknod can be found in so many places!

```
proc mkfifo {f} {
    if [file exists $f] {
        # fifo already exists?
        return
    }

    if 0==[catch {exec mkfifo $f}] return              ;# POSIX
    if 0==[catch {exec mknod $f p}] return
    if 0==[catch {exec /etc/mknod $f p}] return       ;# AIX,Cray
    if 0==[catch {exec /usr/etc/mknod $f p}] return  ;# Sun
    puts "failed to make a fifo - where is mknod?"
    exit
}
```

Suffixes are declared to distinguish between input and output fifos. Here, they are descriptive from the parent's point of view. In the child, they will be reset so that they appear backwards, allowing the following two routines to be used by both parent and child.

```
set  infifosuffix ".i"
set outfifosuffix ".o"

proc infifoname {pid} {
    global prefix infifosuffix

    return "/tmp/$prefix$pid$infifosuffix"
}

proc outfifoname {pid} {
    global prefix outfifosuffix

    return "/tmp/$prefix$pid$outfifosuffix"
}
```

Embedded in each fifo name is the process id corresponding to its disconnected process. For example, process id 1005 communicates through the fifos named /tmp/disc1005.i and /tmp/disc1005.o. Since the fifo names can be derived given a process id, only the process id has to be known to initiate a connection.

While in memory, the relationship between the process ids and process names (and arguments) is maintained in the `proc` array. The array is indexed by process id. For example, if the process id is 1005, the variable `proc(1005)` might hold the string "`telnet  io.jupiter.cosmos`". A similar array maintains the date when each process was started. These are initialized with the following code which also includes a utility procedure for removing process ids.

```
# allow element lookups on empty arrays
set date(dummy) dummy;unset date(dummy)
set proc(dummy) dummy;unset proc(dummy)

proc pid_remove {pid} {
    global date proc

    unset date($pid)
    unset proc($pid)
}
```

When a process is disconnected, the information on this and any other disconnected process is written to the `.dislocate` file mentioned earlier. Each line of the file describes a disconnected process. The format for a line is:

pid#date-started#argv

Writing the file is straightforward:

```
proc pidfile_write {} {
    global pidfile date proc

    set fp [open $pidfile w]
    foreach pid [array names date] {
        puts $fp "$pid#$date($pid)#$proc($pid)"
    }
    close $fp
}
```

The procedure to read the file is a little more complex because it verifies that th process and fifos still exist.

```
proc pidfile_read {} {
    global date proc pidfile

    if [catch {open $pidfile} fp] return

    set line 0
    while {[gets $fp buf]!=-1} {
        # while pid and date can't have # in it, proc can
        if [regexp "(\[^#]*)#(\[^#]*)#(.*)" $buf junk \
                pid xdate xproc] {
            set date($pid) $xdate
            set proc($pid) $xproc
        } else {
            puts "warning: error in $pidfile line $line"
        }
```

```
        incr line
    }
    close $fp

    # see if pids are still around
    foreach pid [array names date] {
        if [catch {exec /bin/kill -0 $pid}] {
            # pid no longer exists, removing
            pid_remove $pid
            continue
        }

        # pid still there, see if fifos are
        if {![file exists [infifoname $pid]] || \
            ![file exists [outfifoname $pid]]} {
            # $pid fifos no longer exists, removing
            pid_remove $pid
            continue
        }
    }
}
```

The following two procedures create and destroy the fifo pairs, updating the `.dislo-cate` file appropriately.

```
proc fifo_pair_remove {pid} {
    global date proc prefix

    pidfile_read
    pid_remove $pid
    pidfile_write

    catch {exec rm -f [infifoname $pid] \
                      [outfifoname $pid]}
}

proc fifo_pair_create {pid argdate argv} {
    global prefix date proc

    pidfile_read
    set date($pid) $argdate
    set proc($pid) $argv
    pidfile_write

    mkfifo [infifoname $pid]
    mkfifo [outfifoname $pid]
}
```

Things get very interesting at this point. If the user supplied any arguments, they are in turn used as arguments to spawn. A child process is created to handle the spawned process.

A fifo pair is created before the fork. The child will begin listening to the fifos for a connection. The original process (still connected to the controlling terminal) will immediately connect to the fifos. This sounds baroque but is simpler to code because the child behaves precisely this way when the user reconnects later.

Notice that initially the fifo creation occurs before the fork. If the creation was done after, then either the child or the parent might have to spin, inefficiently retrying the fifo open. Since it is impossible to know the process id ahead of time, the script goes ahead and just uses 0. This will be set to the real process id when the child does its initial disconnect. There is no collision problem because the fifos are deleted immediately anyway.

```
if {$argc} {
    set datearg [exec date]
    fifo_pair_create 0 $datearg $argv

    set pid [fork]
    if $pid==0 {
        child $datearg $argv
    }
    # parent thinks of child as having pid 0 for
    # reason given earlier
    set pid 0
}
```

If dislocate has been started with no arguments, it will look for disconnected processes to connect to. If multiple processes exist, the user is prompted to choose one. The interaction looks like this:

```
% dislocate
connectable processes:
 #    pid     date started        process
 1    5888   Mon Feb 14 23:11:49  rlogin io.jupiter.cosmos
 2    5957   Tue Feb 15 01:23:13  telnet ganymede
 3    1975   Tue Jan 11 07:20:26  rogue
enter # or pid: 1
Escape sequence is ^]
```

Here is the code to prompt the user. The procedure to read a response from the user is shown later.

```
if ![info exists pid] {
    global fifos date proc
```

```
# pid does not exist
pidfile_read

set count 0
foreach pid [array names date] {
    incr count
}

if $count==0 {
    puts "no connectable processes"
    exit
} elseif $count==1 {
    puts "one connectable process: $proc($pid)"
    puts "pid $pid, started $date($pid)"
    send_user "connect? \[y] "
    expect_user -re "(.*)\n" {
        set buf $expect_out(1,string)
    }
    if {$buf!="y" && $buf!=""} exit
} else {
    puts "connectable processes:"
    set count 1
    puts " #    pid       date started       process"
    foreach pid [array names date] {
        puts [format "%2d %6d  %.19s  %s" \
            $count $pid $date($pid) $proc($pid)]
        set index($count) $pid
        incr count
    }
    set pid [choose]
}
}
```

Once the user has chosen a process, the fifos are opened, the user is told the escape sequence, the prompt is customized, and the interaction begins.

```
# opening [outfifoname $pid] for write
spawn -noecho -open [open [outfifoname $pid] w]
set out $spawn_id

# opening [infifoname $pid] for read
spawn -noecho -open [open [infifoname $pid] r]
set in $spawn_id

puts "Escape sequence is $escape_printable"
```

```
proc prompt1 {} {
    global argv0

    return "$argv0[history nextid]> "
}

interact {
    -reset $escape escape
    -output $out
    -input $in
}
```

The `escape` procedure drops the user into `interpreter` where they can enter Tcl or Expect commands. They can also press ^Z to suspend `dislocate` or they can enter `exit` to disconnect from the process entirely.

```
proc escape {} {
    puts "\nto disconnect, enter: exit (or ^D)"
    puts "to suspend, enter appropriate job control chars"
    puts "to return to process, enter: return"
    interpreter
    puts "returning ..."
}
```

The `choose` procedure is a utility to interactively query the user to choose a process. It returns a process id. There is no specific handler to abort the dialogue because ^C will do it without harm.

```
proc choose {} {
    global index date

    while 1 {
        send_user "enter # or pid: "
        expect_user -re "(.*)\n" {
            set buf $expect_out(1,string)
        }
        if [info exists index($buf)] {
            set pid $index($buf)
        } elseif [info exists date($buf)] {
            set pid $buf
        } else {
            puts "no such # or pid"
            continue
        }
        return $pid
    }
}
```

All that is left to show is the child process. It immediately disconnects and spawns the actual process. The child then waits for the other end of each fifo to be opened. Once opened, the fifos are removed so that no one else can connect, and then the interaction is started. When the user-level process exits, the child process gets an eof, returns from the `interact`, and recreates the fifos. The child then goes back to waiting for the fifos to be opened again. If the actual process exits, the child exits. Nothing more need be done. The fifos do not exist nor does the entry in the `.dislocate` file. They were both removed prior to the `interact` by `fifo_pair_remove`.

```
proc child {argdate argv} {
    global infifosuffix outfifosuffix

    disconnect

    # these are backwards from the child's point of view
    # so that we can make everything else look "right"
    set  infifosuffix ".o"
    set outfifosuffix ".i"
    set pid 0

    eval spawn $argv
    set proc_spawn_id $spawn_id

    while {1} {
        spawn -open [open [infifoname $pid] r]
        set in $spawn_id

        spawn -open [open [outfifoname $pid] w]
        set out $spawn_id

        fifo_pair_remove $pid

        interact {
            -u $proc_spawn_id eof exit
            -output $out
            -input $in
        }

        catch {close -i $in}
        catch {close -i $out}

        set pid [pid]
        fifo_pair_create $pid $argdate $argv
    }
}
```

Expect As A Daemon

When you log in to a host, you have to provide a username and (usually) a password. It is possible to make use of certain services without this identification. finger and ftp are two examples of services that can be obtained anonymously—without logging in. The programs that provide such services are called daemons. Traditionally, a *daemon* is a background process that is started or woken when it receives a request for service.

UNIX systems often use a program called inetd to start these daemons as necessary. For example, when you ftp to a host, inetd on that host sees the request for ftp service and starts a program called in.ftpd ("Internet ftp daemon") to provide you with service. There are many other daemons such as in.telnetd ("Internet telnet daemon") and in.fingerd ("Internet finger daemon").

You can write Expect scripts that behave just like these daemons. Then users will be able to run your Expect scripts without logging in. As the large number of daemons on any host suggests, there are many uses for offering services in this manner. And Expect makes it particularly easy to build a daemon—to offer remote access to partially or completely automated interactive services. In the next section, I will discuss how to use Expect to enable Gopher and Mosaic to automate connections that would otherwise require human interaction.

Simple Expect scripts require no change to run as a daemon. For example, the following Expect script prints out the contents of /etc/motd whether run from the shell or as a daemon.

```
exec cat /etc/motd
```

Such a trivial script does not offer any benefit for being written in Expect. It might as well be written in /bin/sh. Where Expect is useful is when dealing with interactive programs. For example, your daemon might need to execute ftp, telnet, or some other interactive program to do its job.

The telnet program (the "client") is normally used to speak to a telnet daemon (the "server") but telnet can be used to communicate with many other daemons as well. In Chapter 6 (p. 131), I showed how to use telnet to connect to the SMTP port and communicate with the mail daemon.

If you telnet to an interactive program invoked by a daemon written as a shell script, you will notice some interesting properties. Input lines are buffered and echoed locally. Carriage-returns are received by the daemon as carriage-return linefeed sequences. This peculiar character handling has nothing to do with cooked or raw mode. In fact, there is no terminal interface between telnet and telnetd.

This translation is a by-product of telnet itself. telnet uses a special protocol to talk to its daemon. If the daemon does nothing special, telnet assumes these peculiar characteristics. Unfortunately, they are inappropriate for most interactive applications. For example, the following Expect script works perfectly when started in the foreground from a terminal. However, the script does not work correctly as a daemon because it does not provide support for the telnet protocol.

```
spawn /bin/sh
interact
```

Fortunately, a telnet daemon can modify the behavior of telnet. A telnet client and daemon communicate using an interactive asynchronous protocol. An implementation of a telnet daemon in Expect is short and efficient.

The implementation starts by defining several values important to the protocol. IAC means *Interpret As Command.* All commands begin with an IAC byte. Anything else is data, such as from a user keystroke. Most commands are three bytes and consist of the IAC byte followed by a *command* byte from the second group of definitions followed by an *option* byte from the third group. For example, the sequence IACWILL$ECHO means that the sender is willing to echo characters.

The IAC byte always has the value "\xff". This and other important values are fixed and defined as follows:

```
set IAC    "\xff"

set DONT   "\xfe"
set DO     "\xfd"
set WONT   "\xfc"
set WILL   "\xfb"
set SB     "\xfa"     ;# subnegotation begin
set SE     "\xf0"     ;# subnegotation end

set TTYPE  "\x18"
set SGA    "\x03"
set ECHO   "\x01"
set SEND   "\x01"
```

The response to WILL is either DO or DONT. If the receiver agrees, it responds with DO; otherwise it responds with DONT. Services supplied remotely can also be requested using DO, in which case the answer must be WILL or WONT. To avoid infinite protocol loops, only the first WILL or DO for a particular option is acknowledged. Other details of the protocol and many extensions to it can be found in more than a dozen RFCs beginning with RFC 854.[†]

The server begins by sending out three commands. The first command says that the server will echo characters. Next, line buffering is disabled. Finally, the server offers to handle the terminal type.

```
send "$IAC$WILL$ECHO"
send "$IAC$WILL$SGA"
send "$IAC$DO$TTYPE"
```

For reasons that will only become evident later, it is important both to the user and to the protocol to support nulls, so null removal is disabled at this point.

```
remove_nulls 0
```

Next, several patterns are declared to match commands returning from the client. While it is not required, I have declared each one as a regular expression so that the code is a little more consistent.

The first pattern matches `$IAC$DO$ECHO` and is a response to the `$IAC$WILL$ECHO`. Thus, it can be discarded. Because of the clever design of the protocol, the acknowledgment can be received before the command without harm. Each of the commands above has an acknowledgment pattern below that is handled similarly.

Any unknown requests are refused. For example, the `$IAC$DO\(.)` pattern matches any unexpected requests and refuses them. (Notice the parenthesis has a preceding backslash to avoid having "$DO" be interpreted as an array reference!)

```
expect_before {
    -re "^$IAC$DO$ECHO" {
        # treat as acknowledgment and ignore
        exp_continue
    }
    -re "^$IAC$DO$SGA" {
        # treat as acknowledgment and ignore
        exp_continue
    }
    -re "^$IAC$DO\(.)" {
        # refuse anything else
        send_user "$IAC$WONT$expect_out(1,string)"
        exp_continue
    }
    -re "^$IAC$WILL$TTYPE" {
        # respond to acknowledgment
        send_user "$IAC$SB$TTYPE$SEND$IAC$SE"
        exp_continue
```

---

† *TCP/IP Illustrated, Volume 1* by W. Richard Stevens (Addison-Wesley, 1994) contains a particularly lucid explanation of the protocol, while *Internet System Handbook* by Daniel Lynch and Marshall Rose (Addison-Wesley, 1993) describes some of the common mistakes. If you are trying for maximum interoperability, you must go beyond correctness and be prepared to handle other implementation's bugs!

```
    }
-re "^$IAC$WILL$SGA" {
    # acknowledge request
    send_user "$IAC$DO$SGA"
    exp_continue
}
-re "^$IAC$WILL\(.)" {
    # refuse anything else
    send_user "$IAC$DONT$expect_out(1,string)"
    exp_continue
}
-re "^$IAC$SB$TTYPE" {
    expect_user null
    expect_user -re "(.*)$IAC$SE"
    set env(TERM) [string tolower $expect_out(1,string)]
    # now drop out of protocol handling loop
}
-re "^$IAC$WONT$TTYPE" {
    # treat as acknowledgment and ignore
    set env(TERM) vt100
    # now drop out of protocol handling loop
}
}
```

The terminal type is handled specially. If the client agrees to provide its terminal type, the server must send another command that means "ok, go ahead and tell me". The response has an embedded null, so it is broken up into separate **expect** commands. The terminal type is provided in uppercase, so it is translated with "**string lower**". If the client refuses to provide a terminal type, the server arbitrarily uses vt100.

All of the protocol and user activity occurs with the standard input and output. These two streams are automatically established if the daemon is configured with inetd.

Next, the timeout is disabled and a bare **expect** command is given. This allows the protocol interaction to take place according to the **expect_before** above. Most of the protocol actions end with **exp_continue**, allowing the **expect** to continue looking for more commands.

```
set timeout -1
expect                ;# do negotiations up to terminal type
```

When the client returns (or refuses to return) the terminal type, the **expect** command ends and the protocol negotiations are temporarily suspended. At this point, the terminal type is stored in the environment, and programs can be spawned which will inherit the terminal type automatically.

```
spawn interactive-program
```

Now imagine that the script performs a series of expect and send commands, perhaps to negotiate secret information or to navigate through a difficult or simply repetitive dialogue.

```
expect . . .
send . . .
expect . . .
```

Additional protocol commands may have continued to arrive while a process is being spawned, and the protocol commands are handled during these expect commands. Additional protocol commands can be exchanged at any time; however, in practice, none of the earlier ones will ever reoccur. Thus, they can be removed. The protocol negotiation typically takes place very quickly, so the patterns can usually be deleted after the first expect command that waits for real user data.

```
# remove protocol negotation patterns
expect_before -i $user_spawn_id
```

One data transformation that cannot be disabled is that the telnet client appends either a null or linefeed character to every return character sent by the user. This can be handled in a number of ways. The following command does it within an interact command which is what the script might end with.

```
interact "\r" {
    send "\r"
    expect_user \n {} null
}
```

Additional patterns can be added to look for commands or real user data, but this suffices in the common case where the user ends up talking directly to the process on the remote host.

Ultimately, the connection established by the Expect daemon looks like this:

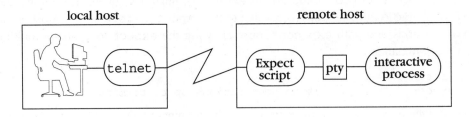

Example—Automating Gopher And Mosaic telnet Connections

Gopher is an information system that follows links of information that may lead from one machine to another.[†] The Gopher daemon does not support the ability to run interactive programs. For instance, suppose you offer public access to a service on your system, such as a library catalog. Since this is an interactive service, it is accessed by logging in, usually with a well-known account name such as "`info`".

Put another way, for someone to use the service, they must `telnet` to your host and enter "`info`" when prompted for an account. You could automate this with an Expect script. Not so, under Gopher. The Gopher daemon is incapable of running interactive processes itself. Instead, the daemon passes the `telnet` information to the Gopher client. Then it is up to the Gopher client to run `telnet` and log in.

This means that the client system has to do something with the account information. By default, the Gopher client displays the information on the screen and asks the user to type it back in. This is rather silly. After all, the client knows the information yet insists on having the user enter it manually. It is not a matter of permission. The client literally tells the user what to type! Here is an example (with XXX to protect the guilty) from an actual Gopher session.

```
+----------University of XXX XXXXXX XXXXXXXX----------+
| Connecting to library.XXX.edu, port 23 using telnet. |
|                                                      |
| Use the account name "info" to log in                |
|                                                      |
|                              [Cancel: ^G] [OK: Enter] |
+-----------------------------------------------------
```

Even Mosaic, with its slick user interface, does not do any better. It looks pretty, but the user is still stuck typing in the same information by hand.

Unfortunately, Mosaic and Gopher clients cannot perform interaction automation. One reason is that there is no standard way of doing it. For instance, there is no reason to

---

[†] While the WWW (e.g., Mosaic) interface is different than Gopher, both have the same restrictions on handling interactive processes and both can take advantage of the approach I describe here.

expect that any arbitrary host has Expect. Many hosts (e.g., PCs running DOS) do not even support Expect, even though they can run `telnet`.

And even if all hosts could perform interaction automation, you might not want to give out the information needed to control the interaction. Your service might, for example, offer access to other private, internal, or pay-for-use data as well as public data. Automating the account name, as I showed in the example, is only the tip of the iceberg. There may be many other parts of the interaction that need to be automated. If you give out the account, password, and instructions to access the public data, users could potentially take this information, bypass the Gopher or Mosaic client and interact by hand, doing things you may not want.

The solution is to use the technique I described in the previous section and partially automate the service through an Expect daemon accessible from a `telnet` port. By doing the interaction in the daemon, there is no need to depend on or trust the client. A user could still `telnet` to the host, but would get only what the server allowed.

By controlling the interaction from the server rather than from the client, passwords and other sensitive pieces of information do not have a chance of being exposed. There is no way for the user to get information from the server if the server does not supply it. Another advantage is that the server can do much more sophisticated processing. The server can shape the conversation using all the power of Expect.

In practice, elements of the earlier script beginning on page 393 can be stored in another file that is sourced as needed. For instance, all of the commands starting with the `telnet` protocol definitions down to the bare **expect** command could be stored in a file (say, `expectd.proto`) and sourced by a number of similar servers.

```
source /usr/etc/expectd.proto
```

As an example, suppose you want to let people log into another host (such as a commercial service for which you pay money) and run a program there, but without their knowing which host it is or what your account and password are. Then, the local server would spawn a `telnet` (or `tip` or whatever) to the real server.

The following example is a script that communicates with the popular FirstSearch system provided by OCLC Online Computer Library Center, a research organization used by more than 17,000 libraries. FirstSearch searches databases such as WorldCat. (WorldCat alone holds more than 29 million records!) Access to FirstSearch costs money so it is appropriate to hide the password while still allowing access. For instance, you could make the service available to your staff this way.[†] Then if they took another job elsewhere, they would not be able to continue using the account, since they never knew the account information and password in the first place.

---

† I will mention one way of doing access control in the next section.

This example merely automates the initial login. You could, of course, do more but this is sufficient to show that there are all sorts of other possibilities.

```
source /usr/etc/expectd.proto
log_user 0              ;# turn output off
set timeout -1
expect                  ;# do negotiations up to terminal type
spawn telnet fscat.oclc.org
expect "authorization*=> "
send "123-456-789\r"
expect "password*=> "
send "jellyroll\r"
log_user 1              ;# turn output on
expect "WELCOME TO FIRSTSEARCH"
```

The script ends as before—removing the protocol patterns and dropping the user into an `interact`.

```
expect_before -i $user_spawn_id
interact "\r" {
    send "\r"
    expect_user \n {} null
}
```

The interface provided by OCLC suffers from the very problem I warned against in Chapter 8 (p. 199). Namely, the interface leaves a window between the time it prompts for the password and disables echoing. This naturally shows up here. Since Expect is so fast, the password is almost always entered in the critical window and echoed. A simple solution is just to sleep for a few seconds. However, this is unreliable. There is no guarantee that any amount of time is enough. A better solution is to absorb the password if it appears. Here is the critical fragment of the script rewritten to do so:

```
expect "password*=> "
send [set password "jellyroll"]\r
expect -re "(.*$password)?(.*WELCOME TO FIRSTSEARCH.*)" {
    send_user -raw $expect_out(2,string)"
}
log_user 1              ;# turn output on
```

If the password appears, the regular expression skips over it. The remainder of the output is matched and sent to the user. Once beyond the password interaction, logging to the standard output is restored, so that it can be done automatically by Expect.

In this example, the script is logging in to another host, and the password appears literally in the script. This can be very secure if users cannot log in to the host. Put scripts like these on a separate machine to which users cannot log in or physically approach. As long as the user can only access the machine over the network through these Expect daemons, you can offer services securely.

Providing the kind of daemon service I have just described requires very little resources. It is not CPU intensive nor is it particularly demanding of I/O. Thus, it is a fine way to make use of older workstations that most sites have sitting around idle and gathering dust.

Telling The System About Your Daemon

Daemons like the one I described in the previous section are typically started using `inetd`. Several freely available programs can assist network daemons by providing access control, identification, logging, and other enhancements. For instance, `tcp_wrapper` does this with a small wrapper around the individual daemons, whereas `xinetd` is a total replacement for `inetd`. `tcp_wrapper` is available from `cert.sei.cmu.edu` as `pub/network_tools`. `xinetd` is available from the `comp.source.unix` archive.

Since anyone using `xinetd` and `tcp_wrapper` is likely to know how to configure a server already, I will provide an explanation based on `inetd`. The details may differ from one system to another.

Most versions of `inetd` read configuration data from the file `/etc/inetd.conf`. A single line describes each server. (The order of the lines is irrelevant.) For example, to add a service called `secret`, add the following line:

```
secret stream tcp nowait root /usr/etc/secretd secretd
```

The first field is the name of the port on which the service will be offered. The next three parameters must always be `stream`, `tcp`, and `nowait` for the kind of server I have shown here. The next parameter is the user id with which the server will be started. `root` is common but not necessary. The next argument is the file to execute. In this example, `/usr/etc/secretd` is the Expect script. This follows the tradition of storing servers in `/usr/etc` and ending their names with a "d". The script must be marked executable. If the script contains passwords, the script should be readable, writable, and executable only by the owner. The script should also start with the usual `#!` line. Alternatively, you can list Expect as the server and pass the name of the script as an argument. The next argument in the line is the name of the script (again). Inside the script, this name is merely assigned to `argv0`. The remaining arguments are passed uninterpreted as the arguments to the script.

Once `inetd` is configured, you must send it a HUP signal. This causes `inetd` to reread its configuration file.

The file `/etc/services` (or the NIS `services` map) contains the mapping of service names to port numbers. Add a line for your new service and its port number. Your number must end with `/tcp`. "#" starts a comment which runs up to the end of the line. For example:

```
secret 9753/tcp     # Don's secret server
```

You must choose a port number that is not already in use. Looking in the `/etc/services` file is not good enough since ports can be used without being listed there. There is no guaranteed way of avoiding future conflicts, but you can at least find a free port at the time by running a command such as "`netstat -na | grep tcp`" or `lsof`. `lsof` (which stands for "list open files") and similar programs are available free from many Internet source archives.

Exercises

1. Write a script that retrieves an FAQ. First the script should attempt to get the FAQ locally by using your local news reading software. If the FAQ has expired or is not present for some other reason, the script should anonymously `ftp` it from `rtfm.mit.edu`. (For instance, the first part of the Tcl FAQ lives in the file `/pub/usenet/news.answers/tcl-faq/part1`.) If the `ftp` fails because the site is too loaded or is down, the script should go into the background and retry later, or it should send email to `mail-server@rtfm.mit.edu` in the form:

   ```
   send usenet/news.answers/tcl-faq/part1
   ```

2. Write a script called `netpipe` that acts as a network pipe. Shell scripts on two different machines should be able to invoke `netpipe` to communicate with each other as easily as if they were using named pipes (i.e., fifos) on a single machine.

3. Several of your colleagues are interested in listening to Internet Talk Radio and Internet Town Hall.[†] Unfortunately, each hour of listening pleasure is 30Mb. Rather than tying up your expensive communications link each time the same file is requested, make a `cron` entry that downloads the new programs once each day. (For information about the service, send mail to `info@radio.com`.)

4. The `dialback` scripts in Chapter 1 (p. 4) and Chapter 16 (p. 351) dial back immediately. Use `at` to delay the start by one minute so that there is time to log out and accept the incoming call on the original modem. Then rewrite the script using `fork` and `disconnect`. Is there any functional difference?

5. Take the `telnet` daemon presented in this chapter and enhance it so that it understands when the client changes the window size. This option is defined by RFC 1073 and is called *Negotiate About Window Size* (NAWS) and uses command byte `\x1f`.

---

† The book review from April 7, 1993 is particularly worthwhile!

NAWS is similar to the terminal type subnegotation except that 1) it can occur at any time, and 2) the client sends back strings of the form:

```
$IAC$SB$NAWS$ROWHI$ROWLO$COLHI$COLLO$IAC$SE
```

where `ROWHI` is the high-order byte of the number of rows and `ROWLO` is the low-order byte of the number of rows. `COLHI` and `COLLO` are defined similarly.

6. You notice someone is logging in to your computer and using an account that should not be in use. Replace the real `telnet` daemon with an Expect script that transparently records any sessions for that particular user. Do the same for the `rlogin` daemon.

## 18

In This Chapter:
- *Tracing Commands And Variables*
- *Peeking And Poking Into Other Processes*
- *A Generalized Debugger For Tcl Programs*

Debugging Scripts

A description of debugging techniques could easily fill an entire book or more—and rightfully so. In any software development, debugging often takes more time than the programming (not to mention design[†]).

The need for debugging is even more exaggerated in Tcl where many people code while thinking. The interpretive nature of the language makes this seductively easy.

Good design principles can help avoid getting stuck in a quagmire. Careful thought can prevent many common traps. In the same way, careful (and imaginative) thought is helpful in solving problems. Some people claim never to use debuggers. I am not one of them, but sometimes it helps to walk away from the keyboard and simply think through what could possibly be happening—or what cannot possibly be happening but is anyway.

Tracing

In this section, I will briefly recap some useful techniques and mention a few more that are very useful for tracking down problems. All of these have to do with tracing control. I will go into other debugging techniques later.

Simple output commands (using `puts` and `send`) can go a long way towards finding problems. However, putting commands in and taking them out is a hassle. You can conditionalize their execution with a variable.

```
if (verbose) {
    puts ". . ."
}
```

---

† Assuming you did any.

Rather than having raw `if`/`puts` commands throughout your code, it is cleaner to isolate them in one place, such as a procedure called `vprint` (for "verbose print").

```
proc vprint {msg} {
    global verbose

    if {$verbose} {puts "$msg"}
}
```

Later if you decide to redirect output to a file or window, you only have to change the one output command in `vprint`.

This idea can be augmented in many different ways. For example, the following definition prints the procedure name before the message.

```
proc vprint {msg} {
    global verbose

    if {$verbose} {
        puts "[lindex [info level -1] 0]: $msg"
    }
}
```

Logging

It is often useful to write information to files so that you can study it later. You can write log files yourself or you can use Expect's logging functions.

The commands `log_user`, `log_file`, and `exp_internal` can all be helpful while debugging. These commands can also be controlled indirectly through procedures similar to the `puts` example above.

I will summarize what these commands do. The `log_user` command controls whether the output of spawned processes is seen. In most scripts, you want to leave this set one way or the other, but it is nice to have the flexibility to turn it off and on during development. The `log_user` command is described further in Chapter 7 (p. 175).

The `log_file` command is related to the `log_user` command. However, `log_file` has almost no uses other than for debugging. The `log_file` command records everything from a spawned process. Even output suppressed via "`log_user  0`" can be recorded. The `log_file` command is further described in Chapter 7 (p. 180).

The `exp_internal` command is another command that is useful only for debugging. The `exp_internal` command enables the printing of internal information, mostly concerning pattern matching. This command was discussed in Chapter 7 (p. 165).

In Chapter 17 (p. 383), I described how to use mail to save information. This technique can be very useful because you can get an immediate indication as soon as the mail has been generated. With the log commands, you have to remember to look at the files they create. For example, in Chapter 1 (p. 13) I described a script that regularly checks a set of modems. If the script encounters a problem that it cannot resolve, it sends mail rather than simply logging the error to a file. This way the problem is brought to an administrator's attention immediately.

Command Tracing

The strace command is yet another command that is useful only for debugging. The command enables the printing of commands before they are executed. Here is what it looks like when commands are traced.

```
expect1.2> set foo [split "a b [expr 10+5]"]
3       expr 10+5
2     split "a b [expr 10+5]"
1   set foo [split "a b [expr 10+5]"]
a b 15
```

Each command is prefixed by an integer describing the depth of the evaluation stack. Each bracketed command increases the evaluation stack. In this example, you can see the expr command being evaluated at the third stack level, the split command being evaluated at the second stack level, and the set command being evaluated at the first level.

Each command is indented by two spaces for each additional level in the stack. The precise level numbers are not that important except as a guide to bounding the amount of information that is produced.

The strace command takes an integer argument that bounds the depth to which commands are traced. For example, the following command traces only commands executed at the first three levels.

```
strace 3
```

This could be useful when there are a lot of subroutines being executed and you want to ignore, for example, many iterations of a loop at some deep level. Unfortunately, this control is not very fine. In practice, I often just use a very high value no matter what kind of script I am using. It is simply not worth the effort of figuring out a precise cutoff. This command is likely to be revised in the future.[†]

---

† The name is particularly likely to change. The s stands for "statement". Once a synonym for "command", "statement" has been relegated to the historical wastebasket.

Given the flag -info, the strace command returns the current depth to which it is tracing.

Variable Tracing

Tcl supports the ability to invoke procedures when variables are read or written. This can be useful in regular programming (for example, Tk makes extensive use of tracing) but it is especially useful during debugging.

For example, the following command traces any assignments to the array expect_out.

```
trace variable expect_out w traceproc
```

The w argument in the command stands for "write". The last argument is a procedure which is called whenever the variable is written (i.e., assigned to). Instead of w, you can also put r (read) or u (unset). A variable is unset when the unset command is used or the variable goes out of scope.

All trace procedures must be declared with three parameters. The first parameter is the variable name, the second is the element name (if the variable is an array), and the third is the letter r, w, or u, depending on if the variable is being read, written, or unset.

The usual thing to do with a trace procedure when debugging is to print out the variable. Here is a trace procedure to do that. The procedure prints the variable name followed by the value. The type argument is ignored since it will always be w in this example.

```
proc traceproc {array element type} {
    upvar [set array]($element) var
    puts "new value of [set array]($element) is $var"
}
```

The trace procedure executes in the context of the scope in which the variable was accessed, so the upvar command is necessary. It gets the variable from the caller's scope, where it is meaningful.

The array name is stored in array and the element name is stored in element. The expression "[set array]($element)" produces the compound name. The more obvious $array($element) would return the value and not the name.

Here is what it looks like when I trace the array expect_out and type the string "hello world" to an expect command that is just looking for "world":

```
expect1.2> trace variable expect_out w traceproc
expect1.3> expect world
hello world
new value of expect_out(0,string) is world
```

```
new value of expect_out(spawn_id) is 0
new value of expect_out(buffer) is hello world
expect1.4>
```

Tracing can also be limited to particular array elements. The following command creates a trace only on the element named buffer in the expect_out array.

expect1.5> **trace variable expect_out(buffer) w traceproc**

Tracing variables that are not arrays is a little simpler. The second argument to the trace procedure is just an empty string and can be ignored. Here is a trace procedure for scalar variables.

```
proc traceproc_simple {v null type} {
    upvar $v var
    puts "new value of $v is $var"
}
```

Using this procedure, you can trace non-array variables. Here are some examples:

```
trace variable spawn_id w traceproc_simple
trace variable timeout w traceproc_simple
```

You can associate the same trace procedure with multiple variables, and you can also associate multiple trace procedures with the same variable. They will all be triggered (sequentially of course). You can even associate the same trace procedure multiple times with the same variable.

Example — Logging By Tracing

The log_file command does not provide any special support for writing the output of different processes to different log files. This can be simulated by tracing the expect_out array. Remember that the spawn_id element identifies the particular spawn id that produced the output.

The following trace procedure writes the value of expect_out(buffer) to a file specific to the spawn id.

```
proc log_by_tracing {array element op} {
    uplevel {
        global logfile
        set file $logfile($expect_out(spawn_id))
        puts -nonewline $file $expect_out(buffer)
    }
}
```

The association between the spawn id and each log file is made in the array logfile which contains a pointer to the log file based on the spawn id. Such an association could be made with the following code when each process is spawned.

```
spawn ...
set logfile($spawn_id) [open ... w]
```

The trace is armed in the usual way:

```
trace variable expect_out(buffer) w log_by_tracing
```

Internally, the `expect` command saves the `spawn_id` element of `expect_out` after the *x*, `string` elements but before the `buffer` element. For this reason, the trace must be triggered by the `buffer` element rather than the `spawn_id` element. A trace triggered on `expect_out(spawn_id)` will see an old value of `expect_out(buffer)`.

In Chapter 6 (p. 149), I described how process output could be discarded if more arrived than was permitted by `match_max`. In fact, a copy of the output is saved in `expect_out(buffer)` before it is removed from the internal buffer. So even if the `expect` command does not pass control to a user-supplied action, the buffer to be discarded can be saved with the `trace` command just shown.

Saving output from the `interact` command in the same fashion is a little trickier. The `interact` command is optimized for speed and there is no automatic saving of the spawn id or buffer. This can be simulated but requires the use of explicit actions and flags.

UNIX System Call Tracing

Before I finish with tracing, I will mention one more tracing aid—for UNIX system calls. Tracing UNIX system calls is totally outside Tcl and yet that is exactly the reason why it is so valuable. Systems calls are precisely the points at which Tcl interacts with the outside world.

By tracing system calls, you can see files being opened and accessed. You can see when your process is sleeping or creating new processes. You can see signals being sent or received. This kind of information is very useful because, after all, programs are run for the side-effects that they have on the outside world. By tracing system calls, you get an idea of all the side-effects that your script is causing.

I will not go into a lot of detail here because so much of this is system specific. However, there are three programs that are particularly useful. `truss` is a very flexible system call tracer that is found on System V derivatives. `trace` is a similar program that is found on BSD-based systems. `strace` is a public-domain version of `trace` that is a lot better than the original. I highly recommend getting familiar with at least one of these tools.

Tk And tkinspect

The Tk extension to Tcl provides commands that are primarily used for the purpose of building graphic user interfaces. However, one Tk command that has nothing to do with graphics is the send command.[†] Tk's send command sends a command from one Tk application to another. The command is evaluated by the second application and returned to the first.

An obvious command to send to an application is "set foo" to find out, for example, what the value of foo is. To do this, all you have to do is send the command from another Tk application. Below, I typed the shell command to start expectk—a program that combines Expect and Tk. Using expectk, I then sent to the application named frogger a request to get the value of the variable named frogcount:

```
% expectk
expect1.1> send frogger set frogcount
17
```

Because X applications typically spend most of their life waiting in an event loop, applications in Tk are almost always ready to respond to send requests. The applications do not have to do anything special to handle them. Most importantly, applications do not have to be stopped to handle them. Tk applications process send requests as they are received. This makes the send command quite useful for debugging. Without any preparation, you can pry into the internal data structures of scripts while they are running!

In fact, you are not restricted to looking at variables. You can change variables. You can execute procedures. You can even redefine procedures as the script is running. Although you may not want to do this last type of operation frequently, all of the commands mentioned previously in this chapter are good candidates for sending to an application that needs to be debugged.

To facilitate the use of send for debugging purposes, I recommend tkinspect. Written by Sam Shen, tkinspect provides a graphic browser to all the global variables and procedures in all the Tk-based applications currently running. You can scroll through variables and values, and change them just by pointing at and editing them using emacs-style commands. At any time, you can send back new values or commands by pressing the send button. tkinspect is so easy to use that you may find yourself using it on *bug-free* programs simply because tkinspect provides a direct view into Tk programs. The Tcl FAQ describes how to obtain tkinspect. For more information on the FAQ, see Chapter 1 (p. 20).

---

† When using Tk, Expect's send command can be accessed as exp_send. For more information, see Chapter 19 (p. 433).

Despite my enthusiasm for send and tkinspect, there are several drawbacks. You can see only global variables. You cannot stop the application to look at variables that are frequently changing. And you may have to switch from using Expect (or some derivative) to Expectk. Chapter 19 (p. 429) explains the changes that are required to run Expect scripts in Expectk.

Tk's send command is really worth exploring. I have brought it up here in the context of debugging, but the ability to have applications send arbitrary commands to each other is very powerful. Although the interprocess communication that send uses is built in to X, Tk brings this capability out in such a way that it is very easy to use. The send command is much more than a debugging tool.

Traditional Debugging

Expect offers a debugging mechanism that is similar to traditional source-level debuggers such as dbx and gdb. From now on, I will call it the *debugger*. This particular debugger is just one of several that are available as separate extensions to Tcl. Read the Tcl FAQ to learn about other Tcl debuggers.

The debugger can be started with the command "debug 1" or by starting Expect itself with the command-line flag "-D". The -D flag is just shorthand for a form of the debug command, so I will talk about debug first.

The debug command can be used to start or stop the debugger. With an argument of 1, the debugger is started. It is stopped with an argument of 0.

```
debug 1
```

When the debugger starts running, it prints the next command to be executed and then prompts you for what to do next. At this point you can do things like single-step the script, set breakpoints, or continue the script. You can also enter any Expect or Tcl commands as well.

The following Tcl commands illustrate that the debugger evaluates Tcl commands as usual.

```
dbg2.1> set m {a b c}
a b c
dbg2.2> llength $m
3
```

The debugger interaction looks a lot like that of the Expect interpreter command. As with the interpreter command, the second number of the prompt is the Tcl history identifier. The first number is the depth of the evaluation stack. In the context of a script, the initial depth of the evaluation stack is 1 but the debugger always introduces a new level to the stack. So the debugger prompts are always 2.*x* or higher.

The `debug` command can appear anywhere in a script. If you have a good idea of where your script is misbehaving, add the `debug` command at that point. If the misbehavior is dependent on some data, put the `debug` command in the appropriate side of an `if` command.

```
if {$a<0} {   ;# code only misbehaves when a is negative?
    debug 1   ;# turn on debugger
}
```

The command-line flag "-D 1" makes Expect execute a "`debug 1`" command before executing any commands in the script. The effect is as if you had made this command the first line in your script. This is probably not where you would actually want to start debugging; however, the flag avoids having to edit the script to manually add the command.

The -D flag also initializes a trap so that if you generate `SIGINT` (e.g., press ^C), the debugger takes control before the next command.

The command-line flag "-D 0" arms the trap without executing the "`debug 1`" command. This is convenient if you want to run your script for a while and then press ^C when you want to take control. If you want to arm a different trap or take some other action upon -D, you can replace the default trap initialization by defining the environment variable `EXPECT_DEBUG_INIT` with an appropriate Tcl command.

If "`debug 1`" is executed from an interrupt handler, control is not passed to the debugger until the next command is about to execute. By using the -now flag, the debugger takes control at the first point at which the interrupt can be fully processed. (See Chapter 14 (p. 318) for more information.)

```
debug -now 1
```

Being able to interrupt a command is particularly useful if the command is of a type that can run for a long time, such as an `expect` command. However, in this situation the debugger may be unable to show the current command, so -now should not be used if it is not necessary. It may be convenient for you to associate the "`debug -now 1`" command with a different interrupt than ^C.

The remainder of this tutorial will assume that the debugger has been started by using the command-line flag "-D 1".

Debugger Command Overview And Philosophy

The debugger commands are:

Name	Description
s	step into procedure
n, N	step over procedure
r	return from procedure
b	set, clear, or show breakpoint
c	continue
w	show stack
u	move scope up
d	move scope down
h	help
\r	repeat last action

The debugger commands are all one letter.[†] This is partly for convenience. Since the debugger is purely an interactive application, commands should be easy to enter. Also, scripts rarely use one-letter commands, so the chances of name conflicts between the debugger and scripted applications is very low.

The command names are very similar and, in some cases, identical to other popular debuggers (e.g., gdb, dbx). Existing Tcl procedures are directly usable, so there are no new commands, for example, to print variables since Tcl already provides such commands (e.g., set, puts, parray).

For the purposes of describing the debugger commands, I will use a script called debug-test.exp. It is shown below. The script does not do anything particularly useful. It merely serves to illustrate how the debugger is used.

```
set b 1

proc p4 {x} {
    return [
        expr 5+[expr 1+$x]]
}

set z [
    expr 1+[expr 2+[p4 $b]]
]
```

---

† The "repeat last action" command is entered by just pressing the return key.

```
proc p3 {} {
    set m 0
}

proc p2 {} {
    set c 4
    p3
    set d 5
}

proc p1 {} {
    set a 2
    p2
    set a 3
    set a 5
}

p1
set k 7
p1
```

If the debugger is started at the beginning of the script, no commands have been executed. Tcl and Expect commands have global scope.

```
% expect -D 1 debug-test.exp
1: set b 1
dbg2.1>
```

When a new command is about to be executed, the debugger prints the evaluation stack level followed by the command. "set b 1" is the first line in the script. It has not yet been executed. "info exists" confirms this.

```
dbg2.1> info exists b
0
```

Stepping Over Procedure Calls

The n command executes the pending command—in this case "set b 1"—and displays the next command to be executed.

```
dbg2.2> n
1: proc p4 {x} {
    return [
        expr 5+[expr 1+$x]]
}
dbg2.3> info exists b
1
```

The command "info exists b" confirms that b has been set. The procedure p4 is about to be defined.

```
dbg2.4> n
4: p4 $b
dbg5.5>
```

The procedure p4 has now been defined. The next command to be executed is p4 itself. It appears in the command:

```
set z [
    expr 1+[expr 2+[p4 $b]]
]
```

The three sets of braces introduce three new levels on the evaluation stack; hence the stack level in which p4 is about to be executed is shown as 4.[†]

Notice that the evaluation stack level does not affect the scope. I am still in the top-level scope and b is still visible.

```
dbg5.5> info exists b
1
```

The argument to p4 is $b. The value of this variable can be evaluated by using set or puts.

```
dbg5.6> set b
1
dbg5.7> puts $b
1
```

Another n command executes p4, popping the stack one level. Additional n commands continue evaluation of the "set z" command, each time popping the stack one level. It is not necessary to enter "n" each time. Pressing return is sufficient. Expect remembers that the last action command was an n and executes that.

```
dbg5.8> n
3: expr 2+[p4 $b]
dbg4.9>
2: expr 1+[expr 2+[p4 $b]]
dbg3.10>
1: set z [
    expr 1+[expr 2+[p4 $b]]
]
dbg2.11>
```

---

† Whether the word "stack" refers to procedure call stack or evaluation stack is either explicit or clearly implied by the context.

It is often useful to skip over multiple commands embedded in a single complex command and just stop the debugger before it executes the last command. The N command does this. Here is what the interaction looks like if I restart the debugging just before the definition of p4:

```
1: proc p4 {x} {
    return [
        expr 5+[expr 1+$x]]
}
dbg2.2> N
1: set z [
    expr 1+[expr 2+[p4 $b]]
]
dbg2.3>
```

Having typed N, the debugger executes the `proc` command but does not stop before *execution* of p4. Instead, the debugger executes all the commands (p4, and `expr` twice) up to the `set` before stopping. The N command is a convenient way of stepping over complex commands such as `if`, `for`, and `source` commands that invoke many other commands at the current scope.

Stepping Into Procedure Calls

The n command executes a procedure atomically. In contrast, it is possible to step *into* a procedure with the s command. (If the command that is about to be executed is not a procedure, then s and n behave identically.)

Imagine that p4 is just about to be executed. After the s command, the debugger stops before the first command in the procedure and waits for more interactive commands.

```
4: p4 $b
dbg5.5> s
7: expr 1+$x
dbg8.6>
```

"expr 1+$x" is the first command to be executed inside of p4. It is nested inside of two brackets, plus the procedure call of p4, so the stack level is increased by three.

s, n, and N take an optional argument in the form of a number describing how many commands to execute. For example:

```
s 2
s 100
s $b
s [expr 2+[p4 $b]]
```

The arguments are evaluated according to the usual Tcl rules because s, n, and N are commands known to Tcl.

The debugger will not interrupt procedures invoked from the command line. This is usually the desired behavior although it is possible to change this.

s, n, and N are action commands. This means that the debugger remembers the last one and uses it if you press return without a command. The arguments are remembered as well. So if you want to execute 10 steps at a time, you need only enter "s 10" once and then press returns thereafter.

Where Am I

In the current scenario, I am about to execute "expr 1+$x" in the procedure p4. I can remind myself of this by displaying the stack of procedure scopes using the w command.

```
7: expr 1+$x
dbg8.6> w
 0: expect -D 1 debug-test.exp
*1: p4 1
 7: expr 1+1
```

The first line of the response describes scope 0. This is the top-level scope of the file itself, and the command used to invoke the program is shown. The second line describes scope 1 which is the invocation of procedure p4. The last line is not a scope but just repeats the evaluation stack level and the command about to be executed.

Notice that when w prints commands, they are displayed *using the actual values of each parameter*. In contrast, when the debugger automatically prints out the next command to be executed, the command is printed as it was originally entered in the script. For example, the debugger initially stopped and printed "expr 1+$w", but the same instruction shows as "expr 1+1" in the output from the w command. Being able to see the values of the parameters this way is exceedingly useful.

The Current Scope

By typing "s 14", the debugger executes fourteen steps. This brings me to the first command in procedure p3.

```
dbg8.8> s 14
4: set m 0
dbg5.9> w
 0: expect -D 1 debug-test.exp
 1: p1
 2: p2
```

```
*3:  p3
 4:  set  m  0
```

The asterisk denotes that p3 is the *current scope*. I can now execute Tcl commands appropriate to the scope of p3. This includes commands that can look or operate directly in other scopes such as `global`, `uplevel`, and `upvar`, but it is simpler yet to move the current scope up and down the stack.

```
dbg5.10> uplevel {set c}
4
```

Moving Up And Down The Stack

The current scope can be changed by the u and d commands. u moves the current scope up, while d moves it down. Interactive variable accesses always refer to the current scope.

```
dbg5.11> u
dbg5.12> w
 0: expect -D 1 debug-test.exp
 1: p1
*2: p2
 3: p3
 4: set m 0
dbg5.13> set c
4
```

Both u and d accept an argument representing the number of scopes by which to move. For example, "u 2" moves from scope 2 to scope 0.

```
dbg5.14> u 2
dbg5.15> w
*0: expect -D 1 debug-test.exp
 1: p1
 2: p2
 3: p3
 4: set m 0
```

An absolute scope is also accepted in the form of "#" followed by a scope number, such as "#3".

```
dbg5.16> u #3
dbg5.17> w
 0: expect -D 1 debug-test.exp
 1: p1
 2: p2
*3: p3
 4: set m 0
```

When an absolute scope is named, either u or d may be used, irrespective of which direction the new scope lies.

Moving the scope does not affect the next script command that is about to be executed. If a command such as s or n is given, the current scope is automatically reset to wherever is appropriate for execution of the new command.

Returning From A Procedure

The r command completes execution of the current procedure. In other words, it stops after the current procedure returns.

```
dbg5.18> r
3: set d 5
dbg4.19> w
 0: expect -D 1 debug-test.exp
 1: p1
*2: p2
 3: set d 5
dbg4.20> r
2: set a 3
dbg3.21> w
 0: expect -D 1 debug-test.exp
*1: p1
 2: set a 3
dbg3.22> r
1: set k 7
dbg2.23> w
*0: expect -D 1 debug-test.exp
 1: set k 7
dbg2.24> r
nowhere to return to
```

Continuing Execution

The c command lets execution continue without having to single-step. In the scenario so far, given a command anywhere, the program would continue until the script ends and the shell prompt appears.

```
dbg2.25> c
%
```

The c command is also useful in other ways. After setting breakpoints, the program can be continued until it hits a breakpoint. The program can also be continued until a signal occurs, such as by pressing ^C.

r and c are action commands just like s, n, and N. Thus, they can be executed by pressing return if they were the previous action command executed. All other commands are not action commands. For example, w is not an action command. If you enter a c command, hit a breakpoint, and then enter a w command, pressing return after that continues the script.

Defining Breakpoints

So far, I have shown how to execute a fixed number of commands or procedure calls with debugger commands such as s and n. In contrast, breakpoints provide a way to stop execution upon a condition. The conditions include:

- line number and filename matching
- expression testing
- command and argument name matching

Now I will demonstrate these conditions and also show how Tcl's trace facility can be used to cause breakpoints.

Breakpoint By Line Number And Filename

Line numbers and filenames are the most common way to specify a breakpoint.[†] This form is correspondingly the most compact. For example, the following command causes execution to break before executing line 7.

```
dbg2.26> b 7
0
```

After creation of a breakpoint, an integer identifying the breakpoint is printed. Later, I will show how this is helpful when you have to keep track of multiple breakpoints.

By default, the line number refers to the file associated with the current scope. A filename may be used to refer to a different file. A colon is used to separate the filename and line number.

```
dbg2.27> b foo.exp:7
1
```

---

† Breakpoints by line number and filename have yet to be implemented as this book goes to press. They will likely be supported in the near future with the syntax shown here.

Breakpoint By Expression

It is possible to break only when an expression is true. For example, the following command causes execution to break only when foo is greater than 3.

```
dbg2.28> b if {$foo > 3}
2
```

Expressions follow the usual Tcl syntax and may be arbitrarily complex.

No breakpointing occurs inside of the evaluation of breakpoint expressions (unless another breakpoint dictates this).

Line numbers and expressions may be combined. Here is the same command as before but augmented with a line number so that execution breaks only when foo is greater than 3 on line 7.

```
dbg2.28> b 7 if {$foo > 3}
2
```

I will show the general form for breakpoints on page 425.

Breakpoint By Pattern Match

It is also possible to define breakpoints by pattern matching on commands and arguments. Regular expressions are introduced by the flag "-re".[†] The following command stops if the string p4 appears within the command about to be executed:

```
dbg2.29> b -re "p4"
3
```

Here are the results of this based on the sample script:

```
% expect -D 1 debug-test.exp
1: set b 1
dbg2.1> b -re "p4"
0
dbg2.2> c
breakpoint 0: -re "p4"
1: proc p4 {x} {
        return [
     expr 5+[expr 1+$x]]
}
```

---

† The debugger permits all flags to be abbreviated to the smallest unique prefix. For example, "-re" can be abbreviated "-r". The usual quoting conventions around patterns should be observed. In this example, the quotes around p4 can be omitted.

```
dbg2.3> c
breakpoint 0: -re "p4"
4: p4 $b
dbg5.4> c
breakpoint 0: -re "p4"
3: expr 2+[p4 $b]
dbg4.5> c
breakpoint 0: -re "p4"
2: expr 1+[expr 2+[p4 $b]]
```

The first breakpoint occurred upon the definition of p4. The second occurred when p4 was called. Two more breakpoints occurred only because p4 was mentioned in the command.

With appropriate regular expressions, any one of these can be selected by itself. For example, to stop only on a definition of p4:

```
dbg2.1> b -re "proc p4 "
```

To stop only on a call to p4 itself:

```
dbg2.2> b -re "^p4 "
```

To stop only on commands which call p4:

```
dbg2.3> b -re "\\\[p4 "
```

The complexity of this last example is somewhat ameliorated by the unlikelihood of it ever being used. I have shown it simply for completeness. The point is, the ability to match on regular expressions is extremely powerful.

Multi-line patterns may be matched in the usual way—using characters such as \n and \r. Using braces instead of double quotes permits the previous pattern to be simplified to "{\[p4   }". However, the braces prevent the possibility of explicitly matching escaped characters such as \n.

Glob-style matching is available by using the flag -gl instead of -re. Because glob patterns match an entire string by default, the equivalents to the previous example look slightly different—anchors are not used and asterisks are required in several places.

To stop only on definitions:

```
dbg2.4> b -gl "proc p4 *"
```

On calls to p4:

```
dbg2.5> b -gl "p4 *"
```

On commands which call p4:

```
dbg2.6> b -gl "*\\\[p4 *"
```

Expressions can be combined with patterns just as they are with line numbers. For example, the following command defines a breakpoint which occurs on a call to p4 but only when foo is greater than 3

```
dbg2.7> b -gl "p4 *" if {$foo>3}
```

Strings which match regular expressions are saved in the array dbg. The part of the command matched by the entire pattern is saved in $dbg(0). Up to nine parenthesized subpattern matches are stored in $dbg(1) through $dbg(9).

For example, the name of a variable being set can be accessed as $dbg(1) after the following breakpoint:

```
dbg2.8> b -re {^set ([^ ])+ }
```

This can be used to construct more sophisticated breakpoints. For example, the following breakpoint occurs only when the variable being set was already set.

```
dbg2.9> b -re {^set ([^ ])+ } if {[info exists $dbg(1)]}
```

Breakpoint Actions

Breakpoints may trigger actions. The default action prints the breakpoint id and definition. It is possible to replace this action with any Tcl command. As an example, the following command defines a breakpoint which prints a descriptive message whenever the variable a is being defined:

```
dbg2.1> b -re "^set a " then {
+> puts "a is being set"
+> puts "old value of a = $a"
+> }
2
```

When run, it looks like this:

```
dbg2.2> c
a is being set
2: set a 2
dbg3.3> c
a is being set
old value of a = 2
2: set a 3
dbg3.4> c
a is being set
old value of a = 3
2: set a 5
```

Each time the breakpoint occurs, the old and new values of a are displayed. Notice that the first time the breakpoint occurred, a was not defined. In this case, $a was meaningless and the `puts` command was not executed. If there had been further commands in the breakpoint, they would also have been skipped.

Implicit error messages generated by actions are discarded. Error messages generated in breakpoint expressions are also discarded. The debugger assumes that such errors are just variables temporarily out of scope.

By default, breakpoints stop execution of the program. It is possible to tell the debugger not to stop by using the commands c, s, n, N, or r from within an action. In this way, breakpoints can be used to trace variables, although Tcl's built-in variable tracing commands perform this particular task much more efficiently.

Here is the trace procedure for simple variables (from page 407) amended with an extra command to interrupt the script if the variable's value ever exceeds 100.

```
proc traceproc_simple {v null type} {
    upvar $v var
    puts "new value of $v is $var"
    if {$var > 100} s
}
```

The s command here still means "step". However, because the script is not being single-stepped to begin with, the s command forces the script back into single-step mode and returns control back to the debugger's interactive prompt at the next command. The n, N, and r commands work similarly.

The following breakpoint prints out the name of each procedure as it is being defined.

```
dbg2.1> b -re "proc (\[^ ]*)" then {
+> puts "proc $dbg(1) defined"
+> c
+> }
0
```

The c command in the last line allows execution to continue after each breakpoint.

```
dbg2.2> c
proc p4 defined
proc p3 defined
proc p2 defined
proc p1 defined
```

The following breakpoint causes the debugger to break after execution of any procedure which has called p4.

```
dbg2.1> b -gl "p4 *" then "r"
```

The following command prints out the string "entering p4" when p4 is invoked. Execution continues for four more steps after that.

```
dbg2.2> b -re "^p4 " then {
+> puts "entering p4"
+> s 4
+> }
```

Multiple breakpoints can occur on the same line. All corresponding actions are executed. At most one debugger command will be executed, however. For example, if breakpoints trigger commands containing both "s 1" and "s 2", only the second (or last in general) will have any effect.

Limitations Of Breakpoint Actions And Interactive Commands

Debugger commands specified in a breakpoint action occur only after all the breakpoint pattern matching and other tests have completed. For example, the following breakpoint appears to print out the old and new values of every variable about to be set.

```
dbg2.1> b -re {^set ([^ ]+) } then {
+> puts "old $dbg(1) = [set $dbg(1)]"
+> n
+> puts "new $dbg(1) = [set $dbg(1)]"
+> }
```

However, the debugger does not execute the next command (i.e., from the n) until the breakpoint action completes. This breakpoint therefore prints the old value twice, incorrectly claiming that the latter is the new value.

```
dbg4.7> c
old a = 2
new a = 2
```

In this case, it is possible to get the new value by just omitting the last puts. The debugger will then automatically print the new value as part of echoing the next command to be executed.

```
dbg4.7> c
old a = 2
2: set a 3
```

This example illustrates a limitation of the debugger. The debugger does not use a separate thread of control and therefore does not allow arbitrary automation of its own commands.

General Form Of Breakpoints

Expressions and actions may be combined. This follows the syntax of Tcl's if-then (but no else). For example, the following command prints the value of foo whenever it is nonzero.

```
dbg2.1> b if {$foo} then {
+> puts "foo = $foo"
+>}
```

The general form of the breakpoint command permits up to one location (specified by pattern, or line number and filename), one expression, and one action. They must appear in this order, but all are optional.

If a location is provided or the if-expression does not look like a line number and/or filename, the if token may be omitted. If an if-expression has already appeared, the then token is also optional. For example, the following two commands have the same effect:

```
dbg2.1> b if {$foo} then {
+> puts "foo = $foo"
+>}
0
dbg2.2> b {$foo} {
+> puts "foo = $foo"
+>}
1
```

When the first argument resembles both a line number and expression, it is assumed to be a line number. The following command breaks on line 17:

```
dbg2.3> b 17
2
```

Listing Breakpoints

If no arguments are supplied, the b command lists all breakpoints. The following example assumes the previous three breakpoints have been set and creates two more. Notice that breakpoints 0 and 1 are identical.

```
dbg2.4> b -re "^p4"
3
dbg2.5> b zz.exp:17 if {$foo}
4
dbg2.6> b
breakpoint 4: zz.exp:23 if {$foo}
breakpoint 3: -re "^p4" if {^p4}
breakpoint 2: b 17
```

```
breakpoint 1: if {$foo} then {
    puts "foo = $foo"
}
breakpoint 0: if {$foo} then {
    puts "foo = $foo"
}
```

Each breakpoint is identified by an integer. For example, breakpoint 4 occurs if foo is true just before line 23 is executed in file zz.exp.

When multiple breakpoints occur on the same line, the actions are executed in the order that they are listed by the b command.

Deleting Breakpoints

A breakpoint can be deleted with the command "b -#" where # is the breakpoint number. The following command deletes breakpoint 4.

```
dbg2.7> b -4
```

All of the breakpoints may be deleted by omitting the number. For example:

```
dbg2.8> b -
```

Help

The h command prints a short listing of debugger commands, arguments and other useful information.

Changing Program Behavior

When the debugger is active, the variable dbg is defined in the global scope. When the debugger is not active, dbg is not defined nor are the debugger commands such as s and n. This allows scripts to behave differently when the debugger is running.

Changing Debugger Behavior

By default, long (multi-line) commands are truncated so that the debugger can fit them on a line. This occurs when the debugger prints out a command to be executed and also in the listing from the w command.

The w command has a -width flag which can change the current printing width. It takes a new width as an argument. For example to display long commands (such as procedure definitions):

```
dbg2.2> w -w 300
```

Because of the parameter substitutions, the w command may try to display extremely lengthy output. Imagine the following script:

```
puts [exec cat /etc/passwd]
```

When the debugger is run, w command output will be truncated unless the printing width is quite large.

```
2: exec cat /etc/passwd
dbg3.1> s
1: puts [exec cat /etc/passwd]
dbg2.2> w
*0: expect -D 1 debug-test3.exp
 1: puts {root:Xu.VjBHD/xM7E:0:1:Operator:/:/bin/csh
nobody:*:65534:65534::/...
dbg2.3> w -w 200
dbg2.4> w
*0: expect -D 1 debug-test3.exp
 1: puts {root:Xu.VjBHD/xM7E:0:1:Operator:/:/bin/csh
nobody:*:65534:65534::/:
daemon:*:1:1::/:
sys:*:2:2::/:/bin/csh
bin:*:3:3::/bin:
uucp:*:4:8::/var/spool/uucppublic:
news:*:6:6::/var/spool/news:/bin...
dbg2.5>
```

When output is truncated, an ellipsis is appended to the end. The default width is 75 which allows some space at the beginning of the line for the procedure call depth information.

By default, no other output formatting is performed. But even short commands can cause lots of scrolling. The following declaration of p4 is less then 75 characters but still takes several lines.

```
% expect -D 1 debug-test.exp
set b 1
dbg2.1> s
1: proc p4 {} {
    return [
        expr 5+[expr 1+$x]]
}
```

The -compress flag with argument 1 tells the debugger to display control characters using escape sequences. For example:

```
dbg2.2> w -c 1
dbg2.3> w
*0: expect -D 1 debug-test.exp
 1: proc p4 {x} {\n\treturn [\n\t        expr 5+[expr 1+$x]]\n}
```

The compressed output is useful for preventing excessive scrolling and also for displaying the precise characters that should be used in order to match patterns in breakpoints.

To revert to uncompressed output, use the same flag with value 0.

```
dbg2.4> w -c 0
```

With no value specified, flags to the w command print out their current values.

```
dbg2.5> w -c
0
dbg2.6> w -w
75
```

Exercises

1. The debugger assumes you use the commands `set` and `parray` for printing scalars and arrays. Write a command named "p" that prints out a variable no matter what kind it is. Add additional features, such as checking the next higher scope or the global scope if the named variable is not found in the current scope.

2. The next chapter describes Tk, a Tcl-based extension for the X Window System. Try using the debugger with Tk. Does it work as you expected?

In This Chapter:

- *Using Expect And Tk Together*
- *A GUI For Setting Passwords*
- *Expecting Process Output In The Background*
- *A Terminal Emulator*
- *Expecting Character Graphics*

19

Expect + Tk = Expectk

Tk provides commands to build user interfaces for the X Window System. With Tk, you can build graphic user interfaces (GUIs) entirely using Tcl and its extensions. In this chapter, I will cover how to use Expect with Tk. Some of the examples are particularly noteworthy. These include a GUI for setting passwords, a terminal emulator, and a mechanism to watch for patterns in character graphic applications.

Tk is one of the most popular Tcl extensions—and deservedly so. Tk provides a layer of abstraction that is quite high-level and yet still provides a lot of flexibility. It is possible to do things much more quickly in Tk than in other toolkits, and even better— it is likely that you will do things with Tk that you never would have even tried without it.[†]

Unlike the Tcl chapter (page 23), I will give only a brief overview of Tk here—it is not the primary focus of this book and is only mentioned a few times in other chapters. Nonetheless, a little knowledge of Tk is necessary to understand the gist of this chapter. I will make up for the lack of a complete introduction by giving a little more information when I use some of the Tk commands for the first time. However, I will skip parts of Tk that are not immediately relevant. For more information, refer to the Tk reference material. For more information on X, refer to the *X Window System Series* from O'Reilly & Associates.

Experienced Tk programmers may skip the introductory material in the next section and go right to the Expectk section beginning on page 432.

[†] Despite my enthusiasm for Tk, it is no longer the only game in town. New interpreted window systems are popping up everywhere. The good news is that many are incorporating Expect-like functionality within them. As an example, Neils Mayer's WINTERP is similar to Tcl and Tk but is based on David Betz's XLISP and OSF's Motif. WINTERP includes the Expect library described in Chapter 21 (p. 491).

Tk — A Brief Technical Overview

Tk provides commands to build user interfaces for the X Window System. For example, the button command creates an object that can be "pushed" analogously to a physical pushbutton. The scrollbar command creates an object that can be manipulated to change the view in other objects. Tk GUIs are built from these and other commands. The actions that Tk GUIs control use the same Tcl commands that you already know.

Widgets

Commands to create objects are simple, and all of the commands follow a similar style. For example, the following command creates a button labelled "Get File".

```
button .getbutton -text "Get File"
```

.getbutton is the name of the newly created button. Any further references to the button in the script are made using this string. Objects such as buttons and scrollbars are called *widgets*.

Commands may be associated with most widgets by using the -command flag. For example, the following command creates a button that when pushed, invokes the getfile command.

```
button .getbutton -text "Get File" -command "getfile"
```

The -command flag can name any Tcl command. This is one of the keys to the power of Tk. The screen layout is defined with simple commands, all in Tk and Tcl. And their behavior is defined with simple commands, also, all in Tk and Tcl. Of course, when used with Expect, any Expect commands may also be given.

Other Widgets And Naming Conventions

Besides push buttons, there are also radio buttons (pushing one in forces others out) and check buttons (they stay in until you push them again). Besides buttons, Tk comes with a variety of widgets such as scrollbars, menus, drawing canvases, etc. Some of these can be used to contain other widgets. For example, a file browser might be made up of a listbox widget and a scrollbar widget, sitting within a frame widget. The frame widget groups other widgets together much like a directory groups files together in the file system. In fact, the analogy is paralleled in the naming convention. The "." in widget names is analogous to a "/" in filenames. The widget .files could be a frame containing the list widget .files.list and the scrollbar widget .files.sb. This naming convention is not required, but it is normally followed if it makes the code simpler to read. Following the analogy, the widget "." represents a top-level window that is not enclosed by anything else.

Each widget name automatically becomes the name of a command to manipulate the widget. For example, the button created in the previous section could be flashed this way:

```
.getbutton flash
```

The size of the listbox widget stored in the variable $lb could be returned this way:

```
$lb size
```

Displaying Widgets

Before widgets can appear on the screen, their relationship to other widgets must be described. For example, two buttons may be displayed inside a frame using Tk's `pack` command as follows:

```
pack .but1 .but2 -in .files
```

The -in flag makes the button widgets appear inside the .files widget. If the hierarchic naming convention is used (described in the previous section), the -in flag and the container widget can be omitted.

```
pack .files.but1 .files.but2
```

The `pack` command decides on the layout and size of the widgets, although additional flags may be used for guidance. The `pack` command is so named because it typically packs widgets together as tightly as possible so as to make the best possible use of the space in the window. Other commands are available to describe widget relationships in different ways, but in this chapter, the examples all use `pack`.

Bindings And Events

Tk's `bind` command describes what actions should be taken when events occur. *Events* include user input (keystrokes, button clicks) as well as window changes (resizes, exposures).

The following `bind` command declares that the `exit` command should be executed when the user enters a Control-C in the widget .files.

```
bind .files <Control-c> exit
```

The next command defines a binding for the first mouse button.

```
bind .files <Button1> {puts "You pressed button 1"}
```

It is also possible to associate events on a class of widgets. The following binding causes all buttons to invoke `highlight_button` when the cursor enters the window.

```
bind Button <Any-Enter> {highlight_button %W}
```

When the event occurs, strings in the action beginning with % are replaced with more event information. For example, %W is replaced with the actual name of the window.

The Event Loop

Tk scripts are similar to X programs in that they are usually event driven. Event-driven programs spend most of their time waiting for events to arrive. As events arrive, they are processed by executing any actions that have been declared with bindings. This simple idea of waiting for events and processing them is known as the *event loop*.

There is no explicit command in scripts where the event loop occurs. The event loop is simply entered after all the commands in the scripts have been read and processed.

Expectk

You can include the Expect and Tk extensions together when you build your Tcl-based application. Alternatively if you have Tk installed on your system, the Expect **Makefile** automatically builds a program called Expectk.

Expectk is a mixture of Expect and Tk. Most of the commands work as before. However, some new commands exist and some old commands have different names.

The most common use of Expectk is to take existing command-line-oriented programs and wrap them with X GUIs. As with Expect, no changes have to be made to the original programs.

Wrapping existing programs avoids several common problems. For example, changing an underlying program requires that you test the result, including features that were working before you touched the program. And it is much more work to test GUIs than to test command-line interfaces. Another problem is version control. If you modify a program, you will have two versions of the original program to maintain—a command-line version and a GUI version. And of course, all of these problems presume that you have the source in the first place, which is often not the case.

Expectk allows you to focus on the GUI, since the original application already exists. This reduces the amount of testing that has to be done and avoids version problems— you will be using the same version of the application whether you use its command-line interface or its GUI interface.

All of the benefits of Tk itself carry through to Expectk. Scripts are much shorter than their compiled equivalents in C or C++. Scripts require no lengthy compilations and can be modified quickly and easily. And the widget library offered by Tk is high-level and compares favorably to more traditional widget libraries. In addition, a GUI builder exists for Tk. Written by Sven Delmas, XF allows you to build a GUI by pointing and clicking, reducing the amount of work required to create the graphical elements and layout of the GUI. The Tcl FAQ describes how to obtain XF. For more information on the FAQ, see Chapter 1 (p. 20).

Expectk can also be useful when creating brand new applications. Many applications do not require an intimate connection to a GUI. By separating the GUI from the back end, you can concentrate on each part separately. Write simple command-line interfaces to the application and you will not have to be debugging X code just to test out your application. Similarly, it is much easier to test a GUI without having to worry about the application code at the same time.

Expectk Scripts

Expectk scripts are executed using the Expectk program. Expectk is very similar to Expect. For example, you can invoke scripts in an analogous way, such as with the command line:

```
% expectk script
```

Expectk scripts may also be executed as:

```
% script
```

if the first line of the script starts with:

```
#!/usr/local/bin/expectk
```

The -- and -f flags work with Expectk just like they do with Expect. However, many of the other flags are different because there are so many additional flags required by Tk and X. For example, as with most X applications, the -display flag allows you to specify an X server. Expectk uses a skeleton framework provided by Tk which is subject to change with little control from Expect. Thus, your best bet to finding out the current list of flags is a quick look at the source.

The send Command

Both Tk and Expect have a command named send.[†] Expectk detects this collision and lets Tk "win" the fight for command names. So if you type "send", you get Tk's send command. Alternate names are provided for any Expect commands that could collide. In particular, Expect commands that do not already begin with "exp" can be invoked by prefixing them with "exp_". For example, Expect's send command can be invoked as exp_send.

---

† I described Tk's send function in Chapter 18 (p. 409) so I will not provide further explanation of it here. Tk's send is implemented using X primitives but is not otherwise intrinsically related to graphics or windows.

```
% exp_send "foo\r"
```

If you accidentally call Tk's send when you want Expect's send, you will see the following error:

```
% send "foo\r"
wrong # args: should be "send interpName arg ?arg ..."
```

The alias exp_send works in both Expect and Expectk, so you can use exp_send all the time if you find it simpler to remember or read. You should also stick with exp_send if you are writing code that is to be portable to both Expectk and Expect.

An Extended Example — tkpasswd

tkpasswd is an Expectk script that creates a GUI for changing passwords conveniently. You might wonder how there could be any value in a GUI for such a trivial program; however, people who change passwords frequently (such as system administrators) will find many benefits. For instance, the GUI provides the same interface whether you are changing local passwords (/etc/passwd) or remote passwords (NIS). The GUI can show accounts in different ways, such as sorted by name or uid. The GUI also highlights accounts that have no passwords—a potential security problem. Lastly, the GUI can reject passwords that are inappropriate. Naturally, all of this is done without modifying the passwd program itself.

Even with these and other features, the script is only 300 lines (of which 60 are empty or comment lines). About 100 lines are related to laying out the graphics. Only about 10 of the lines are directly related to driving the passwd program, but it is worthwhile to examine other parts of the program to see how, for example, the press of a button is translated into a behavior change in the passwd interaction. The script comes with the Expect distribution as an example.

When run, the script displays the image shown on page 435. At the top are several radio buttons which control the script. In the middle is a user browser. Below this are several more buttons and an entry widget in which passwords can be entered.

The script begins with the usual incantation and commentary (trimmed for publication):

```
#!/usr/local/bin/expectk --
# tkpasswd - Change passwords using Expectk
```

The first two buttons choose between a local password database (/etc/passwd) or an NIS database. When either button is activated, the variable passwd_cmd is assigned the list of "passwd" and "cat /etc/passwd" or the list "yppasswd" and "ypcat passwd". The first element in each list is the appropriate UNIX command to set a password, and the second element is the matching UNIX command to read the password database.

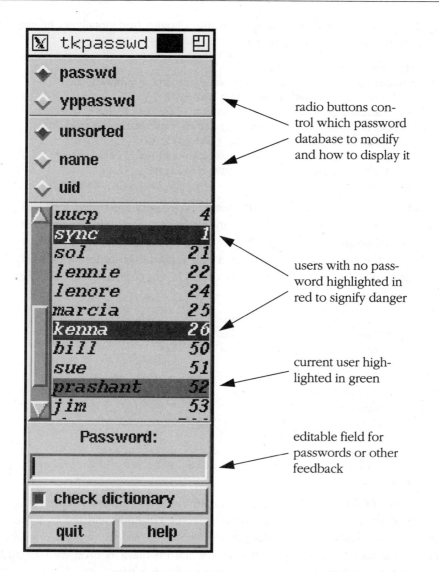

radio buttons control which password database to modify and how to display it

users with no password highlighted in red to signify danger

current user highlighted in green

editable field for passwords or other feedback

Each time a button is pressed, the `get_users` command is also called to reload the correct password database.

I will briefly describe some of the graphical aspects but just for the first set of buttons. This will help to give you more of a feel for Tk if you have never used it.

Both buttons are embedded in a frame with a raised border so that it is easy for the user to see that they are related. "`-bd  1`" means the border is one pixel wide. The "`-anchor  w`" aligns the buttons on the west side of the frame. The `pack` command places the buttons into the frame and then the frame itself is placed on the screen. The

"`-fill x`" makes the buttons and the frame expand horizontally to fill the display. (The actual width is determined later.)

```
frame .type -relief raised -bd 1
radiobutton .passwd -text passwd -variable passwd_cmd \
        -value {passwd {cat /etc/passwd}} \
        -anchor w -command get_users -relief flat
radiobutton .yppasswd -text yppasswd -variable passwd_cmd \
        -value {yppasswd {ypcat passwd}} \
        -anchor w -command get_users -relief flat
pack .passwd .yppasswd -in .type -fill x
pack .type -fill x
```

In another frame, three more buttons control how users are sorted in the display. As before, a value is assigned to a control variable (`sort_cmd`) which conveniently is just the right UNIX command to sort a file. Providing sorted and unsorted displays is important because the NIS database is provided in a randomized order (which usually cries for sorting) while the local database is provided in the original order (and may or may not need sorting).

```
frame .sort -relief raised -bd 1
radiobutton .unsorted -text unsorted -variable sort_cmd \
        -value " " -anchor w -relief flat \
        -command get_users
radiobutton .name -text name -variable sort_cmd \
        -value "| sort" -anchor w -relief flat \
        -command get_users
radiobutton .uid -text uid -variable sort_cmd \
        -value "| sort -t: -n +2" \
        -anchor w -relief flat -command get_users
pack .unsorted .name .uid -in .sort -fill x
pack .sort -fill x
```

In the center of the display is a frame containing a user browser (user list and scroll bar). The users are displayed in a text widget. The currently selected user is displayed in green. Users with no passwords are highlighted in red (to suggest danger). On a monochrome monitor, black on white and white on black is used with an additional border to distinguish between the usual white on black entries.

The default number of users shown is 10 but the window is defined so that the user can increase or decrease it, in which case the user list expands or contracts appropriately. The remainder of the display is fixed.

The width of the users is set at 14—enough for an eight character user name, a blank, and a five character user id. Everything else in the display is fixed to this width and the user is not allowed to change it.

```
frame .users -relief raised -bd 1
text .names -yscrollcommand ".scroll set" -width 14 \
        -height 1 -font "*-bold-o-normal-*-120-*-m-*" \
        -setgrid 1
.names tag configure nopassword -relief raised
.names tag configure selection -relief raised
if {[tk colormodel .]=="color"} {
    .names tag configure nopassword -background red
    .names tag configure selection -background green
} else {
    .names tag configure nopassword -background  black \
        -foreground white
    .names tag configure selection -background white \
        -foreground black
}
scrollbar .scroll -command ".names yview" -relief raised
pack .scroll -in .users -side left -fill y
pack .names  -in .users -side left -fill y
pack .users -expand 1 -fill y

wm minsize . 14 1
wm maxsize . 14 999
wm geometry . 14x10
```

A field within a frame labelled "Password" is provided in which the user can enter new passwords. The focus is moved to the entry field allowing the user to enter passwords no matter where the cursor is in the display. Special bindings are added (later) which allow scrolling via the keyboard as well.

```
frame .password_frame -relief raised -bd 1
entry .password -textvar password -relief sunken -width 1
focus .password
bind .password <Return> password_set
label .prompt -text "Password:" -bd 0
pack .prompt .password -in .password_frame -fill x -padx 2 -pady 2
pack .password_frame -fill x
```

Several more buttons are created and placed at the bottom of the display. Rather than putting them at the top, they are placed at the bottom because it is likely they will be pressed at most once. In contrast, the buttons at the top are likely to be pressed many times.

The first button controls whether passwords are checked against a dictionary. It sets the variable `dict_check` appropriately, and the dictionary is loaded if it has not been already.

```
set dict_loaded 0
checkbutton .dict -text "check dictionary" -variable dict_check \
        -command {
                if !$dict_loaded load_dict
        }
pack .dict -fill x -padx 2 -pady 2
```

A quit button causes the program to exit if pressed.

```
button .quit -text quit -command exit
button .help_button -text help -command help
pack .quit .help_button -side left -expand 1 -fill x -padx 2 -pady
        2
```

A help button pops up a help window describing how to use the program. The actual text is omitted here.

```
proc help {} {
    catch {destroy .help}
    toplevel .help
    message .help.text -text <...help text here...>

    button .help.ok -text "ok" -command {destroy .help}
    pack .help.text
    pack .help.ok -fill x -padx 2 -pady 2
}
```

It is interesting to note that all the preceding code is just to set up the display and takes about a third of the program.

The `get_users` procedure reloads the password database. It is called when any of the top buttons are activated.

After clearing the current list, the procedure executes the appropriate UNIX commands to read and sort the password database. The particular commands are defined by the radio buttons. They select which database to read and how to sort it.

The remainder of the procedure adds the users to the list of names, appropriately tagging any that have null passwords. User ids are displayed as well. User names that have no other information with them are pointers back to the NIS database. They are displayed without user ids but nothing else is done. The script does not have to worry about them because the `passwd` program itself rejects attempts to set them.

```
proc get_users {} {
    global sort_cmd passwd_cmd
    global selection_line
```

```
    global nopasswords ;# line #s of users with no passwds
    global last_line   ;# last line of text box

    .names delete 1.0 end

    set file [open "|[lindex $passwd_cmd 1] $sort_cmd"]
    set last_line 1
    set nopasswords {}
    while {[gets $file buf] != -1} {
        set buf [split $buf :]
        if [llength $buf]>2 {
            # normal password entry
            .names insert end "[format "%-8s %5d" [ \
                    lindex $buf 0] [lindex $buf 2]]\n"
            if 0==[string compare [lindex $buf 1] ""] {
                .names tag add nopassword \
                    {end - 1 line linestart} \
                    {end - 1 line lineend}
                lappend nopasswords $last_line
            }
        } else {
            # +name style entry
            .names insert end "$buf\n"
        }
        incr last_line
    }
    incr last_line -1
    close $file
    set selection_line 0
}
```

At various places in the script, feedback is generated to tell the user what is going on. For simplicity, feedback is displayed in the same field in which the password is entered. This is convenient because the user probably does not want the password left on the screen for long anyway. (Making the password entirely invisible could be done by making some minor changes to the bindings.) The feedback is selected (highlighted) so that it disappears as soon as the user begins to enter a new password.

```
proc feedback {msg} {
    global password

    set password $msg
    .password select from 0
    .password select to end
    update
}
```

The dictionary takes considerable time to load into memory (about 10 seconds for 25,000 words on a Sun Sparc 2) so it is not loaded unless the user specifically activates the "check dictionary" button. The first time it is pressed, this procedure is executed. For each word, it creates an element in an array called `dict`. No value is necessary. Later on, passwords will be looked up in the dictionary just by testing if they exist as an element in the `dict` array—a very fast operation.

Calling the UNIX `grep` command would spread the load out, but it would also expose the password to anyone running `ps`. Instead, I tried my best to speed this procedure up (without resorting to C). Using `split` on the entire file reduced the run-time by about one third from that taken by the more obvious `gets` in a `while` loop. While this can backfire if a file is larger than available memory, it works well with reasonably sized dictionaries.

Since Tcl rescans commands each time they are executed, it is possible to improve performance simply by using shorter commands. (However, the benefit only becomes apparent when there are no other bottlenecks left.) I achieved another 10% increase in speed by temporarily renaming the `set` command to `s`. Interestingly, renaming `dict` to `d` had almost no impact so I left it unchanged. Substituting a single bare character for the "" made no difference at all.

```
proc load_dict {} {
    global dict dict_loaded

    feedback "loading dictionary..."

    if 0==[catch {open /usr/dict/words} file] {
        rename set s
        foreach w [split [read $file] "\n"] {s dict($w) ""}
        close $file
        rename s set
        set dict_loaded 1
        feedback "dictionary loaded"
    } else {
        feedback "dictionary missing"
        .dict deselect
    }
}
```

The `weak_password` procedure is a hook in which you can put any security measures you like. As written, all it does is reject a word if it appears in the dictionary. The mechanism to look up a word was described earlier.

```
# put whatever security checks you like in here
proc weak_password {password} {
    global dict dict_check
```

```
        if $dict_check {
            feedback "checking password"

            if [info exists dict($password)] {
                feedback "sorry - in dictionary"
                return 1
            }
        }
        return 0
    }
```

After entering a password, the `password_set` procedure is invoked to set the password. The interactive command is extracted from the radio buttons and it is spawned. If the prompt is for an "old password", the script queries the user for it and then passes it on. The new password is sent as many times as requested without telling the user. (All passwords have to be entered twice. Short passwords have to be entered four times.) Any unrecognized response is passed back to the user.

```
proc password_set {} {
    global password passwd_cmd selection_line

    if {$selection_line==0} {
        feedback "select a user first"
        return
    }
    set user [lindex [.names get selection.first selection.last] 0]

    if [weak_password $password] return

    feedback "setting password . . ."

    set cmd [lindex $passwd_cmd 0]
    spawn -noecho $cmd $user
    log_user 0
    set last_msg "error in $cmd"
    while 1 {
        expect {
            -nocase "old password:" {
                exp_send "[get_old_password]\r"
            } "assword:" {
                exp_send "$password\r"
            } -re "(.*)\r\n" {
                set last_msg $expect_out(1,string)
            } eof break
        }
    }
```

```
    set status [wait]
    if [lindex $status 3]==0 {
        feedback "set successfully"
    } else {
        feedback $last_msg
    }
}
```

The script is intended to be run by a superuser. Traditionally, the superuser is not prompted for old passwords so no entry field is permanently dedicated in the display for this purpose. However, in case the user *is* prompted, a window is popped up to collect the old password. This also handles the case when a non-superuser tries to change their own password. Trying to change any other password will be trapped by the passwd program itself, so the script does not have to worry about it.

The procedure temporarily moves the focus to the popup so the user does not have to move the mouse. After pressing return, the popup goes away and the focus is restored.

```
proc get_old_password {} {
    global old

    toplevel .old
    label .old.label -text "Old password:"
    catch {unset old}
    entry .old.entry -textvar old -relief sunken -width 1

    pack .old.label
    pack .old.entry -fill x -padx 2 -pady 2

    bind .old.entry <Return> {destroy .old}
    set oldfocus [focus]
    focus .old.entry
    tkwait visibility .old
    grab .old
    tkwait window .old
    focus $oldfocus
    return $old
}
```

Once enough procedures are defined, the script can initialize the user list and radio buttons. Initially, the local password database is selected and displayed without sorting.

```
.unsorted select
.passwd invoke
```

The remaining effort in the script is in handling user input. The global variable selection_line identifies the user whose password is about to be changed. The make_selection procedure scrolls the user list if the selected user is not displayed. Lastly, the selected user is highlighted.

```
proc make_selection {} {
    global selection_line last_line

    .names tag remove selection 0.0 end

    # don't let selection go off top of screen
    if {$selection_line < 1} {
        set selection_line $last_line
    } elseif {$selection_line > $last_line} {
        set selection_line 1
    }
    .names yview -pickplace [expr $selection_line-1]
    .names tag add selection $selection_line.0 \
            [expr 1+$selection_line].0
}
```

The `select_next_nopassword` procedure searches through the list of users that do not have passwords. Upon finding one, it is highlighted. The procedure is long because it can search in either direction and can start searching from the middle of the list and loop around if necessary.

```
proc select_next_nopassword {direction} {
    global selection_line last_line
    global nopasswords

    if 0==[llength $nopasswords] {
        feedback "no null passwords"
        return
    }

    if $direction==1 {
        # get last element of list
        if $selection_line>=[lindex $nopasswords [ \
                    expr [llength $nopasswords]-1]] {
            set selection_line 0
        }
        foreach i $nopasswords {
            if $selection_line<$i break
        }
    } else {
        if $selection_line<=[lindex $nopasswords 0] {
            set selection_line $last_line
        }
        set j [expr [llength $nopasswords]-1]
        for {} {$j>=0} {incr j -1} {
            set i [lindex $nopasswords $j]
            if $selection_line>$i break
        }
    }
}
```

```
        set selection_line $i
        make_selection
}
```

The `select` procedure is called to determine which user has been clicked on with the mouse. Once it has, it updates `selection_line` and the display.

```
proc select {w coords} {
    global selection_line

    $w mark set insert "@$coords linestart"
    $w mark set anchor insert
    set first [$w index "anchor linestart"]
    set last [$w index "insert lineend + 1c"]
    scan $first %d selection_line

    $w tag remove selection 0.0 end
    $w tag add selection $first $last
}
```

The bindings are straightforward. Mouse button one selects a user. ^C causes the application to exit. In the style of emacs, ^P and ^N move the user up and down by one. Meta-n and meta-p invoke `select_next_nopassword` to find the next or previous user without a password. These bindings are defined for the entry field in which the new password is entered. Because this field always has the focus, the user can select different users and enter passwords without touching the mouse.

```
bind Text <1> {select %W %x,%y}

bind Entry <Control-c>{exit}

bind .password <Control-n> \
    {incr selection_line 1;make_selection}
bind .password <Control-p> \
    {incr selection_line -1; make_selection}
bind .password <Meta-n>{select_next_nopassword 1}
bind .password <Meta-p>{select_next_nopassword -1}
```

Using Tk Widgets To Prompt For Passwords

In the `tkpasswd` script, passwords are entered in an entry widget. By default, characters appear in the widget as they are entered. This is not a problem in the `tkpasswd` script; however, other applications typically require passwords to be entered so that onlookers cannot see them. The entry widget has no built-in provision for suppressing the display. Fortunately, though, it is not difficult to simulate the effect.

A number of approaches are possible. However, people have figured out ingenious ways to subvert most of them. For instance, by setting the foreground and background colors alike, the letters cannot be read. However, if you should temporarily leave your workstation, someone could use the mouse to copy the letters out of the widget and paste them into another one where they once again would be visible.

The best approach is to store the password off-screen. The following procedure and bindings store the password in the global variable `password` which should be intialized to an empty string. Asterisks are displayed in the entry widget (`.e`), one for each character entered. If a backspace or delete key is pressed, an asterisk (and the last character in the real password) is removed. Notice how `regexp` is used to delete the last character in the password.

```
proc password_backspace {w} {
    global password

    regexp (.*). $password dummy password dummy
    tk_entryBackspace $w
    tk_entrySeeCaret $w
}

bind .e <Delete> {password_backspace %W}
bind .e <BackSpace> {password_backspace %W}
bind .e <Any-Key> {
    if {"%A" != ""} {
        %W insert insert *
        set password "[set password]%A"
        tk_entrySeeCaret %W
    }
}
```

Even off-screen, the password is not entirely safe. For example, someone armed with a debugger or permission to access your screen could still read the password. To avoid this, once the password has been entered, it should be used and destroyed immediately. For example, a binding for the return key could do that as follows:

```
bind .e <Return> {
    password_set $password          ;# use the password
    set password ""                 ;# destroy the password
}
```

The expect Command And The Tk Event Loop

When waiting inside of `expect` (or `interact`) commands, the Tk event loop is still active. This means that the user can, for example, press buttons on the screen and Tk will respond to the buttons while the script is executing an `expect` command.

While any specific action is being executed from the Tk event loop, the original expect command cannot return. During this time, if the user presses a button that kicks off yet another expect command, the original expect command cannot return until the new expect command returns. (This is true for any command in Tk, not just expect commands.)

If both expect commands read from the same spawn id, the later one will see all the buffered data already received. The new expect command can match data that the original expect command had read but not matched.

All of the descriptions so far are identical to the way Expect works without Tk but in the presence of signals. expect commands that are triggered by signal handlers suspend any currently active expect commands.

The expect_background Command

It is possible to have actions execute whenever input arrives and matches a pattern. This is accomplished using the expect_background command. Patterns declared this way are called *background patterns.* These patterns can match whenever the Tk event loop is active. This is similar to the way Tk's bind command works.

Contrast expect_background with expect. Although only a single expect command can be active at any time, any number of background patterns can be active simultaneously.

The expect_background command takes the same arguments as the expect command. Both commands also handle spawn ids in the same way. So by default, expect_background associates patterns with the current spawn id. Other spawn ids are associated by using the -i flag.

For example, the following command adds any input received from spawn id $shell to the end of the text widget ".text".

```
expect_background -i $shell -re ".+" {
    .text insert end $expect_out(0,string)
}
```

The expect_background command returns immediately. However, the patterns are remembered by Expect. Whenever any input arrives, it is compared to the patterns. If they match, the corresponding action is executed. The patterns are remembered until another expect_background is entered for the same spawn id. For example, the following command effectively cancels the previous expect_background command:

```
expect_background -i $shell
```

Multiple Spawn Ids In expect_background

Multiple spawn ids and patterns can be provided in a single `expect_background` command. Each time a particular spawn id appears, it replaces the previous background pattern associated with that spawn id. It is possible to declare multiple spawn ids together and change or delete some or all of them separately.

Multiple spawn ids are accepted using the "`-i "$id1 $id2 $id3"`" notation or via an indirect spawn id specification (see Chapter 11 (p. 268)). When indirect spawn id lists change, the background patterns are immediately disassociated from the old spawn ids and reassociated with the new spawn ids.

In Chapter 11 (p. 266), I described how the `-info` flag is used to return the association patterns from `expect_before` and `expect_after`. The `-info` flag works with `expect_background` as well.

Background Actions

When a background pattern matches, the associated action is evaluated. Evaluation of the action follows the same rules as for a regular `expect` command. However, inside the action, background patterns for the same spawn id are blocked from further matching. This prevents input that arrived later (i.e., in the middle of an action) from being processed while input associated with the pending action is still being processed.

Any command may be used in the action of a background pattern including another `expect` or `expect_background`. `expect_background` commands allow background patterns from a different spawn id to begin matching immediately—even before the current action finishes. `expect` commands are executed as usual (i.e., immediately), even if they are for the same spawn id as the one associated with the currently executing background action.

It is not possible to wait using both `expect` and `expect_background` for output from the same spawn id at precisely the same time. The behavior in such a situation is undefined.

Example — A Dumb Terminal Emulator

The following script creates two text widgets that work like primitive terminals. One allows interaction with a `telnet` process and the other with a shell. The script has a `bind` command to pass user keystrokes to the processes and an `expect_background` command to handle the output of the two processes.

Notice that the `expect_background` command discards \r characters since output lines ordinarily end with \r\n but the text widget only expects \n as its line terminator. No further intelligence is provided for more sophisticated emulation. For example, absolute cursor motion is not supported. Nonprintable characters appear on the screen as hex escapes.

```
# start a shell and text widget for its output
spawn $env(SHELL)
set shell $spawn_id
text .shell -relief sunken -bd 1
pack .shell

# start a telnet and a text widget for its output
spawn telnet
set telnet $spawn_id
text .telnet  -relief sunken -bd 1
pack .telnet

expect_background {
    -i $telnet -re "\[^\x0d]+" {
        .telnet insert end $expect_out(0,string)
        .telnet yview -pickplace insert
    }
    -i $shell -re "\[^\x0d]+" {
        .shell insert end $expect_out(0,string)
        .shell yview -pickplace insert
    }
    -i $any_spawn_id "\x0d" {
        # discard \r
    }
}

bind Text    <Any-Enter>    {focus %W}
bind .telnet <Any-KeyPress> {exp_send -i $telnet "%A"}
bind .shell  <Any-KeyPress> {exp_send -i $shell  "%A"}
```

Example—A Smarter Terminal Emulator

The previous example was very simple-minded. The characters from the output of the spawned processes were copied to their own text widget. The only attempt at formatting was to handle line endings. Most programs expect more than this. For example, tabs are usually expanded to spaces, and backspaces cause the terminal cursor to move left instead of right.

More sophisticated programs require character addressing. By sending special terminal manipulation character sequences (I will just call them *sequences* from now on), programs can write to arbitrary character locations on the screen. The following terminal emulator supports this. You can use it to run programs such as emacs and vi.

As before, a text widget is used for display. Its name is stored in the variable term. For simplicity, the code only supports a single emulator, assumes a fixed size display of 24 rows of 80 columns, and runs a shell. The following code starts the process and creates the text widget.

```
# tkterm - term emulator using Expect and Tk text widget

set rows 24          ;# number of rows in term
set cols 80          ;# number of columns in term
set term .t          ;# name of text widget used by term

log_user 0

# start a shell and text widget for its output
set stty_init "-tabs"
eval spawn $env(SHELL)
stty rows $rows columns $cols < $spawn_out(slave,name)
set term_spawn_id $spawn_id

text $term -width $cols -height $rows
```

Once the terminal widget has been created, it can be displayed on the screen with a pack command. But this is not necessary. You may want to use the terminal widget merely as a convenient data structure in which case it need never be displayed. In contrast, the following line packs the widget on to the screen in the usual way.

```
pack $term
```

The task of understanding screen manipulation sequences is complicated. It is made more so by the lack of a standard for it. To make up for this, there are packages that support arbitrary terminal types through the use of a terminal description language. So the script has to declare how it would like to hear terminal manipulation requests. The two common packages that provide this are termcap and terminfo. Because termcap has a BSD heritage and terminfo has a SV heritage, it is not uncommon to find that you need both termcap and terminfo. On my own system as delivered from the vendor, half of the utilities use termcap and half use terminfo!

Surprisingly, it is much easier to design a terminal description from scratch than it is to mimic an existing terminal description. Part of the problem is that terminfo and termcap do not cover all the possibilities nor is their behavior entirely well defined. In addition, most terminals understand a large number of sequences—many more than most databases describe. But because the databases can be different for the same terminal from one computer to another, an emulator must emulate all of the sequences whether they are in the database or not. Even sitting down with a vendor's manuals is not a solution because other vendors commonly extend other vendor's definitions.

Fortunately, few sequences are actually required. For instance, most cursor motion can be simulated with direct addressing. This turns out to be more efficient than many relative cursor motion operations as I will explain later.

The following code establishes descriptions in both termcap and terminfo style using the terminal type of "tk". The code succeeds even if termcap and terminfo are not supported on the system. This code actually has to be executed before the spawn shown earlier in order for the environment variables to be inherited by the process.

I will briefly describe the termcap definition. (The terminfo definition is very similar so I will skip those.) The definition is made up of several capabilities. Each *capability* describes one feature of the terminal. A capability is expressed in the form *xx*=*value*, where *xx* is a capability label and *value* is the actual string that the emulator receives. For instance the up capability moves the cursor up one line. Its value is the sequence: escape, "[", "A". These sequences are not interpreted at all by Tcl so they may look peculiar. The complicated-looking sequence (cm) performs absolute cursor motion. The row and column are substituted for each %d before it is transmitted. The remaining capabilities are *nondestructive space* (nd), *clear screen* (cl), *down one line* (do), *begin standout mode* (so) and *end standout mode* (se).

```
set env(LINES) $rows
set env(COLUMNS) $cols

set env(TERM) "tk"
set env(TERMCAP) {tk:
    :cm=\E[%d;%dH:
    :up=\E[A:
    :nd=\E[C:
    :cl=\E[H\E[J:
    :do=^J:
    :so=\E[7m:
    :se=\E[m:
}

set env(TERMINFO) /tmp
set ttsrc "/tmp/tk.src"
set file [open $tksrc w]

puts $file {tk,
    cup=\E[%p1%d;%p2%dH,
    cuu1=\E[A,
    cuf1=\E[C,
    clear=\E[H\E[J,
    ind=\n,
```

```
        cr=\r,
        smso=\E[7m,
        rmso=\E[m,
    }
close $file
catch {exec tic $tksrc}
exec rm $tksrc
```

For simplicity, the emulator only understands the generic standout mode rather than specific ones such as underlining and highlighting. The `term_standout` global variable describes whether characters are being written in standout mode. Text in standout mode is tagged with the tag `standout`, here defined by white characters on a black background.

```
set term_standout 0        ;# if in standout mode

$term tag configure standout \
        -background black \
        -foreground white
```

The text widget maintains the terminal display internally. It can be read or written in a few different ways. Access is possible by character, by line, or by the entire screen. Lines are newline delimited. It is convenient to initialize the entire screen (i.e., each line) with blanks. Later, this will allow characters to be inserted anywhere without worrying if the line is long enough already. In the following procedure, `term_init`, the "`insert $i.0`" operation adds a line of blanks to row i beginning at column 0.

```
proc term_init {} {
    set blankline [format %*s $cols ""]\n
    for {set i 1} {$i <= $rows} {incr i} {
        $term insert $i.0 $blankline
    }
```

For historical reasons, the first *row* in a text widget is 1 while the first *column* is 0. The variables `cur_row` and `cur_col` describe where characters are next written. Here, they are initialized to the upper-left corner.

```
    set cur_row 1
    set cur_col 0
```

The visible insertion cursor is maintained as a mark. It generally tracks the insertion point. Here, it is also set to the upper-left corner.

```
    $term mark set insert $cur_row.$cur_col
}
term_init
```

The `term_init` procedure is called immediately to initialize the text widget.

A few more utility routines are useful. The `term_clear` procedure clears the screen by throwing away the contents of the text widget and reinitializing it.

```
proc term_clear {} {
    global term

    $term delete 1.0 end
    term_init
}
```

The `term_down` procedure moves the cursor down one line. If the cursor is already at the end of the screen, the text widget appears to scroll. This is accomplished by deleting the first line and then creating a new one at the end.

```
proc term_down {} {
    global cur_row rows cols term

    if {$cur_row < $rows} {
        incr cur_row
    } else {
        # already at last line of term, so scroll screen up
        $term delete 1.0 "1.end + 1 chars"

        # recreate line at end
        $term insert end [format %*s $cols ""]\n
    }
}
```

There is no correspondingly complex routine to scroll up because the termcap/terminfo libraries never request it. Instead, they simulate it with other capabilities. In fact, the termcap/terminfo libraries never request that the cursor scroll past the bottom line either. However, programs like `cat` and `ls` do, so the terminal emulator understands how to handle this case.

The `term_insert` procedure writes a string to the current location on the screen. It is broken into three parts. The first part writes from anywhere on a line up to the end. If the string is long enough and wraps over several lines, the next section writes the full lines that wrap. Finally, the last section handles the last characters that do not make a full line. Characters are tagged with the standout tag if the emulator is in `standout` mode.

Each one of these sections does its work by first deleting the existing characters and then inserting the new characters. This is a good example of where termcap/terminfo fail to have the ability to adequately describe a terminal. The text widget is essentially always in "insert" mode but termcap/terminfo have no way of describing this.

One capability of which the script does not take advantage, is that termcap/terminfo can be told not to write across line boundaries. On that basis, this procedure could be simplified by removing the second and third parts. Again, however, programs such as cat and ls expect to be able to write over line boundaries. The term_insert procedure does not worry about scrolling once the bottom of the screen is reached. term_down takes care of that already.

```
proc term_insert {s} {
    global cols cur_col cur_row
    global term term_standout

    set chars_rem_to_write [string length $s]
    set space_rem_on_line [expr $cols - $cur_col]

    if {$term_standout} {
       set tag_action "add"
    } else {
       set tag_action "remove"
    }

    ##################
    # write first line
    ##################

    if {$chars_rem_to_write > $space_rem_on_line} {
       set chars_to_write $space_rem_on_line
       set newline 1
    } else {
       set chars_to_write $chars_rem_to_write
       set newline 0
    }

    $term delete $cur_row.$cur_col \
             $cur_row.[expr $cur_col + $chars_to_write]
    $term insert $cur_row.$cur_col [
       string range $s 0 [expr $space_rem_on_line-1]
    ]

    $term tag $tag_action standout $cur_row.$cur_col \
             $cur_row.[expr $cur_col + $chars_to_write]

    # discard first line already written
    incr chars_rem_to_write -$chars_to_write
    set s [string range $s $chars_to_write end]

    # update cur_col
    incr cur_col $chars_to_write
    # update cur_row
    if $newline {
       term_down
```

```
    }

    ################
    # write full lines
    ################
    while {$chars_rem_to_write >= $cols} {
        $term delete $cur_row.0 $cur_row.end
        $term insert $cur_row.0 [string range $s 0 [expr $cols-1]]
        $term tag $tag_action standout $cur_row.0 $cur_row.end

        # discard line from buffer
        set s [string range $s $cols end]
        incr chars_rem_to_write -$cols

        set cur_col 0
        term_down
    }

    ################
    # write last line
    ################

    if {$chars_rem_to_write} {
        $term delete $cur_row.0 $cur_row.$chars_rem_to_write
        $term insert $cur_row.0 $s
        $term tag $tag_action standout $cur_row.0 \
                                  $cur_row.$chars_rem_to_write
        set cur_col $chars_rem_to_write
    }

    term_chars_changed
}
```

At the very end of `term_insert` is a call to `term_chars_changed`. This is a user-defined procedure called whenever visible characters have changed. For example, if you want to find when the string `foo` appears on line 4, you could write:

```
proc term_chars_changed {} {
    global $term
    if {[string match *foo* [$term get 4.0 4.end]]} . . .
}
```

Some other tests suitable for the body of `term_chars_changed` are:

```
# Test if "foo" exists at line 4 col 7
if {[string match foo* [$term get 4.7 4.end]]}

# Test if character at row 4 col 5 is in standout mode
if {-1 != [lsearch [$term tag names 4.5] standout]} ...
```

You can also retrieve information:

```
# Return contents of screen
$term get 1.0 end

# Return indices of first string on lines 4 to 6 that are
# in standout mode
$term tag nextrange standout 4.0 6.end
```

And here is possible code to modify the text on the screen:

```
# Replace all occurrences of "foo" with "bar" on screen
for {set i 1} {$i<=$rows} {incr i} {
    regsub -all "foo" [$term get $i.0 $i.end] "bar" x
    $term delete $i.0 $i.end
    $term insert $i.0 $x
}
```

The last utility procedure is `term_update_cursor`. It is called to update the visible cursor.

```
proc term_update_cursor {} {
    global cur_row cur_col term

    $term mark set insert $cur_row.$cur_col

    term_cursor_changed
}
```

The `term_update_cursor` procedure also calls a user-defined procedure, `term_cursor_changed`. A possible definition might be to test if the cursor is at some specific location:

```
proc term_cursor_changed {} {
    if {$cur_row == 1 && $cur_col == 0} ...
}
```

By default, both procedures do nothing:

```
proc term_cursor_changed {} {}
proc term_chars_changed {} {}
```

`term_exit` is another user-defined procedure. `term_exit` is called when the spawned process exits. Here is a definition that causes the script itself to exit when the process does.

```
proc term_exit {} {
    exit
}
```

The last user-defined procedure is `term_bell`. `term_bell` is executed when the terminal emulator needs its bell rung. The following definition sends an ASCII bell character to the standard output.

```
proc term_bell {} {
    send_user "\a"
}
```

Now that all of the utility procedures are in place, the command to read the sequences is straightforward. For instance, a backspace character causes the current column to be decremented. A carriage-return sets the current column to 0. Compare this to the code on page 448.

Notice how simple the code is for absolute cursor motion. It is basically two assignment statements. Because it is so simple, there is no need to supply termcap/terminfo with information on relative cursor motion commands. They cannot be substantially faster.[†]

```
expect_background {
    -i $term_spawn_id
    -re "^\[^\x01-\x1f]+" {
        # Text
        term_insert $expect_out(0,string)
        term_update_cursor
    } "^\r" {
        # (cr,) Go to beginning of line
        set cur_col 0
        term_update_cursor
    } "^\n" {
        # (ind,do) Move cursor down one line
        term_down
        term_update_cursor
    } "^\b" {
        # Backspace nondestructively
        incr cur_col -1
        term_update_cursor
    } "^\a" {
        term_bell
    } eof {
        term_exit
    } "^\x1b\\\[A" {
        # (cuu1,up) Move cursor up one line
        incr cur_row -1
        term_update_cursor
```

---

† The definition for nondestructive space might be seen as a concession to speed, but in fact it is required by some buggy versions of termcap which operate incorrectly if the capability not defined. The other relative motion capabilities are assumed by the terminal driver for non-character-graphic tools such as `cat` and `ls`.

```
    } "^\x1b\\\[C" {
        # (cuf1,nd) Nondestructive space
        incr cur_col
        term_update_cursor
    } -re "^\x1b\\\[(\[0-9]*);(\[0-9]*)H" {
        # (cup,cm) Move to row y col x
        set cur_row [expr $expect_out(1,string)+1]
        set cur_col $expect_out(2,string)
        term_update_cursor
    } "^\x1b\\\[H\x1b\\\[J" {
        # (clear,cl) Clear screen
        term_clear
        term_update_cursor
    } "^\x1b\\\[7m" {
        # (smso,so) Begin standout mode
        set term_standout 1
    } "^\x1b\\\[m" {
        # (rmso,se) End standout mode
        set term_standout 0
    }
}
```

Finally, some bindings are provided. The meta key is simulated by sending an escape. Most programs understand this convention, and it is convenient because it works over telnet links.

```
bind $term <Any-Enter> {
    focus %W
}
bind $term <Meta-KeyPress> {
    if {"%A" != ""} {
        exp_send -i $term_spawn_id "\033%A"
    }
}
bind $term <Any-KeyPress> {
    if {"%A" != ""} {
        exp_send -i $term_spawn_id -- "%A"
    }
}
```

Some bindings can be described using capabilities. For instance, the capability for function key 1 could be described in either of two ways:

```
:k1=\EOP:                    termcap-style
:kf1=\EOP:                   terminfo-style
```

The matching binding is:

```
bind $term <F1> {exp_send -i $term_spawn_id "\033OP"}
```

Using The Terminal Emulator For Testing And Automation

This book describes a version of Expect that does not provide built-in support for understanding character graphics. Nonetheless, it is possible to use the terminal emulator in the previous section to partially or fully automate character-graphic applications.

For instance, each expect-like operation could be a loop that repeatedly performs various tests of interest on the text widget contents. In the following code, the entrance to the loop is protected by "tkwait var test_pats". This blocks the loop from proceeding until the test_pats variable is changed. The variable is changed by the term_chars_changed procedure, invoked whenever the screen changes. Using this idea, the following code waits for a % prompt anywhere on the first line:

```
proc term_chars_changed {} {
    uplevel #0 set test_pats 1
}

while 1 {
    if {!$test_pats} {tkwait var test_pats}
    set test_pats 0
    if {[regexp "%" [$term get 1.0 1.end]]} break
}
```

Writing a substantial script this way would be clumsy. Furthermore, it prevents the use of control flow commands in the actions. One solution is to create a procedure that does all of the work handling the semaphore and hiding the while loop.

Based on a procedure (shown later) called term_expect, the rogue script in Chapter 6 (p. 141) can be rewritten with the following code. This code is similar to the earlier version except that instead of patterns, tests are composed of explicit statements. Any nonzero result causes term_expect to be satisfied whereupon it executes the associated action. For instance, the first test looks for % in either the first or second line on the screen. The meaning of the rest of the script should be obvious.

```
while 1 {
    term_expect {regexp "%" [$term get 1.0 2.end]}
    exp_send "rogue\r"
    term_expect \
        {regexp "Str: 18" [$term get 24.0 24.end]} {
            break
        } {regexp "Str: 16" [$term get 24.0 24.end]}
    exp_send "Q"
    term_expect {regexp "quit" [$term get 1.0 1.end]}
    exp_send "y"
}
```

In contrast to the original `rogue` script, there is no `interact` command at the end of this one. Because of the bindings, the script is *always* listening to the keyboard! To prevent this implicit `interact`, remove or override the `KeyPress` bindings that appear at the end of the terminal emulator.

Since the tests can be arbitrarily large lists of statements, they are grouped with braces. For example:

```
term_expect {
    set line [$term get 1.0 2.end]
    regexp "%" $line
} {
    action
} timeout {
    puts "timed out!"
}
```

Timeouts follow a similar syntax as before. A test for an eof is not provided since a terminal emulator should not exit just because the applications making use of it do so. In this example, a shell prompt is used to detect when the `rogue` program has exited.

The `term_expect` procedure lacks some of the niceties of `expect` and should be viewed as a framework for designing a built-in command. Feel free to modify it. Your experiences will help in the ultimate design of a built-in command.

The term_expect Procedure

An implementation of `term_expect` is shown in this section. The code is quite complex and really beyond the level at which this book is aimed. Fortunately, it is not necessary to understand in order to use it. Nonetheless, I will briefly describe how it works. If you follow it all, you are doing very well indeed.

The code assumes that the terminal emulator is available because the text widget maintains the memory of what is on the screen. Although the terminal emulator is necessary, the text widget and, indeed, Tk itself can be obviated by maintaining an explicit representation such as a list of strings representing rows of the terminal. However, even with Tk and the terminal emulator, the timeout and the scope handling makes the code intricate. Without them, the code would be more similar to the fragment on page 458.

Timeouts are implemented using an `after` command which sets a strobe at the end of the timeout period. In order to avoid an old `after` command setting the strobe for a later `term_expect` command, a new strobe variable is generated each time.[†] A global variable provides a unique identifier for this purpose and is initialized separately:

```
set term_counter 0            ;# distinguish different timers
```

The procedure begins by deciding the amount of time to wait before timing out. This is rather involved because it looks in the local scope and the global scope as well as providing a default value. This imitates the behavior of the real `expect` command.

```
proc term_expect {args} {
    set timeout [
        uplevel {
            if [info exists timeout] {
                set timeout
            } else {
                uplevel #0 {
                    if {[info exists timeout]} {
                        set timeout
                    } else {
                        expr 10
                    }
                }
            }
        }
    ]
```

Two unique global variables are used as strobes—to indicate that an event (data or timeout) has occurred. The `strobe` variable holds the name of a global variable changed when the terminal changes or the code has timed out. Later, the code will wait for this variable to change. To distinguish between the two types of events, `tstrobe` is another strobe changed only upon timeout. (It is possible to use a single tri-valued strobe, but the coding is much trickier.)

```
global term_counter
incr term_counter
global [set strobe _data_[set term_counter]]
global [set tstrobe _timer_[set term_counter]]
```

The `term_chars_changed` procedure is modified to fire the strobe. Note the use of double quotes around the body of `term_chars_changed` in order to allow substitution of the strobe command in this scope.

```
proc term_chars_changed {} "uplevel #0 set $strobe 1"
```

---

† Tk 4 promises to provide support for cancelling `after` commands. This would remove the need for separate strobe variables.

The next lines set the strobes to make sure that the screen image can be tested immediately since the screen could initially be in the expected state. The `after` command arranges for the timer strobe to be set later.

```
set $strobe 1            ;# force an initial test
set $tstrobe 0           ;# no timeout yet

if {$timeout >= 0} {
    set mstimeout [expr 1000*$timeout]
    after $mstimeout "set $strobe 1; set $tstrobe 1"
    set timeout_act {}
}
```

If the user omits the final action, the number of arguments will be uneven. Later code is simplified by adding an empty action in this case.

```
set argc [llength $args]
if {$argc%2 == 1} {
    lappend args {}
    incr argc
}
```

If the test is the bare string "`timeout`", its action is saved for later. Both the string and the action are removed from the list of tests.

```
for {set i 0} {$i<$argc} {incr i 2} {
    set act_index [expr $i+1]
    if {![string compare timeout [lindex $args $i]]} {
        set timeout_act [lindex $args $act_index]
        set args [lreplace $args $i $act_index]
        incr argc -2
        break
    }
}
```

Now the procedure loops, waiting for the screen to be changed. A test first checks if the strobe has already occurred. If not, `tkwait` waits. This suspends the loop when no screen activity is occurring. Once the strobe occurs, the rest of the loop executes. If the timeout has occurred or any of the tests are true, the loop breaks so that the action can be evaluated.

```
while {![info exists act]} {
    if {![set $strobe]} {
        tkwait var $strobe
    }
    set $strobe 0

    if {[set $tstrobe]} {
        set act $timeout_act
```

```
    } else {
        for {set i 0} {$i<$argc} {incr i 2} {
            if {[uplevel [lindex $args $i]]} {
                set act [lindex $args [incr i]]
                break
            }
        }
    }
}
```

To keep the environment clean, the global strobe variables are deleted. If a timeout could occur in the future, the unset is similarly scheduled; otherwise the variables are deleted immediately. The term_chars_changed procedure is reset so that it does not continue setting the data strobe.

```
proc term_chars_changed {} {}

if {$timeout >= 0} {
    after $mstimeout unset $strobe $tstrobe
} else {
    unset $strobe $tstrobe
}
```

Finally, the action is evaluated. If a flow control command (such as break) was executed, it is returned in such a way that the caller sees it as well. (See the Tcl manual for more detail on this.)

```
    set code [catch {uplevel $act} string]
    if {$code >  4} {return -code $code $string}
    if {$code == 4} {return -code continue}
    if {$code == 3} {return -code break}
    if {$code == 2} {return -code return}
    if {$code == 1} {return -code error \
                         -errorinfo $errorInfo \
                         -errorcode $errorCode $string}
    return $string
}
```

Exercises

1. Add scroll bars to the terminal emulator on page 447. Make it allow for resizeable text widgets.

2. The terminal emulator is based on an ANSI terminal. Change the emulator so that it emulates a particular terminal that is not ANSI-conforming. This could be useful if you have to interact with a program or service that is hardwired for a terminal type. Make the emulator understand *any* type of terminal.

3. Write a version of the UNIX `script` command that automatically strips out any character graphics as the output is logged to a file.

4. Modify the `term_expect` procedure on page 459 so that it does not require Tk. Use a list of character strings to emulate a Tk text widget. Then try it with an array. Which is faster? Is this what you had expected?

5. Expand on the previous exercise, by emulating multiple terminals. Provide "hotkeys" so that you can switch between different terminal sessions in a single keystroke.

6. Write a script for browsing through the archives of the `comp.lang.tcl` newsgroup. Display the subjects in a scrollable window, allowing them to be ordered by date, subject, or author. Upon selection, download the posting and display it.

7. Modify the script from the previous exercise so that postings may be saved locally or cached so that the script does not have to `ftp` them again if they are selected.

8. Modify the `tkpasswd` script so that it rejects passwords containing fewer than two digits and two alphabetic characters, one uppercase and one lowercase. Use exercise 4 on page 163.

9. On page 444, I showed how to make an entry widget display asterisks instead of the real characters. This provides security while giving useful feedback when entering passwords. Write a procedure that provides this same kind of feedback when entering passwords to the standard input (i.e., when not using Tk).

In This Chapter:
- *Encrypting Directories*
- *Transferring Files*
- *Watching For Unread News*

20

Extended Examples

Examples are an essential component in learning how to program. The explanations in this book are littered with examples. And while many are complete programs, most of them are small.

In contrast, this chapter is composed of several extended examples. Each is a complete Expect script drawing together many different concepts described in other chapters.

Encrypting A Directory

The UNIX `crypt` command encrypts a single file. Because it interactively prompts for a password, `crypt` is a pain to use if you want to encrypt a number of files all at the same time.

The `cryptdir` script, shown here, encrypts all the files in a directory. The current directory is used unless an argument is given, in which case that is used instead. If the script is called as `decryptdir`, the files are decrypted. Here is the beginning where the script figures out what it should do based on its name and arguments.

```
#!/usr/local/bin/expect --

# encrypt/decrypt an entire directory
# optional arg is dirname, else cwd

if {[llength $argv] > 0} {
    cd $argv
}

# encrypt or decrypt?
set decrypt [regexp "decrypt" $argv0]
```

Next, the script queries for a password. If the script is encrypting files, it asks for the password twice. This lowers the chance of encrypting files with an accidentally mistyped password.

```
set timeout -1
stty -echo
send "Password:"
expect -re "(.*)\n"
send "\n"
set passwd $expect_out(1,string)

# wouldn't want to encrypt files with mistyped password!
if !$decrypt {
    send "Again:"
    expect -re "(.*)\n"
    send "\n"
    if ![string match $passwd $expect_out(1,string)] {
        send_user "mistyped password?"
        stty echo
        exit
    }
}
stty echo
```

Once the password is known, the script loops through the list of files encrypting (or decrypting) each one. The suffix `.crypt` is used to store the encrypted version. Not only is this helpful to the user, but the script also uses this convention to avoid encrypting files that have already been encrypted.

```
log_user 0
foreach f [glob *] {
    set strcmp [string compare .crypt [file extension $f]]
    if $decrypt {
        # skip files that don't end with ".crypt"
        if 0!=$strcmp continue
        spawn sh -c "exec crypt < $f > [file root $f]"
    } else {
        # skip files that already end with ".crypt"
        if 0==$strcmp continue
        spawn sh -c "exec crypt < $f > $f.crypt"
    }
    expect "key:"
    send "$passwd\r"
    expect
    wait
    exec rm -f $f
    send_tty "."
```

```
    }
    send_tty "\n"
```

File Transfer Over telnet

The `ftp` program is handy for transferring files but it only works if the remote host is directly reachable via TCP. Suppose you have to `telnet` to a modem pool and then dial out to another modem to reach the remote host. Not only can `ftp` not handle this but neither can a lot of other communications programs. In Chapter 16 (p. 350), I presented a file transfer script that used `rz` and `sz`. Like many other communications programs, `rz` and `sz` require binary copies of their counterpart at each end of the link. If you do not have both, copying one to the other end can be a problem—if it was easy, you would not need the programs in the first place! Even worse, many versions of `telnet` and other programs do not provide 8-bit clean connections. So even if you had `rz` and `sz`, you might not be able to use them over a `telnet` connection.

The script below works over many kinds of links and does not require a copy of itself on the other end. The only assumptions made are that the usual UNIX utilities (such as `cat` and `compress`) exist and that the line is error free. If you do not have `compress`, that can be removed from the script as well. It is used only to speed the transfers.

The script is quite a bit fancier than the `rz/sz` script. This one interactively prompts for file names and other commands.

The script starts off by finding out what the prompt looks like. It then disables the default timeout. The script has a verbose mode so that the user can see what is happening internally. By default this mode is disabled.

```
#!/usr/local/bin/expect --

if [info exists env(EXPECT_PROMPT)] {
    set prompt $env(EXPECT_PROMPT)
} else {
    set prompt "(%|#|\\$) $"      ;# default prompt
}

set timeout -1
set verbose_flag 0
```

As is usually the case, procedures are defined before they are used. Describing the procedures in that order is hard to understand. Instead, I will present the rest of the script out of order.

The final piece of code in the script starts a shell, tells the user about the commands, and then gives control to the user in an `interact`:

```
spawn -noecho $env(SHELL)

send_user "Once logged in, cd to directory to transfer\
        to/from and press: ~~\n"
send_user "One moment...\n"
interact ~~ cmd
```

At this point, the user connects to the remote system using external programs such as `telnet` and `tip`. Once in the remote directory where transfers should take place, the user invokes the cmd procedure by entering "~~". A special prompt appears and a single additional character selects the specific action that should take place such as p for "put file" and g for "get file". The user can enter another ~ to send a literal tilde, ^Z to suspend the process, ? for help, or c to change directory on the local system.

```
proc cmd {} {
    set CTRLZ \032

    send_user "command (g,p,? for more): "
    expect_user {
        g get_main
        p put_main
        c chdir
        v verbose
        ~ {send "~"}
        "\\?" {
            send_user "?\n"
            send_user "~~g  get file from remote system\n"
            send_user "~~p  put file to remote system\n"
            send_user "~~c  change/show directory on local system\n"
            send_user "~~~  send ~ to remote system\n"
            send_user "~~?  this list\n"
            send_user "~~v  verbose mode toggle\
                        (currently [verbose_status])\n"
            send_user "~~^Z suspend\n"
        }
        $CTRLZ {
            stty -raw echo
            exec kill -STOP [pid]
            stty raw -echo
        }
        -re . {send_user "unknown command\n"}
    }
    send_user "resuming session...\n"
}
```

After executing a command, users are returned to the shell. They can then execute more shell commands or enter ~~ to do more file transfers.

The v command is the simplest one that executes a procedure, `verbose`. The procedure just toggles a variable. Another procedure, `verbose_status`, is a simpler version which just tells the user what the value is. It is called if the user asks for help. Finally, there is a `send_verbose` which is called many places in the code. It prints its arguments, but only if the script is in verbose mode.

```
proc verbose {} {
    global verbose_flag

    set verbose_flag [expr !$verbose_flag]
    send_user "verbose [verbose_status]\r\n"
}

proc verbose_status {} {
    global verbose_flag

    if $verbose_flag {
        return "on"
    } else {
        return "off"
    }
}

proc send_verbose {msg} {
    global verbose_flag

    if $verbose_flag {
        send_user $msg
    }
}
```

The c command is the simplest command that interacts with users. It starts by resetting the mode to cooked and enabling echo. This enables users to see what they are typing and fix any typos. Once the new directory is entered, the process sets it with `cd`. (If a user types cd instead of ~~c, only the remote host is affected.) Finally, the terminal mode is reset to how `interact` left it. The `get` and `put` functions handle the terminal mode the same way.

To make this bullet-proof, the `cd` should be wrapped in a `catch`. A lot more error checking could be added throughout the script.

```
proc chdir {} {
    stty -raw echo
    send_user "c\n"
```

```
        send_user "current directory: [pwd], new directory: "
        expect_user -re "(.*)\n" {
            cd $expect_out(1,string)
        }
        stty raw -echo
    }
```

The get_main and put_main procedures get the names of the files to be copied.
They are written here with expect_user commands although gets could have been
used as well. If one name is entered, it is used as both source and destination name.
Otherwise different names are used.

```
    proc get_main {} {
        stty -raw echo
        send_user "g\nget remote file \[localfile]: "
        expect_user {
            -re "(\[^ ]+) +(\[^ ]+)\n" {
                send_user "copying (remote) $expect_out(1,string) to\
                    (local) $expect_out(2,string)\n"
                get $expect_out(1,string) $expect_out(2,string)
            } -re "(\[^ ]+)\n" {
                send_user "copying $expect_out(1,string)\n"
                get $expect_out(1,string) $expect_out(1,string)
            } -re "\n" {
                send_user "eh?\n"
            }
        }
        stty raw -echo
    }

    proc put_main {} {
        stty -raw echo
        send_user "p\nput localfile \[remotefile]: "
        expect_user {
            -re "(\[^ ]+) +(\[^ ]+)\n" {
                send_user "copying (local) $expect_out(1,string) to\
                    (remote) $expect_out(2,string)\n"
                put $expect_out(1,string) $expect_out(2,string)
            } -re "(\[^ ]+)\n" {
                send_user "copying $expect_out(1,string)\n"
                put $expect_out(1,string) $expect_out(1,string)
            } -re "\n" {
                send_user "eh?\n"
            }
        }
        stty raw -echo
    }
```

The `get` and `put` procedures do the real work of transferring the files. They are rather entertaining and illustrate how to do a lot of work with very little in the way of tools.

The `get` procedure gets a file from the remote system and stores it locally. In essence, the script does this by sending a `cat` command to the local system. Locally, a file is created, and as lines arrive, they are written to the new file.

To be able to detect the end of the file, it is first uuencoded which leaves it with an obvious endmarker. This also solves the problem of transferring binary files. Since binary files are no problem, the file is compressed first on the remote system and uncompressed after reception on the local system. This speeds up the transfer.

The process id is used both locally and remotely to prevent collisions between multiple users. Of course, the remote process id is used on the remote side.

It is amusing to note that the conversation on the remote side is done entirely with vanilla UNIX commands, such as `cat` and `stty`—Expect is only required locally.

The `stty` command is sent immediately to disable echo. Later this drastically simplifies what is returned. For example, the echo of the `cat` command does not have to be stripped out from the beginning of the file listing.

The `put` procedure is similar in design to `get` although the details are different. Here, it is critical that echoing be disabled so that the whole file is not echoed back. There is nothing smart waiting to read the file on the other remote system—just `cat`. It suffices to send a ^D to close the file. Of course, the same compression and encoding occurs in `put`; however, it occurs in reverse with the remote system ultimately doing the uudecoding and uncompression.

```
proc get {infile outfile} {
    global prompt verbose_flag

    if (!$verbose_flag) {
        log_user 0
    }

    send_verbose "disabling echo: "
    send "stty -echo\r"
    expect -re $prompt

    send_verbose "remote pid is "
    send "echo $$\r"
    expect -re "(.*)\r\n.*$prompt" {
        set rpid $expect_out(1,string)
    }

    set pid [pid]
    # pid is local pid, rpid is remote pid
```

```
set infile_plain "/tmp/$rpid"
set infile_compressed "$infile_plain.Z"
set infile_encoded "$infile_compressed.uu"

set outfile_plain "/tmp/$pid"
set outfile_compressed "$outfile_plain.Z"
set outfile_encoded "$outfile_compressed.uu"

set out [open $outfile_encoded w]

send_verbose "compressing\n"
send "compress -fc $infile > $infile_compressed\r"
expect -re $prompt

# use label corresponding to temp name on local system
send_verbose "uuencoding\n"
send "uuencode $infile_compressed $outfile_compressed > \
    $infile_encoded\r"
expect -re $prompt

send_verbose "copying\n"
send "cat $infile_encoded\r"

log_user 0

expect {
    -re "^end\r\n" {
        puts $out "end"
        close $out
    } -re "^(\[^\r]*)\r\n" {
        puts $out $expect_out(1,string)
        send_verbose "."
        exp_continue
    }
}

if ($verbose_flag) {
    send_user "\n"              ;# after last "."
    log_user 1
}

expect -re $prompt;# wait for prompt from cat

send_verbose "deleting temporary files\n"
send "rm -f $infile_compressed $infile_encoded\r"
expect -re $prompt
```

```
    send_verbose "switching attention to local system\n\
        uudecoding\n"
    exec uudecode $outfile_encoded

    send_verbose "uncompressing\n"
    exec uncompress -f $outfile_compressed

    send_verbose "renaming\n"
    if [catch "exec cp $outfile_plain $outfile" msg] {
        send_user "could not move file in place, reason: $msg\n"
        send_user "left as $outfile_plain\n"
        exec rm -f $outfile_encoded
    } else {
        exec rm -f $outfile_plain $outfile_encoded
    }

    # restore echo and serendipitously reprompt
    send "stty echo\r"

    log_user 1
}

proc put {infile outfile} {
    global prompt verbose_flag

    if (!$verbose_flag) {
        log_user 0
    }

    send_verbose "disabling echo: "
    send "stty -echo\r"
    expect -re $prompt

    send_verbose "remote pid is "
    send "echo $$\r"
    expect -re "(.*)\r\n.*$prompt" {
        set rpid $expect_out(1,string)
    }

    set pid [pid]
    # pid is local pid, rpid is remote pid

    set infile_plain   "/tmp/$pid"
    set infile_compressed  "$infile_plain.Z"
    set infile_encoded  "$infile_compressed.uu"

    set outfile_plain  "/tmp/$rpid"
    set outfile_compressed  "$outfile_plain.Z"
```

```
set outfile_encoded   "$outfile_compressed.uu"

set out [open $outfile_encoded w]

send_verbose "compressing\n"
exec compress -fc $infile > $infile_compressed

# use label corresponding to temporary name on local
# system
send_verbose "uuencoding\n"
exec uuencode $infile_compressed $outfile_compressed > \
    $infile_encoded

send_verbose "copying\n"
send "cat > $outfile_encoded\r"

log_user 0

set fp [open $infile_encoded r]
while 1 {
    if {-1 == [gets $fp buf]} break
    send_verbose "."
    send "$buf\r"
}

if ($verbose_flag) {
    send_user "\n"          ;# after last "."
    log_user 1
}

send "\004"   ;# eof
close $fp

send_verbose "deleting temporary files\n"
exec rm -f $infile_compressed $infile_encoded

send_verbose "switching attention to remote system\n"

expect -re $prompt      ;# wait for prompt from cat

send_verbose "uudecoding\n"
send "uudecode $outfile_encoded\r"
expect -re $prompt

send_verbose "uncompressing\n"
send "uncompress -f $outfile_compressed\r"
expect -re $prompt
```

```
        send_verbose "renaming\n"
        send "cp $outfile_plain $outfile\r"
        expect -re $prompt

        send_verbose "deleting temporary files\n"
        send "rm -f $outfile_plain $outfile_encoded\r"
        expect -re $prompt

        # restore echo and serendipitously reprompt
        send "stty echo\r"

        log_user 1
    }
```

You Have Unread News — tknewsbiff

biff is a UNIX program that reports when mail is received. In its fancier forms, it can pop up a picture of the sender or play an audio clip. If you receive mail from your boss, for example, you could have biff shout "Red Alert!"

tknewsbiff is a script to do the same thing but for Usenet news. When you have unread news, an audio clip can be played or some other action can be taken. By default, newsgroups with unread news are shown in a window along with the numbers of unread articles. Here is an example:

`tknewsbiff` is quite different from the other examples in this book. The script is customizable by additional Tcl commands supplied by the user. Customizations are stored in the file `~/.tknewsbiff`. A simple version might look like this:

```
set server news.nist.gov
set delay 120
set server_timeout 60
set height 10

watch comp.unix.*
watch *.sources.*
watch dc.dining

ignore *.d
```

The first four commands set variables that control how often `tknewsbiff` checks for news, the news server to check, how long to wait for a response, and the maximum number of newsgroups to display at a time in the window. There are other variables which I will mention later. All are defined using `set` commands.

Next are definitions of which newsgroups to watch. The first command requests that all of the comp.unix groups be watched. Next is a pattern which matches all of the source related newsgroups. Finally, the dc.dining newsgroup (Washington DC restaurant news) is watched.

The `watch` command is just a Tcl procedure which I will show later. Another procedure is `ignore`. The example here causes all discussion groups to be ignored.

The `watch` command supports several flags. The `-display` flag names a command to execute when a newsgroup has unread news. The default action causes the newsgroup in the `newsgroup` variable to be scheduled for display when the window is redrawn. The `-new` flag names a command to execute when unread news first appears in a newsgroup. For example, the following lines invoke the UNIX command `play` to play a sound.

```
watch *.dining  -new "exec play /usr/local/sound/yum.au"
watch rec.auto* -new "exec play /usr/local/sound/vroom.au"
```

By default, `-new` and `-display` are evaluated when more than zero articles are unread. The `-threshold` flag specifies the number of articles after which actions should be evaluated. For instance, "`-threshold 10`" means that the newsgroup will not be displayed until at least 10 articles are unread.

You can cut down on the verbosity of actions by defining procedures. For example, if you have many –new flags that all play sound files, you could define a sound procedure. This allows the –new specifications to be much shorter.

```
proc play {sound} {
    exec play /usr/local/sound/$sound.au
}
```

Using play, the watch commands can be rewritten:

```
watch *.dining -new "play yum"
watch rec.auto* -new "play vroom"
```

The user-defined user procedure is run immediately after the newsgroups are scheduled to be written to the display and before they are actually written. Why is this useful? Suppose unread articles appear in several rec.auto groups and the same sound is to be played for each one. To prevent playing the sound several times in a row, the –new command can set a flag so that in the user procedure, the sound is played once and only if the flag is set.

The user procedure could also be used to start a newsreader. This would avoid the possibility of starting multiple newsreaders just because multiple newsgroups contained unread articles. If started with exec, a check should, of course, be made to verify that a newsreader is not already running. Alternatively, you could send a command to a Tk-based newsreader to switch to a new group or, perhaps, pop open a new window for the new group.

The tknewsbiff Script

The script starts by removing the default window from the screen. The window will be replaced when there is something to be displayed and removed when empty. Since this can happen as news is read or more arrives, two utility procedures are immediately defined and one is invoked. They also keep track of whether the user iconified the window or not.

```
#!/usr/local/bin/expectk --

proc unmapwindow {} {
    global _window_open

    switch [wm state .] \
    iconic {
        set _window_open 0
    } normal {
        set _window_open 1
    }
    wm withdraw .
```

```
}
unmapwindow
# force window to be open when mapped for the first time
set _window_open 1

proc mapwindow {} {
    global _window_open

    if $_window_open {
        wm deiconify .
    } else {
        wm iconify .
    }
}
```

Notice that the variable _window_open begins with an underscore. This is a simple attempt to keep things out of the user's namespace. Anything beginning with an underscore is off-limits to the user (the tknewsbiff man page describes this). On the other hand, the procedures mapwindow and unmapwindow are public. The user can call them directly.

Another utility procedure is defined below. _abort is called when an error is encountered that is too severe for tknewsbiff to continue.

```
proc _abort {msg} {
    global argv0

    puts "$argv0: $msg"
    exit 1
}
```

The environment is now initialized, primarily by giving variables reasonable defaults. The directory in which to find the configuration files is located.

```
if [info exists env(DOTDIR)] {
    set home $env(DOTDIR)
} else {
    set home [glob ~]
}
```

```
set delay                   60
set width                   27
set height                  10
set _default_config_file    $home/.tknewsbiff
set _config_file            $_default_config_file
set _default_server         news
set server                  $_default_server
set server_timeout          60
```

```
log_user 0
```

A few Tk commands define the window that displays the newsgroups. More configuration will take place later when the newsgroups to be displayed are known.

```
listbox .list -yscroll ".scrollbar set" -font "*-m-*" -setgrid 1
scrollbar .scrollbar -command ".list yview" -relief raised
pack .scrollbar -side left -fill y
pack .list -side left -fill both -expand 1
```

Next, the command-line arguments are parsed. The script accepts either a configuration file name or a hostname. If a hostname is given, it is used to find a host-specific configuration file. This enables a user to run multiple copies of tknewsbiff simultaneously, each monitoring news from a different host.

```
while {[llength $argv]>0} {
    set arg [lindex $argv 0]

    if [file readable $arg] {
        if 0==[string compare active [file tail $arg]] {
            set active_file $arg
            set argv [lrange $argv 1 end]
        } else {
            # must be a config file
            set _config_file $arg
            set argv [lrange $argv 1 end]
        }
    } elseif {[file readable $_config_file-$arg]} {
        # maybe it's a hostname suffix for a newsrc file?
        set _config_file $_default_config_file-$arg
        set argv [lrange $argv 1 end]
    } else {
        # maybe just a hostname for a regular newsrc file?
        set server $arg
        set argv [lrange $argv 1 end]
    }
}
```

Once the configuration file is determined, it is read for additional information such as the newsrc location, server name, timeout, etc. The _read_config_file procedure sources the configuration file, allowing any user-written Tcl code to be executed in the global scope. This allows the user complete access to all other procedures and variables in the script, providing tremendous flexibility.

For simple configurations, the user does not have to know much about the syntax of Tcl. For example, commands such as set are common to most .rc files. On the other hand, the sophisticated user can write Tcl code and make tknewsbiff perform in very unusual ways. By providing these hooks, tknewsbiff avoids the burden of having a lot of special-case code. For example, `tknewsbiff` does not have to know how to play sounds on each computer since the user can call any external program to do it via `exec`.

The `watch` and `ignore` commands merely append their arguments to the lists `watch_list` and `ignore_list`. Making `watch` and `ignore` procedures is a little friendlier to the user. People unfamiliar with Tcl might be put off by having to learn about a command named `lappend`. ("What does that have to do with news!?")

The `user` procedure is deleted just in case the user has also deleted it from the configuration file. If they have not deleted `user`, it will be recreated when the file is resourced. If no configuration file exists, the last command in the `_read_config_file` ensures that all newsgroups are watched.

```
proc _read_config_file {} {
    global _config_file argv0 watch_list ignore_list

    proc user {} {}
    set watch_list {}
    set ignore_list {}

    if [file exists $_config_file] {
        # uplevel allows user to set global variables
        if [catch {uplevel source $_config_file} msg] {
            _abort "error reading $_config_file\n$msg"
        }
    }

    if [llength $watch_list]==0 {
        watch *
    }
}

proc watch {args} {
    global watch_list

    lappend watch_list $args
}

proc ignore {ng} {
    global ignore_list

    lappend ignore_list $ng
}

_read_config_file
```

Once the configuration file is read, a few last details are pinned down. The newsrc file can be located and the window can be titled to differentiate it from other `tknewsbiff` instances.

```
# if user didn't set newsrc, try ~/.newsrc-server
# if that fails, fall back to just plain ~/.newsrc
if ![info exists newsrc] {
    set newsrc $home/.newsrc-$server
    if ![file readable $newsrc] {
        set newsrc $home/.newsrc
        if ![file readable $newsrc] {
            abort "cannot tell what newgroups you read - found\
                    neither $home/.newsrc-$server nor $home/.newsrc"
        }
    }
}
# initialize display
set min_reasonable_width 8
wm minsize . $min_reasonable_width 1
wm maxsize . 999 999
if {0 == [info exists active_file] &&
    0 != [string compare $server $_default_server]} {
    wm title . "news@$server"
    wm iconname . "news@$server"
}
```

A number of other procedures are created, and then `tknewsbiff` loops alternating between checking for news and sleeping. In the real script, the procedures have to be defined first, but I will show the loop now because it is easier to understand this way.

```
for {} 1 {_sleep $delay} {
    _init_ngs

    _read_newsrc
    if [_read_active] continue
    _read_config_file

    _update_ngs
    user
    _update_window
}
```

After some initialization, the body of the loop goes on to read the user's newsrc file. This tells how many articles the user has read. `tknewsbiff` then checks to see how many new articles exist. Next, the user's configuration file is read.

Once all the raw data has been collected, `tknewsbiff` decides what actions to take. `_update_ngs` creates an internal description of the newsgroups that contain new articles based on the work earlier in the loop. Prior to updating the visible window, a user-defined procedure, user, is called. This allows the user to look at and play with the internal description. For example, the user procedure could execute an action to start a newsreader.

Now I will describe each procedure. _read_newsrc reads the user's newsrc file. The most recently read article is stored in the array db. For example, if the user has read article 5 in comp.unix.wizards, db(comp.unix.wizards,seen) is set to 5.

```
proc _read_newsrc {} {
    global db newsrc

    if [catch {set file [open $newsrc]} msg] {
        _abort $msg
    }
    while {-1 != [gets $file buf]} {
        if [regexp "!" $buf] continue
        if [regexp "(\[^:]*):.*\[-, ](\[0-9]+)" $buf dummy ng seen]
    {
            set db($ng,seen) $seen
        }
        # 2nd regexp can fail on lines that have : but no #
    }
    close $file
}
```

Next, tknewsbiff checks the number of articles in each group. By default, an NNTP connection is spawned to a news server. However, if the variable active_file exists, the local active file is read instead. Notice how the same code reads the data from either the file or the spawned process.

Each newsgroup is appended to the list active_list. The highest numbered article in each newsgroup is stored in db(*newsgroup*,hi).

```
proc _read_active {} {
    global db server active_list active_file
    upvar #0 server_timeout timeout

    set active_list {}

    if [info exists active_file] {
        spawn -open [open $active_file]
    } else {
        spawn telnet $server nntp
        expect {
            "20*\n" {
                # should get 200 or 201
            } "NNTP server*\n" {
```

```
                        puts "tknewsbiff: unexpected response from server:"
                        puts "$expect_out(buffer)"
                        return 1
                    } "unknown host" {
                        _unknown_host
                    } timeout {
                        close
                        wait
                        return 1
                    } eof {
                        # loadav too high probably
                        wait
                        return 1
                    }
                }
                exp_send "list\r"
                # ignore echo of "list" command
                expect "list\r\n"
                # skip "Newsgroups in form" line
                expect -re "215\[^\n]*\n"
            }

            expect {
                -re "(\[^ ]*) 0*(\[^ ]+) \[^\n]*\n" {
                    set ng $expect_out(1,string)
                    set hi $expect_out(2,string)
                    lappend active_list $ng
                    set db($ng,hi) $hi
                    exp_continue
                }
                ".\r\n" close
                eof
            }

            wait
            return 0
        }
```

The _unknown_host procedure is called if `telnet` fails with that error.

```
    proc _unknown_host {} {
        global server _default_server

        if 0==[string compare $_default_server $server] {
            puts "tknewsbiff: default server <$server> is not known"
        } else {
            puts "tknewsbiff: server <$server> is not known"
        }
```

```
            puts "Give tknewsbiff an argument - either the name\
                of your news server or active file.  I.e.,

            tknewsbiff news.nist.gov
            tknewsbiff /usr/news/lib/active
            \n\
            If you have a correctly defined configuration file\
            (.tknewsbiff), an argument is not required.  See the\
            man page for more info."
            exit 1
        }
```

In the main loop of `tknewsbiff`, the next step is to reread the user's configuration file. This is done so that the user can change it without having to restart `tknewsbiff`.

After reading the configuration file, `tknewsbiff` turns to the job of deciding what to do with all the data. The `_update_ngs` procedure looks through the newsgroup data and figures out which newsgroups should have their `-display` or `-new` actions executed. The code is careful to do actions in the same order that the user specified the newsgroups in the configuration file. Also, actions are not executed twice even if a newsgroup matches two different patterns. Following `_update_ngs` are two utility procedures that calculate whether newsgroup actions should be shown.

```
    proc _update_ngs {} {
        global watch_list active_list newsgroup

        foreach watch $watch_list {
            set threshold 1
            set display display
            set new {}

            set ngpat [lindex $watch 0]
            set watch [lrange $watch 1 end]

            while {[llength $watch] > 0} {
                switch -- [lindex $watch 0] \
                -threshold {
                    set threshold [lindex $watch 1]
                    set watch [lrange $watch 2 end]
                } -display {
                    set display [lindex $watch 1]
                    set watch [lrange $watch 2 end]
                } -new {
                    set new [lindex $watch 1]
                    set watch [lrange $watch 2 end]
                } default {
                    _abort "watch: expecting -threshold, -display or\
                        -new but found: [lindex $watch 0]"
```

```
                    }
                }

            foreach ng $active_list {
                if [string match $ngpat $ng] {
                    if [_isgood $ng $threshold] {
                        if [llength $display] {
                            set newsgroup $ng
                            uplevel $display
                        }
                        if [_isnew $ng] {
                            if [llength $new] {
                                set newsgroup $ng
                                uplevel $new
                            }
                        }
                    }
                }
            }
        }
    }


# test in various ways for good newsgroups
# return 1 if good, 0 if not good
proc _isgood {ng threshold} {
    global db seen_list ignore_list

    # skip if we don't subscribe to it
    if ![info exists db($ng,seen)] {return 0}

    # skip if the threshold isn't exceeded
    if {$db($ng,hi) - $db($ng,seen) < $threshold} {
        return 0
    }

    # skip if it matches an ignore command
    foreach igpat $ignore_list {
        if [string match $igpat $ng] {return 0}
    }

    # skip if we've seen it before
    if [lsearch -exact $seen_list $ng]!=-1 {return 0}

    # passed all tests, so remember that we've seen it
    lappend seen_list $ng
    return 1
}
```

```
# return 1 if not seen on previous turn
proc _isnew {ng} {
    global previous_seen_list

    if [lsearch -exact $previous_seen_list $ng]==-1 {
        return 1
    } else {
        return 0
    }
}
```

The `display` procedure schedules a newsgroup to be displayed. Internally, all it does is to append the newsgroup to the `display_list` variable. The current newsgroup is taken from the global `newsgroup` variable. The `display` procedure is the default action for the `-display` flag.

```
proc display {} {
    global display_list newsgroup

    lappend display_list $newsgroup
}
```

The final procedure in the main loop is `_update_window` which redraws the window, resizing and remapping it if necessary. The procedure `_display_ngs` is a utility procedure which rewrites the newsgroups in the window.

```
proc _update_window {} {
    global server display_list height width
    global min_reasonable_width

    if {0 == [llength $display_list]} {
        unmapwindow
        return
    }

    # make height correspond to length of display_list or
    # user's requested max height, whichever is smaller

    if {[llength $display_list] < $height} {
        set current_height [llength $display_list]
    } else {
        set current_height $height
    }

    # force reasonable min width
    if {$width < $min_reasonable_width} {
        set width $min_reasonable_width
    }
```

```
    wm geometry . ${width}x$current_height
    wm maxsize . 999 [llength $display_list]

    _display_ngs $width

    if [string compare [wm state .] withdrawn]==0 {
        mapwindow
    }
}


# write all newsgroups to the window
proc _display_ngs {width} {
    global db display_list

    set str_width [expr $width-7]

    .list delete 0 end
    foreach ng $display_list {
        .list insert end [
            format "%-$str_width.${str_width}s %5d" \
                $ng [expr $db($ng,hi) - $db($ng,seen)]
        ]
    }
}
```

The newsgroup window is initialized with a few simple bindings. The left button pops up a help window. (The `help` procedure is not shown here.) The middle button causes `tknewsbiff` to stop sleeping and check for new unread news immediately. The right mouse button causes the window to disappear from the screen until the next update cycle. Finally, if the user resizes the window, it is redrawn using the new size.

```
bind .list <1> help
bind .list <2> update-now
bind .list <3> unmapwindow
bind .list <Configure> {
    scan [wm geometry .] "%%dx%%d" w h
    _display_ngs $w
}
```

The user can replace or add to these bindings by adding `bind` commands in their configuration file. For example, here is a binding to pop up an `xterm` and run `rn`:

```
bind .list <Shift-1> {
    exec xterm -e rn &
}
```

Here is a binding that tells rn to look only at the newsgroup that was under the mouse when it was pressed.

```
bind .list <Shift-1> {
    exec xterm -e rn [lindex $display_list [.list nearest %y]] &
}
```

The tknewsbiff display can be further customized at this point by additional Tk commands. For example, the following command sets the colors of the newsgroup window:

```
.list config -bg honeydew1 -fg orchid2
```

After each loop, tknewsbiff sleeps. While it is *not* sleeping, it changes the shape of the cursor to a wristwatch to indicate that it is busy. The _sleep procedure itself is a little unusual. Instead of simply calling sleep, it waits for several characters from a spawned cat process. In the usual case, none arrive and _sleep returns after the expect times out.

However, if the user calls update-now (earlier this was bound to the middle button), a carriage-return is sent to the cat process. cat echoes this as four characters (\r\n\r\n) which is just what the expect in _sleep is waiting for. Thus, tknews-biff wakes up if update-now is run. The cat process is spawned once at the beginning of the process.

```
spawn cat -u; set _cat_spawn_id $spawn_id
set _update_flag 0

proc _sleep {timeout} {
    global _cat_spawn_id _update_flag

    set _update_flag 0

    # restore to idle cursor
    .list config -cursor ""; update

    # sleep for a little while, subject to click from
    # "update" button
    expect -i $_cat_spawn_id -re "....";# two crlfs

    # change to busy cursor
    .list config -cursor watch; update
}
```

```
proc update-now {} {
    global _update_flag _cat_spawn_id

    if $_update_flag return    ;# already set, do nothing
    set _update_flag 1

    exp_send -i $_cat_spawn_id "\r"
}
```

The last things to be done in the script are some miscellaneous initializations. _init_ngs is called at the beginning of every loop, so that `tknewsbiff` starts with a clean slate.

```
set previous_seen_list {}
set seen_list {}

proc _init_ngs {} {
    global display_list db
    global seen_list previous_seen_list

    set previous_seen_list $seen_list

    set display_list {}
    set seen_list {}

    catch {unset db}
}
```

Exercises

1. Use the timeout technique from the `tknewsbiff` script to cause an `interact` to return by pressing a Tk button. Compare this to using a signal.

2. The file transfer script from page 467 assumes very little of the remote host. Modify the script so that it checks for the existence of `rz/sz` (or other tools) on the remote machine and uses them if possible. Similarly, use `gzip` if possible.

3. Most compression programs can read from or write to a pipeline. Use this to reduce the number of temporary files used by the file transfer script.

In This Chapter:
- *Using Expect Without Tcl*
- *The Expect Library*

21

Expect, C, And C++

In the other chapters of this book, I have described how to use Expect with the command-oriented Tcl environment. However, Expect can be used without Tcl. In this chapter, I will describe how to call Expect functions from C by using the Expect library. This library is compatible with C++ as well, and most of the examples are identical between C and C++. For other languages, you are on your own. However, if you know how to call C routines from your favorite language, you should be able to do the same with Expect.

Much of the functions in the library work analogously to their counterparts in the Expect program. Accordingly, it will be very helpful to have some experience with Expect before using the library. Concepts such as spawned processes and glob patterns versus regular expressions are not explained here.

This chapter is not meant to encourage the use of C or C++. Especially for Expect-like programming, working in Tcl is much, much easier than working with C or C++ and their usual edit–compile–debug cycles. Unlike typical compiled programs, most of the debugging of Expect programs is not getting the compiler to accept programs—rather, it is getting the dialogue correct. And this is much faster to do with Tcl.

If you are aware of the trade-offs between C and C++ and Tcl and have good cause to use this library, plow ahead. But if you do not know Tcl and simply want to avoid learning another language, I would suggest taking a step back, reexamining your decision, and giving Tcl a chance. It is more than meets the eye.

For many tasks, the Tcl environment is preferable to that of C and C++. However, C and C++ may be forced upon you if you already have a large amount of software written that uses some other mechanism to provide control over symbol tables and program flow.

For example, you might want to do Expect-like operations from another interpreter such as Basic, Lisp, or Perl. Adding Tcl to those interpreters is just going to make things more complicated. Instead, you can invoke Expect-like operations directly.

Rather than provide bindings for every interpreter under the sun, Expect comes with a library that can be linked with any program. The library has functions that can be used by hand, or with a little glue, added to any interpreter so they can be called in that new language.

In Chapter 22 (p. 518), I will describe how to produce standalone Expect binaries that still use Tcl for control. Often called *compiled*, such programs require no external scripts and are a convenient form to use if you want to package everything in a single file.

Overview

Calling Expect from C and C++ is straightforward. I will omit references to C++ from now on because most of the examples and explanations are identical in both environments. Expect comes as a library that you link with your other object files. The library contains three types of functions. These functions:

- manipulate ptys and processes
- wait for input using patterns
- disconnect the controlling terminal

You need not use these functions together. For example, you can have Expect spawn a process, but then read from it directly (without using patterns). In addition, you can use functions out of the Tcl library (such as the regular expression pattern matcher) or the Expect extension library.

A number of facilities in the Expect program have no analog. Or to put it another way, the Expect library does not provide substitutes for all Expect commands. For example, there is no send function because you can use fprintf or write to do the same thing.

Here is a simple example to create and interact with a process. It may look confusing at first but it will make more sense as you read this chapter.

```
FILE *fp = exp_popen("chess");
exp_fexpectl(fp,exp_glob,"Chess\r\n",0,exp_end);
fprintf(fp,"first\r");
```

The first line runs the chess program. A FILE pointer is returned so that you can interact with the process. The exp_fexpectl function declares a glob-style pattern for which to wait. Finally, the last line sends a string back to the process.

Linking

Linking a program with the Expect library requires only naming the appropriate libraries. The Expect library is called `libexpect.a` and must be supplied when the program is linked. Assuming that it is installed in your system so that the linker can find it, the library is traditionally named from the command line as "`-lexpect`".

For example, if your program is composed of the object files "`foo.o`" and "`bar.o`", they can be linked together as:

```
cc foo.c bar.c -lexpect -ltcl
```

The Tcl library is listed here too. The Expect library "borrows" Tcl's regular expression pattern matcher but nothing else. Rather than shipping yet another copy of the pattern matcher, it is easier just to link with the Tcl library. The Tcl library may be avoided entirely by supplying a replacement for the regular expression pattern matcher.

When the library is used with other languages, it may be desirable to replace the glob or regular expression pattern matchers with different ones. For example, another language may define regular expressions differently than Tcl. Using Tcl's regular expressions with those of another language would be confusing. Unfortunately, there is no standard interface for pattern matchers. A simple solution is to replace calls to the pattern matchers with new calls that follow any of the interfaces used by the Expect library. Because these interfaces are likely to change, they are not formally documented. However, the current interfaces are relatively trivial and should be easily understandable to anyone familiar with popular UNIX pattern matchers.

Include Files

Any files that make references to the Expect library must include the following statement. The statement should appear before any Expect functions are called.

```
#include "expect.h"
```

This statement works for both C and C++ programs.

Some of the Expect library functions work with the C standard I/O package. If you use these parts of the library, you must also include that header as well.

```
#include <stdio.h>
```

If the compiler needs to be told where the Expect include files come from, add an appropriate argument to the compile command. For example, to compile `foo.c`, you might have to say:

```
cc -I/usr/local/include foo.c
```

The precise filename depends on where the include files have been installed. As before, the Tcl include files should also be available. Normally, both the Expect and Tcl include files live in the same directory, so one -I flag should suffice.

Ptys And Processes

The Expect library provides three functions to start new interactive processes. Each of them creates a new process so that its standard input, standard output, and standard error can be read and written by the current process.

exp_spawnl is useful when the number of arguments is known at compile time. exp_spawnv is useful when the number of arguments is not known at compile time. (The third function exp_popen will be described later.) In both cases, the arguments are passed literally—no shell pattern matching is done and no redirection occurs. The shell is simply not involved. I occasionally will refer to these functions generically as the *spawn functions.*

exp_spawnl and exp_spawnv parallel those of the UNIX functions execlp and execvp respectively. The calling sequences are as follows:

```
int
exp_spawnl(file, arg0 [, arg1, ..., argn] (char *)0);
char *file;
char *arg0, *arg1, ... *argn;

int
exp_spawnv(file,argv);
char *file, *argv[ ];
```

In both functions, the file argument is a relative or absolute file specification. No special character processing occurs (such as ~ or * expansion). exp_spawnl and exp_spawnv duplicate the shell's actions in searching for an executable file from the list of directories associated with the PATH environment variable.

The argv parameter in exp_spawnv is made available to the new process as the argv parameter in main. exp_spawnl collects its remaining arguments and then massages them so that they also appear as the argv parameter in main. In both cases, the arguments are copied so that you can later change the pointers or what they point to without affecting the spawned process.

For example, the following command starts a telnet process to the SMTP port of uunet.uu.net:

```
fd = exp_spawnl("telnet",
          "telnet","uunet.uu.net","smtp",(char *)0);
```

Notice that the arg0 parameter is identical to the file parameter. Remember that the file parameter is not part of the argv array in the new main. argv[0] in the new process comes from arg0 in the current process.

In both exp_spawnl and exp_spawnv, the argument list must be terminated by (char *)0. Forgetting the terminating 0 is a common error and typically leads to a core dump.

If the functions are successful, they return a file descriptor. This file descriptor corresponds to the standard input, standard output, and standard error of the new process. You can use the write system call to write to the standard input:

```
write(fd,"foo\r",4);
```

To read from the standard output or standard error, use the read system call.

```
read(fd,buffer,BUFSIZ);
```

A stream may be associated with the file descriptor by using fdopen. In almost all cases, you want to immediately unbuffer the new stream.

```
fp = fdopen(fd,"r+");
setbuf(fp,(char *)0);
```

If an error occurs during exp_spawnl or exp_spawnv, -1 is returned and errno is set appropriately. Errors that occur after a spawn function forks (e.g., attempting to spawn a non-existent program) are written to the standard error of the spawned process and are read by the first read. The rationale for this is described in Chapter 13 (p. 296).

The popen function in the C library accepts a shell command line, runs it, and returns a stream associated with it. Unfortunately, you can only choose to read from or write to a process. You cannot do both.

The Expect library defines exp_popen. It is styled after popen. exp_popen takes a Bourne shell command line and returns a stream that corresponds to the standard input, standard output, and standard error of the new process. Redirection and shell pattern matching are done on the command line. Unlike popen, exp_popen takes no type flag. popen uses a pipe which only supports one-way communication, but exp_popen uses a pty which supports two-way communication. Compare the declarations of popen and exp_popen:

```
FILE *popen(command, type)
char *command, *type;

FILE *exp_popen(command)
char *command;
```

The following statements spawn `telnet`. Some file arguments are listed and the standard error is redirected—not because this makes sense—but just to show that it can be done.

```
FILE *fp;
fp = exp_popen("telnet host smtp *.c 2> /dev/null");
```

Since `exp_popen` returns a stream, you use any of the standard I/O functions to access it. For example, the stream can be written to with `fwrite`, `fprintf`, `fputc`, and others. Here is an example with `fprintf`:

```
char *my_name = "Don";
fprintf(fp,"My name is %s\r",my_name);
```

The stream can be read using `fread`, `fscanf`, `fgetc`, and others. Here is an example with `fgets`:

```
char buffer[100];
fgets(buffer,100,fp);
```

The actual implementation of `exp_popen` is defined in terms of `exp_spawnl`. It is shown below.

```
FILE *
exp_popen(program)
char *program;
{
    FILE *fp;
    int ec;

    ec = exp_spawnl("sh","sh","-c",program,(char *)0);
    if (0 > ec) return(0);

    fp = fdopen(ec,"r+");
    if (fp) setbuf(fp,(char *)0);
    return fp;
}
```

Several variables are made available by inclusion of `expect.h`. They should not be defined or declared but may be read and written.

Two of these variables are set as side-effects of the spawn functions. These are:

```
extern int exp_pid;
extern char *exp_pty_slave_name;
```

The `exp_pid` variable contains the process id of the process created by the spawn functions. The variable `exp_pid` is rewritten each time a spawn function is called so it should generally be immediately saved to another variable.

The spawn functions use a pty to communicate with the process. The variable `exp_pty_slave_name` is the name of the slave side of the pty associated with each spawned process. Put another way, `exp_pty_slave_name` is the name of the tty that the spawned process uses for its standard input, standard output, and standard error.

Here is a program to spawn the `cat` program and print out the process id and tty name of the spawned process.

```
#include <stdio.h>
#include "expect.h"

main(){
    FILE *fp = exp_popen("cat");
    printf("pid = %d\n",exp_pid);
    printf("pty name = %s\n",exp_pty_slave_name);
}
```

When run on my system, this program printed:

```
pid = 18804
pty name = /dev/ttyp3
```

Several other variables control aspects of the spawn functions. They are:

```
extern int exp_console;
extern int exp_ttyinit;
extern int exp_ttycopy;
extern char *exp_stty_init;
```

By default, the pty is initialized the same way as the user's tty (if possible, i.e., if the environment has a controlling terminal.) This initialization is performed only if the variable `exp_ttycopy` is nonzero. It is nonzero by default.

The pty is further initialized to a system-wide default if the variable `exp_ttyinit` is nonzero. The default is generally comparable to "stty sane". `exp_ttyinit` is nonzero by default.

The tty setting can be further modified by setting the variable `exp_stty_init`. This variable is interpreted in the style of `stty` arguments. For example, the following statement repeats the default initialization. If `exp_stty_init` is set to 0, no extra initialization is performed.

```
exp_stty_init = "sane";
```

These three initializations may seem like overkill, but they solve a number of problems. The rationale for all this is described in Chapter 13 (p. 300).

The variable `exp_console` attempts to associate the new pty with the console. If the association is made successfully, any messages to the console are sent to the pty and can be read as the output of the process.

If your system supports the environ variable, you can use this to control the environment of the spawned process. It should be declared as:

```
extern char **environ;
```

The environ variable is an array of character pointers to strings representing the environment variables. (This representation is described in detail in most C texts.) When a new process is spawned, the environ array is copied into the new process and becomes its environment. You may modify the environ table before spawning a process, and the spawned process will get the modified environment.

Most other attributes of a process are inherited according to the "usual" rules of the exec family of functions. This includes things such as user id, group id, current working directory, etc. Signals that are caught are reset to the default action. Lastly, the process is placed in a new process group with a new session id.

It is possible to change attributes in the context of the child process just before the new program is given control (via an exec function) by providing a definition for exp_child_exec_prelude. For example, you might want the child to ignore SIGHUP and SIGTERM. This could be done as follows:

```
void exp_child_exec_prelude() {
    signal(SIGHUP, SIG_IGN);
    signal(SIGTERM, SIG_IGN);
}
```

Allocating Your Own Pty

By default, a pty is automatically allocated each time a process is spawned. It is possible to allocate a pty through some other mechanism (of your own). Conceivably, you could also use a pair of fifos or something similar even though it may not completely emulate tty functionality.

Two variables control pty allocation. They are:

```
extern int exp_autoallocpty;
extern int exp_pty[2];
```

The variable exp_autoallocpty is set to one by default. If you set it to zero, a pty is not automatically allocated by the spawn functions. Instead, the value of exp_pty[0] is used as the master pty file descriptor, and the value of exp_pty[1] is used as the slave pty file descriptor.

The following illustrates pty allocation with the pipe system call. (On traditional UNIX systems, a pipe is a one-way device, so this example is not suitable for most Expect applications. Nonetheless, it serves to demonstrate the calling protocol.) The first statement turns off the automatic pty allocation. The second statement uses the `pipe` system call which conveniently produces two connected file descriptors in the `exp_pty` array. The `exp_popen` creates a `cat` process and uses the two file descriptors in the `exp_pty` array.

```
exp_autoallocpty = 0;
pipe(exp_pty);
exp_popen("cat");
```

When you allocate your own pty, you must also initialize it. The spawn functions do none of the usual pty initializations (e.g., `exp_stty_init` is not used).

After the new process is created, the slave pty file descriptor is closed in the current process and the master pty file descriptor is closed in the spawned process. In the context of the current process, all further communication takes place with the master pty file descriptor (i.e., `exp_pty[0]`).

Whether or not you allocate your own pty, the new process may need to close file descriptors. By default, all file descriptors to processes created by the spawn functions are marked close-on-exec. This enforces the behavior described in the previous paragraph of closing the master pty file descriptor in the spawned process. Other non-spawn-related file descriptors should also be marked close-on-exec so that they can be closed automatically. Alternatively, the function pointer `exp_close_in_child` may be set to a function that closes additional file descriptors. By default, `exp_close_in_child` is 0.

```
void (*exp_close_in_child)();
```

When using Tcl (with or without Expect), the function `exp_close_tcl_files` can be used to close all the files above the standard input, standard output, and standard error to the highest descriptor that Tcl knows about. This is exactly what Expect does. The following statement enables this behavior.

```
exp_close_in_child = exp_close_tcl_files;
```

This behavior is rather crude but often sufficient. A more sophisticated solution requires delving into the Tcl internals and is beyond the scope of this book.

Closing The Connection To The Spawned Process

The Expect library provides no special functions to close the connection to a spawned process. Generally, it is sufficient to call `close`. If you have converted the file descriptor to a stream (or used `exp_popen` which returns a stream), call `fclose` instead.

Once the process exits, it should be waited upon in order to free up the process slot. When convenient, you can wait for the process using any of the wait family of calls. You can also catch SIGCHLD before waiting, or you can ignore SIGCHLD entirely. Further discussion on this can be found in any UNIX system programming text.

As described in Chapter 4 (p. 103), some processes do not automatically terminate when their standard input is closed. You may have to send them explicit commands to exit, or alternatively you can kill them outright. As described above, the exp_pid variable provides the process id of the most recently spawned process.

There is no matching exp_pclose to exp_popen (unlike popen and pclose). It only takes two functions to close down a connection (fclose followed by waiting on the process id), but it is not uncommon to separate these two actions by large time intervals, so providing a new function for this purpose is of little value. Just close the stream using fclose and wait for the process.

Expect Commands

The library provides functions that can be used to read files or streams. Like the Expect program's expect command, the library functions wait for patterns to appear or special events to occur.

There are four functions to do expect-like processing. Two are for handling file descriptors, and the other two are for streams. One of each take lists of arguments similar to exp_spawnl while the others take a single variable argument descriptor similar to exp_spawnv. I will occasionally refer to these functions generically as the "expect functions".

	list of arguments	one variable argument
file	expectl	expectv
stream	fexpectl	fexpectv

Table of expect functions — each function is prefixed with "exp_" in actual use.

The names are mnemonic. Like exp_spawnl and exp_spawnv, the expect functions that end with an "l" take arguments lists, and those ending with "v" take a single variable descriptor. An "f" means that the function reads a stream; otherwise it reads from a file descriptor.

The table shows the short names but these are further prefaced by the string "exp_".[†] For example, the `exp_expectl` function takes an argument list and reads from a file descriptor. A simple example of `exp_expectl` is:

```
exp_expectl(fd, exp_glob, "prompt*", 1, exp_end);
```

This call waits for a prompt to arrive from the file descriptor `fd`. `exp_glob` is the pattern type. It says that the pattern "`prompt*`" is a glob pattern. When it arrives, `exp_expectl` returns the value 1.

More patterns can be expected at the same time by adding them to the argument list.

```
exp_expectl(fd ,exp_glob, "prompt*", 1,
            exp_glob, "another pattern", 2,
            exp_glob, "and another", 3,
            exp_end);
```

The end of the arguments is always marked by `exp_end`. The objects `exp_end` and `exp_glob` are predefined constants of type "`enum exp_type`". This is automatically defined when you include `expect.h`. The public definition of `exp_type` follows. I will mention the other values shown here later on.

```
enum exp_type {
    exp_end,        /* placeholder - no more cases */
    exp_glob,       /* glob-style */
    exp_exact,      /* exact string */
    exp_regexp,     /* regexp-style, uncompiled */
    exp_compiled,   /* regexp-style, compiled */
    exp_null,       /* matches binary 0 */
};
```

The value returned by `exp_expectl` is the number following the pattern that matches. The choice in this example of 1, 2, and 3 is arbitrary. You can associate the same numbers with multiple patterns. In actual code, it is a good idea to use preprocessor definitions to hide the numeric values unless they have some inherent meaning.

Here is an example that looks for a successful login such as from a `telnet` dialogue. When a value is returned, the `switch` statement passes control to an appropriate case. Notice that this example uses macros to hide the real values of the number to be returned. This makes the statement much more readable since each value is used in two places—once in the expect function and once in the `case` statement.

```
switch (exp_expectl(
    exp_glob,"connected",CONN,
    exp_glob,"busy",BUSY,
    exp_glob,"failed",ABORT,
```

---

† In fact, everything in the library is prefaced with "exp_".

```
        exp_glob,"invalid password",ABORT,
        exp_end)) {
case CONN:     /* logged in successfully */
    break;
case BUSY:     /* couldn't log in at the moment */
    break;
case ABORT:    /* can't log in at any moment! */
    break;
case EXP_TIMEOUT:
    break;
}
```

If the expect function times out, it returns EXP_TIMEOUT. Notice that this does not appear in the pattern list. Unlike the Expect program, there is no need to ask for the timeout to be handled. The expect functions do not automatically execute actions—they simply describe what happened. So even though you did not ask for it, you cannot miss the timeout.

The number of seconds in the timeout is determined by the integer variable exp_timeout. If exp_timeout is -1, the timeout is effectively infinite and will never occur. A timeout of 0 is used for polling and is described further on page 508.

There are three other special values that can be returned. EXP_EOF is returned upon eof. -1 is returned if a system call failed or something otherwise horrible occurred. For example, if an internal memory allocation fails, -1 is returned and errno is set to ENOMEM. errno will always be set if -1 is returned.

If the integer variable exp_full_buffer is nonzero, then EXP_FULLBUFFER is returned when the expect function's buffer is full. If exp_full_buffer is zero and the buffer is full, the first half of the buffer is dropped, the second half of the buffer is copied down, and the expect function continues. The buffer is described further on page 504.

All of the special values are small negative integers, so it is a good idea to associate patterns with positive integers although there is nothing in the code that enforces this.

Regular Expression Patterns

Regular expressions can be identified with exp_regexp. Here is the first example from page 501, rewritten to use a regular expression pattern:

```
exp_expectl(fd, exp_regexp, "prompt.*", 1, exp_end);
```

The type of all patterns are always identified explicitly, so different pattern types can be mixed without confusion. Here is an expect call with both glob and regular expression patterns:

```
exp_expectl(fd ,exp_regexp, "prompt.*", 1,
               exp_glob, "another pattern", 2,
               exp_regexp, "and another", 3,
               exp_end);
```

Caching Regular Expressions

The regular expression implementation used by Expect converts the pattern to an internal form that allows strings to be tested very quickly. The conversion procession is known as *compilation*. The compilation itself can cost more in terms of time than is saved later during the pattern matching. But if the pattern is going to be used more than once, compilation can ultimately save a great deal of time.

In the examples so far, the expect functions compile the regular expressions internally. Because input usually arrives slowly, patterns get evaluated many times and the compilation process pays off and time is saved. However, the compiled form is discarded at the end of each expect function. If the function is in a tight loop, this can be wasteful.

You can pass the compiled form to the expect functions by using `exp_compiled` instead of `exp_regexp`. Assuming the compiled form is stored in `fastprompt`, the earlier example might be rewritten this way:

```
exp_expectl(fd, exp_compiled, "prompt.*", fastprompt, 1,
      exp_end);
```

The string-style pattern is still passed, but it is only used for bookkeeping and debugging. The actual pattern matching uses the compiled form.

Patterns are compiled using the function `TclRegComp`. It takes a pattern and returns the compiled form which is of type pointer to `regexp` (a `typedef`). Here is what it might look like when used in a loop:

```
#define PROMPTED 17

char *pat = "prompt.*";
regexp *fastprompt = TclRegComp(pat);

while (1) {
   switch (exp_expectl(fd,
      exp_compiled, pat, fastprompt, PROMPTED,
      exp_end))
   case PROMPTED:
      /* respond to prompt */
   case . . .
}
```

Use `free` to free the memory used by the compiled form when it is no longer needed:

```
free((char *)fastprompt);
```

Malformed patterns cannot be compiled. If `TclRegComp` returns 0, compilation failed. The variable `tclRegexpError` contains an error message describing the problem. Expressed in C, this looks like:

```
fastprompt = TclRegComp(pat);
if (fastprompt == NULL) {
    fprintf(stderr, "regular expresion %s is bad: %s",
            pat, tclRegexpError);
}
```

Exact Matching

The pattern type `exp_exact` identifies a pattern that must be exactly matched in the input. The usual C escapes must be observed; however, no characters are interpreted as wildcards or anchors. Exact patterns are unanchored.

```
exp_expectl(fd, exp_exact, "#*!$", 1, exp_end);
```

The example above returns 1 only if the character stream contains the consecutive sequence of characters "#", "*", "!", and "$".

Matching A Null

By default, nulls (bytes with value zero) are automatically stripped from the spawned process output. This can be disabled by setting the integer variable `exp_remove_nulls` to 0 and reenabled by setting it to 1.

Once null stripping is disabled, nulls can be matched using `exp_null`. A string-style pattern is still passed, but it is only used for bookkeeping and debugging. For example:

```
exp_expectl(fd,
    exp_null, "zero byte", 1,
    exp_end);
```

What Characters Matched

When an expect function returns, the variable `exp_buffer` points to the buffer of characters that were being considered for a match. `exp_buffer_end` points to one character past the end of the buffer. The buffer is null-terminated. If a pattern matches, the variable `exp_match` is set to point into the same buffer but at the position where the pattern first matches. The variable `exp_match_end` points to one past the last matching character. All of these variables are character pointers.

```
char *exp_buffer;
char *exp_buffer_end;
char *exp_match;
char *exp_match_end;
```

The following figure graphically shows the relationship of the pointers to a matched string sitting in a buffer. In practice, it is possible for the match to span the entire buffer.

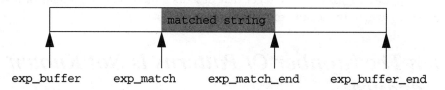

Parenthesized subpatterns from regular expressions have their match information saved but only if the compiled form is used. Each **regexp** object includes the following members:

```
#define NSUBEXP 10

char *startp[NSUBEXP];
char *endp[NSUBEXP];
```

Each subpattern match is defined by a `startp` and `endp` pair. `startp` points to the start of the matching string, and `endp` points to one past the end of the matching string. `startp[0]` and `endp[0]` are identical to `exp_match` and `exp_match_end`. The remaining indices correspond to the parenthesized subpatterns in the original pattern. `startp` is set to 0 if the subpattern did not match.

For example, here is a fragment to print out all of the match information. In the loop, the submatch is temporarily null-terminated so that it can be printed. (The `endp` pointers are always guaranteed to point to writeable memory.) In order to avoid corrupting the string, the character where the null is to be written is temporarily saved and then restored.

```
exp_expectl(fd,
        exp_compiled, pattern, regexp, 1,
        exp_end);
for (i=0;i<NSUBEXP;i++) {
    char save;

    if (regexp->startp[i] == 0) continue;
```

```
        /* temporarily null-terminate the match */
        save = regexp->endp[i];
        regexp->endp[i] = '\0';

        printf("match [%d] = %s\n",i,regexp->startp[i]);

        /* restore old character */
        regexp->endp[i] = save;
    }
```

The expect functions automatically allocate space for `exp_buffer` as required. The variable `exp_match_max` is an integer that describes the maximum length of a string guaranteed to match. By default, `exp_match_max` is 2000.

When The Number Of Patterns Is Not Known In Advance

The `exp_expectl` function is appropriate when the list of patterns is known in advance. At a minimum, the number of patterns must be known in advance.

When the number of patterns can vary, the function `exp_fexpectv` is more suitable. This function is called with only two arguments. The first is a file descriptor. The second is an array of pattern descriptors. The prototype is:

```
    int exp_expectv(int fd, struct exp_case *pats);
```

`struct exp_case` is defined as follows:

```
    struct exp_case {
        char *pattern;
        regexp *re;
        enum exp_type type;
        int value;
    };
```

The information in an `exp_case` structure is exactly the same information that was passed as the direct arguments in `exp_expectl`. The pattern is stored in `pattern`. An optional compiled regular expression is stored in `re`. The `type` element describes the type of pattern and is an `exp_type` enumeration constant (see page 501). As before, the final pattern type must be `exp_end`. Finally, `value` is the integer returned when the associated pattern matches.

`exp_expectv` works slightly differently than `exp_expectl` when the pattern type is `exp_regexp`. In this case, `exp_expectv` compiles each pattern and stores the compiled form in `re`. The compiled form is left accessible in the `exp_case` structure for your use or reuse if `exp_expectv` is recalled with the same patterns. If the type is exp_regexp, then exp_expectv checks if re is initialized before compiling the pattern. The pattern is compiled only if re is not initialized.

When you are done with the regular expression, you must free re in each exp_case that had a regexp, whether you or exp_expectv compiled it.

Expecting From Streams

Both exp_expectl and exp_expectv have analogous functions that work on streams instead of file descriptors. The stream functions have the same names as their file counterparts except that the stream functions have an "f" in the name. This is similar to the distinction between write and fwrite. Both of the stream versions are identical to their file counterparts except that the first argument is a stream instead of a file descriptor.

exp_fexpectl is the stream version of exp_expectl. A simple example looks like this:

```
FILE *fp = exp_popen("telnet");
exp_fexpectl(fp, exp_glob, "prompt*", 1, exp_end);
```

On some systems, the stream versions of the expect functions are much slower than the file descriptor versions because there is no way to portably read an unknown number of bytes without the potential of timing out. Thus, characters are read one at a time. While automated versions of interactive programs do not usually demand high speed, the file descriptor functions are likely to be more efficient on all systems.

You can get the best of both worlds, writing with the usual stream functions (i.e., fprintf) and reading with the file descriptor versions of expect, as long as you do not attempt to intermix other stream input functions (e.g., fgetc). To do this, pass "fileno(stream)" as the file descriptor to exp_expectl or exp_expectv. Fortunately, there is little reason to use anything but the expect functions when reading from interactive programs.

Running In The Background

In Chapter 17 (p. 373), I described how to move a process into the background after it had begun running. A typical use for this is to read passwords and then go into the background to sleep before using the passwords to do real work.

Moving a process into the background is tricky. It also differs from system to system. Fortunately, Expect incorporates this same functionality inside of the spawn routines. Because moving processes into the background is such a common task for programs that use the Expect library, it is available through a separate interface.

To move a process into the background, fork a process, call `exp_disconnect` in the child process, and then call `exit` in the parent process. Here is code to do this:

```
switch (fork()) {
case 0: /* child */
    exp_disconnect();
    break;
case -1: /* error */
    perror("fork");
default: /* parent */
    exit(0);
}
```

Calling `exp_disconnect` disassociates the process from the controlling terminal. If you wish to move a process into the background in a different way, you must set the integer variable `exp_disconnected` to 1. (Initially it is 0.) This allows processes spawned after this point to be started correctly. The `exp_disconnect` function sets `exp_disconnected` to 1.

```
int exp_disconnected;
```

`exp_disconnected` is also shared with the Expect program. If you invoke Expect's `disconnect` command, it will also set `exp_disconnected` to 1.

Handling Multiple Inputs And More On Timeouts

In some cases, you do not want to wait inside of an expect function. Instead, you wait in `select`, `poll`, or an event manager such as those provided by window systems. In this case, give the file descriptor corresponding to the spawned process to the event loop. When the event loop detects that input can be read from the file descriptor, it calls back in some fashion, after which you can call an expect function to test the patterns. You can guarantee that the expect function returns immediately by setting `exp_timeout` to 0. If none of your patterns match, `EXP_TIMEOUT` is returned.

Here is an example using the `select` system call. `select` is directed to watch the file descriptor in `fd`. `select` returns when it finds that there is data to read. `exp_expectl` is then called and it reads the data and performs pattern matching. If none of the patterns match, `exp_expectl` returns `EXP_TIMEOUT` immediately rather than attempting to read more data.

```
#define WAIT_FOREVER (struct timeval *)0

FD_SET(fd,&rdrs);
select(fd_max, &rdrs, . . ., WAIT_FOREVER);
```

```
exp_timeout = 0;
exp_expectl(fd, . . ., exp_end);
```

If `exp_timeout` is nonzero, the expect function can block in the `read` system call while reading from a single file descriptor. Internally, an `ALARM` signal is used to interrupt the `read`. If you define signal handlers, you can choose to restart or abort the `read`. The integer variable `exp_reading` is 1 if and only if the `read` has been interrupted and 0 otherwise. The following statement aborts the `read`:

```
longjmp(exp_readenv, EXP_ABORT);   /* abort the read */
```

The `read` is restarted as follows:

```
longjmp(exp_readenv, EXP_RESTART); /* restart the read */
```

Output And Debugging Miscellany

Some output and debugging controls exist in the library. The variety and flexibility of these are not great because there is not a lot of demand for more development in this area. For instance, interaction debugging is usually done using Tcl, not C.

The controls that exist parallel the commands in the Expect program and extension. They are manipulated using the following variables. All are 0 by default.

```
int exp_loguser;
int exp_logfile_all;
FILE *exp_logfile;
int exp_is_debugging;
FILE *exp_debugfile;
```

If `exp_loguser` is nonzero, the expect functions send any output from the spawned process to the standard output. Since interactive programs typically echo their input, this usually suffices to show both sides of the conversation.

If `exp_logfile` is also nonzero, this same output is written to the stream defined by `exp_logfile`.

If `exp_logfile_all` is nonzero, `exp_logfile` is written regardless of the value of `exp_loguser`.

Debugging information internal to Expect is sent to the standard error when `exp_is_debugging` is nonzero. The debugging information includes every character received and every attempt made to match the current input against the patterns. In addition, nonprintable characters are translated to a printable form. For example, a control-C appears as a caret followed by C. If `exp_logfile` is nonzero, this information is also written to `exp_logfile`.

If `exp_debugfile` is nonzero and set to a stream pointer, all normal and debugging information is written to that stream, regardless of the value of `exp_is_debugging`.

All of these variables directly control their counterparts in the Expect program and extension. For example, the Expect command "`log_user     1`" sets the value of `exp_loguser` to 1.

Pty Trapping

Some systems (notably HPs) require that ptys be *trapped* in order to detect an eof through `select` or `poll`. When trapping is enabled, all `ioctl`s performed by the spawned process on the pty must be acknowledged. This acknowledgment is normally performed automatically when Expect is in one of its expect functions. But occasionally, you may need to explicitly deal with trapping. For example, you might want to change the mode of the slave's pty after it has been started.

The trap and acknowledgment protocols are described in the documentation for your system. I will not describe them here because they can be avoided. This is fortunate, not because they are complex but because they cannot be performed while you are doing something else (e.g., in the middle of an `ioctl` call). The solution is to temporarily disable the trapping.

Trapping can be controlled with `exp_slave_control`. The first argument is the file descriptor corresponding to the spawned process. The second argument is a 0 if trapping is to be disabled and 1 if it is to be enabled.

```
/* disable trapping */
exp_slave_control(fd,0);

/* fiddle with mode of pty */
. . .

/* enable trapping */
exp_slave_control(fd,1);
```

On systems which do not use trapping, `exp_trap_control` turns into a no-op. Thus, if you are concerned about portability to systems which require trapping, use the trap control function.

Exercises

1. Write a program using the Expect library and then rewrite it using the Expect program. Compare the time it took you to write (and debug) both. Compare the size of your

source. Compare the size of the resulting executables. What can you conclude from these comparisons? Repeat this exercise on a significantly larger example.

2. Create a library specifically optimized for `ftp`. It should contain functions to start and stop `ftp`, and to send and expect `ftp` requests. How much simplification can be made over the original expect functions?

3. Create a terminal-emulator widget for Tk. What are the advantages and disadvantages between such a widget and the approach shown in Chapter 19 (p. 448).

In This Chapter:
- Adding Expect To
  Other Tcl-Based
  Programs
- Adding Other Tcl-
  Based Programs
  To Expect

22

Expect As Just Another Tcl Extension

In this chapter, I will describe how to use Expect as just another extension to Tcl. You can wrap it together with popular Tcl extensions such as Tcl-DP, TkSteal, and others. There are two basic approaches you can take to doing this. You can add extensions to Expect, or you can add Expect as an extension to another Tcl-based program.

While most of the material in this chapter will be of interest only to C and C++ programmers, I will also mention a couple of differences in how Expect behaves and can be used when it is combined with other Tcl extensions.

Adding Expect To Another Tcl-based Program

This section describes how to add Expect to another Tcl-based program. I will use the `tclsh` program as an example. `tclsh` is the "Tcl shell" that comes with Tcl. `tclsh` comes with no other extensions, but you can use it as a template for creating a Tcl-based program with other extensions.

The Tcl source directory contains the template in `tclAppInit.c`. Copy this file to a new directory and look inside it at the function `Tcl_AppInit`. You will find the following lines:

```
if (Tcl_Init(interp) == TCL_ERROR) {
    return TCL_ERROR;
}
```

After this line, add code to initialize Expect:

```
if (Exp_Init(interp) == TCL_ERROR) {
    return TCL_ERROR;
}
```

You may want to add other extensions as well. Generally, you can add the extension initializations in any order unless they attempt to use the same command names. In that case, the later extensions "win". The basic Tcl commands are actually created before `Tcl_Init`; however, it must still appear first. Other *XXX*`_Init` functions generally define commands for each extension themselves.

Add a line near the top of the file (anywhere after the include of "`tcl.h`") to include the declaration of `Exp_Init` and other Expect definitions. The include looks like this:

```
#include "expect_tcl.h"
```

Now compile the `tclAppInit.c` file with the following command:

```
cc -I/usr/local/include tclAppInit.c -L/usr/local/lib \
    -lexpect -ltcl -lm
```

You may need to adjust this command depending on your installation. The `-I` flag describes the directory where the include files of Tcl, Expect, and other extensions live. Similarly, the `-L` flag lists where the libraries are. You can have multiple `-I` and `-L` flags. The end of the command names particular libraries. You need the Expect library (`-lexpect`), the Tcl library (`-ltcl`), and libraries for any other extensions. Most systems need the math library (`-lm`) and you may also need others depending on your system. If this does not work, look at the Tcl and Expect `Makefiles` to see what libraries they use on your system.

If the `tclAppInit.c` file compiled and linked, the compiler leaves an `a.out` file in the current directory. It is an executable file that understands Tcl commands, Expect commands, and any other extensions you have defined. You can rename and move this to whatever and wherever you want.

If you are using C++ or if any of the extensions use C++, you will need to make an extra step. You must use C to compile `tclAppInit.c` and C++ for the final command linking everything together into one executable. Some C++ compilers require that the `main` function also be compiled with C++. Because the Tcl library supplies the default `main`, you may need to extract or recreate this and compile it with C++.

It is likely that the idea of a library-based `main` will be revisited in the future. But in all but the simplest of programs, you are likely to want to create your own `main` anyway—for example, so that you can handle flag and file arguments appropriately to your application.

Differences Between Expect And The Expect Extension In Another Program

When using `tclsh` or any other program to which you have added `Exp_Init`, you may encounter differences between it and Expect.

- Command-Line Argument Handling

  Expect defines the behavior of the command-line flags such as `-c` and `-d`. Any other program is not likely to support these. `tclsh` supports only the `-f` flag. Most Tcl programs make other arguments available to the script using the `argv` and `argc` variables as Expect does.

- Signal Handling

  It is possible for other extensions to try and handle signals at the same time that Expect does. However, only one extension can handle the same signal at a time. Multiple extensions may claim to be handling the signal but only one of the signal handlers will be called. Signal definitions should be under control of the user so this should not be a problem.

  The default signal handlers that Expect uses (i.e., `SIGINT`, `SIGTERM`) are not automatically established by `tclsh`.

- Command Names

  Expect commands that share the same names as commands in another extension are usually suppressed (unless the other extension also suppresses its own definition). For example, if another extension defines "`spawn`", it overrides Expect's `spawn`.

  To guarantee that you get Expect's commands, preface them with "`exp_`". For example, when using Tk, "`send`" is Tk's while "`exp_send`" is Expect's. The "`exp_`" versions are always available, even when not using any other extensions, so you can use them all the time if you do not want to worry about switching back and forth.

  Prefixed versions are not provided for Expect commands that already begin with "`exp`" (such as `expect`). For example, there is no such command as "`exp_expect`".

- Exit Handling

  Multiple extensions may attempt to provide exit handlers and similar functionality having to do with the `exit` command. However, only one `exit` command can possibly execute.

  Extensions that provide `exit` commands are unlikely to provide the functionality that Expect does or in the way that Expect does.

Exit handlers declared with "exit   -onexit" can be invoked with "exit -noexit". The terminal modes are also reset, but unlike a plain "exit", control is returned so that additional Tcl or other extension commands can be executed.

- Interpreter Prompting

When typing commands interactively, Expect processes them with the `inter-preter` command. `tclsh` has its own interpreter; however, it is not directly callable as a command. Most other extensions do not provide interactive command interpreters.

Expect's interpreter is similar to `tclsh`'s interpreter in most ways. There only significant difference is in prompting. `tclsh`'s interpreter uses the variables `tcl_prompt1` and `tcl_prompt2` to name functions that produce prompts. Expect's interpreter uses the functions `prompt1` and `prompt2` to generate prompts directly. If you run `tclsh` you will see Tcl's prompts, and if you invoke `exp_interpreter` from `tclsh`, you will see Expect's prompts.

- .rc Files

By default, Expect reads several `.rc` files when it begins running. This is described further in Chapter 9 (p. 221). These files are not read when using Expect as an extension in another program.

Adding Extensions To Expect

You can add other extensions to Expect similarly to the way I described adding extensions to `tclsh`. However, by adding extensions to Expect, you keep aspects of Expect, such as Expect's command-line argument handling.

The Expect source directory contains the template for Expect in `exp_main_exp.c`. Copy this file to a new directory and look inside it at the `main` function. You will find the statements (not necessarily in this order):

```
if (Tcl_Init(interp) == TCL_ERROR) {
    return TCL_ERROR;
}
if (Exp_Init(interp) == TCL_ERROR) {
    return TCL_ERROR;
}
```

Most other extensions can be added by calling *XXX*_Init, where *XXX* is the extension prefix. The actual call should look similar to the ones for Tcl and Expect.

You can generally put the other *XXX*_Init calls in any order unless the extensions attempt to use the same command names. In that case, the later extensions "win". Note that the basic Tcl commands are created before `Tcl_Init`. Other *XXX*`_Init` functions generally define commands for each extension themselves.

Add any include lines near the top of the file (anywhere after the include of "`tcl.h`") as appropriate to your extension.

Compile the `exp_main_exp.c` file with the following command.

```
cc -I/usr/local/include exp_main_exp.c ... \
    -L/usr/local/lib -lexpect -ltcl -lm
```

You may need to adjust this command depending on your installation. The `-I` flag describes the directory where the include files of Tcl, Expect, and other extensions live. Similarly, the `-L` flag lists where the libraries are. You can have multiple `-I` and `-L` flags. The end of the command names particular libraries. You need the Expect library (`-lexpect`), the Tcl library (`-ltcl`), and libraries for any other extensions. Replace the "`...`" with whatever `.o` files or libraries you need. Most systems need the math library (`-lm`) and you may also need others depending on your system. If this does not work, look at the Tcl and Expect `Makefiles` to see what libraries they use on your system.

If the `exp_main_exp.c` file compiled and linked, the compiler leaves an `a.out` file in the current directory. It is an executable file that understands Tcl commands, Expect commands, and any other extensions you have defined. You can rename and move this to whatever and wherever you want.

Note that if you are using C++ or any of the extensions use C++, you will need to make an extra step, using C to compile `exp_main_exp.c` and C++ for the final command which links everything together into one executable.

Adding Extensions To Expectk

Adding extensions to Expectk is very similar to adding them to Expect. This section describes only the differences.

The template `exp_main_tk.c` should be used instead of `exp_main_exp.c`.

Linking requires the Expectk and Tk libraries, so the compile line should look like this:

```
cc -I/usr/local/include exp_main_tk.c ... \
    -L/usr/local/lib -lexpectk -ltk -ltcl -lX11 -lm
```

As with adding extensions to Expect, you may need to adjust this command also. If this does not work, look at the Tcl and Expect `Makefiles` to see what libraries they use on your system.

Creating Scriptless Expect Programs

Expect normally uses a script to control its execution. This means that to run an Expect application, you need both an Expect interpreter and a script.

It is possible to combine the script and the interpreter together, producing a single executable that does not depend on any other files. This executable can be copied to new machines. The machines must be binary compatible and the script must make sense on the new machine. For example, programs that are spawned by the script must exist on the new machine. Stand-alone executables that run a particular script are often called *compiled*, although that is not the usual definition of the word.

Compiled scripts are large. Each one must contain the script plus the executable code for Expect. If you use a single Expect application on a computer, then a compiled script makes sense. If you use more than one Expect application, compiled scripts are just a waste of space. Other than space, there are no significant differences in functionality between compiled scripts and file-based scripts.

To create a compiled Expect script using the `exp_main_exp.c` template, replace all of the calls to the Expect interpretation phase (such as `exp_interpret_cmdfilename`) with a call to `Tcl_Eval`. As an argument to `Tcl_Eval`, pass the string representing the file contents.

```
Tcl_Eval(interp,cmdstring);
```

The string representation of the command must be in writeable memory. One way to guarantee this is to declare it in the following style:

```
static char cmdstring[] = "spawn prog; expect . .";
```

Calling `Tcl_Eval` with a string in read-only memory is a common error. Compare the declaration above with the following entry which allows the string to be placed in read-only memory:

```
char *cmdstring = "spawn prog; expect . ..";   /* WRONG */
```

Any `source` statements must be removed from the command string. Some Tcl extensions make substantial use of files for storing Tcl commands. All of these file references must be removed in the same way as the script file itself.

Functions And Variables In The Expect Extension

Writing C and C++ code that uses the Expect extension is similar to writing C code that uses Tcl. For example, you can call `Tcl_Eval` to execute any Expect or Tcl command.

The following statements spawn a `telnet` process and print the new spawn id. Notice the explicit declaration of `telnet_cmd` as an array instead of a pointer to a string constant. The array declaration guarantees that the characters are put into writeable memory—a requirement of `Tcl_Eval`.

```
char *spawn_id;
char telnet_cmd[] = "spawn telnet";

Tcl_Eval(interp,telnet_cmd);
spawn_id = Tcl_GetVar(interp,"spawn_id",0);
printf("spawn id is %s\n",spawn_id);
```

It is possible to call Expect's commands directly. However, this is a little harder and there is generally no good reason to do so, so it is not documented here.

A number of functions and variables are explicitly made public with C and C++ interfaces. Including the file `expect_tcl.h` gains access to these public symbols. They are defined in this section. Most of them are useful for writing your own `main` customized from Expect or `tclsh`. The descriptions are brief since most of the functional aspects are described in Chapter 9 (p. 213).

The first group of variables are shared by the Tcl-less Expect library, the Expect extension, and the Expect program. In this chapter, only their use in the Expect extension and program will be described.

Shared Variables

```
int exp_disconnected;
```

`exp_disconnected` is initially set to 0. It is set to 1 if Expect's `disconnect` command has been used successfully. Setting `exp_disconnected` to 1 prevents the `disconnect` command from being called.

```
int exp_is_debugging;
```

`exp_is_debugging` mirrors the Expect command `exp_internal`. That is, `exp_is_debugging` contains the most recent value passed as an argument to `exp_internal`. Similarly, the `exp_internal` command reflects the value of `exp_is_debugging`.

```
int exp_loguser;
```

`exp_loguser` mirrors the Expect command `log_user`.

Non-Shared Variables and Functions

The remaining functions and variables are specific only to the Expect program and extension.

`void (*exp_app_exit)(Tcl_Interp *);`

> `exp_app_exit` is a pointer to a function that describes an application-specific handler. The handler is executed after the script-defined exit handler has run. A zero value (the default) indicates that there is no handler.

`FILE *exp_cmdfile;`

> `exp_cmdfile` is a stream from which Expect reads commands.

`char *exp_cmdfilename;`

> `exp_cmdfilename` is the name of a file which Expect opens and reads commands from.

`int exp_cmdlinecmds;`

> `exp_cmdlinecmds` is 1 if Expect has been invoked with Expect (or Tcl) commands on the program command line (using `-c` for example).

`int exp_getpid;`

> `exp_getpid` is the process id of the Expect process itself (not of any spawned processes).

`int exp_interactive;`

> `exp_interactive` is 1 if Expect has been invoked with the `-i` flag or if no scripted commands were invoked when Expect began execution. `exp_interactive` is used to control whether Expect starts its `interpreter` command to interact with the user.

`Tcl_Interp *exp_interp;`

> `exp_interp` points to an interpreter used when no other is available, such as by a signal handler. `exp_interp` is automatically set by `Exp_Init` but may be redefined at any time later.

`int exp_tcl_debugger_available;`

> `exp_tcl_debugger_available` is 1 if the debugger has been armed, typically by a command-line argument.

`char *exp_cook(char *string,int *length);`

> `exp_cook` reads its string argument and returns a static buffer containing the string reproduced with newlines replaced by carriage-return linefeed sequences. The primary purpose of this is to allow error messages to be produced without worrying about whether the terminal is in raw mode or cooked mode.
>
> The static buffer is overwritten on the next call to `exp_cook`.

If the `length` pointer is valid, it is used as the length of the input string. `exp_cook` also writes the length of the returned string to `*length`. If the `length` pointer is 0, `exp_cook` uses `strlen` to compute the length of the string, and `exp_cook` does not return the length to the caller.

`void exp_error(Tcl_Interp *interp,char *fmt,...);`

> `exp_error` is a `printf`-like function that writes the result to `interp->result`. The caller must still return `TCL_ERROR` to tell the Tcl interpreter that an error has occurred.

`void exp_exit(Tcl_Interp *interp,int status);`

> `exp_exit` is comparable to Expect's `exit` command. `exp_exit` calls all the exit handlers (see `exp_exit_handlers`) and then forces the program to exit with the value given by status.

`void exp_exit_handlers(Tcl_Interp *);`

> `exp_exit_handlers` calls any script-defined exit handler and then any application-defined exit handler. Lastly, the terminal is reset to its original mode.

`int exp_interpret_cmdfile(Tcl_Interp *,FILE *);`

> `exp_interpret_cmdfile` reads the given stream and evaluates any commands found.

`int exp_interpret_cmdfilename(Tcl_Interp *,char *);`

> `exp_interpret_cmdfilename` opens the given file and evaluates any commands found.

`void exp_interpret_rcfiles(Tcl_Interp *,int my_rc,int sys_rc);`

> `exp_interpret_rcfiles` reads and evaluates the `.rc` files. If `my_rc` is zero, then `~/.expect.rc` is skipped. If `sys_rc` is zero, then the system-wide `expect.rc` file is skipped.

`int exp_interpreter(Tcl_Interp *);`

> `exp_interpreter` interactively prompts the user for commands and evaluates them.

`void exp_parse_argv(Tcl_Interp *,int argc,char **argv);`

> `exp_parse_argv` reads the representation of the program command line. Based on what is found on the command line, other variables are initialized, including `exp_interactive`, `exp_cmdfilename`, `exp_cmdlinecmds`, etc. `exp_parse_argv` also reads and evaluates the `.rc` files if appropriate.

Exercises

1. In Chapter 19 (p. 440), I described how it took a long time to load the UNIX dictionary into memory using pure Tcl commands. Design and implement an extension to speed that up.

2. Calculate the time that it took to solve the previous exercise. Divide that by the time difference it takes between loading the dictionary with vanilla Tcl commands and your new extension. How many times will you have to load the dictionary before you earn back the time you spent on the previous exercise?

3. The Tcl FAQ lists hundreds of extensions to Tcl. Browse through the FAQ and identify extensions that are useful to you. Download, install, and combine them with Expect.

4. Create your own new extension. If you feel it is of general interest, post a note to the Tcl newsgroup so that others can try it out.

23

Miscellaneous

This chapter contains some commands, concepts, and thoughts that did not fit anywhere else but are still worth mentioning.

Random Numbers

It is occasionally useful to generate random numbers in Expect (e.g., playing a game such as the `robohunt` script does). There is no built-in command to provide random numbers, and it is worth contemplating why not and what to do about it, since the answer generalizes to other questions.

The philosophy of Expect is to *not* provide commands for which there are already numerous solutions. Furthermore, in the case of random numbers, there is no implementation of a random number generator (*RNG*) that will make everyone happy. Different RNGs make compromises between different goals, so your choice of random numbers depend on your reason for using them. Indeed, that is one reason why there are so many RNGs on UNIX.

If there were one RNG wired in to Expect, it would not make everyone happy. Many people care a great deal about the kind of random numbers they get and want to select a particular generator or write their own.

If an RNG is already written as a stand-alone program, run it using `open` or `spawn`. The choice of `open` or `spawn` allows you to get good performance whether your RNG is interactive or non-interactive. If it is non-interactive and generates a stream of random numbers, `open` it and use `gets` to read each new random number. If your RNG is interactive, send the appropriate command as needed and use `expect` to fetch the result. Stand-alone mathematical packages work this way.

If the RNG you want is already written as a C subroutine, you can write a command to call it and then link it in to Expect (see Chapter 21 (p. 491)).

On the other hand, you may not care a lot about the quality of your random numbers—certainly, not enough to relink Expect. You may just want to make sure your program does not run exactly the same way each time. In this case, you can use the following Tcl procedure. It is a linear congruential generator that produces a number x where $0 \le x < 1$. The generator is good enough for many tasks. You can modify the parameters in random for different types of randomness. I chose the parameters here in a very scientific way—by copying them from a book—*Numerical Recipes in C* by Press et al. (Cambridge University Press, 1988). According to Press, the maximum periodicity is period, and the generator passes Knuth's spectral test for 2, 3, 4, 5, and 6. Press also describes more sophisticated RNGs with even better properties.

The package must be initialized by calling random_init with a positive integer seed. It is often sufficient to say "random_init [pid]" since the return value of the pid command changes each time you run your script. You can add yet more randomness by adding elements of the current time to the initialization.

```
proc random_init {seed} {
    global _ran

    set _ran $seed
}

proc random {} {
    global _ran

    set period 259200
    set _ran [expr ($_ran*7141 + 54773) % $period]
    expr $_ran/double($period)
}
```

Once initialized, each call to random returns a new random value.

Example — Generating Random Passwords

mkpasswd is an example script that comes with Expect. mkpasswd generates a new password and optionally assigns it to a user by calling a password-setting program. This automates password creation and assignment while preventing any public exposure of the password.

In order to generate random passwords, mkpasswd uses a variation of the random number procedure above. rand generates a random integer from 0 to $n-1$.

```
proc rand {n} {
    global _ran

    set period 259200
    set _ran [expr ($_ran*7141 + 54773) % $period]
    expr int($n*($_ran/double($period)))
}
```

mkpasswd accepts arguments to control the length and how many digits and letters must be in a generated password. After parsing the arguments, minnum contains the minimum number of digits the password must have. minlower and minupper contain the minimum number of lower and uppercase characters. If the password must be longer than the sum of these variables, they are increased appropriately.

Once the arguments have been handled, the password generation code is simple. In the following fragment, the password is initially created with no characters. Each iteration of each for loop generates a random character of the right type and calls insertchar which adds the character to password.

```
# initialize password
set password ""

# add digits to the password
for {set i 0} {$i<$minnum} {incr i} {
    insertchar [rand 10]
}

# add lowercase letters
for {set i 0} {$i<$minlower} {incr i} {
    insertchar [format "%c" [expr 0x61 + [rand 26]]]
}

# add uppercase letters
for {set i 0} {$i<$minupper} {incr i} {
    insertchar [format "%c" [expr 0x41 + [rand 26]]]
}
```

insertchar itself calls rand as well so that each new character is inserted at a random location in the password.

```
proc insertchar {c} {
    global password

    set password [linsert $password \
        [rand [expr 1+[llength $password]]] $c]
}
```

Since insertion into a list is easier than into a string, `insertchar` maintains the password as a list of characters. Before use, the password must be converted to a string:

```
set password [join $password ""]
```

The Expect Library

In Chapter 2 (p. 68), I mentioned that Tcl provides support for libraries of Tcl procedures. Expect follows the Tcl model. Two directories are provided in which users at your site can create and use publicly-accessible Expect procedures or other data. The directory names are stored in the global variables `exp_library` and `exp_exec_library`.

The `exp_library` directory contains files which are platform-independent. If you have the directory NFS-mounted to multiple computers of different types, all of them can share the same common procedures. In contrast, the `exp_exec_library` directory is specific to a particular machine (and if necessary, different releases of the operating system).

Although scripts are the most common use for these libraries, non-executable data can be stored there as well. For example, in Chapter 13 (p. 291) I mentioned that cat might need a –u flag. Unfortunately, on other systems, the –u flag imposes a performance penalty. So –u should only be used when it is required. One way to detect this is to spawn a cat process, send a character to it, and see if it echoes. Unfortunately, the failure to echo requires an `expect` command to timeout, and this can take a relatively long time in a script. To avoid this, Expect executes this test upon installation and leaves a marker behind in the form of a file for which scripts can test. Because the behavior is dependent upon a particular executable (namely, /bin/cat), the marker is stored in `exp_exec_library` under the name `cat_buffers`. If `cat_buffers` exists, then /bin/cat buffers and the –u is needed to unbuffer it.

In a script, the test looks like this:

```
if [file exists $exp_exec_library/cat_buffers] {
    set catflags "-u"
} else {
    set catflags ""
}
```

The value later might be used as follows:

```
spawn -open [open "|/bin/cat $catflags $fifo" r]
```

The directory names `exp_library` and `exp_exec_library` also appear in the global variable `auto_path` which makes them available to the autoloading facility. If you have generated index files for the Expect libraries, procedures defined there are automatically loaded when you reference them. See the Tcl reference documentation for more information on libraries.

Expect Versions

Like any software, new releases of Expect appear from time to time as features are added and bugs are found and fixed. The `exp_version` command is useful for dealing with version mismatches. It can verify that the script is appropriate for the current Expect executable and prevent the script from continuing if not. With no arguments, Expect reports the current version.

```
expect1.1> exp_version
5.9.0
```

This version may then be placed in your script in an `exp_version` command. If you know that you are not using features of recent versions, you can specify an earlier version.

The version checking is relatively simple and will not catch all incompatibilities, but it will catch many flagrant problems. The checking depends on the way Expect versions are assigned. Expect versions consist of three numbers separated by dots. First is the major number. Unless they are very simple, scripts written for versions of Expect with a different major number will almost certainly not work. In this case, `exp_version` generates an error and returns an appropriate message.

For example, if you are using Expect 5.3.0, you can insert the following command in your script:

```
if [catch {exp_version 5.3.0} msg] {
    puts "warning: $msg"
}
```

If your script is run on a much older version of Expect (e.g., 4.3.0), the script will print a warning that the script was expecting a different version of Expect.

The second number is the minor number. Scripts written for a version with a greater minor number than the current version may depend upon some new feature and might not run. `exp_version` returns an error if the major numbers match, but the script minor number is greater than that returned by `exp_version`.

Third is a number that plays no part in the version comparison. However, it is incremented when the Expect software distribution is changed in any way, such as by additional documentation or optimization. It is reset to 0 upon each new minor version.

The `exp_version` has an `-exit` flag which can be used to force the script to exit rather than return an error. The message explaining the mismatch is sent to the standard output, and the script exits with a return value of 1.

Timestamps

The `timestamp` command is useful for generating time representations in various forms. In its simplest form, `timestamp` with no arguments returns the time in seconds since the *UNIX epoch* (January 1, 1970 UTC).

```
expect1.1> timestamp
759382559
```

To convert the time into other forms, use the `-format` flag with a following string that describes the format. The command returns the string with appropriate substitutions. Generally, substitutions are made for each character preceded by a percent sign. For example, the time of day in 24-hour time is substituted for "`%X`". Anything not preceded by a percent sign is passed through untouched. For example:

```
expect1.1> timestamp -format "The time of day is %X"
The time of day is 17:05:58
expect1.2> timestamp -format "It is a %A in %B"
It is a Monday in January
```

The substitutions are a superset of those defined by the C `strftime` function. The full list supported by Expect is as follows:

`%a`	abbreviated weekday name
`%A`	full weekday name
`%b`	abbreviated month name
`%B`	full month name
`%c`	date-time as in: `Wed Oct  6 11:45:56 1993`
`%d`	day of the month (01-31)
`%H`	hour (00-23)
`%I`	hour (01-12)
`%j`	day (001-366)
`%m`	month (01-12)
`%M`	minute (00-59)
`%p`	am or pm
`%S`	second (00-61)[†]
`%u`	day (1-7, Monday is first day of week)
`%U`	week (00-53, first Sunday is first day of week 1)

---

† *Leap seconds* are occasionally added to correct for the slowing rotation of the Earth.

%V	week (01–53, ISO 8601 style)
%w	day (0-6, Sunday is 0)
%W	week (00-53, first Monday is first day of week 1)
%x	date-time as in: Wed Oct 6 1993
%X	time as in: 23:59:59
%y	year (00-99)
%Y	year as in: 1993
%Z	timezone (or nothing if timezone is not determinable)
%%	a bare percent sign

Any percent sequence not listed here is passed through untouched.

Arithmetic on dates is most conveniently done when everything is represented in seconds either relative to or absolutely from the epoch. A date represented in seconds can be formatted by using the -seconds flag. For example,

```
expect1.1> set time [timestamp]
759443622
expect1.2> timestamp -format %X -seconds $time
15:33:42
expect1.3> timestamp -format %X -seconds [expr $time+1]
15:33:43
```

The time Command

You may want to try different commands and algorithms to compare which is faster. You can use the timestamp command for this, but Tcl provides a built-in command called time which is more convenient.

The time command takes a command to execute and an optional iteration count. It returns a description of the time taken to execute each iteration. As an example, the following command times three iterations of "sleep 7".

```
expect1.1> time {sleep 7} 3
7000327 microseconds per iteration
```

As you can see, each sleep took very close to 7 seconds which is what you would expect. The precise amount of time will vary from run to run depending on what else is executing at the same time, of course. So using a high iteration count can smooth out the difference and provide a more useful answer.

In some cases, it may be useful to run external performance monitors. For example, memory or network usage may be just as important to your application as CPU usage.

Exercises

1. Using the `random` procedure (page 524), write a Tk script that draws a plot of a large number of random values. Use time (modulo the plot width) as the second dimension in the plot. Look for patterns in the plot.

2. Many Tcl extensions come with libraries that are used by the extension itself but are not documented for users. Look through all the Tcl libraries for useful but undocumented utilities.

3. Check the version of Expect that you are running. See if you can find a later one. Do your scripts still work?

4. Use the `time` command and compare "`string match`" against `regexp` doing similar things. Is this reflected in the `-gl` and `-re` flags in the `expect` command?

5. Time the UNIX `sleep` command and compare it to the built-in `sleep` command. At what point is the difference moot? How does this change if you are on a much slower or faster machine?

6. What `timestamp` would exactly duplicate the default output of the UNIX `date` command? Time `date` and `timestamp`.

7. Expect does not have a procedure that does the opposite of `timestamp`—converts a string to a date represented as an integer. Why is that? Write one anyway.

Appendix — Commands and Variables

This appendix is a listing of the commands, flags, and variables built into Expect (not including those provided by Tcl). The listing does not show the complete syntax for each command or flag; this is just an aid to jog your memory as to what is available. Alongside each entry is a brief description and a page number. The page number points to where the command is best described, not necessarily where it first or literally appears.

I have omitted information that is redundant (such as the timestamp substitutions which can all be found on the page which describes timestamp) and the debugger commands (which can be produced by pressing h while in the debugger). I have also omitted commands specific to C and C++ programming since that information is well confined to two short chapters. You can also find all of this in the index.

All of the commands shown here that do not start with "exp" are also callable with the "exp_" prefix. For instance, close can also be called as exp_close.

Commands And Flags

close	close spawned process	Page 101
-i	identify process	249
-slave	close slave of process	295
debug	control debugger	410
-now	start debugger immediately	411
0 or 1	stop or start debugger	410
disconnect	disconnect process from tty	375
exit	exit	35

`-onexit`	declare exit handler	321
`-noexit`	invoke exit handlers but do not exit	321
`#`	exit with this value	35
`exp_continue`	continue `expect` command	145
`-continue_timer`	do not restart internal timer	146
`exp_internal`	control internal diagnostics	166
`-info`	return state	182
`-f`	direct diagnostics to file	173
`0 or 1`	stop or start diagnostics	171
`exp_open`	open spawned process as file identifier	304
`-i`	identify process	304
`-leaveopen`	leave spawned process accessible	305
`exp_pid`	return process id	304
`-i`	identify process	304
`exp_version`	return version of Expect	528
`-exit`	exit if version mismatch	528
version	version needed by script	528
`expect`	wait for pattern	72
`timeout`	match timeout	94
`eof`	match eof	98
`full_buffer`	match full buffer	151
`default`	match timeout or eof	101
`null`	match null	155
`-brace`	arguments are braced	160
`-gl`	glob pattern	109
`-re`	regular expression	109
`-ex`	exact string	134
`-notransfer`	do not update internal buffer	154
`-nocase`	treat input as all lowercase	139
`-i`	identify process	247
`-indices`	save indices of match	124
pattern action ...	pattern action pairs	75
`expect_after`	wait for pattern before others	259
	same flags as for `expect`, plus	
`-all`	return patterns of all spawn ids	266
`-info`	return patterns	266
`-noindirect`	do not return patterns of indirects	269
`expect_background`	wait for pattern in background	446
	same flags as for `expect_after`	
`expect_before`	wait for pattern after others	259
	same flags as for `expect_after`	
`expect_tty`	wait for pattern from terminal	210

	same flags as for `expect`	
`expect_user`	wait for pattern from user	192
	same flags as for `expect`	
`fork`	create child process	374
`inter_return`	return from caller	230
`interact`	pass control of process to user	82
`eof`	match eof	342
`timeout`	match timeout	343
`null`	match null	343
`-brace`	arguments are braced	324
`-re`	regular expression	328
`-ex`	exact string	327
`-input`	input processes	353
`-output`	output processes	353
`-u`	substitute for user process	350
`-o`	process patterns	328
`-i`	identify process	349
`-echo`	echo	333
`-nobuffer`	do not buffer partial matches	337
`-indices`	save indices of match	328
`-reset`	reset terminal mode	344
`-iwrite`	save process spawn id	359
pattern action ...	pattern action pairs	324
`interpreter`	pass control of Expect to user	225
`log_file`	control output saving to file	180
`-a`	save all output	181
`-noappend`	save to beginning of file	180
`-info`	return state	182
`-leaveopen`	treat file as log	180
`-open`	treat file as log	180
file	save output to file	180
`log_user`	control output to screen	175
`-info`	return state	182
`0 or 1`	stop or start output	175
`match_max`	control match buffer size	150
`-d`	default (future processes)	150
`-i`	identify process	249
`#`	new buffer size	150
`parity`	control parity	157
`-d`	default (future processes)	157
`-i`	identify process	249
`0 or 1`	strip or preserve parity	157

`prompt1`	prompt after complete command	228
`prompt2`	prompt after incomplete command	228
`remove_nulls`	control nulls	155
`-d`	default (future processes)	155
`-i`	identify process	249
`0 or 1`	preserve or strip nulls	155
`send`	send string	71
`--`	treat next string as literal	282
`-i`	identify process	247
`-h`	send humanly	278
`-s`	send slowly	275
`-null`	send null	281
`-raw`	do not insert returns	198
`-break`	send break	281
`string`	string to be sent	71
`send_error`	send to standard error	187
	same flags as `send`	
`send_log`	send to log	182
`--`	treat next string as literal	282
`string`	string to be sent	182
`send_tty`	sent to `/dev/tty`	210
	same flags as `send`	
`send_user`	send to standard output	185
	same flags as `send`	
`sleep #`	sleep number of seconds	196
`spawn`	start a process	78
`-console`	treat process as console	300
`-ignore`	ignore signal	310
`-leaveopen`	treat file as spawned process	289
`-open`	treat file as spawned process	289
`-noecho`	do not echo spawn command	298
`-nottycopy`	do not initialize pty like `/dev/tty`	300
`-nottyinit`	do not do sane initialization	300
`-pty`	allocate pty without starting process	293
`strace`	trace statements	405
`-info`	return state	405
`#`	depth to which to trace	405
`stty`	modify terminal parameters	197
`< ttyname`	terminal to modify	204
`raw`	raw mode	198
`-raw`	cooked mode	199
`cooked`	cooked mode	205

-cooked	raw mode	205
echo	echo	199
-echo	no echo	199
rows *[#]*	set or return rows	205
columns *[#]*	set or return columns	205
local-stty-args	execute native stty command	205
system *local-cmd*	execute Bourne shell command	207
timestamp	return timestamp	528
-format	timestamp format	528
-seconds	time source	528
trap	define signal handler	307
-code	code to return	320
-interp	interpreter to use	321
-name	return name of current signal	309
-number	return number of current signal	309
-max	return number of signals	318
action signal-list	action to execute upon signals	309
wait	wait for process to go away	105
-i	identify process	249
-nowait	wait for process in future	106

Variables

any_spawn_id	any listed spawned process	259
argc	number of initial arguments	214
argv	initial arguments	214
argv0	name of script	214
dbg	debugger breakpoint regexp results	422
error_spawn_id	spawn id of standard error	245
exp_library	platform-independent utility scripts	526
exp_exec_library	platform-dependent utility scripts	526
expect_out	results of expect	111
interact_out	results of interact	328
send_human	controls for send -h	278
send_slow	controls for send -s	275
spawn_out	results of spawn	294
spawn_id	currently spawned process	233
stty_init	stty parameters for spawn	300
timeout	maximum time for expect to wait	75

`tty_spawn_id`   spawn id of `/dev/tty`   245
`user_spawn_id`   spawn id of standard input and output   245

Index Of Scripts

This is an index to all scripts or substantial fragments of code.

Symbols

#! rewriting 216

A

aftp 83, 144
anonymous ftp 83, 144
answerback 250, 340
area of circle 36

B

bc 233

C

chdir 469
chess 235, 251, 492
choose 390
command loop 231, 346

D

date 177
desk calculator 233
dialback 3, 350
disconnect 375
dislocate 354, 384
Dvorak 325

E

echo arguments 214
emulating ftp 467
encryptdir 465
encrypting a directory 465
escape 231, 390
exit handler 321
exp_popen 495
expect_four_byte_int 156
Expectk example
 terminal emulator 449
 tknewsbiff 475
 tkpasswd 434

F

factorial 29, 31
fastest machine 253
Fibonacci numbers 34
Fibonacci numbers, recursively 35
file transfer 351
firstline 136, 178
fixline1 216
fsck 8, 339
ftp
 over telnet 467
 put 133
ftpcmd 242, 243
ftp-rfc 186

G

gdb, testing 6
getpass 199, 206

H

hunt, the game of 148

I

idle fakeout 343
inactivity handler 330
interact, complex 361

J

joint control 255

K

keyboard, Dvorak 325
kibitz 255, 355
        under cron 380

L

login 272
lognumber 338

M

mail 383
mapwindow 478
maxtime 98, 100
mkfifo 385
mkpasswd 525

N

news, wakeup on unread 475
noidle 343

O

OCLC 398
Online Computer Library Center 398

P

passmass 154
passwd 5

passwd GUI 434
password
        generator 525
        prompt for 377
        querying on behalf of a program 201
password, query for 199
password_backspace 445
ping 97, 100, 101, 178
preventing bad commands 346
print array elements and values 53
prompt
        default Expect 228
        styles 376
        tset 147
putentry 133

Q

quadratic formula 54
quadratic formula (call by reference) 58

R

racing with rlogin 253
random numbers 524, 525
random passwords 525
reading lines in a file 62
reading lines in a file (fast) 62
reading nulls 156
reconnecting 378
record a session 180
record phone numbers 338
rlogin
        is a test of speed 254
        rsh 118, 119
        with same directory 123
rlogin with same directory 122
rn (read news) 195
robohunt 148
rogue 141, 458
rsh via rlogin 118, 119
rz 351

S

script 180, 337
script, a better version 334
send slowly 277

send_slow 277
set password on multiple machines
        simultaneously 154
SIGCHLD handler 314
SIGTSTP handler 316
SIGWINCH handler 316, 367
slow send 276
slow telnet 152
spawn_ftp 244
split host and domain 137
static variables, emulating 59
stop script after some time 98
su2 179, 200
sum a list 39
sz 351

T
telnet 494
    slow 152
    with same directory 341
ten_chars_per_sec 276
term 460
term_expect *460*
terminal emulator 449
timeallcmds 256
timed reads 77
timed_read 77, 112
timed-read 77
timing all commands 256
tip 196
tkpasswd 434
tkterm 449
traceproc 406
trap all signals 318
tset 147
two users connected to an application 255

U
unbuffer 299
unknown 68
unmapwindow 477

V
verbose 469
vi 104

vprint 404
vrfy 175

W
write 237

X
xkibitz 361
xterm 294

Index

Italicized page numbers denote the most definitive references. Other references denote discussion or examples.

!, 27
    history, 179, 226
−, 27
!!, 179
!=, 27, 482
", 25, 33
#, 24-25, 58, 70, 120, 471, 475, 479, 482, 485-488
    scope identifier, 417
#!, 72, 213, 221, 467
    limited to (usually) 32 characters, 215
    portability kludge, 216, 232
    rewriting, 216
#!/usr/local/bin/expect, 215
    —, 72
#!/usr/local/bin/expectk, 433, 477
#0, 58, 482
$, 7, 24, 57, 73, 107-108, 120-121, 472
    literal, 134
$?, 97
$expect_library/expect.rc, 218, 221
$status, 97, 118
%, 27, 120, 524
    for substitutions in bind actions, 432
%W, 431

&, 66, 372
    disadvantages to disconnect, 377
&&, 27
(\[^\r]*)\r\n, 145
*, 6, 27, 32, 63, 87, 107, 153
    at end of pattern is tricky, 89
    at start of pattern is redundant, 88
+, 27
    as procedure name, 363, 365
+>, 228
., 108
    as widget separator or top-level widget, 430
.*, 107, 116, 331
.*\n, 129
.+, 251
    implicit, 357
.crypt suffix, 466
.cshrc, 11
.dislocate, 386, 391
.expect.rc, 222, 232
.netrc, 11, 22
.newsrc, 481
.o files, 517
.profile, 11
.rc, 22, 221, 232, 516, 521
.rhosts, 13
.tknewsbiff, 476
/, 27, 63, 430
/\X, 329
/bin/cat, 526

/bin/mail, 383
/bin/sh, 61, 211, 292-293, 392
/dev/null, 359, 375
/dev/tty, 210-211, 245, 293
/dev/ttya, 290
/dev/ttyp0, 294
/etc/inetd.conf, 400
/etc/motd, 392
/etc/passwd, 45, 289, 434
/etc/resolv.conf, 84
/etc/services, 400
/tmp, 303
/tmp/fifo, 299
/usr/etc/expectd.proto, 398-399
/usr/etc/secretd, 400
/usr/include/signal.h, 318
;, 24
<, 66, 209, 383, 486
<<, 22, 383
<=, 27
<1>, 487
<Any-Enter>, 431, 457
<Any-Key>, 445
<Any-KeyPress>, 457
<BackSpace>, 445
<Button1>, 431
<Configure>, 487
<Control-c>, 431
<defunct>, 105
<Delete>, 445
<F1>, 457
<Meta-KeyPress>, 457
<Shift-1>, 487
= as procedure name, 365
==, 27, 37, 474
>, 66, 172, 474, 484
>@, 67
?, 32, 63, 91
@, 67
    misbehavior, 302
[, 481
[], 26, 33, 57, 63, 91, 108
    overloading, 91
[^, 108
[^]], 129
[^^], 129

[incr Tcl], 60, 69
\, 8, 63, 91, 109, 470
\ at end of line, *25*
\\$, 118
*, 108
\[, 96, 109
\[^\r]*\r\n, 136
\\, 8, 327
\\\$, 121, 125
\\\r, 327
\\r, 327
\0, 24, 155
\004 (^D), 474
\b, 24, 326
\n, 96, 197, 274, 335
    matching everything but, 113
    newline on output, 71
    on input, 72
\n on output, 79
\octal, 24
\ooo, 326
\r, 5, 79, 326-327
\r\n, 80, 119, 448
    stripping \r, 257
\r~#, 282
\t, 24
\xhex, 24
^, 73, 96, 107-108, 121, 129
    history, 226
    literal, 134
^\, 312
^C, 274, 311, 314, 317, 319, 411
    exit by default, 103
^D, 102, 230, 238, 342, 471
^G, 148, 275, 344
^U, 274, 302
^Z, 240, 274, 316, 346, 371
{, 29
{}, 481
    glob matching, 63
|, 61, 66, 209, 284, 292
||, 27
}, 29
~, 63, 182, 288
~/.dislocate, 384
~/.expect.rc, 218, 221, 521

032 (^Z), 468
−1, 81, 502
1990 Winter USENIX Conference, xxvi
1991 Winter USENIX Conference, xxvii
2>, 293
3Com, 14
7 versus 8-bit connection, 352, 467

A

absolute cursor motion, 456
Academic Press, 20
Accardo, Thomas, xxix
actions, 75
    background, 447
active file, 482
adb, 9
adding extensions
    to Expect, 516
    to Expectk, 517
Addison-Wesley, 19, 394
Advanced UNIX Programming, 305
after, 459, 461–462
aftp, 83, 143, 163, 232
aftp.exp, 293
AIX 3.2, 291
ALARM, 509
Amdahl, 14
anchor, 73
    differences between glob and regular
        expression, 126
and, 27
anonymous ftp, 83
ANSI terminal, 462
answerback, 250, 340
any_spawn_id, 259, 261
APL, 70
append, 46, 49, 56
arbitrary precision arithmetic, 233, 246
Archie, 18, 22
argc, 215, 515
arguments
    do not interpret remaining, 217–218
    varying, 39
argv, 77, 215, 515
argv0, 214–215

arithmetic, arbitrary precision, 246
array, *49*, 362
    information, 52
    names, 52, 367
    size, 52
arrow keys, simulating, 286
asleep, falling, 211
assert, 183
associativity, 28
at, 371
AT&T, 15
atom, 107, 110
auto_path, 526
Autoconf, xxviii
automatic Expect script writer, 270
automation
    of non-UNIX systems, 14
    partial, 8, 82
    total, 4
avoiding echo, 335

B

background, *372*
    actions, 447
    expect library, 507
    patterns, *446*
    processing, 371
backquotes, 78
backslashes, 24, 109, 125
    in patterns, 91
backup, 14
    from cron, 13
Baha'i World Centre, 14
base, change, 234
batch, 371
Baughman, Sue, xxix
Bayona, Miguel Angel, xxix
bc, 233–234, 246
bedroom, spawning, 78
begin standout mode, 450
behavior differences of Expect versus
    Expect as an extension, 513, 515
benchmarking, 529
Betz, David, 429
bg, 240, 371–372
bidirectional

communication over pipes, 305
process pipelines, 292
biff, for news, 475
Bimmler, 331
binaries Expect, 492
bind, 431, 437, 442, 444-445, 448, 457, 487
bindings, 432
for Expect, 492
bold, xxxiii
books
Advanced UNIX Programming, 305
Computer Lib, 121
Internet System Handbook, 394
Numerical Recipes in C, 524
Practical Programming in Tcl and
Tk, 20
Software Solutions in C, 20
Tcl and the Tk Toolkit, 19
TCP/IP Illustrated, Volume 1, 394
X Window System Series, 429
boolean operators, 27
Bourne shell, xxvi, 70
braces, 29, 32
in lists, 40
nesting, 33
open, 33
Bradfute, Todd, xxix
branch, 109-110, 115
break, 34, 141, 228-229, 461, 474
breakpoint
action, 422
limitations, 424
by expression, 420
by line number and filename, 419
by pattern match, 420
defining, 419
deleting, 426
general form, 425
listing, 425
bridges, 14-15
Brighton, Allan, 59
broken pipe signal, 315
Brown, Thomas, xxix
browsing global variables, 409
BSD, 449
buffering

input, 74
interact, 332
output perpetually, 154
bug, OS, 291
button, 430, 438
clicks, 431

C

C, xxv, 70, 491, 513, 517, 519
subroutine, 524
–c, 217-218, 232
c, 418, 423
C language identifier, 108
C shell, xxvi, 70
C++, 491, 513, 517, 519
special instructions for, 514
caching regular expressions, 503
Cambridge University Press, 524
canonical input buffer size, 286
capability, *450*
caret, 73
carriage-return linefeed, 80
cat, 289, 300, 467
command to remote system, 471
–u, 292, 488, 526
cat_buffers, 526
catch, 53-54, 58, 60, 67, 296, 318, 334, 367,
372, 374, 438, 442, 469, 473, 480,
482, 489, 527
catching errors, 53
causing errors, 55
cc, 493
cd, 470
CD-ROM, 17
ceil, 27
CenterLine Software, 14
cert.sei.cmu.edu, 400
change the base of a number, 234
character graphics, 142
output, 283
character translations, 325
check dictionary, 438
checkbutton, 438
chess, 12, 234, 262
timed, 246
with expect –i, 251

with interact, 350
chess.exp, 17
child, 391
    termination signal, 308, 313
CHILDKILLED, 313
chmod, 72, 215
choose, 390
chunking of output, 89-90, 152
Cisco, 14
cl, 450
clear screen, 450
close, 101, 249, 472, 474, 482, 499
    file, 60
    implied at end of script, 102
    –slave, 295, 364
cm, 450
COLUMNS, 450
command
    name clashes, 514-515
    timestamps, 256
    tracing, 405
commands
    debugger, 412
    evaluating lists as, 56
comments, 24, 70
common mistakes, 258, 495, 518
comp.lang.tcl, 21, 463
comp.source.unix, 400
compilation of regular expression, 503
compiled
    Expect, 518
    Expect programs, 492
compress, 467
CompuServe, 275
Computer Lib, 121
Computer Security FAQ, 203
Computerized Processes Unlimited, 21
ComputerVision, 15
concat, 42-43
conference proceedings, 21
connecting to background processes, 381
console output, 300
contacting multiple users, 382
continuation lines, 33
continue, 34, 143, 228, 339, 482
    execution, 418

signal, 308, 316
control structures, *29*
controlling terminal, 245, 372
controlling unreliable processes, 15
converting from floating-point to
        integer, 27
cooked mode, 89
co-processes, xxiv
copying file through firewalls, 15
copyright information, 15
core, 312
cos, 27
Courier, xxxii-xxxiii
cron, 12, 371, 373, 380, 401
    backup, 13
crypt, 2, 200
    directory, 465
cryptdir, 465
csh, 226
C-style real number pattern, 140
cu, 289-290
current scope, *417*
currently spawned process, *234*
Curses, 10
    output, 283
    testing, 458
cursor motion, 456
cursor positioning character
        sequences, 142
Cygnus Support, 15, 21

D
d, 417
daemon, *392*
    telnet, 392
Data General, 14-15
databases, 14
date, 314
    versus timestamp, 530
dbg, 426
dbg array, 424
Dbm, 69
dbx, 410, 412
dc, 234
DCL, 330
deadlock, not a problem, 305

debtron, 355
debug, 411
    1, 410
    –now, 411
debugger, 223, *410*
    commands, 412
    flag abbreviations, 420
    help, 426
    output compression, 428
    output width, 426
    prompt, 410
    repeat last action, 412
    testing, 6
debugging, 403, 509
    disconnected processes, 377
    logfile, 180
    patterns, 165
decryptdir, 465
default, 101
deferring evaluation, 29
defining breakpoints, 419
definitions, xxxii
DejaGnu, 15
deleting
    breakpoints, 426
    files with funny names, 211
Delmas, Sven, 432
demos, 14
destroy, 438
device drivers as programs, 289
diagnostics, 171
    output, 165, 167
    redirecting from shell, 173
dial
    pager, 85
    phone numbers from a list, 85
dialback, 3, 369, 401
    via interact, 350
dictionary
    check, 438
    time to load, 522
diff, 67
Digital Equipment's Western Research
        Laboratories, 19
direct spawn id, *268*
directory encryption, 465

disconnect, 371, *375*, *379*, 388, 401, 519
    advantages over &, 377
disconnected processes
    debugging, 377
    reconnecting, 378
    strategy for getting passwords, 373
dislocate, 17, 230, 354, 390
    example interaction, 388
    manager for disconnected
        processes, 384
DISPLAY, 123
–display, 433, 476
displaying widgets, 431
distance, 59
DO, 393
do, 450
Dodd, David, xxix
dog, 328
domainname, 84
DONT, 393
dos, 328
DOS TSR, 348
dot rc file, 221
DOTDIR, 222, 478
double buffering, 152
down one line, 450
DTR, 196
duck: quack, 117
dumb terminal emulator, 447
dump, 9
    estimating number of tapes, 126
    reprompting, 194
Dvorak, 17, 330, 347
    keyboard, 325
dynamically generating procedures, 232

E
ECHO, 393
echo, 119, 199, 273
    avoidance, 335
    interact, 333, 335
    passwords with asterisks, 444, 463
echo.exp, 215, 219
edit–compile–debug cycle, Expect is
        easier, 491
efficiency, 359, 440

element, 506
else, 31, 478, 483
elseif, 31
Elvis, 96
emacs, xxiv–xxv, 344
    shell, 226, 301
email address pattern, 137
emulator, 448
    dumb terminal, 447
Encore Computer, 15
encrypting a directory, 465
encryption function, 5
end of file, *98*
end standout mode, 450
endp, 505–506
ENOMEM, 502
entry, 437, 442
env, 67, 120
env(PATH), 287
environ, 498
environment variable
    COLUMNS, 450
    DISPLAY, 123
    DOTDIR, 222
    EXPECT_DEBUG_INIT, 312, 411
    EXPECT_PROMPT, 120
    HOME, 222
    LINES, 450
    PATH, 287
    TERM, 373, 450
    TERMCAP, 450
    TERMINFO, 450
eof, *98*, 100, 230, 327, 353, 483
    ignored by some programs, 103
epoch, *528*
error, 55
    general strategy for catching, 225
    reporting, inband protocol, 358
    spawn, 296–297
error_spawn_id, 245
errorCode, 313
errorInfo, 55
errors, 53
    catching, 53
    causing, 55
escape, 390

doubling up, 326
eunuchs, 328, 333
Europe, 157
eval, 56, 59, 341, 368
    expect, 160
    spawn, 99
evaluating
    commands in other scopes, 59
    lists as commands, 56
evaluation stack, 405, 410, 414
event loop, *432*
    expect, 445
event manager, 508
exact, 327
    pattern, 332, 504
exec, 9, 66, 81, 196, 466
    2>, 293
    compress, 474
    cp, 473
    date, 338
    deleting files with funny names, 211
    kill, 296, 308, 345, 367
        –STOP, 346
        –STOP 0, 317, 468
    mv, 67
    play, 477
    rm, 67, 466, 473–474
    tilde substitution, 67
    uudecode, 473
    uuencode, 474
    versus system, 207
    xterm, 295
        –e, 488
execlp, 494
execute command before script, 217–218, 232
execute UNIX commands, 66
execvp, 494
exercises, a note about, xxxiii
exit, 230, 374, 390, 431, 478, 484
    handling, 321, 515
    implied at end of script, 100
    –noexit, 516
    –onexit, 321, 367, 516
    reset terminal, 204

status, 97
    rsh, 117
value, 178
exp_ prefix, 311, 433, 501, 515
EXP_ABORT, 509
exp_app_exit, 520
exp_autoallocpty, 498-499
exp_buffer, 505-506
exp_buffer_end, 505
exp_case, 506
exp_child_exec_prelude, 498
exp_close_in_child, 499
exp_close_tcl_files, 499
exp_cmdfile, 520
exp_cmdfilename, 520
exp_cmdlinecmds, 520
exp_compiled, 501, 503, 505
exp_console, 497
exp_continue, 145, 147-148, 249, 268, 357,
    472, 483
    affects spawn_id, 238
    –continue_timer, 146
exp_cook, 520-521
exp_debug, 311
exp_debugfile, 509-510
exp_disconnect, 508
exp_disconnected, 508, 519
exp_end, 492, 501-503
EXP_EOF, 502
exp_error, 521
exp_exact, 501, 504
exp_exec_library, 526
exp_exit, 311, 521
exp_exit_handlers, 521
exp_expect (no such command), 515
exp_expectl, 501-509
exp_expectv, 506-507
exp_fexpectl, 492
exp_full_buffer, 502
EXP_FULLBUFFER, 502
exp_getpid, 520
exp_glob, 492, 501-503
Exp_Init, 513-514, 516
exp_interactive, 520
exp_internal, 166, 171, 174, 404, 519
    –f, 174

exp_interp, 520
exp_interpret_cmdfile, 521
exp_interpret_cmdfilename, 518, 521
exp_interpret_rcfiles, 521
exp_interpreter, 521
exp_is_debugging, 509-510, 519
exp_library, 526
exp_logfile, 509
exp_logfile_all, 509
exp_loguser, 509-510, 519
exp_main_exp.c, 517-518
exp_main_tk.c, 517
exp_match, 505
exp_match_end, 505
exp_match_max, 506
exp_null, 501, 504
exp_open, 304
    –leaveopen, 305
exp_parse_argv, 521
exp_pclose, 500
exp_pid, 304, 496, 500
exp_popen, 492, 494-497, 499-500
exp_pty, 498
exp_pty_slave_name, 497
exp_readenv, 509
exp_regexp, 501-503, 507
exp_remove_nulls, 504
EXP_RESTART, 509
exp_send, 409, 433, 483, 515
    –i, 489
exp_slave_control, 510
exp_spawnl, 494-496, 500
exp_spawnv, 494-495, 500
exp_stty_init, 497, 499
exp_tcl_debugger_available, 520
EXP_TIMEOUT, 502, 508
exp_timeout, 502, 509
exp_ttycopy, 497
exp_ttyinit, 497
exp_type, 506
    enum, *501*
exp_version, 527
Expect
    adding extensions to, 513, 516
    as an extension, 513
    binaries, 492

bindings, 492
buffering, 74
compiled, 518
experimenting with, 225
finding, 18
in the background, 371
job control, 274
library, 429, 492-493, 510, 514, 517, 526
   in background, 507
   Tcl-less, 519
Makefile, 514
philosophy, xxv
prompt, 71
README, 16
retrieve latest version, 106
running interactively, 221
script, 72
scriptless, 518
send, 433
software distributions, 17
version, 527, 530
with no controlling terminal, 372
expect, 71-72, 345, 357, 466, 471, 482-483
\r\n, 119
argument ambiguity, 159
–brace, 160
braces, 76
common mistakes, 166, 177, 258
control flow in actions, 140
double buffering, 152
–ex, 134
from files, 500
from multiple processes
   simultaneously, 249
from streams, 507
function side-effects, 504
function side-effects picture, 505
–gl, 109-110, 135, 160
–i, 248, 488
   associates with which
   pattern?, 252
   list of spawn ids, 255
   versus spawn_id, 248
indentation, 75
–indices, 124

internal comments, 158
internal timer, 146
library functions, 504
multiple timeouts, 253
–nocase, 139, 211
no-op action, 190
–notransfer, 154
null, 155
output, recording all, 180
pattern-action pairs, 75
–re, 109, 135, 472, 475
regular expression limits, 158
repeating, 145
speed, 148
Tk event loop, 445
expect program, 217-218, 232
–, 218, 224
—, 217-218
#! guidelines, 221
arguments, 214
–b, 217, 224
–c, 515, 520
   multiple occurrences, 219
–D, 311, 410
   0, 411
   enable debugger, 217, 223
–d, 515
   print internal diagnostics, 217, 223
–f, 217, 220
–i, 520
   run interactively, 217, 221
invoking without saying
   "expect", 215
–n, 218, 221
prompt, 232
putting into background, 371
expect.h, 493, 496-497
expect.rc, 521
expect_after, 101, 247, 259-261
actions, 267
–info, 266
expect_background, 446, 448, 456
–info, 447
expect_before, 101, 247, 259-261
actions, 267

–all, 267
   common problems, 264
   complex example, 262
–info, 266
–noindirect, 269
EXPECT_DEBUG_INIT, 312, 411
expect_four_byte_int, 285
expect_out, 7, 297
   tracing, 406
   writing, 243
expect_out(0,string), 73
expect_out(1,string), 111, 236, 473
expect_out(2,string), 111
expect_out(9,string), 111
expect_out(buffer), 73, 96, 111, 124, 408
   tracing, 407
expect_out(spawn_id), 261, 359
expect_out(X,end), 124
expect_out(X,start), 124
expect_out(X,string), 124
EXPECT_PROMPT, 120, 148, 341, 467
expect_tcl.h, 514, 519
expect_tty, 210
   /dev/tty, 210
expect_user, 192, 197, 199, 238, 291, 340,
      345, 372-373, 468, 470
expectd.proto, 398
ExpecTerm, 10
Expectk, 10, 432-433
   –flags, 433
expectl, 500
expectv, 500
experimenting, 225
exposure, widget, 431
expr, 28, 443, 469, 487, 524
expressions, 27, 37
   unquoted strings in, 37
Extended Tcl, 69
extensions, 69, 513
   others, 522

F

factorial, 29
falling asleep, 211
FAQ, *20*
   Computer Security, 203

   script to retrieve, 401
fastest system, find, 253
Faught, Danny, xxix
fclose, 499
FD_SET, 508
fdopen, 495
feedback without echo, 335
fexpectl, 500
fexpectv, 500
fg, 240, 372
fgetc, 496, 507
Fibonacci, 34
fifo, 299, 378
   creation, 388
      nonportable, 385
   eof, 292
fifo_pair_create, 387
fifo_pair_remove, 387, 391
fifos, 246, 292, 356, 378, 498
figure
   expect function side-effects, 505
   interact, 324
      –input/output, 354
      –u, 350
   kibitz, 356
   tknewsbiff, 475
   tkpasswd GUI, 435
   xkibitz, 365
file, 217
   access, 60
   atime, 65
   close, 60
   delete, 67
   dirname, 64
   executable, 65, 298
   exists, 65, 480
   extension, 64, 466
   flush, 61
   gets, 62
   information, 65
   isdirectory, 65
   isfile, 65
   open, 60
   owned, 65
   read, 62
   readable, 65, 479, 481

remove, 67
rename, 67, 70
rootname, 64
seek (to location), 62
size, 65
stat, 66
tail, 64, 479
tell (location), 62
transfer over telnet, 467
type, 65
unique name, 70
writable, 65
write, 61
FILE *, 492
file identifier, *60*
    converting to spawn id, 304
filename
    manipulation, 64
    matching, 63
    reserved, 224
files as spawned processes, 289
filtering bad commands, 346
find, 136
    fastest system, 253
finger, 392
finish, 418
firstline, 305
FirstSearch, 398
fixline1, 216-217
flag, *218*
floor, 27
flush, 61, 304
focus, 437, 442
for, 30, 461, 481
foreach, 39, 238, 367, 466, 484-485, 487
fork, 297, 371, *374*, 388, 401, 508
    non-intuitive side-effects, 374
formal parameters, 34
format, 46, 487, 525
four byte integer pattern, 156
fprintf, 492, 496, 504
fputc, 496
frame, 436-437
fread, 496
freak biological accident many years
    ago, xxix

free, 504
Free Software Report, 15
Frequently Asked Questions List, 20
Frisbee, 381
fscanf, 496
fsck, 1, 8, 339
ftp, 1, 11-12, 22, 78, 80, 103, 185, 189, 336,
    344, 349, 392, 467
    anonymous, 83
    by mail, 19
    directory retrieval, 131-132
    library, 511
    mirror, 270
    prompt, 190
    recursive, 17, 133, 163, 336
    rewriting, 22
    with retry, 143
ftpcmd, 242
ftp-rfc, 17, 187-188
full_buffer, 151
fun stuff, 2
fwrite, 496

G

game
    chess versus chess, 234
    robohunt, 148
    rogue, 142, 458
Garamond, xxxii
GCT, 17
gdb, 2, 6, 410, 412
GEnie, 275
get_old_password, 442
get_users, 438
gethostbyname, 131
getpass, 199, 211
    better version, 206
gets, 62, 304, 474, 482
    stdin, 345, 372
gibberish, due to parity, 157
GL, 69
-gl, 109-110
glob, 63, 67, 478
    patterns, 87, *91*

global, 59, 70, 241, 243, 417, 442-443, 469, 471, 473, 477-478, 480, 482, 484-487, 489, 524
    command, 36
    scope, 413
    variables, 36
glomerular nephritis, 325
GNU C and C++ testing, 15
GNUS, 211
gone fishing!, 2
Goodd party lash night!, 279
Gopher, 392, 397
grab, 442
grep, 440
    avoiding, 438
GUI
    builder, 432
    passwd, 17
guidelines, 221
gzip, 489

H

handler
    exit, 321
    signal, 308
handling errors, 53
hangup, 102
    signal, 308, 314
help, debugger, 426
hexadecimal, 27
    pattern, 106, 108
highlighting, 451
history, 226
    event number, 228
    nextid, 228
    redo, 227
Holst, Wade, 21
Holzmann, Gerard, xxix
HOME, 222
home directory, 182
Hopkirk, Mike, 20
host-independent audio program, 480
hostname, 84
hotkeys, 348, 463
Houdini, 96
HP, 14, 510

HTML browsers and converters, 20
Huebner, Rob, xxix
hugs and kisses, 331
hung pty, 302, 305
hunt-and-peck, 280
HUP, 400

I

–i is supported by most commands, 249
I like cheesecake, 138
IAC, 393
IBM, 14-15
idle workstations, good use for, 400
if, 31, 443, 469, 471, 473-474, 478, 481, 483, 485, 489
ile, 226
illegal instruction, 313
in.fingerd, 392
in.ftpd, 392
inactivity monitor, 347
in-band error-reporting protocol, 358
include files, 493
incr, 30, 366, 461
indigestion, system, 153
indirect spawn id, *268*, 359
inetd, 204, 371, 392, 395, 400
infifo, 378
infinite timeout, 344
infinity, 278
info, 69
    commands, 52
    exists, 51, 218, 366, 413, 481-482, 485
    globals, 52
    level, 52, 60
    procs, 52
    script, 52
info@radio.com, 401
information on current patterns, 266
Init functions, order of, 516
input limit in cooked mode, 274
insecurity, 202
insert mode, 452
integer pattern, 108
inter_return, 229-230, 340, 344
interact, 8-9, 82, 123, 249, 259, 317, 323, 337, 357, 359, 368, 391, 459, 468

argument ambiguity, 160
–brace, 325
break, 339
buffering, 332
character translations, 325
characters that do not match, 331
continue, 339
default action, 341
–echo, 334-335
echo, 333, 335
efficiency, 359
eof, 342, 353
–ex, 327
figure, 324, 354
–i, 349, 351, 353, 360
–indices, 329
–input, 353-355, 358, 360-361, 368
inter_return, 340
job control emulation, 360
matching is different than
    expect, 329
multiple processes, 378
–nobuffer, 337-338, 340
null, 343
–o, 328, 340, 349, 351
optimized for speed, 408
–output, 353-355, 358, 360-361, 368
–re, 329
redirecting to /dev/null, 359
–reset, 317, 344, 346, 355
    to prevent character loss, 346
return, 338-340
returning in the caller, 340
simple patterns, 324
terminal mode, 226
timeout, 343, 353
–u, 295-296, 351-354, 360, 378
    figure, 350
interact_out, 361
interact_out(0,end), 329
interact_out(0,start), 329
interact_out(0,string), 329
interact_out(buffer) does not exist, 329
interact_out(spawn_id), 359
interacting with background
    processes, 381

interactive disconnected processes, 223
Interactive Line Editor, 226
Internet System Handbook, 394
Internet Talk Radio, 401
Internet Town Hall, 401
interoperability, 394
Interpret As Command, 393
interpreter, *225*, 229-230, 341, 363, 368,
    390
    inter_return, 229
    multiple, 321
    prompt, 226-227, 516
interrupt signal, 308
ioctl, 510
italics, xxxii

J

jim, 357
job control, 7, 12, 240
    interact, 360
    shell, 310
    shell-style can't be automated, 240
Jobs, Steve, 176
Johnston, Barry, xxix
join, 45-46, 64, 526
joining lists into string, 45
journals, 21

K

k1, 457
KABORT, 358
KDATA, 358
kdestroy, 376
Kenna, xxix, 435
Kerberos, 5, 13, 376
kermit, 196, 289
kernel-generated stop signal, 316
Kernighan, Brian, xxix
keyboard stop signal, 308
keystrokes, 431
kf1, 457
kibitz, 17, 256, 355, 357-359, 382
    dynamic, 361
    figure, 356
    implementation, 356

−noproc, 380
proxy account, 357
using from other scripts, 380
versus xkibitz, 361
xterm, 294
KILL, 307
kill, 296, 308
−9, 204
signal, 308, 312
−STOP 0, 317
Kimery, Sam, 20
kinit, 376
Kinzelman, Paul, xxix
Knuth, 524
Korn shell, xxiv

L

label, 437, 442
lappend, 43, 49, 364, 461, 483, 485–486
leap seconds, 528
Legalese, 15
Lehenbauer, Karl, 59
Lemis, 18
levels of precedence, 28
-lexpect, 514
−lexpect, 517
Libes family, xxix
libexpect.a, 493, 514
library, 68
    Expect, 492–493, 510, 514, 517, 526
    ftp, 511
    platform-dependent versus -
        independent, 526
    Tcl, 493, 514, 517
limit program to given time, 98
limitations
    input buffer max, 276
    terminal driver, 274
lindex, 38, 133, 443, 479, 484
line kill character, 274
linefeed, 396
line-oriented, 197
LINES, 450
linsert, 44
Lisp, 70
list, 57

append, 43
command, 42
commands can be dangerous, 232
reverse, 70
listbox, 479
listing breakpoints, 425
lists, 38
    are strings, too, 41
    creating, 42
    inserting, 44
    joining lists into strings, 45
    lists of, 40–41
    of spawn ids, 254
    replacing elements, 44
    searching, 44
    selecting elements, 38
    sorting, 45
    spawn ids, 254
    splitting, 45
llength, 38–39, 215, 337, 479, 485–486
    dangerous, 189
lo¿i¿:¿, 157
load_dict, 440
log, 27
    by tracing, 407
log_file, 180, 334, 337, 404
    −a, 181
    −noappend, 180
log_user, 175–177, 179, 249, 285, 298, 364,
        404, 466, 471–474, 510, 519
    −info, 182
logfile, 407
logger, 377
login, 3, 154, 167, 272, 351
lognumber, 338
longjmp, 509
lpc, 231
lpr, 284
lpunlock, 17
lrange, 39, 201, 479, 484
lreplace, 44
lsearch, 44
    −exact, 485
lsort, 45
−ltcl, 517
Lynch, Daniel, 394

M

macho stud language, 3
Mackerras, Paul, 216
mail
  commercial provider, 275
  process, 383
  protocol, 130
  sending from Expect, 383
  verify address, 175
make_selection, 443
Makefile, 514, 517
man pages, xxiii, *19*
manager
  disconnection, 379
  for disconnected processes, 384
Mariano, Adrian, xxix
Martin Marietta, 14
master
  and slave, 294
  pty, *294*
match anything but the given
      characters, 129
match_max, 150, 249, 408
  –d, 150
maxtime, 98, 100, 163, 232
Mayer, Neils, 429
McLennan, Michael, 60
message-of-the-day, 122
meta key, 457
mirror, ftp, 270
miscreant, 121
missing return, 345
mkdir, 66
mkfifo, 385
mkpasswd, 17, 524
modem
  AT command in a loop, 211
  dial, 85
  monitoring usage, 338
  testing and setting, 14
  works by hand but not by script, 196
modulo, 27
monitor
  inactivity, 347
  modem usage, 338
Moore, Jeff, xxix

more, 149
Morse, Will, xxix
Mosaic, 392, 397
  slick but stupid, 397
Motif, 10, 429
Motorola, 14
moving up or down the stack, 417
Mulroney, Lenore, xxix
Mulroney, Sue, xxviii
multiple commands on a single line, 24
multiple processes, 233
  interacting with one another, 234
multi-user control, 17
mv, 67

N

N, 415, 423
n, 413, 415, 423
named pipes, 246
National Cancer Institute, 14
National Institute of Standards and
      Technology, xxviii, 16
NAWS, 401
Negotatiate About Window Size, 401
Nelson, Ted, 121
netpipe, 401
netstat, 401
network
  devices, 14
  pipe, 401
  slow, 152
new features, telling the user about, 336
newgrp, 211
newline, 79
news, unread, 475
newsgroup comp.lang.tcl, 21
NIS, 5, 434
NIST, xxviii, 16
NNTP, 482
nondestructive space, 450, 456
no-op, 190
not, 27
NSUBEXP, 505
NULL, 504
null character, 24, 155, 343, 396, 504

O

O'Reilly & Associates, 429
O'Reilly, Tim, xxix
Obfuscated C and Other Mysteries, 401
Obfuscated C Code Contest, xxvi
OCLC, 398
octal, 27
octal integer pattern, 109
older workstations, good use for, 400
one line pattern, 135
Online Computer Library Center, 398
open, 60, 63, 284, 289, 292, 472, 474, 482,
        523
    pipeline, 526
    w+, 284, 290, 292
    with interactive programs, 284
or, 27
Oracle, 69
order of Init functions, 516
OSF, 429
Ousterhout, John, xxvi, xxviii, 19-20, 28,
        69
outfifo, 378
output
    disabling, 174
    merged with standard error, 175
output chunking, 89-90
overview of Tk, 430

P

p, 428
pack, 431, 435-438, 442, 479
pager, 85
Paisley, Scott, xxv, xxvii
parallel set, 70
parameters, xxxii, 34
parentheses
    for pattern feedback, 111, 115-116
    limit of nine, 116
    override expression precedence, 28
    override pattern precedence, 110
parity, 157, 249, 291
parray, 68, 412, 428
partial automation, 82
pass by reference, *36*, 57
pass by value, *36*

passmass, 17, 155
passwd, 4-5, 7, 200, 436
    executing on multiple hosts
        simultaneously, 155
    GUI, 434
    rewriting, 5
password, 525
    echo with asterisks, 444, 463
    entering twice, 377, 441, 466
    generating random, 524
    prompt, 375
    reuse, 376
    stored in script, 375
password_backspace, 445
PATH, 215, 287
pattern
    any character but], 129
    any character but ^, 129
    any character but a letter, 129
    background, *446*
    backslashes in, 91
    computer generated, 135
    C-style language identifier, 108
    C-style real number, 140
    debugging, 165
    email address, 137
    exact, 327, 332
    four-byte integer, 156
    ftp listings, 132
    ftp prompt, 190
    full_buffer, 151
    hexadecimal, 106, 108
    integer, 108
    longest string not including a
        blank, 129
    ls output, 132
    message-of-the-day, 122
    octal integer, 109
    one and only one line, 135-136
    politics of, 154
    prompt, 119, 121, 125, 147, 167
    range, 91
    readable, 90
    real number, 110
    really slow, 165
    Roman numbers, 106

shell-style, 32, 91
simple, 134
SQL, 135
switch, 133
Tcl integer, 109
timeout (literal), 106, 110
type prefix, 109
pattern match
limits, 149
strategy, 113-114, 130
pattern-action pairs, 75
pclose, 500
Pendleton, Bob, 226
Perl, xxiv-xxv, 70
perpetual buffering, 154
Phelps, Tom, 19
PHIGS, 69
physiologist, 325
pi, 36
pid, 304, 471, 473, 524
pid2whatever, *362*
pidfile_read, 386
pidfile_write, 386
piece, 110
Pike, Rob, 288
ping, 96, 178
pipe, 498-499
bidirectional communication, 305
write failure signal, 308
pipeline, 61, 284
compression through, 489
play audio, 480
politics of patterns, 154
poll, 292, 303, 508
popen, 495, 500
POSIX, 13, 155, 313, 334, 375, 385
stty, 205
POSIX.1, 367
power failure, 307
Practical Programming in Tcl and Tk, 20
precedence, levels of, 28
predefined spawn ids, 245
any_spawn_id, 259
Prentice Hall, 20, 305
Press et al, 524
preventing bad commands, 346

Prime Time Freeware, 17
print array, 68
printf, 497, 521
proc, 34, 438, 445, 468-471, 473, 477-478,
480, 482-487, 489, 524
dynamically generating, 232
procedure, 34
call stack, 414
introduces new scope, 241
recursive, 35
tiny ones are very useful, 242
process, 78
bidirectional pipelines, 292
identifier, 233
procomm, 289
programs
as device drivers, 289
reuse, 288
that ignore eof, 103
prompt, 121, 125, 167
changing, 120, 228, 232, 389
default, 467
ftp, 190
interpreter, 226-227, 516
password, 375
by proxy, 201
patterns, 147
vulgar pattern, 211
prompt1, 228, 362
prompt2, 228
protocol
in-band error-reporting, 358
negotiation, telnet, 395
proxy account, 357
ps, 105, 200
pseudo-random, 278
pseudoterminal, *292*
pty, *292*, 294, 305
allocation, 303, 498
hung, 302
modes, 300
three-step initialization, 301
trapping, 510
ptyfix, 303, 305
puts, 27, 229, 284-285, 304, 412, 472, 478,
483

file, 61
  –nonewline, 61, 284
  versus send, 188, 283
  versus send_user, 182
pwd, 122
Python, xxv

Q

quack said the duck, 117
quadratic formula, 54
quit signal, 308, 312
quotes, xxxiii
quoting conventions, 25

R

r, 418, 423
race condition, 193
radiobutton, 436
random, 278, 524, 530
  number generator, 523
  password generation, 524
random_init, 524
range pattern, 91
rcp, when you cannot use, 351
–re, 109
read, 62, 495
  commands from file, 217, 220
  commands from standard input, 218, 224
  from script, one line at a time, 217, 224
readability, 90
readline (GNU), 226
real number pattern, 110
reap, 105
reasonable error, 279
**reconnecting disconnected
    processes**, 378
recursive
  ftp, 17, 133, 163, 336
  procedures, 35
Red Alert!, 475
redirection
  shell, 173
  standard I/O, 209

regexp, 107, 137, 175, 189, 364, 465, 482, 503
  –indices, 138
  to delete last character in word, 445
  versus string match, 530
regsub, 138, 216
  –all, 139
regular expression, xxviii, 107, 328, 332, 421, 502
  atom, 107
  branch, 109, 115
  caching, 503
  compilation, 503
  figure, 115
  further reading, 20
  limits, 158
  POSIX.2 style, 114
rehash, 72, 215
remote shell exit status, 117
remove_nulls, 155, 249
  –d, 156
remsh, 97
rename files, 70
repeaters, 15
reprompting, 193
Request For Comments, 80
reserved file name, 224
resize, 250, 431
retrieve an RFC, 17, 186
return, 34-35, 143, 228, 230, 339, 363, 368, 418, 442, 469, 483, 485-486
  character on input, 72, 79
  –code, 462
  from interact, 338, 340
  from interpreter, 227
  from procedure, 418
  missing, 345
  multiple values, 58
  value, 26
      overriding, 320
reuse, 288
reverse, 70
rewriting
  ftp, 22
  passwd, 5
rewriting the #! line, 216

RFC
   1073 (Window Size), 401
   854 (Telnet), 80, 393
   959 (FTP), 80
   retrieve, 186
rftp, 17, 133, 163, 336
RHBOMB, 121
rlogin, 2, 126, 200, 316, 340, 351-352, 357,
      402
   daemon, 316
   script, 122
   versus rsh, 118
   with same directory, 122
rlogin-cwd, 17
   for telnet, 341
rlogind, 316
rm, 66
   –f, 334, 475
rn
   behaves oddly in background, 373
   reprompting, 195
RNG, *523*-524
Robbins, Arnold, xxviii
robohunt, 148
robust, 81
Rochkind, Marc, 305
rogue, 141-142, 458-459
rogue.exp, 17
Roman number pattern, 106
Rose, Marshall, 394
round, 27
routers, 14-15
rsh, 97, 126
   exit status, 117
   versus rlogin, 118
rtfm.mit.edu, 401
rup, 232
rz, 352, 369, 467, 489
   over rlogin, 351

S

s, 423
Sandia National Laboratories, 15
sane, 158, 301, 497
Savoye, Rob, xxviii, 15
SB, 393

scalar, *51*
scan, 46-47, 140, 487
   regular to control character, 330
scanf, 140
Scheme, xxv
Schlumberger, 15
Schumacher, Dale, 20
scientific notation, 27
scope
   current, *417*
   global, 413
   identifier, 417
script, 180, 183, 259, 334, 337, 348, 463
   design, 231
   robust, 81
   send_humanly, 285
   with command timestamps, 256
scriptless Expect programs, 518
scrollbar, 430, 437, 479
SE, 393
se, 450
search path, 287
security, 200, 202
   by file protection, 202
   by host protection, 203
   problem, 434
   testing, 14
seek, 62
select, 292, 303, 444, 508
select_next_nopassword, 443
semicolon, 24
SEND, 393
send, 71, 284-285, 433, 466, 471-474
   —, 282
   –break, 282
   –h, 278
      good typist, 280
   humanly, 278
   –i, 248, 271
   long running, 276
   not affected by log_user, 176
   –null, 281
   –raw, 285
   -s, 277
   slow, 275, 277
   Tk, 409

Tk versus Expect, 433, 515
to multiple processes, 272
unknown strings, 283
versus puts, 188, 283
without echo, 273, 276
send –i, 352
send_error, 187, 373
send_human, 278, 281
send_log, 182, 377
send_slow, 277, 281, 285
send_tty, 210, 284, 466-467
send_user, 7, *185*, 198, 284, 335, 337, 340,
        373, 468, 470, 472
    –raw, 198
    translation, 345
    versus puts, 182
sendexpect, 191
sendmail, 130
sequences, *448*
serial interface, 351
    not ready, 196
set, 24, 412, 428, 438, 442, 461, 468, 472,
        476-486, 489
    parallel, 70
setbuf, 495
Sex, xxvi
SGA, 393
shadow passwords, 5
Shaney, Mark V., 288
shape, 279
SHELL, 468
shell
    backquotes, 78
    Bourne, 178
    echo, 119
    has peculiar behavior as daemon, 392
    job control, 7, 372
    limit, 150
    prompt, 273
    rc file, 11
    testing, 7
shell redirection, 173
shell-style, 91
Shen, Sam, xxix, 409
shortcuts, expect_before and
        expect_after, 259

SIG prefix, 309
SIG_DFL, 310, 312, 315
SIG_IGN, 309, 314-315, 498
SIGALRM is reserved, 318
SIGCHLD, 308, 313-314, 366, 500
SIGCLD, 313
SIGCONT, 308, 316-317
SIGHUP, 308, 310, 314, 498
SIGILL, 313
SIGINT, 308-309, 311-312, 317, 319, 515
SIGKILL, 307-308, 312
signal, 274, 489, 498, 509
    9, 307
    avoid if possible!, 307
    evaluation, 318
    generation, *307*
    handler, 308, 515
        problems, 319
    in spawned process versus
        Expect, 310
    power failure, 307
    sending, *307*
    specifications, 307
signal.h, 318
SIGPIPE, 308, 310, 315
SIGQUIT, 308, 312
SIGSTOP, 308, 316, 318
SIGTERM, 308, 312, 498, 515
SIGTSTP, 308, 316
SIGUSR1, 308-309, 312, 317, 319
SIGUSR2, 308-309, 312, 317
SIGWINCH, 308, 315, 361
Silicon Graphics, 14
simulating 500 users simultaneously, 15
simulations, 14
sin, 27
sins, covering up, 187
SIPP, 69
slave, pty, *294*
sleep, 99, 195-*197*, 277
    UNIX versus Expect, 530
slowing rotation of the Earth, 528
smart terminal, 448
    emulator, 448
SMTP, 130, 175, 494
    connect to port, 392

so, 450
sockets, 289
software
    distributions with Expect, 17
    interrupt, 307
        signal, 311
    quality assurance, 14
    termination signal, 308, 312
    testing, 15
Software Solutions in C, 20
sort, 436
source, 36, 68
    $expect_library/expect.rc, do
        not, 218, 221
    ~/.expect.rc, do not, 218, 221
Sparc, 440
spawn, 71, 78, 284, *287*, 337, 351, 388, 488,
        523
    /bin/sh –c for redirection, 292
    absolute versus relative names, 287
    catching errors, 296–297
    –console, 331
    eval, 99
    functions, *494*
    hints, 99
    –ignore, 310, 315
    in the bedroom, 78
    –leaveopen, 290
    multiple processes, 233
    –noecho, 298, 368
    –nottycopy, 301
    –nottyinit, 302
    –open, 289, 292, 304, 379, 482, 526
        tty device, 290
    –pty, 294, 364
    redirection or pipeline, 291
    sh –c, 466
    telnet, 482
    within a procedure is tricky, 100
spawn id
    converting to file identifier, 304
    direct, *268*
    indirect, *268*, 359
    integer representation, 239
    lists, 254
    multiple, 358

    predefined, 245
    separate input buffers, 249
    useful as array index, 239
spawn_id, 233–234, 238, 242, 247, 274,
        360, 407
    affects many commands, 238
    job control, 240
    read implicitly, 241
    returning, 244
    versus –i, 248
    writing, 243
spawn_out(slave,fd), 295
spawn_out(slave,name), 294, 316, 364, 368
Spencer, Henry, xxviii–xxix, 16, 20
split, 45–46, 64
    /etc/passwd, 45
    filename, 45
    versus gets in a while loop, 440
splitting strings into lists, 45
sprintf, 46
SQL, 69
    patterns, 135
sqrt, 27
sscanf, 46
stack, 414
    evaluation, 405, 410
    moving up or down, 417
Standard C, 155
standard error, 172, 245
    sending to, 187
standard I/O buffering, 7
standard input, 72, 245
    redirection, 209
standard output, 172, 245
    disabling, 174
    redirection, 209
        from shell, 173
standout mode, 451
startp, 505
static variables, 59
stderr, correct use of, 188
stdio.h, 493, 497
stepping into procedure calls, 415
stepping over multiple commands, 415
stepping over procedure calls, 413
Stevens, W. Richard, xxix, 394

stop signal, 308, 316
strace, 405, 408
    –info, 406
strategy
    for catching errors, 225
    script design, 231
strftime, 528
string, 46
    append, 49
    command, 47
    compare, 461, 466, 479, 481
    everything is a, 23
    first, 48
    formatting, 46–47
    index, 48
    last, 48
    length, 48
    match, 47, 91, 136, 485
    match versus regexp, 530
    parsing, 46
    range, 48
    reverse, 70
    tolower, 48
    toupper, 48
    trim operations, 48
    trimright, 78, 112, 140
string manipulation, 46
strlen, 521
strobes, 460
struct exp_case, 506
struct timeval *, 508
stty, 198, 204, 206, 251, 290, 302, 315, 325,
        364, 372–373, 471
    <, 290
    –a, 207
    arguments, 205
    columns, 315
    –echo, 199, 205, 274, 290, 294
    echo, 199
    –icrnl, 72
    istrip, 291
    –ocrnl, 348
    POSIX, 205
    –raw, 468, 470
    raw, 290–291, 294, 470
    rows, 315

sane, 301, 377
stty_init, 301
    –istrip, 302
su, 2
    with logging, 183
su2, 178, 200
subpattern, 110
sum, 39
Sun, 440
Sun User Group, 17
superuser, 442
support, 21
suspend
    character, 316
    signal, 308
SV, 449
switch, 32, 133, 137, 231, 477, 484, 501, 503
syslog, 377
system
    call tracing, 408
    inactivity monitor, 330
    indigestion, 153
    versus exec, 207
sz, 352, 369, 467, 489
    over rlogin, 351

T

tag2pid, *362*
talk, 331
Tcl, 11
    abbreviation, 11
    archive, 20
    best and worst things about, 70
    extensions, 21, 513
    idea database, 21
    library, 493, 514, 517, 530
    Makefile, 514
    philosophy, xxv
    pronunciation, 3
    reference material, *19*
    shell, 26, 513
    source directory, 513
    total access to, 231
Tcl and the Tk Toolkit, 19, 28, 69
tcl.h, 514, 517
TCL_ERROR, 513, 521

Tcl_Eval, 227
  argument restrictions, 518
Tcl_Init, 513–514, 516
tcl_interactive, 223
Tcl_Interp, 520–521
tcl_prompt1, 516
tcl_prompt2, 516
tclAppInit.c, 513–514
Tcl-DP, 513
TclRegComp, 503–504
tclRegexpError, 504
tclsh, 26, 513, 515, 519
  –f, 515
  interpreter, 516
TclX, 69
TCP, 467
TCP/IP Illustrated, Volume 1, 394
tcp_wrapper, 400
Tektronix, 14
telephone exchange data collection, 14
tell, 62
telnet, 2, 8, 14, 126, 130–131, 166, 169, 196,
    204, 250, 325, 340, 349, 384, 392,
    397–398, 467–468, 496, 519
  behaves oddly in background, 373
  daemon, 392
    written in Expect, 371, 393
  escape character, 230
  file transfer over, 467
  IAC, 393
  needs code to force exit, 239
  protocol, 393
    negotation, 395
  record session, 402
  slow, 152
  style escapes, 336
  to all different ports, 162
  to multiple hosts, 239
telnet-cwd, 341
ten_chars_per_sec, 276
TERM, 373, 450
term_chars_changed, 454, 460
term_clear, 452
term_cursor_changed, 455
term_down, 452
term_exit, 455

term_expect, 458–459, 463
term_init, 451
term_insert, 453
term_standout, 451
term_update_cursor, 455
TERMCAP, 450
termcap, 286, 449, 452
terminal, *372*
  ANSI, 462
  controlling, 372
  emulate multiple, 463
  emulator, 17
    scroll bars, 462
    testing, 458
  identification code, 250
  mode, 226
  parameters, 158
  servers, 15
  type tk, 450
terminal driver, 72, 119
  buffers, 197
  echo, 273
  limitations, 274
  translations, 274
terminal-generated stop signal, 316
TERMINFO, 450
terminfo, 286, 449–450, 452
testing, 440
  GNU C and C++, 15
  interactive programs, 6
  security, 14
  shell, 7
  software, 15
Testing Foundations, 17
text, 437
  widget, 451, 463
Thompson, Ken, 12, 235
tilde, 288
time, 529
timeallcmds, 256
timed-read, 17, 77, 112, 126, 218
timed-run, 17
timeout, 3, 94–95, 242, 249, 327, 343, 353,
    483
  –1, 81
  as local variable, 488

infinity, 344
  literal pattern, 106, 110
  no association with spawn id, 253
  none, 81
  read implicitly, 241
  variable, 75
timestamp, 257, 303, 528
  versus date, 530
timing
  a read in the shell, 77
  dictionary loading, 522
  other commands, 529
  out, 74
  problems, 153
tip, 4, 196, 282, 288–291, 351, 398, 468
Tk, 10, 283, 409, 429, 432
  debugger, 428
  overview, 430
  send, 409, 433
  suppressing button highlighting, 222
  terminal emulator, 511
  widget hierarchy, 295
tk
  colormodel, 437
  terminal type, 450
tk_entryBackspace, 445
tk_entrySeeCaret, 445
tk_strictMotif, 222
tkinspect, 409
TkMan, 19
tknewsbiff, 17, 475
tkpasswd, 17, 434, 463
  figure, 435
TkSteal, 295, 513
tkterm, 17, 449
  example tests, 454
tkwait, 442, 461
Todd, Bennett, xxix
Tool Command Language, 11
toplevel, 438, 442
tput, 283
tr –d \015, 348
trace, 53, 408
  procedure, 423
tracing, 403
  command, 405

system calls, 380, 408
  variable, 406
transcript, 305
trap, 308
  –code, 320
  –interp, 321
  –max, 318
  –name, 309
  –number, 309
  pty, 510
  SIG_DFL, 310
  SIG_IGN, 309
truss, 380, 408
tset, 147
TSR, 348
TSS HAS GONE DOWN, 121
tty_spawn_id, 245, 372
  unset, 375
ttyp0, 294
TTYPE, 393
typeahead, 195
typescript, 334

U

u, 417
U.S. Department of Commerce, xxviii
UART not ready, 196
unbuffer, 17, 299
uncompress, 81, 473
underlining, 451
underscore convention, 478
unencrypted passwords in files,
      NOT!, 203
unhang a printer, 17
uniquely-named file, 70
University of California at Berkeley, xxvi,
      16
University of Toronto, 16
University of XXX XXXXXX
      XXXXXXXX, 397
UNIX, 14, 375
  versus VMS, 154
unix, 328
UNIX epoch, *528*
unknown, 68, 226, 362
unread news, 475

unset, 53, 367, 462, 489
uplevel, 59, 241, 417, 458, 462, 480, 485
upvar, 57, 241, 244, 417
    #0, 482
USENET Software, 17
user_read, 231
user_spawn_id, 245, 354, 356
user-defined signal, 308, 317
users, contacting multiple, 382
uuencode, 471–472
Uunet, 80, 130, 170

V

variables
    information, 51
    static, 59
    tracing, 53, 406
    unsetting, 53
varying argument lists, 39
verbose mode, 404
verify mail address, 175
versions of Expect, 530
    testing, 527
vi, 344
    autoabbreviation, 326
Virden, Larry, 20
vmess, 328, 333
VMS, 330
    versus UNIX, 154
vms, 328
vprint, 404
vrfy, 175
vt100, 395
vulgar prompt pattern, 211
vxWorks board, 348

W

w, 416–418
    -compress, 428
    –width, 426
wait, 105, 249, 313, 466, 483
    –nowait, 106
    return value, 313
wait for prompts before sending, 79, 81
waiting for a process, 105

watch, 476
weak_password, 440
weather, 17
Weibull distribution, 278
Welch, Brent, xxix, 20
What does that have to do with
    news!?, 480
where am I, 416
while, 29, 231, 339, 479, 482, 484
widget, *430*
    classes, 431
    display, 431
    exposure, 431
    terminal emulator, 511
WILL, 393
Willison, Frank, xxix
WINCH, 367
window
    change event, 431
    size change signal, 308, 315
WINTERP, 429
wm, 437, 477–478, 481, 487
wonders of UNIX, the, 318
WONT, 393
World Bank, 14
World Wide Web, 20
WorldCat, 398
write, 241, 492, 495
    to multiple people, 237
WWW, 20, 397

X

X, 315, 361
    authority file, 124, 126
    client –display flag, 433
    for interprocess communication, 410
    GUI builder, 432
    resize, 250
    window id, 295, 364
X Consortium, 295
X Window System, 10, 222, 283, 428–429
X Window System Series, 429
X11
    R5, 294, 367
    R6, 295
Xerox, 14

XF, 432
xinetd, 400
xkibitz, 361, 384
    figure, 365
    versus kibitz, 361
XLISP, 429
XMODEM, 351
XOX, 331
xterm, 315, 363, 367–368
    –C, 300
    –e, 293
    resize, 250
    –S, 294-295, 364
    vehicle for interhost
        communication, 361
    via kibitz, 294
    window id, 364
xterms, 305

Y
YART, 69
YMODEM, 351
you have unread news, 475
yppasswd, 436

Z
Z (from ps), 105
Z shell, xxiv
ZMODEM, 351
zombie, *105*

About the Author

Don Libes is married to Susan Mulroney, a professor in the Department of Physiology and Biophysics at the Georgetown University School of Medicine. Sue performs research in the area of kidney growth and development. Their well-hydrated daughter, Kenna, has two lovely kidneys.

Colophon

Our look is the result of reader comments, our own experimentation, and feedback from distribution channels. Distinctive covers complement our distinctive approach to technical topics, breathing personality and life into potentially dry subjects. UNIX and its attendant programs can be unruly beasts. Nutshell Handbooks help you tame them.

The animal featured on the cover of *Exploring Expect* is a rhesus monkey, a primate of the macaque genus. Like all macaques, rhesus monkeys live in matriarchal communities made up of several family units, each with a female of reproducing age as its head. Males generally move on to another group when they reach maturity, while females stay with the same group for life. Occasionally, when a group reaches 80 to 100 members, several of the older females will break off, taking their families with them, and start a new group.

The communities are strictly hierarchical, and group behavior patterns help to maintain the hierarchy. Activities such as mutual grooming and "nitpicking" not only serve to appease the higher-ranking members of the group, but also help to reassure the lower-ranking members. If there is a dispute between two members of the group, lower-ranking macaques often take the side of the combatant from the higher-ranking family, in the hopes that this loyalty will place them in higher favor.

One distinguishing feature of macaques is the sac-like pouches in their cheeks, into which a large amount of food can be stuffed. This enables them to gather food quickly in potentially dangerous places, and to eat it later in a safe environment. When ready to eat, they will force the food from the pouch into the mouth by pressing on the cheeks.

Macaques are able to adapt to a wider range of environmental conditions than almost any other animals, with the exception of humans. They live at the heights of the Himalayas and in low-lying flatlands. They can withstand both hot and arid and cold and snowy climates. Macaques adapt particularly well to urban areas, where they often proliferate so well that they become pests. Attempts have been made to relocate macaque populations back into the wild, but they tend to migrate away from the forest and back to the nearest city, where they find an abundance of food.

Because of their physiological similarities to humans, rhesus monkeys are extensively used in scientific experimentation. The rhesus blood factor, or Rh factor, was discovered in rhesus monkeys in 1937, and later in humans, by pathologists Karl Landsteiner and Alexander Solomon Wiener. Rh factors are hereditary red blood cell antigens. Giving Rh-positive blood to a person who is Rh-negative, or vice versa, can cause the body to have a dangerous and possibly fatal defensive reaction. By testing for Rh factors, dangerous mismatches are avoided.

Edie Freedman designed this cover and the entire UNIX bestiary that appears on other Nutshell Handbooks. The beasts themselves are adapted from 19th-century engravings from the Dover Pictorial Archive. The cover layout was produced with Adobe Photoshop 2.5 and Quark XPress 3.3 for the Macintosh, using the Adobe ITC Garamond font. Whenever possible, our books use RepKover™, a durable and flexible lay-flat binding. If the page count exceeds RepKover's limit, perfect binding is used.

The inside layout was designed by Edie Freedman and Jennifer Niederst and implemented by Mike Sierra in FrameMaker using Adobe ITC Garamond and New Courier fonts. The figures were created in FrameMaker by Don Libes. The colophon was written by Clairemarie Fisher O'Leary.

UNIX Tools

Writing GNU Emacs Extensions

By Bob Glickstein
1st Edition April 1997
236 pages, ISBN 1-56592-261-1

This book introduces Emacs Lisp and tells you how to make the editor do whatever you want, whether it's altering the way text scrolls or inventing a whole new "major mode." Topics progress from simple to complex, from lists, symbols, and keyboard commands to syntax tables, macro templates, and error recovery.

UNIX Power Tools, 2nd Edition

By Jerry Peek, Tim O'Reilly & Mike Loukides
2nd Edition August 1997
1120 pages, Includes CD-ROM
ISBN 1-56592-260-3

Loaded with even more practical advice about almost every aspect of UNIX, this new second edition of *UNIX Power Tools* addresses the technology that UNIX users face today. You'll find increased coverage of POSIX utilities, including GNU versions, greater *bash* and *tcsh* shell coverage, more emphasis on Perl, and a CD-ROM that contains the best freeware available.

Tcl/Tk Tools

By Mark Harrison
1st Edition September 1997
678 pages, Includes CD-ROM
ISBN 1-56592-218-2

One of the greatest strengths of Tcl/Tk is the range of extensions written for it. This book clearly documents the most popular and robust extensions—by the people who created them—and contains information on configuration, debugging, and other important tasks. The CD-ROM includes Tcl/Tk, the extensions, and other tools documented in the text both in source form and as binaries for Solaris and Linux.

Perl

Advanced Perl Programming

By Sriram Srinivasan
1st Edition August 1997
434 pages, ISBN 1-56592-220-4

This book covers complex techniques for managing production-ready Perl programs and explains methods for manipulating data and objects that may have looked like magic before. It gives you necessary background for dealing with networks, databases, and GUIs, and includes a discussion of internals to help you program more efficiently and embed Perl within C or C within Perl.

Learning Perl on Win32 Systems

By Randal L. Schwartz, Erik Olson & Tom Christiansen
1st Edition August 1997
306 pages, ISBN 1-56592-324-3

In this carefully paced course, leading Perl trainers and a Windows NT practitioner teach you to program in the language that promises to emerge as the scripting language of choice on NT. Based on the "llama" book, this book features tips for PC users and new, NT-specific examples, along with a foreword by Larry Wall, the creator of Perl, and Dick Hardt, the creator of Perl for Win32.

Mastering Regular Expressions

By Jeffrey E. F. Friedl
1st Edition January 1997
368 pages, ISBN 1-56592-257-3

Regular expressions, a powerful tool for manipulating text and data, are found in scripting languages, editors, programming environments, and specialized tools. In this book, author Jeffrey Friedl leads you through the steps of crafting a regular expression that gets the job done. He examines a variety of tools and uses them in an extensive array of examples, with a major focus on Perl.

Perl

Perl Resource Kit—UNIX Edition

By Larry Wall, Nate Patwardhan, Ellen Siever,
David Futato & Brian Jepson
1st Edition November 1997
1812 pages, ISBN 1-56592-370-7

The *Perl Resource Kit—UNIX Edition* gives
you the most comprehensive collection of
Perl documentation and commercially
enhanced software tools available today.
Developed in association with Larry Wall, the creator of Perl, it's
the definitive Perl distribution for webmasters, programmers,
and system administrators.

The *Perl Resource Kit* provides:

*   Over 1800 pages of tutorial and in-depth reference docu-
    mentation for Perl utilities and extensions, in 4 volumes.
*   A CD-ROM containing the complete Perl distribution, plus hun-
    dreds of freeware Perl extensions and utilities—a complete
    snapshot of the Comprehensive Perl Archive Network (CPAN)—
    as well as new software written by Larry Wall just for the Kit.

Perl Software Tools All on One Convenient CD-ROM
Experienced Perl hackers know when to create their own, and
when they can find what they need on CPAN. Now all the power
of CPAN—and more—is at your fingertips. *The Perl Resource Kit*
includes:

*   A complete snapshot of CPAN, with an install program for
    Solaris and Linux that ensures that all necessary modules are
    installed together. Also includes an easy-to-use search tool
    and a web-aware interface that allows you to get the latest
    version of each module.
*   A new Java/Perl interface that allows programmers to write
    Java classes with Perl implementations. This new tool was
    written specially for the Kit by Larry Wall.

Experience the power of Perl modules in areas such as CGI, web spi-
dering, database interfaces, managing mail and USENET news, user
interfaces, security, graphics, math and statistics, and much more.

Perl in a Nutshell

By Stephen Spainhour, Ellen Siever &
Nathan Patwardhan
1st Edition May 1998 (est.)
450 pages (est.), ISBN 1-56592-286-7

The perfect companion for working programmers, *Perl in a Nutshell* is a comprehensive reference guide to the world of Perl. It contains
everything you need to know for all but the most
abstruse Perl questions. This wealth of information is packed into
an efficient, extraordinarily usable format.

Programming Perl, 2nd Edition

By Larry Wall, Tom Christiansen &
Randal L. Schwartz
2nd Edition September 1996
670 pages, ISBN 1-56592-149-6

Coauthored by Larry Wall, the creator of Perl,
the second edition of this authoritative guide
contains a full explanation of Perl version
5.003 features. It covers Perl language and
syntax, functions, library modules, references, and object-oriented features, and also explores invocation options, debugging,
common mistakes, and much more.

Perl 5 Desktop Reference

By Johan Vromans
1st Edition February 1996
46 pages, ISBN 1-56592-187-9

This is the standard quick-reference guide for the
Perl programming language. It provides a complete
overview of the language, from variables to input and
output, from flow control to regular expressions, from functions
to document formats—all packed into a convenient, carry-
around booklet. Updated to cover Perl version 5.003.

Learning Perl, 2nd Edition

By Randal L. Schwartz & Tom Christiansen,
Foreword by Larry Wall
2nd Edition July 1997
302 pages, ISBN 1-56592-284-0

In this update of a bestseller, two leading Perl
trainers teach you to use the most universal
scripting language in the age of the World
Wide Web. Now current for Perl version 5.004,
this hands-on tutorial includes a lengthy new chapter on CGI programming, while touching also on the use of library modules, references, and Perl's object-oriented constructs.

The Perl Cookbook

By Tom Christiansen & Nathan Torkington
1st Edition April 1998 (est.)
600 pages (est.), ISBN 1-56592-243-3

The Perl Cookbook is a collection of hundreds of
problems and their solutions (with examples)
for anyone programming in Perl. The topics
range from beginner questions to techniques
that even the most experienced Perl programmers might learn from.

How to stay in touch with O'Reilly

1. Visit Our Award-Winning Web Site

http://www.oreilly.com/

★ "Top 100 Sites on the Web" —*PC Magazine*
★ "Top 5% Web sites" —*Point Communications*
★ "3-Star site" —*The McKinley Group*

Our web site contains a library of comprehensive product information (including book excerpts and tables of contents), downloadable software, background articles, interviews with technology leaders, links to relevant sites, book cover art, and more. File us in your Bookmarks or Hotlist!

2. Join Our Email Mailing Lists

New Product Releases
To receive automatic email with brief descriptions of all new O'Reilly products as they are released, send email to:
listproc@online.oreilly.com
Put the following information in the first line of your message (*not* in the Subject field):
subscribe oreilly-news

O'Reilly Events
If you'd also like us to send information about trade show events, special promotions, and other O'Reilly events, send email to:
listproc@online.oreilly.com
Put the following information in the first line of your message (*not* in the Subject field):
subscribe oreilly-events

3. Get Examples from Our Books via FTP

There are two ways to access an archive of example files from our books:

Regular FTP
- ftp to:
  ftp.oreilly.com
  (login: anonymous
  password: your email address)
- Point your web browser to:
  ftp://ftp.oreilly.com/

FTPMAIL
- Send an email message to:
  ftpmail@online.oreilly.com
  (Write "help" in the message body)

4. Contact Us via Email

order@oreilly.com
To place a book or software order online. Good for North American and international customers.

subscriptions@oreilly.com
To place an order for any of our newsletters or periodicals.

books@oreilly.com
General questions about any of our books.

software@oreilly.com
For general questions and product information about our software. Check out O'Reilly Software Online at **http://software.oreilly.com/** for software and technical support information. Registered O'Reilly software users send your questions to: **website-support@oreilly.com**

cs@oreilly.com
For answers to problems regarding your order or our products.

booktech@oreilly.com
For book content technical questions or corrections.

proposals@oreilly.com
To submit new book or software proposals to our editors and product managers.

international@oreilly.com
For information about our international distributors or translation queries. For a list of our distributors outside of North America check out:
http://www.oreilly.com/www/order/country.html

O'Reilly & Associates, Inc.
101 Morris Street, Sebastopol, CA 95472 USA
TEL   707-829-0515 or 800-998-9938
      (6am to 5pm PST)
FAX   707-829-0104

O'REILLY™

International Distributors

UK, EUROPE, MIDDLE EAST AND NORTHERN AFRICA (EXCEPT FRANCE, GERMANY, SWITZERLAND, & AUSTRIA)

INQUIRIES

International Thomson Publishing Europe
Berkshire House
168-173 High Holborn
London WC1V 7AA
United Kingdom
Telephone: 44-171-497-1422
Fax: 44-171-497-1426
Email: itpint@itps.co.uk

ORDERS

International Thomson Publishing Services, Ltd.
Cheriton House, North Way
Andover, Hampshire SP10 5BE
United Kingdom
Telephone: 44-264-342-832 (UK)
Telephone: 44-264-342-806 (outside UK)
Fax: 44-264-364418 (UK)
Fax: 44-264-342761 (outside UK)
UK & Eire orders: itpuk@itps.co.uk
International orders: itpint@itps.co.uk

FRANCE

Editions Eyrolles
61 bd Saint-Germain
75240 Paris Cedex 05
France
Fax: 33-01-44-41-11-44

FRENCH LANGUAGE BOOKS

All countries except Canada
Telephone: 33-01-44-41-46-16
Email: geodif@eyrolles.com
English language books
Telephone: 33-01-44-41-11-87
Email: distribution@eyrolles.com

GERMANY, SWITZERLAND, AND AUSTRIA

INQUIRIES

O'Reilly Verlag
Balthasarstr. 81
D-50670 Köln
Germany
Telephone: 49-221-97-31-60-0
Fax: 49-221-97-31-60-8
Email: anfragen@oreilly.de

ORDERS

International Thomson Publishing
Königswinterer Straße 418
53227 Bonn, Germany
Telephone: 49-228-97024 0
Fax: 49-228-441342
Email: order@oreilly.de

JAPAN

O'Reilly Japan, Inc.
Kiyoshige Building 2F
12-Banchi, Sanei-cho
Shinjuku-ku
Tokyo 160-0008 Japan
Telephone: 81-3-3356-5227
Fax: 81-3-3356-5261
Email: kenji@oreilly.com

INDIA

Computer Bookshop (India) PVT. Ltd.
190 Dr. D.N. Road, Fort
Bombay 400 001 India
Telephone: 91-22-207-0989
Fax: 91-22-262-3551
Email: cbsbom@giasbm01.vsnl.net.in

HONG KONG

City Discount Subscription Service Ltd.
Unit D, 3rd Floor, Yan's Tower
27 Wong Chuk Hang Road
Aberdeen, Hong Kong
Telephone: 852-2580-3539
Fax: 852-2580-6463
Email: citydis@ppn.com.hk

KOREA

Hanbit Media, Inc.
Sonyoung Bldg. 202
Yeksam-dong 736-36
Kangnam-ku
Seoul, Korea
Telephone: 822-554-9610
Fax: 822-556-0363
Email: hant93@chollian.dacom.co.kr

SINGAPORE, MALAYSIA, AND THAILAND

Addison Wesley Longman Singapore PTE Ltd.
25 First Lok Yang Road
Singapore 629734
Telephone: 65-268-2666
Fax: 65-268-7023
Email: daniel@longman.com.sg

PHILIPPINES

Mutual Books, Inc.
429-D Shaw Boulevard
Mandaluyong City, Metro
Manila, Philippines
Telephone: 632-725-7538
Fax: 632-721-3056
Email: mbikikog@mnl.sequel.net

CHINA

Ron's DataCom Co., Ltd.
79 Dongwu Avenue
Dongxihu District
Wuhan 430040
China
Telephone: 86-27-3892568
Fax: 86-27-3222108
Email: hongfeng@public.wh.hb.cn

ALL OTHER ASIAN COUNTRIES

O'Reilly & Associates, Inc.
101 Morris Street
Sebastopol, CA 95472 USA
Telephone: 707-829-0515
Fax: 707-829-0104
Email: order@oreilly.com

AUSTRALIA

WoodsLane Pty. Ltd.
7/5 Vuko Place, Warriewood NSW 2102
P.O. Box 935
Mona Vale NSW 2103
Australia
Telephone: 61-2-9970-5111
Fax: 61-2-9970-5002
Email: info@woodslane.com.au

NEW ZEALAND

Woodslane New Zealand Ltd.
21 Cooks Street (P.O. Box 575)
Waganui, New Zealand
Telephone: 64-6-347-6543
Fax: 64-6-345-4840
Email: info@woodslane.com.au

THE AMERICAS

McGraw-Hill Interamericana Editores, S.A. de C.V.
Cedro No. 512
Col. Atlampa 06450
Mexico, D.F.
Telephone: 52-5-541-3155
Fax: 52-5-541-4913
Email: mcgraw-hill@infosel.net.mx

SOUTH AFRICA

International Thomson Publishing
South Africa
Building 18, Constantia Park
138 Sixteenth Road
P.O. Box 2459
Halfway House, 1685 South Africa
Telephone: 27-11-805-4819
Fax: 27-11-805-3648

O'REILLY™

O'Reilly & Associates, Inc.
101 Morris Street
Sebastopol, CA 95472-9902
1-800-998-9938

Visit us online at:
http://www.ora.com/
orders@ora.com

O'REILLY WOULD LIKE TO HEAR FROM YOU

Which book did this card come from?

_____

Where did you buy this book?
❑ Bookstore   ❑ Computer Store
❑ Direct from O'Reilly   ❑ Class/seminar
❑ Bundled with hardware/software
❑ Other _____

What operating system do you use?
❑ UNIX   ❑ Macintosh
❑ Windows NT   ❑ PC(Windows/DOS)
❑ Other _____

What is your job description?
❑ System Administrator   ❑ Programmer
❑ Network Administrator   ❑ Educator/Teacher
❑ Web Developer
❑ Other _____

❑ Please send me O'Reilly's catalog, containing
a complete listing of O'Reilly books and
software.

Name _____   Company/Organization _____

Address _____

City _____   State _____   Zip/Postal Code _____   Country _____

Telephone _____   Internet or other email address (specify network) _____

Nineteenth century wood engraving
of a bear from the O'Reilly &
Associates Nutshell Handbook®
Using & Managing UUCP.

BUSINESS REPLY MAIL

FIRST CLASS MAIL   PERMIT NO. 80   SEBASTOPOL, CA

Postage will be paid by addressee

O'Reilly & Associates, Inc.

101 Morris Street
Sebastopol, CA 95472-9902